BUSINESS WEEK

Guide to
Mutual Funds

Seventh Annual Edition

Jeffrey M. Laderman
Senior Writer, BUSINESS WEEK

McGraw-Hill

New York   San Francisco   Washington, D.C.   Auckland   Bogotá
Caracas   Lisbon   London   Madrid   Mexico City   Milan
Montreal   New Delhi   San Juan   Singapore
Sydney   Tokyo   Toronto

International Standard Serial Number:
BUSINESS WEEK Guide to Mutual Funds
ISSN 1060-975x

McGraw-Hill

A Division of The McGraw·Hill Companies

1 2 3 4 5 6 7 8 9 0   MAL/MAL   9 0 2 1 0 9 8 7

ISBN 0-07-036774-4

The editor for this book was Susan Barry, the editing supervisor was Jane Palmieri, and the production supervisor was Pamela Pelton. It was set in Century Expanded by North Market Street Graphics.

Printed and bound by Malloy Lithographers, Inc.

CONTENTS

PREFACE

Each and every year, BUSINESS WEEK's annual Mutual Fund Scoreboard issue, The Best Mutual Funds, is one of the best-selling single issues of the magazine. It's easy to understand why. Mutual fund assets now stand at $3.5 trillion, up from just $1 trillion in 1990, and investors can't get enough information about them. Of course, BW isn't the only publication that reports on and rates mutual funds. But we think we're the best. So do the mutual fund executives who were asked by *Securities Industry Management* magazine a few years ago to rate those who rate mutual funds. *SIM*'s survey awarded BW's Mutual Fund Scoreboard an A–, the highest grade of seven publications rated. In its comments, *SIM* gave BW "high marks for being an innovator and for solid editorial comment." The best grade any of the competitors received was a B.

Now the magazine with the best mutual fund scoreboard is proud to bring you the best mutual fund book on the market—the BUSINESS WEEK *Guide to Mutual Funds*, Seventh Annual Edition. This slim, easy-to-read volume is your passport into the dynamic world of mutual fund investing. The new edition has the latest information on 885 equity, 653 bond, and 260 closed-end funds. We tell you all you want to know about mutual funds—which funds are beating the market and their competitors, which funds are delivering the highest returns with the least risk, and which funds have the highest and lowest costs. And we also feature the BUSINESS WEEK ratings. These ratings assess the risk-adjusted returns of each fund with at least five years of performance history against all other funds.

In this latest edition of the fund guide, we bring you a new and much improved way to look at mutual funds. We have reclassified the mutual funds into categories that are more specific and insightful than the traditional industry way of categorizing funds, such as "growth" or "equity–income." In this new system, U.S. diversified equity funds are categorized by both the size of the companies they invest in and the kinds of valuation measures they use to choose stocks. We've added new categories for international funds as well, to better help you navigate the overseas opportunities that mutual funds make available to you. We've overhauled the bond funds classification, too, emphasizing the maturity of the bonds in the portfolio as well as the kind of issuers. And to help you identify the best funds in each category, we've introduced category ratings. They rate funds as compared to others in their category.

We also bring you information not often found in other publications' mutual fund round-ups. We report equity fund total returns both before and after taxes. That's an important distinction since many investors underestimate the impact of taxes on their mutual fund investments. Another feature in our equity scoreboard, "Potential Capital Gains Exposure," assesses what kind of future tax liability a fund may have. We're always looking for new ways to look at the risks of investing in mutual funds, and we have a new one in this year's scoreboard: "Best Quarter, Worst Quarter." These data columns in the equity fund scoreboard review the 20 quarters in the 1992 through 1996 period and identify each fund's best quarterly performance and its worst. That's another way to look at how volatile a fund can be.

The book is basically composed of two parts. In the first part, we pull together the essentials you need to know about mutual funds: how they work and how you can use them. The second part is the BUSINESS WEEK Mutual Fund Scoreboard. The Scoreboard provides a wealth of information about mutual fund performance, costs, and risks that helps you to keep track of your own holdings—and prospect for new ones. The BW ratings are the highlight of the Scoreboard. Funds are rated on the basis of their returns—and their risk.

The book's first chapter is an introduction to mutual funds—why they're popular, what kinds of returns they can provide, and how investors can harness their earning power. Chapter 2 takes a close-up look at the world of mutual funds—equity funds, bond funds, and money-market funds—and describes how they invest your money. This year we've reorganized some of the fund categories to reflect the emergence of new sorts of funds. We'll also look into the closed-end funds, the manic first cousins of mutual funds. They often have higher highs and lower lows than their mutual fund kin.

In Chapter 3 we examine how you buy and sell mutual funds. That includes all you need to know about commissions, or the "load." There are funds that are sold with front-end loads, back-end loads, low-loads, hidden loads, and no-loads. And if you're going to pay a load, we'll help you determine which is the most cost-effective way of doing so. And we also explore new ways for investors to buy funds, such as networks or fund marketplaces developed by Charles Schwab & Co. and others and the increasingly popular adviser-based "wrap" programs.

When you've completed Chapters 2 and 3, you will know about the variety of funds and how you buy them. Then the question is what to buy. Chapter 4 asks you the questions you need to answer to help you build your own investment portfolio of mutual funds. And, of course, once you have your funds you can't just forget about them. So in Chapter 5 we cover how to monitor your funds—making sure they do what you want them to do.

If you've made the right moves, you're making money. And if you're making money, you will have to pay taxes. Chapter 6 explains the special tax rules that apply to how mutual funds report their income to you and how you, the shareholder, report to the Internal Revenue Service. We'll show you how to minimize the tax bite when you're cashing in your gains, and how to make the most of your losses by turning them into tax deductions.

In Chapter 7 we take a closer look at the Scoreboard and how to interpret the information in it. Chapter 8 looks at the most recent Scoreboard—which funds are in ascendancy, which are in decline, and what it means for the coming years. What follows is the Scoreboard itself—a cornucopia of information about nearly 1800 funds. Once you have the basics of mutual funds investing under your belt, the Scoreboard is the perfect place to start your search for the funds that will help you reach your financial goals.

We believe that this book fulfills a function that other mutual fund books do not. Most don't provide anything as complete as the Scoreboard's compendium of ratings, performance history, and costs. Some books that have tabular material, we've discovered, are limited in their scope. They cover Fidelity funds or no-load funds, bond funds or closed-end funds. We cover them all—load, no-load, low-load, Fidelity, and funds offered by scores of other mutual fund managers. If you're trying to identify the best, you have to search far and wide.

| Acknowledgments

The Scoreboard itself is produced for BUSINESS WEEK by Morningstar, Inc. This company takes care of gathering the vast amounts of data from the funds—organizing it and analyzing it in a way that allows us to assign ratings to funds. We'd like to thank the folks at Morningstar, especially John Rekenthaler and Kelly Messman, for their advice and assistance in preparing the Guide.

At BUSINESS WEEK, Senior Writer Jeffrey M. Laderman took charge of writing the book and coordinating the project. Laderman, a Chartered Financial Analyst, has covered mutual funds for more than a decade. He helped to launch the first Mutual Fund Scoreboard in February 1986, and has written the accompanying stories every year since.

Also contributing to the project was Arthur Eves, BUSINESS WEEK's graphics director, who developed the charts and tables that accompany and amplify the text. Senior Editor Seymour Zucker lent his skillful editing and much valued advice to the project. Without his enthusiastic support, and that of Stephen B. Shepard, BUSINESS WEEK's editor-in-chief, and Mark Morrison, the managing editor, this project would not have been possible.

Mutual Funds: The People's Choice

Over the last several years, investors embraced mutual funds with a fervor that even the most optimistic fund executive could not have predicted. Since the beginning of 1991, investors have poured nearly three-quarters of a trillion dollars into mutual funds that invest in stocks and bonds. In the record-setting year 1993, stock or "equity" funds took in a record $128.2 billion; bond or "fixed-income" funds, $113.6 billion. In 1996, the funds nearly broke the record. They took in $223 billion in equity funds, but only $13 billion in bond funds.

Why are people putting billions into mutual funds? Well, nothing sells like success, and for the most part investors have been successful. In 1991, 1992, and 1993, they earned plump returns as interest rates fell, vastly increasing the value of stocks and bonds. In 1994, interest rates shot up, causing losses in bond funds that have effectively stopped the flood of new money ever since. But investors never wavered in their support for equity funds, even when the stock market teetered that year.

Investors who stuck it out during tough 1994 were paid off handsomely in 1995—and then some. The average U.S. equity fund delivered a total return of 32 percent, including appreciation, dividends, and capital gains distributions. Throw in specialty and international funds, and you still get a total return of nearly 27 percent.

And though many investment strategists did not have high hopes for 1996, that too, turned out to be an excellent year for equity funds. The BUSINESS WEEK Mutual Fund Scoreboard shows U.S. diversified equity funds earned a 19.3 percent total return; all equity funds, 17.7 percent. The 25 funds with the highest returns earned at least 33.3 percent for shareholders (Table 1-1). The top bond funds earned just 5.4 percent, victims of a volatile bond market. But the top 25 bond funds still came in with impressive results—the best was up 41.1 percent (Table 1-2).

In the last few years investors also saw some of the foibles of mutual funds. Several portfolio managers were disciplined by regulators for making personal investments that conflicted with their professional duties. One was even dismissed from his job. The actions prompted most companies to tighten up their personnel trading policies, and the fund industry itself developed guidelines about what fund personnel should and should not do with personal trading.

In recent years, fund investors learned a new 4-letter word with 11 letters: "derivatives." These derivatives—financially-engineered investment instruments whose value is "derived" from some other security or index—helped sink two government-mortgage funds and erode principal in dozens more. Money-market mutual funds, which are supposed to be the most risk-averse funds of all, were not untouched by the derivatives mess, either. However, in all but one instance, the funds' management companies absorbed the losses of the handful of money funds adversely affected by derivatives. (In early 1997, yet another fund company stepped in to bail out a money-market mutual fund that had erred the old-fashioned way—it had made an investment that turned out bad because of "financial irregularities" at the company.)

By and large, investors have a lot of confidence in mutual funds. In a summer 1994 BUSINESS WEEK/Harris Poll of mutual fund investors, after much of the year's damage had been done,

TABLE 1-1

EQUITY FUNDS
1996'S TOP RETURNS

Fund	Total return*
PBHG TECHNOLOGY & COMMUNICATION	54.4 %
FIDELITY SELECT ENERGY SERVICES	49.0
FREMONT U.S. MICRO-CAP	48.7
RYDEX OTC	43.1
FIDELITY SELECT ELECTRONICS	41.7
FIDELITY HONG KONG & CHINA	41.0
LONGLEAF PARTNERS REALTY	40.7
INVESCO STRATEGIC GOLD	40.6
OAKMARK SMALL CAP	39.8
INVESCO STRATEGIC ENERGY	38.8
FIDELITY EXPORT	38.6
COHEN & STEERS REALTY	38.5
LEGG MASON VALUE PRIMARY SHARES	38.3
FPA CAPITAL	37.8
MONTGOMERY SMALL CAP	37.3
FIDELITY SELECT HOME FINANCE	36.8
FIDELITY REAL ESTATE	36.2
FIDELITY SELECT REGIONAL BANKS	35.7
STEIN ROE YOUNG INVESTOR	35.1
ARTISAN INTERNATIONAL	34.4
GUINNESS FLIGHT CHINA	34.4
FIDELITY SELECT NATURAL RESOURCES	34.3
VANGUARD SPECIALIZED ENERGY	34.0
SOUND SHORE	33.7
SALOMON BROS. CAPITAL	33.3

*Pretax return, includes reinvestment of dividends and capital gains

DATA: MORNINGSTAR INC.

fully 94 percent said they're somewhat or very confident that their investments are safe and only 24 percent said they planned to scale back their holdings. In addition, the poll's respondents showed they had a fairly realistic view of the risks that go with investing. Asked who is to blame if a mutual fund loses money, 60 percent said "no one." Asked what they would expect if one of their funds lost money, 80 percent said they did not expect anyone to make up the losses.

The sentiments expressed in that poll were certainly borne out in the subsequent two years. Investors continue to stash their savings in mutual funds. With more than one out of four U.S. households owning mutual funds, funds have established their place in family finance alongside the savings account, the checkbook, and the credit cards.

And those not familiar with funds are learning about them at the workplace. Mutual funds are fast becoming a mainstay of a type of pension program called the 401(k) plan. In these sorts of plans, employees—often matched in part by employers—make regular pretax contributions to the plan, which in turn are invested in any one of several choices which may include mutual funds. In 1995, for instance, General Motors Corp. added 38 Fidelity mutual funds to its 401(k) plan. A large percentage of the monthly inflows to mutual funds comes through the workplace.

Sure, novice investors have learned through experience that markets—and mutual fund prices—don't always go up. But taking a longer-term view, investors have been rewarded for taking the higher risks of investing. Indeed, over the long haul, the greater risk to investors is in playing it too safe. Investors who keep long-term funds in CDs and U.S. Treasury bills may be taking a big risk that they won't meet their long-term financial objectives, like a college education for their children or a comfortable retirement for themselves.

Mutual funds are hardly new. They've been a part of the investment world since the 1920s. For most of that time, funds offered one sort of investment—stocks. Bond funds were few, and tax-free bond and money-market mutual funds didn't come along until the 1970s. Even equity mutual funds were only a sideshow on Wall Street. First, individual investors and, later, pension funds held much more sway.

Today, because individuals have put their dollars in the hands of mutual fund managers, mutual funds dominate the stock market. They don't dominate in the sense that they "control" companies. But right now the funds are the most active investors, with the most new money to put to work. Market participants follow the funds' moves very closely. Just consider all the publicity surrounding the trading in the gargantuan Fidelity Magellan Fund. In late 1995, portfolio manager Jeffrey Vinik, in shareholder reports and in press interviews, made complimentary remarks about technology stocks around the same time he was selling them. In November 1995, Magellan sold an estimated $5 billion in tech stocks—and other Fidelity funds likely sold a few billion more. Fidelity critics howled, saying Vinik was trying to talk up the stocks to get a better price on his sales. Fidelity officials said Vinik's statements were his honest opinion at the time they were made but portfolio managers have to be free to change their minds. Indeed, that's what they're paid for. Certainly, portfolio managers must play by the rules, but that doesn't include telling everybody what their next move is going

TABLE 1-2

BOND FUNDS

1996'S TOP RETURNS

Fund ▼	Total return* ▼
FIDELITY NEW MARKETS INCOME	41.4 %
FIDELITY ADVISOR EMERGING MARKETS	40.3
ALLIANCE GLOBAL DOLLAR GOVT.	38.3
GT GLOBAL HIGH-INCOME B	35.9
SCUDDER EMERGING MARKETS INCOME	34.6
MERRILL LYNCH AMERICAS INCOME B	33.8
STRONG HIGH-YIELD BOND	26.9
JANUS HIGH-YIELD	24.1
ALLIANCE NORTH AMERICAN GOVERNMENT	23.1
SALOMON BROS. HIGH-YIELD BOND	21.2
GT GLOBAL STRATEGIC INCOME B	20.3
NORTHEAST INVESTORS	20.2
PACIFIC HORIZON CAPITAL INCOME	19.5
EV MARATHON STRATEGIC INCOME	18.2
PUTNAM CONVERTIBLE INCOME-GROWTH	17.8
PAINEWEBBER HIGH-INCOME A	17.3
PHOENIX HIGH-YIELD A	17.2
DEAN WITTER CONVERTIBLE	17.0
STATE ST. RESEARCH HIGH-INCOME A	16.9
FRANKLIN CONVERTIBLE SECURITIES I	16.3
MAINSTAY HI-YIELD CORPORATE BOND B	15.6
VANGUARD CONVERTIBLE SECURITIES	15.4
AIM HIGH-YIELD A	15.4
HANCOCK HIGH-YIELD BOND B	15.2
ALLIANCE MULTI-MARKET STRATEGY B	15.2

*Pretax, includes reinvestment of dividends and capital gains

DATA: MORNINGSTAR INC.

Mutual funds would still be a financial backwater if not for the millions of individuals who now entrust their hard-earned money to mutual fund companies. It's not always an easy trust to give. Savers who move their money out of a bank or thrift give up federal deposit insurance. Mutual funds have no guarantees.

The growth of the mutual fund industry has even surprised industry officials. In 1990, for instance, an industry-sponsored study estimated the funds would have $2 trillion in assets by 1995 or 1996, and at least $3 trillion by 2000. At year-end 1996, fund assets were nearly at the $3.5 trillion mark (Figure 1-1). Since 1990, the number of funds has nearly tripled, reaching 6270; the number of shareholder accounts more than doubled to 149 million.

The popularity of the funds is more than a bull market phenomenon. After all, many fund investors could just as easily buy stocks and bonds directly, but choose funds instead. Funds are convenient and efficient investment vehicles that give all individuals—even those with small sums to invest—access to a splendid array of opportunities. Mutual funds are uniquely democratic institutions. They can take a portfolio of giant blue-chip companies like Exxon, General Electric, and Philip Morris, and slice it into small enough pieces that most anyone can buy.

Mutual funds allow investors to participate in foreign stock and bond markets which they couldn't do on their own—or would find to be a costly, time-consuming, and logistical quagmire if they tried. International equity funds make investing across national borders no more difficult than investing across state lines. Closed-end funds, which, like mutual funds, are pools of professionally managed investments, allow investors to target their investments into individual nations like Chile, Indonesia, Thailand, and Turkey. (Closed-end funds also offer more conventional stock and bond investments.) There are even closed-end funds that invest in the former Communist nations like Russia—a preposterous notion only about a half-dozen years ago.

Mutual funds have opened up a world of fixed-income investing to people who not too many years ago had few choices other than passbook accounts and savings bonds. Through bond funds individuals can tap into the interest payments from any kind of fixed-income security you can imagine and many you can't. The range goes from U.S. Treasury bonds to collateralized mortgage obligations, adjustable-rate preferred stock, floating rate notes, and even other countries'

to be. That would be detrimental to fund shareholders to whom every portfolio manager has a fiduciary responsibility.

Mutual funds play a critical role in the municipal bond market as well. State and local governments increasingly turn to the mutual funds to buy their bonds and provide the financing needed to operate public services and rebuild the aging infrastructure. And because of the funds, governments are saving billions in interest expense.

Mutual funds are key participants in other markets, too. Through investment in U.S. Treasury securities, mutual funds help to finance the budget deficit. Funds bring fresh capital to the home mortgage market through their purchases of mortgage-backed securities, making it easier and a little cheaper for families to buy homes. And, with investments in high-yield bonds and commercial paper, mutual funds are helping to lower the borrowing costs for corporations.

FIGURE 1-1

THE EXPLOSIVE GROWTH IN MUTUAL FUNDS

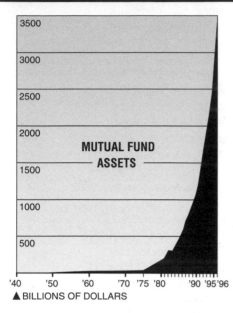

MUTUAL FUND
ASSETS

▲ BILLIONS OF DOLLARS

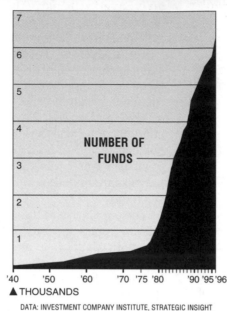

NUMBER OF
FUNDS

▲ THOUSANDS

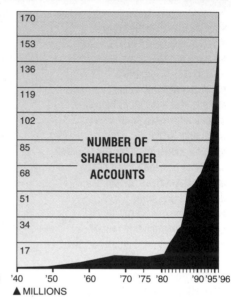

NUMBER OF
SHAREHOLDER
ACCOUNTS

▲ MILLIONS

DATA: INVESTMENT COMPANY INSTITUTE, STRATEGIC INSIGHT

debt—denominated both in U.S. dollars and in other currencies.

After the bond market volatility investors experienced in 1994 and, to a lesser degree, in 1996, a boring old bank account may look pretty good to a yield-oriented investor. Funds are not the same as bank deposits. No one guarantees that your assets will remain intact, let alone grow. Some legislators and regulators have pointed to surveys of bank customers who bought mutual funds at the bank—and think they're insured. The only fund that can be considered as safe as a bank deposit is one investing solely in U.S. Treasury bills. No one should use equity funds for money that they're going to need to buy a house or a car in the near future. But the longer the investment horizon, the lower the risk of losses. Money stashed away for many years instead of months could well go into a mutual fund, or a properly constructed portfolio of funds.

How do you find the right funds? BUSINESS WEEK's *Guide to Mutual Funds*, Seventh Annual Edition, will make it easy for you. In one volume we survey the world of funds, tell you what you need to know about them, help you tailor your own investment plan, and choose the funds that will best fulfill it. Perhaps you would rather invest through a broker or financial planner, relying on their advice. That's fine, too. But don't turn to a salesperson without a solid grasp of mutual

funds yourself. If you enter the world of mutual funds as an educated consumer and avoid the common mistakes (Table 1-3), you can become a successful investor.

What's a Mutual Fund?

A mutual fund is an investment company that pools the money of many individual investors. When the fund takes in money from investors, it issues shares. The price of a mutual fund share is the total net assets—the fund's assets less liabilities—divided by the number of shares outstanding. This figure is also called the fund's net asset value, commonly referred to as "NAV."

Unlike stocks, whose prices are subject to change at each trade, mutual fund NAVs are calculated at the end of each day. To figure their NAVs, the funds use the closing prices of each of the securities in their portfolios. (Bond funds often own securities that trade infrequently and daily prices are hard to come by. These funds use outside services that estimate the bonds' prices.)

A mutual fund is also an "open-end" vehicle. That means the fund doesn't have a fixed number of shares, but issues new shares as it takes in money and redeems them as investors withdraw. This liquidity—the ability for investors to get in and out of the funds easily and at little or no cost—is one of the most important features the funds bring to the financial system. A smaller number of funds are "closed-end" funds. They raise their capital during offering periods, and after that, investors can only get into the fund or out of it by buying or selling the shares on a stock exchange or in the over-the-counter market.

Open-end or closed-end, both types of funds are highly regulated entities, governed by a federal law—the Investment Company Act of 1940. Regulators don't dictate investment policy, but they make sure investment managers adhere to prescribed standards of disclosure, record-keeping, and administration.

As a practical matter, the fund companies police themselves. The U.S. Securities & Exchange Commission has fewer than 150 examiners to check up on thousands of funds. For the most part, the mutual funds have avoided the kind of financial scandals seen on Wall Street and in the thrift business in the 1980s and have a fairly clean record.

The mutual fund format is especially good for those just getting started in the investment game. If you only have $1000 or $2000 to invest, very few stockbrokers or professional money managers are going to bother with you. Those who do will not give you the attention and research support afforded to their more well-heeled clients—nor should you expect it. They have to make a living, and the commission on a small nest egg isn't worth much of their time.

But if you put your money in a mutual fund, the first-string portfolio managers will be working on your mutual fund account. The $1000 investor gets the same attention as the $100,000

TABLE 1-3

FUND INVESTORS' BIGGEST MISTAKES

▶ Buying last year's or last quarter's hottest performer only because it did well.

▶ Ignoring the prospectus—especially the parts on fees and investment policy.

▶ Choosing funds inappropriate for investment goals.

▶ Selecting highest yields without regard for risks.

▶ Losing track of fund performance.

▶ Failure to keep records for investment evaluation and taxes.

investor. That's because the fund's performance is the manager's calling card. Its successes will be chronicled in the media—and so will its failures. That's a powerful incentive for the portfolio manager to give the fund his or her very best efforts.

You might be one of those people who thinks of a mutual fund as an investment for small and unsophisticated investors; that it's okay for investors who are still building their assets, but anyone with an appreciable amount of money moves into direct investment in stocks and bonds. That's not so. Today many investors who could well afford stockbrokers and professional money managers prefer mutual funds. Over the last decade, a few fund companies have developed "sector funds," nondiversified funds that invest in a particular industry or group of industries. Such investment vehicles are designed to look more like stocks than mutual funds and to appeal to investors who might otherwise choose to invest in individual stocks.

Service, convenience, and efficiency all help to explain the growth of mutual funds. But no one would invest in mutual funds if they didn't think they would make money. And, indeed, mutual funds have made huge sums of money for those wise enough to have invested in them.

First Encounters with a Mutual Fund

Many investors first encountered a mutual fund when they bought a money-market fund. In the late 1970s and early 1980s, the interest rates that banks and thrifts could pay savers were set by bank regulators—and they were kept artificially low. Those with $10,000 could pull their money out of the bank and buy Treasury bills, but there was no high-interest vehicle for individuals with less money—until the money-market mutual fund.

The money-market funds revolutionized savings in America. They pooled investors' money and bought the kind of higher-yielding money-market investments that individuals could not get on their own. When short-term interest rates soared to almost 20 percent, the money funds made it possible for anyone to take advantage of the enormous yield. Before the advent of these funds, the only choice a small investor had was a passbook account paying 5 percent.

5

Money funds revolutionized savings in America.

The money-market funds also resuscitated the mutual fund industry, which for years had been suffering from liquidation—investors taking more money out of the funds than they were putting in. By 1982, money-market funds had commandeered about $200 billion in assets. When the great bull market in stocks and bonds got underway, the mutual fund companies had millions of new customers to whom they could pitch their stock and bond funds.

Fund investors were not disappointed. During the 1980s equity mutual funds earned on average an annual total return of 14.9 percent. In one sense, that's terrific. A $1000 investment in the average equity fund at the start of the decade would have grown to a little more than $4000 by the end. But relative to the Standard & Poor's 500 stock index, the yardstick by which money managers are measured, the return is a little thin. The S&P 500, in fact, delivered an average annual total return of 17.5 percent during the decade.

But examine those returns more closely. The S&P 500 is an index, "managed" by a computer. A mutual fund is a portfolio of stocks that needs a manager, who is usually backed up by analysts and some support staff. The fund must keep meticulous records of its own transactions and those of its thousands of shareholders. Account statements need to be prepared and mailed to each of them. There's also the cost of staffing those toll-free phone lines and fees for the auditing and regulatory filings. All this service costs, on average, about 1.29 percent a year of fund assets, or $1.29 per $100 invested. And that comes out of a fund's returns.

Next, consider that most equity mutual funds keep about 5 percent of their assets in cash. In a bull market, cash (Treasury bills and other money-market instruments) has lower returns than stocks. Over the decade, the cash accounted for another half a percentage point in the underperformance.

Finally, remember that the S&P 500 is dominated by large companies—and the average mutual fund owns companies that are much smaller than the General Motors and Exxons of the world. In the 1980s, the stock price performance of the larger companies beat the small-to-medium-sized companies. So there was no way that the average fund could top the S&P 500.

This "underperformance" doesn't seem to have dampened investor enthusiasm for mutual funds. Nor should it. The performance of equity funds still beat money-market and bond funds over the decade and probably gave investors a better return than if they had done nothing with their money. In addition, the average return is just that. Hundreds of funds fared better and 64 even beat the S&P during the decade.

And, even better for mutual fund investors is the fact that the tide seems to have shifted toward small-to-medium-sized companies. From 1991 through 1993, the average U.S. diversified fund, which has more small and midsized stocks than the S&P 500, beat S&P by an average of 3 percentage points a year. In 1994 and 1995, the S&P 500 led the way. For the first half of 1996, the smaller companies were trouncing the S&P 500—and so were mutual funds. But the stock market toppled in the summer, and in the second half of the year, the larger stocks overtook the smaller ones. That trend continued into early 1997.

Moreover, you don't have to settle for average returns. If you choose your mutual funds carefully and keep abreast of your funds' progress by tracking net asset values, reading shareholder reports, and using the BUSINESS WEEK ratings, you can improve your portfolio performance.

One academic study pondered the question, "Do winners repeat?" The academics examined monthly mutual fund returns over a 12-year period and found that they do indeed, as do losers, and concluded that a review of past performance is useful in differentiating one mutual fund from another. Although it may not be wise to buy only the No. 1 performer in any one year, it is indeed advisable to select from funds that have been among the best year after year.

Another study looked at equity mutual funds over a 14-year period and concluded that there is some "persistence" of performance. The researchers found that funds that excelled during one year continued to excel for as long as eight quarters, or two years, more. More important, they concluded that there are ways to identify these mutual funds so investors can put their money into the funds and enjoy the benefit of the funds' expertise.

One way to find the best funds, the ones that exhibit this persistence of performance, is in the BUSINESS WEEK Mutual Fund Scoreboard. The BW ratings take into account a mutual fund's risk as well as its total return over a five-year period. This longer view of performance screens out the one-year wonders. The funds that rise to the top do so with consistently strong risk-adjusted returns.

The Joys of Compound Growth

If you're ever cornered by a mutual fund salesperson, he or she will whip out the "mountain" chart (Figure 1-2). What's really important is not the mountain, but the top line, which depicts the growth of a one-time investment in a mutual fund. The line rises slowly at first, but soon accelerates and appears to jump off the page. The Templeton Funds, for instance, show what would have happened if you had invested $10,000 in the Templeton Growth Fund when it opened for business in November 1954 and instructed the fund to reinvest all dividends and capital gains distributions. Over four decades later, your original $10,000 alone would be worth over $586,000. But with reinvestment of dividends and capital gains, your investment is worth almost $3.38 million, more than five times as much.

FIGURE 1-2

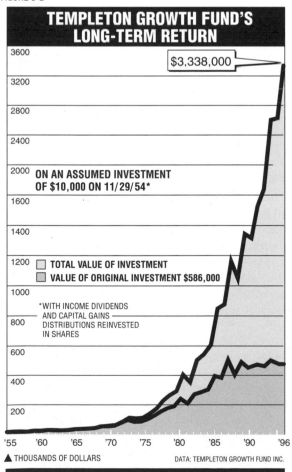

TEMPLETON GROWTH FUND'S LONG-TERM RETURN

$3,338,000

ON AN ASSUMED INVESTMENT OF $10,000 ON 11/29/54*

☐ TOTAL VALUE OF INVESTMENT
▨ VALUE OF ORIGINAL INVESTMENT $586,000

*WITH INCOME DIVIDENDS AND CAPITAL GAINS DISTRIBUTIONS REINVESTED IN SHARES

'55 '60 '65 '70 '75 '80 '85 '90 '96

 THOUSANDS OF DOLLARS   DATA: TEMPLETON GROWTH FUND INC.

Sales hype? Well, the track record is real. Templeton Growth Fund, which was one of the first international funds (that is, funds that invest in non-U.S. stocks), has had an average annual return of 14.3 percent. What is a little exaggerated is the $10,000 investment. The equivalent in today's dollars is more than $50,000. Even today, that's hardly your average mutual fund investment.

The example may be a bit fanciful, but the principle demonstrated in this sort of sales material is simple—the power of compound rates of return. You earn a return on your investment and, if you don't take it out of the fund, you begin to earn returns on your returns. You're probably familiar with a bank certificate of deposit. If you leave the interest in the CD, you earn interest on your interest. Mutual funds don't pay a fixed rate of interest. But if you reinvest profits in more fund shares, you're compounding your returns.

Look at Table 1-4. If you invest $10,000 now, hold on to the investment for 20 years, reinvest your returns, and earn, on average, 11 percent, your nest egg grows more than eightfold—to $80,623. Now look at the return in another way. An 11 percent return on $10,000 is $1100. Over 20 years that totals $22,000. So, after two decades you can account for $32,000—your $10,000 initial investment and the annual return earned on it. The other $48,000 is the return on your returns.

Mutual funds don't guarantee a rate of return. The portfolio managers do their best to deliver the highest rate of return they can and live within their investment objectives. And if a fund does earn, on average, 11 percent a year, it's not earning that every year. Some years the fund might earn twice that amount and other years actually lose money. It's only in retrospect that you come up with nice round numbers like an 11 percent or 14 percent annual rate of return. It's simply an average.

If you want to harness the power of compound rates of return, investing in mutual funds is a convenient and efficient way to do it. Suppose you own some bonds and collect $389 in interest twice a year. You want to reinvest the money, but what can you do with it? You can't buy more bonds because it's an odd amount. You can stash it away in a money-market mutual fund until you have enough to buy another bond. But while the money is sitting in a money-market fund, it's probably not earning what it could in a bond.

A mutual fund makes this process much simpler. If a bond fund pays you $389, or any other such amount, you can (in advance) direct the fund to reinvest the money immediately. You don't

7

TABLE 1-4

THE WONDERFUL WORLD OF COMPOUND INTEREST

Invest $10,000 in year 1

Rate of return	What your investment would be worth at the end of year...					
	5	10	15	20	25	30
7%	$14,026	$19,672	$27,950	$38,697	$52,274	$76,123
8	14,693	21,589	31,722	46,610	68,485	100,627
9	15,386	23,674	36,425	56,044	86,231	132,677
10	16,105	25,937	41,772	67,275	108,347	174,494
11	16,851	28,394	47,846	80,623	135,855	228,923
12	17,623	31,058	54,736	96,463	170,001	299,599

Invest $2,000 a year

Rate of return	What your investment would be worth at the end of year...					
	5	10	15	20	25	30
7%	$12,307	$29,567	$53,776	$ 87,730	$135,353	$202,146
8	12,672	31,291	58,649	98,846	157,909	244,692
9	13,047	33,121	64,007	111,529	184,648	297,150
10	13,431	35,062	69,899	126,005	216,364	361,887
11	13,826	37,123	76,380	142,530	253,998	441,826
12	14,230	39,309	83,507	161,398	298,668	540,585

Invest $200 a month

Rate of return	What your investment would be worth at the end of year...					
	5	10	15	20	25	30
7%	$14,402	$34,819	$ 63,762	$104,793	$162,959	$245,417
8	14,793	36,833	69,669	118,589	191,473	300,059
9	15,198	38,993	76,249	134,579	225,906	368,895
10	15,616	41,310	83,585	153,139	267,578	455,865
11	16,049	43,797	91,772	174,715	318,116	566,046
12	16,497	46,468	100,915	199,830	379,527	705,983

DATA: BUSINESS WEEK

have to worry about odd amounts of money. There is no check stuck in the mail. Your money is at work all the time. The mutual fund will take whatever the amount is, divide it by the current price per share, and give you that many shares. If it's 17.693 shares, so be it, since the fund can sell you fractional shares down to one-thousandth of a decimal place.

The ability to invest odd sums and buy fractional shares makes mutual funds ideal vehicles for savings programs. Millions of mutual fund shareholders, in fact, invest regularly through automatic investment plans. Suppose you want to save $200 a month and invest it in equities. It's not practical to buy $200 worth of stock at a time. Commissions are high on small orders, and there's no way to invest odd amounts that are left over and buy fractional shares of stock on any exchange.

With a regular savings program the compound growth tables look even more alluring. Remember, the numbers are greater because you periodically invest new money in the fund. Put $200 a month into a mutual fund and you can really see the money build up. After 20 years you've put in $48,000. If that money earns an 11 percent average annual return for 20 years, your stake grows to about $174,715. That's nearly $127,000 more than you put in.

The ease and efficiency with which investments compound make mutual funds perfect investments for long-term savings programs like college funds or retirement accounts. That's why mutual funds are the investment vehicle of choice for Individual Retirement Accounts (IRAs). According to figures compiled by the Investment Company Institute, at the end of 1995 mutual fund IRAs held about $410.8 billion in assets, 35 percent of all IRA money. Banks and thrifts together had only a little more than half that amount. In 1985 mutual funds had only 12.5 percent of the IRA pie; banks and thrifts together had over 60 percent of the IRA assets.

Be Realistic About Your Expectations

Remember the Templeton Growth Fund, with the mythical investor whose $10,000 investment of 40 years earlier made him a millionaire? He didn't become a millionaire instantaneously. Invest $10,000, and even if you earn 20 percent a year, it would still take 26 years to turn it into a million. Mutual funds won't get you rich quick, but if you persist in investing, and you invest with funds that are persistently good, your wealth will grow.

Whatever funds you choose for your investment program, you should be realistic in your expectations. Mutual funds are organized to invest in a specific kind of security or a particular market. So if you choose an equity fund that invests in large capitalization stocks, you hope it's going to perform better than the S&P 500. But if the S&P is down 20 percent, you can't realistically expect your fund to be up. If your fund was only down 10 percent, you might be hopping mad at the fund manager. But, in fact, among his peers, he or she would be considered a hero. Likewise, if you're investing in a money-market fund when Treasury bill rates are 5 percent, you shouldn't expect a 10 percent return. The returns generated by the fund won't be terribly different from what happens in the market in which it invests. If you did get 10 percent from that very fund, it would be a sure bet that the fund was not living up to the investment guidelines that all money-market mutual funds must follow.

You also need a little perspective on expectations. Both 1995 and 1996 were extraordinary years for the U.S. stock market, the average gain a whopping 30 percent a year. That's nearly three times the long-term average price gain for large-capitalization U.S. stocks. Many market commentators have argued for the last several years that the stock market is overpriced and bound for a crash, or at least a serious correction. We at BUSINESS WEEK believe there are solid fundamental economic reasons for the stock market's advance,

and that even with the Dow Jones industrial average near 7000, stocks and mutual funds can offer good long-term investment opportunities. However, we recognize—and you should too—that rate of gain in the last two years cannot continue indefinitely. More important, it doesn't have to to make investing pay off.

As an investor, you have no control over the stock or bond markets. But you do have control over your own portfolio of mutual funds. We don't advocate buying and selling funds frequently, trying to catch the ups and avoid the downs of the market (what's known as market-timing, see Chapter 4). But if you select funds with the help of the BUSINESS WEEK ratings, monitor their performance, and keep investments matched to your financial objectives, your long-term investment program will be rewarding.

The World of Mutual Funds

You may know you want to invest in mutual funds, but where do you start? At one time, funds pretty much invested in big U.S. corporations. Period. Today, there are funds that specialize in everything from biotechnology to small Asian companies to municipal bonds issued within the bounds of a single state. The number of funds is so large and investment programs so varied that investors would be overwhelmed without some way to organize the offerings.

This chapter will help you make sense of the thousands of funds—and how they invest your money. To accomplish this, we've broken the chapter into several sections: equity funds, bond funds, and money-market funds. We follow with a section on closed-end funds—a predecessor of the mutual fund that is usually overshadowed by mutual funds and overlooked by investors.

Let's look first at equity funds, those funds that invest in equities, or common stocks. Many of the companies most widely held by equity funds are household names—Philip Morris, IBM, General Electric, General Motors, AT&T, Ford Motor, and Chrysler (Table 2-1). Find the column, "Percent of net assets." Philip Morris, the stock most commonly found in equity mutual fund portfolios, amounts to less than 1 percent of the net assets of all equity fund holdings. Even the 25 largest holdings only amount to 12 percent of equity funds' net assets. That's a sign of the diversity and variety within mutual fund portfolios.

To get a better understanding of equity funds, you have to look closer. The mutual fund industry has traditionally categorized funds by the fund's investment objective as stated in the prospectus, a legal document required by securities law. These are the investment objectives you will find in most mutual fund publications and advertising: "growth," "growth and income," and "small company."

But now, mutual funds have become so diverse in their strategies that the old nomenclature doesn't work anymore. For example, what is a "growth" fund anyway? It's a fund whose "primary aim is to provide capital appreciation (a rise in share price) rather than steady income," according to the *1996 Mutual Fund Fact Book*, which is published by the Investment Company

TABLE 2-1

EQUITY FUNDS

LARGEST HOLDINGS

Stock ▼	Percent of net assets ▼
PHILIP MORRIS	0.93%
GENERAL ELECTRIC	0.67
INTEL	0.64
FEDERAL NATIONAL MORTGAGE ASSOCIATION	0.62
CISCO SYSTEMS	0.55
CITICORP	0.50
CHASE MANHATTAN	0.45
AT&T	0.42
E.I. DUPONT DE NEMOURS	0.41
IBM	0.41
PFIZER	0.41
AMERICAN HOME PRODUCTS	0.41
GENERAL MOTORS	0.41
JOHNSON & JOHNSON	0.38
MERCK	0.38
EXXON	0.37
BRISTOL-MYERS SQUIBB	0.36
MICROSOFT	0.35
WAL-MART STORES	0.34
FORD MOTOR	0.34
CHRYSLER	0.33
BANKAMERICA	0.33
ALLSTATE	0.33
SCHLUMBERGER	0.32
ORACLE	0.31

DATA: MORNINGSTAR INC.

Institute, the fund industry's principal trade association. The problem with that definition is that it's so vague it can be applied to hundreds, if not thousands, of funds.

The truth is that this definition gives an investor little guidance on exactly how the fund actually "grows" the value of your investment. The Janus Twenty Fund takes a fairly traditional growth route, buying stocks in blue-chip growth companies such as Coca-Cola, Nike, and Intel and, most recently, big bank stocks such as Wells Fargo, Chase Manhattan, and Citicorp. The median market capitalization (total market value of a company's shares) of all the stocks in the portfolio is $26.3 billion.

At the other end of the growth-fund spectrum is Lindner Growth Investors, which, judged by its portfolio has little in common with Janus Twenty. Among the largest holdings are Alliant Techsystems, Acordia, Acceptance Insurance, and Noram Energy. Recognize any of these names? Probably not. They're not household names, and they're much, much smaller companies. The median market capitalization is only $520 million, just one-fiftieth that of Janus Twenty.

Are these two funds at all alike? Other than the fact both are growth funds that invest in equities, no. It's not even that one invests in very large companies, the other, small. The companies are very different as well. Janus Twenty's companies sell, on average, at nearly seven times their "book" value, which, simply put, is the value of the company's assets that are "on the books" less the liabilities. It's what the accountants say the company's worth. That may seem high, but the key here is earnings growth, not book value. On that side, Janus's companies are winners—an average 33 percent growth in earnings a year over the last five.

Lindner Growth's companies, on the other hand, sell for just 2.5 times book value. Why so low? Well, these companies are often out of favor with investors. Look at the five-year earnings growth rate—in this case, just 4.5 percent—and you can understand why these stocks are out of favor. So why does the manager of the Lindner Growth fund want to invest in them? The fund manager believes that the stocks are undervalued and certain changes are going on in the companies that will result in the market's ultimately recognizing that value. These changes might be an upturn in earnings, an exciting new product, a corporate restructuring, or perhaps even a merger.

In the investment world, Janus's stocks would be considered a "growth" portfolio; Lindner's, a "value" portfolio. We can also characterize the funds by the median market capitalization of the stocks they hold. Janus is definitely large-cap, Lindner small-cap. Put the two characteristics together, and you get large-cap growth and small-cap value. Those are two very distinct "investment styles," both of which, when executed well, have the capability to make plenty of money for investors.

Of course, not all investment styles do equally well all the time. For instance, Janus Twenty beat Lindner Growth in 1995 and 1996, but Lindner beat Janus in 1992, 1993, and 1994. That's one of the reasons it's important to examine mutual funds by their styles. Properly categorized, style tells you more about how the fund invests than the "investment objective."

Investment style also tells you more about what to expect from your fund. Consider the Janus Enterprise Fund, which, like its sister fund Janus Twenty, has growth as its investment objective. In 1996, the behavior of the two funds was quite different. Janus Twenty made steady gains most of the year, mirroring the rise in the S&P 500. Janus Enterprise, on the other hand, ran ahead of Janus Twenty early in the year, but took a 15 percent dive in the summer, and only recovered about half of that loss by year-end. Total return for Janus Twenty, 27.9 percent; Janus Enterprise, 11.7 percent.

Their investment styles help to explain the differences in performance. Small-cap growth stocks never recovered after the summer correction, as investors flocked to the perceived safety and liquidity of large-cap stocks like those that are in the Dow Jones industrial average and the S&P 500. Small-cap stocks in general, and small-cap growth stocks in particular, were left behind in the big rally, and that hurt funds like Janus Enterprise.

Now doesn't it make more sense to categorize funds by market cap and investment style than by the investment objective of growth? We think so, and so do the mutual-fund experts at Morningstar, Inc., the well-known mutual fund data and research firm that prepares BUSINESS WEEK's Mutual Fund Scoreboard. The folks at Morningstar, in fact, have revamped their fund categories to reflect these investment styles, and so has BW.

These categories are not entirely new. Three years ago, BW started to report investment style in the Scoreboard while still using the old investment objectives for grouping funds. Now we are categorizing funds in the Scoreboard and in this chapter by style. That means it will be easier for investors to compare funds with like investment programs. For example, an investor might have thought a switch from Janus Enterprise to Janus Twenty was warranted, since the two were growth funds, and one obviously was performing a whole lot better. A stylistic approach, on the other hand, reveals that there's a reasonable explanation for disparities in performance. An investor might wish to make the switch anyway, but at least, this way, the investor will do so knowing he or she is picking up a distinctly different sort of fund.

There are other good reasons for looking at funds through this stylistic filter. For instance, most fund investors today own more than one fund, with the idea that some diversification among funds is a good idea. Suppose an investor owned the Kaufmann, Janus Enterprise, Baron Growth & Income, and Robertson Stephens Emerging Growth funds. Using investment objectives to categorize funds, the investor would have a maximum growth, a growth, a growth and income, and a small company fund and think she's getting some diversification. Yet, in a stylistic analysis, all are small-cap growth funds, and it's likely they're making many similar investments. Is that the diversification the fund investor was seeking? A fund investor who is trying to build a diversified portfolio of funds will have an easier time doing it by using stylistic categories than by using the traditional investment objectives.

One more good reason for using market cap/investment style analysis on funds is that it levels the playing field. For instance, fund companies sometimes give their funds names that track one investment objective when the funds actually pursue another. Look at Robertson Stephens Growth and Income Fund. Most growth and income funds strive to produce some dividend payout, so they must invest a good portion of the fund assets in stocks that pay dividends. Such stocks are less volatile than growth stocks that don't pay dividends. Yet in the summer slump of 1996, the fund's portfolio plummeted more like a growth fund than a growth and income fund. The reason: portfolio manager John Wallace does not invest like most growth and income managers. He puts most of the fund's money into high-octane growth stocks that don't

pay dividends. For the income component, he invests in convertible bonds and eschews the conservative dividend-paying stocks commonly found in his competitors' funds. Most of the time, this strategy allows him to outshine the other growth and income fund managers.

Is it right for Robertson Stephens & Co. to call this a "growth and income" fund? Well, the definition of that investment objective is broad enough and vague enough to allow the Robertson Stephens fund to fit within it. But to call it a growth and income fund might stretch credulity a bit, since it neither invests like most of those funds nor produces returns that look like most of the other growth and income funds. When it outperforms other growth and income funds, as it did for most of 1996, do investors really understand it's doing so because it's taking greater risks and investing like a growth fund?

One way of compensating for this sort of unexpected behavior is to ignore the objective listed in the fund's prospectus and put the fund into a different objective group. Morningstar, for instance, has done this on occasion to better describe a fund's behavior. For the last several years, the fund research firm has put Warburg Pincus Growth and Income Common Shares into its growth fund category, even though "income" is in the name. And it seems appropriate. During 1996, the fund paid out only 0.4 percent in yield, which is far less than what would be expected in a growth and income fund.

But moving errant funds into different objectives categories isn't enough if the objective categories themselves are inadequate for today's investment world. Suppose Robertson Stephens Growth & Income Fund were reclassified as a growth fund. An investor still runs into the same kind of problem described earlier with Janus Twenty and Lindner Growth Investors—growth funds themselves encompass a myriad number of investment styles. So, comparing growth funds to growth funds isn't always a fair comparison, either. Robertson Stephens Growth & Income is a growth fund investing in midsized companies, while Lindner Growth Investors invests in small-cap value stocks.

Style-based categories gives investors much better descriptive information about funds than the traditional investment objectives. The style analysis comes right out of the fund's portfolio. Investment objectives come out of a document written by marketing executives and lawyers. Which would you rather trust?

Investment "style" tells the story.

Determining Style

You don't need an MBA to look at the holdings of Janus Enterprise, Janus Twenty, or Lindner Growth Investors and tell whether they're large or small companies. But Morningstar analysts don't rely just on eyeballing the portfolios to determine their median market caps or whether the stocks fall into the growth or value camp. There's a methodology to it.

To determine the appropriate capitalization, the analysts calculate the median market capitalization for all the stocks in the portfolio. Suppose there are 75 stocks in a fund, the analysts will calculate the market cap for each of the companies, and then rank them from high to low. The market cap of stock No. 38 is the median market cap for the fund. It's right in the middle, with an equal number of stocks (Nos. 1 through 37 and 39 through 75) above and below it. Morningstar uses the median rather than the mean (or what we know as an average) because having a few very large stocks (Microsoft, Intel, or Coca-Cola, for instance) can significantly skew the results. If the median market cap of the companies in the portfolio is greater than \$5 billion, it's a large-cap fund; \$1 billion to \$5 billion is a mid-cap fund; and less than \$1 billion, a small-cap fund.

The second part of designating style is to determine whether the fund practices a growth or value approach to investing. Again, the Morningstar analysts go back to the fund portfolio to crunch numbers. First, they calculate a price-to-earnings (p–e) ratio for each stock in the fund. That's the price divided by the most recent 12 months' per-share earning. Then, they weight the p–e by holdings, so that the p–e of a stock that comprises 2 percent of the fund counts twice as much as the p–e of a stock that makes up only 1 percent of the fund. Then they go through the same process to calculate and weight price-to-book value (p–b) ratios for the stocks. A company's book value is its assets less liabilities, or what the accountants would say the company is worth. But few stocks sell at book value, and in a bull market, most sell well in excess of book value. When comparing price-to-book value, the lower the ratio, the cheaper the stock; the higher the ratio, the more expensive the stock. Then as with p–e's, the p–b's are weighted.

The next step is to compare the fund's p–e ratio and p–b ratio to a benchmark. For funds investing in the United States, it's the S&P 500. Here's how it works. Suppose a fund has an 18 p–e and a 2.5 p–b ratio compared to the S&P's 21 p–e ratio and a 3.7 p–b ratio. (Remember, the S&P's p–e and p–b ratios rise and fall depending on the health of the stock market and the level of interest rates. Thus, in a bull market, a fund with a p–e of 15 ends up as a value portfolio, while in a bear market, the same p–e would be associated with a growth-stock portfolio.) The style calculation first divides the fund's p–e by S&P's p–e and gets 0.86; then divides the fund's p–b by S&P's p–b, the result of which is 0.68. Morningstar adds the two quotients, the sum of which in this case is 1.54. If the sum is less than 1.75, the fund is tagged a value fund; above 2.25, it's a growth fund. Should it fall between 1.75 and 2.25, it's a blend of the two, suggesting some characteristics of both value and growth. Since each diversified domestic equity fund is classified in one of three categories of size and style, there are now nine categories (Figure 2-1).

One problem with style-based categories is that some funds temporarily change style. This may not be a deliberate move by the fund managers, just market dynamics. For instance, a successful value manager might find his fund has gone from the value column to the blend column because some of the stocks he bought have appreciated handsomely and are no longer as cheap as value stocks. The manager might still consider himself a value investor, and eventually sell those stocks and replace them with more traditional value investments. That's why Morningstar looks at the fund's stylistic history as well as its current practices, when determining which style category to place a fund into.

FIGURE 2-1

A BETTER LOOK AT YOUR FUNDS

BUSINESS WEEK now categorizes U.S. diversified equity funds in two ways: by the median market capitalization of the stocks it owns and by the relative valuation or "style" of those stocks. It's a system developed by Morningstar Inc.

Funds whose stocks have a median market cap of \$5 billion or more are considered large-cap funds, \$1 billion or less are small-cap, and those in between, mid-cap. To determine each fund's style, the average price–earnings ratios and price-to-book ratios are calculated and compared with the S&P 500. Those with significantly lower-than-average p–e's and p–b's are "value" funds, those higher than average "growth," and those in the middle "blend."

		Investment Style		
		VALUE	BLEND	GROWTH
Median Market Capitalization	LARGE	LARGE-CAP VALUE	LARGE-CAP BLEND	LARGE-CAP GROWTH
	MEDIUM	MID-CAP VALUE	MID-CAP BLEND	MID-CAP GROWTH
	SMALL	SMALL-CAP VALUE	SMALL-CAP BLEND	SMALL-CAP GROWTH

The BW Scoreboard applies this stylistic grouping to diversified funds that invest primarily in the United States. Essentially, all the funds that in the past were categorized as maximum growth, growth, growth and income, equity–income, and small company will now be reclassified as one of the following: large-cap value, large-cap blend, large-cap growth; mid-cap value, mid-cap blend, mid-cap growth; or small-cap value, small-cap blend, small-cap growth. Generally speaking, the large-cap value funds are expected to be the least risky, or volatile; the small-cap growth funds are expected to be the most risky.

There's more to the new categories. The three investment objectives that combine stocks and bonds—asset allocation, balanced, and multiasset global—have been reorganized into two new categories: domestic hybrid and international hybrid (Table 2-2). And whether they are domestic or international, hybrids must have on average no less than 20 percent and no more than 70 percent of their assets in equities. Fidelity Puritan Fund, for instance, is now a domestic hybrid. Merrill Lynch Global Allocation B is an international hybrid.

Morningstar has also refined what is considered a domestic portfolio and what is considered an international portfolio. Funds can have up to 40 percent non-U.S. holdings and still be considered domestic, then slotted into one of the nine categories of domestic funds. A fund must be more than 40 percent non-U.S. to be considered an international fund. Thus, SmallCap World Fund, which you might surmise is an international fund investing in small companies, is now considered a domestic small-cap growth fund since it has only 38 percent of its assets abroad.

There's a new line-up among international funds as well. There's a Latin America category, and what was formerly the Pacific investment objective is split into three categories: Diversified Pacific, Pacific ex-Japan, and Japan. For a fund to be categorized by region, at least 75 percent of its assets much be invested in that region. The other international classifications remain the same. A foreign fund invests almost entirely in non-U.S. markets, though it can have up to 10 percent of its assets in the United States. A world fund is just the opposite, it can invest anywhere and has no less than 10 percent of its money in the United States. Diversified emerging markets funds must have at least 50 percent of their assets in the emerging markets.

What doesn't change in the new fund classifications are the specialty or sector funds. The sector fund categories are communications, financial, health care, natural resources, precious metals, real estate, technology, utilities, and specialty-miscellaneous (the few funds that don't fit into any of the other categories).

TABLE 2-2

THE NEW MUTUAL FUND CATEGORIES VS. THE OLD INVESTMENT OBJECTIVES

New ▼	Old ▼
EQUITY FUNDS*	
Large-cap Value	Maximum Growth
Large-cap Blend	Growth
Large-cap Growth	Growth and Income
Mid-cap Value	Equity-Income
Mid-cap Blend	Small Company
Mid-cap Growth	
Small-cap Value	
Small-cap Blend	
Small-cap Growth	
Domestic Hybrid	Balanced
International Hybrid	Asset Allocation
	Multiasset Global
Diversified Emerging Markets	Diversified Emerging Markets
Foreign	Foreign
World	World
Europe	Europe
Diversified Pacific	Pacific Basin
Pacific ex-Japan	
Japan	
Latin America	
BOND FUNDS	
Long Bonds (Gen.)	Corporate—General
Intermediate Bonds (Gen.)	Corporate—High-Quality
Short Bonds (Gen.)	Corporate—High-Yield
Ultrashort	Government—General
Long Government	Government—Adjustable-Rate Mortgages
Intermediate Government	Government—Mortgage
Short Government	Government—Treasury
Municipal National Long	Municipal—National
Municipal National Intermediate	Municipal—Single-State
Municipal Single-State Long	Municipal—California
Municipal Single-State Intermediate	Municipal—New York
Municipal Short	Convertibles
High-Yield	World Bond
Convertibles	Short-Term World Income
International	
Multisector	

*No change in the specialty equity funds.
DATA: MORNINGSTAR INC., BUSINESS WEEK

Morningstar has reorganized its bond fund line-up as well. The conventional bond fund objectives categorize funds mainly by the kinds of bonds they buy—government, corporates, or municipals. We have adopted the new Morningstar system, which looks at both the type of bonds and the average maturity or duration of the fund's bonds. Long-term bond funds are those with durations (a more refined measure of maturity that we'll discuss later in this chapter) of greater than 6 years; intermediate-term funds have durations of greater than 3.5 years and less than 6 years; short-term funds are those with durations of less than 3.5 years but greater than 1. There's one ultra-short category that encompasses both government and corporate bonds and has a duration of less than a year. Municipal funds are organized into national and single-state long- and intermediate-term categories, but all short-term muni funds, whether national or single-state, are in the same category.

Shuffling the bond fund categories will make selecting bond funds and tracking their returns much easier because it's much easier to see how well funds are performing if you compare them to funds with like maturities or durations. On this count, bond funds have always been a little easier to understand than stock equity funds since many have "long-term" or "intermediate" in their titles. Still, by rating funds in their own categories, investors will be able to see more quickly which long-term U.S. government fund has not only the best return but also the best risk-adjusted return as well.

Not all bond funds fit into these categories. Convertible bonds and high-yield bonds, which in many ways have as much to do with the equity market as interest rates, retain their own categories. There's no further differentiation for intermediate or long-term bonds. Most high-yields (and convertibles, too, since most of them are less than investment grade) fall in the short-to-intermediate-term range. The world bond fund category also remains. It picks up the leavings of the short-term world income category, which has too few funds and assets to keep it alive as a separate classification.

Equity Funds

We'll start with equity funds and look first at the larger, lower-risk diversified sorts, such as the large-cap value funds, and eventually work our way to the more aggressive small-cap growth funds. Then we'll examine the hybrid and specialty funds.

LARGE-CAP VALUE FUNDS

You know you should invest in equity mutual funds, but somehow the volatility of the stock market and the possibility of losing your money scares the daylights out of you. If this describes you, try a fund that invests in large-cap value stocks. Of the nine categories of domestic equity funds, these funds are the least risky and perhaps the most palatable for the anxious investor. Most of the funds in this category were formerly in the growth and income and equity–income investment objectives. They keep one eye on downside risk and the other on a stock's upside potential. Some of the larger and better known funds in this category are Fidelity Equity–Income, Fidelity Equity–Income II, Fidelity Destiny I, Fidelity Destiny II, Vanguard/Windsor, Vanguard/Windsor II, and Washington Mutual Investors. The performing large value fund of 1996 was Legg Mason Value Primary Shares, with a 38.3 percent total return (Table 2-3).

Just because they're cautious, doesn't mean these funds can't perform well. During 1996, the funds earned an average 21.1 percent total return—some 3.4 percentage points better than the average fund. Of the 20 largest equity mutual funds, the only ones to beat the S&P 500 were the two Vanguard/Windsor funds. Both funds carried heavier-than-average weightings of financial and energy stocks, sectors that are both relatively rich in dividends and, in 1996, rich in appreciation as well. Financials boomed on strong earnings and industry consolidation; energy issues zoomed on higher oil prices and an increase in exploration and drilling activity. Legg Mason Value Primary Shares has an exceptionally strong five-year performance because it has had, on average, over 40 percent of its assets in financial stocks during a period in which they recovered from near-death prices. Kemper-Dreman High Return A Fund had as much as a 61 percent allocation to financials over the past five years.

Still, two factors are what make these funds relatively conservative. One is the nature of the stocks they buy. No high-flying semiconductor or software stocks here, but some of the biggest names in American business: Philip Morris, Federal National Mortgage Assn., Citicorp, Chrysler, and IBM (Table 2-4). To most value investors, what makes a stock attractive is that it's cheap. Don't confuse cheap with a low price, like $5 or $10 a share. A share of stock is said to be cheap only when it's measured by some valuation crite-

Large-cap value funds are the least risky.

TABLE 2-3

LARGE-CAP VALUE FUNDS
BEST RETURNS

Period ▼	Fund ▼	Total return* ▼
1996	LEGG MASON VALUE PRIMARY SHARES	38.3%
1994-96	LEGG MASON VALUE PRIMARY SHARES	25.5
1992-96	FIDELITY DESTINY I	19.8
1987-96	FIDELITY DESTINY II	18.9

*Average annual, pretax   DATA: MORNINGSTAR INC.

ria such as the p–e ratio and/or p–b ratio and then compared to a benchmark, like the p–e or the p–b of the S&P 500.

That a stock is cheap—suppose it has a lower-than-average p–e ratio—is no guarantee against losing money, since a cheap stock can always get cheaper. But think of it this way: If the market gets hit with a downdraft, cheap stocks can fall, but usually not as far or as hard as expensive stocks. Chances are, you're going to lose more money if an expensive stock becomes cheap than if a cheap stock gets cheaper.

Another important attribute of large value funds is the emphasis on dividend-paying stocks. Some of the funds, like the two Fidelity Equity–Income offerings, stipulate that at least 65 percent of the stocks in the fund must be dividend payers. There's a reason for this: that a company is able to pay a dividend suggests that it is generating cash above and beyond its needs and is not likely to go broke. That doesn't mean that investing in dividend-paying companies is a cinch. These companies still require monitoring. Sometimes dividend payers fail to recognize their problems, refuse to cut dividends when they should, and get into trouble. Since these are large, highly visible companies, investment analysts usually detect the trouble right away. They advise their clients to sell, and the stock starts to fall in anticipation of a dividend cut.

In recent years, neither investors nor companies themselves have paid much attention to dividends. Investors preferred to buy stocks that had greater growth potential than is available in most dividend-paying stocks. And companies themselves responded to the market's appetite for share appreciation by deploying excess cash to buy back shares rather than hike dividends. Some investors argue it's not a bad thing to do. Dividends are considered ordinary income and are taxed at the same rate investors pay on their salary and interest income, which can be as high as 39.6 percent (and that's just the federal tax). When companies buy back shares instead of boosting their dividends, the only shareholders that get taxed are those who sell their shares. If those shares were held for longer than a year, any profits would be taxed at the more favorable long-term capital gains rate, a maximum of 28 percent.

Since these large value funds generate fully taxable dividend income, many advisers counsel high-income investors to use them only in tax-deferred accounts like 401(k)s and IRAs. In such accounts, there's no tax liability until the investor retires and starts drawing the money out.

Be forewarned that many veteran investors don't take a casual view of dividends. In bear markets, a situation that many of today's investors have not experienced, a steady dividend stream becomes a primary support of a stock or a portfolio of stocks. After all, the only way to make money in stocks is through capital appreciation and dividends. When the appreciation part is in doubt, the security of a dividend payout starts to look a whole lot better.

Even though they buy many of the same big, cheap, dividend-paying stocks, some funds in this category stand out with their own particular quirks. Vanguard/Windsor (which is closed to new investors) is not afraid to concentrate its positions. Its 10 largest holdings amount to some 40 percent of the $16.7 billion portfolio. Oppenheimer Quest Opportunity Value Fund A, which is slightly under $1 billion in size, has 57 percent of its portfolio in its top 10 holdings. That Oppenheimer fund has been a top-rated fund for the last two years. The $783 million Babson Value Fund takes a somewhat different tack, keeping the portfolio to 40 stocks, and trying to keep an equal weighting in each. If portfolio manager Nick Whitridge wants to add a new stock, he must sell

TABLE 2-4

LARGE-CAP VALUE FUNDS
LARGEST HOLDINGS

Stock ▼	Percent of net assets ▼
PHILIP MORRIS	1.32%
FEDERAL NATIONAL MORTGAGE ASSOCIATION	1.09
CITICORP	1.07
CHRYSLER	1.02
E.I. DUPONT DE NEMOURS	1.01
ALLSTATE	0.99
CHASE MANHATTAN	0.98
FORD MOTOR	0.94
ATLANTIC RICHFIELD	0.93
IBM	0.92

DATA: MORNINGSTAR INC.

one—presumably the weakest, or the one that went up the most and is no longer a value.

Some analysts interpret such huge concentrations as risky, since there are more eggs in fewer baskets. Managers of these risk-shy funds see it differently. Good value investments are hard to come by, so when you find them, you have to make the most of them. This buy-and-hold tendency is reflected in the low turnover ratios that are only a little more than half the average for equity funds.

Washington Mutual, part of the American Funds family, has a low turnover as well, perhaps because there aren't that many stocks it can invest in. That's because in making investments, the fund follows the "Prudent Man Rule," a rule for fiduciaries that means every investment in the fund must pass certain quality standards and pay a dividend. According to Morningstar analysts, fewer than 300 stocks are even eligible for investment in the fund.

Lexington Corporate Leaders, another large-cap value fund, also has a rather select portfolio. In fact, it's almost a static portfolio. The fund goes back to 1935 and was set up to invest in 30 stocks its founders thought would prosper for years to come. The portfolio manager has the ability to sell a stock, but cannot add a new name. Still, 23 of the original 30 survive, and they include such companies as Mobil, Procter & Gamble, General Electric, DuPont, and Exxon. Even more amazing, the fund is the leading performer in its category over the last 5- and 10-year periods.

LARGE-CAP BLEND FUNDS

Some investment managers call themselves "value" investors, and others "growth" investors. But you'd be hard pressed to find investment managers who call themselves "blend" investors. The blend fund, however, is sort of the vast middle—the huge category into which fall all the funds that don't strongly gravitate to either side of the investment world. The blend funds have attributes of both the growth and value styles. What makes them a blend is that when the portfolio statistics are calculated, the numbers fall in the middle. According to Morningstar's criteria, the combined p–e and p–b ratios of these funds can be no more than 12.5 percent greater than or 12.5 percent less than the combined p–e and p–b ratios for the S&P 500.

Blend does not have to be bland. The best performer of 1996 was Salomon Brothers Investors O Fund (Table 2-5), up 30.4 percent. (That O class of

TABLE 2-5

LARGE-CAP BLEND FUNDS		
BEST RETURNS		
Period ▼	Fund ▼	Total return* ▼
1996	SALOMON BROTHERS INVESTORS O	30.4%
1994-96	RYDEX NOVA	21.6
1992-96	SAFECO EQUITY NO-LOAD	19.8
1987-96	FIDELITY GROWTH AND INCOME	18.9
*Average annual, pretax		DATA: MORNINGSTAR INC.

the fund is closed. New investors can purchase one of three classes of shares that come with loads.) Large-cap blend is a huge category (the largest of the nine categories of U.S. diversified equity funds), and it includes many highly regarded funds: Fidelity Growth & Income, Investment Company of America, Janus, and T. Rowe Price Equity–Income. That Fidelity offering has long been a winner, with high returns and below-average risk scores. Compared to most of Fidelity's megafunds, it had a strong performance in 1996. With $22 billion in assets, portfolio manager Steven Kaye can't be too nimble, but it's far easier to manage a fund of this size in large-cap rather than small or mid-sized stocks. The largest stocks in this universe include Philip Morris, General Electric, Intel, and Merck (Table 2-6).

Though it's a large-cap blend fund, T. Rowe Price Equity–Income still manages to produce a dividend stream that puts most large-cap value funds to shame. Brian Rogers, portfolio manager for more than a decade, often goes against the conventional wisdom, such as buying electric and telephone utilities when few pros had a good word for them. But more often than not, Rogers's moves pay off. Two other Price offerings in this category, too new to be rated, still bear watching—T. Rowe Price Blue Chip Growth Fund and T. Rowe Price Dividend Growth Fund. Dividend Growth Fund, in fact, has a similar risk profile to Equity–Income, but a much smaller asset base.

Another large-cap blend with an admirable long-term record is the Guardian Park Avenue A Fund. The $1.4 billion fund beat the S&P 500 during the last 1-, 5-, and 10-year periods by using a quantitative stock selection system that chooses stocks through both macroeconomic data and fundamental factors like earnings and valuation. One qualitative factor that may make the fund attractive to some: it's had the same portfolio manager, Charles Albers, for nearly 25 years. One drawback is that the fund has the ability to invest in almost any style, and, indeed, three years ago, it was a small-cap value. So if you're a demon for style consistency, the fund is probably not for you.

But perhaps the most compelling—and sometimes controversial—of the large-cap blend funds is the Vanguard Index Trust 500 Portfolio, which is a fund that invests in such a way as to replicate the S&P 500 index. It's an "index" fund and, in a way, it's an unfund-like fund. Its critics call it "guaranteed mediocrity." Why? Unlike the vast majority of mutual funds, the Vanguard Index Trust 500 Portfolio does not attempt to beat a benchmark, only to match it. (The fund is usually off by no more than one-tenth of a percentage point.) Expenses are ridiculously low, less than one-sixth that of the average equity fund. That's because, since the fund does not pick stocks, there's no need for an army of analysts or on-site visits with corporate executives. And, in effect, the fund is managed by a computer. The irony of all this is that over the last three years this "passive" fund—so called because its managers just follow the S&P 500—has beaten 90 percent of active managers. Part of the reason is the low expenses, but even with expenses excluded, the fund has been a winner.

There's a more fundamental reason for the index fund's strong performance. Both in 1995 and 1996, while small and mid-sized stocks did well, the large-cap stocks performed even better. In both years, Wall Street had fears of a recession and bear market, and big investors shifted money out of the smaller stocks and into the bigger. The reason: In a recession, larger companies have more resources and staying power, and in a bear market, larger company stocks are far more liquid and easier to sell than smaller, lesser-known names.

TABLE 2-6

LARGE-CAP BLEND FUNDS

LARGEST HOLDINGS

Stock ▼	Percent of net assets ▼
PHILIP MORRIS	1.73 %
GENERAL ELECTRIC	1.51
FEDERAL NATIONAL MORTGAGE ASSOCIATION	1.10
INTEL	0.96
E.I. DUPONT DE NEMOURS	0.83
EXXON	0.83
PFIZER	0.82
AT&T	0.78
MERCK	0.76
JOHNSON & JOHNSON	0.74

DATA: MORNINGSTAR INC.

Another reason for the index fund's success is the index fund phenomenon itself. Indexing is far more popular among multi-billion-dollar pension funds than it is among individual investors, who still have a little difficulty grasping the notion that matching a benchmark can give you a superior result. But most of the individuals coming to indexing are coming via pension plans, like the employer-sponsored 401(k) plans. In some respects, index funds perform well just because more and more people are choosing to index. In the case of an S&P index fund, every dollar is spent the same way. The more money that goes into indexing, the more money that gets spent investing in those very stocks that make up the index. Is it any surprise they perform so well?

Does this make an S&P index fund a must-buy investment? It's hard to argue against it. Certainly, many investors can benefit by having some portion of their equity portfolio in an index fund. But viewing the index fund over the last five years alone is a little misleading. The stock market has had an extraordinarily good run, with nothing more than a nearly 10 percent fall in stock prices.

But if the market swooned, the index would not look so good. For starters, there's no safety net. Index funds don't carry cash, which cushions a fall, and unlike active managers, they can't redeploy more of their assets to "defensive" sectors like utilities or food stocks. While these actions by active managers can hold a fund back during a bull market, properly deployed, such actions can soften a downturn. So remember when you are considering index funds, there is that drawback.

Indexing itself does not have to be boring. Look at the Rydex Nova Fund. Though designed for market-timers, Rydex will open the door for anyone with a relatively steep $25,000 minimum investment. By design, the Nova fund seeks investment returns that correspond to 150 percent of the performance of the S&P 500. So if the S&P is up 20 percent, this fund should go up 30 percent. Likewise, if the S&P goes down 20 percent, this fund should go down 30 percent. The fund doesn't always reach that 150 percent goal, but it has exceeded the S&P by a good margin. Rydex runs the fund without a share of stock. It's managed with a combination of cash, bonds, and call options.

Rydex Ursa Fund is an index fund in reverse. It's managed to move in the opposite direction of the S&P 500, so its big fat 12 percent loss in 1996 is neither unexpected nor a sign of portfolio ineptitude. Ursa, the Latin word for "bear," is designed to win in a bear market. Its mission is to move in the opposite direction of the S&P 500. (It's run with a combination of cash, options, and futures.) So if the stock market takes a dive, Ursa should shine.

LARGE-CAP GROWTH FUNDS

For the last several years, Wall Streeters dabbled with small-cap and mid-cap stocks but ultimately fled to the safety of large-cap growth stocks. There was good reason for this. At every hint of a slowing economy, these companies—with a clearly defined, "visible" earnings outlook—seemed more and more attractive in an uncertain economic environment. The major stocks in these funds tended to be larger high-tech companies and defensive consumer stocks like food, drugs, and beverages. In 1996, the best fund in this category, Rydex OTC—an index fund investing in the NASDAQ OTC Composite—earned an enviable 43.1 percent total return versus 21.1 percent for the average large-cap growth fund (Table 2-7).

That Rydex OTC Fund may sound miscast among the large-cap growth funds. After all, OTC stocks generally are smaller companies. But the NASDAQ index is, like the S&P 500, a capitalization-weighted index, so the bigger, more successful companies are the largest and tend to dominate the entire index. The largest holding of the fund is Microsoft, which alone counts for 13 percent of the index. In all, tech stocks account for more than one-third of the index. Indeed, the NASDAQ Composite has become another large-cap index, and its fate is tied to that of the large-cap stocks.

The question to consider when investing in these funds is, how long can these stocks continue their winning streak? The conventional wisdom about successful large companies is that inertia will eventually overtake them. Rapidly growing companies become above-average growers, above-

average turns out to be average. The slowdown in growth is predictable—in theory. The art of investing in these companies is getting the timing of that growth right—to buy at a p–e ratio that's fair relative to the growth rate.

Look at Cisco Systems, a principal manufacturer of servers and related equipment that tie together computer networks. It's the top holding of the large-cap growth funds (Table 2-8). The company has gone from annual sales of nearly $70 million in fiscal 1990 to $4.2 billion in the most recent four quarters. That's about a 100 percent a year gain; during the same time, earnings grew an average of nearly 80 percent. Cisco is still chugging along, but it's no longer growing at the same torrid pace of five years ago. (At that time, you would not have found Cisco in a large growth portfolio, but in a small or mid-size fund.) Now, the earnings growth rate is forecast to be about 30 percent. That's a far cry from what it was, but 30 percent annual earnings growth is nearly four times that of the average big-company stock. At the end of 1996, Cisco sold for about 30 times 1997 earnings, which is about fair value for a stock whose earnings are expected to grow at a 30 percent pace.

But then look at Pfizer, the No. 3 holding, one of the world's leading pharmaceutical companies. At the end of 1996, the stock traded at about 23 times earnings though Wall Street's longer-term earnings forecast called for a 15 percent gain. Does that make Pfizer an overpriced stock? By many measures, it does indeed. Why would a fund manager buy Pfizer at 23 times earnings? One reason is that the manager himself had a much higher forecast than that of the consensus of Wall Street analysts. The other bet is that in a slow-growth economy, the market will eventually award higher p–e ratios to companies whose earnings grow at a faster-than-average pace.

The apparent risks notwithstanding, there's a reason why the market values these companies highly. They are superb companies. Many of these companies, though based in the United States, are world-class leaders with substantial operations outside the United States. Coca-Cola, for instance, has no equal anywhere on the globe, and most of its profits are generated outside the United States. Nor does any semiconductor company even approach Intel. Mutual funds that identify and invest in these sorts of companies early on can make a bundle for their investors.

The exceptionally strong returns earned by these funds may be masking some unrealized risks. These large-cap growth stocks are the

TABLE 2-7

LARGE-CAP GROWTH FUNDS

BEST RETURNS

Period	Fund	Total return*
1996	RYDEX OTC	43.1%
1994-96	ENTERPRISE GROWTH A	21.6
1992-96	ENTERPRISE GROWTH A	19.8
1987-96	AMER. CENT.—20TH CENT. ULTRA INV.	18.1

*Average annual, pretax   DATA: MORNINGSTAR INC.

TABLE 2-8

LARGE-CAP GROWTH FUNDS
LARGEST HOLDINGS

Stock ▼	Percent of net assets ▼
CISCO SYSTEMS	2.72%
INTEL	2.08
PFIZER	1.52
CITICORP	1.50
JOHNSON & JOHNSON	1.47
ORACLE	1.39
GENERAL ELECTRIC	1.39
MICROSOFT	1.30
PHILIP MORRIS	1.24

DATA: MORNINGSTAR INC.

most closely watched on Wall Street (they're the so-called "institutional favorites" you hear about in stock market reports), and they're said to be the most efficiently priced. To stand out in this category, a fund manager has to make some serious "sector" bets, concentrating holdings in a few areas that he or she thinks will do a lot better than the large growth stocks in general. During 1996, for instance, Enterprise Growth A had 35 percent of its assets in technology stocks versus 24 percent for the large-cap growth funds and just 11 percent for the S&P 500. Fortunately, that bet paid off, but it could have been a big depressant on the fund had it not.

Of course, sector weightings aren't everything either. American Century–Twentieth Century Ultra Investors, the giant in this category, had an even larger allocation to technology, nearly 44 percent. But while the fund did not collapse in 1996, it still lagged the S&P 500 by a healthy margin. One explanation may be that this fund is playing out of its league. Until five years ago, it was a small company fund. When it hit paydirt and shot up 86 percent in 1991, the assets ballooned—and the managers were forced to move up to larger and larger stocks. There's nothing wrong with that, except the fund built its reputation on a much smaller asset base and much smaller stocks than it now owns.

The next largest fund in this category, Fidelity Growth Company, is no pipsqueak either, with $9 billion in assets under management. The difference is that Fidelity Growth Fund has always worked in the larger company precincts. Until June 1996, the fund had been run by Robert Stansky, the talented manager who succeeded Jeffrey Vinik at the helm of the giant Fidelity Magellan Fund.

Other noteworthy funds in this category include Dreyfus Appreciation, Harbor Capital Appreciation, IDS New Dimensions, Janus Twenty, and Vanguard U.S. Growth. That Vanguard fund is not to be confused with Vanguard Index Trust Growth Portfolio, which is the "growth" half of the S&P 500. That fund is perhaps most exposed to the dangers of high valuations right now. Vanguard U.S. Growth is a managed fund which, though it's planted firmly in the growth camp, has nevertheless managed to earn above-average returns with just average risk.

Perhaps one of the most interesting of the large company growth funds is Stein Roe Young Investor Fund, a fund with a mission to invest in securities issued by companies that affect the lives of children and teenagers. The idea is perhaps more marketing oriented than market oriented. No doubt Stein Roe marketers thought the fund would be a natural for parents and grandparents to buy for their kids. And, in fact, the company developed sales literature and shareholder reports that even a kid could understand.

The reality is that the fund can invest in almost anything. Its second largest holding is Intel. The connection? Well, Intel chips power nearly all the PCs and lots of kids and teenagers use or own their PCs, no? As a practical matter, it's hard to think of a company with a business that couldn't in some way be linked to kids. (A steel company? This company is a supplier to the automakers, who use it to build cars and minivans that parents use to chauffeur their children.) You don't have to be a young investor to invest in or profit from this fund. The fact is, this fund would have admirable returns under any name.

MID-CAP VALUE FUNDS

It's difficult to generalize about mid-cap value funds, or, for that matter, any kind of mid-cap fund. Funds that fit in one of the corners of the nine-category box—large-cap value, large-cap growth, small-cap value, and small-cap growth—are the most distinctive about how they invest. Look inside the portfolio of a small-cap growth or large-cap value fund, and you won't mistake it for anything else.

But what do you make of, say, Sound Shore Fund, the best-performing mid-cap value of the year (Table 2-9). Among the holdings are Wal-Mart Stores, with a whopping $64.4 billion in market capitalization; Federal National Mortgage Assn., with $40.4 billion; and MCI Communications Corp., with $20.2 billion. But there's also relatively small Toy Biz Inc. ($185 million) and Wolverine Tube ($347 million). Still, of the 24 stocks in the fund, 14 are distinctively mid-cap. They include Amphenol, the fund's second largest holding; Compuware, the fourth; and Echlin, the fifth. All told, Sound Shore's median market cap comes out to $2 billion.

Sound Shore is not at all unusual for a mid-cap value fund. Very often, these funds buy a wide range of stocks, and for these managers, capitalization is not as important as what they consider to be a good investment idea. That's pretty much what you see in Michael F. Price's enormously successful Mutual Series funds—now known as Franklin Mutual Shares Z, Franklin Mutual Qualified Z, and Franklin Mutual Beacon Z (all three rate three upward-pointing arrows). They're three of the five largest funds in this category. Like many mid-cap value funds, Price's funds include a wide range of investments chosen more for their attractiveness as value plays than to meet any market capitalization target. One of Price's big successes of recent years was to take a big stake in the large but undervalued Chase Manhattan Corp. and lobby the management, the board of directors, and, if necessary, other big shareholders into taking action to improve "shareholder value." That's the buzz word for "get the stock price up—or else." In several months' time, Chase agreed to a merger with rival Chemical Banking Corp. to create a bank holding company larger than Citicorp. Even while participating in the megabanking play, the portfolios remained a mid-cap investor.

Price's funds still own a good chunk of Chase Manhattan stock, and because of those funds' size, Chase is the No. 1 holding of the mid-cap value funds, comprising 2.1 percent of total net assets (Table 2-10). Several other of Price's largest holdings also appear on this list: U.S.

TABLE 2-10

MID-CAP VALUE FUNDS	
LARGEST HOLDINGS	
Stock ▼	Percent of net assets ▼
CHASE MANHATTAN	2.08 %
US WEST MEDIA GROUP	1.14
PHILIP MORRIS	1.03
RJR NABISCO HOLDINGS	0.94
FIRST USA	0.81
DUN & BRADSTREET	0.67
MELLON BANK	0.65
AMBAC	0.64
INVESTOR CL. B	0.63
LOCKHEED MARTIN	0.61

DATA: MORNINGSTAR INC.

West Media Group, RJR Nabisco Holdings, and Investor Cl.B. (a Swedish holding company). None of them are particularly mid-cap, but they definitely are value plays.

Another sort of mid-cap value fund is the $4.2 billion Oakmark Fund, a formerly very successful small-cap value fund that, in getting larger, climbed the market-cap ladder. In 1992, the fund's first full year, Oakmark held 40 stocks with a median market cap of a little over $600 million. But then the money came cascading in on the strength of portfolio manager Robert J. Sanborn's superstar returns (30 percent for four months of 1991, followed by 48.9 percent in 1992 and 30.5 percent in 1993). By the end of 1993, the fund had over $1.2 billion, and was heading for mid-cap climes. By 1996, the fund neared $4 billion, 90 stocks, and a median market cap of over $3 billion. Since the fund's charter says nothing about market cap, Oakmark could become a large-cap fund unless Sanborn takes some steps to slow the market cap down.

Many mid-cap value funds have long used "value" in their names, but only recently have some funds started to call themselves "mid-cap" or even "mid-cap value." Pioneer Three Fund changed its name to Pioneer Mid-Cap Fund in February 1996. A few months later, Lord Abbett Value Appreciation Fund was renamed Lord Abbett Mid-Cap Value Fund. What's behind the name changes? One reason is the recognition of investor interest in funds that define their investment style. The other reason may be marketing. Neither the Pioneer nor the Lord Abbett fund had distinguished track records, so there was nothing to lose in changing the names. If

TABLE 2-9

MID-CAP VALUE FUNDS		
BEST RETURNS		
Period ▼	Fund ▼	Total return* ▼
1996	SOUND SHORE	33.7 %
1994-96	GOLDMAN SACHS GROWTH AND INCOME	21.2
1992-96	OAKMARK	25.7
1987-96	STRONG SCHAFER VALUE	16.3

*Average annual, pretax   DATA: MORNINGSTAR INC.

nothing else, it might attract money that's looking for a mid-cap home.

MID-CAP BLEND FUNDS

Many funds will call themselves mid-cap value or mid-cap growth, but it's unlikely a fund company will ever market a fund as a mid-cap blend. Middle of the road in market cap without a distinct value or growth bent? Sounds like a big yawner—or a marketing challenge.

But consider this: the supersized $54 billion Fidelity Magellan Fund looks like a large-cap fund at the moment, but since Morningstar began tracking investment style in 1990, Magellan has been dead center in the nine-box grid. Magellan's had its problems of late: an ill-timed shift into long-term Treasury bonds cost the fund dearly early in 1996 when the stock market rose and the bond market sank, a move that led to the eventual resignation of portfolio manager Jeffrey Vinik. Fidelity's marketing department has presented its superstar fund many ways, but never as a mid-cap blend or even a mid-cap fund. The same goes for Fidelity Contrafund, at $23.8 billion, the second-largest fund in this category and the best-performing fund over the last 10 years (Table 2-11). Part of Contrafund's excellent long-term record actually belongs to Vinik who ran the fund for several years before moving to Magellan. Will Danoff has piloted Contrafund for over six years, which, at Fidelity, is an eternity. The giant fund family usually switches fund manager assignments more frequently than that.

Over the years, Fidelity Magellan built its reputation on savvy stockpicking (some argue that if Vinik had stuck to this and not made a foray into bonds, he'd still be running the fund)—and there's nothing bland about that. Isn't that what mutual funds are all about? It makes a lot of sense that many of the funds run by star stockpickers wind up in this category—they'll go to all corners of the stock market for a good invest-

TABLE 2-12

MID-CAP BLEND FUNDS	
LARGEST HOLDINGS	
Stock ▼	Percent of net assets ▼
U.S. TREASURY NOTE 5.875% 07/31/97	1.07 %
INTEL	0.96
CATERPILLAR	0.90
PHILIP MORRIS	0.74
CHRYSLER	0.74
FEDERAL NATIONAL MORTGAGE ASSOCIATION	0.72
GENERAL MOTORS	0.67
CSX	0.64
U.S. TREASURY BOND 6.25% 08/15/23	0.61
SCHLUMBERGER	0.56

DATA: MORNINGSTAR INC.

ment. And when the composition of those portfolios are calculated, they wind up smack in the middle of the pack.

The holdings of the two big Fidelity funds—together they amount to nearly half the assets in the mid-cap blend category—dominate the list of top holdings (Table 2-12). That's why 2 of the top 10 holdings are various U.S. Treasury bonds. That's the legacy of the large position in Treasury bonds held by Magellan and, to a much lesser extent, Contrafund during 1996. While those Fidelity funds were loaded up on bonds, the average mid-cap blend had less than 2 percent. Chances are, over time, those bond holdings will disappear from the category's top 10.

If the bonds were gone, the stocks left behind don't seem to be mid-cap: General Motors, Chrysler, and Caterpillar are hardly mid-cap companies. But again, there are two ways to be a mid-cap fund: one is to buy mid-cap stocks, the other is to have a wide range in which the median is a mid-cap. When funds take the former tack, their largest holdings can indeed be very large.

A more typical mid-cap fund might be Mairs & Power Growth Fund, a newcomer to the list of three-up-arrow funds. The largest holding is Medtronic, which at $16.5 billion is a smaller large-cap stock. But other top holdings fall squarely in the mid-cap range: BMC Industries, ADC Telecommunications, Saint Paul Cos., and Ecolab. Another long-standing mid-cap player is the Nicholas Fund, a $4.1 billion fund run by the man whose name is on the door, Albert Nicholas. By charter, it's supposed to invest in small-cap and mid-cap companies, and it does. Many years ago, the fund had more of a small-cap cast, but

TABLE 2-11

MID-CAP BLEND FUNDS		
BEST RETURNS		
Period ▼	Fund ▼	Total return* ▼
1996	SALOMON BROTHERS CAPITAL	33.3 %
1994-96	FRANKLIN GROWTH I	21.2
1992-96	FRANKLIN GROWTH I	25.7
1987-96	FIDELITY CONTRAFUND	16.3

*Average annual, pretax   DATA: MORNINGSTAR INC.

with the growth in assets, the fund has tended to own some larger stocks.

Both the Mairs & Power and the Nicholas funds have an attribute that's a little more common in this category than in most others—portfolio managers with lots of longevity. Nicholas has been running his fund since 1969; George Mairs, since 1980. Donald Yacktman started the fund that bears his name in 1992. But that came after a long career running other funds, and he was no babe in the business. Mario Gabelli, whose Gabelli Asset Fund is in this category, is another veteran stockpicker who was a portfolio manager for years before branching out into mutual funds about 10 years ago.

Another marathoner in this category is Kenneth Heebner of CGM Capital Development Fund. He's been running that fund for 20 years. Heebner, known for making bold bets on particular stocks and industry sectors, has an excellent 15-year record. But interspersed in those years are some nasty single-year surprises. In four of those years, he lagged the S&P 500 by more than 10 percentage points, and in 1994, the fund was actually down nearly 23 percent.

MID-CAP GROWTH FUNDS

Scratch beneath the surface of a mid-cap growth fund, and you may just find a successful small-cap growth fund. Many funds, of course, have long plowed the sometimes neglected area of mid-cap stocks, but they never presented themselves as such. Brian W. H. Berghuis, portfolio manager of T. Rowe Price Mid-Cap Growth Fund, is fond of recalling that when his fund started in 1992, the term "mid-cap investing" was barely on Wall Street's radar screen. Berghuis seized the ground because, he felt, investors could earn nearly as much money with mid-caps as small-caps but take on a lot less risk. Berghuis's strategy is to buy the growth stocks when they are in the $500 million-to-$1.5 billion market cap range and let them roll. If this strategy is successful, they'll grow into mid-caps. If you start with mid-caps, the successful ones eventually graduate to the big leagues.

There have always been mid-cap growth funds, though, even if they didn't explicitly present themselves that way. The William Blair Growth Fund, for instance, invests in growth stocks of all market capitalizations, but has always balanced the mix so that it falls smack in the middle. The New Economy Fund does not specifically mention mid-cap companies in its prospectus objective, but it's long been a mid-cap investor.

Some of the better-known mid-cap growth funds certainly didn't start out that way. Look at PBHG Growth Fund, which has the highest 5-year and 10-year returns of the group (Table 2-13). The prospectus allows the fund to invest in companies with either revenues or market capitalizations of up to $2 billion. That's the limit. Until 1995, the fund always managed to keep its median market cap well within the small-cap limits. And, of course, the fund excelled in that tough field, especially in the 1990s. In 1991 and 1995, the fund earned a little better than 50 percent returns.

A fund's success as a small-cap investor leads to a torrent of new shareholders, new money, and the inevitable "market cap creep." With more and more money, fund managers are simply forced to buy larger- and larger-cap stocks to fill the portfolio. Among the better-known mid-caps that grew into this category are Alger Small Capitalization, American Century–Twentieth Century Vista Investors, Fidelity OTC, MFS Emerging Growth B, Putnam Voyager A, and PBHG Growth.

At PBHG Growth, the fund assets grew so much it was remarkable that fund manager Gary Pilgrim could keep the fund focused on small-cap stocks as long as he did. PBHG Growth swelled to $187 million at the end of 1993 from $3 million at the end of 1992. By the end of 1995, the fund had $2 billion in assets, already a sizeable fund for one with a small-cap mission. The fund had been closed for awhile in 1995, but reopened at the start of 1996, and the money rushed in again. By year-end, assets were up to $5.9 billion. Coincidentally, in 1996, PBHG Growth could only muster a 9.8 percent total return, the fund's worst showing in seven years. Perhaps the amount of money has finally overwhelmed the fund's ability to manage it to earn the superior returns to which its shareholders had become accustomed.

TABLE 2-13

MID-CAP GROWTH FUNDS
BEST RETURNS

Period	Fund	Total return*
1996	PBHG CORE GROWTH	33.3%
1994-96	ROBERTSON STEPHENS VALUE + GROWTH	26.1
1992-96	PBHG GROWTH	26.6
1987-96	PBHG GROWTH	21.3

*Average annual, pretax   DATA: MORNINGSTAR INC.

TABLE 2-14

MID-CAP GROWTH FUNDS
LARGEST HOLDINGS

Stock ▼	Percent of net assets ▼
HFS	1.46 %
CISCO SYSTEMS	1.28
COMPUTER ASSOCIATES INTL.	0.87
INTEL	0.83
ORACLE	0.74
MICROSOFT	0.72
HBO & CO.	0.64
ASCEND COMMUNICATIONS	0.63
CASCADE COMMUNICATIONS	0.61
PARAMETRIC TECHNOLOGY	0.61

DATA: MORNINGSTAR INC.

Of course, even if a successful small-cap growth fund is closed to new investors, it still can become a mid-cap fund by virtue of its successes. If enough small-cap stocks flourish, they eventually become mid-caps. Some managers will sell them out of the portfolio at that point, but not all. If you have enough of them, the fund will evolve into a mid-cap investor. That's a result of successful investing

As is much the case with the other mid-cap fund categories, most of the largest holdings are not mid-cap companies themselves (Table 2-14). Only No. 9 of the 10 largest, Cascade Communications Corp., with a market cap of $3.1 billion, is a true mid-cap. HBO & Co. (a health-care management firm, not a cable TV operator), the seventh largest holding, is barely over the large-cap threshold, at $5.4 billion. The largest holding, HFS, a franchiser of hotels and real estate agencies, has a $9 billion market cap.

The mid-cap growth category also contains several quirky funds worth mentioning. One, Merrill Lynch Growth B, earned top returns even while carrying a sizeable cash hoard. While the cash cushions the downswings, the fund manager must work extra hard with the invested assets to overcome the drag of cash in a bull market. So far, portfolio manager Stephen Johnes has been able to pull it off, mainly by concentrating the holdings in sectors which he thinks will outperform.

Another notable is MFS Research A, a fund which one Morningstar analyst says shows that "20 heads are better than one." Kevin R. Peake is the portfolio manager but does not run the fund in the conventional sense. Peake is head of the firm's research department and it's the analysts who contribute the investment ideas to the fund.

It's not by definition a mid-cap fund, but the fund attempts to diversify across a broad spectrum, and so winds up in the mid-cap camp.

The Janus Olympus Fund, which is less than two years old, is one of the more interesting offerings in this category. Portfolio manager Scott W. Schoelzel runs a fairly concentrated portfolio, with only about 40 holdings. He describes the portfolio as a "barbell." The stocks tend to fall in one of two categories—large, well-established companies with steady and visible growth in earnings, or smaller, more rapidly growing, and more risky, companies. The result is a portfolio that mixes Citicorp, Coca-Cola, and Microsoft with hot growth names like Ascend Communications, Biogen, and Netscape Communications. And though the fund is young, the approach looks promising.

SMALL-CAP VALUE FUNDS

When you mention investing in small companies, many people think of an Internet start-up or biotech research firms or faddish specialty retailers or fast-food chains. Now look at the major holdings of Oakmark Small Cap, the best small-cap value fund of 1996 (Table 2-15). There's a manufacturing conglomerate, a machine tool maker, a real estate development, a cable TV operator, and a community bank. Doesn't sound real sexy or cutting edge, does it?

That doesn't mean you can't make money in these stocks. Indeed, a well-run company in a prosaic business can be a big money-maker. These companies don't usually have to worry too much that their new technology will become obsolete in six months or that new competitors are opening their doors every day. That's usually not the case.

Small-cap value stocks—and the funds that invest in them—often run counter to the faster-paced, high fliers that usually make the headlines. When those "momentum" stocks sputter, as they did in the second half of 1996, the small-cap

TABLE 2-15

SMALL-CAP VALUE FUNDS
BEST RETURNS

Period ▼	Fund ▼	Total return* ▼
1996	OAKMARK SMALL CAP	39.8 %
1994-96	FPA CAPITAL	28.2
1992-96	FPA CAPITAL	24.5
1987-96	FPA CAPITAL	21.4

*Average annual, pretax   DATA: MORNINGSTAR INC.

TABLE 2-16

SMALL-CAP VALUE FUNDS
LARGEST HOLDINGS

Stock ▼	Percent of net assets ▼
BANCTEC	0.29 %
ICN PHARMACEUTICALS	0.24
BELDEN	0.23
CHARMING SHOPPES	0.22
UNIVERSAL HEALTH SVCS. CL. B	0.22
ETHAN ALLEN INTERIORS	0.21
ALLIANT TECHSYSTEMS	0.19
FINGERHUT	0.19
FREMONT GENERAL	0.19
AIR EXPRESS INTERNATIONAL	0.19

DATA: MORNINGSTAR INC.

value stocks usually pick up steam. The stock market tends to swing back and forth between favoring value stocks and growth stocks. Over the last 3- and 10-year periods, small-cap growth beat small-cap value. But over the last 1- and 5-year periods, small-cap value held sway.

There's another advantage to owning small-cap value funds. Because the stocks they buy are already "cheap" when measured by traditional yardsticks like p–e ratios, p–b ratios, and dividend yields, the funds tend to be less volatile than the funds that buy the more traditional emerging growth stocks. In effect, these funds are a way to play the small-cap market without wild price swings, a more palatable way to play small-cap stocks for nervous investors.

As a result, small-cap value funds fare a lot better in risk-adjusted ratings than the small-cap growth. In the 1997 BUSINESS WEEK Mutual Fund Scoreboard, seven small-cap value funds earned three upward-pointing arrows, the highest rating for risk-adjusted returns. No small-cap growth or small-cap blend funds made it onto the overall top performers' list.

Small-cap value funds can be a pretty diverse lot, if only because there are so many more companies they can invest in. Large-cap growth funds pretty much all choose from among the same 200 to 300 companies. Even small-cap growth funds tend to be duplicative in their holdings because the managers are mainly seeking the same lightning-like emerging growth companies. But in small-cap value, there are literally thousands of possible investments.

That doesn't mean it's easy to invest in these companies. Many of the stocks are illiquid. That

is, there's little day-to-day trading in the stocks because there are not that many shares to start with, and many of them are "closely held," that is, in the hands of a founder, some family members, or managers. Because of the limitations of this corner of the market, small-cap value funds sometimes face the choice of closing to new investors, or moving up the capitalization ladder. Babson Enterprise, FPA Capital, Franklin Balance Sheet Investment, Heartland Value, and T. Rowe Price Small-Cap Value have dealt with size by closing to new investors. Even Fidelity Low-Priced Stock Fund, a top-rated fund from this category, was closed several times to give the portfolio manager time to digest the cash. That's unusual for Fidelity, where the corporate motto has usually been "size is no object."

Some small-cap value managers break this universe into even smaller segments. Consider the Royce Micro-Cap Fund and Royce Premier Funds. Portfolio manager Charles Royce takes distinctly different approaches to the two. Royce Premier chooses its investments from among 1400 or so small-cap companies with market capitalizations of $300 million to $1 billion. Most small-cap funds and institutional investors stalk that prey, he says, and so it's a fairly efficient market. So with Royce Premier he makes bigger bets, limiting his holdings to about 50 companies and concentrating them in several sectors. For Royce Micro-Cap, he looks to a universe of some 6500 companies, with market caps of between $5 million and $300 million. Since this micro-market is much less liquid, he owns many more stocks—about 150—in a broadly diversified portfolio. Another Royce-run fund, Pennsylvania Mutual Fund, has a mix of the two strategies.

Perhaps because this universe is so diverse, there is far less concentration in the funds' largest holdings (Table 2-16). For instance, the largest holding of the small-cap value funds is Banctec, a company that provides data processing services for small banks. It's just 0.29 percent of the categories' collective holdings. Compare that to the top name in mid-cap value, Chase Manhattan Corp., which commands 2.1 percent of the category's holding. What's more, these major holdings really are small companies. Of the 10 largest, one has a market capitalization slightly greater than $1 billion. The rest are comfortably below that.

SMALL-CAP BLEND FUNDS

If you are only going to invest in one small-cap fund, you may want to go up the middle with a

TABLE 2-17

SMALL-CAP BLEND FUNDS
BEST RETURNS

Period	Fund	Total return*
1996	FIDELITY EXPORT	38.6%
1994-96	G.T. GLOBAL AMERICA GROWTH A	18.1
1992-96	G.T. GLOBAL AMERICA GROWTH A	18.7
1987-96	LEGG MASON SPECIAL INVEST. PRIM.	14.6

*Average annual, pretax   DATA: MORNINGSTAR INC.

small-cap blend fund. Dreyfus New Leaders, for instance, builds its portfolio with two managers who mix value and growth plays. The value manager buys financial and energy stocks, the growth manager, consumer products and health-care companies. But taken as a whole, the blended funds tend to behave a little more like growth funds than value. So they're not exactly the same as buying 50 percent each of a small-cap growth and small-cap value fund. Still, these funds can give investors much of the taste of small-cap growth without quite as much hair-raising volatility.

The best performer in 1996 was the Fidelity Export Fund, up 38.6 percent. For the three- and five-year periods, the best returns of the category were produced by G.T. Global America Growth A (Table 2-17). Investors should be wary of chasing that fund because it's now gone upscale. In January 1997, the fund was renamed G.T. Global America Mid-Cap Growth, given a new management team, and sent off to work the mid-cap universe of stocks.

But Fidelity Export, at least, looks like a good bet to remain a small-cap fund. The fund isn't a small-cap by definition, though its prospectus allows that the companies it invests in will likely have small market capitalizations. The fund's stated mission is to invest at least 65 percent of its assets in North American companies that derive at least 10 percent of their revenues from exported goods or services. Large companies, such as Philip Morris or Procter & Gamble, certainly derive much more of their sales and profits from overseas, but they're not usually exporters. They manufacture their wares all over the world. The idea in this fund is that if a smaller company with far fewer resources than the big firms can develop an export business, it has to be smarter or offer better products.

Other funds in this category are more general and less specific in their investment objectives. Basically, they're just looking for money-making

opportunities in small-cap stocks. Sure, many portfolio managers identify investment "themes," and search for the best stocks to play them. Take, for example, Princor Emerging Growth A, a very close runner-up to G.T. Global America Growth A in three-year returns. The management of that fund believes that the aging of America opens up vast money-making opportunities for financial services and health-care providers. So it maintains larger stakes in financial and health-care companies. That's not so unusual, either. The largest holdings of the small-cap blend funds include health-care, financial, and technology companies (Table 2-18).

The runner-up in five-year returns, Crabbe Huson Special Primary Shares, looks a lot better than it actually is. Those high returns are mainly the product of two sensational back-to-back years, 1992 and 1993, in which the fund logged 33.4 percent and 34.6 percent, respectively—numbers that helped put the little-known Portland, Oregon, investment management company on the mutual fund map. Manager James E. Crabbe even successfully negotiated the volatile 1994 stock market, earning 11.7 percent when most of his peers were in the red. The fund's undoing came in 1995 and 1996, when Crabbe used his ability to sell stocks short. (In a short sale, an investor borrows stock, sells it, and hopes to buy it back at a lower price. In effect, it's a bet that the stock will go down. If the stock goes up, he loses money.) He bet that the technology sector was overpriced and headed for a fall. But he was wrong, and the short positions lost money and dragged down the overall results. The fund's

TABLE 2-18

SMALL-CAP BLEND FUNDS
LARGEST HOLDINGS

Stock	Percent of net assets
KEANE	0.32%
VIVRA	0.26
PHILIP MORRIS	0.23
AMERICA ONLINE	0.22
STANDARD FEDERAL BANCORP	0.21
ORYX ENERGY	0.21
MAGELLAN HEALTH SERVICES	0.21
WESTERN DIGITAL	0.21
CAPITAL RE	0.20
STORAGE TECHNOLOGY	0.20

DATA: MORNINGSTAR INC.

1995 return was a meager 10.8 percent; 1996, a scant 5.9 percent.

The small-cap blend category is where you will find index funds. The Vanguard Group, the largest manager of indexed mutual funds, has several in this category—Vanguard Index Small Cap Stock, which tracks the Russell 2000 stock index, and Vanguard Index Extended Market, which tracks the Wilshire 4500 (which is roughly the 5000 largest U.S. stocks without the 500 at the top of the list). Vanguard Index Small Cap Stock is the "smaller" of the two. The median market capitalization is $555 million, well within the small-cap parameters. The median market cap on Extended Market is $1.2 billion, which, if it continues to grow, may well become a mid-cap fund. Over the last one- and five-year periods, the Small Cap fund outperformed Extended Market, while Extended Market led during the last three years.

While index funds have made mincemeat of stockpicking fund managers in the large-cap arena, the case for indexing among small-cap stocks is not so clear cut. Active managers argue that these stocks are less efficient than big-caps and they can exploit these inefficiencies through good stock selection. The index funds say the higher costs of operating in the small-cap arena wipe out any gains from stockpicking. New research from Morningstar Inc. comes to two conclusions about small-cap index funds. During bull markets, they edge out actively run small-company funds using the same investment style. During bear markets, they lag, and their overall risk–return profiles are equal or slightly worse than those of actively managed rivals.

SMALL-CAP GROWTH FUNDS

Strap on your seat belt, put on a crash helmet. Small-cap growth funds are the most volatile of the nine U.S. diversified fund categories. In theory, this should be the most rewarding kind of fund. The fund managers are investing in small, rapidly growing companies. When these high-octane stocks work, they can make big, big bucks for fund investors. When they flop, by failing to meet an expected profit forecast or bumbling a new product, look out below. There's few buyers for those busted emerging growth stocks when all the small-cap growth managers want to sell. So they sell what they can, and mark down the rest of their holdings.

Still, there's plenty of potential in these stocks and these funds because of some of the simple laws of percentages. There's no limit on how much a successful company can earn or gain in stock value. But in a bum stock, the maximum loss is only 100 percent—few fund managers hold on to a losing situation to that point. A small-cap growth fund doesn't have to hit a home run with every stock; a handful will more than carry the rest of the portfolio to fund stardom in any one year.

The best one-year return belongs to a relative newcomer, as is not uncommon in this neighborhood of funddom—Fremont U.S. Micro-Cap, up 48.7 percent (Table 2-19). Micro-cap stocks—generally speaking, companies with market capitalizations of less than $100 million—were barely on investors' radar screens a few years ago. But in 1996 they appeared like jumbo jets. From January through May, the micro-cap funds racked up year-to-date returns in excess of 40 percent. But then that balloon was pricked and the micro-cap growth stocks, perhaps the riskiest of the riskiest fund category, plummeted. Through superior stock selection, portfolio manager Robert Kern was able to steer Fremont U.S. Micro-Cap around the maelstrom in his corner of the market.

Van Wagoner Micro-Cap, one of the brand new offerings of 1996, was not so lucky. The fund had a strong enough start, up 44 percent by mid-May, with a heavy dollop of initial public offerings (IPOs), a staple of many micro-cap and small-cap growth funds. Like Fremont, Van Wagoner plunged at mid-year. With some recovery in prices, the fund managed to finish the year with a 24.5 percent total return. Still, few Van Wagoner shareholders actually did that well. The fund did not even open for business until early January, so relatively few shareholders had the benefit of the entire rise.

Whether micro-cap funds ultimately pay off remains to be seen. There haven't been enough of them in operation long enough to make any judgments. Several of the older micro-caps, Babson Enterprise and Royce Micro-Cap, work the value

TABLE 2-19

SMALL-CAP GROWTH FUNDS		
BEST RETURNS		
Period ▼	Fund ▼	Total return* ▼
1996	FREMONT U.S. MICRO-CAP	48.7%
1994-96	PBHG EMERGING GROWTH	29.1
1992-96	AIM AGGRESSIVE GROWTH	24.5
1987-96	KAUFMANN	19.3
*Average annual, pretax		DATA: MORNINGSTAR INC.

side of Wall Street. They do not invest in IPOs or hot Internet software companies and do not show a lot of volatility. Capital market theory argues that the highest returns go to those who take the highest risks. By that reckoning, funds like Fremont and Van Wagoner should make money for investors over the long haul.

Most investors, however, may feel more comfortable with more mainstream small-cap growth funds. Sure, at times, they can be heavy investors in volatile market sectors, like technology. But as a group, it pays to shop around. PBHG Emerging Growth, the fund with the best three-year returns, has at times had nearly half the portfolio in tech stocks. But that's not necessarily typical of small-cap growth. The list of the category's largest holdings includes technology, but also health-care, fast-food restaurants, office products, and a regional railroad (Table 2-20).

Still, these funds are not for the faint of heart. Many of the funds practice an investment strategy called "momentum investing," buying the stocks of companies with a high earnings growth rate and great prospects that this will continue—companies with "momentum."

Practioners of this strategy don't believe in buying cheap stocks and selling them when they move up. Their game is to buy what's moving up and sell it when it moves up higher. In other words, "buy high, sell higher." The distinguishing characteristics of the stocks these funds traffic in is their high price-to-earnings ratios. Three funds in this category have average p–e ratios of 50. About one-third of the rated funds in this category have a risk rating of "very high" compared to less than 10 percent of all equity funds.

Among the momentum funds are AIM Aggressive Growth A Fund and the Kaufmann Fund, both the top return funds for the last 5- and 10-year periods, respectively. American Century–Twentieth Century Giftrust Investors had long been a successful momentum player, but in 1996, like many other momentum players, it lost the "mo." This unusual fund, which demands a long-term perspective because it locks shareholders in for a minimum of 10 years, earned only 5.8 percent.

It's important to note that not all small-cap growth funds take their investors on these wild rides. Baron Asset Fund, for instance, has an enviable 20 percent average annual total return for the last five years with only an average risk rating. The Acorn Fund, with a 17.6 percent average annual return, carries only average risk, as does Manager Special Equity Fund, with a 17.4 percent average annual return.

TABLE 2-20

SMALL-CAP GROWTH FUNDS	
LARGEST HOLDINGS	
Stock ▼	Percent of net assets ▼
HFS	0.55%
CASCADE COMMUNICATIONS	0.49
WISCONSIN CENTRAL TRANSPORT	0.46
RATIONAL SOFTWARE	0.41
MCAFEE ASSOCIATES	0.39
DURA PHARMACEUTICALS	0.37
PAPA JOHN'S INTERNATIONAL	0.36
LINCARE HOLDINGS	0.36
OMNICARE	0.35
VIKING OFFICE PRODUCTS	0.35

DATA: MORNINGSTAR INC.

HYBRID FUNDS—DOMESTIC AND INTERNATIONAL

Domestic and international hybrid funds are also new investment categories. There's really nothing new here, just reorganization of the funds formerly classified as balanced, asset allocation, or multiasset global. Basically, they are funds that regularly own equities, but may also mix them with bonds, cash, and sometimes gold. Because these funds offer diversification among types of assets as well as diversification among securities, they have become popular vehicles for retirement plans such as individual retirement accounts (IRAs) and employer-sponsored plans like 401(k)s. Especially in retirement plans that don't offer a wide variety of funds, an asset allocation option can make an appealing choice.

Outside the retirement plan, investors don't really need the hybrid funds. Investors assemble diversified fund portfolios on their own, of course, selecting the desired mix of equity and bond funds, both U.S. and foreign, and adding in gold or real estate funds for diversification. But that doesn't come cheaply. It may take a $10,000 to $20,000 stake to make the minimum purchases in all the kinds of funds you might need. With many of these hybrids, you can get the diversification and breadth of investment with just a minimum investment of a few thousand dollars.

Before investing in some of these retirement-oriented hybrids, investors are asked to complete a questionnaire that helps to determine their risk-taking ability. Then, depending on the score, investors are pointed toward an aggressive, moderate, or conservative asset allocation fund, with the most aggressive usually taking the most risk. Those most aggressive funds are usually recommended to the younger investors. Fidelity is the leader in this product, with its Asset Manager series of funds. Putnam, T. Rowe Price, and Vanguard have also introduced their own versions of the Asset Manager approach. Obviously, over time, the investor is going to have to move from the growth to the middle of the road and, eventually, to the most conservative portfolio. Stagecoach Funds, the mutual fund arm of Wells Fargo Bank, takes a different approach. Stagecoach LifePath Funds have different "target maturities" starting with the year 2000. Investors who will be retiring around 2020, for instance, would choose the 2020 fund, which would gradually adjust its portfolio toward a more conservative mix as its shareholders age. Stagecoach also has a 2040 Retirement Fund, which might make a good choice for someone just getting out of college now.

Not all the hybrids come from the former balanced and asset allocation classes. There are some well-regarded funds that were previously considered all-equity holdings. FPA Paramount Fund, the top-performing domestic hybrid fund of 1996 and the 1987–1996 period (Table 2-21), was a growth and income fund under the old investment objective classifications. Though it's an equity fund, manager William Sams is a "value" investor who will buy bonds or cash if he thinks there's more money to be had there than in equities—and there's often a big chunk of one or the other. Hence, the fund's now a hybrid.

The Third Avenue Value Fund, formerly in the growth-fund investment objective, now resides among the domestic hybrids. This fund, a three-up-arrow performer both in all fund ratings and among the domestic hybrids, has always mixed stocks and bonds, but it's not the typical mix of blue-chip stocks and U.S. government or investment-grade bonds. The securities are often distressed properties. That's just fine, because portfolio manager Martin Whitman is a wiz at ferreting out those which will come back to life and rebound in price. Whitman's type of fund is fairly unique. The only things close to it are the Franklin Mutual Shares and its sister funds.

The majority of domestic hybrid funds are the old "balanced" funds, which are the "sensible shoes" of the mutual fund business—prudent, practical, and, yes, boring. With these funds you get stocks for growth and bonds for income—and a portfolio manager who gets paid to figure out how much of each you need. There's nothing trendy about balanced funds, either. They are among the oldest funds. Vanguard/Wellington Fund opened up shop in 1928, and about a dozen more date back to the 1930s. Invesco Balanced, the best domestic hybrid for the last three years, is a relatively new offering to the category. The fund is just old enough to get a three-year return.

The balanced fund is based on the principle that stock prices and bond prices go in opposite directions. In a booming economy, for instance, stocks rise because of improving corporate profitability. The boom creates increasing demand for credit, so interest rates rise and bond prices fall. In 1996, the economy remained fairly strong, though hardly robust. Long-term interest rates rose about 1 percentage point, which was bad for bonds, though certainly not as bad as the 2-percentage-point rise in 1994. Then, in a recession, the opposite is supposed to happen: Stocks fall and bonds rise. But in the recession of 1990, both stocks and bonds tumbled. And in 1991, 1993, and 1995, both stocks and bonds went up together; and in 1990 and 1994, they fell side by side. The bottom line: Balanced funds on average did not distinguish themselves during 1994 or 1996, nor did they, as a group, suffer embarrassment. On average, their returns were less than those of pure equity funds but higher than those of bond funds.

Balanced funds are far from uniform in their results. Their returns depend on how the portfolio managers fill in the stock and bond portions of their portfolios. In 1996, the funds that had large-cap stocks in the equity portion and cash or short-term bonds in the fixed-income portion did best. Of course, balanced funds are pitched to investors as conservative investments and tend to own blue-chip stocks in most cases. Among the largest holdings are familiar blue-chips like Philip Morris, General Electric, and Bristol-Myers Squibb (Table 2-22).

The balanced funds' long histories may give comfort to some investors. Over the last few

TABLE 2-21

DOMESTIC HYBRID FUNDS
BEST RETURNS

Period ▼	Fund ▼	Total return* ▼
1996	FPA PARAMOUNT	29.4%
1994-96	INVESCO BALANCED	19.6
1992-96	THIRD AVENUE VALUE	18.9
1987-96	FPA PARAMOUNT	16.9

*Average annual, pretax   DATA: MORNINGSTAR INC.

THE WORLD OF MUTUAL FUNDS

TABLE 2-22

DOMESTIC HYBRID FUNDS
LARGEST HOLDINGS

Stock ▼	Percent of net assets ▼
PHILIP MORRIS	1.32 %
GENERAL ELECTRIC	0.93
U.S. TREASURY NOTE 5.875% 3/31/99	0.77
U.S. TREASURY NOTE 7.875% 11/15/04	0.70
AMERICAN HOME PRODUCTS	0.68
U.S. TREASURY NOTE 5.75% 10/31/00	0.62
E.I. DUPONT DE NEMOURS	0.61
BRISTOL-MYERS SQUIBB	0.60
FORD MOTOR	0.56
CITICORP	0.56

DATA: MORNINGSTAR INC.

years, they don't look all that appealing compared to all-equity funds that rode the crest of the bull market. But over the long haul these funds have provided respectable returns with relatively low risk. That's because they tend to live circumscribed lives. For instance, one typical common rule is that the fund have no more than 65 percent of its assets in stocks. It's a good discipline. If rising prices push the stock portfolio up against the limit, the portfolio managers must start unloading stocks in order to balance the holdings. This fits well with an old Wall Street adage, "You can't go broke taking a profit."

While the balanced funds have a long history, the asset allocation funds are relative upstarts. They're sort of hyperactive balanced funds. While balanced funds are generally stocks and bonds, asset allocation funds may add other assets into the mix, including gold, real estate, or commodity-linked securities. What's more, many of the asset allocation funds have the ability to boost a particular class of asset up to 100 percent of the funds. Balanced funds by definition can't take that extreme a position.

Exactly how much of each asset goes into the fund is determined by the fund manager using a sophisticated computer-driven program, and they're not all the same. While equity fund results largely depend on stock selection, the success of asset allocation programs relies on how much of the fund goes into each asset class. Security selection does not play as much of a role in these funds' returns.

To understand the asset allocation fund, you have to take a hard look at Fidelity Asset Manager, with $10.9 billion in assets. Two sister funds,

Fidelity Asset Manager: Growth and Fidelity Asset Manager: Income together claim another $3.3 billion in assets. In the early 1990s, the funds pushed the frontiers away from traditional asset classes like U.S. stocks, U.S. bonds, and money-market funds to include global stocks and bonds from both developed countries and emerging markets. Then portfolio manager Robert A. Beckwitt developed the computer models that set asset allocations for the fund. Once the allocations were set, Beckwitt would usually leave stockpicking to the equity specialists at the firm.

But in reinventing the asset allocation fund, Beckwitt also ventured out into areas relatively new for mutual funds. For instance, he put money in "structured notes"—bonds with interest payments tied to commodity prices. These derivatives—yes, they are derivatives—make good investment sense. They allow a fund to profit from a rise in commodity prices without investing in commodities or futures contracts, which a fund usually cannot do. For several years, Asset Manager earned sensational returns, even while spreading the money around the globe. But all that came unraveled in 1994. Prices for emerging market debt started to topple in January, and after the Federal Reserve started to raise rates in February, the rest of the bond markets—and eventually the stock markets—skidded as well. By April, this wunderfund was down some 7 percent. Beckwitt managed to recoup some of the losses later in the year by unloading bonds—mostly foreign bonds. But the fund, which always had a penchant for Latin America, was hurt by the crash of the Mexican peso and the plunge in Latin American debt. That scotched any hope for getting back in the black, and the fund finished 1994 with a –6.6 percent total return. The fund recovered slowly in 1995 and achieved an 18.2 percent return, well behind the all-fund average.

Stung by the poor performance, Fidelity management removed Beckwitt from the funds in early 1996 and replaced him with a team of three managers, who cobbled together a 12.7 percent return. Relative to the all-fund average, it wasn't as bad as 1995's, but it's still a disappointment. For the three years ending in 1996, the worst three years of the fund's history, Asset Manager earned an average of just 7.6 percent a year versus an all-fund average of 13.8 percent.

Fidelity Asset Manager is considered an international rather than domestic hybrid because, while it can raise or lower its foreign holdings, it must have some at all times. The same goes for its sister fund, Fidelity Asset Manager: Growth, and Merrill Lynch Global Allocation B. Under the old classification system, these funds were multi-asset global funds.

In recent years, international hybrid funds haven't appeared all that appealing. Fidelity Asset Manager: Growth, the best-performing of the international hybrids during 1996, earned just 13.6 percent, well below the all equity fund average of 17.7 percent (Table 2-23). Merrill Lynch Global Allocation B was the best three-year performer, with a relatively tame 11 percent average annual total return. GAM International beat the Merrill fund over the last five years, but Merrill's very low-risk profile allows it to earn three upward-pointing arrows, making it among the best-rated of all funds in the BW Mutual Fund Scoreboard.

The reason for the underperformance is simple. Over the last few years, non-U.S. equity markets generally underperformed U.S. markets, and bonds underperformed stocks. These international hybrids, by charter, invested in both. The largest holdings of the international hybrids tend to be government bonds and blue-chip stocks, except that, in this case, the government that stands behind the bond might be Germany's or Argentina's (Table 2-24).

Though the Fidelity and Merrill funds loom large in the relatively small number of international hybrid funds, there are a few others worth noting. Perhaps the fund in this category admired by most investment advisers is SoGen International, the very low-risk but rewarding fund managed for the last 18 years by Jean-Marie Eveillard. Like Merrill Lynch Global Allocation B, the SoGen (SoGen is short for Société Générale, a large French bank) offering earned the highest rating in the BW Scoreboard. But the fund also beat its peers among the international hybrids, winning a three-up- arrow category rating as well.

The New York–based Frenchman runs an eclectic portfolio. There's no elaborate computer

TABLE 2-24

INTERNATIONAL HYBRID FUNDS	
LARGEST HOLDINGS	
Security ▼	Percent of net assets ▼
REPUBLIC OF GERMANY 7.75% 10/1/04	1.14%
GOVT. OF FRANCE 8.25% 4/25/22	0.94
REPUBLIC OF GERMANY 6.25% 1/4/24	0.92
REPUBLIC OF ARGENTINA 5.25% 3/31/23	0.75
U.S. TREASURY NOTE 6.5% 8/15/05	0.72
PHILIP MORRIS	0.70
U.S. TREASURY NOTE 7.875%	0.66
STORA KOPPARBERG CL. A	0.61
REPUBLIC OF ARGENTINA 6.312% 12/20/23	0.60
REPUBLIC OF GERMANY 7.375% 2005	0.43
REPUBLIC OF ARGENTINA 6.437% 03/31/23	0.42

DATA: MORNINGSTAR INC.

model here. Eveillard is an old-fashioned value investor, and he'll go anywhere in the world to find it. He's not afraid to make unorthodox investments, either. One of its largest holdings, for instance, is the Bank of International Settlements, an institution in Switzerland that serves as a clearinghouse for all the central banks (you know, the Federal Reserve, the Bank of England, the Bundesbank). Its shares sell for far less than the amount of cash and gold bullion that backs each share.

There are clunkers in all fund categories, but in this category you will find one of the real clunkers of the fund universe—the Comstock Partners Capital Value A Fund. The fund logged a –7.4 percent return in 1996, and could only muster a 3.6 percent average annual return for the 1992–1996 period.

The problem with this fund, it seems, is that it's almost always positioned for disaster. For instance, it gained 13 percent in 1990's third quarter, when the average fund lost 15.8 percent. That's because at the beginning of the quarter the portfolio manager had lots of cash, little in stocks, and even had 2 percent of the fund in put options that shot up in value as the Japanese stock market tanked. It really made its mark in 1987, when it dodged Black Monday and managed to turn in a 29 percent return for the year.

Perhaps the point of this fund is to be permanently bearish, giving investors a contrarian holding for their portfolios. But if that's the mission, the fund has not really performed that role, either. If that were the case, the fund would at least have made a modest amount of money in

TABLE 2-23

INTERNATIONAL HYBRID FUNDS		
BEST RETURNS		
Period ▼	Fund ▼	Total return* ▼
1996	FIDELITY ASSET MANAGER: GROWTH	13.6%
1994-96	MERRILL LYNCH GLOBAL ALLOCATION B	11.0
1992-96	GAM INTERNATIONAL A	18.8
1987-96	GAM INTERNATIONAL A	15.5

*Average annual, pretax   DATA: MORNINGSTAR INC.

1994, when bond markets worldwide cratered and stock markets swung wildly. Yet it did not.

INTERNATIONAL FUNDS

We pay up for German-made sports cars and luxury sedans. We sip French and Italian wines and bottled water. Many of our favorite electronic toys like compact disc players, video game machines, and camcorders come from the Pacific rim. We Americans are worldly as consumers but, until a few years ago, we've been parochial as investors. United States stocks make up only about one-third of the market value of world equities, but U.S. investors have, at most, only about one-sixth of their equity assets abroad.

That's changing thanks to mutual funds that make it easy and convenient to invest abroad. Heck, with funds, buying a portfolio of French, Brazilian, and Indonesian stocks is no more difficult than buying a portfolio of U.S. blue-chips. In 1993, international equity funds captured the imaginations—and the money—of millions of U.S. investors, who sent their billions abroad. The number of international equity funds investing abroad shot up from 210 to 344. More important, the assets in those funds rocketed from $42 billion to $104 billion. For many months, one out of every two dollars flowing into equity funds was going international.

Because international funds reach into the far corners of the globe, even many sophisticated investors who pick and choose at home opt for mutual funds when investing abroad. Many international funds are associated with organizations having global investment capabilities, and that gives the funds first-hand information on, say, Japanese banks or German machine-tool companies or Spanish utilities. That's awfully hard to get from your desk in Pittsburgh, Peoria, or Paramus—even with a computer, a modem, and the World Wide Web.

Then, too, accounting standards and tax treatments vary across borders, so the financial reports of Germany's Siemens or Sweden's ABB Brown Boveri and General Electric are not going to be comparable, even if their businesses are. Good equity analysis of non-U.S. companies takes some specialized knowledge most U.S. investors just don't have. Finally, the logistics of buying and selling abroad are daunting—and expensive—and may require several brokers, banks, and other services to process trades. That can be vastly simplified by leaving it all to a fund, where the processes are well-established and performed at institutional rates.

One particular type of international fund that really galloped to the forefront during this decade is the so-called "emerging markets" fund—mutual funds that invest in developing stock markets such as those in Latin America, the Pacific Basin (excluding Japan, Australia, and New Zealand), and even the nascent markets of Eastern Europe. During 1993, for instance, Fidelity Emerging Markets Fund earned an 81.3 percent total return. (Fidelity could not keep up with the demand for prospectuses.) Templeton Developing Markets was up 74.5 percent, and Lexington Worldwide Emerging Markets up 63.4 percent. Funds like Dean Witter Pacific Growth and Merrill Lynch Dragon, which zoomed in on China and the surrounding countries, ran up even higher returns.

But in the markets, risk and reward are intertwined. No fund can earn 80 percent or 50 percent one year—a stupendous reward—without taking risk. To expect that kind of return year after year is unrealistic. And in 1994 the emerging markets and the funds that invest in them got a heavy dose of reality. Fidelity Emerging Growth lost money, down 17.9 percent in total return; Templeton Developing Markets, down 8.6 percent; and Lexington Worldwide Emerging Markets, down 13.8 percent. That was not a disaster given the outsized returns of 1993. But these markets and these funds limped through 1995 as well, and emerging markets were the only category of fund to have negative returns, down an average –5.1 percent. Not until 1996 did these funds reach respectability again, pulling off an 11.1 percent total return. Still, the three-year average annual return was –2.3 percent. The investors who came in at the end of the 1993 boom are still waiting to break even.

Investing overseas via mutual funds is hardly a new idea. The Templeton Growth Fund, for instance, started in 1954 and has posted an average annual return of 14.3 percent over its four decades. Templeton started investing in Japan in the 1950s when the whole notion that it would become the world's second largest stock market (for a period in the late 1980s, it was the largest) seemed absurd. But for many years, the mutual fund industry left international investing to Templeton and a few others. Today, most fund families have at least one international fund and many have multiple offerings.

In fact, international funds have become so diverse that we've split the group into eight categories: two broader groups, foreign and world; diversified emerging markets; two regional

TABLE 2-25

INTERNATIONAL FUNDS
BEST RETURNS

Period ▼	Fund ▼	Total return* ▼
DIVERSIFIED EMERGING MARKETS		
1996	TEMPLETON DEVELOPING MARKETS I	22.5 %
1994-96	TEMPLETON DEVELOPING MARKETS I	4.0
1992-96	TEMPLETON DEVELOPING MARKETS I	12.1
1987-96	LEXINGTON EMERGING MARKETS	8.4
FOREIGN		
1996	ARTISAN INTERNATIONAL	34.4%
1994-96	HARBOR INTERNATIONAL GROWTH	14.8
1992-96	HARBOR INTERNATIONAL	16.5
1987-96	IVY INTERNATIONAL A	12.1
WORLD		
1996	IDEX GLOBAL A	26.8%
1994-96	SELIGMAN HENDERSON GLOB. SMALL A	17.4
1992-96	JANUS WORLDWIDE	17.5
1987-96	TEMPLETON GROWTH I	14.2
EUROPE		
1996	SCUDDER GREATER EUROPE GROWTH	30.9%
1994-96	DEAN WITTER EUROPEAN GROWTH	19.7
1992-96	DEAN WITTER EUROPEAN GROWTH	18.8
1987-96	FIDELITY EUROPE	12.1
LATIN AMERICA		
1996	FIDELITY LATIN AMERICA	30.7%
1994-96	G.T. LATIN AMERICA GROWTH A	-4.9
1992-96	MERRILL LYNCH LATIN AMERICA B	5.4
1987-96	NOT APPLICABLE	
DIVERSIFIED PACIFIC		
1996	PUTNAM ASIA PACIFIC GROWTH	5.8%
1994-96	MERRILL LYNCH PACIFIC B	4.7
1992-96	DEAN WITTER PACIFIC GROWTH	12.8
1987-96	DEAN WITTER PACIFIC GROWTH	12.2
JAPAN		
1996	VANGUARD INTL. EQ. INDEX PACIFIC	-7.8 %
1994-96	VANGUARD INTL. EQ. INDEX PACIFIC	2.3
1992-96	VANGUARD INTL. EQ. INDEX PACIFIC	3.5
1987-96	JAPAN	3.5
PACIFIC EX-JAPAN		
1996	FIDELITY HONG KONG & CHINA	41.0%
1994-96	G.T. GLOBAL NEW PACIFIC A	1.2
1992-96	T. ROWE PRICE NEW ASIA	13.6
1987-96	G.T. GLOBAL NEW PACIFIC A	11.5

*Average annual, pretax   DATA: MORNINGSTAR INC.

groups, Europe and Latin America; and three sorts of funds for the Pacific Basin (Table 2-25). Those categories are Diversified Pacific, Pacific ex-Japan, and one just for Japan.

If you don't own any international fund, your first should come from the foreign or world categories. Sound the same, don't they? Foreign funds invest mainly in the more industrialized countries and mature capital markets, though some do spice the portfolios with emerging markets securities. What's more, they usually specifically exclude U.S. stocks.

World funds, on the other hand, usually have some of their portfolios in U.S. stocks. (One fund, SmallCap World, has 62 percent of its portfolio in the United States, and has historically kept its U.S. component so high that Morningstar classifies it as a domestic small-cap growth fund.) In fact, 4 of the 10 largest equity holdings in this category are Philip Morris, Merrill Lynch, Ford Motor, and Citicorp. They're all U.S. companies, but they all have significant operations around the globe as well. To be a large U.S. company today, you have to be global.

Those stocks are major holdings in several Templeton funds. Templeton is a leading manager of international funds, but what many mutual fund investors don't realize is that Templeton also invests in the United States. Only two Templeton funds explicitly exclude U.S. investments—the Templeton Developing Markets I and Templeton Foreign I.

Does it make a difference to investors? That depends on how you construct your portfolio of funds. Suppose you decide you want to invest 25 percent of your total portfolio outside the United States. You should steer clear of the "world" funds, since such funds may have about one-third of their assets in U.S. stocks. So instead of getting 25 percent of your money abroad, you may get only 16 percent. If you don't mind having the U.S. stocks or you don't care about a precise asset allocation, then don't exclude these investment vehicles. World funds have one advantage over foreign funds. If the U.S. stocks look better to the portfolio manager than foreign markets, he or she can take advantage of those opportunities. That was certainly the case in 1995 and 1996 when U.S. stocks far outpaced the foreign markets.

With international investing, fund managers usually take one of two basic approaches. First, there's the "top-down" method. Portfolio managers look first at the countries, the local economies, and macroeconomic data like growth in Gross Domestic Product, inflation, and employment. Then they look at how that stacks up to the local stock market—is it cheap or dear given the economic backdrop? The funds usually use an international index as a guide and overweight or underweight countries according to their estimation of the stock market prospects. The managers decide on a country allocation—so much percent of the portfolio to Germany, so much to Japan, and fill in the stocks accordingly, or turn that job over to other managers or analysts. The idea is to get the markets right and all else will follow. A leading practitioner of this method is T. Rowe Price International Stock Fund, which earned a 16 percent total return in 1996.

The opposite tack is, of course, the "bottom-up" method, one favored by the Templeton Funds. In bottom-up, the portfolio managers first use various stock selection methods to come up with the companies they want to invest in. The resulting country allocation is the result of stock selection. Thus, the returns of these funds can be quite different from the indexes. For instance, Artisan International Fund, with a 34.4 percent total return in 1996 had 11 percent of its assets in Sweden and 10 percent in Norway. The two Scandinavian countries together make up only a few percentage points of any international index. Had the fund stayed close to an index, it would never have earned those kinds of outsized returns. Had the manager been wrong about Scandinavian stocks, the fund would have been near the bottom of the pack.

The sorts of investments made by European, Pacific, and Latin American funds are self-evident. These funds are not substitutes for foreign funds, but supplements. These regional funds are the sector funds of the international equity world. Each category has a different investment story to tell. Europe, for instance, is developing into one megamarket, with economic barriers falling across the continent. That should make it nearly as easy, for instance, for a Spanish company to sell its products in France and Germany as it is for a New Jersey company to sell in Pennsylvania and New York.

Eventually, this one-market Europe should be a bonanza for businesses and their shareholders. Many of the European funds started up a few years ago, hoping to be reaping those riches by now. But Germany's high interest rates sent rates soaring all over Europe. That depressed business and was deadly for European stocks. In 1993, when interest rates in Europe started to fall, European funds soared for the first time in four years. The following year, rising interest rates worldwide sent many local stock markets reeling. The main reason that European funds finished the year on a plus note was that several European currencies rose against the dollar.

The last two years have been much better for European stock markets. In 1995, currency turmoil and slowing economies on the Continent held these markets in check, but the markets still made gains and the European funds, on average, gained 18 percent. The only markets to thrive were Britain's—which was, like the United States, benefiting from a mergers and acquisition boom—and Switzerland's—as currency-savvy investors fled the German mark for the safety of the Swiss franc. In 1996, the Europe funds put on their best show since 1993, climbing 24.7 percent and even beating the S&P 500. The European stock markets benefited from lower interest rates, corporate restructuring, and economic upswings in Central and Eastern Europe.

On the other side of the globe, Pacific funds have some of the world's worst- and best-performing markets. Look at the Japanese stock market. During the 1980s, the market soared, with the Nikkei stock average going from less than 10,000 in 1980 to nearly 40,000 at the end of 1989. But that's not all. Starting in 1985, the value of the dollar versus the Japanese yen has fallen by nearly two-thirds. That means, even if there had been no appreciation in the price of a Japanese stock denominated in yen, it still would have soared for dollar-based shareholders.

But since 1990, the yen price of stocks has more than halved. Offsetting that somewhat is that the yen is worth more in dollar terms. Still, the currency gains did not overcome sinking stock prices. The bear market in Japan has been devastating for such one-time highfliers as the Japan Fund and G.T. Global Japan Growth Fund. (Both funds had good returns in 1993 and 1994, more because of the stronger yen than because of a bull market in stocks.) In 1996, the best-performing fund in the new Japan category was Vanguard International Equity Index Pacific Fund—and that was down 7.8 percent, beating the average 10.1 percent loss for the group. (It's in the Japan category because Japan, even in its depressed state, makes up about 75 percent of the index that this fund tracks, the Morgan Stanley Capital International Pacific index.) The main reason the fund beat the crowd is that, since it's a Pacific index fund, it still has some 25 percent of its assets outside Japan—something the pure Japan funds don't have.

International funds help diversify a portfolio.

International funds can profit from a weak dollar.

Asia outside Japan is quite another story. Spurred by economic and market reforms in China, the entire region underwent a strong burst of economic growth in the early 1990s. That made a star of the Hong Kong stock market in 1992 and 1993, as Western investors saw it as the door to China. But the China boom spread throughout the region to such nations as Thailand, Indonesia, Singapore, and Malaysia. In 1993, nearly all the stock markets around China's perimeter doubled in local currency terms.

Not surprisingly, those markets plunged in 1994—with Hong Kong stocks down about 31 percent. Now, just imagine what would happen to these markets if the hard-core Communists reasserted control in Beijing and turned the clock back on economic reform. That's the kind of risk that's hard to quantify. Nonetheless, in 1995 Hong Kong stocks rebounded by about 20 percent and climbed another 33.5 percent in 1996. But many of the region's markets, like those in Thailand, the Phillipines, and South Korea, were down and most of the others were flat. For the three years ending in 1996, both the diversified Pacific funds and those excluding Japan had slightly negative average annual total returns.

Your money does not have to travel halfway around the world to get a wild ride. There's always the Latin America funds, which have opened for business over the last several years as many neighboring nations in our hemisphere started to fight inflation, privatize their economies, and invite foreign investment. In 1996, the average Latin America fund earned a snappy 24.3 percent. Even so, the three-year average for these funds is negative 5.3 percent. That tells you 1994 and 1995 were some pretty difficult years.

Indeed, at the end of 1994, the Mexican government devalued the peso after promising investors it wouldn't and set off a near panic in Mexican markets and throughout Latin America. Investors fled Mexico and pulled money out of Argentina and Brazil as well, pushing all these emerging markets into a funk, as well as all the diversified emerging markets funds. Latin stocks comprise a large proportion of those funds, and, along with some successes in the nascent markets of Eastern Europe, were largely responsible for the improvement in the returns of diversified emerging markets funds in 1996.

Sure, international funds may seem risky. But when they're combined with U.S. funds, they actually lower the riskiness, at least as measured by volatility. That's because U.S. funds have a high degree of correlation. When one goes up or down, they all do, though not to the same extent. But non-U.S. markets and funds that invest in them do not have a high degree of correlation. They're more likely to zig when the U.S. funds zag. So if U.S. funds are in a slump, chances are some non-U.S. funds will be doing well. That's why even when the foreign markets were eclipsed by the United States, mutual fund companies were launching new international funds.

International investing makes sense for another fundamental reason. If other countries are enjoying faster economic growth than the United States, it stands to reason that corporate profits are going to be stronger than in the United States. So by investing abroad you get a chance to capture some of that other growth. And you still have the opportunity to invest in industries that have all but disappeared in the United States, such as consumer electronics.

For some investors, the chief worry about international investing is currency risk. That's an important question to ask when shopping for international funds. Some funds do hedge currencies; some don't. You have to read the prospectus for the fund's hedging policy. Here's how a hedge works: Suppose a fund owned $100 million worth of Japanese stocks and the manager believed the yen would decline against the dollar. One way to protect the yen-denominated investment would be to sell $100 million worth of yen in the currency market. That move has the effect of "neutralizing" the yen in the fund. Then, the fund gains or loses on the stock price movement of the Japanese stock—just as it would with a U.S. stock.

But hedging has a cost, even if it's done right. It can be especially costly if it's done wrong. What if, against the forecasts of the currency experts, the yen went up instead of down against the dollar? (That's exactly what happened in 1994.) That hedge, which is supposed to protect the portfolio, would become a money-loser. That's why many funds—such as Templeton, one of the most experienced in overseas investing—don't explicitly hedge. But they will factor a depreciating foreign currency into their portfolio by investing in companies that benefit from the cheaper currency, like exporters.

Sure, there will be times when investors wish they had hedged the currency, like the Mexican currency crisis that began on December 20, 1994. Unable to support the peso at its then level of 3.5 pesos to the dollar, about 29 cents, the Mexican government devalued the currency 15 percent—the first major devaluation in seven years and the first since the international investors and U.S. mutual fund investors sent billions south of the border. Then the currency speculators rushed in and drove the peso down even further in the foreign exchange market. Unable to prop up the currency, the government just let the peso seek its own level. Three weeks later, the peso had dropped to about 17 cents, or 41 percent of its original value.

At first, most of the damage came from currency. But then the Mexican stock market was hit, and other Latin American markets were hit as well because investors feared a repeat of the Mexican situation. By March 1995, Mexico's Bolsa and the Latin American funds had hit their lows and slowly began to rebound. Still, nearly all finished 1995 with huge losses, ranging from –9 percent for Scudder Latin America Growth to –24.6 for Merrill Lynch Latin America B.

Even with currency risk—that the value of your investments will fluctuate because of currency fluctuations—it's still advisable for U.S. investors to place some international funds in their portfolios. If you have all your assets in dollars, you're still not without risk. What if the dollar is falling in relation to other currencies? You may have to kiss off that European vacation, but you can live without that. A weak dollar could mean you spend more for foreign-made goods, some of which have no domestic substitutions. And a weak dollar can even push up prices for U.S.-made goods. Even if you're shopping for a Chevy, your cost for the car can be affected by currency fluctuations. If the dollar falls against the yen, that would probably lead to higher prices for Japanese cars that compete with Chevrolet. If its competitors' prices are going up, General Motors may try to profit by raising prices too. Putting a portion of your assets abroad is as American as baseball, hot dogs, apple pie, and the 4th of July.

PRECIOUS METALS FUNDS

Incredible. Astounding. Mindboggling. No adjectives really do justice to the 1993 performance of the funds specializing in precious metals, or gold funds. Lexington Strategic Investments, the leading gold fund of the group and the leading mutual fund of the year, blasted out a 264.9 percent return. That's probably an all-time record for a mutual fund. United Services Gold Shares, at 123.9 percent, was no slouch either, with a double. The top 25 funds of the year were all gold funds, and the average gold fund delivered a whopping 97 percent return.

But the ensuing years were not so spectacular. Lexington Strategic Investments was still the leader of the pack in 1994, though it was up only 11.3 percent, the only gold fund to make money that year. By 1995, when the average precious metals fund earned a 1.4 percent return, Lexington Strategic was down 14.7, its fortunes so diminished that the fund was no longer large enough to qualify for the BUSINESS WEEK Mutual Fund Scoreboard. By 1996, it lost another 11 percent. United Services Gold Shares, also a hot shot in 1993, took a 24.9 percent dive in 1995 and another 25.5 percent loss in 1996. The long-term results are dismal. A dollar invested in United States Gold Shares 10 years ago is now worth about 45 cents.

If you look at investing in stocks, you can pretty much count on two out of three years to be good ones, so the long-term results will be positive. With gold funds, it's pretty much a toss-up, with bad years perhaps even more likely to come up as good years. For most of the last 15 years, an investor could have made as much money in a money-market mutual fund as in the average gold fund—and taken virtually no risk.

So why would anyone invest in precious metals funds? For years, the conventional wisdom argued that every investor should place 5 or 10 percent of his or her assets into gold or gold mutual funds, which mainly buy gold-mining stocks. Gold was seen as a hedge against inflation, a safe haven in times of international upheaval or economic strife. But the conventional wisdom hasn't seemed to work for quite some time. Gold traded for $370 right before Iraq's 1990 invasion of Kuwait. Ten weeks later, after oil prices had nearly doubled, gold sold at about the same price. For the third quarter of 1990, precious metals funds were the best-performing fund category, but they still returned only 4 percent. And for the year, precious metals funds plunged 23.6 percent. Nor did gold prices react

TABLE 2-26

PRECIOUS METALS FUNDS		
BEST RETURNS		
Period ▼	Fund ▼	Total return* ▼
1996	**INVESCO STRATEGIC GOLD**	40.6%
1994-96	**SCUDDER GOLD**	11.5
1992-96	**SCUDDER GOLD**	15.0
1987-96	**MIDAS**	10.8

*Average annual, pretax DATA: MORNINGSTAR INC.

much in August 1991, at the time of the abortive Soviet coup. So much for "crisis" protection.

An inflation hedge? Perhaps. But for many years real interest rates—that is, interest rates after inflation—have been high. An investor who put money in short-term fixed-income securities could earn a rate of return well in excess of the inflation rate. Compare that to owning gold bullion, which must be insured and stored while it produces no income to offset those out-of-pocket expenses.

Gold prices finally started to move up in 1993, from nearly $300 an ounce toward $400. This was the move that helped to spark the tremendous move in gold mutual funds, and that was a period when global inflation was relatively subdued.

Since then, gold has rallied to the $400 level several times, but could never sustain it. By early 1997, the price was below $350.

The case for having a little money in gold funds is that it's nearly impossible to predict when they're going to zoom. At the end of 1992, on the eve of their spectacular 1993 bull market, the gold funds had a little more than $2 billion in assets, less than half of 1 percent of all money in equity mutual funds. Clearly, those who profited most in the gold rush of 1993 were investors who had a contrarian bent. They had invested in the doggiest of investments on the chance that the pendulum would swing back the other way.

The best explanation for gold's 17.3 percent rise in 1993 was a rather elementary one—supply and demand. For many years, foreign central banks, which are big owners of gold, sold millions of ounces of gold bullion to help shore up their currencies. That supply swamped the market in 1991 and 1992, but the selling abated in 1993. Demand picked up as well, especially in the rapidly growing economies of Asia, where the newly wealthy convert excess cash into gold.

But how does an increase of less than 20 percent in the price of gold translate into a near double for gold mutual funds? For one reason: Gold-mining shares have operating leverage; that is, a little increase in the price of gold can increase their profits handsomely. Here's why. Suppose a mining company can produce gold at a cost of $340 an ounce, and gold sells at $350 an ounce. That's a profit of $10 an ounce. If gold goes to $375 an ounce, the company's cost is still $340, but the profit is $35 an ounce. That's a 150 percent increase in profits on a 7 percent increase in the price of gold (from $350 to $375). That's why, when gold prices are rising, many traders prefer to play the rally via gold-mining shares. Of

TABLE 2-27

PRECIOUS METALS FUNDS	
LARGEST HOLDINGS	
Stock ▼	Percent of net assets ▼
BARRICK GOLD	6.50 %
NEWMONT MINING	5.00
PLACER DOME	3.41
EURO-NEVADA MINING	2.62
GETCHELL GOLD	2.57
SANTA FE PACIFIC GOLD	2.37
HOMESTAKE MINING	2.21
TVX GOLD	2.12
BRE-X MINERALS	2.00
FREEPORT-MCMORAN COPPER/GOLD A	1.95

DATA: MORNINGSTAR INC.

course, the same principle works on the way down. If gold is falling, mining company profits can melt away quickly.

But rising gold prices don't explain all of 1993's gold-fund returns. For that, you have to look at the unfolding political developments in South Africa, a major gold-producing nation, as the white-controlled government agreed to cede power to the black majority. That touched off a huge rally in the South African stock market, where many of the gold-mining companies are traded, as well as a surge in the value of the South African currency. While many precious metals funds own a mixture of South African, North American, and Australian gold stocks, Lexington Strategic Investments and United Services Gold Shares own exclusively South African stocks.

Many thought the remarkable political changes in South Africa would help to narrow the rift in the gold-shares market because many institutional and individual investors have long refused to put money into South African companies, lest it be seen as approval of the former government's racial policies. Now, the South African mining companies are largely ignored because they are high-cost producers.

Indeed, investors are starting to view gold stocks less as inflation plays and more as potential money-making vehicles, the same way they would approach another natural resource like oil, copper, or forest products. The real propellant behind the best-performing precious metals funds like Invesco Strategic Gold, up 40.6 percent, are companies that strike gold (Table 2-26). One of the big hits of 1996 was Bre-X Minerals, a tiny Canadian company that reputedly struck it big in Indonesia. The stock went up over 300 percent—and it's the largest holding of the Invesco fund. In early 1997, the Bre-X stock plunged as doubts were raised about its gold find.

The largest holdings of the gold funds are larger North American producers, such as Barrick Gold, Newmont Mining, and Placer Dome (Table 2-27). As restrictions against South African investments fade away, the striking valuation differences between the South African and non–South African stocks should also narrow.

Putting a little money in precious metals funds is not a bad idea. Most diversified equity funds don't own any gold shares at all, so a precious metals fund helps your total portfolio diversification. And while they are the most volatile of equity funds, precious metals funds live a life of their own. The fluctuations in NAVs have little to do with the ups and downs of the Dow, the S&P 500, or any other stock market indicator. That attribute also improves a portfolio's diversification and lowers its overall risk. It's not easy to find gold funds that shine among the overall universe. But BUSINESS WEEK's new category ratings show the Midas Fund and Scudder Gold as the two with the best risk-adjusted returns.

SPECIALTY FUNDS

Specialty funds are essentially nondiversified mutual funds. They may invest in dozens of companies, but they're all in the same industry or group of industries. When their underlying sectors do well, these funds rise to the top. For a few years, health-care funds led the performance derby. Then it was financial funds, precious metals, technology funds, and, now, real estate. (We've separated precious metals from the other specialty funds because they have very different investment characteristics from most specialized portfolios.) Our specialty group also includes a catchall "miscellaneous" category, which includes such diverse and unrelated sectors as food and agriculture, environmental services, media, and retailing. They're all in the miscellaneous category because there aren't yet enough of any one of them (Table 2-28).

Investment advisers and mutual fund experts often debate whether fund investors should use specialty funds. After all, if you choose a specialty fund, you are making a choice that's left to professional portfolio managers in the more diversified funds. Are you qualified to make that decision? It's a decision that's more typically made by investors who choose stocks for themselves.

TABLE 2-28

SPECIALTY FUNDS
BEST RETURNS

Period	Fund	Total return*
COMMUNICATION		
1996	FIDELITY SEL. DEVELOPING COMMUN.	14.6%
1994-96	FIDELITY SEL. DEVELOPING COMMUN.	15.7
1992-96	FIDELITY SEL. DEVELOPING COMMUN.	19.0
1987-96	FIDELITY SEL. TELECOMMUNICATIONS	17.9
FINANCIAL		
1996	FIDELITY SEL. HOME FINANCE	36.8%
1994-96	FIDELITY SEL. HOME FINANCE	29.2
1992-96	FIDELITY SEL. HOME FINANCE	34.1
1987-96	FIDELITY SEL. HOME FINANCE	21.9
HEALTH		
1996	T. ROWE PRICE HEALTH SCIENCE	26.8%
1994-96	FRANKLIN GLOBAL HEALTH I	27.2
1992-96	VANGUARD SPEC. HEALTH CARE	16.3
1987-96	INVESCO STRATEGIC HEALTH SCIENCE	21.3
NATURAL RESOURCES		
1996	FIDELITY SELECT ENERGY SERVICE	49.0%
1994-96	FIDELITY SELECT ENERGY SERVICE	28.3
1992-96	FIDELITY SELECT ENERGY SERVICE	21.4
1987-96	VANGUARD SPEC. ENERGY	15.0
TECHNOLOGY		
1996	PBHG TECHNOLOGY & COMMUNICATIONS	54.4%
1994-96	FIDELITY SELECT ELECTRONICS	41.2
1992-96	FIDELITY SELECT ELECTRONICS	36.5
1987-96	SELIGMAN COMMUNICATIONS & INFO.	22.5
MISCELLANEOUS		
1996	FIDELITY SELECT RETAILING	20.9%
1994-96	FIDELITY SELECT FOOD & AGRIC.	18.0
1992-96	INVESCO STRATEGIC LEISURE	15.0
1987-96	INVESCO STRATEGIC LEISURE	12.9
REAL ESTATE		
1996	LONGLEAF PARTNERS REALTY	40.7%
1994-96	COHEN & STEERS REALTY SHARES	18.6
1992-96	COHEN & STEERS REALTY SHARES	18.9
1987-96	FIDELITY REAL ESTATE INVESTMENT	11.8
UTILITIES		
1996	PRUDENTIAL UTILITY B	21.2%
1994-96	STRONG AMERICAN UTILITIES	13.1
1992-96	FIDELITY UTILITIES	12.1
1987-96	FIDELITY SELECT UTILITIES GROWTH	11.9

*Average annual, pretax   DATA: MORNINGSTAR INC.

Specialty funds are the middle ground between investing in funds and investing in stocks. In fact, in setting up the vast array of sector funds, Fidelity Investments designed the program to appeal to investors who might otherwise trade stocks. The sector funds are priced every hour during the trading day, and investors can buy or sell at the next hour's prices. (Most mutual funds are priced only after the close of trading, and transactions made before 4 p.m. are executed at the end of the day.)

Though many fund families have some specialty funds in their line-up, none even approaches Fidelity's large menu. For instance, not only is there a financial services fund, but there's a roster of single-industry funds within that: brokerage and investment management, insurance, regional banks, and home finance (savings and loans). There's a fairly broadly chartered technology fund, but Fidelity also manages more narrowly defined funds. Fidelity has separate funds for computers, software, and electronics as well. Fidelity Select Electronics was the best-performing tech fund for the 1994–1996 and 1992–1996 periods. It was also the only technology fund to earn three upward-pointing arrows, both in the all-fund ratings and among other tech funds.

If the fund managers are doing their jobs right, the specialty funds should have the same characteristics as the market sectors they represent. Natural resources funds primarily invest in energy and look the best when energy prices are rising. They're often considered a hedge against inflation, though they didn't look that way during 1994, when inflation was a concern in the financial markets. Utilities funds should be safe and boring, since they buy stocks to collect the dividends. But in 1994, they were anything but safe and boring. Rising interest rates and increased competition in the utility industry wreaked havoc on the utilities—and funds that invest in them.

Specialty funds can only perform as well as the sectors in which they must invest. In 1990 and 1991, all health-care stocks, from tiny biotechnology to big pharmaceutical companies, soared. So did the health funds, which were up 22.5 percent in 1990 and 78.3 percent in 1991. In 1992 and 1993, the stocks fell out of bed. Health funds slid, on average, 11.2 percent in 1992 and eked out a 1.7 percent gain for 1993. In 1994, many sectors of the health industry started to rebound, and the funds performed respectably, up 5.3 percent. In 1995, they surged to the top again, earning a 47.3 percent return and beating out the technology funds.

Even within specialty funds, the strategies can vary a lot. Consider the T. Rowe Price Science & Technology Fund. The fund is mainly high-tech and some medical technology. But it invests not only in the creators and producers of technology, but also in companies that employ technology to their benefit. In 1996, one of its largest holdings was First Financial Management, a provider of data processing services that relies heavily on the application of computer technology.

The Merrill Lynch Technology Fund takes an unorthodox approach to sector investing. Unlike nearly all specialty funds, which remain fully invested in their sectors at all times, portfolio manager James Renck will sell stocks and raise cash if he thinks that's the prudent thing to do. And when he does choose stocks, Renck focuses on a few rather than a broad selection of stocks. The fund has had its moments of brilliance, but the three-year results are poor, an average annual return of 10.7 percent versus the category average of 25.7 percent.

Technology funds have all the sexy companies, but the hottest specialty fund category of 1996 was real estate. These funds invest mainly in real estate investment trusts (REITs), which are not unlike mutual funds. They pool investor's money to invest in real estate. Some REITs are diversified in the kind of property they buy, but others are specialized—shopping centers, multifamily housing, office buildings, or even nursing homes. Real estate funds may also invest in construction or homebuilding companies, but their principal holdings are REITs.

The real estate fund is one sort of specialty fund that investors could comfortably tuck away in their porfolios as a core holding. They really do add diversification to a portfolio. As with gold-mining stocks, most diversified equity funds do not invest in REITs, nor do index funds. (In 1996, Vanguard launched a REIT index fund.)

REITs represent a distinctly different asset class from stocks or bonds. Real estate is, of course, cyclical, but it does not have a high correlation with stocks. So a tumble in the stock market does not necessarily presage a fall in REITs. In fact, early in the summer of 1996, when the stock market was going down at a rapid pace, REITs were climbing.

The other striking characteristic of REITs and the funds that invest in them is that they are mainly income-oriented vehicles. As such, many fund investors would do well to use them in their tax-deferred retirement accounts rather than in taxable accounts where they'll produce taxable income. The difference between REITs and bonds is that REITs are not fixed-payment instruments. An economic boom that would cause interest rates to rise and bond prices to fall would probably also increase rental income, money that ultimately flows back to REIT owners. So REIT funds can be viewed as an inflation hedge for a fixed-income portfolio.

Whether it's technology funds or health-care funds or financial funds, one thing is clear. When specialty funds are on a hot streak, they attract "hot money." Many professional traders track sector-fund prices, just as they keep tabs on individual stocks, looking for the funds with "momentum." When they spot it, they can really pile into a fund. For instance, at the start of 1992, Fidelity Savings & Loan Fund (since renamed Fidelity Home Finance) had $10 million in assets—it was not even large enough to get into the Scoreboard. But the fund was up 15 percent in the first quarter, while the stock market was down 2.5 percent. By March 31, the fund totaled $134 million in assets. Five very profitable years later, the fund has $800 million in assets, suggesting this sort of fund has limited rather than widespread appeal. If it had wide appeal, the fund would have several billion dollars.

With these specialty funds, the more specific the investment mission, the more risk is in the fund. But there's obviously more potential for big gains. If you think health-care funds have excelled, look at the purely biotech funds. Oppenheimer Global Bio-Tech was up 121.1 percent in 1991, the single best fund for the year. (In 1994, Oppenheimer folded the fund and merged it with Oppenheimer Global Emerging Growth Fund.) Fidelity Select Biotechnology Fund was up over 40 percent in 1989 and 1990 and 99 percent in 1991. The same forces that can bring about big gains can take them away, too. Biotech funds were pummeled in 1992 and 1994 and broke even in 1993. The Fidelity fund gained 49.1 percent in 1995, but even so, the five-year average annual return is a paltry 3.1 percent, about a third of the return earned by the average health-care funds.

Still, specialty funds can be a good alternative to trying to pick stocks in hard-to-understand industries. For instance, only a handful of biotechnology companies are real operating companies with marketable products and real sales. For those companies, the tools of financial analysis can work. But most biotechnology companies are research and development operations that don't make any money. To find the winners among

those, an investor would have to have a Ph.D. in molecular biology to figure out which companies were pursuing the research that would be most likely to result in marketable drugs.

This more specialized service may come at a higher price. Specialized funds tend to have somewhat higher expenses, in part because they're smaller and in part because the fund companies can charge them. Fidelity Select portfolios charge combined loads and redemption fees of 3.75 percent. That's not onerous if it's a long-term investment, but it's a high price if you're looking to capitalize on a short-term move. Watch out. This is one area where fees and expenses can really get you.

INDEX AND SOCIAL INVESTING FUNDS

Index mutual funds have been around for 20 years, but only in 1996 did they all of a sudden become hot properties. The Vanguard Index 500, which tracks the Standard and Poor's 500-stock index, took in $8 billion in fresh cash, finished the year with $30.3 billion in assets, and climbed the ladder of size to become the third largest fund. By the time this book comes out, it will no doubt have surpassed Investment Co. of America and become No. 2. Still, that puts it about $20 billion behind the Fidelity Magellan Fund. Yet, with the investor appetite for index funds and the dreary returns from the lumbering Magellan, it would not be at all surprising to find that the Vanguard fund becomes the largest fund within a few years.

Indexing is a method for managing investments, not an investment style in itself. The Mutual Fund Scoreboard categorizes index funds like any other funds, by the nature of the portfolio. The Vanguard Index 500 is a large-cap blend fund; Vanguard Index Small Capitalization Stock, a small-cap blend; American Century Global Gold (formerly Benham Gold Equities Index), a precious metals fund. Most of the time, index funds are easy to spot. They either have "index" in their title, or very low expenses, or both (Table 2-29).

Index funds are mutual funds designed to replicate, rather than beat, the performance of a market index. That's why they're low cost, too. They can be managed by computers. But, isn't accepting an index's return the same as settling for average? Not at all. It's better than not beating the index. And every year many funds fail to beat the indexes. The Vanguard Index 500, which copies the S&P 500, beat the average large-cap

Index funds try to match, not beat, the market.

TABLE 2-29

INDEX AND SOCIAL INVESTING FUNDS

INDEX FUNDS

AMERICAN CENTURY GLOBAL GOLD
AMERICAN GAS INDEX
BT INVESTMENT EQUITY 500 INDEX
CITIZENS INDEX
COMPOSITE NORTHWEST A
DREYFUS MIDCAP INDEX
DREYFUS S&P 500 INDEX
FEDERATED MAX-CAP INSTL.
FEDERATED MINI-CAP
FIDELITY MARKET INDEX
FIDELITY U.S. EQUITY INDEX
GALAXY II LARGE CO. INDEX RETAIL SHARES
GALAXY II SMALL CO. INDEX RETAIL SHARES
GALAXY II U.S. TREASURY INDEX RETAIL SHARES
MAINSTAY EQUITY INDEX A
SCHWAB 1000
SCHWAB INTERNATIONAL INDEX
SCHWAB SMALL CAP INDEX
SSGA S&P 500 INDEX
STAGECOACH CORPORATE STOCK A
T. ROWE PRICE EQUITY INDEX
VANGUARD BALANCED INDEX
VANGUARD BOND INDEX INTERMEDIATE-TERM
VANGUARD BOND INDEX SHORT-TERM
VANGUARD BOND INDEX TOTAL MARKET
VANGUARD INDEX 500
VANGUARD INDEX EXTENDED MARKET
VANGUARD INDEX GROWTH
VANGUARD INDEX SMALL CAP STOCK
VANGUARD INDEX TOTAL STOCK MARKET
VANGUARD INDEX VALUE
VANGUARD INTL. EQUITY INDEX EMERGING MARKETS
VANGUARD INTL. EQUITY INDEX EUROPEAN
VANGUARD INTL. EQUITY INDEX PACIFIC
VICTORY STOCK INDEX

SOCIAL INVESTING FUNDS

ARIEL APPRECIATION
CALVERT SOCIAL INVESTMENT MANAGED A
CALVERT STRATEGIC GROWTH A
CALVERT WORLD VALUE INTERNATIONAL EQUITY A
CITIZENS INDEX
DREYFUS THIRD CENTURY
PARNASSUS
PAX WORLD

DATA: MORNINGSTAR INC.

blend fund in the one-, three-, and five-year periods ending in 1996. During the same periods, it also beat the average U.S. diversified fund and the average equity fund. Is it any wonder that index funds are so popular?

In part, the Vanguard index fund's edge comes from low expenses. The Vanguard fund has an expense ratio of 0.20, or 20 cents per $100. The average large-cap blend fund takes $1.16 per $100 in expenses; the average equity fund, 1.29 percent. So, right off the bat, the S&P index fund has nearly a 1 percentage point edge. But be forewarned. While all S&P 500 index funds have the same stocks, they don't all own the same return. The difference is expenses. Vanguard charges only the cost of running the funds; others charge much higher rates. The comparable index fund offered by Dreyfus levies a 0.55 expense ratio; Fidelity and T. Rowe Price, 0.45 percent.

Index funds also have another advantage that works especially well in bull markets. They are always fully invested in stocks. In fact, one of an index fund manager's main responsibilities at the end of the day is to make sure the net new cash (inflows less outflows) is invested in the index stocks all in the right proportions. That's the only way to insure that all the fund shareholders' money is earning the index returns.

Conventional equity funds don't run fully invested. There's always 4 or 5 percent of their assets in cash, as it sometimes takes awhile to find places for the new money. This is especially a problem with value funds that are picky about where they put the money.

Of course, the main reason index funds look so good now is that the U.S. stock market has been in a bull market for over six years. In a bear market, cash is a cushion against declining prices. Since index funds don't carry cash, there is no downside protection. If the S&P 500 were to undergo a serious correction, many investors—some of whom have come to think the S&P 500 is "riskless"—will have a shocking revelation about the other side of index funds.

Index funds, though they have average returns, actually have above-average BW ratings. That's because, to get a positive rating, a fund must beat the S&P on a risk-adjusted basis. Since many funds fail to do that, they drop to the "average" rating. If enough of them do that, the index funds get pushed up to one upward-pointing arrow, an above-average rating. That plus the low cost factor make a compelling case for index-fund investing.

But fund analysts question whether all index funds have such an advantage over managed funds. The S&P 500 fund is successful because the market for big-cap U.S. stocks is very efficient. It's hard for portfolio managers and analysts to add value to an S&P-like fund. Away from the 500, though, markets are far less efficient, and smart stock picking can pay off. Thus, indexing may not be as good an idea in other investment categories, such as small-cap stocks or foreign markets.

In emerging markets, for instance, good stock picking should outperform an index. But in 1995, Vanguard International Equity Index Emerging Markets Portfolio was slightly in the black, up 0.5 percent. That made it the best diversified emerging markets fund of the year. In 1996, the fund earned a 15.8 percent return, easily beating the 11.1 percent category average. How could that be? George U. Sauter, the chief of Vanguard's index funds, says that while it's true that the smaller markets are less efficient, the trading and management costs are much higher. That means the cost of exploiting those inefficiencies wipe out any excess return from those investments.

And there are cases where indexing just hasn't worked. The Vanguard International Index Equity Pacific Portfolio has been a poor performer among the Asian funds because some 75 percent of it, like the Morgan Stanley Capital International Pacific Index, is invested in the long-suffering Japanese stock market. Most "managed" Pacific funds did better by underplaying or ignoring Japanese stocks.

"Social investing" or "socially responsible" funds, like index funds, cut across a number of categories. The Dreyfus Third Century Fund is a large-cap growth fund; Parnassus Fund is small-cap value; and Pax World Fund, despite its name, is a domestic hybrid. What characterizes these funds is not so much what they do, but what they don't do: They don't invest in defense, tobacco, alcohol, or gaming industries.

And that's not all. Many of these funds screen potential investments for their labor relations, minority employment practices, and attitudes toward women. Companies with questionable track records are also excluded. The same principles carry over to fixed-income investments as well. Pax World won't even invest in U.S. Treasury bonds because the proceeds could be used for military purposes.

In recent years, some of the social investing funds have done well. Pax World and Dreyfus Third Century were top-rated in the early 1990s. That doesn't mean social investing is a superior method of stock picking. It's just that in the 1987–1991 period, drug and health-care companies, which are naturals for social investing funds, performed much better than steel and oil companies, which are much less likely to be part of social investing funds. In recent years, the returns have been all over the lot, suggesting it's more a case of stock selection than social philosophy. Dreyfus Third Century did well in 1995 and 1996, but Parnassus Fund fared relatively poorly in both years despite a strong market. Indeed, social investing screens were never meant to enhance returns, but to assure investors who care about it that their money would not be used to support industries or practices they don't like.

For years, social investing funds were "South Africa free." Because of the country's apartheid policies and white minority rule, they certainly did not make any direct investments in South Africa nor would they invest in any company that had business there. Now, with apartheid abolished and blacks able to participate in political life, it's no longer taboo to invest in that country or in companies that do business there.

Bond Funds

When interest rates go up, bond prices go down. When rates decline, bond prices shoot up. Understand that, and you're well on your way to understanding bond, or fixed-income, mutual funds.

Look at Table 2-30. Consider a bond that pays a 7 percent coupon and matures in 10 years. If rates go down 1 percentage point to 6 percent, the price of the bond climbs to 7.44 percent. Should rates rise by a like amount, the bond

TABLE 2-30

HOW CHANGES IN INTEREST RATES AFFECT BOND PRICES				RATES FALL 1%, PRICES RISE BY... / RATES RISE 1%, PRICES FALL...
MATURITY ▶ COUPON	1 YEAR	5 YEARS	10 YEARS	30 YEARS
5%	0.97% / −0.96	4.49% / −4.27	8.18% / −7.79	17.38% / −13.80
6%	0.96% / −0.95	4.38 / −4.16	7.79 / −7.11	15.45 / −12.47
7%	0.96% / −0.94	4.27 / −4.06	7.44 / −6.80	13.84 / −11.31
8%	0.95% / −0.94	4.16 / −3.96	7.11 / −6.50	12.47 / −10.32

DATA: T. ROWE PRICE ASSOCIATES

declines 6.80 percent in value. As you can see from the table, the longer the maturity, the more sensitive the bond is to changes in interest rates. If rates on a 30-year bond were to rise 1 percentage point, the bond would drop 11.31 percent in price. The five-year bond would only be nicked by a 4.06 percent drop.

The relationship between interest rates and bond prices is one of the most fundamental in all of finance. Yet how many of the millions of investors who flocked into bond funds in the 1991–1993 period really understand that? For instance, an investor who purchased Vanguard Fixed-Income Long-Term U.S. Treasury Portfolio at the beginning of October 1993 suffered a 17 percent decline in net asset value over the next year. That was softened somewhat by the fund's 7 percent yield, but the bottom line was ugly—a –10 percent total return. Investors may not like it, but will accept that kind of behavior from stocks. But from bonds?

If understanding the inverse relationship between interest rates and bond prices (and bond fund NAVs) isn't hard enough, now the bond-fund investors also have to grapple with the "D" word, derivatives. These have been around for years but hit the headlines during 1994 when their quickly sinking prices caused big trouble for some corporations, public investment funds, and yes, a few, but just a few, mutual funds.

Simply put, a derivative is a financial instrument the value of which is derived from some other source. Take, for instance, a "structured note" with an interest payment tied to the price of copper. To price the note you have to know the interest-rate formula, and that's dependent on the price of copper.

If the price of copper goes up, so will the interest payments and the price an investor would pay for the note. If copper slides, so will the note. There's nothing especially risky or suspicious about that.

Derivatives can be used to speculate in stocks, bonds, or commodity-market movements. Options limit the potential loss; futures do not. But most derivatives can be used in a way to hedge portfolio risk. Selling Treasury bond futures, for instance, can protect a bond-fund portfolio from losses related to rising interest rates.

The problem with derivatives comes when they're used to speculate on the direction of the financial markets rather than to hedge against adverse moves—and the portfolio manager's bet turns out wrong. And if the derivative is leveraged, too, the loss is further magnified.

The leverage might work like this. During the three years of falling interest rates, many large investors—mutual funds included—bought "inverse floaters," bonds structured so that their interest payments actually increased as rates went down. But because of the way these bonds were engineered, the inverse floater's interest rate may go up 3 or 4 percentage points for every 1 percentage point drop in the regular rate. Naturally, as short-term rates dropped 4 percentage points over the period, some of these bonds were paying out very juicy yields—sometimes in excess of 20 percent. But the flip side is that when interest rates started to rise—as they did in 1994—the bond's payout started to decline, also 3 or 4 percentage points down for every percentage point the regular rates went up. Since such securities are priced based on their payout, the prices for such leveraged derivatives just melted away.

The derivative debacle of 1994 underscored another problem. Many of the derivatives created in the early 1990s from mortgage-backed securities did not behave as the financial engineers' computer models had predicted. For instance, Piper Jaffray Institutional Government Income Fund and Managers Intermediate Mortgage Fund—both managed by Piper's Worth Bruntjen—plunged and racked up a 25 percent decline in total return in 1994's first quarter. The two funds, chock full of mortgage-backed derivatives, fell, in part, because many of the unusual securities did not behave as expected. For instance, Bruntjen's financial models predicted that the interest-only and principal-only securities would neutralize each other. If one went down, the other would go up in value. Instead, in the chaotic, declining market, both sorts of securities went down in price. The Piper fund ended the year with a –28.8 percent total return, the Managers fund, nearly as bad, went down 25 percent.

Computer models can "value" a security, but at the end of the day, when a mutual fund has to price its portfolio, what counts is the market price. When the bond market rout began, market prices were far below theoretical prices—and for good reason. There were hordes of investors who wanted to unload these mortgage derivatives, but scant few buyers willing to step up. Losses were so bad in the PaineWebber Short-Term U.S. Government Fund that to preserve its credibility with investors and brokers, Paine Webber spent some $268 million to buy unmarketable securities—known on the Street as "kitchen sink" bonds—from the fund. That, incidentally, did not

Derivatives can enhance a fund's returns.

make the shareholders whole, but simply lessened their losses. For the year, the fund had a −4.9 percent total return.

What is so daunting to bond-fund investors is that even if they do their homework and study the portfolio, it's hard to spot the derivatives. No portfolio manager is going to point to a security—often the underlying issuer is a government-affiliated issuer like Federal National Mortgage Association or Federal Home Loan Mortgage Corp.—and say, "This is a derivative security, the price of which can be extremely volatile under rapidly changing market conditions." Usually, investors will look at the credit quality of the issue—which is excellent with these two issuers—and figure the investment is secure. With these derivatives, there's no question that in the end they will pay off at maturity. But the problem is that a portfolio manager may have paid a price figuring on a five-year payback, but after rates rose, the estimated payback period might have shot up to 25 years. So the security takes a double price hit—because it's now a longer maturity and it's paying a less-than-market interest rate.

Of course the derivative minefield can be treacherous for an investor who, until a few years ago, kept most of his or her money in the bank. Fortunately, most bond funds do not—and never have—used the exotic derivatives. But to be sure, Randall Merk of American Century Benham Funds suggests that an investor quiz the broker or fund's sales agent about the use of derivatives in the fund (Table 2-31).

For all the public brouhaha over derivatives, most bond funds don't invest in derivatives and, in 1994 and 1996, lost money the old-fashioned way. Interest rates rose, and the price of the bonds went down accordingly. How much they declined depended on the average maturity of the portfolio, a figure that you can find in the BUSINESS WEEK Mutual Fund Scoreboard. But you can also obtain that figure from bond-fund shareholder reports, or just by calling the fund company. The average maturity is nothing more than the weighted average of the maturities of all the bonds held by the fund. And the maturity of the bond is merely the number of years left until the bond will be redeemed by its issuer for its full, principal value.

Maturity is a revealing piece of information. The longer the maturity, the more sensitive the bond prices are to changes in interest rates. And buying the golden credit of the U.S. Treasury is no safe haven from fluctuating bond prices. U.S. Treasury bonds, in fact, are considered to have no

TABLE 2-31

WHAT TO ASK A MUTUAL FUND MANAGER ABOUT DERIVATIVES

What percentage of the fund is in derivatives?
Be wary if it's any more than five percent. Most of the funds that ran into trouble had anywhere from 15 to 40 percent.

How are the derivatives used?
Ideally, they're used for hedging. Be wary if the fund is using them to juice the yield. Watch out if interest-only (IO) and principal-only (PO) derivatives are paired off and declared to be perfectly hedged. Experience shows that may not be the case.

Is anyone paying attention to what the fund manager is doing?
The fund management company and the fund's board of directors should be aware of what the portfolio manager is doing and monitoring the use of derivatives.

How are the derivatives priced?
The fund should be using an impartial, third-party service to price derivative securities for purposes of calculating the day's net asset value.

How have the derivatives benefited or hurt the fund in the past?
If the fund hasn't used them before, you might avoid that fund. Do you want the fund manager to get his education in derivatives using your money?

DATA: AMERICAN CENTURY BENHAM FUNDS, BUSINESS WEEK

credit risk, so their values are solely a function of the changes in rates. (High-yield, or junk bond, funds are also affected by interest rates, but less so. When the economy is strong, corporate cash flows increase, and so does the ability for companies to pay their debt. So high-yield bonds usually take a little less of a hit from rising rates than do highly rated investment grade bonds.)

As a rule, the net asset value of a fund comprised of long-term bonds will fluctuate more than a fund of intermediate-term bonds. And a short-term bond fund is the least volatile of the three. Table 2-32, for instance, which comes from the Vanguard Group, sums up how changes in interest rates would affect some of its bond funds. In general, short-term funds like the Vanguard Short-Term Corporate Bond Portfolio keep their average maturities below 3 years; intermediate funds like the Vanguard Bond Index fund, in the 3- to 10-year range; long-term funds have maturities over 10 years; and many, like the Vanguard Fixed-Income Long-Term U.S. Treasury Bond Portfolio, keep the average in the 20- to 25-year range.

Maturity is a good measure of the potential price volatility of a government or general bond fund. But it doesn't tell the whole story. Two bonds, or bond funds, with the same maturity may not necessarily have the same duration, and

TABLE 2-32

HOW INTEREST RATES AFFECT BOND FUNDS

VANGUARD PORTFOLIO ▼	AVERAGE MATURITY ▼	EST. IMPACT OF INTEREST RATE CHANGE ON NET ASSET VALUE			
		−1% ▼	−2% ▼	+1% ▼	+2% ▼
SHORT-TERM CORPORATE BOND	2.7 yrs.	2.2%	4.4%	−2.7%	−4.4%
TOTAL BOND MARKET INDEX	8.8 yrs.	4.6	9.3	−4.6	−9.3
LONG-TERM U.S. TREASURY	20.1 yrs.	9.5	19.1	−9.6	−17.4

DATA: VANGUARD GROUP OF INVESTMENT COS.

as such they won't react to interest rate changes in the same way. Bond fund managers pay close attention to duration in running their funds, but the concept is not well-known or understood among lay investors. Most bond fund managers will give shareholders information on yields and maturities in their funds, but ask a shareholder representative about duration and you might just stump them.

The calculation of duration is complex, but the principle behind it is not. Duration looks at a bond as a series of cash payments (interest payments and the bond redemption at maturity are considered payments). The duration formula calculates a "present value" for each payment, adds them up, and estimates how long it would take the bondholder to recover his or her entire investment in today's dollars.

Suppose Bond Fund A and Bond Fund B have portfolio maturities of 15 years and they yield 6.5 percent. But Fund A owns bonds issued when rates were lower: they have lower interest payments and they sell at a discount to their redemption value, say 90 cents on the dollar. Fund B has bonds that were issued when rates were higher and now sell for 110 cents on the dollar. Fund A has the higher duration because, since it has lower cash payments, it will take longer for the investor to recover his or her money. Fund B, whose bonds pay out more income, has a lower duration.

Is low duration better than high? That depends on your market outlook. When interest rates are falling, high duration bonds and bond funds will do better. The lower interest rate gives all the future cash flows a higher present value. When rates are rising, lower duration is less vulnerable to loss.

Sometimes investors who worry a lot about fluctuations in net asset value choose to keep their money in short-term bond funds or stick with money-market funds. In a money-market fund the principal is steady, but the yield, or interest rate, is very volatile. That's just the opposite of the long-term fund, where the NAV can be volatile, but the interest is steadier. If you depend on your investments to generate a certain amount of income, you will need to use intermediate- or long-term funds. The returns from shorter-term funds may be too unpredictable.

When investing in bond funds, it's also important to note the difference between owning, say, a bond fund and owning bonds directly. Most bonds pay interest twice a year, at predetermined dates and at a predetermined amount. A 20-year, $1000 bond with a 7 percent interest rate will make a $35 payment every six months for the next 20 years. That's not the case with a managed bond fund.

Most bond funds make an income distribution monthly, and it may or may not be the same every month. The funds don't earn the same amount of money every month because they rarely have the interest coming in in 12 equal payments. And many bond funds just pass on whatever they've earned during the month, after taking out fund expenses.

But some funds have shareholders who take the income in cash rather than reinvest it. And many of those shareholders like a steady payout. So in those cases, the fund managers attempt to smooth out the income distributions and pay a set amount. Suppose the fund managers settle on a payout of 10 cents per share per month, which may be reasonable given the interest earnings on the portfolio. Some months the fund earns more, some months less, but on average the fund can afford to pay out $1.20 over the year.

Now suppose interest rates fall. Thousands of new shareholders are buying into the fund because they heard about the 10 cents per share per month distribution. But the fund can't invest the new money at as high a rate as before, and the earnings of the fund drop. Inevitably, the income payout must drop too. A mutual fund must pay out its earnings, but it can't pay what it doesn't earn. If, in a period of falling interest rates, someone tries to sell you a bond fund with an unusually high monthly payout, beware. The payout may not be sustainable—or the fund is making the payment out of capital, not income. If that's the case, the fund is chipping away at its net asset value.

This loss of net asset value can be significant. To test just how much, the analysts at Morningstar Inc. looked at the change in fund NAVs for 181 government and high-quality corporate bond funds from November 1, 1986 to September 30, 1994. The significance of those two dates is that the interest-rate environments at the two points were near identical, with the long-term interest rate on U.S. government bonds at about 8 percent. If bond funds behaved like bonds, the net asset values in 1994 should have been around the same as in 1986.

But that was not the case at all. The average fund was down 7.6 percent, and with 14 funds, the NAV loss exceeded 15 percent. The reason, concluded Morningstar, was that the funds were stretching to pay the highest possible yields. And in doing that, they emphasized premium bonds—those are bonds whose interest payments were set when rates were higher. So a 20-year government bond with an 11.25 percent coupon will, in a period when a new bond with the same maturity fetches about 8 percent, sell at a "premium"—in this case, $1294 for a bond with a $1000 face value. Even so, the bond pays $112.50 a year, and even on a $1294 investment, that's an 8.7 percent current yield ($112.50 divided by $1294). But here's the catch: Every year, the value of the bond will decline as it gets closer to maturity. So the yield to maturity is much closer to 8 percent—the current rate of interest.

The high-coupon strategy allows a higher current payout, and that's very important to bond funds that are sold by brokers and salespersons, because, as they say in the business, yield sells. Those same bond funds often have much higher than average expenses and so must seek higher yields to be able to pay them and also provide their shareholders a competitive rate of return. And some portfolio managers defend the practice, especially if it has delivered a good total return.

A fund that overachieves on the income side may be okay if it's in an individual retirement account (IRA) or other tax-shelter plan. But it doesn't make much sense for many taxpaying investors. The interest is taxable in the year it's paid and at ordinary income tax rates. If the high-yield strategy has also delivered capital losses (remember the average 7.6 percent NAV loss over eight years), investors will eventually be able to deduct them. But the future tax savings from long-term capital losses will be worth far less than the current tax bite from the higher-yield funds.

There's another major difference between direct ownership of bonds and owning shares in a bond fund. If you own a 10-year bond, you know that next year it will be a 9-year bond; in 2 years, an 8-year; and so forth. In 10 years, it will mature. Though interest rates may go up and down in the interim, the maturity of your portfolio of bonds gets shorter every year. The price volatility should decrease with the shortening of the portfolio's maturity. Bond funds, on the other hand, never "mature." If a fund's policy is to keep its maturity around 10 years, it will keep trading the bonds in the portfolio to do just that. Investors can't "shorten" their maturities without switching to another fund. And that could trigger capital gains taxes, even if the investments are in municipal bond funds.

The basic relationship between average maturity and volatility of bond funds holds true no matter whether your fund is taxable or tax-free, government or corporate. The net asset values of funds that invest in U.S. government securities are almost entirely dependent on interest rate movements.

The creditworthiness of the issuer comes into play—but in a small way—with investment-grade corporate and municipal bonds. Investment-grade corporate and municipal bonds are those rated AAA, AA, A, or BBB by Standard & Poor's, or Aaa, Aa, A, or Baa by Moody's Investor Services (Table 2-33).

Anything less than investment grade is "junk" debt, more charitably known as "high-yield" debt. The junk segment of the bond market is where credit considerations may even overwhelm interest rate movements in the pricing of securities. The highest ratings in the junk sector, sometimes also referred to by the oxymoron "quality junk," are BB and B. Some of the quality junk companies are formerly blue-chips that have taken on enormous amounts of debt in leveraged buyouts, takeovers, or other financial restructurings. Then there's CCC and on down to D—for default, or bonds no longer making interest payments. That would include the bonds of companies in bankruptcy.

Since interest rates are the driving force in the bond market, the variations in returns from bond funds are not as dramatic as those from equities. Take, for instance, the municipal bond funds. During 1994, the single worst year in the bond market in 60 years, the best muni fund delivered a total return of 2.4 percent; the worst, −20.4 percent. That's a range of nearly 23 percentage points. By contrast, equity funds are far more heterogeneous. Interest rates, though they play a role, are only one of many fundamental forces

> Bond funds, unlike bonds, never "mature."

TABLE 2-33

A GUIDE TO BOND CREDIT RATINGS

RATING		
S&P	**MOODY'S**	
AAA	Aaa	Amoco, Bell South, Exxon, and General Electric are a few of the dwindling number of borrowers in this very exclusive club.
AA	Aa	Here's where you'll find AT&T and many other phone companies. Also Coca-Cola, McDonald's, and Wal-Mart Stores.
A	A	Tough times a few years ago sent IBM's credit rating down along with its stock price. The quality is still high.
BBB	Baa	The lowest rating a bond can receive and still be considered an investment-grade security.
BB	Ba	The highest ranking for junk bonds, sometimes known by the oxymoron, "quality junk."
B	B	Many highly leveraged companies are in this category, which suggests some doubt about borrower's ability to pay.
CCC	Caa	Includes the debt of retailer Levitz Furniture and the airline USAir.
CC	Ca	Just another rung down the credit ladder, with increasing possibility for default.
C	C	The pits. At Moody's this means default.
D	na	Interest and/or principal is in arrears.

DATA: BUSINESS WEEK

that affect stocks. So returns from equity funds have a much greater variation. During 1994 the best equity fund delivered a 35.3 percent return; the worst, –50.3 percent—a range of nearly 87 percentage points.

Although these statements are generalizations, they become even more true when you hone in on funds with similar goals. True, Vanguard Fixed-Income Long-Term U.S. Treasury Fund, with an average maturity of 21 years, is going to get nailed if interest rates rise. But so will the net asset values of all long-term government bond funds.

So, in a sense, bond funds are much more targeted in their mission than equity funds. Portfolio managers for equity funds typically have far

more choice of what stocks to invest in than bond fund managers have choice of bonds. And even in declining stock markets, there are always a few industries or companies that will run counter to the trend. A dramatic breakthrough with a genetically engineered drug will send a biotechnology stock climbing, no matter what's happening to the Dow Jones industrial average. Find enough of the winners and equity fund managers can still buck a downtrend.

But bond fund managers work from a pool of securities that are far more homogeneous. If you manage the Merrill Lynch Federal Securities Fund, you have to invest in U.S. government debt or government-backed debt. How different are the results going to be from other government bond funds?

Bonds and bond funds entail some other risks as well. First, there's call risk. Most corporate and municipal bonds give the issuer the right to redeem the bonds or "call" them after about 5 years in the case of corporates, 10 in the case of long-term municipal bonds. If interest rates have dropped by the time a bond becomes callable, issuers will call the bonds and refinance them at a lower rate. (It's basically the same idea as refinancing your home mortgage to take advantage of lower interest rates.)

Calls are bad news for bondholders. True, the bondholders collect a premium for their bonds: The issuer may pay $1030 or $1050 for a $1000 bond. But that's small consolation to the bondholders who will have to reinvest the proceeds at a lower rate of interest. A mutual fund with a large number of callable bonds might find itself in that quandary. Part of a bond fund manager's job is to steer around such obstacles. One way around the call problem is to buy bonds whose coupons are so low that they're unlikely to be called. The easiest solution, of course, is U.S. government bonds, which can't be called.

Whether or not a bond is callable, the bond or bond-fund investor also faces reinvestment risk. Remember, a bond provides the investor a series of interest payments over a set number of years, and the reinvestment of that money is part of the total return from investing in bonds. (If you take the money out when it's paid, there is no reinvestment.) The risk in reinvestment risk is that rates will decline over the life of the bond, and the cash from the periodic interest payments will be reinvested at lower and lower rates. The antidote to reinvestment risk is to invest in zero coupon bonds. These bonds don't pay interest. Instead they are sold at discount to face value. The difference between the purchase price and the maturity value is the interest. Since there is no cash to reinvest, there is no reinvestment risk.

Another sort of risk is "event risk." There's not too much heard about it nowadays, but it was big back in the 1980s. Event risk was the danger that an investment grade bond would turn into a lower quality bond through an event like a hostile takeover or a management-led leveraged buyout.

In trying to understand bond funds, it helps to think of them as similar to specialty or "sector" funds found among equity mutual funds. Diversified equity funds have wide latitude in what they can invest in. Specialty funds target particular investments. Bond funds tend to "specialize" in a certain sector, like a long-term government securities fund or a short-term municipals. This specialization puts more responsibility on the investor. If you choose to invest in a long-term bond fund and interest rates shoot up, there isn't much the portfolio manager can do to keep the NAV from falling. The best he or she can do is try to contain the damage.

What's also important to remember when looking at bond funds is the difference between a fund's yield and its total return. Total return includes the yield plus or minus changes in net asset value. Suppose a fund has a 12 percent yield but only a 2 percent total return. You can surmise that the fund lost 10 percent of its asset value during the year. Likewise, in an up market, a fund's total return should exceed the yield owing to an upturn in bond prices. If you're comparing bond funds, be sure to compare yields with yields and total returns with total returns.

Given these caveats, let's look at categories of bond funds in the BUSINESS WEEK Mutual Fund Scoreboard. As with equity funds, we've overhauled many of the categories, organizing them by maturity as well as the issuers of the bonds in the portfolio. The funds in the general bond category mainly invest in investment-grade and government debt. We break them down into four groups by maturity: long, intermediate, short, and ultrashort. U.S. government bond funds are classified as long, intermediate, or short. Among the municipal bond funds, there's one short-term category. Long-term and intermediate-term municipal funds are divided into national (with bonds from all across the country) and single-state (with bonds from a single state, usually of interest only to taxpayers of that state).

The more specialized categories are largely the same as before: high-yield, convertibles, and multisector. International bond funds now incorporate the short-term world income funds. Those funds have been dwindling away to the point where there aren't enough of them to sustain their own category.

As with the equity funds, the new categories are meant to sort the funds into groups by the way they invest, not necessarily what they say about themselves. As such, you will find funds that, judged by their names, seem to be in the wrong category. For instance, Strong Government Securities is in the general bond intermediate category because it fails to meet the intermediate government fund hurdle of having at least 80 percent of the portfolio in government securities. Despite its name, Fidelity Intermediate Bond Fund falls in the short-term category. That's because its average duration is 3.2 years, while the cut-off for intermediate funds is 3.5 years.

LONG-TERM BOND FUNDS

If you choose to invest in a general long-term bond fund, you're probably putting your money into one of the most volatile sorts of bond funds. Only long-term government funds are more risky. The risk here, of course, is not credit risk, which comes to mind when most people think about borrowers and lenders. It's interest-rate or market risk, the chance that the fund's net asset value will slide around with fluctuations in interest rates. Funds in this category have an average maturity in excess of 10 years and an average duration of 6 or more years. Roughly speaking, a fund whose bonds have an average duration of 6 years will fall 6 percent for a 1 percentage point rise in interest rates, and rise 6 percent for a 1 percentage point fall. But most of these funds have durations in excess of 10 years.

That said, why do investors choose these funds? In general, the longer the maturity of a bond, the higher the interest rate. That's one of the underlying principles of investing in bonds. Indeed, though it does not happen every year, over the last five years, the average long-term bond fund topped the intermediates and short-terms. In the last year, the volatility in the long-term bond market knocked these funds around and the average fund lost money, even after adding back income distributions.

These funds certainly maintain a very high credit quality, so they should hold up relatively well in an economic slowdown or recession. Better than one-quarter of their holdings are U.S. government or government-backed securities. Another sort of blue-chip investment is

Bond funds have very specific goals.

"sovereign" bonds, or dollar bonds issued by foreign governments with high credit ratings and interest payments in dollars. Only about 10 percent of the holdings are below investment grade. On the other hand, the ability of a general bond fund to dabble in the lower-quality issues can help prop a fund's results when interest rates are rising. That's one of the reasons Alliance Bond Corporate Bond B was able to earn 9.3 percent in 1996, nearly tripling the category average.

But the real superstar of this category is the Loomis Sayles Bond Fund (Table 2-34). The $538.2 million fund led its peers in total return for the last one-, three-, and five-year periods. It's also the only general long-term bond fund to win three upward-pointing arrows in the Scoreboard and it's also garnered a three-up-arrow rating in its category. As you might expect, Loomis Sayles Bond is no generic long-term fund, and its portfolio manager, Daniel J. Fuss, is no run-of-the-mill manager. Fuss is quite active, moving money around to take advantage of inefficiencies in the fixed-income markets.

Though he maintains an average credit quality that is still investment grade, at times Fuss will lace the portfolio with less than sterling credits. In 1996, for instance, he seized on the resurgence of emerging markets debt and put some in the portfolio to improve returns. Unlike many bond fund managers, Fuss sees rising rates as an investment opportunity. Falling rates can provide windfall profits in the short term, but they lower future returns because money earned by the bonds is reinvested at lower rates.

Another standout in this category is Invesco Select Income Fund. It also earned a top category rating, but takes a somewhat different approach. Loomis Sayles's bonds tend to concentrate around the BBB credit rating, or just above the junk bond threshold. Invesco Select Income fared well recently because it had about half its assets in high-yield debt, but maintained an average investment grade quality because it offset

TABLE 2-34

LONG-TERM FUNDS (GEN.)
BEST RETURNS

Period	Fund	Total return*
1996	LOOMIS SAYLES BOND	10.3%
1994-96	LOOMIS SAYLES BOND	11.8
1992-96	LOOMIS SAYLES BOND	14.3

*Average annual, pretax   DATA: MORNINGSTAR INC.

that by placing about one-third of its assets in AAA-rated bonds.

INTERMEDIATE BOND FUNDS

The general corporate intermediate bond fund category is a broad one, encompassing a wide variety of bond-picking investment styles. What ties these funds together is their focus on a portfolio with an investment-grade credit rating, an average maturity between 4 and 10 years, and average durations of between 3.5 and 6 years. Those duration figures give you a way to assess risk. Simply put, an intermediate fund with an average duration of 5 years has half the interest rate sensitivity as one with a 10-year duration. Since intermediate funds generate yields that are 80 to 90 percent that of the long-term funds, it's no wonder that many more investors opt for intermediate maturities. You get most of the yield with much less of the risk.

Intermediate funds don't usually make big bets. Their portfolios tend to revolve around a benchmark, the Lehman Brothers Aggregate Bond Index. That index has a duration of around 5 years, so the portfolio managers who really expect a fall in rates might buy longer-term, higher-yield bonds in order to push their duration out to 6 years. Those who anticipate higher rates might sell longer-term bonds in order to shorten the maturity to 4.5 or even 4 years.

In late 1996, judging these funds by their largest holdings might have suggested they were government bond funds. That's because, after a long, extended economic expansion, the yield on investment-grade corporate debt is not much greater than that of Treasuries. In such situations, bond managers might say corporates are "rich" and Treasuries "cheap." What that means is that investors can switch into Treasuries—which have no credit risk—from corporates, without having to give up much yield in return. In a recession, when investors fear corporations may not have the means to pay their debts, that gap is much wider.

Bond fund managers pay close attention to those gaps—in bond parlance, they're quality spreads. They track the yield differentials between many kinds of bonds and often make trades when the historical relationship gets out of whack. To stock market investors, that's like betting on grass growing. But in the bond fund world, a manager's compensation can depend on beating the next guy or an index by a couple of one-hundredths of a percentage point. In that context, those trades can be worthwhile.

TABLE 2-35

INTERMEDIATE-TERM FUNDS (GEN.)

BEST RETURNS

Period	Fund	Total return*
1996	SUNAMERICA DIVERSIFIED INCOME	12.4%
1994-96	STRONG CORPORATE BOND	9.3
1992-96	STRONG CORPORATE BOND	10.8

*Average annual, pretax   DATA: MORNINGSTAR INC.

Strong Corporate Bond Fund, the fund with the highest returns over the last three- and five-year periods, rarely gets far away from its duration benchmark (Table 2-35). Instead, the managers add value to the portfolio by paying close attention to those differentials between sectors of the bond market and even unusual gaps between individual issuers. This results in perhaps three times the amount of trading that takes place in the average intermediate fund, but it's been profitable trading nonetheless. The fund earns three upward-pointing arrows when rated against other intermediate funds.

Federated Bond Fortress Fund also earns the highest category rating. But it does so with bigger bets. When the portfolio manager anticipates a faster economic growth, he shortens the duration and lowers the credit quality. When he anticipates slower growth, it lengthens duration and upgrades credits. The returns are strong because, over the last five years, the manager has managed to make the right calls at the right times. But if it doesn't, the fund might get a nasty double whammy, both from the wrong interest rate and the wrong credit quality calls.

If you don't want to worry about managers making the right call, this category also includes the Vanguard Bond Index Fund Total Bond Market Portfolio. That mouthful is a bond index fund managed to replicate the return of the Lehman Bros. Aggregate Bond Index. The fund employs the same indexing approach as with equity funds and earns its keep by not trying to second-guess the market and keeping expenses to a minimum.

Indexed bond funds have not caught on in the bond market as in the equity market. Part of the reason is that investors just aren't interested in bond funds these days. The other reason, perhaps, is that these funds haven't so convincingly beaten the managed bond funds. For the last one-, three-, and five-year periods, the Vanguard Bond Index Fund Total Bond Market Portfolio beat the average fund only in the three-year period, and only by 0.3 percentage point a year. Vanguard also has a separate intermediate-term bond index fund, as well as a short-term index fund.

SHORT BOND FUNDS

As bond funds go, short-term funds are the least volatile. To qualify for this category, the maturities usually must be between 1 and 5 years, and the durations between 1 and 3.5 years. But in absolute terms, they're still pretty safe. Sure, a 1 percentage point hike in interest rates could knock 3 percent off a fund with a duration of 3 years. But in the short maturities, such hikes are infrequent.

Since these funds are fairly restricted regarding what they can do with maturities, they try to make their mark through bond selection. These funds generally invest in a wide variety of fixed-income instruments—from Treasuries and investment-grade corporates to high-yield and emerging markets debt. In most cases, the funds are restricted as to the portion of their assets that can go into the less creditworthy issues.

At a time when longer-term bonds are falling in price, these funds can deliver relatively attractive returns. In 1996, for instance, a year that experienced several sharp swings in long-term rates, the short-term funds turned in some attractive returns. The average short-term general bond fund earned a 5 percent total return, which handily beat the intermediate's 3.7 percent return and the long-term's 3.3 percent return. That was the reverse order of 1995, a bullish year for bonds in which the longest maturities made the most money.

The best short-term bond fund of 1996 was Alliance Short-Term Multi-Market A, with a fat 13.4 percent return (Table 2-36). Before you rush to buy it, be forewarned that it's an atypical short-term fund, a refugee from the now-disbanded short-term world income fund category. No doubt the fund got some help from short-term emerging markets debt. But like

TABLE 2-36

SHORT-TERM FUNDS (GEN.)

BEST RETURNS

Period	Fund	Total return*
1996	ALLIANCE S-T MULTI-MARKET A	13.4%
1994-96	HOTCHKIS & WILEY LOW DURATION	7.9
1992-96	STRONG SHORT-TERM BOND	6.5

*Average annual, pretax   DATA: MORNINGSTAR INC.

many funds with big one-year returns, it also has some rather unpleasant results in its past. Even including the sharp 1996 results, the fund has a five-year average annual return of only 3.3 percent, which is less than what an investor could have earned in money-market funds with a lot less cost and risk.

Far more conventional and better choices in this category are Harbor Short Duration Fund and Strong Short-Term Bond, both of which earned the highest category ratings. The Strong portfolio has been in the top quartile of its category five of the last six years. The fund keeps an investment grade credit quality, but has the ability to put up to 25 percent of the assets in bonds rated BB. For most of the last few years, the ability to buy the higher yield, lesser credits has helped boost the returns of the fund.

ULTRASHORT BOND FUNDS

The ultrashort category is the newest addition to the bond fund portion of the BUSINESS WEEK Mutual Fund Scoreboard. This relatively small category takes in ultrashort corporate funds, like Strong Advantage Fund and Neuberger & Berman Ultra Short Bond Fund, and the adjustable-rate mortgage funds that were previously in the government category. The two types of funds have very different investment programs but they share an important common characteristic—a portfolio duration of less than one year. The idea behind these funds is to earn a higher return than a money-market fund without taking a whole lot more risk.

Strong Advantage Fund, the best performer of the last five-year period, is one of the oldest of the ultrashort funds (Table 2-37). With $1.4 billion in assets, it's also the largest of the funds. Volatility is kept to a minimum. Portfolio manager Jeffrey A. Koch, who's run the fund since 1991, keeps the duration at 6 months. That's not a whole lot more than a money-market fund. He seeks the extra yield by venturing out into the lesser credits where money-market funds typically don't go. That's because money-market funds are managed to keep their net asset values (NAVs) constant at $1 per share. Strong Advantage does not have a lot of variation in NAV, but it's not obliged to stay at a fixed rate. During 1996, the fund earned a total return of 6.7 percent and paid out income distributions of 6.2 percent, which means the fund actually went up about half a percent in NAV.

Neuberger & Berman Ultra Short Bond Fund used to follow a similar strategy, but did not venture out to the lesser credit. But the fund

TABLE 2-37

	ULTRASHORT BOND FUNDS	
	BEST RETURNS	
Period	Fund	Total return*
1996	PIPER ADJ. RATE MORTGAGE SECS.	6.8%
1994-96	STRONG ADVANTAGE	5.9
1992-96	STRONG ADVANTAGE	6.8

*Average annual, pretax   DATA: MORNINGSTAR INC.

recently changed its investment policy to extend duration to between one and two years. So despite its name, Morningstar plans to move this fund to the short-term category.

The other members of this group are the funds that invest in adjustable-rate mortgages. In theory, a mutual fund that owns nothing but adjustable-rate mortgages (ARMs) should be a pretty safe, conservative offering. Most of the ARMs are issued by government-sponsored enterprises like Federal National Mortgage Assn. and Government National Mortgage Assn., so credit is not an issue. And since most ARMs reset their interest rates at least once a year, the effective maturity is no more than a year. So even though the net asset values of ARMs funds fluctuate, they shouldn't fluctuate much—and ARMs still provide a higher rate of interest than a money-market mutual fund.

In reality, many of these funds have been disappointments. If anything, these short-maturity funds should have distinguished themselves in 1994's bear market by at least completing the year with a positive total return. But the average ARMs fund fell far short, and, in fact, only 5 of the 12 ARMs funds in the Scoreboard had positive results.

The bear market disappointment might have been more palatable if the funds really outperformed during the bull markets. But in the three-year period of falling interest rates, only in 1991 did the funds—and there were only six at the time—really stand out, earning 10.5 percent total return and beating the average taxable money-market fund by 5 percentage points. Spotting sharp 1991 returns, fund-management companies rolled out new ARMs funds, and by the end of 1992 the number of funds had risen to 32 and assets more than doubled to $20 billion; the total return wound up being less than half that of the year before.

The culprit then was falling interest rates. Because ARM securities have higher yields than, say, short-term Treasuries, they typically sell at a premium. So an ARM with a 6 percent yield may sell for $1050, or 105 in bond parlance. But then interest rates go down, and at the next reset, the yield falls to 5 percent. Now the ARM may sell for only $1030, or 103. The fund's shareholders lose that $20 out of net asset value.

But that's not the only problem posed by the ARMs funds. Like conventional mortgage funds, falling rates often encourage homeowners to refinance. That means every ARM purchased at 103 or 105 is paid off at 100. Fund shareholders have to eat the losses, too. Not surprisingly, rising interest rates proved problematic as well. In 1994, for instance, short-term rates ran up so fast and so far that the built-in adjustments did not bring the yields of many ARMs up to competitive rates of interest. The result—sagging prices for ARMs securities.

Although ARMs funds are not the magic investment that many had hoped for, they still can offer a decent return with a modest amount of risk. Whether they delight or disappoint depends on what investor expectations are. Investors who are concerned about stability of NAV should seek out the "purest" ARMs funds they can find—those that invest in government-backed ARMs only. Stay clear of those that mix in other privately issued ARMs securities. If trouble sets in, there is no market for them.

Even when ARMs funds stick to top drawer issuers, it's not certain they are a great deal for the investor. Given that most of these funds have been through an entire interest-rate cycle (down and then back up to the starting point), it has become clear that there still remains a big gap between the theory and the practice of ARMs investing. Rather than put, say, $10,000 in an ARMs fund, an investor might achieve better results by putting $5000 each in a money-market fund and a short-term U.S. government bond fund (a plain vanilla fund without derivatives). Or better yet, put the entire amount in a well-seasoned ultrashort bond fund like Strong Advantage Fund.

LONG GOVERNMENT FUNDS

Long-term government bond funds are not for the faint of heart. Sure, the U.S. government guarantee may comfort the investor worried about the creditworthiness of borrowers. But because government bonds have no credit risk, they are totally creatures of changes in interest rates. And since the long government funds own bonds with average maturities in excess of 10 years and durations of more than 6 years, they

TABLE 2-38

LONG GOVERNMENT FUNDS

BEST RETURNS

Period	Fund	Total return*
1996	HANCOCK SOVEREIGN U.S. GOVT. A	1.2%
1994-96	AMER. CENT.—BENHAM TARGET 2015	9.5
1992-96	AMER. CENT.—BENHAM TARGET 2020	10.6

*Average annual, pretax   DATA: MORNINGSTAR INC.

are the most sensitive to changes in interest rates. When rates fall, such as what happened in 1995, these funds earned an average 24.4 percent total return. That's something more like you would expect from stocks. In 1994 and 1996, when rates rose, the total returns were –7.1 percent and –1.9 percent, respectively. The best performer in the fund category, Hancock Sovereign U.S. Government Income Fund A, earned a 1.2 percent return (Table 2-38). Remember, those are returns after adding back the income distributions. The net asset value of these funds fell anywhere from 7 to 14 percent.

While these funds' fates are largely determined by interest rates, there is still some room for portfolio managers to maneuver. If the manager believes that interest rates will decline, he or she can move fund assets into longer maturity bonds with higher duration. If it looks like interest rates are heading higher, the manager can sell bonds to "shorten" the maturity and duration. Managers can't avoid declining bond prices altogether, but can take steps to lessen the damage, such as investing in "premium" bonds. Those are bonds that sell at a price in excess of their value at maturity because their coupons or interest payments are higher than those of the current rates. When rates go up, such bonds tend to hold their value better.

If the fund is a general government bond fund instead of one restricted to Treasuries, the manager has the ability to pick up some extra return by investment in government-backed mortgages or government-agency issued bonds. As a practical matter, the government stands behind them, but because they're not Treasuries, they tend to pay somewhat higher interest rates.

The most extreme—and volatile—sorts of long-term government funds are those of American Century–Benham Target Maturities series, which invest in zero-coupon bonds. These bonds sell at a fraction of their par value, $1000, and mature in their target year at $1000. There are no interest payments in the interim. The "interest" from a zero-coupon bond is just the difference between the purchase price and $1000. There are six of these funds, with maturities in 2000, 2005, 2010, 2015, 2020, and 2025. The last three are perhaps some of the most volatile in the entire bond fund universe.

There's no bond more sensitive to changes in interest rates than a zero-coupon bond. Go back to the idea of duration. A 30-year bond with a 7 percent coupon has a duration of around 11 or 12 years. A 30-year zero-coupon bond has a duration of 30 years. There are no interest payments between now and year 30, so the value of the bond is determined by the present value of that redemption payment of so many years away. In 1993, a year in which long-term interest rates declined to the lowest level in decades, the fund maturing in 2020 had gained as much as 40 percent by October, but then declined to finish the year with a still sharp 35.6 percent gain. In 1994, when interest rates shot up quickly, that same fund lost 17.7 percent in net asset value. In 1995, the fund shot up an amazing 61.3 percent.

In periods of falling interest rates, the zero-coupon funds will invariably be the best performers. Of course, they'll likely be the worst when interest rates rise. As short-term trading vehicles, these funds make some sense. They're no-load and can be bought and sold with a telephone call. But as long-term investments, even Benham management admits you're better off in a regular zero-coupon bond.

Suppose you're going to be 65 in 2020, nearly 25 years away. You decide to put your individual retirement account funds into zero-coupon bonds that mature that year, a reasonable thing to do. The best bet would be to pay the broker's commission, for once you do, you won't pay another nickel for the next 25 years. But if you buy the zero-coupon mutual fund, you'll be hit for 0.60 to 0.70 percent in expenses each year.

(Zero-coupon bonds or bond funds only make sense in a tax-deferred account. Though they pay no cash interest, the Internal Revenue Service says the zero earnings "accrete" interest every year as they get closer to maturity. So you have to pay taxes on the interest every year, though you don't collect it for years to come. Some people use them for children's accounts, and invest in the series that matures when the child is college age. If a child is paying tax at his or her parents' rate—and many now do—the zeros may not be worthwhile for him or her, either. Right now, only minors 14 and older have their income taxed at their own tax rates.)

Not surprisingly, this long-term government fund category is a relatively small one in number of funds and assets under management. Most bond investors are risk-averse anyway, so why invest in bonds that at times can exhibit the same volatility as equity funds? General long-term bonds are risky, too, but they can moderate a little of the interest-rate sensitivity by investing in lower-grade corporates or non-U.S. issues, which respond to changes in credit quality and not just rates. Long-term government funds are creatures of fluctuating interest rates.

INTERMEDIATE GOVERNMENT FUNDS

If you listen to the business and financial news on television and radio, the announcers will, along with the Dow Jones industrial average, give the bond market a mention: "The interest rate on the benchmark 30-year U.S. Treasury bond declined one-tenth of 1 percent today. . . ." Investors pay a lot of attention to the 30-year government bond, but that's no more the bond market than the price of Coca-Cola or General Electric is the stock market. The government bond market is by and large a market of intermediate-term securities.

There's another good reason for investors to choose intermediate-term over long-term bond funds. They provide nearly as much return for about one-third to one-half less risk. That's certainly the case in the bond market, in which the yield on a 10-year bond is usually around 90 percent or more of that of the 30-year bond. And the same goes for mutual fund returns. For the 3 years ending in 1996, the intermediate-term funds earned nearly 90 percent of the return earned by long-term funds, and the same goes for the 10-year record.

Some of these government funds rely mainly on Treasuries and U.S. agency issues, others emphasize mortgage-backed securities. The advantage of those that have only Treasury and U.S. agency issues is that the income produced by those bonds is exempt from state and local income taxes. Mortgage-backed securities have no such exemption, even those issued by government agencies like Government National Mortgage Assn. (GNMA or "Ginnie Mae"), or government-related companies like Federal National Mortgage Assn. (FNMA or "Fannie Mae") or Federal Home Loan Mortgage Corp. (FHLMC or "Freddie Mac").

Still, mortgage-related funds tend to dominate this category. Many are recognizable as such, with "GNMA" or "Mortgage Securities" in their titles. But not all. The $10.1 billion Franklin U.S.

Zero-coupon bond funds are the most volatile of all bond funds.

Government Securities I invests solely in government-guaranteed mortgages. But aren't mortgages mainly long-term, like 15 or 30 years?

Indeed they are, but rare is the person who sticks with one mortgage for 30 years and pays it off in its entirety. Most people pay much sooner, either when they sell the house or refinance and take out a new mortgage. Most mortgage-backed securities issued by the Government National Mortgage Assn. are backed pools of individual mortgages, and the "average life" of a GNMA is about 12 years.

Intermediate government funds may sound fairly generic, but they take different approaches to investing. Note, for instance, State Street Research Government Income A does not have "U.S." in front of the word "government." The fund's prospectus says it will usually have at least 65 percent of its assets in U.S. government securities. What about the rest? In 1996, at least, it was Australian and Israeli government debt. In all, 28 percent of the portfolio was in something other than U.S. government securities.

An investor would also expect a government income fund to preserve capital, but that's not necessarily the case. Some funds say their objective is preservation of capital and current income, or current income consistent with preservation of capital. Some say current income alone, with no mention of capital preservation. There is a difference. To maximize current income, a fund can take steps that put a part of its capital at risk.

That's certainly the case with Franklin U.S. Government Securities I. It's a popular fund because it has one of the highest yields in the bond fund universe, even when compared to high-yield corporate issues with far higher coupons. (The yield in 1996 was 7.3 percent.) The fund achieves this by investing in current coupon GNMA securities (those whose mortgages pay at the going rate at the time of purchase). Most investors recognize that higher interest rates will damage the NAVs. But mortgage holders prepay higher-rate mortgages too quickly, the fund suffers capital losses, and the NAV drops. During 1996, the fund paid out 7.3 percent in cash, but the total return was only 4.6 percent. That comes out to about a 2.7 percent loss in net asset value.

Of course, the Franklin fund was not the only intermediate government fund to lose capital in 1996. Even the best performer, Lexington GNMA Income, with a 5.7 percent total return and a 6.4 percent yield, suffered some NAV erosion (Table 2-39). Because it's relatively small, only $133.7

million, the Lexington fund is more of a niche player. It invests in GNMA project loans rather than mortgages on single-family homes and earns some incremental returns that way. It also makes occasional forays into Treasury bonds to bet on the direction of interest rates, which can also add to the return when the bets turn out right.

Fidelity Mortgage Securities, which earned the best returns over the three- and five-year periods, doesn't make bets on the direction of rates. Portfolio manager Kevin Grant keeps the duration of the fund in line with that of the Salomon Bros. Mortgage Index. Instead, the manager makes targeted investments in sectors of the mortgage market he thinks are undervalued, like balloon-note mortgages or securities backed by commercial properties. Both Fidelity Mortgage Securities and Fidelity Spartan Ginnie Mae, another fund managed by Grant, are among the top-rated funds in the intermediate government category.

To understand how mortgage securities work, think of your own situation. Most of these funds invest in home mortgages, just like yours. You make a mortgage payment every month to a bank, thrift, or mortgage company. You don't send your payment to a mutual fund. But it's likely that the original lender has sold your mortgage and is now merely collecting payments and forwarding the proceeds less a small service charge, of course.

Your mortgage, along with hundreds of others, might be pooled together into a mortgage-backed security—and such investments are the principal holdings of the government—mortgage funds. Mutual funds are among the major buyers of mortgage-backed securities. In that sense, they have a role to play in supporting home ownership. Who knows? You may invest in a mutual fund that owns a security that includes your mortgage.

Either way, Fannie's, Freddie's, and Ginnie's mortgage-backed securities are prized by in-

TABLE 2-39

INTERMEDIATE GOVERNMENT FUNDS		
BEST RETURNS		
Period ▼	Fund ▼	Total return* ▼
1996	**LEXINGTON GNMA INCOME**	5.7%
1994-96	**FIDELITY MORTGAGE SECURITIES**	7.9
1992-96	**FIDELITY MORTGAGE SECURITIES**	7.2
*Average annual, pretax		DATA: MORNINGSTAR INC.

Over time, mortgage funds should outperform Treasuries.

vestors. Their credit quality is considered just a shade under that of pure Treasury securities. If borrowers default, the federal agencies guarantee interest and principal. And the federal government stands behind the agencies. Yet the yields are about 1 percentage point higher than Treasury bonds. In 1989, the yield advantage went as high as 1.7 percentage points, as the ailing thrift industry dumped billions in mortgages to raise capital.

Some mortgage-backed securities are bonds, with pools of mortgages serving as collateral. Many are mortgage pass-through certificates and they're like owning the mortgages themselves. A growing segment of this market is collateralized mortgage obligations, better known as CMOs. In a broad sense, all CMOs are derivatives. But not all CMOs are volatile securities that can blow a big hole in a fund's net asset value. However, to understand the mortgage derivatives, you should first understand how the underlying mortgages work.

Despite the sometimes odd behavior of mortgage-backed securities, the mortgage funds are still governed by the immutable laws of fixed-income investing. When interest rates go up, the value of existing mortgages goes down. But there's another dynamic at work, too. The interest, and a small part of the principal, is paid monthly and is predictable. But mortgagors can pay off their principal at any time. A certain amount of prepayment is always figured into the price of a mortgage security. But what is unsettling to the mortgage market—and to funds that invest in mortgage securities—is when the expectations about principal repayment suddenly change.

Here's why. The mortgage-backed market operates on the assumption that a pool of 30-year mortgages will have an "average life" of 12 years. Most people move or refinance their homes well before they pay off a mortgage. But a change in interest rates also alters the expected life of a mortgage-backed security. If that life expectancy drops to 10 years—or lengthens to 15 years—the price of the securities can change dramatically.

Suppose you buy a house and finance the deal with an 8 percent mortgage. And that mortgage, in turn, is owned by some investors through a mortgage-backed security with an 8 percent coupon. You plan to trade up to a larger house in five years, but that doesn't change anything because other mortgagees have no plans to move at all.

Five years go by and you're ready to move, but interest rates shoot up to 10 percent. Your plans are now on hold. You can't sell your house, because the higher interest rates have depressed the housing market. In addition, you are reluctant to take on a mortgage at 10 percent. Instead of selling your home and paying back the mortgage, you stay in the house for a few more years.

At the same time, the investors who hold your mortgage are also hurt. Like all fixed-income instruments, the higher interest rate lowers its value. But in addition, you and many others have delayed your moving plans. That means you will be holding on to your 8 percent mortgages longer. So this security, originally assumed to have a 12-year expected life, now has a 15-year expected life. Higher rates and a longer life make the security less desirable.

But suppose interest rates had dropped to 6 percent. The owners of your mortgage are happy because they're getting 8 percent from you while new mortgages are fetching only 6 percent. But then you sell your house, pay off the 8 percent mortgage, and buy another house with a 6 percent mortgage. Other homeowners in your mortgage pool also sell or refinance their homes to take advantage of the 6 percent rate.

That means the principal gets repaid faster than originally expected, and the security with a 12-year life expectancy now looks like a 10-year. If rates were going up, the mortgage holders would like the faster payback. But with rates heading down, the last thing they want is principal coming back to them. That principal was earning 8 percent. Reinvested in a new mortgage-backed security, the principal would fetch only 6 percent. As mortgage rates come down, one of the major problems for mortgage-fund managers is minimizing prepayment risks.

Got it so far? Now let's look at CMOs and mortgage derivatives. To understand this, go back to how CMOs are created. Investment bankers start with a pool of underlying mortgage securities, like GNMAs. Suppose an underwriter has $200 million worth of mortgages. That represents two cash flows. One is a predictable one, the interest and partial principal payment that homeowners make each month. The other cash flow is the prepayments, or principal that gets paid back early, either from homeowners' selling their homes or refinancing their mortgages. The sponsor of the CMO will look at all the cash flows the mortgages produce and then carve them up to suit different investors.

For those investors who want the more predictable stream of payments, the CMO bankers will take half the mortgage pool, or $100 million, and create a series of "planned amortization class" bonds (PACs). These bonds will behave much like conventional bonds, with regular cash flows. Such bonds will work fine for most bond funds. Generally, these funds also carry a lower interest rate than the underlying mortgages. That's the price these investors pay for predictability. Two-to-three year PACs will work fine in bond funds with two-to-three year maturities. Seven-year PACs are fine for long-term bond funds.

Then come the PAC II and PAC III bonds. Their cash flows are far less certain (II's are more certain than III's) since they get paid after all the PACs are paid. That makes them inherently more risky than PACs, and as such they have higher interest rates (some of the yield held back from the PAC bonds is assigned to the PAC II's and III's). But PAC II's or PAC III's are also far more volatile than PACs, and probably should be shunned by most bond funds.

Risk-averse investors should also avoid the funds which invest heavily in interest-only securities (IOs) or principal-only securities (POs). Those are mortgage-backed securities which pay either interest from a pool of underlying mortgages or principal from a pool of underlying mortgages, but not both. Both are volatile in periods of rapidly changing interest rates. In addition, the risk-shy should avoid funds which are heavy investors in inverse floaters, which are floating rate securities whose payouts go up when rates go down. Their main problem is that when rates go up, their payouts—and prices—melt away. Finally, cautious fund investors should be wary of "Z" bonds, which have the most erratic payout schedule of all the mortgage-backed securities.

Many of those derivatives—inverse floaters, POs, and Z bonds—were responsible for several of the worst bond-fund wrecks of 1994: Piper Jaffray Institutional Government Income, with an ugly 28.8 percent loss for the year, and Managers Intermediate Income Fund, with an almost as ugly 25.1 percent loss. The basic problem was that those derivatives plunged in value when interest rates shot up, far faster than conventional mortgages and bonds would have. Added to that was the fact that many of these securities had been leveraged—purchased with borrowed money—meaning the funds were even more susceptible to higher rates and falling bond prices.

How good are mortgage funds as investments? That depends on other market conditions. Millions of shareholders poured into government mortgage funds in the mid-1980s as interest rates tumbled. Their government imprimatur and higher yields were appealing. But high-coupon mortgage securities usually lag behind bond market rallies because investors are reluctant to pay up for high-yielding mortgages when the conditions are ripe for homeowners to pay them off. On the other hand, when the bonds are beginning to falter, mortgages often hold up better than bonds because what principal does come back gets reinvested at higher rates. Held over an "interest-rate cycle"—a period when rates go up, down, and return to the starting point—the mortgage funds should outperform the pure Treasury funds by about 1 percentage point a year.

SHORT GOVERNMENT FUNDS

Short-term government bond funds fill the gap between the inviolable safety of the money-market and the calculated risk-taking of the intermediate sort. By and large, the market risk of these funds is roughly half that of the intermediates, and a lot less than that of the long-terms. Not a whole lot of market risk, but not a whole lot of reward, either. During 1996, a difficult year for the bond market, they earned 4.3 percent total returns, beating the intermediates and trouncing the long-term government funds. But the yield paid out was over 5 percent, suggesting that even in these low-risk vehicles, you can suffer a capital loss.

To qualify for this category, the maturities usually must be between 1 and 5 years, and the durations, between 1 and 3.5 years. That, plus the constraints of a government fund, doesn't leave room for funds to differentiate themselves. But leave it to the fund managers. There's a lot more diversity in investment approach than you might think. The Vanguard Group even has two entries in this category: Vanguard Fixed-Income Short-Term U.S. Treasury Securities and Vanguard Fixed-Income Short-Term Federal Securities. The difference? The Treasury fund invests only in Treasury, the Federal, in all U.S.-issued securities except Treasuries. The Federal portfolio has a slightly higher yield and total return.

Though many ARMS funds are in the ultra-short category, some show up here as well. Look at Federated ARMS Institutional Fund. The fund with the highest return of 1996, 6.5 percent (Table 2-40), usually stays at the low end of the duration range, between 1 and 1.5 years. That helped during 1996 when interest rates were rising. But the fund management team earns some extra money through opportunistic investments in corners of the ARMS market thought to be undervalued.

Short-term bond funds have little market risk.

TABLE 2-40

SHORT GOVERNMENT FUNDS		
BEST RETURNS		
Period	Fund	Total return*
1996	FEDERATED ARMS INSTITUTIONAL	0.6%
1994-96	IDS FEDERAL INCOME	5.8
1992-96	EV TRADITIONAL GOVT. OBLIGATIONS	19.5

*Average annual, pretax   DATA: MORNINGSTAR INC.

IDS Federal Income, the fund with the best three-year showing, takes an approach that's fairly unusual for a short-term fund. The manager doesn't confine himself to the short end of the spectrum, but chooses from a variety of U.S. agency and mortgage-related securities, some with decades to go to maturity. From these securities, he gets a higher yield than he would from a strictly short portfolio but he also gets the duration of an intermediate fund, about 4.5 years. To bring the duration down, he uses futures and options. Those derivatives have a "negative duration" of 2.3 years. The result is a fund with a duration around 2.2 years, well in the range of a short-term fund.

Yet another approach, practiced by AIM Limited Maturity Treasury Retail Shares, is what's called "laddering." (Actually, this strategy can be and is done with intermediate- and long-term bonds as well.) The fund buys two-year Treasury notes and sells them off after owning them for about a year. Then it buys more two-year notes. The duration ends up around 1.4 years and changes little. The net asset value remains fairly steady, and the fund usually earns excellent risk-adjusted returns. It's one of the funds with three upward-pointing arrows in its category.

The laddering approach is so simple that many investment advisers say there's no point to doing it within the confines of a mutual fund, especially a U.S. Treasury fund. The portfolio manager isn't performing any credit analysis or interest-rate forecasting. Why pay a management fee? Investors can buy the Treasuries themselves—they're easily purchased through frequent Treasury auctions—and do much the same as the portfolio manager is doing. With $5000 or less to invest, a short-term government fund might make more sense. But if you would put $20,000 or more into a short-term government fund, you could ladder a portfolio yourself. Divide your money into thirds, buy a one-year, a two-year, and a three-year note. One year from now, replace the note that's about to mature with a new three-year note. A mutual fund is not always the best way to an investment need.

HIGH-YIELD FUNDS

High-yield bonds and the mutual funds that invest in them make most other sorts of bonds look like pikers. Since 1991, they have trounced investment grade bonds by a wide margin. Even looking at 10- and 15-year records, which include a vicious bear market in 1989 and 1990, the high-yield funds still look significantly better. You have to wonder why anyone would ever invest in a government or investment-grade security.

Well, here's the rub. High-yield bonds are legally bonds. The issuer, or borrower, promises to pay interest at particular times and at a particular interest rate. And because of those fixed-rate payments, these bonds have some sensitivity to changes in interest rates. But the truth is even if these securities look like bonds, they behave more like stocks. Every year in this decade when the stock market has been strong, so has the high-yield bond market. And even in 1994, when the stock market was barely profitable, the high-yield bonds beat stocks by a few percentage points. Martin Fridson, chief of high-yield research at Merrill Lynch & Co., confirmed our suspicions about the true nature of high-yield bonds. He looked at the monthly returns of high-yield bonds from 1985 though 1996 and found that the returns on high-yield bonds correlate with the stock market about 52 percent of the time versus a 41 percent correlation with the 10-year U.S. Treasury bond.

If it's not a stock, but doesn't really behave like a bond, what is a high-yield security? It's evolving almost as a separate and distinct asset, the inclusion of which in a portfolio can help to diversify risks and enhance returns. In short, many investors should consider adding one of these funds to their portfolios. Who wouldn't have liked to have owned Strong High-Yield Bond Fund in 1996, the best high-yielder of the year. It earned a 26.9 percent total return (Table 2-41). Or look at Northeast Investors Trust. Over the last five years, the fund earned an average annual total return of 15.9 percent. That's 0.7 percentage point better than the S&P 500.

How high are the yields? That's a moving target, depending on the general level of interest rates. When the high-yield, or "junk," bond market was flat on its back in 1990, many big issues traded at yields 10 or more percentage points higher than the comparable Treasury rates. In early 1997, the yields were perhaps 2

TABLE 2-41

to 3 percentage points higher, and high-yield bond funds had yields (after expenses) of about 8 percent. Many investors argue that high-yields are too low to make them attractive. Perhaps so, but they are also a lot safer securities now than they were then. It's somewhat analogous to the people who, when the Dow Jones hit 5000, said the stock market was overpriced. When the Dow hit 7000, those who declined to invest paid a heavy opportunity cost.

One thing is for certain: the returns from high-yield bond funds from here on out cannot match those earned over the last five years. Ernest Monrad, portfolio manager of Northeast Investors Trust, recalls that in 1990 he snapped up R.J. Reynolds bonds at 20 percent yields. So he collected a fat coupon payment to start with, and the bonds eventually appreciated in price as well, giving a substantial total return. But now, Monrad, like most other high-yield managers, buys bonds mostly in the 8 to 9 percent range. So the fund is starting with a much lower income component. A bond with an 8.5 percent coupon still might go up in value, but it's probably not going to make the gains that can be had when a bond is selling to yield at twice that rate. But investors might still consider putting some money in these sorts of funds. Says Monrad: "All things being equal, you start off with an 8 percent or 9 percent return. With stocks, the dividend yield is less than 2 percent. You have to depend on appreciation to do better. And income is more reliable than stock price appreciation."

High-yield bond funds were originally pitched to income-oriented investors, who still own large amounts of them. But they should be equally, if not more, attractive to stock market investors as "high-yield equity." At least equity fund buyers would probably take their sometimes volatile performance more in stride. Since these funds pay out a large portion of their profit as income, most investors would probably fare better if they held high-yield bond funds in their tax-deferred accounts, such as IRAs or 401(k)s.

So why do these bonds behave a lot like stocks? They're responding to many of the same forces in the economy. Since the 1990–1991 recession, the economy has been on a relatively slow but steady upward climb. Business conditions improved. Companies got leaner and meaner. Productivity increased. Corporate cash flow and profits zoomed.

All of that is great for stocks, and it's great for high-yield bonds, too. Here's why: The issuers of high-yield bonds are often less mature companies or those with a lot of debt. They pay higher interest rates because they are riskier borrowers. There's a greater chance with these companies that they'll default—or fail to make their interest payments. But when business is good and the companies make money, they become stronger financially and more creditworthy borrowers. Fewer issuers default on their bonds. (The average default rate is about 3 percent a year. For the last several years, the rate was about 1 percent—another reason this market has performed so well.) With better credit ratings, the prices of their bonds will also go up. The investors win two ways—bond prices go up and they collect a very healthy interest payment to boot.

A good economy is good for high-yield bonds. It's not always good for investment-grade bonds, because interest rates often go up. Higher rates do hurt the high-yield bonds somewhat, but that can be offset by improved credit quality. What would really derail the high-yield bond market is a recession (it would be hard on stocks, too). That's when business goes into a tailspin, and that's especially rough on less mature, debt-heavy companies. The reason high-yields have looked so strong in recent years is that we haven't had a recession. But that doesn't mean we won't in the future, either. The last recession hit just as the high-yield market was imploding from the excesses of the 1980s. It wasn't pretty.

The character of the high-yield market has changed a lot over the last 20 years—and it's still evolving. Until the late 1970s nearly all junk bonds were "fallen angels," bonds of once investment-grade companies that had fallen upon hard times. But then, investment banker Michael R. Milken of Drexel Burnham Lambert pioneered the idea of original-issue junk bonds. First, Milken used the bonds to raise money for capital-hungry emerging growth companies. Later, corporate raiders tapped the junk bond market to raise funds to take over big companies or to finance leveraged buyouts—purchases of companies that are made with mostly borrowed funds.

In the 1990s, there's been little takeover or LBO-related junk bond issuance. Instead, many of the new bonds come from new companies borrowing for the first time or established borrowers refinancing high-interest-rate debt.

The original premise behind junk bond investing is simple. Though these securities were riskier than high-quality bonds, the vast majority continued to make interest payments. So, although investing in a few junk bonds may be a dicey proposition, a well-diversified portfolio of junk bonds would be a tempting dish. In such a portfolio the regular income would more than make up for the losses from the occasional default. So mutual funds made a natural vehicle for investing in junk bonds.

The high-yield funds captured investors' attention—and their dollars—in the mid-1980s when interest rates on government and investment-grade bonds fell into the single digits. While the yields in junk bond funds averaged 3 to 4 percentage points higher than those from high-quality funds, the difference between the total returns on junk funds and investment-grade funds was less striking: 22 percent total return (yield plus capital appreciation) for junk funds in 1985 versus 20.6 percent for high-quality funds. In 1986 and 1987, the total returns were nearly identical. The high-yield funds were paying out more in interest, but the investment-grade funds did a better job on maintaining their net asset values.

Those numbers suggest that investors bought junk bond funds for their yields and were not really looking at total return. Only in 1988 did the total returns from junk bonds beat investment-grade bonds decisively—12.6 percent versus 7.6 percent. That was more than reversed in the junk bond debacle. In 1989, for instance, junk funds had an average return of 1.5 percent versus 11.9 percent for high grades. In 1990, junk bonds had a –12.3 percent return versus 17.4 percent for high-quality funds.

What happened to the junk bond market? For starters, Drexel Burnham Lambert—the investment bank that controlled nearly half the market—started to falter in 1989. The firm and Milken, its junk bond chieftain, were under investigation by federal authorities for securities laws violations stemming from the insider trading scandals of the 1980s. (Milken ultimately pleaded guilty to some securities laws violations and spent time in a federal penitentiary.) Drexel's powers and prowess faded, and the firm finally went into bankruptcy in early 1990. The empires

of some big junk bond issuers teetered or collapsed under mountains of debt. Finally, new federal laws prevented savings and loans from buying junk bonds and forced those that already owned them to divest. That further depressed demand for the bonds and increased supply.

An investor exodus from high-yield funds exacerbated the junk market's woes. To meet redemptions, fund managers often sold their "quality" junk, because it could be sold. That left portfolios in even worse shape. After Drexel's demise, some funds had virtually untradeable bonds. As an underwriter, Drexel agreed to make a market for the bonds it brought public. But other brokers didn't have any such obligation to Drexel clients. They could choose which bonds they wanted to trade and ignore the others. As a defensive measure, those funds that had the flexibility added some U.S. Treasury securities. Though lower in yield, managers hoped they would help stem the erosion in net asset value. And if the fund needed to sell bonds to meet redemptions, Treasuries are the most marketable securities in the world.

Junk bond investing was a good idea carried to speculative and dangerous excesses. Not every investor in junk funds got creamed in the bear market. Some high-yield bond funds, such as Invesco High-Yield, Phoenix High-Yield, and Value Line Aggressive Income, managed to keep an even keel, and their shareholders suffered little on a total return basis.

While high-yield bond funds can deliver equity-like returns, they can also have some equity-like changes in their NAVs. For instance, on November 22, 1995, Harrah's Jazz company filed for Chapter 11 bankruptcy, causing bond prices to plunge. Keystone High-Income (B-4) Fund lost 2.6 percent in NAV that day; Paine Webber High-Income Fund, 2.2 percent; and Fidelity Spartan High Income Fund and Fidelity Capital and Income Fund, 1.9 percent each.

Junk bond funds, like equity funds, encompass many investment styles. As a result, their portfolios—and their returns—are far more varied than, say, government or municipal funds. Most high-yield funds now have the lion's share of their assets in "B"-rated bonds. Some, like Phoenix High-Yield, have also gone into global emerging markets—bonds of such countries as Mexico, Argentina, Morocco, and Thailand—in their search for a high yield. That paid off handsomely in 1993 when the fund earned a 21.5 percent total return. But the fund stayed abroad too long in 1994, and the fund's return sank to –28 percent.

High-yield funds can diversify any portfolio.

At least two other junk bond funds damaged by emerging market debt were Keystone America Strategic Income B, down 10.3 percent, and T. Rowe Price High-Yield, down 8 percent.

Then there's the more conservative sort, like Nicholas Income and Vanguard Fixed-Income High-Yield Corporate Portfolio, which stress higher-rated bonds and have lower highs and higher lows than the Phoenix fund. The Vanguard fund, by charter, must have 80 percent of its assets in bonds rated B or better. Northeast Investors Trust takes yet another path. It invests in the junkiest junk—the fund is invested almost entirely in credit B or below, or unrated. The fund can also boost its income by leveraging the fund, borrowing money to buy bonds on margin, thereby increasing the income.

A more conservative approach isn't necessarily less risky. For instance, when the junk bond market, like most bond markets, fell in October 1992, the total return for Fidelity Capital & Income was –1 percent. The higher-quality Vanguard fund had a 2.5 percent fall. Why the difference? The prices for the Fidelity fund's bonds are dependent on each company's situation. The prices for higher-quality junk bonds are more interest-rate sensitive. Each approach to junk fund investing carries its own risks. They're not all the same.

CONVERTIBLE FUNDS

If you think the high-yield bonds are really stocks in disguise, consider convertible bonds. They are issued as bonds, with a set interest payment schedule and a promise to redeem by a certain date. The interest rate is a lower rate than you might expect the issuer to pay. But there is a sweetener here that should more than compensate for that lower rate—the bondholder has the option to convert the bonds into a specified amount of stock in the issuing company at a specified price. So when stocks do really well, convertibles do too. And if the stock of the issuing company doesn't reach its conversion price, the investor always has some interest income from the investment.

Both 1995 and 1996, strong years for the stock market, were sweet years for convertibles. Convertible bond funds were the best-performing category of bond fund—and they were best in three-year and five-year performance as well. Oppenheimer Bond Fund for Growth M, the best fund over the five-year period, earned a 16.8 percent total return (Table 2-42). That even beat the S&P 500.

TABLE 2-42

CONVERTIBLE BOND FUNDS		
BEST RETURNS		
Period ▼	Fund ▼	Total return* ▼
1996	OPPENHEIMER BOND FOR GROWTH A	16.8%
1994-96	PUTNAM CONVERTIBLE INCOME-GROWTH	12.7
1992-96	PACIFIC HORIZON CAPITAL INCOME A	19.5

*Average annual, pretax   DATA: MORNINGSTAR INC.

Yet even when convertible funds do well, they usually don't attract much investor attention. The funds are rather small, and new start-ups are rare. They suffer perhaps because convertibles, which have attributes of both stocks and bonds, are little appreciated by pure stock or pure bond investors. Yet they seem to have a role to play in an equity portfolio. With dividend yields on stocks so low, they make a good addition to the portfolio of a more conservative equity investor, perhaps supplanting the role once played by equity–income funds. For the bond investor, the convertibles can actually smooth out the volatility of a portfolio that's overly sensitive to interest rates. Convertible bonds have only a 20 percent correlation with investment grade bonds, so they definitely do bring diversification to an income-oriented portfolio.

While both high-yield bond funds and convertible bond funds seem to take more of their cues from stocks than from bonds, the two sorts of funds are not really duplicative. In theory, at least, the conversion feature to equity gives convertibles an unlimited return. High-yield bonds, on the other hand, are still fixed-income instruments—and the gains are limited by the interest payment and how the difference between your purchase price and the bond's redemption value.

The issuers are not the same, either. The companies that issue convertible bonds are smaller, more rapidly growing concerns, often in growth industries like high technology and health care. They are looking to keep borrowing costs down because they need money for growth. Those that issue high-yield debt tend to be more mature companies which don't need or are not growing fast enough to need to expand their shareholder base. So, in effect, an investor bringing convertible funds and high-yield funds into his or her portfolio is adding a lot of diversification.

The convertible bond market is not a large one. In fact, it's only about one-quarter the size of the high-yield bond market. Sometimes, even the portfolio managers of the relatively few convertible bond funds have a hard time finding the right bonds. So under certain market conditions, some funds create "synthetic convertibles" by pairing straight debt and call options on the issuer stock. (After all, a convertible bond is merely the combination of a straight bond and a call option on the issuer's stock.) And some funds just park their money in straight debt or equity when they don't like what's happening in the converts market.

INTERNATIONAL BOND FUNDS

Just a dozen years ago, it wasn't too hard to guess which international bond fund would be the best of the year. There were only two, and they both invested in investment-grade foreign debt. Emerging markets debt mutual funds, which are red-hot now, had not yet been invented. Nor had short-term world income funds, a sort of fund that tried—and ultimately failed—to earn high short-term yields without any currency risk.

Today, you will find all three sorts of funds within the international bond fund category, a new grouping that marries the former world bond and short-term world income fund classifications. What all of these funds have in common is that they must have at least 40 percent of their assets in foreign-issued bonds. But that's it. There's a wide variety of investment strategies, ranging across the risk spectrum. Some, like American Century–Benham European Government Fund, own only bonds issued by the major European nations and AAA-rated corporations. Goldman Sachs Global Income A, one of the funds that earned a three-up-arrow category rating, goes heavy on hedging. Franklin Templeton Hard Currency Fund is really a foreign money-market fund. The portfolio's average maturity is always around six months, and the fund never hedges currency exposure. The idea behind the portfolio is to invest in the currencies of low-inflation countries as a hedge against inflation in the United States. Nowadays, the fund holds lots of U.S. securities, which says a lot about inflation in the United States and the strength of the dollar.

Of course, the most alluring funds nowadays are the emerging markets debt funds. Not surprisingly, the best-performing international fund of 1996 was Fidelity New Markets Income Fund, with a 41.4 percent total return (Table 2-43). Only about 7.2 percent of that return was income. Most came from capital gains. It was the kind of return that most equity fund managers would have loved to have earned. The fund earned the high return with investments in such nations as Argentina, Brazil, Ecuador, Panama, Mexico, Poland, and

TABLE 2-43

INTERNATIONAL BOND FUNDS		
BEST RETURNS		
Period	Fund	Total return*
1996	FIDELITY NEW MARKETS INCOME	41.4%
1994-96	SCUDDER EMERGING MARKETS	13.9
1992-96	GLOBAL GOVERNMENT PLUS A	9.8

*Average annual, pretax   DATA: MORNINGSTAR INC.

even Russia. Scudder Emerging Markets Income Fund, the best performer of the last three years, had much the same winning portfolio.

The reason the 1996 returns were so high—far surpassing emerging markets equity funds—was that the funds were rebounding from a bear market that started in 1994 and ran through early 1995. That bear market hit these young funds hard. First came the hit from the rapidly rising interest rate environment. Later came the Mexican peso crisis. In just three weeks, the Fidelity New Markets Income Fund dropped 23.2 percent and G.T. Global High-Income A, 19.6 percent, and they're geographically diversified funds. Alliance North American Government Income Fund B, with a heavy weighting in Mexico, dropped a whopping 28.6 percent. Even though the currency devaluation was contained to Mexico, investors lost their nerve and fled many other markets, driving down prices for emerging market debt everywhere.

You probably have a sneaking suspicion that "emerging markets" is a 1990s euphemism for Third World debt, the scourge of lenders in the 1980s. You're right. Most of the debtors are indeed former deadbeats, and many emerging markets bonds are actually repackaged and restructured bank loans.

The idea behind investing in emerging markets debt is that these countries have cleaned up their acts economically. They've restructured their economies, allowed for privatization of state-owned industries, lowered trade barriers, and welcomed foreign capital. In short, they became much better creditors than they had been. Indeed, portfolio managers who run these funds hone in on such factors as inflation, unemployment, and government fiscal and monetary policy before buying only those countries or "credits" that are clearly on the road to economic reform. The profit for emerging markets debt funds is not only in the higher interest rates, but also in price appreciation of the bonds as other investors recognize the improved credit quality and pay up for the bonds. In that sense, they're somewhat analogous to junk bond funds, and, indeed, many junk bond funds also dabble in these markets.

Currency changes play a part in these funds, too, but usually not as much as you think. Many emerging nations peg their currencies to the U.S. dollar or issue dollar-denominated debt, so currency-induced fluctuations in the fund may well be less than in traditional world bond funds. But when a Third World currency collapses, watch out below.

With the more conventional international bond funds, currencies count for more than credit quality. The argument for international bond investing is the same as it is for investing in foreign stocks—diversification. But non-U.S. bonds do not always zig while the other markets zag. The 1994 bear market in bonds was a global, not just a U.S., bear market. As such, it was hard to find any short-term world income or world bond funds that excelled in 1994, when a U.S. investor would really have appreciated it. Likewise, in 1995, these funds went up along with U.S. bond funds, but nobody complains about that.

What makes foreign fixed-income securities alluring sometimes is when interest rates are higher abroad than they are at home. That makes the yields attractive in themselves. But you have to factor in if the dollar is appreciating against British pounds and German marks. What if your fund is earning 9 percent on its German bonds and the mark appreciates 9 percent against the dollar? Your total return is 18 percent.

But what happens if the dollar appreciates or the other countries' currencies depreciate? That's what happened in 1992. U.S. investors in world bond funds earned, on average, total returns of only 2.8 percent—that's after the yield. PaineWebber Global Income Fund, for instance, paid out a yield of nearly 7 percent, but wound up the year with a total return of 1.3 percent. Investors lost nearly 5 percent of their net asset value during the year.

Or, what happens when the dollar falls, making foreign bonds more valuable, yet the international bond fund you own is plodding along because of a hedging strategy? Indeed, that's what happened in early 1995, when the dollar plunged, especially against the German mark and the Japanese yen, yet very few international bond funds were able to profit on that. That's because they had used the foreign exchange market to "convert" their marks into dollars, a strategy that pays off when the dollar goes up against the mark. But if the mark goes up against the dollar, and the fund has sold its marks, there's no money to be made. Yet most world bond funds employ strategies that do just that.

Why? Most international bond funds are sold as low-risk yield vehicles, not as total return investments. And one way to keep the risk low is to neutralize the foreign currency exposure. But a fund that does that is also undercutting much of the diversification advantage investors get from going global.

MULTISECTOR BOND

Can't decide what kind of bond fund you want? Maybe you don't have to. Try a multisector bond fund. By their charters, they are supposed to keep their money in three types of fixed-income investments: U.S. government bonds or government-backed mortgage securities; foreign debt, both government and private issue; and high-yield corporates, or "junk" bonds. Most of the funds have a benchmark or "neutral" allocation of one-third of assets to each of the three sectors. Then, the portfolio manager is permitted to diverge from that depending on the investment opportunities in each.

The mix makes a lot of sense. U.S. government bonds are high in credit quality, but are the most sensitive to interest-rate risk, or the changes in bond prices that come from changes in interest rates. High-yield corporates are less interest-rate sensitive, but more credit-sensitive. A strong economy might send interest rates up on government bonds, but should also improve the cash flow, and, hence, credit quality, of high-yield bonds. Foreign bonds, even if they are dollar denominated, bring diversification to the mix, since the movements of many foreign economies and bond markets do not correlate to that of the United States.

Though these funds try to maintain somewhat of a balance among the bond sectors, the managers do tilt them to take advantage of perceived market opportunities. During 1996, the best opportunities were in high-yield and foreign

TABLE 2-44

MULTISECTOR BOND FUNDS		
BEST RETURNS		
Period	Fund	Total return*
1996	EV STRATEGIC INCOME	18.2%
1994-96	HANCOCK STRATEGIC INCOME	8.7
1992-96	KEMPER DIVERSIFIED INCOME	12.2
*Average annual, pretax		DATA: MORNINGSTAR INC.

bonds—especially those with emerging markets debt. The best multisector performer of 1996, EV Marathon Strategic Income (Table 2-44), earned its high return with a generous helping of Latin American and Eastern European debt and a minimum of U.S. government issues. In 1995, when U.S. interest rates plummeted, AIM Income A took the top spot because it had a heavy slug of U.S. securities, and long-term ones at that. They deliver the highest total returns in a falling interest rates environment.

The AIM fund is a little different from most of the multisectors. It tends to own longer-term securities with higher durations. The average multisector fund looks to earn its money from sector allocations, not interest-rate bets. Most keep their durations around 4 or 5 years, giving them volatility characteristics of intermediate funds. If funds are going to make interest-rate bets, they'd better be on the right side. Janus Flexible Income Fund started 1996 with a duration of 7, which proved troublesome in the first quarter when interest rates jumped up. The manager quickly shortened the duration to 4, but the damage was largely done. The fund finished the year with a 6.4 percent return, well below the sector's 9.8 percent average.

MUNICIPAL BOND FUNDS

No one likes higher taxes. No one, that is, except the people who sell and manage municipal bond funds. When Bill Clinton was first elected, the "muni" market cheered. His tax hikes for upper-income taxpayers make the muni alternative look better than ever. The income from muni bond funds can't be touched by the Internal Revenue Service as long as the interest income comes from tax-exempt securities issued by state and local governments and authorities. Right after the Republican sweep of Congress in the 1994 elections, muni bond prices slumped. One explanation: the GOP's campaign promises to lower taxes. Lower taxes make munis less attractive. Just about the time munis started to recover from that GOP Congress, millionaire publisher Steve Forbes started campaigning for the Republican presidential nomination. His chief rallying cry was the "flat tax," a "one rate fits all" plan that's anathema to the municipal bond crowd. The lower tax rates go, the higher yields tax-exempt bonds have to pay to attract investors.

A tax-exempt security typically sports a lower yield than a taxable security of comparable maturity and credit quality. All things being equal, their returns are lower than those on comparable

taxable funds, though at times, like 1996, muni funds can outperform taxable funds (Table 2-45). That's because investors will accept a lower rate in return for the tax exemption. In deciding whether to invest in a muni or taxable bond fund, the key question to ask is, "What is the taxable equivalent of the yield on a muni fund?" The answer to that question depends on your marginal tax rate. The higher the rate, the better a muni looks compared to a taxable fund. (If you're talking about a tax-deferred retirement account, always choose the higher yielding taxable bonds.)

When marginal tax rates were first slashed in 1982, some predicted that tax-exempt bonds would lose their attraction. Prior to that, the top tax rate on individual income was 50 percent, so a 7 percent muni bond payout was the same as a 14 percent taxable bond. But after the 1986 tax act, which introduced a 28 percent top rate, the 7 percent coupon was worth only 9.72 percent in a taxable bond.

But the muni never lost its appeal to investors. The 1986 tax bill that cut rates also scotched

TABLE 2-45

MUNICIPAL BOND FUNDS		
BEST RETURNS		
Period ▼	Fund ▼	Total return* ▼
MUNICIPAL NATIONAL LONG		
1996	UNITED MUNICIPAL HIGH-INCOME	6.9%
1994-96	SMITH BARNEY MANAGED MUNIS A	6.6
1992-96	SMITH BARNEY MANAGED MUNIS A	9.0
MUNICIPAL NATIONAL INTERMEDIATE		
1996	LIMITED TERM TAX-EX. BOND AMER.	4.5%
1994-96	LIMITED TERM TAX-EX. BOND AMER.	5.0
1992-96	VANGUARD MUNI. INTERMEDIATE	7.1
MUNICIPAL SINGLE-STATE LONG		
1996	FRANKLIN CA HIGH-YIELD MUNI. I	6.2%
1994-96	SMITH BARNEY CA MUNICIPALS A	6.4
1992-96	PRUDENTIAL CA MUNI. CA INCOME A	8.4
MUNICIPAL SINGLE-STATE INTERMEDIATE		
1996	VANGUARD CA TAX-FREE INS. INTERM.	5.4%
1994-96	DUPREE KY TAX-FREE INCOME	4.8
1992-96	DUPREE KY TAX-FREE INCOME	7.1
SHORT MUNICIPAL		
1996	STRONG MUNICIPAL ADVANTAGE	4.9%
1994-96	USAA TAX-EXEMPT SHORT-TERM	4.4
1992-96	THORNBURG LIMITED-TERM NATIONAL A	12.2

*Average annual, pretax   DATA: MORNINGSTAR INC.

many of the tax shelters high-income individuals used to cut their tax bills. The muni was the one tax haven left. More important, shelters only delay paying taxes. The interest income generated by municipal bonds is always tax-free, and so is interest income that an investor receives from a muni bond fund. However, not all the income generated by the fund is tax-exempt. If the fund is adept at trading bonds, and earns some capital gains, those gains (net of losses) will be passed on to investors as a capital gains distribution, taxable at the capital gains rate.

It's possible that muni funds may start to generate fully-taxable ordinary income as well. That's because the 1993 tax act changed the law so that the money earned when bonds bought at discount to par are redeemed at par will be considered ordinary income—taxable at the investor's highest rate. Before the changes, that difference would have been considered capital gains, taxed at a lower rate. Not surprisingly, Wall Street and mutual fund lobbyists are trying to change that law.

Even so, muni bond funds make sense for many investors. The top federal tax bracket is 36 percent, and for an elite few, a millionaire's surcharge raises it to 39.6 percent. Municipal bonds almost always beat taxables for investors in the highest brackets. But muni yields have been so high at times that muni funds are attractive to investors in lower tax brackets too. To get the maximum return, investors need to compare muni and taxable funds, adjusting for the tax exemption. For instance, in February 1996, the Vanguard Fixed-Income Long-Term U.S. Treasury Fund was yielding 5.93 percent, while the Vanguard Municipal Bond Long-Term Fund was yielding 4.92 percent. What's the better buy? Suppose you're in the 31 percent marginal tax bracket. You merely subtract 31 percent of the yield from 5.93 percent and you get a 4.09 percent yield after taxes. Obviously, the muni fund offers a better yield.

There's another way to look at this. Start with the number 1 and subtract your marginal tax bracket from it: 1 minus 0.31 (31 percent is also expressed as 0.31) equals 0.69. Next, divide that number into the tax-exempt yield. Divide 4.92 percent by 0.69 and you get 7.13 percent. So, unless you can get a return of at least 7.13 percent in a taxable investment of like quality, the muni is the better deal.

Though muni bond income is free from federal taxes, states tax muni income from bonds issued in other states. Neither the New Yorker investing in

a California bond nor the Californian with the New York bond will owe federal tax on the interest, but he or she will owe state income tax. In states with low income tax rates, that may not matter. But in high tax states like California and New York, the extra tax can cut into your returns.

So the mutual fund folks have come up with an antidote for that, too—single-state municipal bond funds. By restricting investment to the investor's home state, these funds generate income that's exempt not only from federal taxes but from state and city income taxes as well. For the tax-weary folks of New York City, a New York bond fund is said to be "triple-tax-exempt." The largest municipal fund of all, in fact, is the Franklin California Tax-Free Income Fund. It's also one of the oldest, dating back to 1977.

No longer do you have to live in a big, heavily populated state to have a single-state fund to call your own. Single-state funds abound in 42 states and Puerto Rico, though New Yorkers and Californians have the most funds to choose from (Table 2-46). If a state isn't represented, it may be because the tax laws are not amenable to it. If there's no state income or personal property assessment that taxes financial holdings, there's no need for a single-state muni fund—though Texas has 24 of them anyway. Illinois, for instance, does have a state income tax, but does not exempt interest earned from most Illinois municipal bonds. So there's no particular advantage for an Illinois taxpayer to invest in most Illinois bonds.

The big drawback of single-state funds is just that: All the bonds come from a single state and

TABLE 2-46

STATES WITH SINGLE-STATE BOND FUNDS

State	Funds	State	Funds	State	Funds
ALABAMA	8	MARYLAND	44	PENNSYLVANIA	75
ARIZONA	43	MASSACHUSETTS	124	PUERTO RICO	1
ARKANSAS	11	MICHIGAN	59	RHODE ISLAND	3
CALIFORNIA	169	MINNESOTA	45	SOUTH CAROLINA	20
COLORADO	26	MISSISSIPPI	4	SOUTH DAKOTA	1
CONNECTICUT	27	MISSOURI	20	TENNESSEE	26
FLORIDA	103	NEBRASKA	2	TEXAS	24
GEORGIA	32	NEW HAMPSHIRE	1	UTAH	5
HAWAII	17	NEW JERSEY	61	VERMONT	2
IDAHO	6	NEW YORK	138	VIRGINIA	72
INDIANA	1	NEW MEXICO	8	WASHINGTON	6
IOWA	3	NORTH CAROLINA	45	WEST VIRGINIA	6
KANSAS	9	NORTH DAKOTA	4	WISCONSIN	15
KENTUCKY	16	OHIO	60		
LOUISIANA	12	OREGON	19		

DATA: MORNINGSTAR INC.

Tax-free bond funds sometimes generate taxable gains.

rise and fall on the financial condition of the state, its local governments, and bond-issuing authorities. In December 1994, the muni market in general and the California market in particular were rocked when Orange County disclosed it had what was eventually determined to be about $2 billion in losses in its investment portfolio, a fund (not a mutual fund) in which Orange County and many smaller jurisdictions had money that was needed to service their debt.

Within days, the county filed for bankruptcy, which put all debt service in doubt and sent bond prices into a skid. The NAV of the Franklin California Tax-Free Fund, the largest California muni fund, dropped 1.32 percent. Franklin California Insured Tax-Free Income Fund took the same percentage hit, even though bond insurers would step in to make up any payments Orange County borrowers missed. In contrast, the nationally diversified Franklin Federal Tax-Free Income Fund fell, too, but only 0.8 percent.

Insured funds are popular with New York investors as well, since the Empire State also seems to undergo a fiscal crisis every few years. Ironically, in New York as in many other states, high-quality bonds of well-known issuers aren't always a safe harbor. When the muni market gets the shakes, the first bonds to get dumped are those of the highest quality. They're the most liquid. Provided they don't default, the lesser credits and lesser known names seem to hold up relatively well. They don't go on the auction block. That's why the relatively unknown Rochester Fund Municipals excels. The fund knows its upstate issuers well, and buys obscure or unrated issues that the big fund families miss. Many muni funds that have "high-yield" in their names achieve that objective just by seeking out the higher interest rates of the little known issuers.

If you've decided to invest in tax-exempt funds, you still have to make the same kinds of decisions you make with taxable funds. Do you want a fund with short-, intermediate-, or long-term bonds? Is there a single-state fund for your home state, and is the yield competitive? We have reorganized the muni fund classifications along maturity and geographic lines. They are municipal national long, municipal national intermediate, municipal single-state long, municipal single-state intermediate, and municipal short, which takes in both national and single-state funds. Funds that invest in insured bonds usually say so in their names. Those that invest in junk-rated or unrated municipal bonds generally use "high-yield" in their names.

The menu of muni offerings is broad, so a good fund can make use of it to diversify a portfolio, both geographically and by the type of project the bonds finance. General obligation (GO) bonds—those backed by the credit and taxing power of the issuer—are only a small part of the muni bond line-up. Far more numerous are revenue bonds, which are paid off by rentals, fees, tolls, and the like from roads, bridges, tunnels, arenas, ballparks, water works, sewage treatment plants, power plants, parking structures, housing, and hospitals.

Revenue bonds are riskier than GOs—after all, the project's revenue can easily fall short of projections. That's a risk with nonessential public projects like arenas and stadiums. Suppose a project runs far over budget or is never completed? That's what happened with the Washington Public Power Supply System in the early 1980s, which failed to complete or build several nuclear power plants that it financed with revenue bonds.

If your fund manager has done some savvy bond trading and racked up some capital gains, the fund will have to make a capital gains distribution too. Sorry, capital gains from tax-free bonds are taxable. But such distributions are infrequent. Still, investors who don't want capital gains should stick to yield-oriented funds that emphasize bonds selling at a premium, or above par. Such funds don't climb as much in a falling rate environment, nor do they melt as quickly if interest rates climb.

Like their taxable counterparts, muni funds are creatures of interest rates. But munis don't move in lock-step with Treasuries either. At times they can be more volatile. In the spring of 1987, when interest rates rose swiftly in the government bond market, investors swamped the muni fund managers with demands for redemptions. With insufficient cash on hand to meet them, muni funds had to sell bonds into a falling market in order to meet redemptions. Since the municipal bond market is far less liquid than the Treasury bond market, even big institutional investors must take huge discounts in price in order to sell bonds quickly. Between mid-March and mid-April 1987, the T. Rowe Price Tax-Free Fund lost 9.22 percent of its net asset value.

On the other hand, sometimes the muni market will outperform taxables. In 1988, for instance, government bonds finished the year about where they started. The muni bonds, in contrast, gained about 6 points, or $60 per $1000 bond. Why? A shortage in supply combined with a pickup in demand from shell-shocked equity investors. Supply and demand of muni bonds does have an effect on prices and, in turn, on yields. In 1992 and 1993, muni funds outdistanced the taxables, even though the muni market was flooded with record new issuance. That's because demand was so strong. In 1994, the supply of new bonds dropped to nearly half. But with rising interest rates and tax-law changes affecting the treatment of market discount bonds, demand—thus prices—dropped even more. As a result, on a total return basis, muni funds did far worse than taxables.

Money-Market Funds

Money-market mutual funds are a breed apart from stock and bond funds. Their principal difference is that they keep their share prices at a constant $1 per share. They're able to do this because they invest in very short-term debt instruments. Usually, price fluctuations in those investments are so small that funds can maintain their constant dollar price. Thus, a money-market mutual fund account will look a lot like a bank account.

As with bond funds, there are taxable and tax-free money-market funds. The taxable funds come in several categories, depending on the kind of investments they make (Table 2-47). U.S. Treasury-only funds invest in just Treasury securities. They have the lowest yield but are considered the safest. Then comes those that invest in Treasuries and repurchase agreements, a sort of loan that's backed by Treasuries. The next category invests in U.S. Government agency securities, such as those issued by Federal National Mortgage Assn. and Student Loan Marketing Assn. The general purpose funds may invest in all of the above, but also seek higher yields from bank-issued instruments and short-term corporate debt. Tax-exempt funds invest in the short-term instruments issued by state and local governments.

TAXABLE FUNDS

In 1981, when short-term interest rates were in the high teens, money-market funds looked like the dream investment. Interest rates on bank deposits were regulated, and passbook accounts—the province of the small investor—paid about 5.5

percent. The average money-market fund paid nearly 17 percent! That's when Americans who never heard of mutual funds got their introduction to them. And it was because of the high yields of the money funds. During the 1980s and into the 1990s, as interest rates headed south, so did the returns from money-market funds (Figure 2-2). And as returns continued to drop, so did investor interest and media attention.

Well, money-market funds are back on investors' radar screens. True, the dramatic rise in short-term interest rates and the consequent volatility in bond funds made money funds look a lot more attractive in 1994 than they had looked in years. But what drew the public attention to money funds again were shocking revelations that some 15 sponsors of 35 money-market funds put up $769 million to avoid "breaking the buck," that is, having to reprice the money-fund shares (kept constant at $1 NAV) because of investments gone bad. Among those bailing out their own funds were Bank of America, Kidder Peabody, United Services, and Value Line. No one came to the rescue of the tiny Community Bankers U.S. Government Money Market Fund, and the fund broke the buck and liquidated for 94 cents on the dollar.

TABLE 2-47

MONEY-MARKET MUTUAL FUNDS: THEY'RE NOT ALL THE SAME

Money-Market Fund	Comments	Yield*
100% U.S. TREASURY	Highest safety, but lowest yields. Interest is subject to federal tax, but is exempt from state and local income taxes in most states.	4.71 %
U.S. TREASURY AND REPO'S	Invests in repurchase agreements, in which a bond dealer sells securities, agreeing to buy them back on a certain date at a higher price. Difference between two prices is the interest.	4.77
U.S. GOVERNMENT & AGENCIES	May also invest in securities issued by U.S.-backed agencies such as Federal National Mortgage Assn. Agency paper is highly-rated and has nearly the same as credit quality as U.S. Treasuries.	4.79
GENERAL PURPOSE	Can also buy high-quality commercial paper of corporations and non-insured bank-related investments, which adds some credit risk. A few "second tier" funds purchase lower-quality paper for a higher yield (5.09%).	4.89
TAX-FREE	Invests in short-term municipal securities, such as tax anticipation notes. Exempt from federal taxes, but not state and local taxes. State-specific funds avoids taxes for taxpayers of those states (2.91%).	2.94

DATA: IBC/DONOGHUE'S MONEY FUND REPORT, BUSINESS WEEK   *1996

FIGURE 2-2

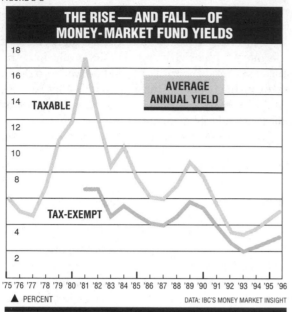

THE RISE — AND FALL — OF MONEY-MARKET FUND YIELDS

TAXABLE

AVERAGE ANNUAL YIELD

TAX-EXEMPT

'75 '76 '77 '78 '79 '80 '81 '82 '83 '84 '85 '86 '87 '88 '89 '90 '91 '92 '93 '94 '95 '96

▲ PERCENT

DATA: IBC'S MONEY MARKET INSIGHT

Tax-exempt money-market funds hit the news, too, after Orange County, California declared bankruptcy. *Money Market Insight*, an industry publication, estimated that sponsors of at least "25 major funds" sought regulators' permission to buy Orange County securities from their funds, lest the securities stop making interest payments. Some sponsors like Franklin and Putnam bought the securities from the funds, while Alliance Capital backed them up with a letter of credit (which would pay off if the securities didn't). Benham and Calvert funds also provided guarantees. In all cases, the fund managers were trying to avoid breaking the buck.

Breaking the buck is the money-fund managers' and the regulators' worst nightmare. Investors recognize that stock and bond funds can fluctuate in NAV, but money funds are not supposed to do so. Usually, the funds invest in instruments that are so short in maturity that the portfolio fluctuations are minute, and thus, the fund can maintain its net asset value at $1 per share. The small profits and losses in the portfolio can be accounted for by varying the payout. If there's a small capital gain, the fund can just pass it along as a little extra yield. By the same token, small losses in principal can be absorbed by the income stream, resulting in a slightly lowered payout. Many funds use an accounting method that allows them to carry the securities on their books at cost. Under those rules, assets don't fluctuate in value at all.

What went wrong in 1994 was that some funds had invested in derivatives such as inverse floaters or "structured notes" which were engineered to pay higher yields in a falling interest-rate environment. When interest rates spiked up, these derivatives plunged in price and could no longer be valued at 100 cents on the dollar. These derivatives worked fine for the funds as interest rates fell, since they allowed the funds to pay higher yields than they otherwise would. But when rates started climbing, these derivatives' yields fell and the funds could not sell the derivatives without taking a large loss that would break the buck. The SEC later issued rules about what money funds could not invest in, which included the same sort of securities that had caused the problems.

It was not the first time that investments gone sour threatened to break the buck. That happened when a few funds, in stretching for yield, bought "junk" commercial paper that went into default. In both cases, the two sponsors, T. Rowe Price Associates and Value Line, Inc., bought the commercial paper from the funds at the funds' cost, and the parent company, not the money fund, took the loss. In response, the SEC tightened regulations on credit quality of fund investments. Still, credit problems do pop up. In early 1997, Mercury Finance Co., which makes used car loans, had serious financial problems that had not been properly disclosed. One rating agency had rated Mercury's commercial paper (very short-term notes) investment grade, while nearly all others considered it in the second tier. While many money-market funds won't invest in such "split-rated" securities, Strong Heritage Money Market Fund did. When the depths of Mercury's problems came out, Strong Capital Management stepped in and bought the commercial paper from the funds. Had it not done so, the fund would have "broken the buck."

Since the mutual fund industry and the SEC have long adopted the $1 per share practice for money funds, a money-market fund statement ends up looking a lot like that of a bank account. If you have 15,271 shares, you also have $15,271. Interest earned each day is usually credited daily. The payments are technically "dividends," but they are the functional equivalent of interest. And since the funds behave an awful lot like bank accounts, it's not surprising that many people use them in just that way. There's one big difference, though, and that's the reason for the emphasis on safety—money-market mutual funds are not government-insured.

In general, money-market fund yields have been higher—on average about 1 percentage point more—than bank money-market deposit accounts. As short-term rates shot up in 1994, the yield advantage over bank money-market deposit accounts increased to the point where money funds were paying more than double bank money-market account rates and even more than six-month certificates of deposit. That's because money-market funds pass along to their investors all they earn—less expenses, of course. A bank money-market deposit account is an administered rate. The bank decides what it will pay on deposits. Though they are somewhat linked to the general level and direction of interest rates, banks tend to pay only what they must to maintain the deposits. That is, if they even want or need to maintain them. If loan demand is weak, as it was for most of 1991 and 1992, banks can always lower their interest rates enough to encourage depositors to take their money elsewhere.

Most money-market funds offer some kind of checking privileges too. However, since they usually require a minimum check amount of several hundred dollars, you'll need a conventional checking account as well. If you want check-writing privileges, be sure to read the portion in the prospectus that describes the program. Not only can there be restrictions on the minimum amount of the check, but also on the number of checks written each month.

But as an investor, you're probably not very concerned with check-writing—though it's handy to have, even if you don't make much use of it. To make your life easier, you'll probably want to have money-market fund accounts with fund groups in which you have other mutual funds.

So, if you have several Franklin, Putnam, or Scudder funds, you might find it convenient to keep a money-market fund there. Suppose you wanted to invest $10,000 in an equity fund, but spread it over a year's time. You might start with $1000 in the equity fund and put the balance in one of the money-market funds. If you set it up with telephone switching privileges, you can gradually shift from the money fund into the stock fund with a series of phone calls.

In the same way, the money-market fund is a good parking place for your money. If you're switching out of a stock or bond fund, you can park the cash in the fund group's money fund while you're deciding what to do next with your money. If you like the fund's yield better than the prospects for stock or bond funds, you may decide to let the money sit. With a money-market fund, your assets are not idle. They earn interest every day.

Since there's a great deal of similarity in investment policy and services, investors who spend considerable time shopping for stock or bond funds pay little attention to their money-market funds. Though there are differences in the quality of the money-market instruments in which money funds invest, by and large those differences are not great. If you're otherwise weighing the risks of a growth fund versus a balanced fund, the difference between money funds is trivial.

If you look at money-market-fund yields that are published in the newspaper financial sections every week, it looks like there can be as much as two percentage points of difference in yields. But that can be deceptive. In the very short term, yields are volatile and any week's yield will depend on the various maturities of the fund.

The shorter the maturity, the faster the yield will respond to changes in interest rates. Suppose one fund has an average maturity of 30 days and another has 15 days. If interest rates rise in the next two weeks, the yield on the 15-day fund is going to go up faster. That's because the fund has more investments maturing sooner and will be able to roll them over at higher interest rates. But if interest rates fall during the period, the longer maturity fund fares better, because it will hold onto its higher-yielding investments much longer.

As a result of the fluctuations in rates and portfolio maturities, week to week the differentials look big. But over a year's time those differences smooth out. In fact, *Income & Safety*, a newsletter that tracks money-market funds, says that the difference between the highest- and lowest-yielding fund in any year is about 0.9 percentage point. That means that, if you had a $10,000 average balance, and you had the worst-yielding fund, you would receive only $90 less income than from the very highest-yielding fund. Of course, the larger the average balance in your money-market fund, the more you want to focus on the yield. That 0.9 percentage point spread on a $100,000 account is $900—and that's not insignificant.

Still, the search for yield has its limitations. Returns are far more homogeneous in money-market funds than in stock or bond funds. That's because money-market funds must live within fairly narrow strictures set down by industry practice and the Securities & Exchange Commission. Funds mainly invest in U.S. Treasury bills, repurchase agreements, certificates of deposit, bankers acceptances, and commercial paper. But

Money funds have strict investment guidelines.

it's also obvious from the events of the last year that perhaps not all funds—at least not the ones that got into trouble—were investing solely in these tried-and-true instruments. Following is a brief description of each.

U.S. Treasury bills. These are short-term obligations of the U.S. government, which come in three-month, six-month, and one-year maturities. Individual investors can buy these on their own, but there's a $10,000 minimum. Other U.S. government agencies also raise short-term funds in the money-markets from time to time. Their securities are also permissible in many funds. Those include the Farm Credit Bank, Federal National Mortgage Association, Federal Home Loan Mortgage Corporation, and the Student Loan Marketing Association.

Repurchase agreements. "Repo's," as they're commonly known, are short-term borrowings using U.S. government securities as collateral. They work like this. A bank or securities dealer has an inventory of Treasury bonds it needs to finance for, say, 20 days. Sometimes the term of the loan is merely overnight. The dealer borrows from a money-market fund and gives the fund securities as collateral for the loan. The arrangement is called a repurchase agreement because the borrower agrees to "repurchase" the collateral by paying back the loan. The credit on the line is the bank's or dealer's, but as long as the fund can claim the securities in case of default, the credit quality is considered high.

Bank certificates of deposit. Most people are familiar with CDs, but the funds invest in "jumbos"—CDs over $100,000 which are not insured by the FDIC. The creditworthiness of the bank is the only thing that backs them up. Sometimes money-market funds invest in Eurodollar CDs, which are dollar-based CDs issued by European, usually London, branches of U.S. banks. The interest rates are usually a little higher than those of domestic CDs. Yankee CDs are issued in the United States by branches of foreign banks.

Banker's acceptances. These instruments are irrevocable obligations of the banks that issue them, so their quality is similar to that of a bank's certificate of deposit. Acceptances are created as a financing tool for international trade, but holders of the acceptances can raise cash immediately by selling them into the money market. Money-market funds often buy them.

Commercial paper. As a less costly alternative to bank borrowings, many large corporations raise funds through commercial paper, or short-term IOUs. There is no collateral behind commercial paper. The only backing is the creditworthiness of the issuer.

If you look behind the yields available on these sorts of instruments, you can see why all money-fund yields lie within a tight range. In early 1996, for instance, three-month T-bills yielded 4.8 percent; high-grade commercial paper, 5.0 percent; and CDs, about 4.8 percent. In that interest rate environment, the average taxable money fund yield was 4.9 percent. There's no way a money fund could earn even 7 percent, especially since money funds have management fees and other expenses as well.

With yields in a narrow range, there's little value a portfolio manager can add by actively trading assets. So the major determinant in performance is overhead. All money funds are sold without sales fees, but in choosing a fund be sure there are no hidden sales fees, known in the mutual fund trade as "12(b)-1" fees, coming out of the portfolio. In selecting a fund also be sure to choose one where the total expenses—management fees and other costs such as printing, mailing, and auditing—come to less than 0.50 percent. That's important because what you earn from the fund is the gross yield less expenses. And when yields are low, expenses play an even greater role. Remember, 0.50 percent on a 5 percent yield is 10 percent of the income. Sometimes fund companies waive all or part of their fund expenses in order to boost the yield. And then they advertise that higher yield as a draw for the fund. If someone's willing to subsidize your investments, why not? Just be sure to ask for how long the waiver is expected to continue. Most funds will guarantee a fee waiver through a certain time, but they often extend them. And even when fund sponsors start to implement the fees, they usually don't take them all at once but phase them in over time. Flex-Fund Money Market Fund, part of the Flex Funds Group, takes yet another approach. The fund's goal is to deliver a yield that's in the top 10 percent of all money-market funds, and the fund sponsor will waive all or part of the expenses to assure the fund's place at the top.

All this begs the question, "Should you invest in a money-market fund based on yield and expenses?" Historically, this has been the best way to go, though in the last few years credit and maturity risks have emerged as major concerns as well.

To ward off potential problems in the money funds, the Securities & Exchange Commission has pulled in its reins in recent years. First of all, the regulators lowered the ceiling on the maximum average maturity of a money-market fund portfolio to 90 days from 120 days. In general, the shorter the maturity of a security or a portfolio, the lower the risk of owning it.

Then, the SEC also came down hard on credit quality. Funds can no longer invest in below-investment-grade commercial paper. And no more than 5 percent of the fund can be invested in the lower tier of investment-grade paper, that which is rated A-2 by Standard & Poor's and P-2 by Moody's.

Finally, in the wake of the 1994 derivatives crises, the SEC banned several sorts of derivatives from money-market funds mainly because their values can change drastically given a change in interest rates. Those off limits to money funds are inverse floaters, leveraged floaters, CMT (Constant Maturity Treasury) floaters, floaters whose interest rates are capped, and floaters whose resets lag changes in short-term interest rates. All of these instruments gained popularity as interest rates came down. That's because with these instruments, payouts actually increased or decreased at a slower rate. Of course, when interest rates started moving up, these floaters' payouts shrank—and so did their values.

With the banning of the most dangerous derivatives, the most cautious investors can probably sleep comfortably using a U.S. government money-market fund. The securities are free of credit risk but have lower yields than the general purpose funds. Still, in times of economic uncertainty, many fund analysts say going for the governments is advisable, even if you have to settle for a lesser return.

It's not even a certainty that one has to give up any yield. By careful fund shopping it's possible to find some government funds with better yields than those which also include bank CDs and commercial paper. Moreover, even if you switch from a general purpose to a government money-market fund in the same fund family, the difference in yields may not be more than 0.30 or 0.40 percentage point. That's a small price to pay if you're worried about credit quality.

U.S. government funds also have another virtue that's sometimes overlooked. Just as the federal government doesn't tax interest earned by investing in state and local government debt, most state and local governments don't tax interest earned on federal government debt. If you are in a high-tax state like New York or California, that exemption can effectively add as much as 1 percentage point to the yield.

Not all government funds qualify for this tax treatment. Interest from repurchase agreements doesn't count because the income is coming not from the government securities but from the borrower who is posting the securities as collateral for a loan. If this is the case, you might consider a money-market fund that holds only U.S. Treasury securities.

TAX-EXEMPT FUNDS

Tax-exempt money-market funds have many of the same characteristics and features as taxable money funds: short-maturity securities, liquidity, and check-writing privileges. But what makes these different—and so alluring to many investors—is that the income is out of the Internal Revenue Service's reach.

These funds escape taxes by investing in a variety of short-term instruments that are issued by state, county, and municipal governments and public authorities. For instance, most communities collect taxes several times a year, but their need for cash doesn't totally conform to that tax collection schedule. So they may issue tax anticipation notes, which are short-term borrowings meant to carry the municipality or agency over until the tax receipts roll in. In a like fashion, there are bond anticipation notes—issued as temporary financing until long-term bonds can be sold—and revenue anticipation notes, which may keep a government unit in operation until other revenue such as a federal grant is collected.

The tax-free money funds also rely heavily on "put bonds" and variable-rate demand notes. In either security the interest rate is reset frequently, sometimes in as short a period as seven days. If the fund manager doesn't like the new interest rate, he or she can always give them back or "put" the bonds back to the issuer for redemption.

Such bonds are rarely put back. The rates are set so that they are competitive with the current rates in the tax-exempt market. Such bonds, which are often backed with a bank letter of credit to assure investors the money will be there to redeem them, almost always trade at par. That makes them especially good investments for money-market type funds that strive to hold their net asset values constant at $1. In fact,

Tax-exempt money funds may offer competitive yields.

investment bankers devised these floating-rate securities largely to meet the needs of tax-exempt money-market funds.

When looking at tax-free funds, remember that the income is not necessarily out of the reach of state and local tax officials. States usually exempt income from municipal securities issued in their state, but don't give a hoot about those issued by others. So a general purpose tax-exempt money-market fund may not be totally tax free. The only part of the income that your state income tax authorities will waive is that which is from your own state. If you're a Michigan resident and 5 percent of the income generated by your tax-free fund came from Michigan securities, the Michigan tax folks will still take a bite of the other 95 percent of your supposed tax-free income.

For many people, that may not be much of a bother. If the local tax is minimal, the tax-free fund may still be a great deal. But if you live in California, Connecticut, Massachusetts, Michigan, Missouri, New Jersey, New York, Ohio, or Pennsylvania, you can find tax-free money-market funds that invest in short-term securities of governments and public authorities in those states. All the income passes to the shareholders untaxed by any governmental authority.

In the early 1990s, rates on conventional money funds had dropped so low that they were almost the same as tax-free funds. But in 1996, that was not the case. The average taxable money fund yield was 4.99 percent; for tax-free funds the figure was 2.99 percent. For all investors, the aftertax return on the taxable fund was higher than the tax-exempt returns. But this is not always the case. Investors need to regularly monitor the two rates. In general, the closer they are to one another the more attractive the tax-free fund becomes.

The most important consideration when looking at tax-free money funds is your overall tax bracket. The bigger the bite from the federal, state, and local taxing authorities, the better a tax-free fund is going to feel. A New York City resident paying the top marginal tax rate is going to find the yield on a "triple-tax-exempt" money-market fund (the "triple" comes from the fact that it's free from federal, state, and city income taxes) attractive. In early 1996, some New York tax-exempt money funds were as high as 3 percent. That's the equivalent of 5.62 percent for a New York City resident in the highest federal, state, and city income tax bracket.

Single-state tax-free funds suffer some drawbacks, mainly lack of diversification. If the state

you live in is undergoing fiscal woes, that will reflect back in the marketplace for all municipal securities issued in that state. Remember the Orange County bankruptcy and the effect on California muni bond funds? Though the NAVs did not fluctuate, many California tax-exempt money funds also had Orange County securities. Franklin Resources, for instance, the parent company of Franklin Funds, didn't wait for bad news. It bought $7.1 million in unsecured Orange County debt from two of its California tax-free money-market funds, just in case the securities failed to pay off.

Another problem with single-state funds is a potential shortage of investments. What if money pours in faster than the portfolio managers can find creditworthy investments? For a while in 1990 Fidelity bought some non-Massachusetts securities for its Massachusetts tax-free fund and also had to go out of state at one time to fill the portfolio of the Spartan New Jersey Tax-Free Fund. That means a small portion of the funds' earnings will wind up subject to state income tax. Though the practice was permitted according to the prospectus, investors certainly thought their fund earnings would be entirely tax-exempt income.

Closed-End Funds

One of the hottest stocks on the New York Stock Exchange in the last few years was not even an operating company. The stock was the Turkish Investment Fund, which shot up 171.3 percent in 1993. The Turkish Investment Fund is one of several hundred closed-end funds. These funds, whose format actually predates mutual funds by more than 100 years, are similar to mutual funds in that they are professionally managed portfolios of securities and are regulated by the same laws.

Many mutual fund management companies run closed-end funds too, and for many of those funds the portfolios look a lot like their mutual fund counterparts. The returns from the best closed-end funds are much like the returns from regular mutual funds (Tables 2-48 and 2-49).

Long overshadowed by mutual funds, closed-end funds had a resurgence in the late 1980s. After the 1987 stock market crash, stockbrokers could not interest their clients in anything much except closed-end bond funds. In 1988, for instance, more than $21 billion went into those

If you pay high taxes, consider a tax-exempt money fund.

TABLE 2-48

CLOSED-END EQUITY FUNDS

BEST RETURNS

Period ▼	Fund ▼	Total return* ▼
1996	**TEMPLETON RUSSIA**	83.9%
1994-96	**FIRST FINANCIAL**	35.7
1992-96	**FIRST FINANCIAL**	44.3
1987-96	**FIRST FINANCIAL**	24.7

*Average annual net asset value, pretax   DATA: MORNINGSTAR INC.

funds. And in 1989, as investors became caught up in the sweeping changes in Europe and Asia, they scrambled to buy closed-end equity funds—like the Spain Fund—that were dedicated to investing in foreign markets. In fact, in 1989 closed-end "single country" funds were 3 of the top 10 performers on the New York Stock Exchange. (The Asia Pacific Fund was No. 4; the Thai Fund, No. 5; the Germany Fund, No. 10.) In 1993, about $17.3 billion was raised for 123 closed-end funds: $15.3 billion for 99 bond funds and $2 billion for 24 equity funds.

In the last few years, however, closed-end funds have all been ignored by investors. Unlike regular mutual funds, mutual-fund managers don't usually spend money to promote them. With investors going wild for regular funds, the closed-end funds get no attention. Brokers tend only to recommend them to customers when they're new and pay a higher commission. Once established, the commission drops, so the brokers turn their attention elsewhere. Even when performance is relatively good, these funds are often starved for investor attention.

The big difference between closed-end funds and mutual funds lies in how investors get their money into and out of them. Mutual funds are "open-ended." When investors want to buy into a fund, the fund management company issues new shares at the fund's net asset value plus a sales charge if the fund is a "load" fund. So if the net asset value is $10 a share, and you invest $10,000, the fund management company will credit you with 1000 shares. When you want to sell your 1000 shares, the fund management buys them back from you at the prevailing net asset value.

Closed-end funds raise capital differently. Suppose a fund management company wants to start a new venture, the Closed-End Fund. The management company hires an investment bank, which organizes the underwriting and finds buyers for the soon-to-be-issued shares. The investment bank gets commitments from investors for

$100 million. So the fund goes public, selling new shares at $10 each (that's the typical starting price), and the fund issues 10 million shares—and that's all. If someone wants to buy or sell shares in the Closed-End Fund after the initial underwriting is completed, he or she has to do it as with any stock: on the stock exchange where it trades.

Is that a big deal? It can be. Suppose the Closed-End Fund portfolio managers are very savvy and the net asset value of the fund goes to $15. An investor decides to take profits and asks her broker to sell the shares. But the broker reports back that he can only get 13½, or $13.50 a share.

True, the portfolio's worth $15, and $13.50 is 10 percent less than what the stock is worth. But the fund company isn't going to redeem the shares, and the only way to liquidate them is to find a buyer. And there's no law that a seller has to receive NAV. The seller can get only what a buyer will pay.

That's not an unusual case. Closed-end equity funds typically sell at a discount to their underlying net asset value, a discount that in the past has been as large as 40 percent. With closed-end bond funds, the discounts are smaller, but they can still move into the double digits. Right after their initial offerings, closed-end funds tend to trade at modest premiums to their net asset values. But often within four to six months they're trading at discounts to their NAVs. That's why most investment managers counsel investors never to buy initial offerings of closed-end funds.

A close look at the mechanics of the closed-end fund shows why they tend to trade at discounts to their NAVs. Go back to the initial public offering. Suppose Closed-End Fund goes public at $10 a share. Out of each $10, about 75 cents goes for underwriting fees and other selling expenses, leaving only $9.25 of the net asset value. Or, turn it around this way: At $10 a share, the fund is selling at an 8 percent premium to its net asset value. That makes it an overpriced stock from the start. Fees and expenses for bond funds usually eat up about 4 to 5 percent of the initial offering price.

There are two ways for the fund's share price to go up. The obvious way, of course, is through superior management. A winning portfolio will boost the net asset value, and that will more or less carry the fund shares upward (though not necessarily dollar for dollar). The other way is for investors who missed the initial offering to bid up the shares on the market.

But there won't be that many investors to bid up the shares. With most closed-end funds, the

TABLE 2-49

CLOSED-END BOND FUNDS

BEST RETURNS

Period	Fund	Total return*
1996	LATIN AMERICA DOLLAR INCOME	49.4%
1994-96	GLOBAL PARTNERS INCOME	15.3
1992-96	NEW AMERICA HIGH-INCOME	19.5
1987-96	FIRST AMERICA PRIME INCOME	15.3

*Average annual net asset value, pretax   DATA: MORNINGSTAR INC.

size of the offering is a function of how much the brokers can sell. Sure, the underwriters might plan a $100 million offering, but if the sales force brings in $300 million in orders, they'll boost the issue to $300 million. That means nearly all the initial demand for a closed-end fund is met on the offering. After the fact, there are few investors who want to buy shares who haven't already done so.

Then, for a few months, the investment bank that underwrote the fund usually buys shares to keep the price up. But sooner or later, the investment bank goes on to underwrite Closed-End Fund II. The brokers start calling clients to talk up the new fund, not to solicit orders for the Closed-End Fund. They can earn a much larger commission on a new fund than they can earn from taking an order for the existing one.

Meanwhile, some of the original investors in the Closed-End Fund start to sell, and there aren't many buyers for the shares. Prices begin to fall and eventually slip below net asset value. Studies show that after four months the average discount for a domestic equity fund is 10.3 percent, and for a single-country equity fund, 11.4 percent. Bond funds seem to hold up better. They trade at an average discount of only 0.12 percent.

Fund managers don't spend money to promote existing closed-end funds as they do with the open-end mutual funds. If they advertise an open-end fund, the new dollars brought into the portfolio will generate additional management fees. Since closed-end funds can't add new dollars to their portfolios, managers have no incentive to advertise.

Closed-end funds can raise additional capital through "rights" offerings, and many did in 1993. In such offerings, existing shareholders are issued rights to buy new shares at a set price, usually a small discount to net asset value. If shareholders choose not to buy, they can sell the rights to other investors who may want them.

Many fund analysts and investors have been critical of rights offerings for several reasons. First, fund managers usually launch the rights offerings at the wrong time. The closed-end bond funds that did so in 1993 used the proceeds to buy bonds while interest rates were nearing a low point—thus making bonds "expensive." By adding a lot of newly purchased lower-yielding bonds to a portfolio with a lot of higher-yielding bonds, rights offerings dilute the funds' earnings and thus work to the disadvantage of the shareholder. The best time to be loading up on bonds is when yields are high, not low. But you rarely see rights offerings in the throes of a bear market, such as the one bond funds were in in 1994.

But shareholders are not the primary concern in a rights offering. The principal beneficiaries of these deals are the investment bankers, who underwrite them, and fund management companies, whose income is based on assets under management. The more money they can lure into the fund, the more money they will make. The other complaint is that the rights offerings are often "coercive." That means that if investors want to maintain their same proportion of ownership in the fund and their share of the income, they have no choice but to invest.

Investor-friendly fund managers are those that take steps to bolster fund share prices if they drop to a large discount to their net asset value. Some funds now have provisions that allow them to buy back their own shares on the market if the discount widens to 10 percent or more. And often the ploy works. For instance, the Franklin Multi-Income Trust, which invests mainly in junk bonds and utility stocks and uses borrowed money to do it, was trading at a 31 percent discount to its NAV near the end of the third quarter of 1990. Then Franklin Resources, the fund's advisers, announced a share buyback. Two weeks later, the shares traded at a slight premium.

And, should the discounts prevail for too long, many funds have new provisions that allow the shareholders to vote to convert to an open-end fund. Once that happens, the discount disappears because investors can then take their money out at net asset value. Just look at the T. Rowe Price New Age Media Fund. The fund sold at around a 20 percent discount to net asset value for over two years. Some investors lobbied to convert the fund into a mutual fund. In February 1997, the directors agreed to do it. The stock price jumped immediately, narrowing an 18 percent discount to 5 percent.

At times, some closed-end funds have traded at enormous premiums, too. Stockbrokers will remind you of that if you rebut their closed-end fund sales pitch. After all, remember the Spain Fund, which at one point in time traded at a premium of 144.5 percent of net asset value. What this means is that investors were willing to pay more than $24 a share for every $10 in assets. Such misvaluations don't last for long. Less than a year later, Spain Fund was trading at a discount of 10 percent to net asset value.

Shares of some single-country funds used to command premiums in the marketplace because they had a "franchise" that couldn't be duplicated. Sometimes closed-end funds trade at a premium because the underwriters could not satisfy all the demand for an issue. But most franchises have disappeared as competitive funds start up and many emerging markets open their doors to foreign investors.

For all the caveats about closed-end funds, they can be smart buys, especially when you might otherwise invest in the open-end fund with a similar investment style (sometimes even the same fund manager). As portfolios, view them much like conventional funds and judge their investment savvy by the same criteria.

Like the open-end mutual funds, the closed-end funds break down into the same categories as do equity and bond funds. That allows investors to make better comparisons to see if some closed-end fund might better fulfill a role in a portfolio than an equivalent mutual fund.

Since there are so many open-end analogs of closed-end funds, why bother with the closed-ends? If the closed-end is selling at a large discount to the open-ends, it may offer a better opportunity. Suppose you're interested in a growth fund in health care so you zero in on H&Q Health Care Investors. The portfolio looks good, as does the track record. In addition, the shares sell, for argument's sake, at a discount of 17 percent from net asset value.

To know if a closed-end fund's discount makes it a buy, the discount has to be compared to its historic range. A 17 percent discount may look good, but perhaps the shares have sold at a 35 percent discount as well. As it turns out, H&Q Health Care Investors traded in a range between net asset value and a 19 percent discount to NAV. That fact says the fund is trading relatively cheaply, and it may be a good time to buy.

In fact, an investor who is bullish on health-care stocks may do much better in the specialized closed-end fund than in an open-end portfolio.

The closed-end fund gives you more upside potential. And here's how. Suppose you buy H&Q, with an NAV of $12, for $10 a share. (In that case, the fund is selling at nearly a 17 percent discount.) Then the stock market starts to rally, health-care stocks do well, and the health-care portfolio climbs 20 percent. So now the net asset value of the fund is $14.40 ($12 plus 20 percent). If the fund still had a 17 percent discount, H&Q Health Care Investors would trade at $12.45. But if health-care stocks were especially strong, investors would become more willing to bid up for the closed-end fund and the discount on the fund would narrow and perhaps disappear.

Suppose that at the end of a year, the discount on H&Q narrows to 5 percent. There's already an appreciation of 20 percent in the portfolio, which brings the NAV to $14.45. Discount that by 5 percent, and the selling price is $13.68. (Since shares trade in eighths of a dollar, round that out to $13.63, or 13⅝.) The original investment was $10 a share and selling at $13.63 represents a 36 percent return (before commissions). An open-end health-care fund might have had only a 20 percent gain. In a bull market the narrowing of a discount on a closed-end fund can give an investor an extra edge.

Of course, if the market turns down, that premium/discount works just the other way. What if the portfolio lost 20 percent of its value and the discount widened to 25 percent? The $12 NAV would then be worth only $9.60—and a 25 percent discount from that is $7.20. The portfolio declined 20 percent, but because of the widening discount the fund price is off 28 percent. In a bear market investors in closed-end funds may be hit harder than regular mutual fund investors.

So much for funds bought at discounts. Let's look at what happens when funds are purchased at a premium. Suppose you buy a fund on the initial offering for $10 a share. After underwriting fees and such, only $9.25 is left for NAV. So, in effect, you pay an 8 percent premium. Let's say the portfolio managers do a good job and the portfolio climbs 20 percent to $11.10. But instead of a premium the fund now sells at a 2 percent discount. If you sell, all you can get is $10.87. So the portfolio went up 20 percent, but the investor could realize less than 9 percent. You're taking an extra risk if you buy closed-end funds selling at a premium to net asset value.

All told, because of differences between share price and NAV in closed-end funds, many fund investors may choose to avoid them altogether and stick with the more familiar and somewhat

> Discounted closed-end funds can be smart investments.

Avoid buying a closed-end fund at a premium.

simpler open-end variety. But there are times when closed-end funds can be the better buy. Mario Gabelli, Charles Royce, and Martin Zweig are just a few investment managers who run both closed- and open-end funds. If you would consider investing in one of their open-end funds, perhaps you should consider a closed-end fund that's selling at a discount.

Look, for instance, at the open-end Royce Value Fund and the closed-end Royce Value Trust. The two have the same portfolio managers and many of the same stocks since they both specialize in value investing in small-to-medium-sized companies. The difference is that the closed-end fund usually sells at a discount. That means that with the closed-end fund you get $1 worth of stock for perhaps 90 or 95 cents. With the open-end fund you get $1 worth of stocks for $1.

Watch out when buying closed-end funds during "crisis" situations. Suppose you thought the sell-off in Latin American was way overdone and you wanted to do some smart contrarian investing. Naturally, a closed-end Latin equity fund selling at a 10 percent discount to NAV might seem better than a similar open-end fund selling at NAV. But individuals, not institutions, dominate the trading in closed-end funds, and they may be slower to react to the news of the day. In the early stages of the Mexican currency crisis, the share prices for closed-end funds did not fall as quickly as the underlying NAVs. For instance, three weeks after the Mexican financial crisis began, prices for Latin American closed-end funds had only dropped about half that of the open-end funds. That means in a falling market the discount actually narrowed rather than increased, and before long, the funds were trading at large premiums to their net asset value. So the best bet is to wait until the market stabilizes, or just stops falling, and let the discount settle down.

If you own closed-end funds, you should also keep your eye on any open-end clones. Sometimes there's money to be made by trading a closed-end fund at a premium for a similar mutual fund. Templeton Emerging Markets, a closed-end fund, has the same portfolio manager and investment policy as the open-end Templeton Developing Markets Fund. But Templeton Emerging Markets spent most of 1992 trading at an average premium to net asset value of 25 percent. The open-end fund would have been the better buy—even after paying the load. In 1993, in fact, John Templeton himself unloaded his shares of the closed-end Templeton Emerging Markets Fund

at a premium of 25 percent over net asset value, and reinvested the proceeds in the open-end fund.

Fund companies such as Franklin, Massachusetts Financial Services, Oppenheimer, and Putnam also operate closed-end bond funds with investment goals similar to their open-end bond portfolios. Bond funds can trade at discounts to NAV, but usually not to the extent of equity funds.

Investing in a closed-end bond fund that's selling at a discount to NAV may result in a higher yield than in a comparable open-end bond fund. Suppose there are open-end and closed-end bond funds with the same manager and similar portfolios. Both have NAVs of $10 per share and a 20 cents per quarter payout. The open-end fund has a yield of 8 percent. But the closed-end fund trades at $9.50, a 5 percent discount to NAV. Buy the closed-end fund, and the same payout becomes 80 cents a year—an 8.4 percent yield. Less money for the same payout results in a higher yield.

The other time to consider closed-end bond funds is when interest rates are falling. When short-term interest rates drop, investors seek to maintain their yields by pulling money out of money-market funds or CDs and buying long-term bond mutual funds. But such a strategy is often self-defeating. What money comes pouring into open-end funds during a time of falling interest rates will be invested at a lower interest rate than the "older" money. That lowers the average yield of the fund and dilutes returns for all shareholders. Closed-end bond funds, because they don't take new money into the portfolio, don't suffer from this sort of dilution problem (unless, of course, the management launches a rights offering).

Buying closed-end bond funds in a period of falling interest rates has some pitfalls, too. After all, a falling-rate environment is a bull market for bonds, so the market prices for closed-end bond funds may trade up to a premium to net asset value. In 1993, for instance, the ACM Government Income Fund sold at a premium as high as 10.9 percent to the value of its portfolio. In that case, the buyer paid $1.09 for every $1 worth of bonds. Moreover, the fund is only earning interest on $1 worth of bonds. So the investor, in effect, is buying a bond at a premium.

But there's a big difference between buying a bond at a premium and a bond fund at a premium. With the bond fund, the investor has all the interest rate risk of a bond, but something more. An investor in a U.S. Treasury or investment-grade bond knows what the interest payment is going to be. On the other hand, bond fund "dividends"—they're technically dividends even though the payout is earned from interest—can be cut, and often are, in a period of declining interest rates. Funds that don't cut—and aren't earning the dividend—could end up making a nontaxable distribution. That's not a freebie, like interest on municipal bonds. A nontaxable distribution means the fund never really earned the money it distributed, so the distribution is considered a return of the investor's own capital. That can be especially annoying to investors who paid a premium for their bond funds. The money comes back at net asset value.

Investors in many closed-end bond funds might be lured by high yields that are produced with leverage. Here's how the funds work. Suppose the funds raise $200 million from investors for regular closed-end bond fund shares. The bond fund then sells perhaps $100 million in preferred stocks—typically to corporations or other institutional investors. The preferred shares pay a dividend that can be either a fixed or a variable interest rate.

So now, the leveraged bond fund can invest $300 million instead of $200 million. Suppose the fund can invest the money to produce an 8 percent interest rate, while paying an average 5 percent rate on the preferred shares. The $200 million earns $16 million a year. The $100 million earns $8 million, less $5 million paid to the preferred stockholders. So the $100 million nets an extra $3 million for the common stockholders. Instead of $16 million in income, the fund earns $19 million. So far, so good.

But what happens if the interest rates climb and bond prices tumble? The portfolio losses to the leveraged fund will be magnified. In the junk bond debacle of 1989 and 1990, among the most battered junk bond funds were those that had leveraged the portfolio. In addition, if the rate on the preferred shares moves up higher than the interest payments on the bonds in the portfolio, the bond fund could be in the position of having to pay the preferred shareholders out of the common shareholders' capital.

The moral of the story: If a closed-end bond fund seems to promise a return that's higher than what the market bears, you have to ask how the fund produced it.

Buying and Selling: The Essentials

Until recently, buying mutual funds was an "either or" business. You either bought them through a salesperson—a stockbroker, financial planner, or sometimes a dually-licensed life insurance agent—or you bought them direct from the mutual fund company. If you bought through a salesperson, you paid a sales charge or "load," a fee that compensates the salesperson for selling you the fund. If you bought directly from the fund company, there was no salesperson, so the fund was purchased "no load," without that fee.

In essence, the load and no-load arrangements represented two ways to distribute funds, and most fund companies followed one or the other. Companies such as Alliance Capital, Franklin, Putnam, and Templeton are load-fund groups, and sell through brokers, sometimes called "broker-dealer" funds. (These funds also include the brokers' in-house proprietary products, such as Merrill Lynch's mutual funds.) Janus, T. Rowe Price, Scudder, and Vanguard are no-load groups, sold without the presence of an intermediary. Instead, they are sold through the mail, toll-free telephone lines, and, in some cases, walk-in investor centers. A few, like Fidelity and Dreyfus, though mainly no-load, developed and sold load funds as well.

Now, new ways to invest in mutual funds are emerging, which are neither load nor no-load. One model is the mutual-fund network, the oldest, biggest, and best-known of which is Charles Schwab & Co.'s Mutual Fund Marketplace. The network addresses one of the drawbacks of investing in multiple funds of several no-load companies: You must maintain relationships with numerous fund companies, and keep track of paperwork for every company with which you deal. Plus, the network makes moving money from, say, a Janus to a Scudder fund as easy as moving from one Janus fund to another. Of course, those who run these networks are in it for the

money, and with no-load funds, who's going to pay the firm that runs the network? Some fund groups, such as Invesco, Janus, Strong, and American Century find this distribution arm so compelling that they pay the networks a small annual fee, about 0.25 to 0.35 percent of assets under management, for bringing them customers.

The networks made simple what was previously difficult—managing diverse portfolios of no-load funds. The networks also made it possible for many brokers to leave the major brokerage firms and set up shops on their own. Instead of selling Franklin and Putnam funds with loads attached, they switched to the no-load networks. Instead of collecting a commission for selling a particular fund, they manage a portfolio of commissionless funds, assessing an annual "management fee." Many load-fund companies, not wanting to miss out on this business, now make their funds available no-load to investors who buy through advisers who charge fees. And the big brokerage firms, seeing the popularity of fee-based mutual fund investing, are changing their ways as well. Now major brokerage firms like Merrill Lynch, Smith Barney, and Prudential Securities are offering large numbers of funds, load and no-load, on a fee-only basis.

A little confusing? First, let's take a few steps back.

What You Need to Know About Loads

For most of their history, mutual funds were sold by salespeople working for the fund companies, brokerage firms, and insurance companies. And for most of that time, the funds came with a stiff "load," or commission. Today, most funds sold by brokers are commonly known as "load" funds.

For many years the load was an 8.5 percent up-front sales charge that lobbed a big chunk of money right off the top of an investment. That meant that out of a $1000 investment, $85 would go toward commissions and only $915 into investments. The 8.5 percent charge usually applied to investments of less than $10,000. For large amounts the sales charge would start to scale back and might even disappear after, say, $1 million. A few fund groups even levied a load on the reinvested dividends and capital gains, though the regulators kept it a tad lower than the initial front-end load. True, the commission seemed high, but salespeople would remind investors that, unlike stocks and bonds, it was only paid on purchase—not again when the investor sold the fund.

There are many more load than no-load funds. That's because many funds need brokers to bring them investors. Some no-loads with excellent track records never really attracted investors—until they added loads. That allowed them to pay brokers to sell their funds. The first year AIM Weingarten was a load fund, assets under management increased by about $98 million, or 58 percent. For instance, the Pasadena Growth Fund switched from no-load to a 3 percent load to encourage brokers to sell the fund. But, says Roger Engemann, the portfolio manager, the 3 percent load proved too small to get the brokers excited about the fund. Then, on the advice of a major brokerage firm, the fund boosted the load to 5.5 percent—and sales took off. The fund more than doubled its assets in less than a year.

In 1992, mutual fund regulators on the U.S. Securities & Exchange Commission staff proposed negotiated loads—allowing fund companies, brokers, and investors to dicker over price. After all, stock commissions have been negotiable since 1975—why not funds? The fund industry howled, and the SEC commissioners didn't press it. The matter died.

NO-LOAD FUNDS

In the early 1970s, the stock market plummeted, and so did mutual fund sales. To shake off the slump, some companies started to sell their funds direct to investors without a sales charge—"no load." No-load funds weren't brand new then, either. But the early no-loads were started by investment counseling firms like T. Rowe Price for accounts deemed too small for individual management, and were not widely marketed.

But along with the no-loads came liberalized rules on mutual fund advertising. Then fund management companies like Dreyfus and Fidelity began dropping the loads from some funds, and when new funds were launched they came without loads. Money-market funds, which drew millions of new investors into mutual funds in the 1970s, were also sold no-load. Their popularity also worked to the advantage of the no-load fund families.

Until the mid-1980s the mutual fund universe was split between the "loads," which stuck with their 8.5 percent sales charges, and the no-loads. Then the load funds, feeling investor resistance to the stiff fees, started lowering their sales charges. Now, there are only a handful of funds with 8.5 percent loads. Most of the load funds have dropped their fees to the 4 to 6 percent range. Increasingly, they have also offered funds with different methods to pay the sales charge, the "back-end load" and the "level load."

BACK-END LOADS

They call it a back-end load, "redemption fee," "exit fee," or, technically, the "contingent deferred sales charge." The fee starts at 4 or 5 percent of the value of the funds you're selling, depending on the fund. If you sell your shares in the first year, you pay the full charge. In the second year, your exit fee drops by 1 percentage point, and so on. By the fifth or sixth year the redemption fees are usually gone, so if you're truly a long-term investor, you may never pay that fee.

Back-end loads were first introduced in the mid-1980s. But this alternative didn't really take off until the late 1980s, when Merrill Lynch introduced "dual pricing." Dual pricing creates two classes of shares for each fund: "A" shares, which carry a one-time up-front load, and "B" shares, which carry the back-end load. Now dual pricing is widespread among brokerage house proprietary funds, and even among the independent fund managers that sell through brokers. While many use the A and B share method, a few, such as Eaton Vance, offer a separate line-up of funds with back-end loads.

During the 1980s, as the load funds lowered up-front sales charges and introduced back-end loads, some no-load companies were going the opposite way. Fidelity Investments, for instance, slapped "low-loads"—2 or 3 percent sales charges—on funds that were previously sold no-load. Fidelity didn't use the load to pay brokers, but to pay for its extensive advertising.

A no-load fund may have hidden sales fees.

But by the 1990s, even though the mutual fund industry enjoyed record sales, investors were resisting loads. Strong Funds, which had low-loads on its equity funds, dropped them altogether in late 1992. Fidelity now waives its low-loads on most funds purchased in retirement accounts (Magellan and Select Portfolios are excluded). In recent years, some load funds with hot performance, such as Oberweis Emerging Growth, switched to no-load, and Heartland Value Fund dropped its front-end load in favor of a back-end load and eventually went no-load. (There are still a few going in the opposite direction. Evergreen Funds switched to loads after the fund management company was acquired by a bank.)

Just because a fund is no-load does not mean there are no fees. For instance, the Vanguard Group levies "transaction fees" on its index funds ranging from 0.5 percent to 1.5 percent, depending on the fund. The difference between this fee and most loads is that the proceeds go to the fund, not to the fund sponsor. The fee is to offset the transaction costs of investing the money. (In most funds, that cost is not explicit but indirect and it is reflected in the price that a fund pays for securities.) At the same time, the Vanguard index funds levy a $2.50 per quarter "maintenance fee" on accounts with less than $10,000 in them. That takes care of reports, statements, and the like. In most funds, that cost ends up on the line itemized as "other expenses."

Some no-loads charge redemption fees, too, but they're usually meant to discourage short-term trading. Vanguard has a 1 percent redemption charge on its Specialized Portfolio series of funds to discourage short-term trading. The Lindner Fund and the Lindner Dividend Fund take a 2 percent redemption fee on shares sold within 60 days of purchase. The Pennsylvania Mutual Fund levies a 1 percent exit fee on shares redeemed within a year of purchase.

Since the wide variation in loads has so muddled the distinction between load funds and no-loads, the terms don't mean so much anymore. In fact, the Investment Company Institute, the fund industry's trade association, looks at funds by the method used to distribute them, not by the sales charges. There are "sales force" funds—those sold to investors through sales folks—and "direct marketing" funds—those sold by the management companies directly to investors (Table 3-1).

"HIDDEN LOADS"

If the loads, low-loads, and no-loads aren't confusing enough, consider the "12(b)-1" fee, or what

TABLE 3-1

THE BIGGEST FUND MANAGERS
AND HOW THEY SELL THEIR WARES

Fund management company	Assets Billions*	Direct sales No-load, Low-load, and institutional	Sales force Load and deferred
FIDELITY	$429.7	●	●
VANGUARD	235.6	●	
AMERICAN FUNDS	174.4		●
MERRILL LYNCH	172.9	●	
FRANKLIN/TEMPLETON	139.8		●
PUTNAM	117.7		●
DEAN WITTER	79.9		●
DREYFUS	79.1	●	●
SMITH BARNEY	78.8		●
FEDERATED	71.0	●	●
T. ROWE PRICE	64.6	●	
AIM MANAGEMENT	58.3		●
AMERICAN EXPRESS (IDS)	58.2		●
OPPENHEIMER FUNDS	56.8		●
AMERICAN CENTURY	50.8	●	
PRUDENTIAL	46.7		●
SCHWAB	42.9	●	
VAN KAMPEN AM. CAP.	42.1		●
ALLIANCE CAPITAL	40.5		●
KEMPER	39.5		●

*As of Dec. 31, 1996. Excludes all variable annuities and off-shore funds.

DATA: STRATEGIC INSIGHT, BUSINESS WEEK

some commentators call the "hidden load." The 12(b)-1 charge, named for the U.S. Securities & Exchange Commission rule which enabled funds to levy it, is, like loads, meant to help defray marketing and distribution costs. Sales force fund companies can use the 12(b)-1 revenues to compensate brokers for their selling efforts. Direct marketing companies, on the other hand, use the money to pay for advertising. At least half of all funds levy some sort of 12(b)-1 fee.

What's very different about this charge is how it is collected from the shareholders. Instead of paying the charge once when investors buy the fund (front-end load), or when they sell it (back-end load), investors pay this fee from the fund's assets. In that sense, the 12(b)-1 charges are treated just like the fees shareholders pay for portfolio management, administration, auditing, printing, postage, and other expenses.

There are limits on 12(b)-1 fees. The fee—which must be disclosed in the prospectus—has a maximum of 0.75 percent of assets per year, or 75 cents per $100 of assets plus a 0.25 percent "service fee," for a total of 1 percent. Many funds, in fact, charge less. Many sales-force companies

A 12(b)-1 fee can erode your profits over time.

with front-end loads also offer funds with back-end loads and 12(b)-1 fees. Many no-load funds have 12(b)-1 fees, too, but the charge is usually much smaller than with a sales-force fund. The rules say that a fund that calls itself "no-load" can have a 12(b)-1 fee of no more than 0.25 percent. Funds with 12(b)-1 charges are noted in the BUSINESS WEEK Mutual Fund Scoreboard.

One percent may not sound like much, but think about it this way. On a $10,000 investment, that's $100 in the first year. But you have to pay 1 percent every year you're in the fund. And, providing that the fund is increasing in value, that 1 percent represents more money each year. Rules enacted in 1992 are designed to put a cap on 12(b)-1 fees so that investors don't pay more in such fees than they would have had they paid an 8.5 percent load. But that cap pertains to the entire fund and not to any individual investor. According to experts, the 12(b)-1 fee on a fund that is not growing would eventually hit the cap. But a fund that's taking in new money may never hit its cap. So investors in those funds may end up paying the 12(b)-1 fee indefinitely.

Confusing enough? It's getting worse. Alliance Capital is one of a number of fund companies that have A, B, and C classes of shares for all its stock and bond funds. The A shares carry a 4.5 percent up-front load. The B shares have an ongoing 1 percent annual 12(b)-1 charge and a declining back-end load. For equity funds, the back-end load is 4 percent in the first year, declining 1 percentage point a year, and disappearing in the fifth year. For fixed-income funds, the back-end load starts at 3 percent and disappears in the fourth year.

The C shares charge neither front- nor back-end loads—they just level a 1 percent a year fee. That's perhaps why it's called the "level-load" fund. Like the 12(b)-1 fee, this level load comes out of the fund's assets every year. You might call it the "forever load." Introduced just a few years ago, some fund executives thought they would quickly outpace both front- and back-end shares in new sales, but that hasn't been the case. According to Morningstar, Inc., 60 percent of the level-load funds have less than $5 million in assets, and 25 percent less than $500,000. Perhaps it's because the shares probably are neither the best deal for investors, nor for the commissioned salespeople who sell them.

Although most fund companies call their front-end load shares "A," back-end load shares "B," and level-load shares "C," don't assume all A's, B's, or C's are alike. In some fund groups, for instance,

the C shares are for institutional investors, or reserved for investors who come to the fund via an employer-sponsored retirement plan.

Some companies, like Neuberger & Berman and Oppenheimer Management, use the "Y" designation for institutional shares. But not all use "Y" that way. Evergreen Funds, for instance, uses Y to designate shares purchased when the fund was still a no-load fund company. New shares are in A, B, and C classes. Some fund managers create multiple classes of shares and call them institutional or "trust" shares. In most cases, those are shares that are distributed through bank trust departments. "Retail" shares are for individual investors.

And what about "Class II" shares? Franklin Funds announced that plan in early 1995. These shares are an alternative to front-end loads, but have a totally different payment structure: Investors would pay a 1 percent load at time of purchase, and another 1 percent of assets if they sell the fund within 18 months. Class II shareholders would also pay higher 12(b)-1 fees of 0.65 percent for bond funds and 1 percent for equity funds.

And mutual fund companies are always coming up with new ways to sell mutual funds, too. One method that's catching on is the "hub and spoke" or "master and feeder" fund arrangement. It works like this: A fund company sets up and manages, for example, a government bond fund. That's the hub. Since this company distributes directly to individual investors, it opens a no-load government bond fund. But instead of owning government bonds, the fund owns shares in the hub, which is a government bond fund. Next, the fund company thinks banks might want to sell this government bond fund to their customers. So it creates another spoke, perhaps with the bank's name on it, sold with a 4 percent load.

The process can go on and on, creating spokes for sales through different distribution channels—institutional investors, retirement plans, and offshore investors—all feeding into the same hub. The advantage of this arrangement is that it's cheaper to run one large, centralized hub portfolio than several smaller funds. That savings should be passed on to the investors in the form of lower expenses.

Investors, for the most part, may not even realize their fund is the spoke of a hub. And, if they're satisfied with results, they may not care. But suppose you paid a load for a spoke fund, while others bought the same hub for a lesser load, or even no load. Right now, a broker selling you a spoke has no obligation to tell you there's another spoke for the same hub with a different pricing scheme. So you may well ask.

Loads, low-loads, hidden loads. Does this mean you forgo all of them and just concentrate on no-load funds? Not necessarily. What is important is that those who invest in mutual funds understand the sales charges, exit fees, and ongoing distribution fees and how they affect the total return from their investments. The U.S. Securities & Exchange Commission, for the most part, has been fairly vigilant on fee disclosure. Their philosophy has been to provide investors with all the information and let the buyer decide. But that puts the burden of fathoming the fee structure back on the fund buyer.

To Load or Not to Load?

Why would anyone buy a load fund? In most cases you can find a no-load analog of most any load fund. True, there are some excellent load funds, but there are also great no-loads. And portfolio performance has nothing to do with whether you paid a broker to sell you the fund. So if you're going to go to the trouble of researching mutual funds at all, you might as well buy no-loads, right?

Perhaps. That's a question only you can answer for yourself. If you're reading this book, it may be because you want to take these decisions into your own hands. You don't want to use a broker, financial planner, or investment adviser. But it's a mistake to dismiss load funds out of hand. If you do, you're cutting yourself off from a large part of the mutual fund universe and many excellent investment opportunities.

When the only alternative to the no-load was an 8.5 percent load, the scales tipped heavily toward the no-load. But today there are former no-load funds that sell with 2 and 3 percent low-loads, and former full-load funds with 4 percent loads. And then there's the back-end load, which many investors never have to pay.

In determining whether to pay a load you have to consider how long you anticipate staying with the fund. Everyone's financial plans are subject to change, of course. And if yours do, most load fund families have a wide range of portfolios to choose from, just like no-loads. And intrafamily switches, such as moving from a Putnam interna-

tional bond fund to a Putnam government bond fund, can usually be done without paying another load. Increasingly, some load-fund groups, like Fortis and Prudential, will let investors switch funds out of other load funds and into theirs without paying a new load. Of course, that's not going to help you if you will end up owing the fund a redemption fee. So if you want to retain the flexibility of moving to other funds of other managers, consider taking the charge up front.

If your investment is for your retirement nest egg or your toddler's college education, a load should not stand between you and the best possible fund. After all, even an 8.5 percent load—and there are very few of them left—over a 10-year holding period works out to less than 1 percent per year. That kind of sales burden can be easily overcome in the performance of an exceptional load fund versus a mediocre no-load.

But most investors are not faced with a choice of 8.5 percent versus no charge. What about choosing between A and B shares? Suppose you're interested in the MFS Emerging Growth Fund. The A shares have an up-front 5.75 percent load, which is fairly stiff in today's market. The B shares, on the other hand, have no up-front load. But there are 12(b)-1 fees amounting to 1 percent a year, and a back-end load that's 4 percent in the first and second year, but then declines 1 percentage point a year until it disappears in the seventh year. What's the best buy?

Depends on your assumptions for your holding period and the rate of return on your investment. If you assume a $10,000 investment and an average annual return of 10 percent a year, the B shares provide better returns up until year 8, even if you redeem and trigger the back-end load. According to Multiple Class Calculator, a software program developed by Money Marketing Inc., the B shares earn more money until year 8, when the A shares nudge them out by $9. After that, the advantage goes to the A shares, but not by much. In year 10, the A shares only beat the B shares by $14. And the higher the assumed return, the longer the B shares retain their edge.

What if you have three choices, as is the case with MFS Emerging Growth's sister fund, MFS OTC Fund (Table 3-2). That fund has A, B, and C shares. The C share has neither an up-front nor back-end charge, but levies 1 percent a year forever. Suppose you go with the same $10,000 investment and assume a 10 percent average annual return. In the early years, the C shares work out best. That's because there is neither a big bite up front, nor one on the back end. For

Differences between load and no-load funds are blurring.

TABLE 3-2

PAY THE LOAD NOW, LATER, OR FOREVER?

MFS OTC Fund has three classes of shares. "A" shares have a traditional front-end load of 5.75%, and a 1.36% expense ratio. "B" and "C" shares have expense ratios, 2.43% and 2.36% respectively, because of the higher 12(b)-1 fees. "B" shares have a 4% redemption fee if you cash out in the first or second year, 3% in the third and fourth, 2% in the fifth, and 1% in the sixth year. Assuming a $10,000 initial investment and a 10% average annual return, which shares make most sense?

Year-End	A shares	B shares	B, if redeemed	C shares
1	$10,239	$10,757	$10,357	$10,764
2	11,124	11,571	11,171	11,586
3	12,085	12,447	12,147	12,472
4	13,129	13,389	13,090	13,424
5	14,264	14,403	14,203	14,450
6	15,496	15,493	15,393	15,554
7	16,835	16,666	16,666	16,742
8	18,289	17,928	17,928	18,021
9	19,870	19,477	19,477	19,398
10	21,586	21,160	21,160	20,880

DATA: MONEY MARKETING INC.

instance, in year 2, the C shares are worth $11,586 versus $11,124 for the A shares and $11,571 for the B shares before redemption, $11,171 after.

But the A shares have a much lower expense ratio than the B or C shares. And over time, that gives the advantage to A-share investors. In year 7 and beyond, the advantage swings to the A-share owners; they have a $169 advantage over B-share holders, and a $93 advantage over C-share holders. By year 10, the A-share holders are $427 ahead of the B-share holders, and $706 over the C-share holders. Obviously, the C shares, which are the cheapest in the earlier years, could end up costing the most if the investment is truly a long-term one. Perhaps the C shares are appropriate if, at the start, you believe the investment will be redeemed in the first few years. Still, many people have a hard time swallowing that chunky up-front sales load. If that's the case, B shares may make the best choice under certain conditions. MFS, for instance, will automatically convert B shares into A shares after the customer has passed the period in which a back-end charge might be levied, usually six years. That way, the investor is also relieved of the heavier 12(b)-1 burden that's in the B shares.

In weighing a load versus a no-load fund, you should also consider the fund's investment parameters. For instance, equity funds generally have broad charters and often disparate results. So even if both funds are growth funds, the differences in returns of growth funds are great and having the "right" fund is important. Paying a modest load for an equity fund that's demonstrated superior results may be better than buying just any no-load.

At the other extreme, short-term bond funds all maintain a fairly similar portfolio, and the differences in returns from one fund to the next are small. So it doesn't make sense to pay a load for a short-term bond fund when there's little likelihood that it will show any better performance than a no-load fund.

There is at least one reason to pay a load—to compensate a broker or financial planner for the time he or she spends meeting with you and monitoring your investments. Perhaps a recommendation for one equity fund does not merit paying a 5.75 percent load. But if a financial planner takes the time to tailor a portfolio of funds for you, he or she has to be paid. The load is one way to do it.

There are other ways as well. Many financial planners, for instance, put their clients' money into no-load funds and then levy an annual fee for the entire portfolio, perhaps 1 or 2 percent. That's not necessarily a better deal for investors, either. If you are investing for more than a few years, you might be better off paying your planner by investing in load funds—providing the planner still delivers good service long after being paid. Six percent off the top of the initial investment may sound steep, but if the fund managers have sliced off 1 percent a year for 10 years, you've paid a whole lot more.

Keep in mind, too, that while it's common practice to refer to a fund as a "4 percent load" or a "6 percent load," not everyone pays the full freight. If the fund carries a sales charge, there are ways to minimize the costs. Most load-fund groups have fee schedules that slide downward for progressively larger investments. Typically, purchases up to $10,000 carry the maximum load. Before making a large investment in a load fund, ask the broker about the next "breakpoint," the dollar amount necessary to qualify for a lower load. In some cases, it might be worth making an extra $1000 or $2000 investment to qualify for the lower sales charge. At the high end, the sales fee often drops to 1 percent—or even totally disappears on major investments of $1 million or more.

Suppose you plan to invest $15,000, but you won't be able to put the money in all at once. Check with your broker to see if the fund management company will let you sign a letter of intent. In such an agreement you pledge to invest over a 13-month period a specified amount which, if invested at one time, would qualify for a reduced sales charge. If you fail to fulfill the letter of intent, you'll owe the fund the difference between the sales charges you've paid and what you should have paid. The company can take the money from your account.

If you're spreading your investments over several funds in the same load-fund group, many funds will give you the same break as if the investment were made in one fund. And all the funds don't have to be for the same account. If you're investing for your personal funds, your IRA, a spousal IRA, and some custodial accounts for the kids, you can probably get a discount that takes in the total investment. But you have to ask.

Mutual Fund Networks

If you opened a stock brokerage account and invested in, say, 10 stocks, you could buy, sell, and keep track of them through one account. It used to be nearly impossible to do the same with mutual funds, except if you kept your investments to one fund family. You could mix and match multiple funds in one account using a commissioned broker or financial planner, but you would still be limiting yourself to a little more than half the fund universe. You would not be able to include, say, T. Rowe Price or Vanguard offerings, since they don't pay commissions to brokers.

Mutual funds are not as interchangeable as stocks, but thanks to the emerging mutual fund networks, they're heading that way. You can think

TABLE 3-3

FUND-SHOPPING THROUGH DISCOUNT BROKERS	
	Toll-free phone
ACCUTRADE	800-882-4887
AMERICAN EXPRESS FINANCIAL DIRECT	800-658-4677
K. AUFHAUSER & CO.	800-368-3669
BARRY MURPHY & CO.	800-221-2111
FIDELITY BROKERAGE SERVICES	800-544-0214
NATIONAL DISCOUNT BROKERS	800-888-3999
NATIONSBANC INVESTMENTS	800-926-1111
QUICK & REILLY	800-221-5220
SEAPORT SECURITIES	800-221-9894
CHARLES SCHWAB & CO.	800-435-4000
VANGUARD BROKERAGE SERVICES	800-992-8327
WATERHOUSE SECURITIES	800-934-4443
JACK WHITE & CO.	800-323-3263

DATA: BUSINESS WEEK

of the networks as sort of a family of fund families. The discount brokerage firm of Charles Schwab & Company originated the network concept more than a decade ago in a program called Mutual Fund Marketplace (MFM) (Table 3-3), and it now has more than $75 billion in fund assets. MFM has over 2000 funds, most of which would be recognizable to investors as no-load funds. But for most of them you have to pay a small transaction charge. Within MFM, there's also a program called One Source, through which investors can buy some 650 funds with no fee. The broker is paid by the fund company, often through a 12(b)-1 charge.

For the other no-load funds, you pay a fee to the broker. For trades up to $15,000 in size, the fee is 0.7 percent of the investment. The fee is 0.2 percent on the next $15,001 to $100,000, and 0.08 percent on everything over $100,000. A $10,000 trade costs $45 and a $25,000 trade, $75. Schwab officials say that, on average, clients in the Mutual Fund Marketplace program end up paying commissions of about 0.3 percent of the amount invested. Investors can get a 10 percent discount by conducting their trades by an automated phone line or by computer link.

So why would anyone pay Schwab to invest in a fund that doesn't charge commissions? If all you ever planned to do was to buy that one fund, there's no good reason. And the commission structure makes the purchasing of no-load funds uneconomical for small trades or monthly investing programs. The transaction fee is 0.7 percent for sums up to $5000, which is $35. But it will cost you $39 anyway. That's because Schwab, like most stockbrokers, has a minimum transaction charge—and in Schwab's case, it's $39. If you're stashing away a couple of hundred dollars a month in a fund, you would do better to deal directly with the fund. You don't want to spend $39 to invest $200.

Many investors like the convenience of the Schwab program even if they have to pay the fees. Rather than a statement and an account with every fund, Schwab delivers a consolidated statement. At tax time there's one Form 1099. If you want to sell one fund and redistribute the proceeds into three other funds, you can effect the change with one phone call instead of several. If you're switching funds, there's a $15 fee for the fund you're switching out of and the regular commission for the one you're going into. In One Source, investors are permitted 15 free trades a year, as long as the funds have been held more than 90 days.

There's another advantage, too. There are some excellent funds with high minimum investments. Two highly regarded bond funds, PIMCO Low Duration and PIMCO Total Return, require minimum investments of at least $500,000 to open an account. But invest through Schwab and you can buy in for as little as $1000. Schwab lowers thresholds because it maintains an "omnibus" account with each no-load fund. That means that PIMCO treats all Schwab customers as one account. Schwab, in turn, keeps track of how many shares of that account belong to each customer. So Schwab can offer lower minimum investments because it is pooling funds from a large number of clients.

Schwab has even extended the Mutual Fund Marketplace program to load funds like American, Colonial, Franklin, Pioneer, Putnam, and Templeton. But the regulations bar brokers from discounting the loads. Still, buying load funds through Schwab or one of its competitors may appeal to investors who want the funds but do not want to deal with the full-service brokers who usually sell them.

Fidelity Investments' FundsNetwork program is similar to Schwab's, offering 3300 no-load and load funds, 600 of them without a transaction fee. Transaction charges are two-part, a base fee plus a variable fee depending on the size of the transaction. For investments of up to $5000, the fee is $17.50 plus 0.8 percent of the principal. For a $3000 purchase, that works out to $41.50. Following the commission schedule, the fee on a $1000 investment would work out to $25.50, except there's a $28 minimum. Several other discount brokers run broad-based mutual fund programs like Schwab's. Jack White & Company has some 4500 no-load and low-load funds. The minimum charge is $27 per trade on trades of up to $5000, $35 for trades of $5001 to $25,000, and $50 for trades in excess of $25,000. Jack White also has a no-fee service with, at last count, 850 funds. That's by far the largest no-fee network.

Load-fund investors may also check out Jack White's CONNECT System. It allows investors to buy load funds without paying loads. Instead, there's a flat $200 fee, no matter how large the purchase.

Suppose an investor would like to place $25,000 in a fund with a 4.5 percent front-end load. That would take $1125 off the top of the investment. The CONNECT charge for the sale would be a flat $200. CONNECT places the buyer's offer on an electronic bulletin board and looks for a seller. CONNECT pays half the fee, or $100, to the seller as an incentive to sell through the Jack White system instead of cashing out

through the fund company. And CONNECT can't guarantee that it can match up willing buyers and sellers on the spot, or even on the day that the order is placed. But the system is expected to become part of a securities dealer's electronic bulletin board, which will enable Jack White to attract fund buyers and fund sellers.

Advisers and "Wraps"

The emerging mutual fund networks are doing more than changing the way many individuals buy and sell funds. They're changing the way brokers and investment advisers conduct their businesses as well. Over the last few years, thousands of brokers have left brokerage firms, where they got paid for their advice through commissions, and have opened up their own firms where, instead of charging commissions, they levy a fee based on the client's assets under management.

Instead of selling traditional load funds from companies like Alliance Capital, Franklin, and Putnam, they channel their clients' money into no-load funds through the networks. They're putting so much in, in fact, that some load-fund groups—not wanting to miss this burgeoning market—make their funds available no-load through the networks to the advisers' clients. Total assets under the control of fee-based advisers amount to nearly $200 billion. The portion of those assets in mutual funds is an estimated $45 billion, according to Cerulli Associates, Inc.

Fee-based advisers don't get paid for selling any particular fund—only for their advice. Of course, in theory, a traditional load fund performs the same function. The difference is that instead of paying the salesperson at the time of sale, the client pays the salesperson over time. Perhaps more important, in a traditional load fund, the salesperson is paid the same no matter how the investment performs, and you may never hear from him or her again.

With an asset-based fee arrangement, the salesperson is, in effect, on the "same side of the table" and you're in a long-term relationship. If the advice is good, the assets under management grow, and so does the adviser's annual fee. Conversely, if the client loses money, so does the adviser. Paying an adviser through asset-based fees is not necessarily cheaper than traditional loads, and indeed, could wind up being more expensive. But it should only be more if the fund performs well. Most people don't mind paying for good advice.

Keep in mind, too, that fee-based arrangements only work out well if the fee is kept under control. Many independent advisers charge in the range of 1 to 1.5 percent of assets, and, the larger the account, the lower the percentage. Most major brokerage firms have a similar arrangement, called the "wrap" account—so-called because it wraps all costs into one price. But the fees may be as high as 3 percent. For a portfolio of mutual funds, that's much too high since the fee mainly covers fund selection and monitoring. The actual stockpicking—which is far more complex—takes place within the mutual funds themselves, and that's paid for through the funds' operating expenses.

The fee-based arrangement isn't for everyone. For starters, do you need or want the help? If you feel comfortable and have the time to do it yourself, you don't need an adviser. If you'd like one—but don't have a minimum $25,000 to invest, it may be hard to find an independent adviser to take your account. Even with a 1.5 percent fee, the account might only generate $400, which probably does not come close to covering the annual cost. Some advisory firms, in fact, want a $100,000 to $200,000 minimum investment. If you can't meet those minimums, and want an adviser, you will have to pay steep hourly rates or go for traditional load-fund products. If you're successful, you may eventually accumulate enough money to switch to an asset-based arrangement.

Considering hiring an adviser to manage a portfolio of mutual funds? Lots of people are doing it, even those who have the savvy to invest the money themselves. Many of those who have the ability just don't have the time. Many people find investment advisers the same way you find other professionals—through referrals and recommendations from friends, relatives, and coworkers. But don't hand over your money to anyone without a thorough investigation—sometimes known as "due diligence" in the investment world—of your own.

Many people who give investment advice, sell securities, and manage money are registered with the U.S. Securities & Exchange Commission. That may sound august, but it means little and assures nothing. All it takes to become an SEC-registered adviser is to complete a lengthy form and pay the $150 fee. No examinations are required, and there is no requirement for education in investment theory and practice. The SEC's Form ADV, which advisers must complete, asks about education, professional credentials, work experience, and the like, but having none of that is no bar to getting the registration. That's why it's imperative to ask an adviser for a copy of his or her ADV. The law requires that he or she provide you with Part II, which describes the investment program, fees, and charges. But ask for Part I as well. The SEC can investigate investor complaints against registered advisers, but as far as regular audits, they are few and far between—on average, once every four decades.

All but a handful of states require investment advisers to register, and many also require they pass some national examinations. But the tests usually deal with the rules and regulations of dealing with clients. They don't test for the adviser's knowledge and understanding of the investments. There are private organizations and professional associations that do that, such as the Association for Investment Management and Research, which awards the Chartered Financial Analyst designation, and the College of Financial Planning, which grants the Certified Financial Planner certificate. If the adviser has one or more such designation, it's definitely a plus. And don't take the adviser's word for it. You may want to call the professional group yourself to verify the credentials.

Most advisers have a track record they can show you. But it's not necessarily going to be useful information. Putting on the best show, the adviser might show you a sample portfolio with what seems to be a high return. But that portfolio might have been devised for a client with far more risk-taking ability or tolerance than you have. So if you are a conservative investor, ask to see what the adviser has done for someone more like yourself. And a really good adviser won't take your word for it that you're a conservative investor. He or she should ask probing questions and perhaps give you a little written quiz to get a better sense of your risk-taking ability. Most people can take more risk than they think they can, and as a result short-change themselves in the long run. A good adviser will spot that and encourage you to correct it.

Once you have decided on an adviser, make sure you understand what services—such as regular consultations and monthly or quarterly reports—the adviser is going to provide, what it's going to cost, and how payment will be collected. Then, the adviser will open up an account for you,

Before hiring an adviser, check references and credentials.

probably with a brokerage firm that has a mutual funds network. The account must be in your name, not the adviser's. You should give the adviser the power to make buy and sell decisions for the portfolio. After all, that's the point of having an adviser. But make sure you receive the confirmation slips and brokerage statements that show the activity in the account. Do not give the adviser the power to take money out of the account. Only you should be able to do that.

Buying on Margin

The convenience and simplicity of the mutual fund networks have also made them popular with mutual fund "market-timers," investors who move assets around, following rigorous technical formulas, trying to capture upside moves in the stock market while steering clear of downdrafts. For more aggressive investors, the program allows the purchase of mutual funds on "margin."

Margin buying works this way. Suppose a fund investor thinks stocks are about to stage a big rally and thinks highly of the Janus Mercury Fund. She decides to invest $10,000 in that fund. If the fund goes up 25 percent in the next six months, the investment is worth $12,500, and the investor can cash out at a profit of $2500. But if the investor buys on margin, she could invest $20,000 in the fund: $10,000 is her money and $10,000 is a loan from the brokerage firm. The interest rate on the loan is usually the broker's loan rate (a figure similar to a bank's prime rate) plus anywhere from 0.5 to 1.5 percent, depending on the size of the loan.

If the fund goes up 25 percent, the leveraged investor's holding climbs to $25,000, and if she sells it, there is a 50 percent return on the original $10,000 investment—a $5000 profit. Well, not quite. Remember, the investor took a loan from the broker to buy the shares. Suppose she borrowed $10,000 for six months at 10 percent interest. That comes out to $500. All told, the investor nets (before commissions) $4500 on her original $10,000. In a cash account that does not use margin, the net profit would be $2500.

But not all margin plays work out so well. What if the value of the investment remained unchanged for six months? Then the margin investor is out the interest. Worse yet, the fund headed south instead of north and declined by 25

percent. So the $20,000 investment is now worth $15,000. What if the margin investor sells at that point? She owes the broker the $10,000 originally borrowed and $500 interest to boot, leaving her with $4500 out of an initial $10,000 investment. Don't use margin buying unless you know exactly what you're doing and can stand the loss.

Prospecting the Prospectus

Nobody wants to read a prospectus. It's a legal document that describes a mutual fund, often in legal and financial terms that may sound awfully technical. But the language is precise for a reason. The SEC has strict guidelines about what the fund can say about itself and how it must present information on past performance, expenses, and fees. Remember, the SEC's approval of a prospectus is only that. It is not an endorsement of any particular investment.

If the prospectus looks daunting today, it's only a shadow of what it was just a few years ago. It's easier to read; its figures are easier to compare; and there's a lot less bulk. Most of the objective information you need is in there: sales charges and fees, investment policy, and administrative matters like the procedure for redeeming shares or switching into other funds. If the fund has an operating history, the prospectus will provide historical data too. What the prospectus won't have is a glowing recommendation from a sales rep or a complimentary article from a financial publication. That may be included in sales literature that's stuffed into the same envelope.

Believe it or not, prospectuses are improving. Direct marketers like Fidelity, who don't have salespeople to explain their funds to investors, are making efforts to both simplify the prospectus and, as much as the lawyers allow, explain things in "plain English." In fact, with the blessings of the SEC, eight fund companies are currently providing vastly simplified "plain English" prospectuses that fit neatly on two sides of an 8½-by 11-inch piece of paper—with room to spare.

Simplifying a prospectus is never easy because it's a document that's trying to serve two purposes. Its stated objective is disclosure, informing investors how a fund invests and operates. But it's also a document that mutual fund company lawyers design as a litigation shield, making sure

Don't let the prospectus scare you.

the fund managers will be able to run the fund without inviting lawsuits.

STATEMENT OF ADDITIONAL INFORMATION

There's plenty of detail in the prospectus, but the investor can also ask the fund to send the Statement of Additional Information (SAI). This bulkier presentation is more of what prospectuses used to be. It covers the same ground as the prospectus, but in far more detail. For instance, the prospectus for the Fidelity Magellan Fund (dated May 20, 1995) is 30 pages, set in double columns, double-spaced, with charts and tables. Each page is 8⅜ by 5⅜ inches in size. That's a fairly slim mutual fund prospectus. The SAI for the same fund is twenty-two 8½- by 11-inch pages—single-spaced, largely unbroken by charts and tables.

How do they differ? The prospectus, for instance, has a heading worded "Adjusting Investment Exposure," followed by two paragraphs outlining in summary form that the fund can use "various techniques" to increase or decrease its exposure to changes in security prices, interest rates, foreign exchange, and other factors that affect security prices. In contrast, Magellan's SAI details those techniques in two single-spaced, 8½- by 11-inch pages.

For most investors, the prospectus will suffice. But you should be aware of the SAI. In a 1991 case decided in a federal appellate court in New York, the judges ruled investors are responsible for knowing what's in the Statement of Additional Information. An investor challenged a fee that he said wasn't in the prospectus. The court said it was—but in the SAI. And since the existence of the SAI was noted in the prospectus and is legally part of the prospectus, he could not claim he was unaware of the charge. In Magellan's case, the mention of the SAI is right on the cover of the prospectus, along with a toll-free telephone number which a prospective investor can call to obtain it.

State securities administrators, who oversee the activities of securities firms at the state level, have been urging fund investors to request SAIs and urging the SEC to require more detailed information in the prospectuses so investors don't have to read both documents. The SEC's Division of Investment Management, which regulates mutual funds, has resisted any moves that might fatten up the prospectuses. If the prospectus is a little-read document now, it will be even less so if it is a thicker and more detailed document.

TAKING A CLOSER LOOK

Don't let the prospectus unnerve you. The financial matters and investment policies may be unique. But much of the other material is boilerplate and doesn't vary much from fund to fund. And not all of it is pertinent to every investor. As long as your planned investment isn't for your Individual Retirement Account or other tax-deferred program, you don't need to read the IRA section in the prospectus.

When thumbing through the prospectus, look for important statistical nuggets like the fund's results and expenses. The documents plainly outline all sales charges, deferred sales charges, redemption fees, exchange fees, management fees, 12(b)-1 fees, and other pertinent expenses. There will also be a condensed financial history of the fund. (Most of these data are also available in the BUSINESS WEEK Mutual Fund Scoreboard.)

Want to take a closer look? Go to Figures 3-1 and 3-2, which are pages four and five from the Fidelity Magellan Fund (the prospectus is dated May 20, 1995). Look at the expense summary. You can see the maximum sales charge, 3 percent. The introductory note tells you on what pages you can find more detailed information on the sales charge. For instance, under certain circumstances, the sales charge can be waived.

You can also see in plain language that there is no sales charge on reinvested dividends, and no deferred sales charges or fees for exchanges (that is, moving money from fund to fund within a family of funds). There is also a $12 annual account maintenance fee for accounts with less than $2500—and it applies across the Fidelity universe.

True, the cost of servicing small accounts is high (it pretty much costs the same to service a $2500 account and a $250,000 account), but fund companies don't bear that cost, the funds do. So in theory, at least, any maintenance fee should go to the fund, not the fund company. But that's not the case here. Putting the $2500 minimum into Magellan may not protect you from the maintenance fee, either. After paying the 3 percent load, that $2500 investment is only $2425. And what if the value declines after you invest? One way to avoid the fee is to sign up for the Automatic Account Builder program, which allows smaller initial investments as long as you make them regularly.

Financial statements give a sense of the fund.

FIGURE 3-1

Expenses

Shareholder transaction expenses
are charges you pay when you buy, sell, or hold shares of a fund. See pages 18 and 24-30 for an explanation of how and when these charges apply. Lower sales charges may be available for accounts over $250,000.

Maximum sales charge on purchases (as a % of offering price)	**3.00%**
Maximum sales charge on reinvested distributions	**None**
Deferred sales charge on redemptions	**None**
Exchange fee	**None**
Annual account maintenance fee (for accounts under $2,500)	**$12.00**

Annual fund operating expenses

are paid out of the fund's assets. The fund pays a management fee that varies based on its performance. It also incurs other expenses for services such as maintaining shareholder records and furnishing shareholder statements and financial reports. The fund's expenses are factored into its share price or dividends and are not charged directly to shareholder accounts (see page 13).

The following are projections based on historical expenses, and are calculated as a percentage of average net assets. A portion of the brokerage commissions that the fund paid was used to reduce fund expenses. Without this reduction, the total fund operating expenses would have been 0.99%.

Management fee	.75%
12b-1 fee	**None**
Other expenses	.21%
Total fund operating expenses	**.96%**

Examples: Let's say, hypothetically, that the fund's annual return is 5% and that its operating expenses are exactly as just described. For every $1,000 you invested, here's how much you would pay in total expenses if you close your account after the number of years indicated:

After 1 year	**$ 40**
After 3 years	**$ 60**
After 5 years	**$ 81**
After 10 years	**$144**

These examples illustrate the effect of expenses, but are not meant to suggest actual or expected costs or returns, all of which may vary.

 Understanding Expenses

Operating a mutual fund involves a variety of expenses for portfolio management, shareholder statements, tax reporting, and other services. As an investor, you pay some of these costs directly (for example, the fund's 3% sales charge). Others are paid from the fund's assets; the effect of these other expenses is already factored into any quoted share price or return.

Then come the operating expenses. The introductory note explains what goes into the charges. The management fee, which can vary depending on the fund's performance, is estimated to be 0.75 percent, or 75 cents per $100. "Other" expenses, which include such administrative costs as maintaining shareholder records and furnishing reports and financial statements, amount to another 0.21 percent.

If you add up all the fund operating expenses, they amount to 0.96 percent, or slightly less than 1 percent of the fund's net assets. So what does that mean to your bottom line? You can find that right below, which shows the cumulative impact of sales charges and expenses. If you invest $1000, and earn 5 percent a year, you've spent $40 on sales and operating expenses in the first year; $60 after 3 years, and up to $144 after 10 years. Actually, a 5 percent assumed rate of return for this fund is absurd, and if that's all you thought you could earn, you certainly would not invest in it. However, that's not the point. The SEC requires funds to use that reporting format account to make it easier for investors to compare fees and expenses.

If the fund is brand new, be sure to check whether the fund management company is subsidizing the fund's overhead or waiving management fees. Don't snub these funds—if someone's going to give you a free lunch, take it. But free lunches don't last forever. It's common for fund management companies to subsidize money-market and bond funds when they're trying to build assets, and they'll often do it for equity funds as well. If the fund company absorbs 0.50 percentage point in expenses, it can really make a money-market or bond fund stand out. And, of

FIGURE 3-2

Financial Highlights

The table that follows is included in the fund's Annual Report and has been audited by Coopers & Lybrand L.L.P. independent accountants. Their report on the financial statements and financial highlights is included in the Annual Report. The financial statements and financial highlights are incorporated by reference into (are legally a part of) the fund's Statement of Additional Information.

Selected Per-Share Data

Years Ended March 31	1986	1987	1988	1989	1990	1991	1992	1993	1994	1995
Net asset value, beginning of period	$ 37.69	$ 55.34	$ 59.85	$ 44.10	$ 52.92	$ 58.60	$ 64.84	$ 68.13	$ 68.44	$ 69.72
Income from Investment Operations										
Net investment income	.49	.42	.63	1.09	1.35	1.39	.81	1.20	.61	.27
Net realized and unrealized gain (loss) on investments	19.59	11.39	(6.64)	8.63	9.39	8.10	9.21	9.18	7.92	5.22
Total from investment operations	20.08	11.81	(6.01)	9.72	10.74	9.49	10.02	10.38	8.53	5.49
Less Distributions										
From net investment income	(.65)	(.46)	(.72)	(.90)	(1.24)	(.83)	(1.30)	(1.25)	(.75)	(.14)[D]
From net realized gain	(1.78)	(6.84)	(9.02)	—	(3.82)	(2.42)	(5.43)	(8.82)	(6.50)	(2.63)[D]
Total distributions	(2.43)	(7.30)	(9.74)	(.90)	(5.06)	(3.25)	(6.73)	(10.07)	(7.25)	(2.77)
Net asset value, end of period	$ 55.34	$ 59.85	$ 44.10	$ 52.92	$ 58.60	$ 64.84	$ 68.13	$ 68.44	$ 69.72	$ 72.44
Total return [A,B]	56.59%	24.26%	(9.64)%	22.26%	20.32%	17.26%	16.48%	17.06%	12.94%	8.21%

Ratios and Supplemental Data

	1986	1987	1988	1989	1990	1991	1992	1993	1994	1995
Net assets, end of period (In millions)	$ 6,086	$ 9,890	$ 8,440	$ 9,627	$13,162	$14,808	$19,824	$24,886	$33,119	$39,803
Ratio of expenses to average net assets	1.08%	1.08%	1.14%	1.08%	1.03%	1.06%	1.05%	1.00%	.99%[C]	.96%[C]
Ratio of expenses to average net assets before expense reductions	1.08%	1.08%	1.14%	1.08%	1.03%	1.06%	1.05%	1.00%	1.00%[C]	.99%[C]
Ratio of net investment income to average net assets	1.95%	1.18%	1.33%	2.13%	2.54%	2.47%	1.57%	2.11%	1.07%	.39%
Portfolio turnover rate	96%	96%	101%	87%	82%	135%	172%	155%	132%	120%

[A] The total returns would have been lower had certain expenses not been reduced during the periods shown.
[B] Total returns do not include the one time sales charge.
[C] FMR has directed certain portfolio trades to brokers who paid a portion of the fund's expenses.
[D] The amounts shown reflect certain reclassifications related to book to tax differences.

course, that's the point. The yield looks alluring, and the money flows in.

But watch out. The prospectus must disclose the full fee structure even if shareholders are not paying it. The point is, you should be aware of what the fees are and what they would be if they were paid. Without the waiver, some of these funds may not look as attractive as others with no waiver, but lower expenses. You can put the money in and take the free lunch. But be ready to leave if and when full rates are levied.

The financial statements also give you some feeling for the fund. The numbers may look scary, but they're really pretty simple. Go to Figure 3-2. Start with the last column, which is for the fiscal year ending March 31, 1995. The top line, net asset value, beginning of the period, tells you just that—what a fund share was worth on April 1, 1994, the start of the fiscal year. Seven lines down, you come up with net asset value at the end of the period, $72.44. The steps in between explain how the fund got from the beginning NAV to the end-of-period NAV.

Start with "net investment income." That's 27 cents a share. It's what's left from stock dividends and interest from fixed-income or money-market holdings after paying for fund expenses. Such expenses include fund managers, record-keeping, postage, auditing, and legal fees. That 27 cents is available for distribution to Magellan shareholders. Of course, that's not a lot of money, considering the NAV is over $70 a share. But Magellan's primary goal is growth of capital, not generation of income. What it collects in income is purely secondary to the fund's main goal.

In a fund like Magellan, the big money is made from capital gains. Look at the line "net realized & unrealized gain (loss) on investments." When a mutual fund sells a security at a profit, it has a "realized" gain; when it sells at a loss, it's a realized loss. If a fund continues to hold stocks that are worth more than the fund paid for them, the stocks represent unrealized gains. Likewise, stocks in a portfolio that are valued at less than their cost are unrealized losses. To get "net" gains, the fund tallies the gains and losses, both realized and unrealized. If the number is positive, as it is here, the fund had net gains. If negative, net losses. In fiscal 1995, the Fidelity Magellan Fund had net gains of $5.22 per share. That, plus net investment income, gives you the next line, "total from investment operations" of $5.49 per share.

Now, if the fund made no distributions during the year, the NAV at the end of the year would be $72.44. But funds, of course, must make distribu-

tions to preserve their unique tax status (see more on that in Chapter 6). So go to the next section, "less distributions." The next line tells you there was 14 cents a share in income distributions. But wait! The fund earned 27 cents in net investment income. Well, fund distributions for tax purposes are made on a calendar year basis, and for book purposes, on a fiscal year basis. So since Magellan keeps a different fiscal year, the distributions aren't usually the same. Nonetheless, that 14 cents came out of each fund share in fiscal 1995, so it's recorded here. Then there was a distribution of $2.63 a share in net realized gains, for a total of $2.77. Subtract $2.77 from $75.21 (what NAV would be if there had been no distributions) and you get the end-of-year NAV, $72.44.

Look for a moment at net realized and unrealized gains for fiscal year 1991. The fund actually had a higher per-share gain, $8.10 versus $5.22 for fiscal 1995, but a slightly smaller capital gains distribution, $2.42 versus $2.63. That tells you that in 1991, at least, most of the gains were unrealized, that is, the fund kept more of its profitable positions without selling them.

The next group of figures, "ratios and supplemental data," should help compare this fund to others. Ratio of expenses to average net assets is 0.96 percent for fiscal year 1995, which is a little less than average for equity funds. Now, the footnote indicates that the fund management company has recaptured part of the brokerage commission rebates (known in the investment business as "soft dollars") to pay for some fund expenses. However, this is not terribly significant, since the next line shows that without such rebates the expense ratio would have been 0.99 percent. Before moving on, look at the expense ratio and how it changes from year to year. The number is trending downward. That's to be expected, since the Fidelity Magellan Fund is by far the largest equity fund and should have some economies of scale in its operations that benefit its shareholders. Be wary of funds in which this ratio is moving up.

The last line, "portfolio turnover rate," 120 percent, means that securities amounting to 1.2 times the total assets of the fund changed hands during the year. That means if a fund had $100 million in assets, the value of the securities that "turned over" during the year amounted to $132 million. Now remember, this is the Fidelity Magellan Fund, which had an average of $36.5 billion in assets during this fiscal year. Roughly, that's securities trades with a face amount of nearly $44 billion. (There's more about portfolio turnover in Chapter 7.)

INVESTMENT POLICY

After the financials, the prospectus turns to the investment objective. In the Magellan prospectus, for instance, the section is called "Investment Principles and Risks." The investment policy section will outline the overall strategy, the permitted investments in the broadest of terms (i.e., stocks or U.S. government or government-guaranteed securities), and restrictions, if there are any.

For a fund with a descriptive name (i.e., a fund that says small company or health care or North America in its name), pay particular attention to what else the fund can do. For instance, in early 1995, a group of shareholders filed a lawsuit against the Alliance North American Government Income Fund, which suffered severe losses during the Mexican currency crisis. The lawyers' complaint? The fund name said it was North American, but the fund had invested in Argentina, which, of course, is in South America. But the prospectus noted that only 65 percent of the fund had to be in North American debt obligations—and the fund met that condition. (In addition, in reports to shareholders, the fund had advised them of the Argentine holdings—yet another reason to read those shareholder reports.)

Pay careful attention to the investment objective and how the fund managers plan to achieve it, especially the kind of risk they might undertake (with your money). Be forewarned. Most fund prospectuses are written in a way that gives fund managers the widest latitude and discretion.

Some funds try to boost returns by trading futures and options contracts or other derivatives. That must be spelled out. Is preservation of capital the utmost priority? Don't assume it is, even if the investment is a government bond fund. Some sacrifice net asset value in order to deliver a high payout, and it says so—though not in such blunt language.

The information in this section helps to describe the fund's character. First Eagle Fund of America, for instance, says it will pursue capital appreciation with a flexible investment strategy that may include junk bonds, foreign securities, restricted securities (illiquid securities that are not publicly traded), and "special situations"—opportunities that may arise from liquidations, reorganizations, mergers, material litigation, technological breakthroughs, or new management and management policies. More-over, First Eagle may buy and sell options and futures contracts and even "leverage its assets for securities purchases"—that's another way to say the fund buys on margin. If you'd sleep better with a fund that invests solely in well-known blue-chips, First Eagle is probably not for you.

SHAREHOLDER SERVICES

Look for services and conveniences. The standard ones are automatic investment and reinvestment of dividends and capital gains distributions. They'll be described in the prospectus. Most money-market funds and many bond funds also offer check-writing privileges. But those that do will often require that you write a check of $500 or $1000 at the least, so don't plan on using these funds to pay at the supermarket. Convenient as they are, such privileges are no substitute for a conventional checking account. (United Services Treasury Securities Cash Fund is a U.S. money-market fund with no minimum check size, and no limit on the number of checks written.)

Automatic investing is an arrangement you set up between the fund company and your bank. You can make periodic investments from your checking account to a designated mutual fund. It's an excellent way to accumulate capital, and unlike a contractual arrangement that some funds still market, you can stop or alter the program at your discretion without any penalty.

Most fund groups ordinarily roll over the dividends and capital gains into new shares. That's one of the major benefits of investing in mutual funds. By reinvesting your earnings you have the opportunity to compound the growth rate of the fund. It's the same idea as earning interest on your interest.

Be sure to indicate on your application what you want done with the dividends and distributions. Those using funds for income sometimes take the dividends in cash or have them deposited into their money-market funds and reinvest the capital gains. If you give no indication at all, the funds will reinvest all the proceeds. If you're a long-term investor, reinvest.

> Make sure the fund's investment goals match yours.

Redemptions

Putting money into a mutual fund is simple. Fidelity Investments' walk-in centers, for instance, make investing easy by having personnel on hand to field questions, take applications, and accept checks. But though you can invest at one of these locations as though you were making a deposit at a local bank, you can't make a "withdrawal" on the spot. The money must come through regular channels, either a check by mail or by bank wire.

Getting money out isn't quite as simple as putting it in. But there's a whole lot less bother to taking money out if you plan for it on the way in. Some investors are surprised to find a $5 exchange or redemption fee taken out of their proceeds when they get their account statement. But if you've read about the fund's redemption procedures in the prospectus ahead of time, it should not be a shock. It has to be in the fee table, along with information about sales charges, 12(b)-1 fees, and the like.

Most funds offer telephone redemption privileges. But that's not something to request on the day you want the money. It's best to do it when setting up the account. If you have an existing account that doesn't have telephone switching privileges, request the form that permits it. And don't assume that if some funds in a family of funds offer telephone redemption, all the funds in the group do. Several of the Vanguard equity funds, for instance, are off-limits to telephone switches.

Even when a fund offers telephone redemption there may be limits on the amount of money that can be withdrawn or the number of switches within a given period. Plan on following the advice of a mutual fund timing service? Ask if the fund group has any qualms about letting frequent switchers into their funds. (That's something you won't find in the prospectus but will have to ask a fund representative yourself.) Sometimes fund groups permit intrafamily telephone switches from an equity fund to a bond fund or money-market fund, but may restrict telephone withdrawal from the fund group. Depending on the amount of money involved (sometimes it's any-

thing over $5000), the fund company may want written instructions.

Obtaining quick access to your funds is especially important with money-market funds since they're most often used as liquid assets or "rainy day" emergency money. All money-fund accounts should be set up with telephone redemption privileges.

Ask for check-writing privileges too. Even if you don't use the checks for regular bill-paying, the checks provide quick access to your account. Most funds can transmit funds by wire to your bank, but again that's not something to negotiate over the phone on the day you need the money. If you want this service, the fund will ask for the appropriate banking information on the application. There's usually a charge for the service as well as a minimum amount of money that must be wired.

Pay particular attention to a fund group's rules on withdrawals. They're not all the same. For many funds a signature on a redemption letter may not be enough. The company may require that the signature (and that of any other person whose name is on the account) be "guaranteed." A signature guarantee is an endorsement that verifies that the signature is genuine. The guarantor will compare the authenticity of the signature to one already on file. You're supposed to sign the letter in the presence of the guarantor.

Many funds accept guarantees from commercial banks or savings institutions that are members of the Federal Deposit Insurance Corporation or brokerage firms that are members of the New York Stock Exchange. Some may accept others like state-insured thrifts and federally insured credit unions, but ask the fund service personnel first. A notary public's seal is usually unacceptable.

Getting
money out of
a fund takes
planning.

Building an Investment Portfolio

You've been reading about some of the new wonder drugs on the market, and you give your doctor a call. "Doc, these new drugs sound great. How about writing me some prescriptions for the two or three that you think are best?" Sounds absurd, doesn't it? First you have to know what ails you before you get a prescription.

Yet many investors choose their investments the same way. They hear about a hot-performing fund, or a fund with a novel investment twist, and jump in. What they need to do first is examine their financial goals and decide what exactly they are trying to achieve through their investments (Table 4-1). Only then can they make a sensible choice from the multitude of investment opportunities. There are hundreds of excellent mutual funds out there, but not every one of them—even those with the highest BUSINESS WEEK ratings—is appropriate for every investor.

Determining Your Financial Goals

The 35-year-old physician with two preschool-aged children needs to build capital—and has time on her side. She would probably benefit from an all-equity portfolio, with the number of funds depending on how much money she was starting with. With $10,000 or so, she might go for five funds: a large-cap blend fund such as the Vanguard Index 500, which tracks the S&P 500; a mid-cap blend fund such as Mairs & Power Growth Fund or a mid-cap value fund like Strong Schafer Value Fund; a small-cap value fund such as Royce Micro-Cap; a small-cap growth fund such as Baron Asset Fund, Acorn Fund, or PBHG Emerging Growth; and a foreign fund such as Janus Overseas, T. Rowe Price International, or Templeton Foreign. With, say, $40,000 to $50,000 in assets, she might add large-cap growth and large-cap value funds to supplement or supplant the index fund and a diversified emerging markets fund to supplement the international component.

The 45-year-old computer programmer, having built some savings through aggressive investing, may have to settle for a lower return to steady his investment portfolio. He's about to embark on years of college tuition payments for his children and he wants to be sure the money will be there when he needs it. So he's keeping at least one year's worth of tuition and room and board payments in an ultrashort bond fund like the Strong Advantage Fund. He's lightened up a bit on the more aggressive small-cap and mid-cap growth funds. Now, less volatile funds like Vanguard/Windsor II Fund, Fidelity Equity-

TABLE 4-1

BEFORE INVESTING, CONSIDER...

▶ Do you need current income from your investments?

▶ How soon will you need the proceeds of your investments?

▶ How will inflation affect you?

▶ How much risk are you willing to take?

▶ How will taxes affect your investments?

▶ What kind of temperament do you have for investing?

Income, and Third Avenue Value Fund have more appeal to him. He still owns international funds, which make up 25 percent of his portfolio. And, except for the college money that's tucked away in the ultrashort bond fund, it's still an all-equity portfolio.

The 55-year-old lawyer is finished with his children's education and is now socking it away for retirement about 10 years hence. He still has 80 percent of his portfolio in equities, but only about 10 percent is in the volatile small-cap growth funds. As his tolerance for risk has lessened, he's tilting more of his equity investments to the value categories—small-cap value, mid-cap value, and large-cap value. On the international side, he also has value-oriented funds, such as Tweedy Browne Global Value.

His friend, also 55, is a corporate executive who fears that cutbacks might cost him his job and force him into early retirement. He too is moving from more aggressive equity funds to tamer funds such as T. Rowe Price Equity-Income. For the fixed-income portion of the portfolio, he chooses less volatile intermediate-term bond funds like American Century-Benham GNMA Income and Harbor Bond.

Mutual funds, like all investments, are only means to an end, not an end in themselves. They're used to accumulate a down payment for your first home, as an educational fund for your children, or as a nest egg for your retirement. So before you choose the investment vehicle, you need to assess what goal you want to achieve through your investments. If you go to a travel agent, the first question is, "Where do you want to go?" not "Which airline do you want to fly?"

The conventional wisdom says younger people should take on the most risky investments and gradually shift over to less risky investments as they age. By the time they're retired they should be into income-producing vehicles almost entirely. But the conventional wisdom is too general to serve everybody's needs. If you're in your late twenties, and saving to buy a home, you don't have decades to wait. You'll need money-market funds and short-term bond funds to help you achieve that objective. You may have a two-track investment plan. Keep taxable assets in the shorter-term investments and keep the long-term investments, like growth-oriented equity funds, in your IRA.

Likewise, many retirees shift too quickly into income-producing investments, whether they need them or not. Younger retirees, in particular, might do best if they stick with equities when

The younger you are, the more risk you can take.

their various pensions and other sources of retirement income suffice. Life expectancy is going up, and retirees in their early sixties may live well into their eighties. That means they need to increase their capital faster than the rate of inflation. They're going to need equity investments to do that.

To help choose the most appropriate funds for an investment program, you should first answer the following series of questions.

DO YOU NEED CURRENT INCOME FROM YOUR INVESTMENTS?

If you're the kind of person who needs to spend the interest from your certificates of deposit, you need current income. Most investors for whom current income is a priority are retirees, but not exclusively. Sometimes families may have some investment capital, obtained perhaps through an inheritance, but need to use it to generate income to meet expenses. A single parent, for instance, may need income from investments to supplement other sources.

Figure how much income you need from your investments. Start with an estimate of how much regular income you need in total, and then subtract all other sources, such as salaries, pension payments, Social Security payments, and the like. Suppose you need $50,000 a year, and all other sources produce $40,000. Your portfolio will have to produce $10,000. Long-term interest rates are around 6.6 percent, and yields on stocks are, on average, less than 2 percent. You'll need at least $150,000 invested in long-term bonds (or bond funds) to produce $10,000. But if you have $300,000 you can count on, the other $150,000 could be invested for capital appreciation. That will enable you to build a larger portfolio for the day when $10,000 won't be enough.

If you have a regular income from your job that meets your needs, current income should not even be a consideration. You should emphasize investments that shoot for capital gains, not income. Sure, you balance the two. But remember, investments that maximize current income, like money-market mutual funds, provide no capital gains. And many bond funds that maximize current income will, at times, suffer capital losses.

These guidelines are not inviolable absolutes. When short-term interest rates are high, say 12 percent, a money-market mutual fund is going to be a hard investment to beat. The return would be so large and the risks so minimal that no other investment would look competitive.

HOW SOON WILL YOU NEED THE PROCEEDS OF YOUR INVESTMENTS?

Identifying the right time horizon goes a long way toward finding the right funds. If you're saving for a goal 15 years distant—like college tuition for a preschooler—you can rely on equity funds to carry the weight of reaching your goals. Over long periods of time they outperform bond and money-market funds. For periods of less than 10 years, short- and intermediate-term bond funds have to play a greater role in the portfolio. Cash that's going to be tapped in a year or less should be invested in a money-market fund.

Some people fail to grasp the importance of the time horizon. What is the long term, they say, but a series of short terms back to back? So why not just invest short term and continue to reinvest over and over again?

Here's why. In the 70 years that records have been kept, U.S. Treasury bills—the safest short-term investment around—have delivered an average annual return of 3.7 percent, and long-term government bonds, 5.1 percent. During the same period the total return on common stocks—capital appreciation plus reinvestment of dividends—averaged 10.7 percent per year. The story is much the same if you look at only 30 years. Fixed-income returns are higher, but they still lag well behind equities.

The time horizon is easy to quantify. If it's 1997 and your child starts college in 2007, his or her education fund has a time horizon of 10 to 14 years. If you're 40 now and have a 401(k) retirement plan at work, the 401(k)'s time horizon is at least 19 years (you can start withdrawing funds at age 59½), but it's more likely to be 27 or 30. Think of the time horizon as a balance sheet: The assets are your investments, the liabilities are the expenses to be funded in future years.

HOW WILL INFLATION AFFECT YOU?

Since your investment dollars will ultimately be used to "purchase" goods or services some time in the future, then inflation, the erosion of purchasing power, is an important matter that must be considered in your investment portfolio. If you don't take the impact of inflation into account in your investment planning, you risk being ravaged by its effects.

Think of it this way. You invest $1000 in a 30-year U.S. government bond paying 6.6 percent interest. You collect $66 a year (actually, $33 every six months), and in 30 years you get back your $1000. Suppose that for now the $33 semi-annual payment buys you and your spouse dinner at a modestly priced restaurant (and you don't order alcoholic beverages and you skip dessert).

What will it buy in 10 years? If inflation is modest, say only 3 percent, that $33 will be $24.50 in today's money. So, in 10 years, what bought dinner for two now may buy lunch for one—maybe. What about the principal? If inflation averages only 3 percent a year for the next three decades, the $1000 will have only about $412 worth of purchasing power. Maybe dinner for one, if you're lucky.

To inflation-proof a mutual fund portfolio, you have to buy equity funds, especially small company funds. Common stocks and small company stocks have shown over the long haul that they beat the Consumer Price Index hands down. True there are times—like the 1970s—when inflation knocks the socks off the stock market. Stocks in general don't usually beat inflation in periods when inflation is accelerating. But small company stocks can do well in inflationary periods if the companies' growth rates outpace inflation.

International stock and international bond mutual funds should also help guard a portfolio from the ravages of inflation. In periods of inflation, the dollar tends to drop in value against foreign currencies. This in itself feeds inflation because U.S. consumers must pay more dollars for imported goods. But when the dollar goes down in value, assets denominated in foreign currencies go up. So to the extent you have money in foreign assets, you have a hedge against the declining value of your dollars.

HOW MUCH RISK ARE YOU WILLING TO TAKE?

As the jocks will tell you, "No pain, no gain." Well, in the investment world the pain is the risk and volatility. We don't seem to mind when the Dow Jones industrial average shoots up 100 points in a day, but we're very unhappy when it's down that much. People say they don't like volatility and risk, but what they're really telling you is that they don't want their investments to go down. Nobody ever complained when their investments went up.

Most investors are so risk averse that they fail to make objective judgments. Taking risks isn't easy. Psychologists studying how people make financial decisions have found that most will shy away from risks, even when the odds dictate otherwise. Many people pay a premium in the form of a lower return on their investment for the greater certainty of preserving that capital.

To best fight inflation, invest in equity funds.

That's because most people are more influenced by their fear of losses than by the prospect of gains. Behavioral psychologists, in fact, find that the pain of a loss looms twice as large as the pleasure of an equivalent gain. Even if the odds are 50-50, the average person will take a risk only if he or she can win twice as much as he or she can lose.

Investors often avoid risks because they're more influenced by recent history than by a long run of events. For most of 1987, investors couldn't get enough of the stock market. From January through August, the Dow industrials gained over 800 points. The fact was, as the Dow climbed, it became very risky. Stocks entered the overvalued zone in terms of corporate earnings, book value, and dividend yields. But as the market went up, people paid little attention to those risks.

Then the market crashed, losing 508 points on October 19, 1987. More than one-fifth of the market value of Corporate America was washed away in six and a half hours. In the following weeks stocks were marked down by more than a third from the summer's high, yet no one wanted the merchandise. They were afraid, or waiting for the 50-percent-off sale. Of course, the weeks after the crash, in retrospect, were the time to buy. Yet investors were far too scared to do so.

If you're like most investors, you've erred on the side of caution. You have probably underestimated the amount of risk you can take (like having too much in money-market funds relative to your investment goals) and are paying for it dearly in lost opportunities. It's a serious matter when it comes to pension savings. When companies give employees the option of directing how their pension funds are to be invested—the nub of the increasingly popular 401(k) plans—they tend to choose fixed-income investments. Younger employees, in particular, need stocks if they are to have enough on which to retire. When companies direct the pension plan investments, they place 60 to 70 percent of the assets in stocks.

If you have a long time horizon, your ability to take risks is greatly enhanced. Here's why. The long-term return from owning stocks is 10.7 percent, about twice as high as from bonds. But, of course, stocks don't achieve that return year-in and year-out. In 1995 and 1996, for instance, the stocks in the Standard & Poor's 500 stock index racked up a total return (price appreciation plus dividends) of 37.5 and 22.9 percent, respectively, and 1991 was a banner year as well, with a 30.4 percent gain. In 1992, the return was a more modest 7.6 percent; in 1993, the return was 10.1 percent; and in 1994, only 1.3 percent. Over the last six decades the best year was 1933—in the depths of the depression. Stocks gained 54 percent. The worst year was two years earlier, in 1931, when stocks lost more than 43 percent of their value. Since World War II the best year was 1954, up 52.6 percent; the worst, 1974, down 26.5 percent.

Though any one year's results can be a stunner, over time the law of averages takes over. In any one year, statisticians estimate, the probable return from common stocks is between −10 percent and +30 percent. But over a five-year period, that expected range of returns narrows considerably—from +1 percent to +19 percent. And over 20 years, the range of expected returns is +5.5 to +14.5 percent. Simply put, the more years in your average, the more likely your results will look like the long-term average.

HOW WILL TAXES AFFECT YOUR INVESTMENTS?

Most investment advisers would caution you against making an investment solely because it shelters you from taxes. For many years lots of buildings were built because investors coveted the tax-sheltering attributes of commercial real estate. That they had tenants for the buildings was only a secondary consideration. The best investments are those that make sound economic sense.

But once you've identified a good investment idea, you should see how it stands up to the tax system. To do that, you have to know—or have a pretty good approximation of—what your marginal tax bracket is. And don't forget to include the impact of state and local income taxes as well.

Suppose your combined federal and state marginal tax bracket is 35 percent. What that means is that for every additional $1 in income, the tax folks siphon off 35 cents. So you have to start asking yourself, "How much do I want to bring in, and how much can I defer?"

When it comes to the taxes, mutual funds don't have a whole lot of leeway. The tax laws say a fund must pay out 98 percent of its net income and realized capital gains each year (that's net after deducting the expenses of running the fund). A fund that yields 5 percent may leave shareholders with only 3.25 percent after they've paid taxes.

If you want to minimize taxes, concentrate on small-cap and mid-cap growth funds. For one, the sorts of stocks these funds buy pay few or no dividends. And if the portfolio manager has a policy of holding stocks for the long term, he or she is not going to do a lot of trading. Trading and, more importantly, profits from trading produce gains that must be passed on to shareholders. Some fund advisers recommend index funds because of their ultra-low turnover. The only time they sell a stock is when it is removed from the index, an infrequent occasion.

In the matter of bond and money-market funds, it's always wise to examine whether a lower-yielding tax-free fund will provide a greater aftertax return than a taxable one. Table 4-2 walks you through the calculation of how to know whether a tax-free investment will provide a better return than a taxable one.

Of course, if you're investing within the confines of a tax-deferred account, like an individual retirement account, you don't give a hoot about taxation. There's no tax until you start withdrawing from the plan years in the future. About the only thing you need to remember is: Tax-free securities don't belong in a tax-deferred plan.

WHAT KIND OF TEMPERAMENT DO YOU HAVE FOR INVESTING?

Looking at income needs, taxes, time horizons, and the like, it's easy to come up with an objective conclusion such as: I should put 70 percent of my money in small-cap and mid-cap growth funds. All well and good. You understand the rationale and fully accept the notion that, with your time horizon, the riskier, higher-return vehicles should deliver the best results.

But if you're the sort of person who shudders at the thought of losing a piece of your principal, who worries about every twist and turn of the stock market, who would become stressed out if your investment went south for a while, this investment program is not for you. If you like the plan, but your spouse doesn't, it's not worth straining a marriage. If 70 percent is too heavy a concentration in equities, see if you can start with 25 percent in a stock mutual fund. If you (or your spouse) can get comfortable with that, then you can always increase the percentage of your assets in equities. Don't be ashamed to move cautiously. Advice comes from others, but the money that's invested on that advice is yours.

Research on how people make investment decisions has turned up some interesting observations that may help you examine your ability to take investment risks. In her work on the psy-

chological characteristics of individual investors, Marilyn MacGruder Barnewall, a financial consultant, describes the "passive investor" and the "active investor."

Passive investors—and most people fall into this category—have a greater need for security than tolerance for risk. In fact, they usually perceive risks to be greater than they are. These people typically have come by their wealth "passively"—by inheritance or by risking others' capital to achieve their wealth. Included in this group are most corporate executives and most people who are employed by others. This is not to

TABLE 4-2

WHAT'S A SINGLE-STATE MUNI BOND FUND WORTH TO YOU?

State	FEDERAL MARGINAL TAX RATE				State	FEDERAL MARGINAL TAX RATE			
	28%	31%	36%	39.6%		28%	31%	36%	39.6%
ALABAMA	31.6	34.5	39.2	42.6	MISSOURI	32.3	35.1	39.8	43.2
ARIZONA	31.0	34.6	39.6	43.0	MONTANA	35.9	38.6	43.0	46.2
ARKANSAS	33.0	35.8	40.5	43.8	NEBRASKA	33.0	35.8	40.5	43.8
CALIFORNIA	34.7	37.4	42.0	45.2	N. HAMPSHIRE	31.6	34.5	39.2	42.6
COLORADO	31.6	34.5	39.2	42.6	NEW JERSEY	30.5	35.4	40.1	43.4
CONNECTICUT	31.2	34.1	38.9	42.3	NEW MEXICO	33.7	36.9	41.4	44.7
DELAWARE	33.0	35.8	40.4	43.8	NEW YORK	32.9	35.7	40.4	43.7
DIST. OF COL.	34.8	37.6	42.1	45.3	N. Y. CITY	35.3	38.1	42.6	45.8
GEORGIA	32.3	35.1	39.8	43.2	N. CAROLINA	33.0	36.4	41.0	44.3
HAWAII	35.2	37.9	42.4	45.6	N. DAKOTA	36.6	39.3	43.7	46.8
IDAHO	33.9	36.7	41.2	44.6	OHIO	32.0	35.4	40.5	43.8
INDIANA	31.2	34.0	38.8	42.3	OKLAHOMA	35.2	37.9	42.4	45.6
IOWA	35.2	37.9	42.4	45.6	OREGON	34.5	37.2	41.8	45.0
KANSAS	33.6	36.3	41.0	44.3	PENNSYLVANIA	30.0	32.9	37.8	41.3
KENTUCKY	32.3	35.1	39.8	43.2	RHODE ISLAND	33.5	36.9	42.3	46.2
LOUISIANA	30.1	35.1	39.8	43.2	S. CAROLINA	33.0	35.8	40.5	43.8
MAINE	33.4	36.9	41.4	44.7	TENNESSEE	32.3	35.1	39.8	43.2
MARYLAND	33.4	36.2	40.8	44.1	UTAH	33.2	35.8	40.5	43.8
MASS.	36.6	39.3	43.7	46.8	VERMONT	33.0	36.3	41.8	45.6
MICHIGAN	31.2	34.0	38.8	42.3	VIRGINIA	32.1	35.0	39.7	43.1
MINNESOTA	33.8	36.9	41.4	44.7	WEST VIRGINIA	32.7	35.5	40.2	43.5
MISSISSIPPI	31.6	34.5	39.2	42.6	WISCONSIN	33.0	35.8	40.4	43.8

Suppose you are a Californian with a combined federal and state marginal tax bracket of 42%. What's the tax-equivalent yield for a California municipal bond fund yielding 5%? Here's the calculation:

$$\frac{\text{Tax-free yield}}{1 - \text{Combined marginal tax rate}} = \text{Tax-equivalent yield}$$

$$\frac{5}{1 - (0.42)} = \frac{5}{0.58} = 0.0862 \text{ or } 8.62\%$$

The 5% yield would be the equivalent of an 8.62% taxable yield.

DATA: FRANKLIN RESOURCES, BUSINESS WEEK

suggest that those who work for salaries do nothing for them, but the investment capital at stake in their enterprise is not theirs—and that's a critical factor. Passive investors are more likely to use brokers, investment advisers, or financial planners.

Active investors, on the other hand, are individuals who have earned their own wealth in their lifetimes. Barnewall says these people understand how to take risks and have a higher tolerance for risk than a need for security. In fact, they often underestimate their risks. Their tolerance for risk is high, she says, because of a strong belief in themselves. They usually feel most comfortable with investments which they "control." So, for some active investors, mutual funds may be unappealing since the funds' portfolio managers are the ones calling the shots on what stocks to buy and sell. On the other hand, the mutual fund universe is diverse enough to offer many choices and timing decisions, so an active investor can still achieve a lot of control. Nonetheless, direct sales funds would probably be more appealing to active investors than those sold through brokers or other intermediaries.

Of course, no one is totally one thing or the other. Passive investors may maintain, say, 70 percent of their investments in relatively secure products like certificates of deposit, money-market funds, and bond funds, with the other 30 percent in more risky ventures like growth funds. Active investors may do just the opposite.

The investment counseling firm of Bailard Biehl & Kaiser takes a different approach to sizing up investors' ability to take risk. Their work identifies four sorts of investor profiles: "adventurer," "celebrity," "individualist," and "guardian." Adventurers are just that. They like risk and they often make intuitive judgments. Celebrities are the trendies—fashion followers wanting to do what's hot rather than what's best. Individualists are the entrepreneurial sort and take a rational, methodical approach to most everything they do. Then there's the guardians, who are nervous about preserving their wealth and seek guidance in doing so.

Do you recognize yourself in one of these categories? Are you an adventurer? If so, you may need to practice a little self-restraint. Before embarking on a financial adventure, be sure you have enough of your assets under a fairly conservative investment program. Celebrity? You need restraint too. Your history is probably one in which you've made a lot of investments, but have

not earned much to show for it. Individualists, as it turns out, often make the best investors.

Putting It All Together

Okay, you now know what you want from your investments and have a good idea of what kind of investor you are. You still need to choose a mutual fund portfolio. And with over 6000 funds (including money-market funds) available, the job is not easy. But don't be overwhelmed by it. Think about your favorite supermarket. There are thousands of items on its shelves and in the refrigerated and freezer cases, but does that fact prevent you from shopping? You choose what you need and virtually ignore the thousands of items you don't need. True, the supermarket is familiar ground, while the mutual fund market is not. Yet with a good shopping list and smart shopping skills, it's possible to assemble an ideal portfolio of funds.

What you need is an idea of the categories of funds you want and in what proportions. In theory, the higher-risk funds should provide the higher rewards, though that's over a multiyear period. You certainly can't make that generalization for short-term results. To get an idea of how the various categories of funds stack up on risk, look at Figure 4-1. Keep this chart of relative risk in mind as you design and assemble a portfolio of funds.

The risk spectrum here goes from 0 to 9. Money-market funds, for purposes of this exercise, will be assumed to have zero risk. The riskiest funds here are precious metals funds, which are well ahead of the next two risky funds, Latin America and technology. (These calculations are based on the last five years of performance.) The most volatile of the diversified funds, small-cap growth, is still far less risky than precious metals and Latin America. The equity funds that mix in bonds and cash, the hybrid funds, have a much lower risk profile, between 2 and 3. Among the specialty funds, utilities funds have similar risk characteristics. They're all a little riskier than any of the bond funds, which pretty much cluster between 1 and 2.

First, before making an investment, be sure you have a cash reserve that totals a minimum of six months' living expenses. Set it aside in a

> Before investing, be sure you have a cash reserve.

FIGURE 4-1

MUTUAL FUNDS RISK SPECTRUM

Are specialized funds riskier than diversified equity funds? How much risk is there in bond funds compared to equity funds? Here's a chart that can help investors understand the relative risk of various types of mutual funds. The risk scale goes from 0 to 9, with 0 defined as no risk. Money-market funds are not on the chart, since there are no fluctuations in their net asset value (NAV). Some specialized funds, like technology and precious metals, are at the high end of the risk spectrum. The NAVs of these funds can fluctuate sharply.

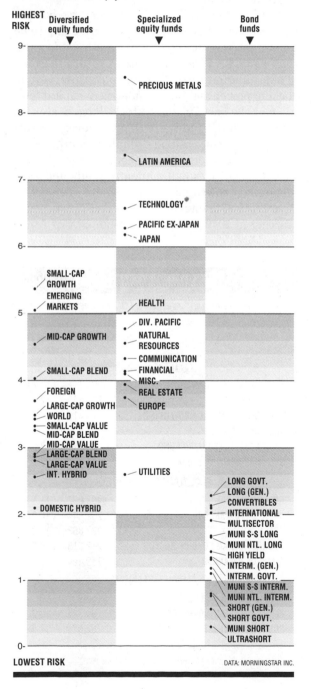

DATA: MORNINGSTAR INC.

money-market mutual fund. That's not part of the long-term investment program. It's a rainy-day account, and if you tap into it, be sure to replenish it. If you're in a high tax bracket, you might consider using a tax-free money-market fund instead of a taxable one.

YOUR ASSET ALLOCATION PLAN

When you're ready to invest, you need an "asset allocation" plan. That's just a strategy on how to divvy up your money. A sample asset allocation plan may recommend placing 50 percent of the portfolio in U.S. equities, 30 percent in bonds, 10 percent in foreign stocks, and 10 percent in foreign bonds.

Many money managers devise allocations with elaborate computer models that make the whole process look about as simple as performing the calculations to guide a spacecraft to Mars. Most of the popular personal finance software programs also perform this function. Many mutual fund companies will also give you software that will do the same, usually putting you through a quiz, adding up points, and recommending an asset allocation plan based on your score. Some of the more sophisticated programs will allow you to set minimum or maximum allocations, such as no less than 10 percent or more than 50 percent, for various sorts of asset classes (for our purposes, large company mutual funds, small company funds, international funds, etc.). It then crunches the numbers, spitting out a range of asset mixes that go from the safest to the riskiest.

Some of the programs describe the probability of achieving or exceeding your goal over several time periods. One hint: Don't take the first allocation that pops up. If the program allows it, tinker with the choices and the parameters until you get something that "feels" right. What happens if I add more stocks? Change my time horizon? Once you have a plan, it's easy to implement it through mutual funds. Growth and income funds fit big stocks; small company funds fit little stocks; international funds fit foreign stocks; money-market funds fit Treasury bills, etc.

There are other ways to get help in devising your plan. If you are working with a broker, financial planner, or investment adviser, that's part of his or her job. Even the direct marketing fund companies are now helping investors with asset allocation. Firms like Dreyfus, Fidelity, T. Rowe Price, Scudder, and Vanguard, to name a few, all offer various worksheets, computer software, consultations, and seminars.

ACHIEVING YOUR FINANCIAL GOALS

The right asset allocation plan starts with the financial goal. Are you trying to accumulate a specific amount of money? Perhaps you want to be able to send your four-year-old to a top-drawer private college, which, in today's dollars, costs about $30,000 a year for tuition, books, and living expenses. How much will you need?

Hold on to your hat. Assume that costs will rise at 9 percent a year, since educational expenses have continued to run far in excess of the Consumer Price Index. Today's $30,000-a-year college costs will be about $100,000 a year 14 years hence, when your preschooler starts college.

How are you going to get that money? To fund a $100,000 expense, you'll need 100 zero-coupon Treasury bonds that mature in 2011. In early 1997, such bonds had a yield of 6.94 percent, and would cost $379 each, nearly $38,000 for the lot. (Zeros are sold at a discount to face value and mature at par.) And that would only take care of one year's education. What about the other three? Graduate school? And other children?

But if you could earn a higher rate of return on your investments, you wouldn't need to put as much up front right now. True, the long-term return from stocks is only 10.7 percent, but suppose that through savvy mutual fund investments you could earn 2 percentage points more? Then you would only have to put up a little less than $20,000 to get $100,000.

If you don't happen to have a spare $20,000 either, you're going to have to start a regular savings and investment program. The college fund planning kits available from many fund companies and brokerage firms will help you determine how much you'll need and how much you have to save per month or per year to achieve that goal. For instance, if you can earn an average 10 percent return, saving about $250 a month—for the next 14 years—will get you $90,000. But if, through more aggressive and riskier investments, you get an average 12 percent return, your $250 a month should come out to around $107,000. Of course, that only covers one year of college. But look at it this way: As you and your child or children get older, you should be putting more money away each month. The more you put away, the more you'll earn.

SAVINGS FOR RETIREMENT

And what about savings for retirement? Projecting how much you're going to need in 25 years to carry you through another 20 or so after that may seem pointless. But many mutual fund companies, brokerage firms, and financial planners have worksheets or software that can walk you through the exercise. You don't have to be an actuary, nor do you have to know what your grocery bill will be in the year 2020. Expenses are calculated in today's dollars, and they are later multiplied by an inflation factor. Based on your current nest egg and how much you can expect it to grow, the worksheet will tell you how much a year you have to save in addition to reach your retirement goal.

But let's face it. The longer your time horizon, the less accurate specific targets are going to be. You might just approach the investment in a way that would let you earn a rate of return in excess of the inflation rate. That should preserve purchasing power and build some extra capital too.

Over the past 70 years, stocks have beaten the inflation rate handily, with an average return that is 7 percentage points higher than the Consumer Price Index. Small company stocks, the sort you find in small company funds and some maximum growth mutual funds, did even better, 9 percentage points higher. Over a 57-year period starting in 1940, Investment Company of Amer-

TABLE 4-3

THE LONG, LONG HAUL

What would have happened to $1000 invested in each of these funds for the period, Jan. 1, 1940–Dec. 31, 1996?

	Total value ▼	Average annual total return* ▼
EQUITY FUNDS		
INVESTMENT CO. OF AMERICA	$926,112	12.7%
FIDELITY FUND	861,645	12.6
KEYSTONE STRATEGIC GROWTH K-2	794,416	12.4
SELIGMAN GROWTH	709,775	12.2
LORD ABBETT AFFILIATED FUND	706,651	12.2
SELIGMAN COMMON STOCK	645,387	12.0
BALANCED FUNDS		
DELAWARE FUND	$403,092	11.1%
AMERICAN BALANCED	232,544	10.0
CGM MUTUAL	222,863	10.0
GEORGE PUTNAM FUND OF BOSTON	212,013	9.9
ALLIANCE BALANCED	149,404	9.2
BOND FUNDS		
KEYSTONE HIGH INCOME B-4	$158,937	9.3%
LORD ABBETT U.S. GOVERNMENT SECS.	94,724	8.3
SCUDDER INCOME	62,085	7.5

*Pretax return, includes reinvestment of dividends and capital gains

DATA: CDA/WIESENBERGER, MORNINGSTAR INC.

ica achieved an average annual return of 12.7 percent (Table 4-3). The comparable inflation figure during that time was 4.4 percent. According to Wiesenberger Investment Companies Service, five other funds also earned 12 percent or more per year.

Bonds, on the other hand, have only topped the inflation rate by 2 percentage points. But some bond funds that have been around for 57 years have fared far better: For the period 1940 through 1995, Keystone High-Income B-4 averaged 9.3 percent and Lord Abbett U.S. Government Securities, 8.3 percent.

True, bonds in general have not given much inflation protection, but it's quite possible that bonds will provide better returns in the future. That's because a fundamental shift has taken place in the capital markets and the way that interest rates are determined. Prior to 1979 the Federal Reserve—the U.S. central bank and traffic cop for the money that flows through the economy—would look at the economy, decide what the interest rate should be, and then try to manage the money supply in such a way as to achieve that rate.

That approach often fueled inflation since the Fed, though independent, was always under political pressure to keep interest rates down. The central bank often erred by keeping interest rates too low, which, in itself, is a contributing factor to inflation. But in the 1980s the Fed—and the rest of the world's major central banks—changed course, concentrating on the appropriate supply of money for the state of the economy. With tighter controls on the creation of money, the central bankers now let market forces determine interest rates.

The bright side of this more volatile world of bonds is that the "real" rates of return—what you're left with after counting the effects of inflation—have been high for the past decade and are likely to remain so. During the 1980s, for instance, the real rate of return on long-term government bonds was as high as 6 percentage points. While that abnormally high number did not last, it's a good bet the real rates will stay well in excess of the 1.4 percent rate experienced over the last six decades.

One new development that bears watching is the Treasury's new inflation-indexed bonds. These long-term bonds, issued in early 1997, pay a low interest rate, around 3 percent, which remains the same for the life of the bond. The inflation adjustment is made to the principal. Right after they were issued, several mutual fund companies announced plans to launch funds to invest in them.

It's too soon to tell if these bonds are a good investment or not. But one thing is certain. The upward adjustments in the value of principal will be taxed as income, even though there is no payout. Thus, these sorts of bonds and bond funds should be held in a tax-deferred account only. Otherwise, you end up paying taxes on what some people call "phantom" income.

LOOK TO YOUR HORIZON

Since stocks remain the best long-term investments, mutual fund investors with long time horizons should invest heavily in equity funds. So start with the premise that investors in their twenties and thirties, and perhaps even through their forties, should invest in equity mutual funds. Their investment horizons are 20 years or more.

Those whose horizons are between 10 and 20 years—say the 40- to 50-year-olds—might begin to lower their risks by moving some of their assets into more conservative equity funds and some bond funds. Even at retirement, investors shouldn't shy away from equities. With improved medical care, many persons in their mid-sixties might well live another 20 years. These people are still going to need to keep some equities. If they convert everything to fixed-income investments early in their retirement, they may produce more income now but risk not having enough capital later.

Figure 4-2 lays out five different portfolio mixes for five different decades of life. Suppose you're in your early thirties. Your investment horizon is at least 30 years or so, you can tolerate a good deal of risk, and you need inflation protection. So you split your money into four pieces, putting equal amounts into large-cap, mid-cap, small-cap, and foreign funds. Within those groupings, choose both growth and value funds.

By your forties you may want to come down a notch in the riskiness of your equity funds. Perhaps now you would trim back the equity funds and use that portion of the allocation for high-yield bond funds. These funds bridge the stock and bond world, and exhibit characteristics of each (see Chapter 2). They can generate a return close to the long-term return from stocks, but with more income and less volatility. Since these funds' relatively large payouts are subject to ordinary income tax, these funds are best used in the confines of a tax-deferred retirement-type account.

The fifties are peak years for investment.

FIGURE 4-2

BUILDING A MUTUAL FUND PORTFOLIO FOR YOUR NEEDS

THE 20s Single or married, the investment horizon calls for growth-oriented funds. Still, if you are yet to purchase a home, you will need some of your assets in a low-risk fund like a short-term bond fund. If you already have a home, consider the sample portfolio for the 30s.

40% MONEY-MARKET OR SHORT-TERM BONDS
20% LARGE-CAP
20% SMALL-CAP OR MID-CAP
20% FOREIGN

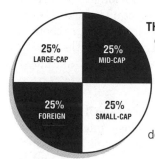

25% LARGE-CAP
25% MID-CAP
25% FOREIGN
25% SMALL-CAP

THE 30s Married, with small children, and you already have purchased a home. You're starting on a long-term investment program. College bills are a dozen or more years ahead of you, and retirement is decades away.

THE 40s You're more secure financially, but you have a more cautious investment program now. College may be a near-term expense. Retirement is still 20 or so years away. So the asset mix changes, and you introduce more conservative vehicles like high-yield bond funds, and short- or intermediate-term bond funds. That lowers the portfolio risk, but still provides long-term growth.

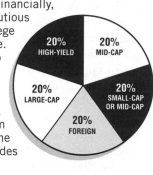

20% HIGH-YIELD
20% MID-CAP
20% LARGE-CAP
20% SMALL-CAP OR MID-CAP
20% FOREIGN

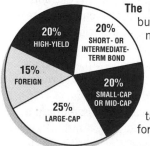

20% HIGH-YIELD
20% SHORT- OR INTERMEDIATE-TERM BOND
15% FOREIGN
20% SMALL-CAP OR MID-CAP
25% LARGE-CAP

The 50s You're still married, but you're empty nesters now. The children are grown, and finished or nearly finished with their educations. You are in your peak earning years, and should take advantage of that to sock it away for retirement.

THE 60s You're retired, but don't run from the equity funds. Hopefully, you have many, many years ahead of you, and will need to grow your capital. Only equities can do that.

DATA: BUSINESS WEEK

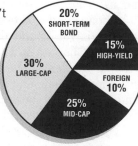

20% SHORT-TERM BOND
15% HIGH-YIELD
FOREIGN 10%
25% MID-CAP
30% LARGE-CAP

For most people, the fifties are peak years for saving. Your earnings growth may have flattened out at this point, but often children are grown and educated, so your expenses have gone down. Disposable income grows and so does your ability to invest. At this point many people are more interested in socking it away than rolling the dice, so they come to depend more on fixed-income investments. You may keep your equity investments intact, but start to put new investment dollars into tax-free municipal bond funds.

For new retirees, the best investment advice is: Don't shorten your time horizon very much. If you put too much money into current income producers like money-market funds or short-term bond funds, you risk depleting your capital when it should be growing. And remember, too, that although $1 per share net asset value of money-market funds appears solid, the income produced by those $1 shares is quite volatile.

Suppose you've decided to put 40 percent into large-cap funds, 40 percent into mid-cap and small-cap funds, and 20 percent into international funds. How many funds do you need? One from each category? Two? You may decide that no fund should have more than 20 percent of your assets, so you choose two funds each for the growth and maximum growth portions of the portfolio and one international fund. If your entire stake were, say, $10,000, you might put $2000 each into two growth funds, $2000 in each of two more aggressive funds, and $2000 in one international fund—for five funds in all. If you have $50,000, you might want to introduce a few more funds into your portfolio.

Once you get started in mutual funds there are so many good opportunities that you may be tempted to invest in a lot of different funds. There's no sin in that by itself, but keep in mind that if you own a dozen funds when half a dozen would do, you're also burdening yourself with more paperwork. If you're using load funds, concentrating your investment dollars will allow you to qualify for discounts on the sales charge that aren't available to you if you're always investing small amounts. Finally, except for some specialty funds, most mutual funds are diversified to start with, so piling fund upon fund gives you little added benefit.

If the whole notion of a personalized asset allocation plan seems like overkill, there are alternatives. For instance, there's the "fund of funds" approach to asset allocation. T. Rowe Price has two Spectrum funds. Spectrum Growth divvies up your money among other Price equity funds and Spectrum Income does the same for fixed-income funds. The Vanguard STAR Fund tries to strike a balanced portfolio through investment in other Vanguard stock and bond funds. Fidelity Investments has a worksheet that helps you decide how much risk you can tolerate. The exercise leads you toward one of three asset allocation funds: Fidelity Asset Manager or Fidelity Asset Manager: Income, a slightly more conservative choice; or Fidelity Asset Manager: Growth, the most aggressive of the trio (see Chapter 2).

Several funds companies, Fidelity and Stagecoach are a few, also have rolled out "life cycle" funds. Rather than your having to make the moves from the more aggressive to the more conservative funds as you age, these funds have a target "maturity." You choose the fund whose target maturity is around the time you want to retire. That way the fund's style of management mellows out with age, and you, in theory, don't have to worry about changing funds as you get older. It's an interesting concept, but there is no long-term record yet with these sorts of funds.

Using the Scoreboard Ratings

The BUSINESS WEEK Mutual Fund Scoreboard will help you to find the funds you need. All things considered, look for the funds with the highest ratings—three upward-pointing arrows and two upward-pointing arrows are the two top categories. Then comes one upward-pointing arrow, followed by "average." Finally, there are downward-pointing arrows, with three down arrows being the worst rating. (Read more about the ratings in Chapter 7.)

You'll quickly notice that there are lots of funds without ratings. These funds are too new to be rated. That is, they don't have the five-year track record to qualify for a rating (three years for closed-end funds). Should you invest in them anyway? Many investment pros advise against it. There are enough long-lived funds in most fund categories that you don't need to use a fledgling fund.

If you buy funds through a broker or financial planner, no doubt you'll get a call to invest in a "hot" new mutual fund. There's no hurry. Remember, mutual funds are open-ended, and funds constantly take in new investments and create new shares. (If the broker is soliciting for

a new closed-end fund, hang up the phone. Chances are, you'll be able to buy it cheaper six months to a year later. For further information, refer to Chapter 2's section on closed-end funds.)

Suppose you're getting a pitch for a technology fund and the time seems right to invest in technology. But there are already plenty of existing funds to choose from—and these funds have track records. If the fund is so unique that no alternative exists, you should be even more wary of putting your money down. The garbage dump of the investment business is strewn with great concepts that worked in theory—but not in practice.

Fund management companies often start new funds after an investment idea becomes hot. High-tech stocks, for instance, dazzled investors when the 1980s bull market took off in mid-1982. But technology funds that raised large sums during that period stumbled badly in subsequent years. More recently, short-term world income funds opened for business in the early 1990s, seeking to capture the high short-term yields from abroad. The funds' high payouts were like manna to yield-starved U.S. investors until the European currency system came unglued in 1992—and chewed up the net asset values of these funds. The same thing happened with emerging markets debt funds in 1994.

One way to avoid problems is to adhere to an old rule of thumb in the fund business: Don't invest in a mutual fund until it has a five-year track record. Paying heed to this dictum would have saved investors from some of the newer "concept" funds—like short-term world income funds—which no doubt come to market when the concept is hot. True, it's near impossible for the average investor to look at the prospectus for such a fund and say it won't work. But time is a good test. The concept came undone within three years.

There are times to consider a new fund and waive the rule. Suppose the portfolio manager of a fund you already own and like starts a new fund. You may well follow him or her. A mutual fund is only a shell, an investment vehicle, and has no life of its own other than what its manager gives it. So following a respected manager can make sense.

On the other hand, beware of funds run by market "gurus." Some popular market soothsayers have learned the hard way that prognostication and portfolio management are very different skills, and that if you have one skill, you don't necessarily have the other. In mid-1987, for

Beware of funds run by market "gurus."

instance, Shearson Lehman Brothers launched a fund managed by its superstar stock market strategist, Elaine Garzarelli. In the first few months, Garzarelli made a brilliant call. She left the market in September and largely steered clear of the October 19, 1987 crash.

That well-publicized fact drew in even more investors. At the end of 1987 the fund totaled $685.5 million. But in 1988 Garzarelli missed the stock market's rebound. In fact, the fund lost 13 percent in net asset value while the S&P was up about 16.5 percent. The fund continued to trail the stock market and investors left in droves. Finally, in June 1994, the fund's sponsor, Smith Barney, Inc. (which had acquired the fund in 1993), proposed to merge it into another fund, without Garzarelli at the helm. The remaining shareholders approved the proposal and the remaining $129 million in assets were folded into another Smith Barney fund.

Even if you limit your shopping list to top-rated funds, you may have a hard time finding two- and three-up-arrow mutual funds in every category of fund. That's why the BW Scoreboard now carries a second rating, one based on risk-adjusted performance of funds in the same category. With these category ratings, it's possible to identify the best funds in sectors of the market that are performing poorly relative to other sorts of funds. For instance, most precious metals funds have terrible ratings when compared to all funds. But if you are interested in a precious metal fund, these category ratings allow us to identify the best of the lot.

LOAD OR NO-LOAD?

If you want to work with a broker or a financial planner who's also a broker, you may be restricted to the funds that they sell. You pay the salesperson either through the front-end load, or through higher 12(b)-fees. (See Chapter 3.) A fast-growing alternative to the traditional brokerage arrangement is the fee-only adviser. Even some large brokerage firms are offering this option today. Under these arrangements, you purchase load funds at net asset value. You compensate the adviser through an annual fee based on the amount of assets under management.

If you want to run your account yourself, choose no-loads. Why pay for advice you don't want? You can invest by contacting the fund companies directly. That's fine if you want to invest all in one family, but it's cumbersome if you want to mix and match funds from different families. That's where the mutual fund networks really

make sense. You can open an account with Schwab or Fidelity, buy funds from a large number of fund companies, and do it all through the brokerage firm—one account number, one phone number, one statement.

A MINIMUM INVESTMENT?

Suppose you have $2000 to invest in each of five funds. You call the toll-free telephone number for the funds to get a prospectus and sales material. But remember to ask about the initial investment. Direct-sales funds, in particular, usually have higher minimum investments than broker-sold funds. Many direct-sales funds carry minimum initial purchases of $1000 for equity funds and $2000 to $3000 for fixed-income funds. Broker-sold funds usually have minimum buy-ins in the $250–$500 range. Both types of funds usually lower the threshold significantly for IRA or other retirement accounts, or for investors who enroll in a monthly investment plan.

Building and Rebuilding Fund Portfolios

In assembling your own portfolio, it's often useful to look at others' portfolios. The point is not necessarily to use the same funds in the same way, but to see the kinds of funds professionals use for particular purposes and in what proportions. You can also try to understand some of the logic that goes into these decisions. For example, what about a portfolio for a college-bound toddler? Table 4-4 presents one from Debra B. Silversmith of Sterling Partners in Denver, Colorado. It's for a 3-year-old whose grandparents invest $10,000 in her name. Silversmith recommends a portfolio weighted toward funds that emphasize small and midsize companies whose growth prospects are higher than those of the companies in the S&P 500. "Over time, the higher growth rates should lead to greater fund performance," she says.

That's true, as long as you select funds whose managers are skilled at playing the growth-stock game. As the table shows, for the 40 percent of the portfolio dedicated to smaller company stocks, she chooses Baron Asset Fund and the Kaufmann Fund. Baron, which has outperformed its competitors for nearly 10 years, is light on technology stocks. Kaufmann Fund, on the other hand, carries a heavy complement of tech stocks. Both are run by veteran portfolio managers, not rookies. For mid-cap companies, Silversmith selects the Oakmark and Strong Opportunity funds. Oakmark, a top-rated fund, is a mid-cap value fund, a good offset to the more growth-oriented Baron and Kaufmann. Its BW all-fund rating is three up arrows.

Looking abroad, she chooses Warburg Pincus International Equity Fund Common Shares, "a good mix of developed and emerging market stocks." She especially likes the fact that the fund has more of an emphasis on developing markets than most general foreign funds. It seems to have a better handle on the tricky Pacific rim markets as well. "[Portfolio manager] Dick King has built a fine staff for this fund," says Silversmith. "If you were going to buy one foreign fund, this is it."

Silversmith thinks this portfolio could earn an average annual return of 14 percent a year. If she's right—and that's an ambitious goal—the $10,000 will grow to more than $70,000 when this preschooler turns college freshman. Private college already costs nearly $30,000 a year, so good fund choices are not enough. Her parents will need to add money over the years. For additional investments, Silversmith would allocate the money in the same proportions.

FUNDS FOR A 401(K)

Employees often freeze when they're asked to choose from five or six investment options in their companies' 401(k) plans. So consider the plight of the General Motors Corp. employees, who can select from among 50 Fidelity mutual funds. That's where adviser James B. Kruzan of Investment Management & Research Inc. in Clarkston, Michigan, spotted a business opportunity. He advises GM employees on fund selection for their 401(k)s.

Take, for instance, a 43-year-old executive who has amassed $50,000 in his 401(k), but has it invested in low-return fixed-income funds. He'd like to have an equity portfolio but hasn't a clue which funds to choose and in what proportions.

Since the employee is 25 years from retirement, Kruzan recommends a fairly aggressive mix that he believes will beat the S&P 500 by an average 2 percentage points a year: 40 percent for funds that buy small-cap stocks, 20 percent for mid-cap, 10 percent for large-company, and 30 percent for foreign stocks. That's the outline, and it's a plan that could be fulfilled by scores of funds, not just Fidelity's. But for the GM clients, Kruzan selects

TABLE 4-4

FOUR FUND EXPERTS GO SHOPPING FOR YOU

HEAD START ON A COLLEGE FUND

Investment adviser Debra Silversmith suggests this portfolio for a 3-year-old whose grandparents put $10,000 in her name to launch a college fund. They're all no-load funds, available through the big discount brokers or directly from the fund companies.

FUND	ALLOCATION
OAKMARK	20%
STRONG OPPORTUNITY	15
KAUFMANN	20
BARON ASSET	20
WARBURG PINCUS INT'L. EQUITY COMMON	25

AN ALL-FIDELITY 401(k) PORTFOLIO

Adviser James Kruzan counts many General Motors managers among his clients, and many of them look to him for help in choosing among the 50 Fidelity mutual funds in GM's 401(k) plan. This allocation plan is for a 43-year-old with $50,000 in his 401(k), but could as easily be used by anyone wanting an all-Fidelity line-up.

FUND	ALLOCATION
FIDELITY LOW-PRICED STOCK	16.0%
FIDELITY EMERGING GROWTH	12.0
FIDELITY OTC	12.0
FIDELITY MID-CAP STOCK	20.0
FIDELITY DIVIDEND GROWTH	5.0
FIDELITY GROWTH & INCOME	5.0
FIDELITY DIVERSIFIED INT'L.	9.0
FIDELITY EMERGING MARKETS	9.0
FIDELITY CANADA	6.0
FIDELITY EUROPE	6.0

GAME PLAN FOR A ROLLOVER IRA

Financial planner William Young suggested this portfolio for a 50-year-old single woman who is leaving a job with a $100,000 lump-sum payment that will be rolled over into an IRA. As a commission-based adviser, Young sells load funds. He recommends shares with up-front loads, since they are cheapest in the long run.

FUND	ALLOCATION
PUTNAM GROWTH & INCOME A	20%
GUARDIAN PARK AVENUE A	20
MFS RESEARCH A	15
SMALLCAP WORLD	15
TEMPLETON FOREIGN CLASS I	30

FOR THE GOLDEN YEARS

Madeline I. Noveck recommends this portfolio for a 62-year-old with a $500,000 lump-sum pension payment. This retiree has other income sources, and needs to generate $7500 a year from this nest egg. Noveck uses both load and no-load funds.

FUND	ALLOCATION
FIDELITY ADVISOR GROWTH OPPORTUNITY A	7.5%
HARBOR CAPITAL APPRECIATION	7.5
SIERRA EMERGING GROWTH A	4.0
THIRD AVENUE VALUE	4.0
IVY INTERNATIONAL A	23.0
COHEN & STEERS REALTY SHARES	8.0
FIDELITY ADVISOR FOCUS NATURAL RESOURCES T	7.0
VANGUARD F/I SHORT-TERM CORPORATE BOND	7.0
HARBOR BOND	18.0
T. ROWE PRICE INTERNATIONAL BOND	9.0
MONEY-MARKET FUND (YOUR CHOICE)	5.0

DATA: BUSINESS WEEK

from the Fidelity menu. For the most aggressive funds, he chooses Fidelity Low-Priced Stock, Fidelity Emerging Growth, and Fidelity OTC. For the mid-cap slot, he picks Fidelity Mid-Cap Stock. The big-stock slice splits between Fidelity Growth & Income and Fidelity Dividend Growth.

Kruzan then divides the international portion into four parts, allocating 9 percent each to Fidelity Diversified International and Fidelity Emerging Markets. Two regional funds, Fidelity Canada and Fidelity Europe, get 6 percent each. Kruzan says the Canadian fund is as much a natural resource fund as a country fund, since natural resources make up a large part of Canada's economy. He likes the Canadian fund and thinks U.S. investors often overlook their northern neighbor. "The slow growth, low interest rate environment that is so good for our market should benefit our biggest trading partner as well," he says.

For ongoing contributions, Kruzan suggests 30 percent in Fidelity Dividend Growth and Fidelity Low-Priced Stock and 20 percent in Fidelity OTC Fund. He proposes allocating 20 percent of the monthly contribution to Fidelity Pacific Basin—which is not part of the portfolio makeover. "That allows you to use these funds' higher volatilities to your advantage by buying more shares at bottoms and fewer at tops," says Kruzan.

THE ROLLOVER IRA

With companies shrinking their payrolls, long-time employees often walk away with six-figure pension distributions and no idea of how to invest them. "That's the kind of help many of our new clients need," says William S. Young of First Financial Group in Towson, Maryland.

Look at the example of a 50-year-old single woman with $100,000. She's not a gambler, but she is willing to take as much risk as her adviser thinks is appropriate. So Young devised an all-equity portfolio with moderate risk. "With at least 10 years to go before retirement, you can go with an all-stock portfolio," says Young. "In all the 10-year periods since World War II, bonds have beaten stocks less than 10 percent of the time."

Unlike Silversmith, who is paid a percentage of assets under management, Young earns his pay from commissions—and so chooses from the load funds. And when a fund has front-end or back-end shares, he recommends the up-front "A" or "I" shares, because they're most cost-effective for long-term investors.

Young's prescription is simple: five funds, with near-equal weightings. He eschews the latest highflier funds for those that he believes show "consistency of results." The first two holdings, Putnam Growth & Income A and Guardian Park Avenue are "core" funds, with Putnam having a "value" (higher dividend, low price–earnings ratio) approach, while Guardian is more growth-oriented. He also likes Guardian's quantitatively driven stock selection system. "It's proven and disciplined," he says. Young also recommends MFS Research A, a growth fund whose stocks are chosen by research analysts, not portfolio managers. "The fund's not dependent on any one manager's skill," he says. Still, the fund has beaten the market over the last three and five years. "It's an underappreciated gem."

The remaining 45 percent of the portfolio goes to SmallCap World and Templeton Foreign I funds. That may appear to be a bit too heavy on foreign stocks. But SmallCap World, despite its name, has only about 38 percent of its assets abroad. That, combined with Templeton Foreign, puts the portfolio's overseas investments at 36 percent.

EQUITY FUNDS FOR RETIREMENT

Retirement is no reason to drop equity investments. In fact, the longer you hope to live, the more you're going to need them. That's the approach adviser Madeline I. Noveck of Novos Planning Associates Inc. in New York takes in constructing a $500,000 portfolio for a 62-year-old recent retiree.

Noveck works with a large palette of funds, both no-load and load, since that affords more and better investment options. If she uses a load fund, the portion of the commission paid her is credited against her regular asset-based fees. Noveck's list is long, with 11 funds. But she's working with more money, which usually requires more funds. And the client has two needs: the generation of about $7500 a year to supplement his current retirement income and capital appreciation so there will be enough to fund the next 20 years or so in retirement. She believes her portfolio can beat the S&P 500 return but with less volatility.

Like our other advisers, Noveck covers every segment of the stock market. For large- to mid-cap stocks, she chooses the Fidelity Advisor Growth Opportunities A and Harbor Capital Appreciation funds; and for smaller companies, Sierra Emerging Growth A and Third Avenue Value Funds. For foreign investments, she opts for Ivy International A, a large-cap fund focusing mainly on Europe but with some exposure to Japan and emerging markets. She'd like to have

Retirees need equity funds, too.

FIGURE 4-3

RESTRUCTURING A PORTFOLIO OF FUNDS

BEFORE

The "Cranes," a couple in their early 40s, held $544,051 in taxable and tax-deferred retirement accounts—more than 80% of it in 15 equity mutual funds. Working with Lou Stanasolovich of Legend Financial Advisors, they decided to scale back their equity holdings about 60%. Stanasolovich analyzed the funds for investment style and performance and developed a new investment plan.

Pie chart (BEFORE):
- INTERNATIONAL EQUITIES 16.5%
- CASH AND MONEY-MARKET FUNDS 19.2%
- DOMESTIC EQUITIES 64.3%

AFTER

Stanasolovich slashed domestic equities to 23.5%, mainly by cutting large-cap stocks. He added small growth and value funds to the mix and put in new mid-cap funds. He unloaded several international funds—but boosted the allocation in total by adding to several existing positions and bringing in others. About 8% went toward low-risk short-term bond funds, 14% into domestic bond funds. In international bond funds, he selected both investment grade and low-quality. For further diversification, he introduced real estate funds and a risk-arbitrage fund.

Pie chart (AFTER):
- RISK-ARBITRAGE 3.3%
- INTERNATIONAL BONDS 6.6%
- REAL ESTATE 7.7%
- DOMESTIC BONDS 14.0%
- INTERNATIONAL EQUITIES 21.7%
- CASH AND SHORT-TERM BONDS 23.2%
- DOMESTIC EQUITIES 23.5%

	Allocation (%)	Investment Category
DOMESTIC EQUITIES†		
BERGER 100	2.9	MID-CAP GROWTH
NEUBERGER & BERMAN MANHATTAN	1.0*	MID-CAP BLEND
T. ROWE PRICE CAP. APPREC.	4.4*	MID-CAP VALUE
JANUS TWENTY	2.9	LARGE-CAP GROWTH
AMER. CENT.-20th CENT. ULTRA INV.	8.2	LARGE-CAP GROWTH
GROWTH FUND OF AMERICA	10.0*	LARGE-CAP GROWTH
CGM MUTUAL	6.0	LARGE-CAP VALUE
AMERICAN MUTUAL	11.3*	LARGE-CAP VALUE
WASHINGTON MUTUAL INVESTORS	8.1*	LARGE-CAP VALUE
T. ROWE PRICE EQUITY-INCOME	5.5*	LARGE-CAP VALUE
INVESCO INDUSTRIAL INCOME	3.6	DOMESTIC HYBRID
INTERNATIONAL EQUITIES		
SMALLCAP WORLD	8.8*	SMALL-CAP GROWTH**
MONTGOMERY EMERGING MARKETS	0.7	DIV. EMRG. MKTS.
OAKMARK INTERNATIONAL	0.8	FOREIGN
EUROPACIFIC GROWTH	6.2*	FOREIGN

†Includes 0.4% in stocks   *Funds in tax-deferred retirement accounts   **Advisors considers this an international fund, while Morningstar puts it with domestic funds.

	Allocation (%)	Investment Category
SHORT-TERM BONDS		
PILGRIM AMERICA PRIME RATE**	4.4%	ULTRA SHORT
PIMCO LOW DURATION	3.7	SHORT TERM
DOMESTIC EQUITIES†		
BERGER SMALL CO. GROWTH	5.5	SMALL-CAP GROWTH
ROYCE MICRO-CAP	3.7	SMALL-CAP VALUE
VAN WAGONER MID-CAP	5.5*	MID-CAP GROWTH
FRANKLIN MUTUAL BEACON Z	2.8*	MID-CAP VALUE
JANUS TWENTY	2.9	LARGE-CAP GROWTH
NEUBERGER & BERMAN GUARDIAN	2.8	LARGE-CAP VALUE
INTERNATIONAL EQUITIES		
OAKMARK INTERNATIONAL	3.8	FOREIGN
ACORN INTERNATIONAL	2.8	FOREIGN
WARBURG PINCUS INT. EQ. COMM.	2.4	FOREIGN
IVY INTERNATIONAL A	2.4*	FOREIGN
SOGEN OVERSEAS	1.8*	FOREIGN
MORGAN STANLEY EMRG. MKTS. A	5.0	DIV. EMRG. MKTS.
MONTGOMERY EMERGING MARKETS	3.7*	DIV. EMRG. MKTS.
DOMESTIC BONDS		
NORTHEAST INVESTORS	5.3*	HIGH-YIELD
PIMCO TOTAL RETURN	4.9*	INTERMEDIATE-TERM
LOOMIS SAYLES BOND	3.7*	LONG-TERM
INTERNATIONAL BONDS		
PIMCO FOREIGN	4.4*	INTERNATIONAL BOND
SCUDDER EMRG. MKTS. INCOME	2.2*	INTERNATIONAL BOND
REAL ESTATE		
COHEN & STEERS REALTY SHARES	2.9*	REAL ESTATE
HEITMAN REAL ESTATE-INSTL.	2.9*	REAL ESTATE
CGM REALTY SHARES	1.8*	REAL ESTATE
RISK ARBITRAGE		
MERGER FUND	3.8*	MID-CAP BLEND

†Includes 0.4% in stocks   *Funds in tax-deferred retirement accounts
**Closed-end fund
Percentages may not equal 100 because of rounding.

DATA: LEGEND FINANCIAL ADVISORS INC., MORNINGSTAR, INC.

Harbor International, a no-load that is closed to new investors. But Ivy International shares the same portfolio manager, so it will do. "The portfolio manager (Hakan Castegren) is worth it," she says.

Noveck also places money in funds that don't correlate to the market in general and thus diversify the portfolio. For instance, she allocates 7 percent to Fidelity Advisor Focus Natural Resources T, a gold and natural-resources fund. Cohen & Steers Realty Shares and T. Rowe Price International Bond are in the portfolio for the same reasons. Five percent goes to a money-market fund ("choose one with a high yield") both for diversification and liquidity.

The realty fund has another job—to provide current income. That, plus the income from Harbor and Vanguard bond funds, should provide the $7500 a year the client needs now—with a few dollars to spare. The distributions from the other funds, says Noveck, should be reinvested. That keeps the investor's capital at work for another day.

RESTRUCTURING A PORTFOLIO

So you have a few funds tucked away in an IRA to which you haven't contributed for years. Several funds are still sitting in a 401(k) at a former employer. Then there's a sheaf of funds you've bought yourself over the last few years, listening to tips from fund fanciers at work and from your own perusings of the covers of the personal finance magazines. Does this describe you or someone you know?

Many people have mutual fund portfolios, but they were never planned out, chosen in a way to cover a particular range of investment styles or asset classes. That doesn't mean they haven't made money. In a bull market, most anything can do well.

Still, even if you have a collection of funds that have done well, it may not be the optimal mix for you. The best portfolio for you depends on your tolerance for risk in the value of your portfolio. Look at the "Cranes," a couple in their early 40s who sought the assistance of Lou Stanasolovich of Legend Financial Advisors Inc. in Pittsburgh for restructuring their portfolio (Figure 4-3). Through IRAs, Keogh plans, and other mutual fund investments, they had accumulated a $544,051 portfolio that was 80 percent in equities.

Like many investors who came to funds during the 1990s, the Cranes had never seen their investments mauled in a bear market. When Stanasolovich showed them what happened to their funds during the 20 percent market decline in 1990, they decided to slice their equity allocation to 60 percent. So Stanasolovich reviewed the portfolio, came up with a new asset allocation plan, and chose the best funds to implement it. He was able to work with some of the funds they already had. But he sold many of the equity holdings to make room for bond and real estate funds he thought were necessary to balance out the portfolio. He also placed most of the bond and real estate funds inside the tax-deferred retirement accounts. That way, he minimized the taxes on the income they produce. In a like manner, he tried to do much of the selling that needed to be done in the retirement accounts, thereby dodging capital gains taxes. Keep that in mind if you have restructuring of your own to do.

What Stanasolovich did was to drastically reduce the domestic equity allocation, the part of the Crane's holdings that was most vulnerable to a decline in the U.S. stock market. He took the allocation down from 64.3 percent to 23.5 percent. He also reduced the number of domestic equity funds from 11 to 6, and changed all but one, the Janus Twenty Fund. The old portfolio was over-weighted in large-cap stocks. In restructuring, Stanasolovich introduced small-cap and mid-cap holdings as well.

In the makeover, Stanasolovich also increased the international equity exposure and introduced international bonds. He chose PIMCO Foreign, an institutional fund that's open to clients of investment advisers. That fund buys mainly investment-grade bonds. Scudder Emerging Markets Income, on the other hand, invests in emerging markets debt, much of which is the equivalent of junk bonds.

The new portfolio got a domestic junk bond fund, Northeast Investors, and investment grade short-term, intermediate-term, and long-term bond funds. One short-term bond fund, Pilgrim America Prime Rate Fund, is actually a closed-end fund trading on the New York Stock Exchange. The fund invests in bank debt that's pegged to the prime rate, so if interest rates go up, so does the fund's yield.

To further diversify the portfolio's asset mix, Stanasolovich introduced three real estate funds: Cohen & Steers Realty Shares, CGM Realty Shares, and Heitman Real Estate, an institutional fund. Though they were the best performing sector funds in 1996, over long periods of time real estate funds have low correlations with the U.S. stock market. He also put a small amount of money into the Merger Fund, a risk-arbitrage fund that has a stock market correlation that's even lower than the real estate portfolios.

Making Your First Investment

You've got your investment goals, you know which funds you want to buy, and you're rarin' to go. But then you hesitate and freeze. Fear and doubt set in. You wait; you do nothing; you miss many opportunities.

Here's how to get off the mark. If you're a long-term investor, buying today, next week, or next month may not make much difference to

Good fund portfolios require planning.

your results. If you could perfectly predict stock market tops and bottoms, it would make a difference. But let's face it, if you could do that, you wouldn't be dabbling in mutual funds. You'd be playing the futures or options markets and making a bundle.

When you choose to plunk down your money can matter. But it's not because you have a hunch about the direction of the market. If you are dealing with a taxable investment, you should avoid a mutual fund or closed-end fund just before a dividend or capital gains distribution. Here's why. Funds are required to distribute nearly all of their income and realized capital gains (more about that in Chapter 6). The funds' distribution policies vary. Some equity funds pay out income dividends quarterly (bond funds often pay monthly) if they earn dividends or interest. Capital gains, if there are any, are usually declared once a year, mostly in December. You can find out distribution dates by calling the fund's toll-free line.

Suppose you invest $10,000 in a fund with an NAV of $10 per share and you get 1000 shares. Then, a few days after your investment, the fund declares a capital gains distribution of $1 per share. What happens is this: Each share pays out $1, so the NAV drops to $9 per share. Your 1000 shares are now worth $9000 (assuming there has been no other change in NAV). You reinvest the distribution and that $1000 gets you another 100 shares. So you still have an investment worth $10,000.

But you also have a tax liability. The $1000 distribution is taxable to you, but did you really earn it? Was your capital invested long enough for the managers to earn that kind of money? The gains were earned on money invested long before your money ever found its way to the fund. By investing in advance of the distribution, you wind up being taxed on something you didn't earn. You would have been better off waiting until after the distribution. Before you make a sizable investment in a fund, it's always smart to call to find out if any dividends or distributions are forthcoming.

So, for tax reasons, it does matter when you invest. For pure investment purposes, the advantages of timing are not so obvious. The question seemed particularly compelling in August 1989, when the Dow Jones industrial average raced past the 2722 point—the highwater mark that had been reached on August 25, 1987. Between August 1987 and August 1989 there was a 1000-point decline—508 of it on October 19, 1987—and a remarkable recovery. Had the investors who bought equity mutual funds on August 27, 1987 bounced back, too?

BUSINESS WEEK asked Morningstar, Inc., which provides the data for the Mutual Fund Scoreboard, to measure equity fund performance between August 25, 1987 and September 1, 1989, when the Dow had closed at 2752. The survey covered 727 funds and looked at the total returns generated during a two-year period.

The mutual funds, for the most part, did an admirable job for their shareholders—even those who, in retrospect, had invested on perhaps the worst day of the year, if not the decade. Approximately 80 percent of the funds broke even or better. More than 400 funds, or 56 percent, beat the 9 percent return that could have been earned by investing in the Dow stocks during that time. About 300 funds, more than 40 percent, beat the 13 percent total return of the Standard & Poor's 500 stock index during that period. The average U.S. diversified equity fund returned 11 percent. Counting all equity funds—including international and specialty portfolios—total returns averaged 9.6 percent, slightly above the return on the Dow.

The folks at T. Rowe Price mutual fund group conducted a test to measure the impact of timing. Suppose you were a diligent investor and every year you put $2000 into the stocks of the S&P 500. But you were also the world's worst market timer. It seems that every year you managed to invest your $2000 in the stock market at the high for the calendar year.

Well, even if your timing is lousy, there's still a payoff to your discipline. Between 1969 and 1989, the period of the study, the investor who picked the worst day of each year to invest still did well. From his or her $40,000 in contributions ($2000 a year for 20 years), the hapless market-timer amassed a stake of $175,422, an 11.4 percent average annual return. Of course, the perfect timer—the person who invested two grand at the lowest point of each year—did much better. The perfect investor wound up with $226,365, a 13.5 percent average annual return. Granted, there's a $50,000 difference between the best and the worst timer, but as a practical matter most investors' results would be at neither extreme.

There are other ways to ease yourself into mutual funds. Suppose you have a lump sum of $25,000 to invest, but you're leery of doing it all at once. Why not break the total pie into smaller slices, say, $5000 each, and feed them into your mutual funds gradually over the next year? You put $5000 into the funds at first, and the other

For tax reasons, it does matter when you invest.

Dollar-cost averaging is a contrarian strategy.

$20,000 into a money-market fund. You have four more "payments" to make before you're totally invested. Put the next $5000 slice in three months from now, and another $5000 each at six months, nine months, and one year. That way, if the market is lower at some time in the next 12 months, you have an opportunity to get in at lower prices.

Though most investors fear a plunging equity market, the bond market can also give them a jolt. Fixed-income investors usually stampede into bond funds when interest rates are falling, anxious to hold onto yields that are slipping away. But at the same time, as a portfolio's yield is going down, the prices of its bonds are going up. That means investors chasing yields are also buying heavily into a rising market.

It may not be necessary to chase intermediate- and long-term bonds. Odds are you'll see today's prices and yields again in the next few years. Between 1987 and 1994, for instance, the long-term rate on U.S. government bonds has fluctuated between 5.8 and 10.2 percent. At the low end, bond prices were said to be "high"; with the higher yield, bond prices were said to be "low." Stock prices, in theory, have no upside boundary. Stocks have infinite lives and their potential is tied to the success of the company.

But bonds have finite lives and what they can pay investors is fixed. So bond prices are constrained by the level of interest rates. Over time, the range of interest rates will vary, but you can bet there will be a trading range. When the economy is booming, rates go up; when the economy is slumping, rates come down. As long as there is a business cycle, there are going to be fluctuations in interest rates.

Dollar-Cost Averaging

If you're feeding a bankroll into mutual funds over time, what you're really engaging in is a time-honored practice called "dollar-cost averaging." This investment strategy is simple. You invest a fixed number of dollars at periodic intervals, usually monthly or quarterly. When the price of the investment is low, your fixed dollar investment buys more. When prices are high, the same amount of dollars buys less. But so long as the total return of your investment is in a generally rising trend, dollar-cost averaging will almost ensure that your average cost per

share will be less than the current price. If you're part of a 401(k) plan or some other savings incentive plan, you're already practicing dollar-cost averaging.

Let's look at this a little more closely. Suppose you want to invest $200 a month in an equity mutual fund. You've arranged with your bank for an electronic transfer of the money from your checking account once a month on the day of your choice.

To see how this works, let's look back at how a monthly investment program would have fared (Table 4-5). Suppose an investor put $200 a month into American Century-20th Century Ultra Investors starting in January 1992.

At the start of the program, the price per share was $17.34. So in the first month the investor bought 11.534 shares (that's 200 divided by 17.34). By the beginning of February, the NAV had climbed to $17.61. That means he already has a small paper profit in his first shares, but he gets slightly fewer shares for his next $200—this time, only 11.357. The relationship between share price and shares purchased is simple: the higher the price, the fewer the shares purchased; the lower the price, the more the shares purchased.

As you can tell from the share price, this fund rocketed from the time of the first purchase in 1992 and peaked in November, 1995, at $28.16 a share. Of course, the net asset value did not go up in a straight line. In fact, in 1992, shortly after beginning the investment program, the price went as low as $14.55. But with the discipline of monthly investing and a long-term investment horizon, that worked to the investor's advantage. When the price was $14.55, his $200 bought more shares. When the price finally rebounded, he owned more shares on which to profit. All told, the investor had accumulated 535.908 shares from the monthly investments and two capital gains distributions. At the end of four years, the investor had an average profit of $6.49 per share, or $3478, in an account worth $13,992.56.

If you think about it, dollar-cost averaging is a contrarian investment strategy. When the prices are low—indicating that investors are not buying stocks—dollar-cost investors are buying stocks, and they're getting more shares. When the bulls are running, these investors are still buying. But the fixed-investment plan restrains them from any wild excesses, such as stepping up investments when the market is roaring or dropping out entirely when stocks are sagging. Bull market or bear market, they're investing the same

TABLE 4-5

HOW DOLLAR-COST AVERAGING WORKS FOR FUND INVESTORS

In January, 1992, an investor decided to start a program of dollar-cost averaging. He selected American Century–20th Century Ultra Investors, and decided to invest $200 on the first business day of every month, and reinvest any dividends or capital gains if and when they're paid.

1992 SUMMARY Invested $2400, purchased 152.164 shares at an average cost of $15.77 per share

Date	Price/Share	Shares purchased	Total shares
January	$17.34	11.534	11.534
February	17.61	11.357	22.891
March	17.39	11.501	34.392
April	16.19	12.353	46.745
May	14.93	13.396	60.141
June	15.50	12.903	73.044
July	14.58	13.717	86.761
August	15.27	13.098	99.859
September	14.55	13.746	113.605
October	14.59	13.708	127.313
November	15.56	12.853	140.166
December	16.67	11.998	152.164

No income or capital gains distribution

1993 SUMMARY Invested $2400, purchased 124.837 shares at an average cost of $19.23 per share

Date	Price/Share	Shares purchased	Total shares
January	$17.29	11.567	163.732
February	18.30	10.929	174.661
March	16.55	12.085	186.745
April	17.36	11.521	198.266
May	17.53	11.409	209.675
June	19.43	10.293	219.968
July	19.93	10.035	230.003
August	20.11	9.945	239.949
September	21.45	9.324	249.273
October	21.99	9.095	258.368
November	21.89	9.137	267.504
December	21.06	9.497	277.001

No income or capital gains distribution

1994 SUMMARY Invested $2653.51, purchased 129.043 shares at an average cost of $20.56 per share

Date	Price/Share	Shares purchased	Total shares
January	$21.18	9.443	286.444
February	22.66	8.826	295.270
March	22.18	9.017	304.287
April	20.71	9.657	313.944
May	21.25	9.412	323.356
June	20.46	9.775	333.131
July	19.24	10.395	343.526
August	19.60	10.204	353.730
September	20.41	9.799	363.529
October	20.16	9.921	373.450
November	21.07	9.492	382.942
December	20.04	9.980	392.922
Dec. 17, paid a capital gains distribution of $0.6452 per share, or $253.51	19.32	13.122	406.044

1995 SUMMARY Invested $3061.80, purchased 129.864 shares at an average cost of $23.58 per share

Date	Price/Share	Shares purchased	Total shares
January	$19.61	10.199	416.243
February	19.49	10.262	426.505
March	20.26	9.872	436.376
April	20.95	9.547	445.923
May	21.28	9.398	455.321
June	22.19	9.013	464.334
July	24.14	8.285	472.619
August	26.10	7.663	480.282
September	26.55	7.533	487.815
October	27.25	7.339	495.155
November	28.16	7.102	502.257
December	27.86	7.179	509.436
Dec. 16, paid a capital gains distribution of $1.2991 per share, or $661.81	25.00	26.472	535.908

After four years, the investor has invested $9600 out of his pocket, plus another $915.31 from reinvestment of distributions. He owns 535.908 shares at an average cost of $19.62 per share. On Dec. 31, 1995, the price per share is $26.11. The total investment is worth $13,992.56.

DATA: AMERICAN CENTURY INVESTORS, BUSINESS WEEK

amount. As long as you hold on for the long term (the average annual return for stocks is over 10 percent) and you choose a well-managed fund, dollar-cost averaging should pay off handsomely.

For sure, the investor who put in a lump sum of $9600 (the total out-of-pocket cost) back in January, 1992 would have far surpassed the investor who put in $200 a month. In fact, his account would be worth $15,523. But that misses the point. Not everyone has a big lump sum to invest, but most people can come up with some monthly contribution.

Switch Funds! The Timing Game

Mutual fund purveyors have always cultivated the image that their wares are long-term investments. Of course, long-term doesn't mean the same thing to all people, but most of us would agree that long-term is at least more than a year, and probably a few beyond that.

However, during the last decade or so, the fund management companies have also made it quick and simple to purchase and redeem funds. It's become so easy to move large sums of money by telephone that some now use mutual funds for trading, which has a much shorter time horizon than investing. What most of these traders are trying to do is to employ a strategy called "market-timing."

The object of the game is to get your money invested early in a market upswing and to get your profits out before the downturn. Traders have long done this with individual stocks and, more recently, with options, futures, and no-load mutual funds. No-load equity funds seem to be made for market-timing. They already are, like the market, a diversified basket of stocks. And getting in and out is cheap and easy.

The idea of market-timing is appealing. Everyone wants to participate in rallies and dodge the declines. Many newsletter advisers and telephone hotline tipsters run market-timing advisory services, but you have to be skeptical about whether they're worthwhile or if the principle is even sound.

Take a look at the records of the market-timers. One timing system used by the newsletter *Systems and Forecasts* racked up a 15.8 percent average annual total return in the 10-year period ending December 31, 1996, according to the *Hulbert Financial Digest* (Table 4-6). That may sound good, but it's only half a percentage point a year better than the return of the S&P 500. Only three timing models beat the broader Wilshire 5000 index or the average U.S. diversified fund during that period. More important, about 100 mutual funds did better, among them Fidelity Contra-fund, FPA Capital, Janus, Kaufmann, Mutual Shares Z, and PBHG Growth.

The record shows that market-timing is no sure thing. What's perhaps even more surprising is how poorly some of the newsletters—which charge subscribers several hundred dollars a year for "advice"—actually performed. Following the advice of the *The Professional Tape Reader*, a market-timer would have ended up with less than a 5 percent average annual return. He or she could have done better than that in a money-market fund with a lot less trouble.

More importantly, market-timing results represent gross returns before taxes. Market-timing with taxable funds—that is, anything outside an individual retirement account or other such tax-deferred retirement plan—would hardly be worth the trouble. Every switch is what the accountants call a "taxable event." Assuming that you were making profitable trades over the last 10 years, you might have paid as much as a 50 percent tax on the gains (prior to 1987). And that's before state and local income taxes, too.

Academic studies of market-timing cast doubt on its efficacy. In the mid-1980s, two University of

TABLE 4-6

THE MARKET-TIMING GAME

Newsletter	Portfolio/ timing system	Average annual total return*
SYSTEMS AND FORECASTS	"Time Trend"—100% Cash on Sells	15.80%
MARKET LOGIC	Seasonality Timing System	15.76
INVESTORS INTELLIGENCE	Fidelity Mutual Funds (Equity)	14.84
BOB BRINKER'S MARKETIMER	Aggressive Growth Mutual Funds	12.95
FABIAN PREMIUM INVESTMENT	Equity/Cash Switch Plan	12.38
MUTUAL FUND INVESTING	Growth Portfolio	12.31
THE MARKETARIAN LETTER	Mutual Fund Portfolio for Traders	11.50
MUTUAL FUND FORECASTER	Trader's Corner Portfolio	11.32
MUTUAL FUND STRATEGIST	Mirat Growth Portfolio	10.67
FUND EXCHANGE		10.13
PERSONAL FINANCE	Mutual Fund Port./Short-Term Trad.	9.85
INVESTECH	Mutual Fund Advisor	8.50
STOCKMARKET CYCLES	Fidelity Select Switchers	8.50
GROWTH FUND GUIDE	Timing Only: Mutual Fund Alloc.	8.36
PROF. TIMING SERVICE	Mutual Fund Model Portfolio	8.21
ELLIOTT WAVE THEORIST	Investors/100% Cash on Sells	7.70
BOB NUROCK'S ADVISORY	Tech. Mkt. Index/100% Cash on Sells	6.31
PROFESSIONAL TAPE READER	Long-Term Model/100% Cash on Sells	4.98

BENCHMARKS

STANDARD & POOR'S 500	Total Return	15.24 %
WILSHIRE 5000	Total Return	14.67
U.S. DIVERSIFIED EQUITY FUNDS	Total Return	14.30
ALL EQUITY FUNDS	Total Return	13.40

*Jan. 1, 1986-Dec. 31, 1996   DATA: *HULBERT FINANCIAL DIGEST,* MORNINGSTAR INC.

Calgary professors determined that an investor who accurately predicted every bull and bear market from 1926 to 1983—buying stocks at the beginning of bull markets and switching to Treasury bills at the onset of bear markets—earned an 18.2 percent average annual return, even assuming a 1 percent commission was paid on each trade.

By comparison, the buy-and-hold investors only earned an 11.8 percent average annual return during the same period. But no market-timer has a perfect record. What if your market-timing was right about 50 percent of the time? Too bad. If so, your average annual return would have dwindled to 8.1 percent. To beat the buy-and-hold investor, the professors concluded, the timer would have had to be right 70 percent of the time.

One of the problems with market-timing is that the stock market typically makes large gains in relatively short periods, followed by longer periods when not much seems to happen at all. Rushmore Funds, for instance, looks back at the performance of the S&P 500 index during the 1980s. For the entire decade, the average annual return was 17.6 percent. But if you take out the 10 days when stocks made their largest gains, the average annual return drops to 12.6 percent. Take out the 20 best days for stocks, and the return is only 9.3 percent. The point is, if you're not invested during those short bursts of activity, you can miss a lot of the potential rewards.

Or look at the T. Rowe Price New Horizons Fund, one of the oldest and largest of the funds specializing in small companies. In 1990, the fund's sponsors calculated that 80 percent of the gains over the prior 30 years, or 120 quarters, actually occurred in 12 of the quarters. So to time that kind of fund successfully, you would have had to have been invested in the fund during only 12 of 120 quarters. Unless you can tell with absolute certainty which quarters are the critical ones, buy-and-hold would be a better strategy.

There's no better example of this than the first quarter of 1991. The New Horizons Fund rocketed up 28 percent in just three months. Yet at the end of December 1990, the economy was in recession and war was about to erupt in the Persian Gulf. If your assets had been in a money-market fund then, would you have shifted them into stocks, given the gloomy atmosphere?

Though the numbers suggest the odds are against them, market-timers keep trying. But sometimes market-timing can be downright disruptive and harmful to long-term investors. Sup-

pose you're a portfolio manager running a $100 million fund. You normally keep about 5 percent of your assets in cash to meet redemptions and seize upon new investment opportunities.

Then some market-timers start pumping money into your fund. If the timers are following a variety of trading systems, that might not be so bad since they would not all trade at the same time. But suppose a market-timing adviser who had a wide following among both institutions and individuals moves to a particular mutual fund, bringing along about $10 million in assets. At first you are delighted, as it's a vote of confidence in your abilities. (It also pleases the bosses, since the greater the number of dollars in the fund, the more management fees it generates.) Everything goes along swimmingly, and in six months or so the fund goes up 20 percent. The market-timer's followers see their collective $10 million increase to $12 million.

But one day the market-timer says switch—and all of a sudden his or her followers want their money out. The fund has $6 million in U.S. Treasury bills that can be sold to raise cash, and another $1 million in new money came in that day. But to redeem $12 million, you have to sell $5 million worth of stocks. That may not be all bad, since it never hurts to take a profit. But what if your game plan—successful thus far—had called for buying, not selling? Or what if it isn't a particularly good time to sell? Trading has a cost, too, that comes out of the fund's assets. If timers make excessive switches in and out of a fund, it could hurt the returns left for the other shareholders.

As much as management companies love to "gather assets," from time to time they have quietly invited market-timers or suspected market-timers to take their business elsewhere. For instance, the Kaufmann Fund, which invests in many small, emerging growth companies, once returned a $25 million check to a wealthy investor. Lawrence Auriana, one of the portfolio managers, said he feared what would happen when this investor asked for his money back all at once. Auriana said the fund might have to dump stocks just to redeem that big shareholder's account, which could be detrimental to the other shareholders. Auriana says there are market-timers in the fund, but they don't have enough fund shares to be disruptive.

So many fund sponsors now discourage market-timers from investing in their funds that one relatively new fund manager, Rydex Series Trust, decided to tailor its funds for timers and

Some fund companies may turn away frequent switchers.

invite the switchers in. Rydex Nova Fund is the bullish fund that timers buy when they think stocks will go up. It's a souped up index fund, which buys mainly in stock-index futures and options to keep liquidity high and transaction costs down. Nova also has an extra weighting of call options that makes it more volatile than the S&P index itself—so anyone buying this fund had better be right.

Rydex Ursa is the bears' fund, designed to rise in NAV as stock prices head south. That's because this fund sells index futures and buys put options, both of which yield gains as stocks stumble. (In that sense, it can be used not only by timers but by anyone looking to hedge against a decline in the market.) To keep out the small fry, Rydex requires a minimum $25,000 investment.

Market-timing pays only if you're very, very good at it—and then, only if you don't have to pay taxes on the gains. Mutual funds work best when used as long-term investments. No matter what kind of calendar you use, two days is not the long term.

Monitoring Your Mutual Funds

So now you have a portfolio of mutual funds—which, in effect, gives you a group of top-drawer professional money managers to work for you. And those managers are backed up by scores of staff members who can turn up information and analysis that you could never hope to assemble on your own.

Ah, it would be nice if you could leave your mutual funds on autopilot and watch your fortune just mount up. But nothing is that perfect. Many mutual funds can be buy-and-hold investments, but none of them are buy-and-forget. To keep on top of your mutual fund portfolio takes some of your time. Fortunately, it's not a lot of time. An hour or two a month would probably take care of most investors' needs.

Most people keep tabs on their funds by following them in the financial pages of their daily newspapers. But there are other ways as well. Computer buffs can access mutual fund prices through many on-line services or at a myriad of websites on the Internet. Many popular money-management programs download the data directly into your computer. Nearly all fund companies maintain toll-free phone numbers that allow you to check on prices and your account status.

Tracking Funds in the Financial Pages

Mutual fund prices are quoted daily in *The Wall Street Journal, Investors Business Daily,* and just about any newspaper that carries daily financial tables. In addition, Sunday newspapers usually have the mutual fund tables that summarize the high, low, and last price for the week. Not every single fund makes it into the newspapers. To qualify, the fund needs a minimum of 1000 shareholders or $30 million in assets.

Until a couple of years ago, most newspapers carried the same mutual fund tables. The funds are presented alphabetically by fund family, followed by several columns of fund prices, all represented in dollars and cents. There's net asset value, followed by the offer price, which is the NAV plus the load for funds sold with front-end loads. The last column is the daily price change, which, for most mutual funds, usually amounts to pennies per day. In addition, there are letters that serve to footnote such features as 12(b)-1 plans, redemption fees, or an income or capital gains distribution. Over 600 newspapers still carry this basic table, which is distributed by the Associated Press.

But now, some newspapers are starting to vary their mutual fund tables. From Monday through Thursday, *The Wall Street Journal,* for instance, shows three basic features—NAV, NAV net change from previous day, and year-to-date return. On Fridays, the tables are expanded to show the last four-week, and one-, three-, and five-year periods. In addition, the funds get a letter grade for their one-, three-, and five-year showings. An "A" puts their performance in the top 20 percent of funds with the same investment objective. An "E" puts them in the bottom 20 percent. In addition, the *Journal's* Friday tables include data which change little from week-to-week—investment objective, maximum initial sales charge, and expense ratio. The *Journal's* data come from Lipper Analytical Services, Inc.

Some major newspapers, including *The New York Times* and *Chicago Tribune,* carry a new version of the fund tables developed by Morningstar, Inc. *The New York Times* version, for instance, carries the previous day's NAV only, along with a percentage price change, not the price change in dollars and cents. Otherwise, the remaining data also change daily. On Tuesday, it's maximum sales charge; Wednesday, one-year total return; Thursday, three-month return; and

Daily price changes are small for funds.

Friday, year-to-date return. On Saturdays, funds with at least three years of performance history get a return/risk rating. The return rating goes from 1 to 5, 1 being the lowest relative return among funds with the same investment objective. The risk rating also goes from 1 to 5, 5 being the lowest risk and 1 the highest risk. Thus, a fund with a 5/1 rating would have terrific returns achieved with very high risk.

Even newspapers with new formats follow some of the same conventions. The fund tables are organized alphabetically by fund family (from AAL Mutual to Zweig Funds), and then alphabetically within families. Fidelity is so large that its funds are broken into several groups, such as Fidelity Investments (where you'll find Magellan, Puritan, and the best-known Fidelity products), Fidelity Selects (the specialty portfolios), and Fidelity Spartan (a line of low-overhead funds). Not all funds are parts of families. But they're still integrated into the tables in alphabetical order.

If you're familiar with stock tables, you'll notice that mutual fund tables are different. Mutual fund pricing, for instance, goes down to the penny—$8.71, or $15.46, or $65.03, or whatever. Stock price quotes typically move in quarters or eighths—an eighth is 12.5 cents—and for stocks below $5, you'll sometimes see sixteenths—units of 6.25 cents.

Day to day, the movement of mutual funds seems almost glacial. Pick up one of the daily tables and scan the righthand column, headed by "NAV chg" or "Change in net asset value." The changes are usually small: "1.02, 2.03, 1.01, 2.07, 1.04." If the stock market has made a big move up or down that day, those numbers will usually show greater changes, but by and large the movements are small.

There are several reasons for this. First, mutual funds are highly diversified pools of assets and not all the securities move in the same direction at the same time. For example, if there are 100 stocks in a fund, the change in net asset value is the difference between the 50 that went up that day, the 40 that went down, and the 10 that had no change at all.

Whatever the market's move, the mutual fund tables appear to mute the effect. Take a look at the stock market's activity on December 21, 1995. The Dow Jones industrial average went up to 5097 from 5059, a 0.75 percent move. Suppose your mutual fund behaves much like the Dow, and has a net asset value of $15. A 0.75 percent gain on $15 is 11 cents. Even big moves in the stock market don't look like a lot in mutual funds—a 2 percent gain or loss on the Dow industrial average would be about 100 points. In this hypothetical mutual fund, it's only about 30 cents.

Look at the mutual fund table that appeared in *USA Today* on December 22, 1995—which reported results of December 21 (Figure 5-1). The Dow Jones industrial average climbed 0.75 percent. The NAV of the Fidelity Blue Chip Growth Fund ("BluCh" in the table under the boldface heading "Fidelity Invest") closed at $30.50, a 19-cents-per-share gain. That may sound pretty good, but it's only 0.63 percent, slightly below the return of the Dow for that day.

If you had scanned down a few more lines to check out Fidelity Stock Selector ("StkSlc"), you would also have seen a 19 cent gain. But Stock Selector did better than Blue Chip because its gain was 19 cents on top of a lower NAV of $21.80. So Stock Selector's gain was 0.87 percent. Don't let those cents fool you. What counts is the level of the NAV before you measure the change. To get the previous day's NAV, add back the losses or subtract the gains from the current day's NAV. Some newspapers even report the day's percentage gain.

Watching your bond funds rise and fall can be like watching the grass grow. The 30-year U.S. Treasury bond—the benchmark by which the bond market is most commonly measured—was 6.09 percent, down 0.02 percent for the day. So there was very little change in the bond funds. The Vanguard Fixed-Income Long-Term U.S. Treasury Fund, which is most sensitive to changes in bond prices, did not move enough even to create a 1 cent change in the fund's NAV.

INTERPRETING THE FUND TABLES

Many newspapers use the presentation shown in Figure 5-1. The first column is the NAV, based on December 21 closing prices. The second column is the change in the NAV from December 20, expressed in dollars and cents. The third column, "YTD%," is the year-to-date performance, which is change in net asset value plus reinvestment of dividends and capital gains distributions.

Note how the fund tables are organized. Most funds are listed within families such as AAL Mutual, AARP Investment, and so on. Then they're alphabetical within those families. The tables include both stock and bond but not money-market mutual funds. Funds not part of large fund groups are listed alphabetically along with the fund families, but they will be listed in regular type while the fund families are in boldface.

Look at the listings and you'll see some single letters after the fund names. A capital letter, usually A or B, attached at the end of the fund name usually denotes a class of share. Under Fidelity Advisory, for instance, you will find A, B, and I shares. A shares have a front-end load, B shares a back-end load with redemption, and I shares are for institutional investors. Or look at Galaxy Funds Retail and Galaxy Funds Trust. Retail shares are for individual investors, trust shares for bank trust customers. Whether the fund family uses a letter, or "retail" and "trust," the underlying portfolios are the same. What's different is how the fund shareholder pays for the fund. When the returns of two classes differ, it's because differing amounts of fees are taken out of the fund. (See Chapter 3 for a discussion of multiple classes of shares.)

Then there are various lowercase letters used throughout the table. The "n" means the fund is no-load. The "p" indicates that the fund levies a 12(b)-1 fee for distribution expenses. (Need an explanation? See Chapter 3.) Some funds have an "r." That indicates a redemption fee. How much? That's not in the table, but it's an indication that if you sell your fund for the NAV listed in the table, you may not collect the full amount. You'll also see many funds with "t" accompanying them. That footnote tells you that both "p" and "r" apply to this fund.

The footnotes "p," "r," and "t" are there all the time. They describe an ongoing characteristic or policy of the fund. But on occasion you may see an "x," "e," or "s." The "x" may be familiar from the stock tables. It means the fund just paid a dividend. Investors buying after the fund has "gone

FIGURE 5-1

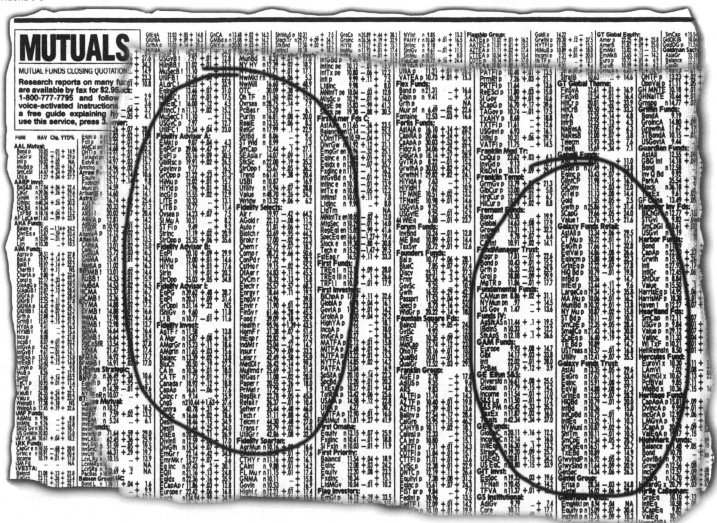

ex-dividend" do not collect that dividend. Often the fund appears to decline in net asset value. But the decline may only reflect that money was paid out of the fund. If a fund pays a 10-cents-a-share dividend, and goes down 5 cents a share on the ex-dividend date, that means the fund would have risen a nickel a share had the dividend not been paid.

When a fund pays a capital gains distribution, the symbol is an "e" instead of an "x." No matter, the effect on the fund pricing is the same. The "s" works the same way as an "x," except that it means the dividend is paid in stock instead of cash.

There may be some funds with no NAVs after their names. This usually means the fund company didn't yet have the price available when the National Association of Securities Dealers came to collect it. The day after the October 1987 stock market crash, the fund table was strewn with blanks. That frightened many people, who thought their funds had been wiped out.

Money-market fund quotes are not usually in daily newspapers. They can be found on Thursdays (they're released on Wednesday) and sometimes in Sunday newspapers, too. Net asset value for money funds is assumed to be held constant at $1 a share, thus there's no point in reporting it. What is reported in the money-market fund table is the annualized yield for the last 7-day period. If it's 4.88 percent, that doesn't mean the fund paid 4.88 percent over the last 7 days, but that the rate paid, held constant over a year, would be 4.88 percent. If the newspaper also includes 30-day yield, compare the two. If the 7-day is higher than the 30-day yield, it's because interest rates have gone up. If the 7-day yield is less than the 30-day yield, rates have come down.

Another useful figure in the money-market fund table is the average maturity. That figure is quoted in days. Consider the $41 billion Merrill Lynch CMA Money Fund, the largest money-market fund. In early 1997, the fund had a 71-day average maturity. Of course, the money-market funds have billions in securities maturing every day. But a 71-day average maturity means that the average of all the maturities in the fund is 10 weeks. The Kemper Money Market Portfolio had an average maturity of 31 days, or a little more than 4 weeks. The industry average at the time was 53 days.

Okay, so now short-term interest rates rise. Which fund will deliver more yield to its shareholders? The Kemper fund, for sure, because it will take about a month before all the money is rolled over and reinvested at higher rates. In contrast, it will take 2½ months for the Merrill fund to gain full advantage of the higher rates. The Merrill fund's yield will go up more slowly.

Now suppose interest rates come down. The investors in the Merrill fund will hold on to the higher yields longer. The yield from the Kemper portfolio will come down in about half the time. In fact, the Merrill fund, with what is a long maturity for a money-market mutual fund, was fully expecting a drop in short-term rates.

The maturities of money-market funds are not static either. When portfolio managers anticipate that interest rates will fall, they buy longer-maturity securities for the portfolio, hoping to hold on to the higher rates longer. In like manner, they shorten maturities in anticipation of rising interest rates. Some investors track the ups and downs of portfolio maturities as market indicators. If the average maturity lengthens, that represents the collective opinion of hundreds of fund managers that rates are heading down. It may not be right, but it tells you what the conventional wisdom is.

Keeping track of closed-end funds is a little trickier. You can find the share prices every day under the appropriate stock market listing— New York Stock Exchange, American Stock Exchange, or the NASDAQ National Market System (over-the-counter market). But what you see is the per-share price, which, as you know, is usually different from net asset value.

The NAVs of closed-end funds are generally reported in the financial pages once a week. Closed-end funds usually report NAVs on Friday and you can find them in the newspapers over the weekend (Mondays in *The Wall Street Journal* and *Investors Business Daily*).

Keeping Score

The whole point of watching your funds' performance is to make sure that they are doing what's expected of them. Fund managers might have all the best intentions, but they're human, too.

The first thing investors want to know about a fund is the total return—for the quarter, for the year, or for any other period. The total return—appreciation plus reinvestment of dividends and capital gains—allows investors to compare a fund's performance to that of a benchmark index like the S&P 500, and also to other funds.

> Closed-end funds report NAVs once a week.

TABLE 5-1

FIGURING MUTUAL FUND RETURNS

Suppose that on the first business day of 1993 you bought Twentieth Century Heritage Investors Fund at a net asset value of $9.31. Late in the year, the fund distributed $0.5738 per share to investors. At year's end, the NAV was $10.61. What's the fund's return for the year?

$$\frac{\text{Final NAV} + \text{Distributions} - \text{Starting NAV}}{\text{Starting NAV}} \times 100$$

$$\frac{\$10.61 + \$0.5738 - \$9.31}{\$9.31} \times 100$$

$$= \frac{1.8738}{9.31} \ (100) = 0.2013 \ (100) = 20.13\%$$

HOW TO COMPUTE YOUR TOTAL RETURN

Suppose you invest $2000 in a mutual fund and you reinvest the dividends and capital gains distributions of $325. At the end of the year, your account is worth $2415. In this example, you don't need to add in the distributions--they're already accounted for in the current value. If you take the distributions in cash, you need to add them back as in the first example.

$$\frac{\text{Current value of shares} - \text{initial investment}}{\text{Initial investment}} \times 100$$

$$= \frac{\$2415 - \$2000}{\$2000} \ (100) = \frac{415}{2000} \ (100)$$

$$= 0.208 \ (100)$$

$$= 20.8\%$$

DATA: AMERICAN CENTURY FUNDS, BUSINESS WEEK

Computing the total return is simple. Let's look at the case of American Century-20th Century Heritage Investors (Table 5-1). Suppose you invested your money on the first business day of 1993. Heritage had a net asset value of $9.31 per share. On the last day of the year, the NAV was $10.61. And during the year, the fund paid dividends and capital gains distributions amounting to $0.5738 per share.

Here's how to figure the fund's return. Start with the final NAV, $10.61. Add in the distributions of $0.5738. That brings the total to $11.1838. Next, subtract the initial NAV, or $9.31. That amounts to $1.8738 per share, which is the fund's "profit" for the year. Next, divide the $1.8738 profit by the starting NAV, $9.31, which comes to 0.2013. To turn that into a percentage, just multiply by 100. The total return is 20.13 percent.

Though this calculation covered a one-year period, the method works for any time period. The key to taking an accurate measurement is to remember to include all the dividends and distributions.

But the total return is a measure of how well the portfolio managers performed. That doesn't necessarily tell you how well your own investment is doing. For instance, if you paid a load or sales charge, that won't be reflected in the total return calculation that uses NAV. So here's a way to calculate your own return.

Suppose you invested $2000 in a mutual fund and reinvested dividends and capital gains distributions of $325. At the end of the year, your account is worth $2415. To figure your return, take the value of your shares at the end of the period—$2415. If the fund has a back-end load or redemption fee that applies to you, and you're considering selling the account, you should subtract that from the current value of the shares.

Next, subtract your initial investment. If you paid a load, that's already figured into the initial investment. If you reinvest dividends and capital gains, there's no need to add them back. They're counted in the current value of your shares. If you don't reinvest and you take distributions in cash, you have to add them back to the current value figure. Then take the difference, $415, and divide that by the initial investment, $2000. That yields 0.208, so multiply that by 100 to come up with 20.8 percent.

Suppose you are investing in a mutual fund on a monthly schedule. Then the calculation starts to get a little stickier. To get an exact return, you need to use a complex method called the internal rate of return, which accounts for the timing of the investments into the fund. Leave that to the professionals, or to a computer program that can provide it. You can get a rough approximation of your return by calculating your average cost per share (see "Dollar-Cost Averaging" in Chapter 4). Do all the numbers have you breaking out in a cold sweat? Calm yourself. With a pocket calculator, a pencil, and paper, you can do it yourself just fine.

Let the Computer Do It

You certainly don't need a computer to keep track of your mutual funds. But if you do have a personal computer and are willing to take the time to master new software, there are a number of money and investment management programs that simplify the "keeping up" process. Some of the better-known commercial software in this category is Quicken, Managing Your Money, and Simply Money. If you're adept at using the spreadsheet programs like Microsoft Excel or Lotus 1-2-3, you can create your own portfolio record-keeping systems.

The programs allow an investor to set up multiple portfolios: yours, your spouse's, the IRA, the kids', each with an unlimited number of investments. You could also treat each mutual fund as a portfolio. Fund investors might find it convenient to organize portfolios by the fund family—like Fidelity or Franklin—or by the broker who handles the account—like Dean Witter or Paine Webber.

Computer power is particularly handy for investors who make frequent purchases and regular reinvestment of dividends and capital gains. If you invest monthly and reinvest the income and distributions, you will be making 12 to 16 transactions a year. By entering each one into the computer program, the investor knows exactly how many shares of each investment he or she has, what it's worth, and what the average cost is.

More important, the programs show each transaction individually as well as what the profit or loss is on that particular investment. Suppose the overall investment is in the black, but several purchases of funds were made at higher prices and are in the red. These programs will flag those transactions—which is awfully helpful for tax-planning purposes.

Among the tax-oriented programs, CompuVest is an excellent choice. It can calculate your "cost basis" the three different ways that are accepted by the IRS (more on that in Chapter 6), allowing you to select the one that's most advantageous. (CompuVest sells for $34.95, including shipping, and can be returned within 30 days. Call 1-800-532-2392.) Another excellent new entry in this category of software is TaxTracker for Windows (available for $49 from the No-Load Fund Shareholders Assn., Inc., 1-800-966-5623). Though designed for the fund investor, TaxTracker is easily adaptable for stocks and bonds as well. Another feature here that's not in most financial software is an internal rate of return calculator. That will allow you to make a more sophisticated measure of your investment performance. You can also order the program at the Internet address (http://www.manhattanlink.com).

Mutual Funds Online

If you have a computer and a modem, you probably already subscribe to one of the online services, such as America Online or to an Internet access service (Table 5-2). The online world is emerging as a valuable tool for tracking, researching, and keeping up with mutual funds. America Online's Mutual Fund Center includes the ability to conduct transactions for participating funds. BUSINESS WEEK Online, also on AOL, features the Mutual Fund Corner, a place where all BW's stories on or about mutual funds are collected. Morningstar, Inc., the company that provides the data for the BW Mutual Fund Scoreboard, has its own online section as well, featuring monthly updates on more than 6500 funds and a library of excellent articles on fund investing from Morningstar's publications. Both BW and Morningstar have lively message boards where fund aficionados can ask questions—not only of BW and Morningstar folks, but of each other. CompuServe carries CDA/Wiesenberger's screenable database on 4700 funds, and you can also download Morningstar and Value Line reports for a surcharge. Prodigy's fund database comes from Micropal, Inc., and Prodigy also carries another service which enables users to chart mutual fund NAVs. All three major online services provide daily net asset value information and access to brokerage firms should you choose to invest in funds online.

The three major services also provide access to the Internet and the World Wide Web, which opens up vast new resources—and a lot of worthless information as well. We've already screened some of the offerings, and there are excellent home pages worth checking out. Start with NetWorth, a centralized starting point, which contains information from 30 fund companies. To get beyond the first pages, you have to register, but it's free. You'll get a password. You can keep a portfolio online, download shareholder reports, interviews with fund managers, and even fund prospectuses. (Stuff a prospectus in a computer file and save a tree.) NetWorth also allows you to download data to Quicken and other personal finance software. Other good fund-stops include Mutual Funds Magazine, Schwab, Fidelity, and Vanguard. For fans of closed-end funds, the Internet Closed-End Fund Investor offers some great information and tools which are not readily available elsewhere online.

Fund investors who venture online should also join the newsgroup, "misc.invest.funds." That's a message board where fund folks meet to ask questions, exchange opinions, and gather insight into mutual funds. Want to know why your hot fund was down 2 percent last week when the market fell less than 1? Post the question. Someone might have the answer—and that person may even be from the mutual fund company.

A computer can simplify keeping up with your funds.

TABLE 5-2

FUND "SURFING" ONLINE

The Internet

NetWorth
Fund information for more than 30 companies, with links to many home pages. Can also download data to Quicken and other personal finance programs. Service is free, but requires registration.

http://networth.galt.com

Mutual Funds Interactive
Good commentary, profiles and chat, plus market news, fund quotes, and portfolio tracking. Be sure to bookmark this site.

http://www.fundsinteractive.com/

Morningstar
Snappy new site, with loads of fund research to help you plan a portfolio. Links with brokerage firms let you invest as well. Service is free, but requires registration.

http://www.morningstar.net

Mutual Fund Investor's Corner
Sponsored by the Mutual Fund Education Alliance, a trade association of the direct-marketed (mainly no-load) funds. Fund info limited to that of members companies, but that's mainly what the do-it-yourself investor would want anyway.

http://www.mfea.com

FundAlarm
Maintains data on 500 funds (mainly those over $500 million), and tracks the funds vs. various benchmarks. Is one of yours a "three alarm" fund, and therefore should be dumped?

http://www.FundAlarm.com

Mutual Funds Magazine
Includes current and past stories from the magazine, and a screenable database of funds.

http://www.mfmag.com

SEC EDGAR Database
The U.S. Securities & Exchange Commission's electronic database, for those who want to read the official mutual fund filings.

http://www.sec.gov/edgarhp.htm

Schwab Online
The cyberdoor to the nation's largest discount brokers, which includes information on Schwab's popular Mutual Fund Marketplace and OneSource programs.

http://www.Schwab.com

Fidelity Investments
The home page for the nation's largest fund company and for its brokerage firm. Plenty of performance info, and prospectuses as well.

http://www.fid-inv.com

Jack White & Co.
Discount broker with the most number of funds, 4200 at last count. Website is not as slick as some, but if you want fund selection, no one offers more.

http://pawws.com/jwc/jwms.html

Vanguard Mutual Funds
Quiz yourself on your mutual fund knowledge, but don't worry if you don't do too well. You can enroll in the Vanguard University where you can learn how to build portfolios of funds, guided by the works of John C. Bogle's, founder and chairman.

http://www.vanguard.com

IBC Money Fund Monitor
The place to go for the latest information on money-market mutual funds. The site also includes news and commentary on the money-market activity, interest-rate developments, regulatory issues, and fund strategies. Carries data on more than 1200 taxable and tax-free money-market.

http://www.ibcdata.com

Internet Closed-End Investor
A great online service for an often-overlooked investment vehicle—the closed-end fund. Fund data, charts, screening capability, and more. Some services free, some require subscription.

http://www.icefi.com/

Newsgroups: misc.invest.funds
Want another opinion about some fund or funds? Scan the postings in this Internet-wide message board. If you can't find it, ask the question yourself. You'll get plenty of answers.

Online Services

America Online
Mutual Fund Center is a great jumping off point, collecting info on funds from around AOL and the Internet. Other funds-stops include Morningstar, American Association of Individual Investors, and BUSINESS WEEK Online's Mutual Fund Corner. Sage, a site whose motto is "Making Sense of Mutual Funds," is a winner—and an AOL exclusive. Call 1-800-641-4848.

CompuServe
FundWatch by *Money Magazine* includes reports from CDA/Wiesenberger, has ability to screen database. Morningstar and Value Line reports also available. Call 1-800-848-8990.

Prodigy
Comprehensive mutual-fund data provided by Micropal, with weekly updates. Another service, charts fund NAVs. Mutual Fund Center has daily price quotes and news about mutual funds and fund companies, provided by Dow Jones. Call 1-800-PRODIGY.

DATA: BUSINESS WEEK

When Your Fund Is Ailing

You're tracking your funds, diligently keeping records of weekly prices, remembering to count distributions in your returns. Then you start to notice that one of your funds is slipping. The stock market is moving up modestly but this fund is heading south.

The long-term record is still exceptional, and you're a long-term investor. So you stick with the fund—and watch it slip away. Now you're not only lagging the market, but you're losing real money. What do you do?

You're facing the most difficult question in all of investing: When do you jettison a fund that's in a funk? Suppose you sell and it turns out to be the bottom of the decline. You might regret it later. Maybe you paid a load to get into the fund, and so are reluctant to leave now. Sometimes people just refuse to admit they made a bad investment—there's too much ego involved. So they're slow to sell when perhaps they should.

Before pushing the "sell" button on a poorly performing fund, ask some questions about it. The most important: How is the fund doing relative to its market sector and peer group? Suppose the S&P 500 delivered a total return of 10 percent over the previous period and your small-cap growth fund gained only half that much. The question is: How much better did the other small-cap growth funds perform? Perhaps your fund, while dragging behind the market, did well among its peer group. So besides comparing your fund to the market, compare your fund to its peers.

If you had owned a high-yield bond fund in the latter half of 1989 and 1990, you may have been dismayed by plunging net asset values. At that time, no junk fund was going to look good. And the question wasn't, "Do you want to own this junk fund or another junk fund?" but "Do you want to invest in a junk bond fund at all?" You may have invested in one of the better junk bond funds. But you have to compare yours to others to know that.

Sometimes you make a bet without realizing it, and the failure of the investment is not entirely the manager's. If you buy a long-term government bond fund, the investment won't succeed unless long-term interest rates come down—or at least stay flat. If they go up, your fund is going to falter. You may choose to sell out,

but don't replace your fund with another long-term bond fund at the same time. If you're attracted by the long-term results of these sorts of funds, then you just stick with them, through good times and bad.

An investment in narrowly defined funds such as technology or health care or Latin American equities or emerging markets debt is a good bit riskier than in a broad-based fund with a wide menu of portfolio options. If you own a Latin equity fund and the value of the Mexican peso plunges, as it did in late 1994, you can't blame the portfolio manager for not beating the S&P 500. You might expect him to beat his peers, but certainly a Latin fund could not be expected to dodge such a macroeconomic event entirely.

What was your motivation in choosing this investment? If you were trying to seize upon a trading opportunity, like a big rally in Latin American stocks, you might as well sell, since the opportunity didn't materialize. If you bought to diversify your portfolio and to take advantage of a long-term growth opportunity, you should hold on nonetheless—and perhaps even increase your investment. If you bought the fund to diversify your holdings, don't fret. Chances are some of your other funds are doing quite well.

Before you jettison a mutual fund, you have to remember that few funds do well under all market conditions. What you should expect is that gains in up periods outweigh the losses in the down periods. The Vanguard/Windsor Fund is a case in point. The fund, then managed by John B. Neff, fared only about half as well as the S&P 500 in 1989 and fell more than twice as much as the market during 1990. Neff's "value" style of investing, which has proved successful for years, leads him to buy out of favor, high-dividend-paying stocks like autos, banks, and insurers. Those were among the worst-performing stock groups of the year. But the history of Neff's style of investing is that when the tide turns his way, he more than makes up for downswings. That's starting to happen. In 1992, Windsor more than doubled the returns of the S&P 500; in 1993, it nearly doubled the market index. And even in the difficult year of 1994, the fund finished slightly behind the total return of the S&P 500, but ahead of most mutual funds. In 1995, Neff's final year, the fund gained 30.1 percent. In 1996, under the guidance of Charles Freeman, the fund gained 26.4 percent.

What if value funds performed well—but Windsor didn't. Then you may have good reason to fire the fund. Indeed, it's because the best fund managers run into downdrafts that you diversify your mutual fund investments. That's why you might offset Windsor with, say, the Janus Fund or T. Rowe Price Blue Chip Growth, which choose companies for their earnings growth rather than value characteristics. If Windsor tried to boost its returns by loading up on small stocks of fast-growing high-tech companies, that too would be reason enough to dump the fund. Ask the professionals who advise pension funds on selection of investment managers: The only sin worse than underperforming the market is not following your stated investment program.

In short, don't dump a fund just on performance alone. Compare your fund to an appropriate market index, like the S&P 500; the S&P MidCap 400; or for small-cap stocks, the Russell 2000. Foreign funds can be compared to the foreign market indexes, such as those published by Morgan Stanley or Goldman Sachs. Bond funds should be compared to an appropriate bond index, depending on the maturity of the fund. Lehman Bros., Merrill Lynch, and Salomon Bros. all have numerous bond indexes for every segment of the bond market—corporates, Treasuries, global, mortgage-backed, and by maturity, too—short-, intermediate-, and long-term.

You can compare equity funds by their investment category. You can find that information in the BUSINESS WEEK Mutual Fund Scoreboard. All funds with the same investment style, such as "large-cap value" or "medium-cap growth," would make a good peer group. The same goes for bond funds.

Let's say you were comparing two small company funds, Invesco Emerging Growth, up 23.3 percent in 1993, and Heartland Value Fund, which earned 18.8 percent. Both funds beat the Russell 2000. But Heartland, with the lesser return, may actually have done a better job for its shareholders. Following a "small-cap value" investment style, its manager beat the 17 percent average return for all small-cap value funds. Invesco, following a "small-cap growth" style, was a laggard. The average small-cap growth fund was up 26.6 percent in 1993.

Keep in Touch with Your Fund

When you buy a mutual fund you are, in effect, "hiring" an investment manager to do a job for you, such as investing in small- to medium-sized companies. So to oversee your fund portfolio, you have to make sure your managers are doing what they told you they would do. If you invest in a small company fund, you don't want the manager spending your money on IBM, AT&T, and GE.

Funds do change gears, but they're supposed to notify you. As a shareholder, you're entitled to get periodic reports—at least semiannually, though many report quarterly as well. But the information in a report may be quite dated by the time you see it. Funds have 90 days after the close of their fiscal half and full fiscal year to deliver shareholder reports. Still, even a somewhat dated report can be informative.

Shareholder reports vary in their content and presentation. The Gintel Fund, for instance, has a very simple report, but it's quite informative nonetheless (Figure 5-2). All fund reports will

FIGURE 5-2

GINTEL FUND
Status of Investments
September 30, 1995
(Unaudited)

Common Stocks		Purchase Cost	Market Value	Per Share Cost	Market	% of Net Assets
150,000	Federal National Mortgage	$8,108,946	$15,525,000	54.06	103.50	15.9
355,000	Checkpoint Systems	2,846,216	9,363,125	8.02	26.38	9.6
150,000	Union Camp	6,750,336	8,643,750	45.00	57.63	8.9
700,000	Chart Industries	3,321,550	6,125,000	4.75	8.75	6.3
665,000	Oneita Industries, Inc.	8,414,133	5,652,500	12.65	8.50	5.8
150,000	Capstead Mortgage	2,932,501	4,781,250	19.55	31.88	4.9
90,000	Schering-Plough Corp.	2,147,611	4,635,000	23.86	51.50	4.8
100,000	FirstFed Michigan	868,021	3,512,500	8.68	35.13	3.6
50,000	DuPont	2,798,852	3,437,500	55.98	68.75	3.5
50,000	Phelps Dodge	2,992,527	3,131,250	59.85	62.63	3.2
48,000	Fluor	2,223,496	2,688,000	46.32	56.00	2.8
100,000	Singer Co.	2,497,273	2,662,500	24.97	26.63	2.7
52,500	Weyerhaeuser	2,101,374	2,395,313	40.03	45.63	2.4
100,000	New Park Resources	1,946,258	1,750,000	19.46	17.50	1.8
100,000	Vertex, Inc.	1,550,000	1,725,000	15.50	17.25	1.8
25,000	Johnson Controls	1,195,851	1,581,250	47.83	63.25	1.6
25,000	Tyco International	1,278,937	1,575,000	51.16	63.00	1.6
75,000	Price/Costco	1,011,188	1,284,375	13.48	17.13	1.3
30,000	Black & Decker	750,260	1,023,750	25.01	34.13	1.0
20,000	Pepsico Inc.	696,562	1,020,000	34.83	51.00	1.0
100,000	OHM Corp.	693,749	900,000	6.94	9.00	0.9
25,000	WorldCom	608,749	803,125	24.35	32.13	0.8
25,000	OrNda Healthcare	433,750	531,250	17.35	21.25	0.5
	Miscellaneous Securities	4,355,479	4,447,601			4.6
	Total Investments	$62,523,619	89,194,038			91.3
	Cash and Short-Term Investments		8,482,994			8.7
	NET ASSETS		**$97,677,032**			**100.0**
	NET ASSET VALUE PER SHARE		**$15.77**			
	INCREASE IN NET ASSET VALUE PER SHARE YEAR-TO-DATE		**26.6%**			

FIGURE 5-3

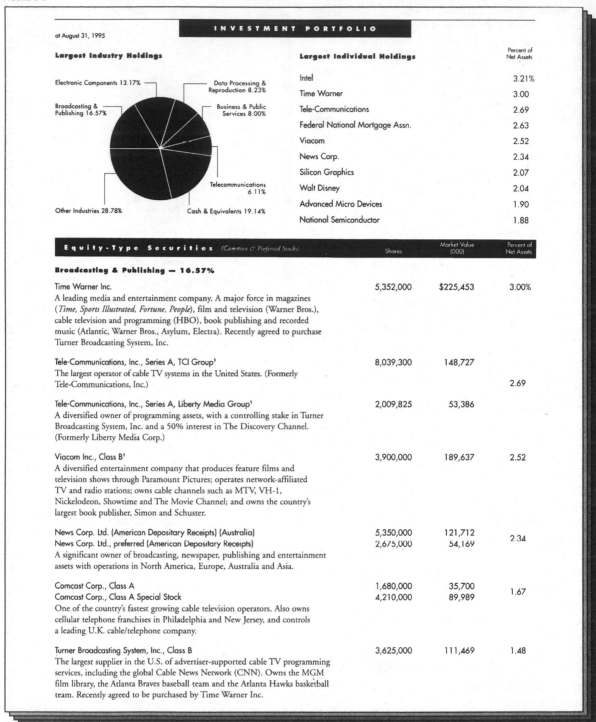

at August 31, 1995

INVESTMENT PORTFOLIO

Largest Industry Holdings

Electronic Components 13.17%
Data Processing & Reproduction 8.23%
Broadcasting & Publishing 16.57%
Business & Public Services 8.00%
Telecommunications 6.11%
Other Industries 28.78%
Cash & Equivalents 19.14%

Largest Individual Holdings	Percent of Net Assets
Intel	3.21%
Time Warner	3.00
Tele-Communications	2.69
Federal National Mortgage Assn.	2.63
Viacom	2.52
News Corp.	2.34
Silicon Graphics	2.07
Walt Disney	2.04
Advanced Micro Devices	1.90
National Semiconductor	1.88

Equity-Type Securities *(Common & Preferred Stocks)*	Shares	Market Value (000)	Percent of Net Assets
Broadcasting & Publishing — 16.57%			
Time Warner Inc.	5,352,000	$225,453	3.00%
A leading media and entertainment company. A major force in magazines (*Time, Sports Illustrated, Fortune, People*), film and television (Warner Bros.), cable television and programming (HBO), book publishing and recorded music (Atlantic, Warner Bros., Asylum, Electra). Recently agreed to purchase Turner Broadcasting System, Inc.			
Tele-Communications, Inc., Series A, TCI Group[1]	8,039,300	148,727	
The largest operator of cable TV systems in the United States. (Formerly Tele-Communications, Inc.)			2.69
Tele-Communications, Inc., Series A, Liberty Media Group[1]	2,009,825	53,386	
A diversified owner of programming assets, with a controlling stake in Turner Broadcasting System, Inc. and a 50% interest in The Discovery Channel. (Formerly Liberty Media Corp.)			
Viacom Inc., Class B[1]	3,900,000	189,637	2.52
A diversified entertainment company that produces feature films and television shows through Paramount Pictures; operates network-affiliated TV and radio stations; owns cable channels such as MTV, VH-1, Nickelodeon, Showtime and The Movie Channel; and owns the country's largest book publisher, Simon and Schuster.			
News Corp. Ltd. (American Depositary Receipts) (Australia)	5,350,000	121,712	
News Corp. Ltd., preferred (American Depositary Receipts)	2,675,000	54,169	2.34
A significant owner of broadcasting, newspaper, publishing and entertainment assets with operations in North America, Europe, Australia and Asia.			
Comcast Corp., Class A	1,680,000	35,700	
Comcast Corp., Class A Special Stock	4,210,000	89,989	1.67
One of the country's fastest growing cable television operators. Also owns cellular telephone franchises in Philadelphia and New Jersey, and controls a leading U.K. cable/telephone company.			
Turner Broadcasting System, Inc., Class B	3,625,000	111,469	1.48
The largest supplier in the U.S. of advertiser-supported cable TV programming services, including the global Cable News Network (CNN). Owns the MGM film library, the Atlanta Braves baseball team and the Atlanta Hawks basketball team. Recently agreed to be purchased by Time Warner Inc.			

show the market value of a security on the day of the report. But Gintel's also discloses the purchase price of the investment. That's a line-by-line report card on how the fund manager is doing.

The Gintel Fund lists its stocks by their value of the holding in the portfolio. Federal National Mortgage Association (more commonly known by its nickname, "Fannie Mae") is by far the largest holding, with 150,000 shares. What makes it the largest is not the number of shares, but the market value of those shares (price times the number of shares) which, the statement shows, is $15,525,000. Now compare that to the purchase cost of $8,108,946, and you can also see that the fund has a tidy profit, a near double, in the stock. If thinking in millions is a little unwieldy, Gintel reports per-share cost and market value, too. By disclosing cost, this fund also shows its losing positions—stocks whose market value is now below the fund's cost. By comparing cost and market value, you can see that just two (Oneita Industries, Inc. and New Park Resources) of the 23 holdings are in the red.

But that cost information isn't always in the reports. Typically, the reports show the security and its market value on the date of the report. The American Funds group, for instance, doesn't provide the shareholder's costs, but does a good job in portfolio reporting. Look at Figure 5-3, from the 1995 Annual Report of Growth Fund of America. At the top, there's summary information on major industries in which the fund is invested, and the 10 largest holdings. Without reading any further, the shareholder can see how his or her money is deployed. For instance, broadcasting and publishing is the largest industry sector in the portfolio, commanding 16.57 percent of the assets, and the second largest is electronic components, with 13.17 percent.

Then look at "Largest Individual Holdings." The single largest holding in the portfolio is Intel Corp., the world's leading semiconductor company, and thus, an "electronic components" company. Two other semiconductor manufacturers, Advanced Micro Devices, Inc. and National Semiconductor Corp., are No. 9 and No. 10 in the top 10. Broadcasting and publishing companies command the second, third, fifth, sixth, and eighth largest positions.

If you want more information, there's plenty to follow. Look down the page. The first broad category listed is "Broadcasting & Publishing." And under that heading, the companies are listed according to the market value of the investment. Time Warner Inc., worth $225,453,000 at the time of the report, is first, commanding 3 percent of the entire portfolio. Next are two different classes of shares in Tele-Communications, Inc. What's informative about this report is the description of the individual companies, something that is not often provided in mutual fund literature.

Most reports include a letter to shareholders from the president of the fund management company or from the portfolio manager. The letter typically discusses market conditions, though by the time you get the report the quarter will be long past. Twice a year, the fund is supposed to provide you with a copy of the portfolio. You don't

FIGURE 5-4

T. Rowe Price
T. Rowe Price Associates, Inc., 100 East Pratt Street, Baltimore, MD 21202

James S. Riepe
Managing Director

Dear Shareholder:

All of the T. Rowe Price mutual funds will hold shareholder meetings in 1994 to elect directors, ratify the selection of independent accountants, and approve amendments to a number of investment policies.

The T. Rowe Price funds are not required to hold annual meetings each year if the only items of business are to elect directors or ratify accountants. In order to save fund expenses, most of the funds have not held annual meetings for a number of years. There are, however, conditions under which the funds must ask shareholders to elect directors, and one is to comply with a requirement that a minimum number have been elected by shareholders, not appointed by the funds' boards. Since the last annual meetings of the T. Rowe Price funds, several directors have retired and new directors have been added. In addition, a number of directors will be retiring in the near future.

Given this situation, we believed it appropriate to hold annual meetings for all the T. Rowe Price funds in 1994. At the same time, we reviewed the investment policies of all of the funds for consistency and to assure the portfolio managers have the flexibility they need to manage your money in today's fast changing financial markets. The changes being recommended, which are explained in detail in the enclosed proxy material, **do not alter the funds' investment objectives or basic investment programs**.

In many cases the proposals are common to several funds, so we have combined certain proxy statements to save on fund expenses. For those of you who own more than one of these funds, the combined proxy may also save you the time of reading more than one document before you vote and mail your ballots. The proposals which are specific to an individual fund are easily identifiable on the Notice and in the proxy statement discussion. If you own more than one fund, please note that **each fund has a separate card. You should vote and sign each one**, then return all of them to us in the enclosed postage-paid envelope.

Your early response will be appreciated and could save your fund the substantial costs associated with a follow-up mailing. We know we are asking you to review a rather formidable proxy statement, but this approach represents the most efficient one for your fund as well as for the other funds. Thank you for your cooperation. If you have any questions, please call us at 1-800-225-5132.

Sincerely,

James S. Riepe
Director, Mutual Funds Division

CUSIP#779572106/fund#065

have to second-guess the portfolio manager, but a quick scan might tell you a few things. If the fund is supposed to invest in small, fast-growing companies—and you don't recognize many of the companies' names—then the fund manager is probably pursuing what he or she promised to pursue. If you have a high-quality bond fund and you find it's peppered with junk bonds, you ought to ask a few questions. Don't be bashful. Call the fund management company and ask for an explanation.

The quality of shareholder reports varies widely. Some fund managers are brutally frank when they have had a period of bad performance; others are elliptical or evasive, and never admit head-on when their results are poor. Charles Freeman, portfolio manager of the Vanguard/ Windsor Fund, includes a report card on his performance by comparing the performance of major fund holdings with their industry group. It's a practice he carried on from his predecessor, John B. Neff. For instance, in the 1996 annual report, Freeman gave himself an A for his investments in energy and insurance and an A+ for his investments in technology. But he awarded himself an F for his investments in aluminum, chemicals, paper, and steel companies. Few funds are as informative and frank as Windsor, though Vanguard, in general, provides fairly complete reports.

Morningstar's analysts also rate funds' reports to shareholders. They look at the amount of financial information—above and beyond what's required by law—and the presentation. Is it organized in a reader-friendly manner? Can the shareholder learn something about the investment from the reports?

Morningstar discovered that good funds don't necessarily earn A's and B's on their reports. But they also found that poor performers rarely have great reports, either. In general, Morningstar discovered a positive correlation between superior equity-fund shareholder reports and the returns these funds achieve.

In a 1993 study, for instance, Morningstar found that 45 funds with A ratings on their shareholder reports had five-year average annual returns of 20.8 percent. Funds with B-rated

FIGURE 5-5

T.RowePrice **We Need Your Proxy Vote Before April 20, 1994**

Please refer to the Proxy Statement discussion of each of these matters.

THIS PROXY WHEN PROPERLY EXECUTED WILL BE VOTED IN THE MANNER DIRECTED HEREIN BY THE SHAREHOLDER. IF NO DIRECTION IS MADE, THIS PROXY WILL BE VOTED FOR ALL PROPOSALS.

Please fold and detach card at perforation before mailing.

1. Election of directors. **FOR** all nominees listed below (except as marked to the contrary) ☐ **WITHHOLD AUTHORITY** to vote for all nominees listed below ☐**1.**

(INSTRUCTION: TO WITHHOLD AUTHORITY TO VOTE FOR AN INDIVIDUAL NOMINEE STRIKE A LINE THROUGH THE NOMINEE'S NAME IN THE LIST BELOW.)

Leo C. Bailey   Donald W. Dick, Jr.   David K. Fagin   Addison Lanier   John H. Laporte   John K. Major
Hanne M. Merriman   James S. Riepe   Hubert D. Vos   Paul M. Wythes

2. Approve changes to the Fund's fundamental policies. **FOR** each policy listed below (except as marked to the contrary) ☐ **ABSTAIN**☐**2.**

If you do NOT wish to approve a policy change, please check the appropriate box below:

☐ (A) Borrowing	☐ (E) Purchasing Securities	☐ (I) Investment Companies	☐ (M) Ownership of Securities
☐ (B) Commodities & Futures	☐ (F) Real Estate	☐ (J) Purchasing on Margin	☐ (N) Illiquid Securities
☐ (C) Lending	☐ (G) Senior Securities	☐ (K) Oil & Gas	☐ (O) Short Sales
☐ (D) Single Issuer	☐ (H) Control	☐ (L) Options	☐ (P) Unseasoned Issuers

3. Ratify the selection of Coopers & Lybrand as independent accountants. **FOR**☐ **AGAINST**☐ **ABSTAIN**☐**3.**

4. I authorize the Proxies, in their discretion, to vote upon such other business as may properly come before the meeting.

CUSIP#779572106/fund#065

T. ROWE PRICE OTC FUND, INC. **MEETING: 8:00 A.M. EASTERN TIME**

THIS PROXY IS SOLICITED ON BEHALF OF THE BOARD OF DIRECTORS

The undersigned hereby appoints John H. Laporte and James S. Riepe, as proxies, each with the power to appoint his substitute, and hereby authorizes them to represent and to vote, as designated below, all shares of stock of the Fund, which the undersigned is entitled to vote at the Annual Meeting of Shareholders to be held on Wednesday, April 20, 1994, at the time indicated above, at the offices of the Fund, 100 East Pratt Street, Baltimore, Maryland 21202, and at any and all adjournments thereof, with respect to the matters set forth below and described in the Notice of Annual Meeting and Proxy Statement dated March 9, 1994, receipt of which is hereby acknowledged.

Please sign exactly as name appears. Only authorized officers should sign for corporations. For information as to the voting of stock registered in more than one name, see page 3 of the Notice of Annual Meeting and Proxy Statement.

Dated: ______________________, 1994

____

____

Signature(s)

CUSIP#779572106/fund#065

reports had an 18.1 percent average annual return for the five-year period. The funds with reports rated B through D all had average annual returns around 15.5 percent. There were only six funds that flunked. But these funds with F-rated reports had nothing much to say for themselves. Their five-year average annual return was a skimpy 4.7 percent.

There are other times that you hear from a fund. Every time the prospectus is updated, you should get a new copy. That's to keep in your files. If there has been some major change in policy, such as imposition of a load or 12(b)-1 fee, or a change in redemption procedures, it should be highlighted or noted to investors in a separate letter.

Finally, most mutual funds are corporations, registered in various states and governed by the laws of that state. If the state requires annual meetings, your fund will send you a proxy statement, a proxy card, and an invitation to the meeting. At the least, the proxy will have a ballot for election of the fund directors and the hiring of the auditors.

If the fund management contract is up for renewal as well, you'll be asked to approve that, along with any changes in fees or sales charges. Shareholders also may be asked to okay mergers and changes in investment management firms, and do such routine things as elect directors (from a list of nominees) and ratify the board's choice of auditors. If there is any change in investment policy, it should also be a ballot question. For instance, many domestic equity funds have changed policy to allow investment in foreign securities, usually with a limit on the percentage of fund assets that can be invested abroad. If you're against that in principle, then vote no. But the overwhelming chances are that you'll be outvoted.

Is it really necessary to raise fees in an era when funds are bulging with new money? After all, fund managers' fee incomes increase with the size of their funds. The larger the fund, the more the managers collect. But put yourself in the management company's shoes. The best time to ask for a raise is when business is going gangbusters. Shareholders may not be so generous during a bear market.

Other than the serious business, such as approving fees, it's easy to dismiss the proxies as not even being worth your time to read and consider. But don't toss them out—not even seemingly innocuous proxies from money-market funds (Figures 5-4 and 5-5). Vote, sign, and return them in the postage-prepaid envelope. You don't have to vote yes, and you can abstain. But it's critical to return the proxy because the funds need a quorum to hold a meeting. (In signing the proxy, you give persons named on the statement the ability to vote your shares as you direct.) You have as many votes as you have shares. If a fund fails to obtain enough proxies for a quorum, it will have to conduct another mailing. And shareholders bear the cost of proxy solicitation.

Few funds have meetings anymore. Many conduct votes by proxy without convening a meeting. The meeting is an opportunity to ask questions of fund managers, but there probably isn't anything you're going to learn in person that you couldn't find out from a phone call or letter to the shareholder services department.

When the Fund Manager Changes

One of the toughest questions in mutual fund investing is what to do when the portfolio manager changes, especially "star" managers like Peter Lynch, who piloted the Fidelity Magellan Fund to tremendous successes and took an early retirement from fund management in 1990. Of course, Lynch's departure was big news. But how do you know if there's been a change in portfolio managers?

For starters, the management company has to tell you in the fund documents. That's a new development in fund regulation because, until a few years ago, funds were under no obligation, and many preferred not, to tell. And, in case you haven't picked up on it before, BUSINESS WEEK Mutual Fund Scoreboard also notes when the portfolio manager of an equity fund has changed.

Does a change in leadership matter? It depends on the sort of fund. With a money-market fund and even many bond funds, the manager may not matter much at all. And some fund management companies, such as the American Funds and American Century Investors, take a team approach to investment management, so one portfolio manager may hardly be missed. Vanguard/Windsor's Neff stepped down at the end of 1995, but was succeeded by Charles T. Freeman, a deputy who spent 25 years at his side. That fund's investors should be fairly confident of a continuity in investment style.

But that's not always the case. With many equity funds the manager has a lot of latitude. When Peter Lynch retired from the Fidelity

> Shareholder reports vary widely in quality.

Magellan Fund, mutual fund analysts were split over whether to sell. Six months after Lynch's departure, those who sold looked smart. It wasn't that Morris Smith, Lynch's successor, fumbled. Just weeks after he took over the reins, the stock market went into a swoon. True, Magellan underperformed a poorly performing market. But the fund is so large, and owns so many stocks, that it's quite possible that the performance in the second half of 1990 may not have been much different had Lynch remained at the helm.

In 1991, when the stock market rallied, so did Magellan, up 41 percent for the year. But early in 1992, Smith, citing a need for a break, left the fund, too. Jeffrey Vinik, Smith's successor, trailed the market, too, early in his tenure, and some analysts wondered whether it was time to leave the fund. But Vinik also had an excellent track record (he formerly ran Fidelity Contrafund and Fidelity Growth & Income Fund). In 1993, in fact, Magellan posted a 24.7 percent total return, more than doubling the return of the S&P 500—one of the best relative performances since the early 1980s, when the $31.7 billion fund was less than $1 billion in size. In 1996, Vinik invested 20 percent of the fund in Treasury bonds—and the bond market sank. He left the fund at the end of May. He was succeeded by Robert E. Stansky, another top manager.

Neither Lynch's, Smith's, nor Vinik's departure was fatal for Magellan because Fidelity has an exceptional pool of managerial talent and an army of talented research analysts. In fact, the company changes fund managers fairly frequently. In 1996, however, the changes became quite frequent. The company made a slew of changes in the spring to try to improve sagging performance. Later in the year, manager departures resulted in further shifts. More than half the equity funds got a new manager during 1996. The net impact remains to be seen.

Perhaps to protect against the investors' following a star manager out the door, many fund companies have been naming co-managers to funds. The idea, at least, is that if one manager leaves, the second provides continuity and the fund company can say the same management is in place. So when Carlene Murphy Ziegler, co-manager of the Strong Opportunity and Strong Common Stock, resigned in 1994, co-manager Dick Weiss was still in place, along with Marina Carlson, who had been named as an additional co-manager earlier in the year.

Still, many investment managers and financial planners switch funds when a well-regarded fund manager leaves. There have been no definitive studies yet, but Morningstar, for example, uncovered some interesting anecdotal evidence in late 1990. It looked at five managers who switched funds and measured how the old funds had done since the switch versus how the new funds performed under the star managers. In all five cases, investors following the manager to the new fund would have done better.

But there's anecdotal evidence to the contrary as well. Donald Yacktman built an enviable record with Selected American Fund, but left Selected in early 1992 to set up the Yacktman Fund. The results, so far, have been mixed. Yacktman's reputation was enough to draw in $70 million or so in the first six months, a decent start considering that Yacktman did not have a large fund company or marketing muscle behind him. But the investment returns were a different story. In 1993, his first full year in operation, Yacktman Fund was down 6.6 percent. In 1994, the growth stocks he favored rebounded and his fund was up 8.8 percent, and he logged a 29 percent return in 1995. In 1996, he beat the S&P 500, earning a 26 percent return.

Yacktman's departure from Selected American also spurred an unusual chain of management. Selected Financial Services, the management company, replaced Yacktman with another manager. Unhappy with the performance, the independent directors of the fund—members of the board of directors who were not Selected employees—voted to dismiss Selected as the management company and hired Shelby Davis, the highly regarded manager of the Davis New York Venture Fund, to run the fund. (Davis retired in 1997, but his son runs the fund.)

Sometimes there's a change when the ownership of a fund management company is taken over. In 1992, for instance, Franklin Resources, which owns Franklin Funds, took over the Templeton fund company, but left the Templeton fund managers in place, since Franklin bought Templeton in part for its investment expertise. No need to change. When T. Rowe Price Associates took over the USF&G funds, it folded most of them into already existing T. Rowe Price funds. So those fund investors got new managers. In cases like that, investors may want to review the record of the new managers. In late 1993, Pioneering Management, the company that manages the Pioneer family of funds, took over five Mutual

A change in portfolio managers can be significant.

of Omaha funds, but did not merge them into its own funds. Instead, in all but one municipal bond fund, Pioneer installed its own portfolio managers. In such a case, find out which other funds your new manager has run and check out his or her records.

Mutual Fund Mergers

For the most part, if a fund does a reasonable job of meeting its investment objectives, the management company isn't going to tinker with success. Most of the time it's poorly performing funds or funds in poorly performing sectors of the stock market that get a makeover. Often, the makeover is simply merging the weaker fund into a stronger one.

A mutual fund merger can take place in one of several ways. For instance, several funds within the same family may be combined. That's what is usually done with small, poorly performing funds. Such funds are in a Catch-22 situation. Since they're very small, they tend to have higher overhead and expense ratios, which cut into their total returns. And without strong returns, they are unable to attract new investments—and so they remain small.

For all the new funds that have started up in recent years, there have been many quietly merged out of existence, too. Oppenheimer Management Corporation has been a hotbed of mutual fund mergers. With the required approval of shareholders, in 1991 Oppenheimer merged its Ninety-Ten and Premium Income funds into the Oppenheimer Asset Allocation Fund. The merged funds both used options to generate income, albeit not too successfully. The Asset Allocation Fund is not an income fund per se, but it does try to maintain a steady growth and a regular dividend stream. In that case, the investment objectives of the survivor fund were not significantly different from the merged funds' objectives. Oppenheimer also merged two laggard growth stock funds, Directors and Regency, into the better-performing Oppenheimer Target Fund. The track record that remains for fund analysts and investors to see is that of the surviving fund. The records of the losers vanish and are no longer an embarrassment to the fund company.

In 1994, Oppenheimer was reorganizing funds again. The company (with shareholder approval, of course) renamed the Oppenheimer Global Bio-Tech Fund—the top-performing fund of 1991—the Global Emerging Growth Fund, giving the fund a much broader investment mandate. Then it merged the smaller Oppenheimer Global Environmental Fund into the Emerging Growth Fund. Oppenheimer officials said the company made the switches to get out of the sector fund business. Because of bear markets in both sectors, neither fund was flourishing—or attracting new money. As an emerging growth fund, of course, the fund could invest in biotech and environmental companies, as well as a whole lot more.

Another sort of merger is when a small fund family leaves the business entirely and turns over the funds' management to a major management company. Some of the companies that gave up fund management over the last several years had funds with combined assets of less than $100 million.

Then there's the "rationalization" merger, when two companies combine and try to streamline the fund offerings by merging like funds. That's what happened in 1994, when Smith Barney Inc. merged 12 funds—including five money-market mutual funds—it had picked up in the Shearson acquisition. Among those merged was the underperforming Smith Barney Shearson Sector Analysis Portfolio, run by Wall Street guru Elaine M. Garzarelli, folded into what is now Smith Barney Strategic Investors.

The best bet is that you will see more fund company mergers in the next few years as industry growth slows and companies combine to achieve more economies of scale. Fund companies are also combining to broaden their product lines. That's some of the motive behind the 1994 merger of Van Kampen Merritt, a fixed-income group, with American Capital, which is more of an equity-fund manager. In 1996, the combined company was purchased by Morgan Stanley, which managed mainly international funds. But in 1997, Morgan Stanley agreed to merge with Dean Witter Discover & Co., and Dean Witter has a wide range of funds.

Many of these fund-company linkups will no doubt result in mergers at the fund level. If your fund is merged into another fund, it's probably for the better. Small, poorly performing funds have difficulties improving their returns, and a

Investors may benefit from a mutual fund merger.

merger into a stronger fund can be a godsend. You get new fund shares for the old in a tax-free exchange. The new management company usually folds the acquired funds into its own, trying to match up funds with similar objectives.

In 1990, for instance, the Vanguard Group merged its Explorer and Explorer II funds (both technology funds), and changed the investment objective of the combined fund to invest in emerging growth companies. (Such changes must be made with the approval of the shareholders.) This might dismay shareholders who invested in Explorer because of its technological bent. On the other hand, if Explorer had been successful, Vanguard wouldn't have changed it.

Vanguard also merged the poorly performing Vanguard High-Yield Stock Fund into its Vanguard/Windsor Fund. In this case, merged shareholders shifted into a fund with a slightly more aggressive investment posture, a somewhat better track record, and a portfolio 100 times as large. One thing was familiar, though. John Neff ran both funds.

Change Objectives, Change Funds

Investors' objectives, their ability to assume risks, and their income needs change over time—usually in a gradual and predictable way. But sometimes the changes are abrupt, such as the loss of a job or the death of a spouse. Should objectives change, investors might find that, while their maximum growth fund has done a good job, it is no longer an appropriate investment for them.

Likewise, changes in tax status may also dictate a shift in funds. As income increases, so should the relative attractiveness of tax-exempt bond and money-market funds. Once in retirement, an investor might find that taxable bond funds offer more return even after paying taxes. These sorts of shifts don't need to happen all at once, and in fact might best be accomplished in stages. If moving funds results in a capital gains tax liability, the investor might want to spread the move out over several tax years.

Taxes and Record-Keeping

By now, you're gung ho on mutual funds. Strong returns, smart management, diversification, low costs, and ease of investing make them wonderful investments. What's the catch? For all the conveniences of investing in mutual funds, there is one big drawback. Depending on the funds you choose, you just may generate a blizzard of paper. Tempted as you may be to ignore or throw away those confirmation statements, don't. At some time you may sell shares of a fund or liquidate all your holdings in the fund. Then you're going to need those records.

Each time you make an investment in a fund, you'll get a statement from the fund management company (Figure 6-1). It will show the date and amount of the investment, the dollar price per share, the number of shares purchased, and the total number of shares in the fund. Redemptions trigger more paper. Switch dollars from, say, a long-term bond fund to a money-market fund, and you may get three statements: one from the bond fund showing the redemption of shares, one from the money-market fund showing a new investment, and another statement indicating an exchange has taken place.

Suppose you are making monthly investments as part of your own dollar-cost averaging program. That's 12 statements a year. And every year the statements should be cumulative. That is, the year's first statement shows a balance forward and the number of shares carried over from the previous year. Then, after the January purchase, you'll get a statement showing the January account activity. In February, it will show February and January. In March, you get all three months, and so forth. By December you should have the entire year's transactions on one statement. So one way to cut down on the file space is to toss out the previous 11 months' statements, as long as you have an up-to-date record of the account activity.

Remember, too, that your investments and redemptions are not the only transactions that generate paper. Every time the fund pays a dividend or capital gains distribution, another statement goes into the mail. Many bond and some stock funds, like the fund in Figure 6-1, make distributions monthly. That can trigger more paper, too. It's enough to make you want to buy growth-oriented equity funds, since most of them make distributions only once a year.

Now, imagine a fund which you bought on several occasions and at various prices, whose shares you sold a few times, also at various prices, and whose earned distributions were reinvested in the funds—also at various prices. You have tons of paper to start with. But your biggest headache isn't paper—it's taxes.

No, even the computer won't stop the blizzard. A good software program will help you keep track of the information and make it easier to manage. But the postal service is going to keep on delivering the statements. And the information on each of them has to be entered properly into the program.

Mutual Funds' Special Tax Status

Understanding mutual funds and taxes takes a little extra effort. There's a set of rules that governs how the mutual fund must behave to keep its special tax status. (The rules apply to closed-end funds, too.) And then, once the fund has paid out its earnings, it's up to the shareholders to keep track of them properly. If you miss reporting a dividend or capital gains distribution (the fund sends out 1099-DIVs telling you exactly how much), you're likely to get a letter from the IRS and a bill for the taxes due—plus interest and a penalty.

FIGURE 6-1

Investment Account Statement / 1995 CALENDAR YEAR

THE **Vanguard** GROUP
OF INVESTMENT COMPANIES ®

YEAR-TO-DATE DECEMBER 31, 1995 - PAGE 4 OF 11

VANGUARD FLAGSHIP SERVICE
P.O. BOX 1103 * VALLEY FORGE, PA 19482-1103

SAMPLE SHAREHOLDER
123 MAIN STREET
ANYTOWN PA 19191-1919

ACCOUNT VALUE
$195,933.48

FUND NUMBER   39
ACCOUNT NUMBER   12345678901
STATEMENT NUMBER   12345678

Vanguard
FIXED INCOME
SECURITIES FUND
**Short-Term
Corporate Portfolio**

M MCCONNELL   8632 F/S

ACCOUNT SERVICE
CALL 1-800-345-1344

Trade Date	Transaction Description	Dollar Amount	Share Price	Share Amount	Shares Owned
	BALANCE AT - DEC 31, 1994		10.30		28,494.600
01/26	CK-WRITING REDEMP 1004	-2,262.00	10.37	-218.129	28,276.471
01/26	SWP REDEMP FUND EXPRESS	-6,000.00	10.37	-578.592	27,697.879
01/31	INCOME DIVIDEND REINVEST	1,516.45	10.40	145.813	27,843.692
02/24	SWP REDEMP FUND EXPRESS	-6,000.00	10.50	-571.429	27,272.263
02/28	INCOME DIVIDEND REINVEST	1,420.19	10.53	134.871	27,407.134
03/09	CK-WRITING REDEMP 1006	-41,014.13	10.52	-3,898.682	23,508.452
03/24	SWP REDEMP FUND EXPRESS	-6,000.00	10.56	-568.182	22,940.270
03/31	INCOME DIVIDEND REINVEST	1,387.19	10.54	131.612	23,071.882
04/07	PURCHASE BY CHECK	15,000.00	10.57	1,419.111	24,490.993
04/26	SWP REDEMP FUND EXPRESS	-6,000.00	10.61	-565.504	23,925.489
04/30	INCOME DIVIDEND REINVEST	1,333.75	10.59	125.944	24,051.433
05/01	CK-WRITING REDEMP 1007	-27,075.59	10.59	-2,556.713	21,494.720
05/02	CK-WRITING REDEMP 1008	-4,400.00	10.60	-415.094	21,079.626
05/26	SWP REDEMP FUND EXPRESS	-6,000.00	10.73	-559.180	20,520.446
05/30	CK-WRITING REDEMP 1009	-2,500.00	10.75	-232.558	20,287.888
05/31	INCOME DIVIDEND REINVEST	1,205.48	10.75	112.138	20,400.026
06/12	PURCHASE BY CHECK	60,000.00	10.73	5,591.799	25,991.825
06/26	SWP REDEMP FUND EXPRESS	-6,000.00	10.78	-556.586	25,435.239
06/30	INCOME DIVIDEND REINVEST	1,320.29	10.75	122.818	25,558.057
07/31	INCOME DIVIDEND REINVEST	1,468.81	10.15	144.710	25,702.767
08/25	SWP REDEMP FUND EXPRESS	-6,000.00	9.95	-603.015	25,099.752

PAID THIS CALENDAR YEAR	Income Dividends	or	Tax Exempt Income	+	Short-Term Gains	+	Long-Term Gains	=	TOTAL DISTRIBUTIONS

	OCTOBER	NOVEMBER	DECEMBER
30 DAY YIELD	6.20%	6.20%	6.31%
SHARE PRICE-TRADE DATE	$9.27 - 10/27/95	$10.73 - 11/29/95	$8.64 - 12/28/95
DISTRIBUTION PAYABLE DATE	11/01/95	12/01/95	01/02/96

Remember, if you sell shares of a fund, the fund company also has to report the proceeds of the sale to the IRS. That means you will have to account for that transaction as well. You won't forget to do it, since the fund will remind you with form 1099-B. (Like the 1099-DIV, you get one copy, the IRS gets the other.) There may be taxes due, or you may actually have a loss that can be applied as a deduction against them. Without good records, you could end up paying too little in taxes and get caught, or, worse yet, paying more tax than necessary.

Let's start with the tax status of the mutual fund itself. Remember, most mutual funds are also corporations, and shareholders of corporations, in effect, pay tax twice. The corporation pays taxes on its earnings and, if any of the earnings are paid to shareholders as dividends, they're taxed again as part of shareholders' income. But mutual funds escape this double taxation. The fund is treated as a "conduit"—all the income and responsibility for paying the tax on that income pass through the fund to its shareholders.

To keep their special tax status, mutual funds have to live within rigorous rules. There are requirements about diversification. For instance, a fund can't hold more than 10 percent of the outstanding voting stock in a particular company. Mutual funds must also distribute at least 90 percent of their taxable income—dividends and net short-term capital gains. (Tax-exempt funds must distribute 90 percent of their tax-exempt income.)

There's also what's known as the "short-short" rule, which says that no more than 30 percent of the funds' gross income can come from securities held for less than 90 days. For example, the now-defunct Smith Barney Shearson Sector Analysis Fund ran afoul of this a few years ago. The fund had opened for business in 1987 and made a splashy debut. Not only did it sidestep the market crash, but the fund's manager had also purchased put options—which soared in value as the market tanked. She quickly sold the options and reaped significant short-term gains. The gains were so great that the fund ended up violating the short-short rule. So, for that fiscal year, the fund ended up having to pay tax that nicked about 15 cents off the fund's NAV.

Mutual funds must distribute 98 percent of their income and dividends—and do it in the calendar year in which they are earned. In addition, the funds must distribute 98 percent of their net realized capital gains—both short- and long-term capital gains. A fund that fails to meet this distribution test can be hit with a 4 percent excise tax on the undistributed income.

How much a fund distributes in income and capital gains has direct bearing on its aftertax return. (More on aftertax returns in Chapter 7.) Suppose two mutual funds have the same pretax total return. One made no income or capital gains distributions, because it did not buy dividend-bearing stocks and tended to hold rather than trade the stocks in the portfolio. The second fund had the same total return, but about half of it came in the form of distributions. The one that made no distributions would have the higher aftertax return. Of course, if the fund is held in an IRA or other tax-deferred plan, the distributions don't matter. But if the account is taxable, a fund's history and policy of making distributions is a real concern in deciding whether to invest in a particular fund.

When looking at the distributions, remember that not all are taxed equally. Distributions of dividends, interest income, and short-term capital gains are taxed at the same rate at which the shareholder's earned income is taxed—and that can be as high as 39.6 percent. Long-term capital gains—and they're long-term if they were generated by investments held for more than a year—get more favorable tax treatment: The maximum rate is 28 percent, no matter how high the shareholder's regular tax rate is.

Many funds, especially those that practice a buy-and-hold investment strategy, often have huge unrealized and undistributed capital gains in their portfolios. Morningstar, Inc. measures these gains and expresses the magnitude as a percentage of the fund's total holdings. BUSINESS WEEK now includes this number in the Scoreboard under the heading "Untaxed Gains" (see Chapter 7).

Suppose a fund has an untaxed gain of 30 percent. That means 30 percent of the portfolio is unrealized capital gains. If the fund were liquidated tomorrow at $10 a share, the locked-in profits would be unlocked or "realized" in tax terms, and $3 would come back to shareholders as a capital gain. Some investors are wary of funds with high untaxed gains because they think they may be stuck paying tax on the capital gains earned long before they went into the fund.

Sometimes mutual funds have realized net losses, rather than realized gains. But tax rules do not allow mutual funds to distribute their losses to their shareholders. However, the funds can carry the losses forward for eight years and use them to offset future taxable gains. Some bond funds are in that position right now. As those markets recover, the funds are able to offset their gains with these losses.

That may not assuage those who watched their funds undergo partial meltdowns, but it does suggest an investment strategy. Provided a fund meets all your other criteria, investing in a fund with tax losses makes sense. Some other investors realized the loss, but as a new investor to the fund you can get the benefit of the gains they shelter.

Though fund directors can vote to make the distributions at any time, tax considerations result in distributions piling up toward the end of the year. Some funds have a policy of making quarterly income distributions and some may make capital gains distributions at least once during the year. But if a fund has any income or gains to distribute, you can count on most funds making payouts in December. Sometimes the distribution may even be declared on December 31 and not paid until January. That doesn't get shareholders out of paying taxes on it for the year that ended in December.

Mutual fund companies usually mail form 1099-DIVs to shareholders by the end of January. This form reports dividend distributions, capital gains distributions—broken out to show those that are short-term and those that are long-term—and, if applicable, taxes paid to foreign governments. (That may come into play in international funds.) Nontaxable distributions should

> Mutual fund distributions bunch up at year-end.

be noted here, too. Check the figures against your own records and make sure they're correct. The numbers you see on the form are the same numbers that the IRS is going to see.

Ducking the Distribution

It's a good idea to start checking with funds around Thanksgiving to ask about upcoming distributions. A customer service representative will usually know if a distribution is planned. Sometimes the fund management company will announce the exact date and the per-share distribution rate. Some will give shareholders who ask an estimate of the time and the amount to be paid. You may have to keep calling until you get the information. The funds themselves often don't know the date and size of the distribution until late into the year.

Remember the brouhaha around the Fidelity Magellan Fund in late 1994? What had happened was that Fidelity, as is common practice, told investors in November that Magellan would make a $4.32 per-share capital gains distribution in December. No doubt some Magellan investors may have made tax-related moves, such as selling Magellan or taking losses in other funds to shelter the Magellan gain. Three weeks later, Fidelity said oops, we made a mistake. There isn't going to be a distribution.

The incident was a stunner, not because anybody lost any real money, but because the large estimation error—in excess of $2 billion—was in the largest equity fund and was made by the largest mutual fund management company. But fortunately, such errors about distributions are rare and, needless to say, Fidelity and others are going to be double, triple, and quadruple checking those estimates in the future.

There are several good reasons to obtain the distribution information near the end of the year. First, if you are planning any new fund investments, you have to be careful about purchasing shares right before the distribution dates. You could end up getting a distribution of profits earned long before you ever invested in the fund (see Chapter 4).

You may also want to get out of a fund ahead of the distribution date, for much the same reason. For instance, just look back at 1996. Suppose you had invested in a small-cap growth fund in the spring. Pretend for a moment you paid $10 a share.

Then move ahead to early December when the fund has lost 20 percent of what you paid for it. But remember that early in the year the market rallied. What if the fund manager had used the rally to take some profits amounting to $1 per share? The fund would have to distribute those profits before the end of the year. If you still owned the fund, you would be hit with a taxable distribution of capital gains. You would be stuck paying taxes on gains, but your investment, so far, is actually showing a loss.

That's why you should consider selling the fund before the distribution. If you do so, you can realize a tax-deductible loss. Then you have one of two alternatives. If you want to remain fully invested, you can switch to a fund with a similar investment policy—but after that fund has made its distributions for the year. Or, you can stay on the sidelines for 31 days and then return to your fund. The risk in that ploy is that the fund will go up in price a bit before you can get back in. The IRS says you have to wait 31 days before buying back a fund sold for a tax loss—otherwise the loss will be disallowed as a deduction.

Tax Swapping

As the year rolls to a close, some investors like to do "tax swapping." The term comes from the bond market, but can apply to any investment. The idea is to look for a fund in which you may have an unrealized loss and then sell the fund to take the loss and generate a tax deduction. At the same time, you move a like amount of money into a mutual fund with characteristics similar to the one just sold (Table 6-1). The idea is to take advantage of your losses—make the best of a bad situation—while keeping your investment program in place.

Swapping within the same fund family is easiest. In large fund families there is often more than one fund with similar objectives. You may want to switch the Fidelity Contrafund for the Fidelity Magellan Fund. They're both mid-cap blend funds. Fidelity Equity–Income and Equity–Income II, as their names might suggest, are also interchangeable.

Load fund investors should find it most practical to remain within their fund groups. Investors are usually able to switch load funds without paying another load, as long as the load of the new

TABLE 6-1

SAVING ON TAXES BY SWAPPING FUNDS

If you have a loss in a mutual fund, you may want to sell it for a tax loss. If so, you may want to shift the money into a similar fund so as not to change your investment goals. The funds within each grouping have similar investment policies and risk profiles. They can make suitable swaps.

FUNDS	COMMENTS
FIDELITY CONTRAFUND FIDELITY MAGELLAN JANUS MERCURY JANUS OLYMPUS	Contrafund is probably most like Magellan for those who want to switch under the Fidelity umbrella. Likewise, these Janus funds are similar enough to do the same.
FIDELITY EQUITY-INCOME FIDELITY EQUITY-INCOME II VANGUARD/WINDSOR VANGUARD/WINDSOR II	Clone funds can make good swap candidates. These Fidelity equity–income funds are fairly similar. Likewise, the two Vanguard funds invest in large-cap value stocks.
FIDELITY EMERGING MARKETS LEXINGTON WORLDWIDE EMERGING MARKETS T. ROWE PRICE INTERNATIONAL SCUDDER INTERNATIONAL	The two emerging markets funds, though offered by different companies, should be similar enough for tax-swapping. The T. Rowe Price and Scudder international funds have similar portfolio characteristics.
TEMPLETON GROWTH TEMPLETON VALUE TEMPLETON WORLD	Many Templeton equity funds are interchangeable. The Developing Markets, Foreign, Real Estate, and Small Companies funds are unique, and are not interchangeable with each other nor other Templeton funds.
BABSON ENTERPRISE II FIDELITY LOW-PRICED STOCK HEARTLAND SMALL-CAP CONTRARIAN ROYCE VALUE	These funds are all from the small-cap value category. Their companies are usually prosaic rather than cutting edge, but that doesn't mean they can't make money for mutual fund shareholders.
AIM CONSTELLATION AIM GROWTH AMER. CENT.–20TH CENT. VISTA INVESTORS BERGER 100	These funds comb the market for companies with earnings momentum, and they try to hang on to them as long as earnings growth is accelerating. The AIM funds are load, American Century and Berger, no-load.
BABSON BOND FIDELITY INTERMEDIATE BOND VANGUARD BOND INDEX TOTAL MARKET	Swapping bond funds is easier than equity, since these funds usually have easily identifiable investment characteristics such as maturity, credit quality, and tax status.
INVESCO HIGH-YIELD T. ROWE PRICE HIGH-YIELD VANGUARD FIXED-INCOME HIGH-YIELD	All high-yield, or junk bond funds, are not alike. These all have the reputation for investing in "better quality" junk bonds.

DATA: MORNINGSTAR INC., BUSINESS WEEK

fund is less than or equal to the old one. For instance, if an investor moves her money from a fund on which she paid a 4 percent load into another fund in the same family that has a 5.5 percent load, she will probably have to pay only a 1.5 percent load to make up the difference.

Some advisers discourage investors from swapping funds purely for tax purposes. If a swap triggers redemption fees or new sales charges, that has to be figured in to determine whether there would be any benefit from the trade. If, on the other hand, you can justify selling one fund and buying another as a good investment decision, then the ability to save some money on taxes takes a little of the bite out of the loss.

What's My "Cost Basis"?

Mention the term "cost basis," and eyes glaze over. But it's not a big deal. It's just a measure of how much money you put into an investment. If you bought 100 shares of General Motors at $40 per share and paid the broker a $50 commission, your cost basis is $40.50 per share, or $4050.

In just the same way, loads and redemption fees work their way into the cost basis for funds. If you paid a 6 percent load when you bought the fund, that was already figured into your purchase price. So you don't need to adjust for that. Suppose you sell shares and there's a 1 percent redemption fee. If your shares were sold for $5000, a 1 percent exit charge would take $50 out of your proceeds. So your net is $4950, not $5000.

What's complicated about mutual fund record-keeping is that most people don't buy nice round lots, like 100 shares. Many invest a nice round amount, like $1000 or $10,000. Odds are that most shareholders end up with some odd number of shares, with fractional shares rounded off to three decimal places.

Those who reinvest dividends and capital gains must count them when computing their cost basis. Reinvesting a taxable distribution is the same as putting new money into the fund. Forget to include those distributions in the cost basis, and you can wind up paying too much tax. For the most part, investors or their tax advisers are usually on their own when calculating their cost basis. Many companies are starting to provide average cost data—and that's a big help. But hold on to your records, you may need to do it yourself.

What if you don't have good records? Most fund companies will help to reconstruct transaction history records by providing copies of past statements. Depending on the fund, and how many years' worth of data you need, you may be charged a nominal fee for the service.

Suppose you sell all the shares in a mutual fund account. It's easy to compute your cost basis. Add up all the money you invested either directly or through dividend reinvestment. That's the total cost. Then, divide that sum by the number of shares you have. That's the average cost per share. To figure your gain or loss, subtract the cost from proceeds of the sale. If you have shares in the account that are both long-term (held for more than one year) and short-term (less than a year), be sure to note that, even if you use the same cost basis for both kinds of shares. This information is reported on Schedule D of the 1040, the individual's tax return. (This method of computation is also known as the "average cost" or "single-category" method, and we'll come back to it later.)

You can take this average cost approach a step further, to the "double-category" method. Under this tax treatment, you calculate separate cost bases for the long-term shares and for the short-term shares. This method demands extra work, but may be worthwhile for investors who are in tax brackets of 31 percent or higher. (For single taxpayers, that's taxable income of $53,500 or

more; for married persons filing jointly, $89,150 or more.) That's because while the tax rate on short-term gains is the same as on your salary and investment earnings like dividends and interest, the rate on long-term capital gains is capped at 28 percent. If you have gains, most likely the biggest gains are in the shares held long-term, so you should allocate most of the gains to these shares. If you use the average-cost method, you'll end up putting more of the gain on the short-term shares, and that will result in a bigger tax bite.

The tax situation gets stickier if some but not all the shares are sold. Look at Table 6-2. Suppose that on October 25, 1994 the fund's NAV is $10.25, your average cost is $11.11 per share, and you're considering selling some shares. You think you have a taxable loss of $0.86 per share. But that's only if you liquidate the entire account.

If you make a partial redemption and don't specify any specific method you wish to use to calculate your gains and losses, the IRS will assume the first shares in are the first shares out. Suppose you ask the fund for a $2000 redemption. That would result in the sale of 195.122 shares ($2000 divided by $10.25). The IRS would assume those shares were from the first 200 shares bought on February 15, 1993 at $10 per share. Even though you have a loss on the entire investment, selling those shares even at October 25's depressed price would result in a small taxable gain.

But there are alternatives. You could sell shares in a way that would generate a tax-deductible loss. Go back to your average cost per share, $11.11. You can use the single- or double-category methods to calculate the tax liability on partial redemptions. (Remember that you have to note which method you're using on your tax return.) Sell $2000 worth of shares by the single-category method and, instead of a gain, you get a tax loss of $168. That's better, isn't it?

Finally, there's the "specific shares" method, which is perhaps the best approach. But it takes some planning. You must designate in writing which shares are to be sold, and do so in advance of the transaction. The advantage of this method is you can pinpoint the highest-cost shares, those purchased on June 2 and September 28, 1993, and July 6, 1994. The share prices paid on all three dates are higher than today's NAV. By selling these shares, you can redeem $2951, with a tax deductible loss of $549.

Don't forget that with the specific shares method—as with all the options—once you choose to redeem shares in a fund under this

Good records are really valuable at tax time.

TABLE 6-2

CALCULATING TAXABLE GAINS AND LOSSES

On Oct. 25, 1994, the net asset value, or per-share price, is $10.25. The total value of your holdings is $6427.04. You are thinking about selling a part of your shares in the fund. There are several ways to compute your tax consequences. Your goal should be to minimize the tax bite.

Date of Purchase	Amount	Price/ Share	Shares purchased	Total shares
Feb. 15, 1993	$2000,00	$10.00	200.000	200.000
June 2	1000.00	11.75	85.106	285.106
Sept. 28	1500.00	12.25	122.449	407.555
Dec. 15	Income distribution $0.15 per share and capital gains of $1 per share			
Reinvest income	6.13	10.90	5.608	413.163
Reinvest capital gains	407.00	10.90	37.931	450.554
May 10, 1994	1000.00	10.40	96.154	546.708
July 6	1000.00	12.45	80.321	627.029
Totals	**$6968.69**		**Avg. price/share**	**$11.11**

If you are selling all the shares, you can choose from these methods:

SINGLE-CATEGORY Take the average cost of your shares, $11.11, and deduct the $10.25 that your shares are worth now. That's a loss of $0.86 per share. If all the shares have been held either long-term (more than a year) or short-term (less than a year) the loss would be 627.029 times $0.86, or $539.24. But in this case, 407.555 of the shares are long-term, and 219.474, short-term. Multiply each by $0.86, and you get a $350.50 long-term capital loss and a $188.75 short-term capital loss.

DOUBLE-CATEGORY In the prior method, you calculate an average cost and apply it equally to long-term and short-term shares. In the double-category method, you calculate an average cost for the long-term and an average cost for the short-term shares. There are 407.555 long-term shares that cost $4500, for an average cost of $11.04. These shares now show a $0.79 per share loss, for a long-term loss of $321.97. The others have an average cost of $11.25 per share, and show a $1 per share loss. The total short-term loss is $219.47.

If you are selling some but not all the shares, choose from these methods:

AVERAGE COST Using the single-category method to redeem $3000, you end up selling 292.683 shares at a loss of $0.86 each, for a long-term loss of $251.71. It's a long-term loss because the rules say that the oldest shares come out first.

SPECIFIC SHARES Direct the fund to sell the costliest shares, those bought on June 2 and Sept. 28 of 1993 and July 6, 1994. The June 2 shares are now worth $872.34, for a loss of $127.66; the Sept. 28 shares, $1255.10, for a loss of $244.90. Both are long-term losses. The July 6 shares, purchased for $1000, are worth $823.29, for a short-term loss of $176.71. Total redemptions, about $2951 with $949 in tax-deductible losses.

FIRST-IN, FIRST-OUT If you don't tell your mutual fund company which shares to sell, the IRS will assume the oldest shares are sold first. In the above example, the first 200 shares have a cost basis of $10 each. If you sell those shares at $10.25, you have a taxable gain of $0.25 a share on those first 200, or $50, even though the total investment is in the red. This is the least desirable method.

DATA: BUSINESS WEEK

method, all future redemptions must use the same method. You can't use specific shares this year and the single-category method next year.

Investors using the single-category or double-category methods to compute taxes should attach a note to their tax returns saying so. Those using first-in, first-out or the specific shares methods need not do so, but should maintain their records in case of an audit.

Keep in mind that there are rule changes from time to time, so it's best to consult with your accountant or tax adviser. It's also a good idea to call the Internal Revenue Service to get a free copy of Publication No. 564, "Mutual Fund Distributions," for the official treatment of the subject.

Tax-Deferred Investing

IRAS

Mutual fund companies make great places to open up individual retirement accounts (IRAs) and other retirement programs. The companies offer professional management, diversification, and a bent for long-term investing. Mutual fund executives love to rake in retirement dollars, since the money tends to stay in place and generate fees for years. Most fund management companies will shower you with plenty of literature on IRAs and the like, and they also have specialists on hand to explain some of the finer, more technical aspects of the programs. Fidelity Investments will even waive sales charges on many of its equity funds for IRA accounts.

Mutual fund companies manage a little more than $1 out of every $3 in IRAs, according to the Investment Company Institute. That's a larger share of the market than is held by either banks, savings and loans, or insurance companies. What the IRA holder gets from a mutual fund that he or she doesn't get from a depository institution is an enormous variety of investment options. (Remember, though, that mutual funds are not insured.) The only mutual funds that don't make good IRA investments are tax-exempt funds. If the interest is free from taxation, what's the point of sheltering it? It's better to shelter higher interest from otherwise taxable bond funds.

Not only does an IRA help save money for retirement, it produces tax savings, too. Taxpayers who qualify (more about that later) can put away up to $2000 a year tax free. That is, the $2000 is deducted from adjusted gross income in figuring your income tax. What's more, the earnings of your IRA are not taxed until you withdraw funds. So you don't have to worry about investing in a fund the day before a capital gains distribution or choosing the optimal method to compute your cost basis. Your cost basis is always zero.

If you never paid tax on the money you put into a plan, you pay tax when it comes out. Every dollar you put into a mutual fund IRA (or any IRA for that matter) and every dollar it earns while it's in the IRA is fully taxable when it comes out. Taxpayers can start withdrawing money from their IRAs when they are 59½ years old, and must start withdrawals by the time they are 70½.

Taxpayers have over $1 trillion salted away in IRAs of all sorts, but unfortunately, many people are no longer making contributions. That's because the 1986 federal tax reforms—which lowered tax rates—cut back on eligibility. Between 1982 and 1986—the golden era of IRAs—all income earners could put up to $2000 a year into a retirement account and deduct the contribution from their income.

The 1986 act changed the program significantly. Now, a person who is covered by an employer-sponsored retirement plan, or whose spouse is covered by such a plan, has stricter eligibility requirements. To take advantage of the full $2000 deduction (a married couple with one spouse working outside the home can go up to $4000), taxpayers must have an adjusted gross income of no more than $25,000 for a single or $40,000 for a married person filing jointly. The deduction phases out for singles with incomes between $25,000 and $35,000 and couples with incomes between $40,000 and $50,000, though the law allows for some nondeductible IRA contributions. Singles with incomes above $35,000 and couples in excess of $50,000 cannot contribute to deductible IRAs but may be eligible to contribute up to $2000 ($4000 for couples) a year to nondeductible IRAs. In such an IRA, the contribution is not deductible but, as in a deductible IRA, the earnings are not taxed until the money is withdrawn. Those not covered by employer-sponsored retirement plans can still salt away up to $2000 a year tax free no matter what the income level.

Millions who no longer contribute to IRAs still have the accounts. Perhaps you have an IRA at a local bank earning a measly rate of interest. You can move the account to a mutual fund or group of funds. Ask the mutual fund company to send you the applications and the transfer documents, and give them to the institution from which you wish to withdraw your IRA. (If you withdraw a certificate of deposit before maturity, you may owe a penalty to the bank.)

The bank will send you the funds, or you can instruct the institution to transfer the funds directly to the new mutual fund company. Make sure the money is reinvested in another IRA within 60 days, or the government will assume you made a premature withdrawal and hit you for tax and a penalty. Moving an IRA from one institution to another is called a "rollover."

Persons who will be receiving their pension benefit in a lump sum distribution because they're either retiring or changing jobs are especially in need of some advance planning. Unless the money is transferred directly from the employer into an IRA or other qualified pension plan, the distribution will be subject to a 20 percent withholding tax. Those hit with the special tax then have 60 days to put the money into an IRA rollover—or face additional taxes, including a 10 percent penalty for persons less than 59½ years old. If you need help with a rollover, most any mutual fund company will walk you through it.

Pay IRA fees out of your checkbook.

Whatever sort of tax-deferred retirement account you have with a mutual fund company, you may have to pay an annual IRA "custodial" or "maintenance" fee. The fee, which takes care of the additional paperwork of an IRA, is typically $10 a year per fund (or much higher at a full-service brokerage firm), but competition for the retirement accounts is so keen that many companies are starting to waive the custodial fee for all accounts over a certain size, say $5000 or $10,000.

Many mutual fund companies send a bill for the annual fee. If the bill's not paid by the due date, the management company will deduct it from the account. If you don't get a bill, ask the fund company when the fee is due. Make plans to pay the fee out of your checkbook and not out of the retirement account. Since contributions to IRAs are limited, you don't want to take anything out of the account if you can avoid it.

KEOGH PLANS

The IRA isn't the only kind of retirement program offered by mutual fund companies. Funds also hold about one-third of the money invested in retirement plans by the self-employed. Commonly known as Keogh plans, these plans are far more generous, allowing the self-employed to stash away as much as 20 percent of their income, up to $30,000, and deduct it from the current year's taxes. These are far more complicated than the simple IRA, and get even trickier when the self-employed person has employees, too. Consult an accountant or tax adviser before starting one of these programs.

There are several varieties of Keogh. The program that allows the largest contribution (and highest deduction) is least flexible, and the contribution must be made every year. Other programs are less demanding, but the maximum contribution is less, too. There's also the Simplified Employee Pension—Individual Retirement Account, otherwise known as SEP or SEP-IRA. The employer can contribute up to $30,000, or 15 percent of the employee's compensation, whichever is less.

401(K) PLANS

Mutual funds offer the increasingly popular 401(k) plan. Unfortunately, as an employee, you cannot start a 401(k) program for yourself; your employer has to do it. You can ask the company to offer a plan with the investment options coming from a mutual fund family. One of the features that makes 401(k)s different from conventional corporate pension plans is that the employee gets

to choose how the money is invested. That's why mutual funds make excellent homes for 401(k) plans. Look at the array of choices (though not every fund in every group of funds may be eligible for the program). Mutual funds can also service 403(b) plans, which are similar to the 401(k), except they are exclusively for the employees of certain charitable organizations or public school systems.

In such plans, an employee can choose to place up to 10 percent of his or her income (subject to a limit which is adjusted annually) in the 401(k) plan. The employee's taxable income is then reduced by the amount of money contributed to the account. In addition, employers often "match" employee contributions in part or in full. The earnings of the 401(k) account are also tax-deferred until the money is withdrawn at retirement.

VARIABLE ANNUITIES

Imagine owning a mutual fund that paid interest, dividends, and capital gains, and not having to pay any tax year to year. You can't take the money out until you're at least 59½, or you pay a tax penalty, and perhaps a penalty to the fund company, too. Isn't this a mutual fund IRA? No, but you're close.

It's a variable annuity, and it's growing in popularity. Most major mutual fund companies offer variable annuities or manage variable annuity investment for insurance companies. The prime customers for variable annuities are mutual fund investors within 20 years of retirement who have assets they can sock away until then and who can benefit from the tax deferral on investment income. Many baby-boomers already fit that category, and more will in coming years.

The variable annuity probably sounds a lot like an IRA or a 401(k) plan, but with several critical differences. For starters, the contributions are not tax deductible. But unlike the IRA or 401(k), there is no limit to what an investor can put into the annuity.

What's also important is that the costs of investing in a variable annuity can be significantly higher than in comparable mutual funds. Depending on the annuity plan, the investor who cashes out before retirement may still pay a load, or a redemption or surrender charge. The redemption charge for some annuity products can be as high as 10 percent—and that's before any tax consequences. Don't invest in these annuities unless you're 99 percent sure you're not going to need the money for at least a decade. In

Variable annuities look much like mutual funds.

addition, the portfolio management expenses may be higher for annuity funds than they are for comparable mutual funds, since the annuity funds are usually smaller in size and don't enjoy the same economies of scale.

Finally, there's an annuity charge or "wrapper," which pays for a guarantee provided by an insurance company. The guarantee, which on average costs 1.24 percent per year, merely assures the investor's heirs that in case he or she dies while the annuity is in force, the annuity will be worth at least as much as what was put in. (That's why variable annuities have to be offered by a life insurance company.)

This feature would have come in handy for the heirs of someone who had invested in a variable annuity with equity funds in January 1994, and died in April, when the investment might have been worth 20 percent less. As a practical matter, this insurance is only worthwhile in the first few years of the investment.

After all, if the annuity is worth less than the investment after 10 or 20 years, you chose the wrong annuity. Annuity buyers can't elect to waive this guarantee. It's the distinguishing feature that makes it an annuity—a life insurance product that allows the earnings to build up on a tax-deferred basis. Some annuities now have a "step-up" provision which keeps raising the guaranteed death benefit. But that isn't free. Such annuities have higher fees.

The variable annuities may look—and behave—much like mutual funds, but the terminology is a little different. A mutual fund that's connected to a variable annuity is a "subaccount." There are no fund shares in a variable annuity; instead, the worth of the investment is tracked in "accumulation unit value," which, for practical purposes, is the same thing. The average variable annuity has seven subaccount options.

Because of the higher fees and surrender charges, the variable annuity only makes sense as a truly long-term investment. It is often sold as a tax shelter (remember the earnings of the investment are not taxed until withdrawal), but it's really best used as a long-term savings vehicle.

Morningstar classifies the variable annuity subaccounts as it does for equity and bond mutual funds. But there are a few exceptions. All the domestic equity categories are the same, except for specialty subaccounts. There are only enough subaccounts to justify natural resources, real estate, and utilities categories. All other specialized funds are lumped into an "unaligned" grouping. For international equity, Morningstar uses the broader foreign, world, diversified emerging markets categories and international hybrid categories, and foregoes the regional funds. Among the bond subaccounts, there's long-, intermediate-, and short-term general bond and government bond categories, plus high-yield, international, and money-market. For yield-oriented investors, most variable annuities also have a "fixed" account option, which works much like a bank CD.

Selecting a variable annuity takes all the same savvy as choosing a mutual fund—and then some. You are not only buying an investment vehicle, but an insurance wrapper as well. And you can often get many of the same investment funds inside different wrappers. For instance, Fidelity Retirement Reserves is a series of variable annuity portfolios that are managed much like their Fidelity mutual fund counterparts. You can call a Fidelity 800 number or drop in at a Fidelity investor center and obtain the prospectus and the application for the Fidelity variable annuity with the insurance wrapper coming from Fidelity's own insurance company.

But Fidelity also makes those same funds available in other insurors' products. The top-performing Fidelity VIP Fund Equity–Income subaccount is available in 94 different variable annuity products offered by Aetna Life & Casualty, Life of Virginia Commonwealth, Nationwide Life Insurance, and dozens of other companies. What's different? For one, the service. If you buy the annuity direct from Fidelity, you're pretty much on your own. On the other hand, if you buy the fund through an annuity sold by a life insurance agent, you get the agent to help you choose the fund and monitor performance.

What else is different? The cost. Most annuities are sold without a front-end load. But the redemption fees and insurance costs can vary greatly. (Portfolio expense, the cost of running the investment itself, is the same no matter which insurance company offers the fund.) If you invest in the Fidelity Equity–Income annuity subaccount through Fidelity's Retirement Reserves variable annuity, the insurance expense is 1 percent a year, contract fee $30 a year, and there's a 5 percent declining surrender charge in the first year, declining 1 percent a year for five years. Purchased through Nationwide's Best of America annuity, the contract fee is $30. But the other charges are much higher: 1.40 percent a year for insurance expense, and a surrender charge starts at 7 percent and declines 1 percent a year for seven years.

If you're seriously considering an annuity and don't need a salesperson to help you, look into the

> Watch out for high fees on variable annuities.

low-cost annuity products from Vanguard, Scudder, T. Rowe Price, and Charles Schwab. There are no loads or surrender charges on the policies. Insurance expenses are low, too—0.85 percent in the Schwab plan, 0.70 percent in Scudder, and 0.55 percent in T. Rowe Price. Vanguard and Schwab charge a $25 a year contract fee, while Scudder and T. Rowe Price don't charge at all. Minimum investments are $2500 at Scudder, $5000 at Schwab and Vanguard, and $10,000 for T. Rowe Price.

Before investing in any variable annuity, compare the annuity's investment options to a similar, taxable mutual fund. You may find the higher charges and loss of financial flexibility may weigh heavier in your decisions than the opportunity to defer taxes on the fund's earnings. If you would choose a maximum growth or small company fund for the annuity, the deferral may not be worth it. Most aggressive funds don't earn enough dividend income to distribute, and capital gains distributions are not that frequent. Want a government bond fund for your variable annuity? In that case, don't even bother. Buy municipal bond funds. The income is tax-exempt, there are no annuity charges to pay, and you can get your money out when you want it, without paying a tax penalty.

Variable annuities make most sense for investment options that would generate a lot of income in a taxable account—like high-yield bond and equity-income funds. They're also practical if you are an investor who likes to make frequent shifts between investments—moves that become taxable events when done outside the tax shelter of an annuity or qualified retirement program.

In pitching a costly annuity, some salespersons will play up the annuitizing feature. They'll say that when it's time to swap the nest egg for an annuity—a guaranteed stream of payments—their company is the most generous. That may be so, but you don't have to buy their variable annuity. When you're investing for retirement, buy the variable annuity that makes the most investment sense. When it comes time to annuitize, you can always switch the money to another company. And many annuities never get annuitized—people take a lump sum, make periodic withdrawals, or leave the money to their estate.

Using the BW Scoreboard

The BUSINESS WEEK Mutual Fund Scoreboard works like a road map of the mutual fund world. It provides tons of information about returns, fees, sales charges, and risk that should help you avoid hazards and dead ends on your financial journey. But even with the best of road maps, you still need to have some map-reading skills. That's the point of this chapter.

The equity Scoreboard takes in 885 equity funds. That's not every one. We don't include funds that are only open to institutions. Nor do we include more than one class of shares of funds with multiple share classes. The variation between share classes of the same fund is a function of fees, not portfolio performance. The underlying investments are the same. After excluding the institutional funds and duplicative classes of shares, we rank the remaining funds in descending order by asset size. This year, the smallest fund is Prudential Global Genesis B, with $131.3 million.

The bond fund Scoreboard takes in 653 funds. They're selected by asset size too, though the selection process is designed to include categories, like international and convertible, in which the size of the funds tends to be smaller. As with equities, we screen out institutional funds and duplicative classes of funds. The closed-end fund Scoreboard has 120 equity funds and 140 bond funds.

At the start of each Scoreboard there's a summary description of the sort of data that are under each column heading. In this chapter we'll take a more in-depth look at some of the headings. For a thorough discussion of the terms under the heading "Objective," please refer to Chapter 2.

Ratings

The first column after the fund's name is the overall rating. Three upward-pointing arrows is the highest accolade, signifying superior performance. Two upward arrows is very good, and one, above average. Then comes average (abbreviated as "AVG"), which you can also read as neutral. Next come the subpar categories: one downward arrow for below-average performance, two for poor performance, and three for very poor performance (Figure 7-1).

There are many funds with returns that look very good, yet their ratings are average at best. At the same time, there are highly rated funds with seemingly so-so returns. The reason for this is simple. BUSINESS WEEK ratings don't merely reward funds for winning the year's best-performance contest. You don't need a ratings system for that because the returns tell all. What the BW ratings system asks is not only how much money a fund made for its shareholders, but also how much risk the fund took in the process.

In rating fund performance we define risk as the potential for losing money. In the strict sense, risk goes both ways. A fund can be said to have high risk if it is volatile—net asset values swing wildly to the upside as well as the down. But as a practical matter, an investor would not complain if a fund appreciated twice as fast as the S&P 500. He or she may accept—but won't like—the fact that the fund has fallen twice as much as the S&P 500. So the ratings, which are calculated by Morningstar, Inc., don't penalize a fund for upside volatility.

To come up with fund ratings, we measure a fund's last five years of returns. (For closed-end funds, we measure the last three years.) For the overall BW rating, the returns are calculated assuming that you paid the maximum sales charge, or load, if applicable. Obviously this gives the no-load funds a head start on the load funds, since an investor who pays a 5 percent up-front sales charge has to earn 5.26 percent just to break even. (That's right, 5.26 percent. A 6 percent load would reduce a $1000 investment to

FIGURE 7-1

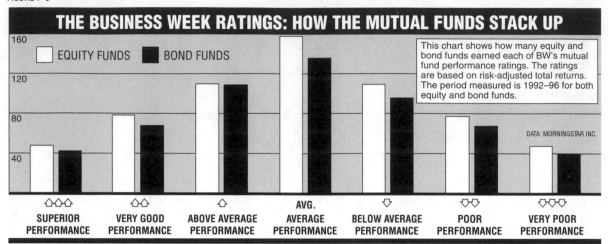

THE BUSINESS WEEK RATINGS: HOW THE MUTUAL FUNDS STACK UP

□ EQUITY FUNDS   ■ BOND FUNDS

This chart shows how many equity and bond funds earned each of BW's mutual fund performance ratings. The ratings are based on risk-adjusted total returns. The period measured is 1992–96 for both equity and bond funds.

DATA: MORNINGSTAR INC.

| △△△ SUPERIOR PERFORMANCE | △△ VERY GOOD PERFORMANCE | △ ABOVE AVERAGE PERFORMANCE | AVG. AVERAGE PERFORMANCE | ▽ BELOW AVERAGE PERFORMANCE | ▽▽ POOR PERFORMANCE | ▽▽▽ VERY POOR PERFORMANCE |

$950. To get back to $1000, the investor would have to earn 5.26 percent.)

If a fund hasn't been in operation long enough to be rated, we still report on it, provided it meets the asset size criteria. We insist on a minimum track record before we rate a fund so we can track the fund's behavior under varying economic conditions. For instance, the 1997 equity fund ratings cover the period 1992 through 1996. We see fund performance under a variety of conditions: a drawn-out economic recovery, a robust expansion, and slower but steady growth; a bout of falling interest rates and rising ones; and disinflation and fears of an acceleration of inflation.

To derive the BW rating, we start with the fund's five-year total return. (These numbers are under the column heading "Average Annual Total Returns (%)." We then adjust the pure performance number by subtracting the "risk-of-loss" factor. (See the section, "Risk," later in this chapter.)

The funds are then rated based on a statistical distribution. The top 7.5 percent of the funds get the highest rating, three up-arrows. The next 12.5 percent of the funds get two up-arrows, and the following 17.5 percent, one up-arrow. Then there's the group in the middle—the average funds. This is the largest group, with 25 percent of the ratings. The ratings are symmetrical on the negative side: There are as many funds with three down-arrows as there are with three up-arrows. There is an exception. To get a positive rating, an equity fund must also beat the S&P 500 on a risk-adjusted basis.

The risk adjustment can change a fund's place in the line-up considerably. Adjusting high-return funds for their high risks might bring them down to the middle of the pack. Likewise, more modest performers with very low risk profiles often end up a lot higher in the relative standings after the adjustment is made.

The bond fund Scoreboard rates municipal bond funds against other muni funds rather than comparing them to all the other bond funds, which are taxable. If not for the separation, muni funds would always be at a disadvantage since, as tax-exempts, their yields are lower than those of comparable taxable bonds.

For most of the Scoreboard's history, the three-up-arrow equity funds have tended to have low or very low risk ratings. But in the late 1980s, the Japan Fund and Merrill Lynch Pacific Fund, for instance, captured top honors for several years even with their high risk levels. The same thing happenned with some technology and health funds in the 1990s. Their performances were so strong that even the fairly stiff risk-of-loss factor wasn't enough to knock them out of the top ratings group.

Should you invest in only the top-rated funds? It's a good place to start your search. But don't end it there. Suppose your investment plan shows you have a long time horizon and a good tolerance for risk. Then you would want to have some small-cap growth, mid-cap growth, and foreign funds as well. But right now, there are no small-cap growth, mid-cap growth, or foreign funds with three-up-arrow overall ratings. That will not always be the case, but it is now, owing to the market conditions of the last several years.

That's why we have developed category ratings as well. We approach category ratings the same way as overall BW ratings. The only difference is that the funds are rated against one another within a single category instead of against all other Scoreboard funds. This second layer of ratings makes it easier to identify funds with good risk-adjusted returns compared to their peers, even if they are not particularly good compared to all funds.

The most extreme case of this is, of course, the precious metals funds. Every one of the 14 funds has a three-down-arrow rating when compared to all funds. But comparing these funds only to one another, we find two that earned three upward-pointing arrows, the Midas Fund and the Scudder Gold Fund. Then there's United Services Gold Shares, which has a three-down-arrow category rating as well. That makes it about the worst of the worst in the Scoreboard.

Not everyone wants to invest in a precious metals fund. But these category ratings have more mainstream applications as well. For instance, in the 1992–1996 period, not one growth fund, either small-cap, mid-cap, or large-cap, earned three up-arrows for the overall rating. But investors still want to own these sorts of funds, and the category rating helps to identify the best of them. There are three large-cap growth, five mid-cap growth, and three small-cap growth funds with three-up-arrow category ratings. And with the category ratings, we have also identified three foreign and two world funds with superior returns. We've done category ratings with bond funds as well.

There is a caveat with category ratings. There aren't ratings for every category. To calculate category ratings, a category needs to have at least seven funds (we have seven levels in the ratings system) with five years of performance data (the number of years we require for ratings). In the 1997 Scoreboard, we had 10 diversified emerging markets funds, but only six with five years of performance history. As a result, we could not perform a category rating on these funds. But we should be able to do so in 1998, when we rate returns for the 1993–1997 period.

What if the overall BW rating of one of your funds declines? That's not necessarily a sign that you should dump the fund. Sometimes funds will decline in ranking not so much from their own performance, but from the relatively stronger returns of others. What you should check is whether the fund is underperforming the other funds in its category. Then, you have to do a little investigation as to why the fund underperformed, and you may determine you want to sell.

The one problem with this ratings system is endemic in all performance measurements. They are based on past performance, which is not necessarily the best predictor of the future. But we do know that there is a tendency for winners to repeat and for funds' risk profiles to stay fairly constant. Depending on the funds, the investment style can be constant as well. In that sense, a thorough assessment of past performance can be useful in investing for the future. The past may not be perfect, but it's the only data we have. What counts is how you use it.

Size

For many years the conventional wisdom held that great mutual funds grew into mediocre ones. Here's why. Suppose a fund manager builds an enviable track record with a small fund. The fund gets bigger through appreciation of the assets. But, more important, investors begin to notice it or the fund manager buys big ads to herald his or her success. Money pours in and the fund manager who was a whiz with a $10 million portfolio now has to find enough attractive stocks to fill a $100 million portfolio.

Rapid growth of assets can sometimes undermine the very success that generated the growth. Perhaps a portfolio manager can keep performing nearly as well at $100 million, but can he or

TABLE 7-1

THE LARGEST EQUITY FUNDS

Fund	Assets (Millions)*
FIDELITY MAGELLAN	$53,988.7
INVESTMENT COMPANY OF AMERICA	30,875.5
VANGUARD INDEX 500	30,331.9
WASHINGTON MUTUAL INVESTORS	25,374.5
FIDELITY GROWTH & INCOME	23,896.5
FIDELITY CONTRAFUND	23,797.9
FIDELITY PURITAN	18,501.7
AMERICAN CENTURY—20TH CENT. ULTRA INV.	18,418.6
VANGUARD/WINDSOR	16,738.1
INCOME FUND OF AMERICA	16,192.2
VANGUARD/WELLINGTON	16,189.7
JANUS	15,890.3
EUROPACIFIC GROWTH	15,726.6
VANGUARD/WINDSOR II	15,700.0
FIDELITY ADVISOR GROWTH OPPORTUNITIES T	15,527.9
FIDELITY EQUITY-INCOME II	15,238.4
FIDELITY EQUITY-INCOME	14,258.9
NEW PERSPECTIVE	12,895.0
PUTNAM FUND FOR GROWTH & INCOME A	12,305.5
DEAN WITTER DIVIDEND GROWTH	12,151.2

*As of Dec. 31, 1996   DATA: MORNINGSTAR INC.

she sustain the pace at $500 million? That depends on the manager and the nature of the stocks invested in. If his or her success has been built on finding little gems and buying them before they're "discovered" by Wall Street, it's going to be difficult. The manager might find enough of them to make an impact on a $100 million portfolio. But the available supply of great little stocks is not going to expand. If anything, the supply could diminish, as others, seeing the success, rush to buy the same sorts of stocks. At $200 million, the portfolio manager is going to have a tough time finding the same kind of investment opportunities that made the fund so successful when it was below $100 million.

The portfolio manager will usually have to start making investments in companies larger than those on which he or she built this reputation. That isn't necessarily bad, but it does change the nature of the portfolio. Or, to get enough small stocks into the portfolio, it might be necessary to lower the standards for the kinds of stocks bought. That isn't good.

If the fund primarily invests in blue-chip and large-capitalization stocks, a fund's size is less of a problem. A $1 billion blue-chip fund may not be any less nimble than a $100 million one. And for fixed-income funds, in which the fund's expenses often make the difference between superior or mediocre results, size can be a help rather than a hindrance.

Of course, the legendary Peter Lynch challenged that wisdom with Fidelity Magellan Fund. Mutual fund analysts and the financial press had predicted the fund's stellar performance would poop out when the fund reached $1 billion in assets. Before Lynch retired in 1990, the fund was nearly $14 billion. In 1993, for instance, Fidelity Magellan had more than doubled the return of the S&P 500—and it started the year with $22.3 billion. By year-end, the fund was at $31.7 billion. True, Magellan's best days came before it was a billion-dollar fund. But since then its record has been far better than funds a fraction of its size. By the end of 1995, Magellan was $53.7 billion.

While Fidelity Magellan is still the largest fund by far, there are some other fast-growing megafunds. The assets of Investment Co. of America, the second-largest fund at $20.9 billion (Table 7-1) grew by 20 percent in 1996. And though bond funds are, on average, larger than equity funds, none comes close to Magellan in size (Table 7-2).

There are some drawbacks to being a small equity fund. Expense ratios for small funds are

TABLE 7-2

THE LARGEST BOND FUNDS

Fund ▼	Assets (Millions)* ▼
FRANKLIN CA TAX-FREE INCOME I	$13,685.9
FRANKLIN U.S. GOVERNMENT SECURITIES I	10,001.8
VANGUARD FIXED-INCOME GNMA	7,398.8
FRANKLIN FEDERAL TAX-FREE INCOME	7,032.0
BOND FUND OF AMERICA	7,002.4
DEAN WITTER U.S. GOVERNMENT SECURITIES	6,422.4
VANGUARD MUNI. INTERMEDIATE-TERM	6,122.9
IDS HIGH-YIELD TAX-EXEMPT A	5,927.8
AARP GNMA & U.S. TREASURY	4,826.1
FRANKLIN NY TAX-FREE INCOME I	4,770.7
VANGUARD F/I SHORT-TERM CORPORATE	4,587.5
MERRILL LYNCH CORPORATE HIGH-INCOME	4,528.6
FRANKLIN HIGH YIELD TAX-FREE	4,309.6
KEMPER U.S. GOVERNMENT SECURITIES A	3,966.2
OPPENHEIMER STRATEGIC INCOME A	3,667.1
DREYFUS MUNICIPAL BOND	3,603.7
VANGUARD F/I HIGH-YIELD CORPORATE	3,563.5
VANGUARD F/I LONG-TERM CORPORATE	3,412.0
PUTNAM HIGH YIELD A	3,263.2
KEMPER MUNICIPAL BOND A	3,254.9
PUTNAM CA TAX-EXEMPT INCOME A	3,174.4
FIDELITY INTERMEDIATE BOND	3,079.7
KEMPER HIGH-YIELD A	3,032.2
VANGUARD BOND INDEX TOTAL	2,952.8
NUVEEN MUNICIPAL BOND R	2,836.3

*As of Dec. 31, 1996   DATA: MORNINGSTAR INC.

almost invariably higher. That's because every fund has certain fixed costs like legal, audit, and registration fees that don't vary much with the size of the fund. Since small funds have fewer assets over which to spread these fixed costs, shareholders in small funds bear higher expenses than those in larger funds.

One other note about asset size. Along with the one-year total return figure, asset size can be used to ascertain how much new money has been added to the fund over the last year. Suppose the fund assets grew 50 percent over the last year. If the fund had a 30 percent total return, figure that 30 percent of the growth came from appreciation and 20 percent from new investments.

If the fund had grown only 20 percent, that's an indication that more dollars went out than came in. This rough calculation works pretty well for equity funds, in which income and capital gains distributions are left to be reinvested. However, it may not work so well for bond funds, since investors who use them to supplement their incomes take the distributions in cash.

Fees

The sales charge is a critical matter for fund investors. Load, no-load, or low-load, it's all here. Some funds have a redemption charge instead of an up-front load. If so, the maximum redemption fee will be under this heading, along with an asterisk noting that it's a redemption fee rather than front-end load. All you need to know about sales charges is in Chapter 3.

Expense ratios are different from sales charges (Table 7-3). Whether or not a fund has a sales charge, it still costs to keep it going. Out of the fund's assets come ongoing costs for management, administration, printing, postage, lawyers, auditors, and the like. These costs are totaled and divided by the net assets in the fund. That's how funds come up with an expense ratio. Paying a load doesn't exempt shareholders from paying expenses, nor do no-load funds necessarily have higher expenses that make up for the lack of load.

Remember the hidden loads—the 12(b)-1 charges—discussed in Chapter 3? Just to recap, the 12(b)-1 fee—named for the SEC ruling that permitted it—allows fund management companies to dip into their assets to pay "distribution" costs. These funds can be used for advertising or marketing expenses, and often they're used to compensate brokers for selling the fund. Chances are, if the fund has an expense ratio of over 2 percent, it's either very small or it levies a 12(b)-1 fee. Those who take such fees are noted in the Scoreboard.

In general, smaller funds have higher expense ratios. That's because they have fewer assets over which to spread their costs. International funds have higher expenses than domestic, since operating overseas is more costly than at home. Some funds may show up with 0.00 percent expenses. That usually means the fund is new, and the management company is waiving fees and absorbing expenses to help the fund get started. In general, the equity funds with the lowest overhead are index funds. That's because index funds have virtually no management cost. The fund manager merely buys the stocks that are in the index, and sells them if they are dropped from the index. A computer can monitor the portfolio to make sure it's behaving like the underlying index.

The average expense ratio for the funds in the equity Scoreboard varies slightly year to year. (In 1996 it was 1.29 percent.) What this means to you is simple. About $1.29 out of every $100 goes toward expenses. Bond fund expenses, on aver-

TABLE 7-3

EXPENSE RATIOS: EQUITY FUNDS

Fund ▼	HIGHEST Expense ratio* ▼	Fund ▼	LOWEST Expense ratio* ▼
ALGER CAPITAL APPRECIATION	3.43%	T. ROWE PRICE SPECTRUM GROWTH	0.00%
PUTNAM INT'L. NEW OPPORTUNITY B	2.72	VANGUARD LIFESTRAT. CONSERV. GROWTH	0.00
MERRILL LYNCH LATIN AMERICA B	2.71	VANGUARD STAR	0.00
NEW USA GROWTH	2.69	VANGUARD LIFESTRAT. MODERATE GROWTH	0.00
AIM GLOBAL GROWTH B	2.64	VANGUARD LIFESTRAT. GROWTH	0.00
NEW ENGLAND STAR ADVISERS B	2.57	VANGUARD LIFESTRAT. INCOME	0.00
MERRILL LYNCH DEVELOPING CAPITAL MARKETS B	2.56	SSGA S&P 500 INDEX	0.18
MERRILL LYNCH HEALTHCARE B	2.55	VANGUARD INDEX GROWTH	0.20
MFS WORLD EQUITY B	2.55	VANGUARD TAX-MANAGED GROWTH & INCOME	0.20
ROBERTSON STEPHENS CONTRARIAN	2.54	VANGUARD INDEX 500	0.20
ARTISAN INTERNATIONAL	2.50	VANGUARD BALANCED INDEX	0.20
INVESCO ADVISOR MULTIFLEX C	2.50	VANGUARD INDEX VALUE	0.20
ALLIANCE TECHNOLOGY B	2.48	VANGUARD TAX-MANAGED CAP. APPREC.	0.20
EV MARATHON GREATER CHINA GROWTH	2.47	VANGUARD INDEX EXTENDED MARKET	0.25
RIGHTIME	2.47	VANGUARD INDEX TOTAL STOCK MARKET	0.25
DEAN WITTER PACIFIC GROWTH	2.45	BT INVESTMENT EQUITY 500	0.25
MFS WORLD GROWTH B	2.45	VANGUARD INDEX SMALL CAP	0.25
ALLIANCE PREMIER GROWTH B	2.43	VANGUARD/WINDSOR	0.29
KEYSTONE INTERNATIONAL	2.42	FEDERATED MAX-CAP INSTL.	0.31
DEAN WITTER WORLDWIDE INVESTMENT	2.41	VANGUARD/WELLINGTON	0.33

*1996, funds with little or no expenses may be funds of funds or subsidized by the fund companies   DATA: MORNINGSTAR INC.

TABLE 7-4

EXPENSE RATIOS: BOND FUNDS

Fund — HIGHEST	Expense ratio*	Fund — LOWEST	Expense ratio*
NEW YORK MUNI	3.64%	T. ROWE PRICE SPECTRUM INCOME	0.00%
ALLIANCE NORTH AMERICAN GOVT. INC. B	3.33	STRONG MUNICIPAL ADVANTAGE	0.00
G.T. GLOBAL HIGH-INCOME B	2.40	STRONG SHORT-TERM GLOBAL BOND	0.00
ALLIANCE MORTGAGE SECURITIES INC.	2.37	VANGUARD BOND INDEX INTERM.-TERM	0.20
ALLIANCE GLOBAL DOLLAR GOVT. B	2.37	VANGUARD MUNICIPAL SHORT-TERM	0.20
ALLIANCE MULTI-MARKET STRATEGY	2.29	VANGUARD BOND INDEX SHORT-TERM	0.20
VAN KAMPEN AMER. CAP. GLOBAL GOVERNMENT B	2.27	VANGUARD BOND INDEX TOTAL MARKET	0.20
NORTHSTAR HIGH TOTAL RETURN B	2.25	VANGUARD CA TAX-FREE INS. INTERM.-TERM	0.20
MFS INTERMEDIATE INCOME B	2.23	VANGUARD PA TAX-FREE INS. LONG-TERM	0.20
EV MARATHON STRATEGIC INCOME	2.18	VANGUARD MUNICIPAL LONG-TERM	0.20
MERRILL LYNCH AMERICAS INCOME B	2.13	VANGUARD FL INSURED TAX-FREE	0.20
MFS MUNICIPAL INCOME B	2.13	VANGUARD CA TAX-FREE INSURED LONG-TERM	0.20
SUNAMERICA U.S. GOVERNMENT SECURITIES B	2.13	VANGUARD MUNICIPAL INSURED LONG-TERM	0.20
MAINSTAY CONVERTIBLE B	2.10	VANGUARD MUNICIPAL INTERM.-TERM	0.20
GT GLOBAL STRATEGIC INOME B	2.07	VANGUARD MUNICIPAL HIGH-YIELD	0.20
SUNAMERICA DIVERSIFIED INCOME	2.06	VANGUARD NJ TAX-FREE INS. LONG-TERM	0.21
SUNAMERICA HIGH-INCOME B	2.06	VANGUARD MUNICIPAL LIMITED-TERM	0.21
KEYSTONE STRATEGIC INCOME B	2.05	VANGUARD OH TAX-FREE INS. LONG-TERM	0.21
COLONIAL STRATEGIC INCOME B	2.00	VANGUARD NY INSURED TAX-FREE	0.21
KEMPER SHORT-TERM GOVERNMENT B	1.97	DREYFUS 100% U.S. TREAS. LONG-TERM	0.25

*1996, funds with little or no expenses may be funds of funds or subsidized by the fund companies   DATA: MORNINGSTAR INC.

age, run about 1.03 percent for taxable funds, 0.80 percent for tax-free funds.

All things being equal, a lower expense ratio is better than a higher one. But if an equity fund has built up a strong track record, even with a high-end expense ratio, that's no reason to shun it. Fund performance is reported net of expenses. Thus, if the fund runs up high costs and still turns out impressive results, so be it. The only caveat is that when the fund hits a downdraft—and all do—a high overhead is going to make it even more painful.

Bond fund investors should be especially sensitive to expense ratios, looking first to funds with the lowest ones and steering clear of those with the highest (Table 7-4). That's because bond fund returns are typically in the single-digits. If the fund earns 7 percent and eats up 1 percent in operating expenses, it will only deliver 6 percent to shareholders. That may not sound like much overhead, but one out of every seven dollars earned by the fund—14 percent of the earnings—was chewed up in overhead. On the other hand, if an equity fund earns 50 percent, few investors are going to care if the expense ratio was 1 or even 2 percent.

If the fund manager is subsidizing the fund's overhead in any way, it's useful to know what the expense ratio would be if the fund were paying its way entirely. Such subsidies don't last forever, and one day shareholders will have to pay the full freight. For several years Dreyfus Corp. and Fidelity Investments waged a fierce battle between two big money-market funds, using waivers of management fees to boost yield and make their funds more attractive. If that's the case, the fund prospectus should spell out how much the fees would be without the subsidy. That might give a more realistic picture of the fund.

Total Return: Pretax and Aftertax

Total return is the fund's appreciation, including reinvestment of dividends and capital gains. The equity fund Scoreboard shows pretax and aftertax returns for 1996 and, if applicable, the average annual pretax and aftertax returns for the 3-, 5-, and 10-year periods. In the bond fund Scoreboard, the total returns are reported under the "Performance" heading. If your money was invested for the entire year and you added no new money, only reinvesting the dividends and capital gains, this reported total return should be your actual return too. If the money came in at any other point during the year, or if you made multiple investments in the fund, your own results will be different.

Yield is the fund's dividend payout as a percentage of its assets. It does not include capital gains distribution. This figure will be high in bond funds (it's under the "Portfolio Data" heading) and relatively low for equity funds. Most small-cap growth and mid-cap growth funds often have no yield at all, since the funds invest in companies that reinvest their profits for expansion rather than pay them out as dividends.

Sometimes a bond fund's total return will be less than the payout. That means that the NAV declined during the prior year. If a bond fund is paying out a yield higher than its total return, the fund's income distributions may be a return of your principal. Such payouts, also known as return of capital, are tax free. Don't cheer about it. It's not a freebie. In effect, you're getting your own money back because the fund couldn't earn a real return on it. Of course, the income distribution just may be a lot higher than the total return because of a loss in principal—that was not uncommon during 1996.

In the equity Scoreboard, you will also find aftertax returns. These figures are the same as the total return, less federal income taxes. Of course, not every fund shareholder pays the same tax rate. So for purposes of calculating aftertax returns, we've used the highest tax rate on income and capital gains that was in effect during the period. Since 1991, we have kept the top rate at 31 percent even though rates have gone higher for some shareholders. So few taxpayers pay the higher rate that it doesn't make much sense to use it for calculations that a large number of mutual fund investors will have to use.

If taxes affected all equity funds equally, there would not be much point to showing these numbers. But exactly how taxes affect funds depends on how the fund earned its returns. As you remember from Chapter 6, mutual funds have to pass along essentially all of their net dividend, interest, and realized capital gains during the year in which they are earned. (There is no tax due on income and capital gains generated by funds in qualified retirement programs like IRAs, Keoghs, and 401(k) plans.)

Take a fund that invests in a lot of high-dividend stocks. Those dividends are part of the fund's return, and will be passed along to investors every year. That means those dividends will be part of a taxable distribution even if, like most fund shareholders, you choose to reinvest the dividends in new fund shares. Suppose a fund earns a dividend yield of 6 percent and appreciates 6 percent, for a total return of 12 percent. Assuming the fund makes no capital gains distributions (it wouldn't have to unless it sold stocks at a profit), you could say that half the fund's return was taxable to you. If you are in the 31 percent bracket (and for simplicity, set aside state and local income taxes), the aftertax return would be 10.14 percent. How so? After taxes, the 6 percent yield is 4.14 percent. Add that to the 6 percent appreciation, and the return comes to 10.14 percent.

Next, suppose a fund is up 12 percent from capital appreciation, and there is no dividend or income distribution. If half of that return were a capital gains distribution, then, assuming the gains were long-term (held by the fund for more than a year), that 6 percent would be taxable at the maximum capital gains rate of 28 percent. That distribution comes out to 4.32 percent after taxes, dropping the aftertax return to 10.32 percent.

Now suppose the fund earned a 12 percent total return, but paid out no taxable dividend or capital gains distributions. In that case, the aftertax return is the same as the pretax return but that doesn't mean you don't pay taxes on your gains. You pay taxes when you or the fund earns income or realizes capital gains. If your fund is able to increase its net asset value without making distributions, that's fine as long as you own the fund. But should you sell the fund, you'll be hit with a taxable gain at that time. Equity mutual funds can help you defer taxes, but not avoid them.

How much attention you have to pay to aftertax returns depends on your tax bracket and investment needs. If you're in the 28 percent bracket, these figures will overstate the tax bite. If you're in the 36 percent or 39.6 percent brackets, the tax impact will be understated. If you're trying to minimize taxes, seek funds whose aftertax returns are fairly close to the pretax results. That means there was little tax impact. You might also steer clear of funds that rely heavily on bonds and dividend-paying stocks. But keep in mind when choosing funds that minimize taxable

The potential tax bite may influence your choice of funds.

income that you may be taking on more risk. Funds with higher payouts tend to be more conservative and more stable funds.

Trend

The current and historical results give absolute performance. For equity funds, "Trend" looks at how a fund performed relative to other funds in each of four 2½-year periods over the last 10 years. For bond funds, each box is a 1-year period.

The boxes read from left to right, so, in the equity tables, the box farthest to the left represents the period that runs from 7½ to 10 years past. (For the 10 years ending December 31, 1996, that box covers the period running from January 1987 through June 1989.) The box on the right is the most recent 2½-year period. Each box is either one-quarter, one-half, three-quarters, or totally filled. These gradations are also known as quartiles.

Suppose the fund's boxes look like this: second level, first level, third level, and fourth level. This means that in the first period the fund's performance put it in the bottom half of all funds. Actually, since the one-quarter marker allows us to place a fund in the bottom 25 percent of all funds, this half designation means the fund fell somewhere between the 25th and 50th percentiles. If the box is only one-quarter filled, the fund was dragging bottom during that period.

But in the last five years this fund seems to have picked up. Perhaps there was a change of management, or the market became more favorable toward this fund's investment style. In the third period, the fund is at the third level, indicating that the results fell into the 50th to 75th percentiles. Finally, in the most recent period, the fund has been a leader among funds—up there in the top 25 percent of all funds.

Remember, the "Trend" figure measures relative performance, not the absolute performance discussed under total returns. If the market goes through a few bad years, even the top-quartile funds may have had absolute returns that looked pale. Conservative equity funds are more likely to show up near the top in tough times; the more aggressive funds will show better relative performance in boom times.

One more thing. The "Trend" clues you in about the consistency of performance. Is it erratic or does it always stay around the same level? Fidelity Magellan has good years and some not so good years, but most of the time, it has been a filled-box performer in the Scoreboard's "Trend" column.

Portfolio Data

The next set of data looks inside each fund's portfolio. The first column, "Turnover," is a measure of trading activity. To arrive at this number, we take the lesser of purchases or sales and divide it by average monthly assets. So if the lesser of the two is $50 million, and the average fund assets are $100 million, the turnover ratio is 50 percent—which happens to be a moderate figure. (A fund's prospectus will contain its exact turnover ratio.)

The funds are then ranked by those numbers in descending order. Next, the funds are assigned a rating from "very high" down to "very low," using a statistical distribution similar to that for the BUSINESS WEEK mutual fund ratings.

High turnover could mean higher expenses. High turnover could also mean higher taxes. That's because mutual funds must distribute their net capital gains to shareholders, and funds that trade are presumably taking lots of gains. In contrast, low turnover funds tend to hold onto their winners and let them ride. There's no tax due until the fund sells the holdings. Funds with very high turnover tend to be small-cap growth, mid-cap growth, and even some large-cap blend funds. Funds with "very low" turnover are rather diverse, including precious metals, utilities, and, of course, all sorts of index funds.

While "Turnover" measures a fund characteristic over a period of time, the next three columns are snapshots of the portfolio. The item, "% Cash," shows the portion of the fund's portfolio that's not invested in stocks or bonds. A fund with a relatively low cash level, say 2 or 3 percent, is said to be "fully invested." If a fund has a double-digit cash level, it usually indicates the fund manager is wary of the market, or can't find the kinds of investment opportunities he or she likes. On occasion, this figure will be negative. That could mean one of two things. Funds that own stocks purchased on "margin"—that is, with borrowed funds—usually show a negative cash figure. But few funds actually buy on margin. More likely, the fund has just paid out a capital gains distribution.

Next comes "% Foreign," an item new to the Scoreboard. The idea in including this data is that

"Trend" measures a fund's relative performance.

many U.S. diversified funds do own a small measure of foreign stocks. Suppose you had chosen Putnam Diversified Equity B to fill in the mid-cap growth portion of your portfolio. By looking at this column, you will find the fund has 33 percent of its assets abroad, which could be enough to make you wonder if this fund is the optimal mid-cap growth fund for your portfolio. Likewise, this item of info is a way to check up on how international your international funds really are. SmallCap World, for instance, has only 38 percent of its assets abroad.

Then comes the "P–E Ratio," or price-to-earnings ratio. With equities, the p–e ratio is the price of the stock divided by the last 12 months' earnings per share. A stock that sells at 50 and has earned $2.50 per share has a p–e of 20. Another way to interpret the p–e is, "How many dollars do you have to pay for each $1 of earnings?" In that analysis, a 20 p–e tells you it costs $20 to "buy" every $1 of earnings.

Investment analysts use p–e's as a measure of value. Stocks with low p–e's are said to be "cheap," and high p–e's, "expensive." For the stock market as a whole, the average p–e over time is about 14; in bull markets, that average can climb over 20, and in bear markets, it can dip into the single digits.

The price–earnings ratio for a mutual fund is simply the average of the p–e's of the stocks in the fund, weighted by the size of the holdings. Suppose a fund has just two stocks: $90 million of bank, with a p–e of 10, and $10 million worth of software company, with a p–e of 50. The average of the two numbers, 10 and 50, is 30. But 90 percent of the fund is in the stock with a p–e of 10, and 10 percent is in the stock with a lofty 50. So take 90 percent of 10, or 9, and add to it 10 percent of 50, or 5 percent. The weighted average p–e is 14.

Stocks with high p–e's often have no dividends or low dividends because the companies are growing so fast they need to reinvest all their profits. Low-growth companies, like automakers, utilities, and oil producers pay relatively high dividends. High p–e funds are not going to generate a lot of dividends. Low p–e stocks are often a mainstay of growth and income and equity–income funds.

Stocks—and funds—with relatively high p–e's are considered riskier than those with low p–e's (Table 7-5). That's because Wall Street has high hopes for such companies and will be quick to dump them if they disappoint. If the investment

TABLE 7-5

EQUITY FUNDS: PRICE–EARNINGS RATIOS

HIGHEST		LOWEST	
Fund	Price–earnings ratio*	Fund	Price–earnings ratio*
CALVERT STRATEGIC GROWTH A	55	FRANKLIN UTILITIES I	14
PBHG SELECT EQUITY	52	FRANKLIN INCOME I	14
AMERICAN CENT.–20TH CENT. VISTA INVESTORS	52	COLONIAL UTILITIES B	15
FIDELITY SELECT AMERICAN GOLD	51	KEMPER-DREMAN SMALL CAP A	15
IAI EMERGING GROWTH	50	OAKMARK SMALL CAP	15
HANCOCK SPECIAL EQUITIES B	50	CENTURY SHARES	15
ROBERTSON STEPHENS EMERGING GROWTH	50	GT GLOBAL EMERGING MARKETS A	15
AMERICAN CENT.–20TH CENT. GIFTRUST	50	FRANKLIN BALANCE SHEET INVMT.	15
PBHG EMERGING GROWTH	49	FEDERATED UTILITY A	16
PBHG TECHNOLOGY & COMMUN.	47	PRINCOR WORLD A	16
PUTNAM OTC EMERGING GROWTH A	47	LEGG MASON TOTAL RETURN PRIMARY	16
PBHG CORE GROWTH	46	MERRILL LYNCH CAPITAL B	16
PARKSTONE SMALL CAP INV. A	46	INVESCO STRATEGIC FINANCIAL SVCS.	16
PBHG GROWTH	46	PENNSYLVANIA MUTUAL	16
JANUS ENTERPRISE	46	AMERICA'S UTILITY	16
INVESCO EMERGING GROWTH	46	T. ROWE PRICE LATIN AMERICA	16
PIMCO ADV. INNOVATION C	45	COLONIAL GOBAL UTILITIES A	16
GOVETT SMALLER COMPANIES A	45	FIDELITY SELECT REGIONAL BANKS	16
BT INVESTMENT SMALL CAP	45	PIONEER II A	16
AMERICAN CENT. GLOBAL GOLD	44	COMSTOCK PARTNERS STRATEGY O	17

*1996

DATA: MORNINGSTAR INC.

world assigns a low p–e to a company's stock, expectations are already low. Funds with low p–e stocks are thought to be less risky than those with high p–e stocks.

The next column, "Untaxed Gains," is also a revealing feature. This figure shows what percentage of the portfolio is unrealized capital gains and undistributed gains (see Chapter 6). Suppose a $500 million fund acquired its holdings at a cost of $400 million. There's $90 million in unrealized gains, and $10 million in realized yet undistributed gains. All together, that's 20 percent of the portfolio. Suppose you buy the fund today, and the manager liquidates the entire portfolio tomorrow (that almost never happens). Twenty percent of the money that comes back to you will be capital gains on which you will owe tax.

Just because the figure may be high doesn't mean you should avoid the fund. The figure is very high for Century Shares, 67 percent, but that's because the fund is a long-term investor that holds on to stocks for years. A high potential gains figure is also a sign that the fund has been successful. A fast-growing fund will probably have a low figure because the fund assets will likely be increasing much faster than its portfolio profits.

Funds which have suffered large losses often have negative capital gains exposure. That's because although mutual funds have to distribute realized capital gains to shareholders, they're not permitted to distribute realized losses. Instead, the losses are retained within the fund, and used to offset or "shelter" capital gains. Buying a fund with large losses can be a smart move, if you think the fund is poised to make gains. Certainly, investors who bought high-yield bond funds in 1991 had the benefit of large losses incurred during the 1989–1990 collapse of the junk bond market. And in 1993, many precious metals funds ran up big gains and sheltered them with losses built up over many years. But before buying a fund for the sheltering power of its capital losses, you should be convinced that the fund's fortunes are on the mend. Otherwise, you're just buying another money-losing fund.

The column "Largest Holding" is also telling. Though most funds hold dozens, if not hundreds, of stocks, the largest holding often signals the investment style. If the largest holding is Exxon, Procter & Gamble, or General Electric, you know the fund likes large, strong, and well-established companies. If the largest holding is an obscure high-tech company you've never heard of, that's a tipoff, too. You can bet that the second, third, and other holdings are not Exxon, P&G, and GE.

Ask the fund to send a shareholder report that has the entire portfolio. Of course, that's only a snapshot of what the portfolio looked like on a particular day. In fact, a portfolio is dynamic. Even if the names don't change much, the numbers do, since the prices of the holdings can change every day. But the "personality" of the fund, as shown through the kind of investments it makes, doesn't change.

The "% Asset" that follows "Largest Holding" tells you how much of the fund is made up of this stock. If it's 10 percent (and that would be high), a 10 percent move in the underlying stock would, all things being equal, show up as a 1 percent move in the fund.

In the bond fund Scoreboard, there's an item called "Maturity." Like p–e's in the equity fund Scoreboard, maturity tells you something about the nature and risk profile of the fund. In the bond business maturity is simply the time until the bond matures or pays back the principal, or face amount. Maturity for a bond fund is simply the average of the maturities of the bonds in the fund, weighted according to the market value of those securities.

As a rule, the longer the maturity of a fund, the more volatile it is, and the greater the risk. Funds with longer maturities fare well when interest rates fall, but they're battered when rates rise. Shorter maturity funds do just the opposite. They may lose a bit when rates rise, but not nearly so much as the longer-term funds.

Keep in mind that there is one major difference between maturity of bonds and maturity of bond funds. The maturity of a bond is declining all the time. A 30-year bond issued 10 years ago is a 20-year bond today, and will be a 5-year security in 15 years. In that sense the riskiness of a bond declines as it gets closer to maturity.

A bond fund, on the other hand, never matures. The maturity does change, but does so by the decision of its portfolio manager. If the goal is to keep the fund's maturity at 15 years, for instance, the manager has to keep juggling the bonds and the mix of bonds so as to produce that average result.

Risk

For our Scoreboard we define risk as the potential for losing money. There are other

"Maturity" is an indicator of a bond fund's risk.

ways to define it, but for you as an investor it's the most significant way. If your mutual fund is volatile—if its net asset value is subject to sharp fluctuations—it's risky. You're probably not going to get too upset about sharp moves to the upside. But you're not going to like it when the NAV nosedives.

The BUSINESS WEEK ratings focus on downside risk. To determine a fund's risk, we first measure a fund's total return for each month in the five-year measurement period. Total return is the change in net asset value, plus any distributed dividends and capital gains. Suppose the net asset value of a fund drops from $12.50 per share to $12.25 during the month and there were no dividend or capital gains distributions. The fund's total return was –2 percent.

The next step is to calculate that month's Treasury bill rate of return—what you could have earned by taking on no risk at all. If the annualized T-bill rate was 3 percent, the one-month return is 3 percent divided by 12, or 0.25 percent. Then we take 2 percent away from 0.25 percent and get –1.75 percent.

When a fund returns less than the T-bill rate, the result will always be a negative number. Then all the negative numbers are added up and divided by the number of months in the period. So, suppose that in a 60-month period a fund underperforms in 24 months. The negative numbers for each of those months are added up and divided by 60.

The farther fund performance falls below the T-bill rate, the greater the average negative number will be. And the greater the number, the higher your risk of losing money in a mutual fund. This risk-of-loss factor is also subtracted from a fund's total return over the entire period to come up with the BUSINESS WEEK rating.

For the risk column, the Scoreboard translates these numbers into one of five categories of risk. The funds with the greatest risk of loss numbers get the "very high" designation. That classification is followed by "high," "average," "low," and "very low." The funds at each extreme—the very highest and very lowest—are highlighted in Tables 7-6 and 7-7.

We've added a new feature to the risk column this year, showing the best and worst quarters of the last five years or 20 calendar quarters. We only include this data for funds with five years of performance history. These figures can show you the range of quarterly results over a common period, so you get a sense of how volatile the fund can be.

Keep in mind, many of these funds have probably had bigger quarterly ups and downs than you see in the table, but we only look at the last five years. Otherwise, funds that were around during the stock market crash of 1987 would look a lot worse than those that weren't. That wouldn't be a fair comparison. When you look at this data, you're judging the best and worst quarters under the same set of market conditions.

Here's how you might use it. Consider Fidelity Low-Priced Stock Fund and Fidelity Magellan Fund. (It's easy to compare them because they're next to each other in the Scoreboard.) Fidelity Low-Priced Stock Fund's best quarter was the fourth of 1992, up 12 percent, and its worst, the fourth of 1994, down 1.3 percent. Fidelity Magellan Fund, on the other hand, had higher highs and lower lows: a 15.8 percent gain in the second quarter of 1995 and a 4.5 percent loss in the second quarter of 1994. The differences are pretty dramatic. You could also have surmised there was a difference by looking at the risk rating before the best quarter, worst quarter statistics. Fidelity Low-Priced Stock Fund has a "low" rating, while Fidelity Magellan Fund has an "average" rating.

TABLE 7-6

RISKY BUSINESS
FUNDS WITH "VERY HIGH" RISK

ALGER SMALL CAPITALIZATION	HANCOCK GLOBAL TECHNOLOGY A
AMERICAN CENT.–20TH CENT. GIFTRUST	IAI EMERGING GROWTH
AMERICAN CENT.–20TH CENT. ULTRA INV.	INVESCO PACIFIC BASIN
AMERICAN CENT.–20TH CENT. VISTA INV.	INVESCO STRATEGIC GOLD
AMERICAN CENT. GLOBAL GOLD	INVESCO STRATEGIC HEALTH SCIENCE
DEAN WITTER DEVELOPING GROWTH	JAPAN
DEAN WITTER PACIFIC GROWTH	KEYSTONE PRECIOUS METALS HOLDINGS
FIDELITY EMERGING MARKETS	KEYSTONE SMALL CO. GROWTH (S-4)
FIDELITY PACIFIC BASIN	MERRILL LYNCH LATIN AMERICA B
FIDELITY SELECT AIR TRANSPORT	MIDAS
FIDELITY SELECT AMERICAN GOLD	MFS EMERGING GROWTH B
FIDELITY SELECT BIOTECHNOLOGY	OBERWEIS EMERGING GROWTH
FIDELITY SELECT DEVELOP. COMMUN.	OPPENHEIMER DISCOVERY A
FIDELITY SELECT MEDICAL DELIVERY	OPPENHEIMER GLOBAL EMERGING GROWTH A
FIDELITY SELECT PREC. METALS & MINERALS	OPPENHEIMER GOLD & SPECIAL MINERALS A
FIDELITY SELECT SOFTWARE & COMPUTERS	PACIFIC HORIZON AGGRESSIVE GROWTH A
FIDELITY SELECT TECHNOLOGY	PBHG GROWTH
59 WALL STREET PACIFIC BASIN EQUITY	PIMCO ADV. OPPORTUNITY C
FORTIS GROWTH A	PIONEER GROWTH A
FOUNDERS DISCOVERY	ROBERTSON STEPHENS EMERGING GROWTH
FRANKLIN GOLD I	SAFECO GROWTH NO LOAD
GT GLOBAL HEALTH CARE A	T. ROWE PRICE NEW ASIA
GT GLOBAL NEW PACIFIC A	T. ROWE PRICE JAPAN
GT LATIN AMERICA GROWTH A	

DATA: MORNINGSTAR INC.

TABLE 7-7

NOT SO RISKY BUSINESS
FUNDS WITH "VERY LOW" RISK

AMERICAN BALANCED	INVESCO ADVISOR FLEX C
AMSOUTH BALANCED	INVESCO TOTAL RETURN
BERWYN INCOME	LINDNER DIVIDEND INVESTORS
CAPITAL INCOME BUILDER	LONGLEAF PARTNERS
COLUMBIA BALANCED	MERGER
COMPOSITE BOND & STOCK A	MERRILL LYNCH GLOBAL ALLOCATION B
DELAWARE A	MFS TOTAL RETURN A
DODGE & COX BALANCED	MFS WORLD TOTAL RETURN A
EVERGREEN BALANCED Y	MUTUAL BEACON Z
EV TRADITIONAL INVESTORS	MUTUAL QUALIFIED Z
EXCELSIOR INCOME & GROWTH	MUTUAL SHARES Z
FEDERATED STOCK & BOND A	NEW ENGLAND BALANCED A
FIDELITY ASSET MANAGER	OAKMARK
FIDELITY BALANCED	OPPENHEIMER ASSET ALLOCATION A
FIDELITY GROWTH & INCOME	OPPENHEIMER DISCIP. ALLOCATION A
FIDELITY PURITAN	PHOENIX STRATEGIC ALLOCATION A
FOUNDERS BALANCED	PHOENIX INCOME & GROWTH A
FRANKLIN BALANCE SHEET INVESTMENT	PIONEER EQUITY–INCOME A
FRANKLIN EQUITY INCOME I	PIONEER INCOME A
FRANKLIN INCOME I	PUTNAM BALANCED RETIREMENT A
FREMONT GLOBAL	RIGHTIME BLUE CHIP
GATEWAY INDEX PLUS	ROYCE PREMIER
GEORGE PUTNAM OF BOSTON A	T. ROWE PRICE BALANCED
IDS DIVERSIFIED EQUITY–INCOME A	T. ROWE PRICE CAPITAL APPRECIATION
IDS MUTUAL A	T. ROWE PRICE EQUITY–INCOME
INCOME FUND OF AMERICA	SAFECO INCOME NO-LOAD

DATA: MORNINGSTAR INC.

The best/worst quarterly statistics could help you compare funds with the same risk ratings. Look at Fidelity Low-Priced Stock Fund and the Royce Micro-Cap Fund. Both are small-cap value funds, have the highest BW overall rating, and are low in risk. Royce Micro-Cap Fund has a 13.3 percent best quarter (incidentally, it was the fourth quarter of 1992 as well) and a –3.6 percent return in the second quarter of 1992. That's a little wider range of returns than the Fidelity fund, especially on the downside. If you are concerned about downside risk, there has been a little more in the Royce fund.

Specialized funds usually have bigger swings than the diversified funds. The best quarterly return in the 1997 Scoreboard was the 46.2 percent recorded by Invesco Strategic Gold Fund in 1996's first quarter. Its worst showing was –21.3 percent in the fourth quarter of 1994. But funds that invest in merging growth companies, characterized by high price–earnings ratios, can also have wide swings. Oberweis Emerging Growth Fund, for instance, was up 22.4 percent in the fourth quarter of 1992 after being down 20.4 percent in the second quarter of the same year.

One thing these "worst quarter" figures don't show you is how the funds behaved in a bear market. There hasn't been one in the past five years. But as the statistics show, many funds went through some pretty ugly periods in 1992 and 1994, bad enough to give you a taste of the bear. Take each of your fund's worst quarter returns and double it. If you can live with that kind of one-quarter loss for one of your funds, you're ready for whatever the markets may give you.

Are Three Great Years in a Row Really Possible?

At the beginning of 1996, most investment professionals did not have high expectations for the stock market. After all, in 1995, the stock market had gone up 37.5 percent, the best annual performance in two decades. The thinking was that you couldn't get two in a row. But markets have a way of surprising. The Dow Jones industrial average breached 6000, finishing the year at 6448.3. (The Dow broke 7000 in mid-February 1997.) That turned out to be a 26 percent gain. The Standard & Poor's 500, a much broader index, logged a 22.9 percent gain. U.S. diversified equity funds gained an average of 19.3 percent; the average equity fund, 17.7 percent. Corporate earnings, always an important driver for stocks, continued to post strong gains through the year. Merger and acquisitions activity, another sure-fire catalyst for rising stock prices, raced along at a blistering and record pace.

What was perhaps even more surprising about the stock market's strong showing in 1996 was that the bond market was not supportive. From start to finish, the yield on the benchmark 30-year U.S. Treasury bond went from 6 percent to 6.6 percent. But at midyear, the yield had gone to 7.2 percent, came back down to 6.4 percent in the fall, and crept its way higher. (By March 1997, the yield stood at 6.8 percent.) Needless to say, that kind of interest-rate volatility wreaked havoc on intermediate-term and long-term bond funds. The average taxable bond fund earned a 6.5 percent total return. That average includes the double-digit returns earned by convertible, high-yield, and international bonds. Look at the more mainstream government and investment-grade corporate funds, and the average return is just 3.4 percent. The average tax-free fund earned 3.7 percent.

Bond funds may have disappointed, but equity funds still shined brightly. The stock market performed so well that the question of the day for investors seemed to be whether it was time to take their profits off the table. After all, if the stock market is up over 30 percent in one year and over 20 percent in the next, isn't it doomed to disappoint investors in the third year? Not necessarily. It all depends on what's going on in the United States and the global economy. The economic backdrop that helped produce the remarkable returns—relatively low interest rates and low inflation—is still very much in place and will not be dislodged easily.

And the financial system is flush. For starters, there's the cash pouring into mutual funds, which in turn flows to the stock market. During 1996, investors put $223 billion into equity mutual funds. The rush continued in 1997, with the equity funds taking in nearly $50 billion in January and February alone. Investor interest in bond funds, on the other hand, is almost nonexistent. True, bond funds took in $13 billion in 1996, but nearly all the money went to high-yield bond funds, which are a close cousin of equities. Investment-grade bond funds and tax-free bond funds continued to suffer from net withdrawal of assets.

The lessons of 1996? For starters, patience is rewarded. If you make a long-term commitment to invest, you should basically stick with it for the long term, and not let short-term market forecasts push you out of the market. That also reinforces one of the lessons of the difficult year, 1994: Although mutual funds can provide attractive returns over long periods of time, they don't necessarily provide them in each and every year. Lesson No. 2? You really can't predict in which years they will or will not perform.

Equity Funds

So many funds. So many great returns. But it was a great year. Certainly, there are some flukes that never shined before and never will again. So you want funds with staying power. They don't have to shoot out the lights every year. You just want some funds that have shown they can do well over a longer period of time. Just as important, you want funds that will provide a good return for the amount of risk they took with your money.

That's why a good place to start your fund search is the list of 48 funds that earned three upward-pointing arrows, the highest rating for risk-adjusted total return over the last five years (Table 8-1). Many of these funds, like Fidelity Low-Priced Stock, Heartland Value, Lindner Dividend Investors, SoGen International, T. Rowe Price Equity–Income, and the Franklin Mutual Series three—Mutual Beacon, Mutual Qualified, and Mutual Shares funds—are familiar to BUSINESS WEEK readers. A few, like Longleaf Partners, the Merger Fund, and T. Rowe Price Small-Cap Value Fund are closed to new investors. But there are plenty of worthy funds with open doors—Babson Value Fund, Mairs & Power Growth Fund, Oakmark Fund, Royce Micro-Cap Fund, Royce Premier Fund, Sound Shore Fund, and the Strong Schafer Value Fund.

Most of these three-up-arrow funds did not rise to the top because they scored the highest absolute returns. What separates BW's ratings from others' is that they're based on risk-adjusted total return. That adjustment can bring a highflier down to earth or propel a steady plodder to the top.

If you're concerned about buying into equity mutual funds after the market has had such a large run, you should appreciate this list of funds; 41 of the 48 top funds have either low or very low risk. In addition, most of them practice a "value" investment style. They buy stocks with below-average price-to-earnings ratios and price-to-book ratios, as opposed to "growth" stocks, which have higher growth rates but higher p–e and p–b ratios.

These value funds don't grab the attention that dynamic growth funds sometimes command, but they have generally outperformed the growth funds over the past five years. Even more important, they often earn high ratings because they're less volatile than the growth funds. In that sense, they may make better investments. "Our data shows that growth funds have higher long-term returns, but I suspect investors make more money in value funds," says John Rekenthaler, publisher of *Morningstar Mutual Funds*, a biweekly publication that reports on mutual fund performance. "Because the funds are less volatile, investors tend to hold onto them longer and let the profits roll. With growth funds, they often buy when they've already gone up and sell when they're down."

Which of these funds will work best for you depends on a number of variables, like your age, your stomach for risk, and even your tax bracket. The Lindner Dividend Fund, for instance, is a blend of high-dividend common stocks, convertible securities, and junk bonds that, when combined, produce a portfolio with very low risk. (Though officially a domestic hybrid fund, the stock portion of the fund falls in the mid-cap value category.) Its mission is to generate dividend income, and it does that well. During 1996, this stock-and-bond mixture yielded 6.1 percent, a higher payout than many pure bond funds. Berwyn Income Fund, another three-up-arrow portfolio, is much the same sort of investment as Lindner. It generally invests at least 80 percent of its assets in income-producing securities, and that can include dividend-paying stocks. In 1996, the fund had a 6.3 percent yield.

But before you invest in a fund like Lindner Dividend or Berwyn Income, remember that dividend income, like the interest you earn from a bank account, is taxable at your ordinary tax rate. So if you're in the 31 percent federal tax bracket, nearly a third (more perhaps, if you're also subject to state income tax) of what the fund pays to you in dividends eventually goes to the Internal Revenue Service.

That's why we include aftertax returns in the equity portion of the BW Mutual Fund Scoreboard. For instance, from the Scoreboard you learn that Lindner Dividend earned an 11.5 percent total return in 1996, which fell to 8.7 percent after paying taxes on the dividends. Berwyn Income's 14 percent total return dropped to 10.7 percent after taxes. (The aftertax return is estimated using a 31 percent tax rate on dividends and a 28 percent rate on capital gains distributions.) Over five years, Lindner's 12.8 percent average annual return fell to 10 percent after taxes, and Berwyn's 14.2 percent shrank to 11.1 percent.

Obviously, if you're in the 36 percent or 39.6 percent tax brackets, you may want to avoid excellent funds like Lindner Dividend or Berwyn Income. There's one exception: if you are considering this sort of fund for a tax-deferred invest-

ARE THREE GREAT YEARS IN A ROW REALLY POSSIBLE?

ment plan like an individual retirement account. In that case, these funds are great, offering high, steady income coupled with low risk.

This year's top performers' list has plenty of funds with low or very low risk that still beat the S&P 500. Such funds can be good plays for investors whose long-term objectives call for an equity-like rate of return but who have a hard time living with the day-to-day volatility of the stock market. Franklin Mutual Beacon Z, Franklin Mutual Qualified Z, and Franklin Mutual Shares Z are also in that category. Those funds are fairly unique in the fund world.

At the core is a "value" strategy, buying out of favor stocks that may not look good by the earnings alone, but have strong assets, franchises, or some other attributes that could change the situation. And Michael F. Price, who runs the funds, is a proactive investor in lobbying for change at undervalued companies. In spring of 1995, his funds bought 6.2 percent of the stock of the Chase Manhattan Bank and lobbied the bank's managers to take steps to improve the bank's performance and stock prices. The funds' moves were widely credited with forcing Chase to merge with its New York rival, Chemical Banking Corp., to create America's largest bank.

But perhaps what this trio of funds is best noted for is its bankruptcy investments. Sounds scary, huh? Not really. Bankruptcies are only scary before they happen, not after. The funds usually buy bankrupt companies' bonds and bank notes, which creditors are only too happy to sell when they are not paying interest, take active roles in the restructuring of the companies, and cash out when the companies are reorganized. The funds also invest in private securities and risk-arbitrage, investing in mergers and takeovers. These funds are laggards when the market is redhot and the stocks of rapidly growing companies lead the way. That certainly was the case in 1995 and the first half of 1996. But over the long haul, the funds have beat the market handily—and they are fairly unique.

The only caveat here is that Price sold the funds to the Franklin Templeton Fund group in late 1996. That's why these funds are now the "Franklin Mutual" funds. Price collected about $610 million upfront and an incentive package that can give Price another $200 million within five years if the funds meet certain growth targets. Price signed a five-year employment contract that ties him to the firm until 2001, but he does have the option to work part-time after the first year.

If you invest now, will he stick around to manage the funds? Probably so. First, Price put $150 million from the sale back into the funds, and he also took a portion of his payment in Franklin Resources stock. And then there's the $200 mil-

TABLE 8-1

TOP-PERFORMING EQUITY MUTUAL FUNDS

These equity mutual funds stand out among all funds with three upward-pointing arrows in the BUSINESS WEEK Mutual Fund Scoreboard. To get this rating, they needed to deliver superior risk-adjusted total returns over the past five years.

Fund	Average annual total return*	Investment category	Risk
AARP GROWTH & INCOME	15.9%	Large-cap Blend	Low
BABSON VALUE	18.6	Large-cap Value	Low
BERWYN INCOME	14.2	Domestic Hybrid	Very low
DODGE & COX BALANCED	14.0	Domestic Hybrid	Very Low
EXCELSIOR INCOME & GROWTH	16.3	Mid-cap Blend	Very low
FIDELITY ADV. GROWTH OPPORTUNITY T	17.8	Large-cap Blend	Low
FIDELITY DESTINY I	19.8	Large-cap Value	Low
FIDELITY DESTINY II	19.6	Large-cap Value	Low
FIDELITY EQUITY-INCOME	17.3	Large-cap Value	Low
FIDELITY EQUITY-INCOME II	17.0	Large-cap Value	Low
FIDELITY GROWTH & INCOME	17.2	Large-cap Blend	Very low
FIDELITY LOW-PRICED STOCK	20.8	Small-cap Value	Low
FIDELITY PURITAN	14.8	Domestic Hybrid	Very low
FIDELITY SEL. ELECTRONICS	36.5	Technology	High
FIDELITY SEL. HOME FINANCE	34.1	Financial	Average
FIDELITY SEL. REGIONAL BANKS	27.0	Financial	Average
FIDELITY VALUE	19.0	Mid-cap Value	Low
FIRST EAGLE FUND OF AMERICA	21.5	Mid-cap Value	Average
FOUNDERS BALANCED	14.3	Domestic Hybrid	Very low
FRANKLIN BALANCE SHEET INVESTMENT	18.9	Small-cap Value	Very low
FRANKLIN MUTUAL BEACON Z	19.5	Mid-cap Value	Very low
FRANKLIN MUTUAL QUALIFIED Z	19.6	Mid-cap Value	Very low
FRANKLIN MUTUAL SHARES Z	19.1	Mid-cap Value	Very low
HANCOCK REGIONAL BANK B	27.4	Financial	Low
HEARTLAND VALUE	22.0	Small-cap Value	Average
IDS DIVERSIFIED EQUITY-INCOME A	15.4	Large-cap Value	Very low
INCOME FUND OF AMERICA	13.1	Domestic Hybrid	Very low
LINDNER DIVIDEND INV.	12.8	Domestic Hybrid	Very low
LONGLEAF PARTNERS	19.9	Mid-cap Blend	Very low
MAIRS & POWER GROWTH	19.4	Mid-cap Blend	Average
MERGER	10.8	Mid-cap Blend	Very low
MERRILL LYNCH GLOBAL ALLOCATION B	12.7	Int'l. Hybrid	Very low
OAKMARK	25.7	Mid-cap Value	Very low
OPPENHEIMER QUEST OPPORTUNITY A	18.5	Large-cap Value	Low
T. ROWE PRICE CAPITAL APPRECIATION	13.5	Mid-cap Value	Very low
T. ROWE PRICE EQUITY-INCOME	17.1	Large-cap Blend	Very low
T. ROWE PRICE GROWTH & INCOME	16.4	Large-cap Blend	Low
T. ROWE PRICE SMALL-CAP VALUE	18.8	Small-cap Value	Low
ROYCE MICRO-CAP	17.9	Small-cap Value	Low
ROYCE PREMIER	14.7	Small-cap Value	Very low
SAFECO INCOME NO LOAD	14.9	Large-cap Value	Very low
SCUDDER GROWTH & INCOME	15.8	Large-cap Blend	Low
SKYLINE SPECIAL EQUITIES	20.7	Small-cap Value	Average
SMITH BARNEY PREMIUM TOTAL RETURN B	13.5	Large-cap Value	Very low
SOGEN INTERNATIONAL	12.9	Int'l. Hybrid	Very low
SOUND SHORE	18.8	Mid-cap Value	Low
STRONG SCHAFER VALUE	18.4	Mid-cap Value	Low
THIRD AVENUE VALUE	18.9	Domestic Hybrid	Very low

*1992–1996 pretax returns, includes appreciation plus reinvestment of dividends and capital gains

DATA: MORNINGSTAR INC.

159

lion performance bonus. All told, that's probably enough to keep Price interested in the funds' fate. And while Price is the chief, he's also backed by a talented analytical staff well-versed in his ways. Also, if you invest in these funds now, it's going to cost you more. Franklin is a load-fund group, while prior to the acquisition the funds were no-load. Investors who owned shares before the Franklin takeover own the "Z" shares, which entitle them to continue to invest in Price's funds no-load.

If you don't want to pay a load for the Franklin Mutual funds, you might consider two no-loads with a similar approach and three upward-pointing arrows: Third Avenue Value Fund and First Eagle Fund of America. Third Avenue Value's veteran "vulture" investor Martin J. Whitman and its returns are very similar to those of the Franklin Mutual funds. The main difference is that Whitman, with far less money to manage than Price, invests in much smaller companies, and with a higher bond component, ends up in the domestic hybrid category. Like Price's funds, First Eagle Fund of America falls more in the mid-cap than small-cap climes and also engages in some risk arbitrage to enhance returns. Unlike either of Price's funds, the fund also has the ability to leverage (buy securities with borrowed money), which it does—albeit sparingly. Managed by the team of Harold J. Levy and David L. Cohen, First Eagle actually beat Price's returns in the last one-, three- and five-year periods.

Of course, if you prefer the low-risk or low-volatility funds, you inevitably run into many funds which generate at least some income. That, in part, is what makes them lower risk. Securities that provide an income stream, on balance, have a little less volatility than those that don't.

NEW FACES AMONG THE TOP-RATED FUNDS

One of the most interesting things about the BW Scoreboard is that you sometimes find a little-known fund that rises to the top through our rigorous selection process. Babson Value Fund, one of the funds that earned an overall rating of three up-arrows for the first time, trolls among the large-cap value stocks. It's the kind of fund that's buying unloved stocks even when they're still in the headlines. "Kmart was a terrible performer when we owned it in 1995," says Nick Whitridge, who has run the fund since 1984. "But it was one of our best performing stocks of 1996." Whitridge runs a concentrated portfolio, with just 40 stocks

and a strict buy-and-sell discipline that keeps turnover to a minimum. No new stock can be added unless the fund sells an existing one. The fund earned a 22.7 percent return in 1996 and an 18.6 percent total return for the 1992–1996 period.

Mairs & Power Growth Fund, another top-rated fund, is also new to the Scoreboard. Only in the last year did it become large enough to be included. Headquartered in St. Paul, Minnesota, the fund is an arm of the Mairs & Power investment counseling firm. George A. Mairs III, grandson of the firm's founder, has run the mutual fund for 17 years. The fund's 1996 return of 27.8 percent not only beat the S&P handily, but its 3-, 5-, and 10-year results do as well. In addition to beating the S&P 500 over these multi-year periods, this mid-cap blend fund has also beaten the S&P in each of the last 7 years. That's a feat few funds have accomplished.

The fund is certainly not a regional fund by charter, but by practice the fund has a heavy Minnesota accent. About 80 percent of the fund's holdings, including 5 of the top 10 holdings, are based in the upper Midwest. Mairs is most comfortable in investing in companies he knows well, and that's why he has so much local exposure. The other reason is that once he gets something he knows and likes, he sticks with it. Portfolio turnover is about 5 percent a year versus about 80 percent in the average equity fund. Even as the fund nearly doubled in assets in 1996, two of the three new stocks he added were Minnesota companies, and the third, Burlington Northern, has major operations in the state.

Another top-rated fund that's making its first appearance on the BW Scoreboard is the Sound Shore Fund. Like the Mairs & Power Growth Fund, it is part of an investment counseling firm rather than a large mutual fund company. T. Gibbs Kane Jr., one of the fund's two managers, says an important factor in the fund's success, like Babson Value, is its focus on 40 stocks. "When we're right about a stock, we own enough of it to make an impact on the fund's returns," says Kane. The challenge for Sound Shore and for Mairs & Power now is to stay focused on their investment discipline in the face of the inevitable onslaught of money that's sure to come their way.

Strong Schafer Value Fund is not making its first appearance in the Scoreboard, but it's the first time it's had an overall rating of three upward-pointing arrows. Since joining the Strong family of funds a couple of years ago, the fund has nearly quadrupled in size. But manager

David Schafer is a disciplined investor who seems to have handled the swelling asset base without diluting his return. In 1996, Strong Schafer Fund earned a 23.2 percent return, and for the 1992–1996 period, an 18.4 percent total return.

The Strong Schafer Value Fund, like Babson Value and Sound Shore, limits the number of stocks in the portfolio, now to about 45 (this number will probably creep up as the fund soaks up new money). Schafer buys stocks with below average p–e ratios but an above average earnings growth rate and diversifies the fund with about 20 percent foreign exposure. P–e's in most foreign markets are below those in the United States.

Furthermore, Schafer does not allow cash to build up. That's not easy to do when the money is pouring in. Keeping cash down is good in a bull market, but could be dangerous when the bears are in charge. The no-cash policy means that whenever he wants to invest in a new stock, he must sell one of the existing positions to raise the money. As a result, he must constantly cull the weakest stocks out of the portfolio or take profits in those that have become fully valued. But like many value managers, Schafer is an infrequent trader, and so the portfolio turnover is low.

Two funds from the Royce family of funds are also making their first appearance on the top-performers' list this year—Royce Micro-Cap Fund and Royce Premier Fund. Portfolio manager Charles M. Royce is no rookie to mutual funds, but some of his funds have been in a slump for several years. Now, he's back on top with these small-cap value funds, which usually invest in somewhat prosaic companies that lack the pizzazz and high valuations of software or Internet stocks. The difference between these two funds is one of market capitalization of the stocks in the funds.

Royce Premier concentrates on the "larger" small-caps, the universe of about 1400 companies with market capitalizations between $300 million and $1 billion. "That's where most mutual funds and institutional buyers go when they want to invest in small-caps," says Royce. That, he says, is a fairly efficient market, and to make money there, "you need to take bigger bets." To that end, Royce Premier keeps the portfolio limited to about 50 stocks concentrated in just a few sectors. The fund earned an 18.1 percent total return in 1996, and a 14.7 percent average annual return for the 1992–1996 period.

Royce Micro-Cap Fund stalks completely different prey: the 6500 public companies, most of them little-known, with market caps between $5 million and $300 million. Since the micro-cap market is much less liquid, Royce takes a totally different tack. He holds 150 stocks in a broadly diversified portfolio. The fund earned a 15.5 percent return in 1996 and a 17.9 percent average annual return over the last five years.

Another portfolio manager with two top-rated funds is Robert Hoffman, lead portfolio manager for the AARP Growth & Income Fund and the Scudder Growth & Income Fund. Hoffman heads a three-manager team at Scudder, which has the fund management contract for the American Association of Retired Persons (AARP). Both large-cap blend funds are almost entirely the same, except for one thing. Scudder Growth & Income Fund owns tobacco stocks. The AARP Growth & Income Fund, in deference to the wishes of the AARP, does not. The two funds' five-year average annual returns are virtually the same.

Both funds follow a strategy called "relative dividend yield," buying dividend-paying stocks when their yields are high relative to their yield histories. "The yield is usually high because the stock is out of favor," says Hoffman. "When the yield becomes relatively low, it's usually because the stock price is going up." The sell signal for a stock usually comes when the yield is low. The fund ends up in the blend category because he buys stocks when they are considered value investments and holds them as they evolve into growth investments.

CATEGORY RATINGS GIVE FUNDS ANOTHER LOOK

As investors start to look at their funds as a unified portfolio, they may be concerned that some of their funds aren't getting good overall ratings. That's certainly been the case for the last few years with most international funds. Foreign markets have lagged the U.S. markets so most funds investing abroad have fared poorly when judged alongside funds that invest at home. Or consider the large-cap growth, mid-cap growth, and small-cap growth fund categories. Not one fund from any of those three earned three up-arrows in overall rating. Still, a diversified portfolio should contain some of those funds. But which ones?

That's why we now rate funds within their categories as well as against all funds (Table 8-2). The same risk-adjustment methodology applies to these ratings. A fund needs five years of performance history to qualify for a rating, which

"Growth" funds lag the "value" funds in BW ratings.

runs the gamut from three up-arrows to three down-arrows. The difference, though, is that we need at least seven funds with five-year histories in a category to rate the category. As such, only 20 of our 28 categories have category-rated funds. But all the major domestic and international categories do have ratings.

For instance, in the world category (international funds that can also invest in the United States), Janus Worldwide Fund and Templeton Growth Fund I earned three-up-arrow ratings. Both funds are "bottom-up" international equity investors. What that means is the fund managers choose the stocks first, rather than choosing the

TABLE 8-2

THE BEST PERFORMERS IN THEIR CATEGORIES

Rating funds by category, we awarded these funds three up-arrows. They earned the highest risk-adjusted returns when compared with their peers. Not all categories have ratings, since some lack enough funds with five-year returns to perform a ratings analysis.

	Average annual total return*
LARGE-CAP VALUE	
BABSON VALUE	18.6%
FIDELITY DESTINY I	19.8
FIDELITY EQUITY–INCOME	17.3
FIDELITY EQUITY–INCOME II	17.0
OPPENHEIMER QUEST OPPORTUNITY A	18.5
LARGE-CAP BLEND	
AARP GROWTH & INCOME	15.9%
FIDELITY ADV. GROWTH OPPORT. T	17.8
FIDELITY GROWTH & INCOME	17.2
GUARDIAN PARK AVENUE A	19.4
T. ROWE PRICE EQUITY–INCOME	17.1
T. ROWE PRICE GROWTH & INCOME	16.4
PUTNAM FUND FOR GROWTH & INCOME A	16.2
SCUDDER GROWTH & INCOME	15.8
LARGE-CAP GROWTH	
DREYFUS APPRECIATION	13.5%
PHOENIX GROWTH A	10.5
VANGUARD U.S. GROWTH	12.9
MID-CAP VALUE	
FRANKLIN MUTUAL BEACON Z	19.5%
OAKMARK	25.7
MID-CAP BLEND	
EXCELSIOR INCOME & GROWTH	16.3%
LONGLEAF PARTNERS	19.9
MAIRS & POWER GROWTH	19.4
MERGER	10.8
MID-CAP GROWTH	
WILLIAM BLAIR GROWTH	15.1%
FIDELITY BLUE CHIP GROWTH	16.6
MERRILL LYNCH GROWTH B	20.1
MFS RESEARCH A	18.4
PUTNAM VISTA A	17.8
SMALL-CAP VALUE	
FIDELITY LOW-PRICED STOCK	20.8%
FRANKLIN BALANCE SHEET INVESTMENT	18.9
SMALL-CAP BLEND	
GABELLI SMALL-CAP GROWTH	15.0%
T. ROWE PRICE OTC SECURITIES	16.9

	Average annual total return*
SMALL-CAP GROWTH	
ACORN	17.6%
BARON ASSET	20.0
MANAGERS SPECIAL EQUITY	17.4
FOREIGN	
EUROPACIFIC GROWTH	13.4%
HARBOR INTERNATIONAL	16.4
MANAGERS INTERNATIONAL EQUITY	14.0
WORLD	
JANUS WORLDWIDE	17.5%
TEMPLETON GROWTH I	15.0
EUROPE	
DEAN WITTER EUROPEAN GROWTH	18.7%
DOMESTIC HYBRID	
BERWYN INCOME	14.2%
FIDELITY PURITAN	14.8
FOUNDERS BALANCED	14.3
INCOME FUND OF AMERICA	13.1
LINDNER DIVIDEND INVESTORS	12.8
THIRD AVENUE VALUE	18.9
INTERNATIONAL HYBRID	
SOGEN INTERNATIONAL	12.9%
FINANCIAL	
FIDELITY SELECT HOME FINANCE	34.1%
HEALTH	
VANGUARD SPECIALIZED HEALTH CARE	16.3%
NATURAL RESOURCES	
FIDELITY ADV. FOCUS NATURAL RESOURCES T	20.7%
PRECIOUS METALS	
MIDAS	20.5%
SCUDDER GOLD	15.0
TECHNOLOGY	
FIDELITY SELECT ELECTRONICS	36.5%
UTILITIES	
FIDELITY UTILITIES	12.1%
INVESCO STRATEGIC UTILITIES	11.3

*1992–96, pretax returns, includes reinvestment of dividends and capital gains

DATA: MORNINGSTAR INC.

market or country where the stock trades or the company is domiciled. In the other strategy—"top down"—funds make allocation bets on various countries depending on their macroeconomic and market outlooks and buy stocks to fill in the allocations. Not that the country doesn't matter, of course, in the bottom-up strategy. It's just not the overriding concern.

"The companies I like most," says Helen Young Hayes, manager of the Janus Worldwide Fund, "have a produce or service that's exportable. That way, they're not bound by the local economy." But she doesn't rule out purely local companies, like Telebras, the Brazilian telecommunications giant, if the growth propsects are strong. Janus Worldwide Fund earned 26.4 percent in 1996 and 17.5 percent a year for the five years ending in 1996. In both periods, Hayes beat the S&P 500. The fund earned one up-arrow for an overall rating, as did the Templeton Growth I Fund. Hayes also manages the Janus Overseas Fund, which is categorized as a foreign rather than a world fund, because it does not invest in U.S. stocks. That fund gained 28.8 percent in 1996, but does not yet have a long enough track record for a rating.

The foreign funds with three-up-arrow category ratings are EuroPacific Growth Fund, Harbor International, and Managers International Equity Fund. The first two are also bottom-up funds. Managers International Equity is split between two managers. One, John Rensberg of Lazard Freres Asset Management, is a traditional bottom-up stock-picker. The other, William Holzer of Scudder, Stevens & Clark, takes an approach that's more like top-down managers. He first identifies important global trends and then finds the stocks that can capitalize on them. Harbor International is closed to new investors, but portfolio manager Haken Castegren also runs Ivy International, a load fund.

The category ratings will help you to identify the best of the large-cap, mid-cap, and small-cap growth funds, none of which earned three up-arrows in overall ratings this year. Among large-cap growth funds, there are three: Dreyfus Appreciation Fund, Phoenix Growth Fund A, and Vanguard U.S. Growth Fund.

The fund with the highest absolute returns of the three is Dreyfus Appreciation Fund, with a 13.5 percent total return for the last five years and a 25.7 pecent return for 1996. The portfolio manager for Dreyfus Appreciation is Fayez Sarofim, whose eponymous firm runs billions of dollars for big institutional investors like pension funds and endowments. The fund has a strictly blue-chip portfolio, loaded up on such successful multinationals as Coca-Cola, General Electric, and Merck. Coke, in fact, makes up 5 percent of the fund. With the market up so strongly in the last two years, these stocks have pretty rich valuations, and if the market goes into a tailspin, this fund can be vulnerable.

Among the mid-cap growth funds, there's five funds with category ratings of three up-arrows—William Blair Growth, Fidelity Blue Chip Growth, Merrill Lynch Growth B, MFS Research A, and Putnam Vista A. The highest absolute return for the ratings period belongs to Merrill Lynch Growth B, a 20.1 percent average annual return. That's even 1.7 percentage points better than the next highest.

Merrill Lynch Growth Fund for Retirement and Investment, the full name of the fund, sounds sort of staid. But the portfolio is anything but that. Of late, most of its assets have been concentrated in just two sectors—technology and energy. In 1996, at least, both fared well, and the fund earned a 28.4 percent return for the year. This is no sector fund, but when the portfolio manager finds an investment theme he believes in, he is not bashful about making a long-term commitment to it.

MFS Research A, on the other hand, is much more diversified and does not bear the hand of such a strong-willed manager. In fact, MFS Research A is essentially run by committee. The equity analysts at Massachusetts Financial Services Co. pick the stocks for the fund. It's not just that the fund had a lucky year. This unusual portfolio management structure was put in place more than five years ago and the record has been admirable ever since. So much for all the jokes about committees.

Among the small-cap growth funds, the top-rated funds are the Acorn Fund, Baron Asset Fund, and the Managers Special Equity Fund. Baron Asset Fund is an exceptional fund, able to compete effectively in the small-cap growth arena without loading up on the volatile technology stocks. In fact, Baron Asset has only 5 percent of its portfolio in technology while the average small-cap growth fund has a 25 percent weighting. Baron Asset isn't immune to pullbacks in the small-cap sector. During the summer of 1996, the fund sank 11 percent in several weeks. Still, the fund recovered enough to log a 22 percent gain for the year. The average small-cap growth fund earned only 16.6 percent (Table 8-3).

The other two top-performing small-cap growth funds are also worth noting. The Acorn Fund, led

MFS Research, a winning fund, is run by a committee.

TABLE 8-3

EQUITY FUND PERFORMANCE

U.S. diversified equity funds didn't beat the S&P 500 in 1996, but they made enough to keep their shareholders happy. International funds earned good returns, too, as long as they stayed out of Japan.

Category	Average annual total return*				1996's Best performer
	1996	1994–96	1992–96	1987–96	
REAL ESTATE	34.0%	13.2%	15.0%	11.8%	Longleaf Partners Realty
NATURAL RESOURCES	31.0	17.3	15.0	11.7	Fid. Sel. Energy Svc.
FINANCIAL	29.7	22.9	24.5	18.2	Fid. Sel. Home Finance
EUROPE	24.7	14.5	13.3	9.7	Scudder Greater Eur. Growth
LATIN AMERICA	24.3	-5.3	5.3	NA	Fidelity Latin America
SMALL-CAP VALUE	21.8	14.9	16.5	13.6	Oakmark Small Cap
LARGE-CAP VALUE	21.1	17.3	15.7	14.0	Legg Mason Value Prim.
LARGE-CAP GROWTH	21.1	16.2	12.0	14.6	Rydex OTC
TECHNOLOGY	20.9	25.7	23.8	18.2	PBHG Tech. & Comm.
SMALL-CAP BLEND	20.7	13.6	15.2	13.5	Fidelity Export
MID-CAP VALUE	20.5	15.4	15.7	13.4	Sound Shore
LARGE-CAP BLEND	20.0	16.4	13.6	13.4	Salomon Bros. Investors O
MID-CAP BLEND	19.1	15.5	14.6	14.5	Salomon Bros. Capital
WORLD	17.6	10.4	11.7	11.3	Idex Global A
SMALL-CAP GROWTH	16.6	17.1	15.3	16.0	Fremont U.S. Micro-Cap
MID-CAP GROWTH	16.1	15.8	14.1	15.2	PBHG Core Growth
FOREIGN	16.0	7.9	10.9	9.9	Artisan International
PACIFIC EX-JAPAN	15.9	-1.3	11.3	11.5	Fidelity Hong Kong & China
HEALTH CARE	14.2	20.4	9.6	18.9	T. Rowe Price Health Sci.
DOMESTIC HYBRID	13.0	11.5	11.1	11.2	FPA Paramount
DIV. EMERGING MKTS.	11.7	-2.3	10.4	8.4	Templeton Developing Mkts.
SPECIALTY-MISC.	11.0	10.3	13.2	15.8	Fidelity Sel. Retailing
INTERNATIONAL HYBRID	11.0	7.0	10.2	10.7	Fidelity Asset Mgr. Growth
UTILITIES	10.2	8.8	9.9	10.3	Prudential Utility B
PRECIOUS METALS	8.1	-0.5	9.2	5.5	Invesco Strategic Gold
COMMUNICATION	7.7	9.3	16.3	16.2	Fidelity Sel. Dev. Comm.
DIVERSIFIED PACIFIC	1.8	-0.8	8.8	6.0	Merrill Lynch Pacific B
JAPAN	-10.2	-0.3	0.8	3.5	Vang. Intl. Eq. Indx. Pacific
U.S. DIVERSIFIED FUNDS	19.3	16.1	14.5	14.3	
ALL EQUITY FUNDS	17.7	13.8	13.5	13.4	
S&P 500	22.9	19.7	15.2	15.3	

*Pretax return, including appreciation plus reinvestment of dividends and capital gains
NA=Not available

DATA: MORNINGSTAR INC.

since 1970 by Ralph Wanger, takes a more global view than many small-cap players. Wanger tries to identify important themes and looks for the small-cap companies that are best poised to exploit them. That leads the fund to look abroad as well. For the last several years, the fund has been a laggard in

its category in large part because of its foreign holdings. In early 1997, the fund still had 20 percent of its assets abroad. Even with the drag of the foreign holdings, the fund still has a risk-adjusted return that puts it at the top of its category.

The other fund, Managers Special Equity Fund, is divided among three portfolio managers from three different investment firms. Gary Pilgrim, manager of the PBHG Growth Fund, practices an investment style of buying emerging growth stocks with a lot of "momentum." They also have high p–e ratios, and when they falter, a lot of downside risk. Timothy Ebright runs his portion as a micro-cap value fund, not unlike Charles Royce. The third manager, Andrew Knuth, is a "growth-at-a-price" investor among the larger small-cap stocks. "Growth-at-a-price" investors will pay up for growth, but not chase the shooting stars that Pilgrim and others do. The three different management approaches make the fund a good choice for an investor who wants just one small-cap growth fund in his or her portfolio.

THE SURPRISE OF 1996: REAL ESTATE SHINES

As a mutual fund category, real estate funds have only been around a few years. A few funds, like giants Cohen & Steers Realty shares and Fidelity Real Estate Investment, have been around for awhile, but the vast majority of funds are spanking new. Given the performance in 1996, up 34 percent (Table 8-3), there's going to be a whole lot more funds and money in them in the next few years. In 1996, Vanguard even opened up a REIT index fund.

Real estate funds scored big returns because, in part, of new demand for the real estate investment trusts (REITs). These trusts are not unlike mutual funds, except they own office buildings, shopping malls, nursing homes, hotels, apartments, and other sorts of properties. The income for REITs is rent, which the REITs pass on to shareholders after taking out operating and finance expenses. When a REIT's properties are doing well, the rental income goes up—and so do the dividends to shareholders. REITs benefit both from the growth in the value of the underlying properties and growth in rental income. Some REITs are diversified, but many specialize in one kind of real estate investment.

What was unique about the REIT sector in 1996 was that every subsector did well, especially the retail sector, which had suffered for several years from overbuilding and a retailing slump.

Hotel REITs are also riding high, as is the lodging industry. The glut of hotel rooms created in the late 1980s has been used up and many cities are actually short on first-class hotel space. And not a lot of new building is going on. That bodes well for the hotel REITs going forward.

Among the real estate funds, Cohen & Steers Realty Shares and Fidelity Real Estate Investment Fund are REIT investors only, while Longleaf Realty Partners and CGM Realty (that's not yet big enough to be in the Scoreboard, but probably will be in 1998) take a more aggressive tack, investing in building and construction companies as well. Such funds usually have lower yields.

Most investors really don't need specialty funds, since buying a technology or health fund is usually duplicative of something that's already in the diversified funds they own. But not so with REITs, which are little owned by conventional mutual funds. As such, real estate funds bring a diversification to a total fund portfolio. Real estate is also considered a hedge against inflation. Although inflation has not been a serious problem for the last several years, it's still a risk that investors may want to hedge against by keeping at least a small portion of their portfolios in REIT funds. Of course, precious metals funds used to be considered an inflation hedge, but they're far more volatile and lack the dividend stream the REITs offer. Even if inflation is not a problem, REITs can make money just from the normal course of the real estate business.

Interestingly enough, the second-best-performing fund category in 1996 was natural resources. The funds in this category are also considered inflation hedges, and inflation was not a serious problem. But energy prices did rise in 1996, helping the oil company stocks. Oil and gas exploration picked up as well, greatly benefiting the energy service companies. The best-performing natural resource fund, in fact, was Fidelity Select Energy Service, with a 49 percent total return. The broader Fidelity Select Energy was up a none-too-shabby 32.4 percent. Of the other major sectors, financial funds were up 29.7 percent, even in the face of higher interest rates. The financial funds soared along with bank earnings and takeover fever in the banking industry. Technology stocks weathered some rough spells during the year, but tech funds still finished with a 20.9 percent total return.

Among the international sector funds, the stars were Europe and Latin America. European stocks rallied along with the United States. In Great Britain, like the United States, corporate profits were strong and so was mergers and acquisition activity. The driver on the continent was better earnings and lower interest rates. Even in the face of a rising dollar, the European funds gave shareholders a 24.7 percent return for 1996, and a 14.5 percent return for the last three years.

Latin America, up 24.3 percent, is quite a different story. Last year was a comeback from two disastrous years. Mexico, the leading Latin American market, finally started to revive, and the Mexican government even paid off the loan the United States made to it back in the throes of the peso crisis a few years back. Still, investors in Latin funds have a way to go to catch up. The three-year return for Latin America funds was –5.3 percent. That means $10,000 invested in a Latin America fund at the beginning of 1994 was worth a little less than $8500 at the end of 1996.

The revival in Latin America was a main factor behind the comeback in the diversified emerging markets funds. They earned, on average, an 11.7 percent total return in 1996. Also contributing to these funds' returns were a bounceback in China, a surge in Hong Kong, and some smart returns from Eastern Europe, especially Russia. China's rebound helped the Pacific ex-Japan category. But the diversified Pacific funds, which include the long-suffering Japanese stocks, could only muster a 1.8 percent total return. The Japan category was still a disaster, as investors lost money both on the stocks and on the sinking yen. The Japan funds had an average return of –10.2 percent. After seven years of horrific performance, you would think the Japan stock market would have made a comeback already. Buying a Japanese fund could be the best contrarian bet of the year.

Bond Funds

Suppose the bond market staged a rally and nobody came. That's what happened during 1995. Well, given what happened in 1996, it's probably just as well no one showed up. Interest rates rose, the bond market gyrated, and bond fund returns were mediocre at best. The average taxable bond fund earned a 6.5 percent return, but that includes convertible, high-yield, international, and multisector funds, which in themselves include high-yield and international bonds. The "plain vanilla" government and investment-

Real estate and resource funds soared, even with low inflation.

grade corporate bond funds earned total returns of just 3.2 percent. When the total return is less than the yield from the funds as it is here, that's a good indication that the net asset value of the bond funds eroded as well. The average tax-free fund actually did better than investment-grade taxable bonds, earning a 3.7 percent total return.

Are bond funds really so repugnant that investors won't put money into them anymore? By some reckonings, yes. "There's been a staggering amount of volatility considering the low

TABLE 8-4

TOP-PERFORMING BOND MUTUAL FUNDS

These funds stand out among all bond funds in the BUSINESS WEEK Mutual Fund Scoreboard. They earned three upward-pointing arrows, meaning they achieved superior risk-adjusted total returns over the last five years.

Fund	Average annual total return*	Investment category
AIM HIGH-YIELD A	13.3%	High Yield
CALVERT TAX-FREE RESERVES LTD.-TERM A	4.2	Muni. Short
COLONIAL HIGH-YIELD SECURITIES A	13.8	High Yield
DEAN WITTER HIGH-YIELD SECS.	15.0	High Yield
DREYFUS SHORT-INTRM. MUNI. BD.	4.8	Muni. Short
EATON VANCE INCOME OF BOSTON	12.6	High Yield
FEDERATED HIGH-INCOME BOND A	12.9	High Yield
FEDERATED HIGH-YIELD	12.1	High Yield
FIDELITY SH.-TRM. MUNI. INST.	4.3	Muni. Short
FIDELITY ADV. HIGH-YIELD T	14.6	High Yield
FIDELITY CAPITAL & INCOME	14.7	High Yield
FIDELITY SPARTAN HIGH-INCOME	15.6	High Yield
FIDELITY SPARTAN SHORT-INT. MUNI.	5.1	Muni. Short
FIRST INVESTORS FUND FOR INCOME A	13.1	High Yield
FIRST INVESTORS HIGH-YIELD A	13.2	High Yield
FLAGSHIP LTD.-TERM TAX-EXEMPT A	6.0	Muni. Natl. Interm.
FRANKLIN AGE HIGH INCOME I	12.9	High Yield
FRANKLIN HIGH YIELD T/F INC. I	8.2	Muni. Natl. Long
KEMPER HIGH-YIELD A	13.0	High Yield
LIMITED TERM NY MUNICIPAL A	6.9	Muni. Single-State Interm.
LOOMIS SAYLES BOND	14.3	Long (General)
MAINSTAY HI-YIELD CORP. BOND B	15.8	High Yield
MERRILL LYNCH CORP. HI-INC. B	12.0	High Yield
NORTHEAST INVESTORS	15.9	High Yield
NORTHSTAR HIGH-YIELD T	14.1	High Yield
NUVEEN MUNICIPAL BOND R	6.8	Muni. National Long
OPPENHEIMER BOND FOR GROWTH M	16.8	Convertibles
OPPENHEIMER CHAMPION INCOME A	12.9	High Yield
T. ROWE PRICE T/F HIGH-YIELD	7.7	Muni. National Long
T. ROWE PRICE T/F SH.-INTM.	4.9	Muni. Short
PUTNAM CONVERT. INCOME-GROWTH A	15.2	Convertibles
SELIGMAN HIGH-YIELD BOND A	14.9	High Yield
SIT TAX-FREE INCOME	7.1	Muni. National Long
SMITH BARNEY MUNI. LTD. TERM A	6.1	Muni. National Interm.
STATE ST. RESEARCH HIGH-INC. A	13.7	High Yield
THORNBURG INTERM. MUNI. A	7.3	Muni. National Long
THORNBURG LTD.-TERM NATL. A	5.7	Muni. Short
UNITED MUNICIPAL HIGH-INC. A	8.6	Muni. National Long
USAA TAX-EXEMPT SHORT-TERM	4.9	Muni. Short
VAN KAMP. AM. CAP. HI-YLD MUN. A	7.7	Muni. National Long
VANGUARD MUNI. LIMITED-TERM	5.0	Muni. Short
VANGUARD MUNI. SHORT-TERM	4.0	Muni. Short

*1992–96 pretax returns, includes reinvestment of dividends and capital gains   DATA: MORNINGSTAR INC.

level of interest rates," says Kenneth J. McAlley, head of the fixed-income division at U.S. Trust Co. and senior portfolio manager for several Excelsior bond funds. "It's hard to see the next turn of events that will bring people back to bond funds."

The bond funds' recent past performance won't do the job. Even over the last five years, taxable bond funds earned an average annual total return of 7.6 percent, about half that of the average return of U.S. diversified equity funds. What's more, there's a growing—and healthy—realization among mutual fund investors that equity funds are the backbone of an investment program. If you are to keep your money invested for a period of at least 10 years, equity funds make the optimal investment.

But today's unloved investment often has a way of becoming tomorrow's darling. That makes bond funds worth more than just a look. They demand serious consideration. And equity-fund investors whose portfolios are teeming with bull-market profits might well consider a little diversification into bonds.

If it's time to go back to bonds, which bond funds do you buy? You can start with examining the 42 funds on the top performers' list (Table 8-4). This list would put a big smile on the face of Michael R. Milken, the one-time junk bond king of Wall Street. Twenty of the funds are high-yield bond funds, which invest in bonds rated below investment grade—the sort of securities Milken popularized in the 1980s. The theory behind junk bonds is that while there's greater risk of default, higher yields more than make up for occasional bad bonds.

What's also noteworthy about the top performers' list is what's not on it: a government bond fund. That's got nothing to do with the furious budget battle going on in Washington or the fear of a default. One reason for this poor showing was that the devastating 1994 bond market hit government debt the hardest, lowering returns and raising risk ratings. But even without 1994, government bond funds are not compelling. In the corporate or muni markets, smart credit research and good portfolio management can pay off. But in the government market, the most efficient securities market in the world, there are few inefficiencies to uncover and little value added by fund managers, especially after taking into account sales charges and ongoing fund expenses.

Still, if you want to invest in a government bond fund, we now have category ratings that will help you identify those which earned the

ARE THREE GREAT YEARS IN A ROW REALLY POSSIBLE?

highest risk-adjusted returns in each category. To derive these ratings, we go through the same process as with the equity fund category ratings.

The category ratings are particularly useful to the opportunistic investors. Suppose you are convinced that long-term interest rates will soon begin to fall, and fall hard. Under those circumstances, the best investment is a long-term government bond fund. But the best overall rating you will find for a long-term government fund is two downward-pointing arrows, the second worst of all ratings. But what if you rate the long-term government bond funds against each other instead of against all taxable funds. Checking the category ratings, you will find the Dreyfus 100% U.S. Treasury Long-Term Fund is the best, with three upward-pointing arrows. Table 8-5 lists 49 funds which are tops in their categories.

This year's Scoreboard identifies one long-term bond fund, though, that really is unique—it earned a three-up-arrow, all-fund rating. That means the fund was able to nudge into the top category against high-yield funds which collect bigger interest payments and have, on average, shorter maturities. That fund is Loomis Sayles Bond Fund.

Daniel J. Fuss, Loomis Sayles's portfolio manager, orchestrated a 14.3 percent average annual

TABLE 8-5

THE BEST PERFORMERS IN THEIR CATEGORIES

Rating bond funds by category, we awarded these funds three up-arrows. They earned the highest risk-adjusted returns when compared to their peers.

	Average annual total return*			Average annual total return*
SHORT (GENERAL)			**MULTISECTOR**	
HARBOR SHORT DURATION	5.1%		KEMPER DIVERSIFIED INCOME A	12.2%
STRONG SHORT-TERM BOND	6.5		**INTERNATIONAL**	
INTERMEDIATE (GENERAL)			GLOBAL GOVERNMENT PLUS A	9.8%
FEDERATED BOND FORT.	10.5%		GOLDMAN SACHS GLOBAL A	8.1
FPA NEW INCOME	8.8		PRUDENTIAL INT. GLOBAL INCOME A	8.9
T. ROWE PRICE SPECTRUM INCOME	8.9		**MUNICIPAL SHORT**	
STRONG CORPORATE BOND	10.8		DREYFUS SHORT-INTERMEDIATE MUNI. BD.	4.8%
LONG (GENERAL)			**MUNICIPAL NATIONAL INTERM.**	
INVESCO SELECT INCOME	9.0%		FLAGSHIP LTD.-TERM TAX-EXEMPT A	6.0%
LOOMIS SAYLES BOND	14.3		**MUNICIPAL NATIONAL LONG**	
SHORT GOVERNMENT			FRANKLIN HIGH YIELD T/F INCOME I	8.2%
AIM LTD. MAT. TREASURY RET.	5.0%		NUVEEN MUNICIPAL BOND R	6.8
ASSET MGMT. ADJUSTABLE RATE	5.2		T. ROWE PRICE TAX-FREE HIGH-YIELD	7.7
FEDERATED ARMS INSTL.	4.7		SIT TAX-FREE INCOME	7.1
NEW ENGLAND ADJ. RATE U.S. GOVT. A	4.8		THORNBURG INTERMEDIATE MUNI. A	7.3
INTERMEDIATE GOVERNMENT			UNITED MUNICIPAL HIGH-INCOME A	8.6
AMERICAN CENT.-BENHAM GNMA	6.6%		VAN KAMPEN AM. CAP. HI-YIELD MUNI. A	7.7
CARDINAL GOVERNMENT OBLIGATIONS	5.8		**MUNI. SINGLE-STATE INTERM.**	
FIDELITY MORTGAGE SECURITIES	7.2		LIMITED TERM NY MUNICIPAL A	6.9%
FIDELITY SPARTAN GINNIE MAE	6.4		**MUNI. SINGLE-STATE LONG**	
LEXINGTON GNMA INCOME	6.4		AMERICAN CENT-BEN CA. MUNI. HIGH-YLD.	7.9%
VANGUARD FIXED-INCOME GNMA	6.7		FIDELITY SPARTAN PA MUNI. INC.	7.5
LONG GOVERNMENT			FRANKLIN AL TAX-FREE INC. I	7.1
DREYFUS 100% U.S. TREASURY LONG-TERM	7.5%		FRANKLIN AZ TAX-FREE INC. I	7.0
CONVERTIBLES			FRANKLIN GA TAX-FREE INC. I	7.0
OPPENHEIMER BOND FUND FOR GROWTH M	16.8%		FRANKLIN FL TAX-FREE INC. I	7.1
HIGH YIELD			FRANKLIN MA INS. TAX-FREE INC. I	6.8
FIDELITY SPARTAN HIGH-INCOME	15.6%		FRANKLIN NY TAX-FREE INC. I	7.3
MAINSTAY HI-YIELD CORP. BOND B	15.8		FRANKLIN PA TAX-FREE INC. I	7.2
NORTHEAST INVESTORS	15.9		PRUDENTIAL CA MUNI. CA INC. A	8.4
SELIGMAN HIGH-YIELD BOND A	14.9		PUTNAM NY TAX EXEMPT OPPORT. A	6.8

*1992–96, pretax returns, includes reinvestment of dividends and capital gains

DATA: MORNINGSTAR INC.

total return while keeping the fund long-term in its maturities and 65 percent of its assets in investment-grade securities. Fuss earned a return that's more like that of high-yield bonds. Few other long-term bond funds even come close.

To earn those returns, Fuss works with a wide array of fixed-income instruments, including foreign bonds and convertible bonds. "We have much less correlation with the bond market than our average maturity and credit quality would lead you to think," says Fuss. And he says he wouldn't mind a spike in interest rates to 7.5 percent, from today's 6.8 percent, a prospect that would make most bond-fund managers blanch. Says Fuss: "That would create a lot of discount bonds, and we love discount bonds."

HIGH YIELD LOOKS GREAT, BUT . . .

Before you rush to high-yield funds, remember that you're viewing them under near ideal conditions. Over the past five years, the period for the 1997 ratings, junk bonds have had the wind at their backs. Interest rates fell, allowing many issuers to refinance; corporate cash flows swelled, improving issuers' ability to service their debt; and the economy, though slow at times, continued to grow and stayed clear of recession. And the default rate on junk bonds plummeted as well.

Keep in mind, too, that the junk funds earned high marks because their 1989–1990 bear market is no longer in the ratings period. The best example of a fund that benefits from this turn of the calendar is Dean Witter High-Yield Securities, with a 15.0 percent average total annual return. In 1990, the fund had a horrendous –40.1 percent return. Its standout five-year return was launched in 1991, when the market rebounded and the fund amassed a smashing 67.2 percent return. The fund also beat the competition in 1992 and 1993, but has been a laggard since.

Managers of the top-rated high-yield funds acknowledge that things have gone well since 1991 and are mindful that things might not always be so bright. To that end, some of the high-yield funds have become "defensive," moving money into bonds of higher-rated issuers and into industries that are less sensitive to the ups and downs of the economy. Still, if the high-yield bonds go into a bear market, it won't be as bad as the 1989–1990 period. Back then, the preponderance of bonds were issued by more leveraged companies and had higher interest rates. Now, the companies are less leveraged, more creditworthy, and, on average, paying lower interest rates than back then.

Indeed, interest rates on high-yield bonds have come down so much that they're now in the 8-to-9-percent range, and don't seem very high yield at all. Some investment advisers ask if it's even worthwhile to invest in high-yields when the rates relative to government bonds are so low. But that's not the point. Because high-yield bonds don't have a strong correlation with bond funds in general, adding a high-yield fund to an income oriented portfolio makes some sense.

High-yield bond funds can supplement and diversfy an equity fund portfolio as well. With the yield on stocks a measly 2 percent, a stock market investor who's looking for a little more income might find the high-yield funds a good alternative to stocks—more income and a little less appreciation. Any one of the 20 high-yield funds on the top performers' list would make a good candidate for investment. The highest-rated of these highly rated funds are the four that received three up-arrows when compared to other high-yield funds. They are Fidelity Spartan High-Income, MainStay Hi-Yield Corporate Bond B, Northeast Investors, and Seligman High-Yield Bond A.

CONVERTIBLES MOVE TO THE FAST LANE

If high-yield bonds do well in a robust stock market, consider the convertible bonds, the best-performing category of bond fund for the last one-, three-, and five-year periods (Table 8-6). These securities have yields that are 3 to 4 percentage points below that of high-yield bonds. But convertible bonds offer something else in return—the ability to convert the bond into equity. A conventional bond is limited in how much it can appreciate; not so for convertibles that turn into equity.

Indeed, convertible bond funds behave more like stocks than even high-yield funds. Yet unlike stocks, the interest-bearing coupon on the bond does soften some of the downside risk. Considering that a large number of convertible bond issuers are emerging growth companies that don't pay dividends, the convertible bond can be a lower-risk alternative to emerging growth equity funds. "We've been able to get convertibles that go up about 75 percent as fast as the underlying stock, but go down only about half as much, and that's a pretty good trade-off," says Hugh H. Mullin, co-manager of Putnam Convertible Income Growth A Fund, one of the two convertible bond funds to earn overall ratings of

> "High-yield" yields look relatively low, yet investors seek them.

three up-arrows. The other top-rated convertible fund is Oppenheimer Bond Fund for Growth A, which is also the top-rated fund when compared to all other convertible bond funds.

No doubt there would be more convertible bond funds, if only there were more convertible bonds. In the world of securities, they're a fairly rare breed. The entire market value of the converts is $120 billion, compared to about $500 billion for high-yield bonds and the $8 trillion market value of the U.S. equity market. But success tends to spawn copycats in the investment business, and as convertible bonds have done well, no doubt investment bankers are trying to convince clients to issue more convertible bonds.

RICHES FROM ABROAD

The average international bond fund earned a respectable 12.8 percent total return in 1996. But the three-year average annual return is just 6.1 percent a year, and the five-year return, only 6.8 percent a year. What you can surmise from that string of numbers is that up until 1996, there had been some poor returns. Indeed, for several years, the emerging markets debt funds racked up nothing but losses, battered first by higher interest rates and later by the Mexican currency and debt crisis. All during that period, many of the emerging markets nations continued to prosper, institute economic reforms, and make their debt payments.

And almost as fast as they went out the door, the thundering herd returned and drove the prices for emerging markets debt ever higher. Fidelity New Markets Income Fund, the year's leading international bond fund, earned a 41.4 percent total return with exotic investments such as Russian bank bonds. The fund's manager, John Carlson, made a bold move and bought the bonds prior to Boris Yeltsin's reelection, making a big and winning bet on the outcome. The major holding of the fund, though, is a Latin American core with equal parts of Mexican, Argentine, and Brazilian debt, all markets back from the near-dead.

The funds that invest in the developed international markets didn't have such a spectacular year. Rising interest rates hurt global funds that usually carry a good chunk of U.S. bonds, and a generally rising dollar dampened funds like American Century—Benham European Government Bond and T. Rowe Price International Bond Fund, neither of which hedge currencies. Still, even the higher grade international bond funds managed to make the average U.S. government bond fund look pretty lame.

A SO-SO YEAR FOR MUNI FUNDS

The story for municipal bond funds is much the same as it is for taxable funds. Interest rates rattled this market during 1996 as well, and bond prices suffered. As a rule, the shorter the maturity of the fund, the better it performed. In some respects, the muni funds did a little better. Both national and single-state long-term funds outdistanced the long-term U.S. government funds. But the lure of the stock market was so strong it was even difficult to get investors interested in tax-free bond funds. As a result, more money went out of tax-exempt funds than went in.

In all, 1996 was a relatively tame year for the municipal bond market. There were no big disasters, like the Orange County, California, bankruptcy that rocked the market in late 1994. And the dreaded "flat tax" idea faded with Steve Forbes's shot at the GOP nomination for president. The flat tax, a reform of the tax code that puts everyone in the same tax bracket, is anathema to the muni bond crowd. They depend on

TABLE 8-6

BOND FUND PERFORMANCE

The best returns came from funds that track the stock market the most—convertibles and high-yield bonds. International funds did well, too, thanks to lower rates and higher prices for emerging markets debt.

| Category | Average annual total return* | | | Best performer for 1995 |
	1996	1994–96	1992–96	
CONVERTIBLES	14.5%	10.6%	13.3%	Pacific Horizon Captl. Inc. A
HIGH YIELD	14.1	8.6	12.6	Strong High-Yield Bond
INTERNATIONAL	12.8	6.1	6.8	Fidelity New Markets Income
MULTISECTOR	9.8	6.7	8.8	EV Marathon Strategic Income
ULTRASHORT (GEN.)	5.7	4.3	4.8	Piper Adj. Rate Mortgage Secs.
SHORT (GEN.)	5.0	4.8	5.2	Alliance S/T Multi-Market A
SHORT GOVERNMENT	4.3	4.6	5.1	Federated ARMS Instl.
MUNI SHORT	4.1	4.0	4.8	Strong Municipal Advantage
MUNI S.S. INTERM.	4.0	4.5	6.4	Vanguard CA Tax-Free Ins. Interm.
MUNI NATL. INTERM.	3.8	4.3	6.1	Limited Term Tax-Ex. Bd. Amer.
INTERMEDIATE (GEN.)	3.7	5.6	7.4	SunAmerica Diversified Inc. B
MUNI NATL. LONG	3.7	4.4	6.8	United Municipal High-Inc. A
MUNI S.S. LONG	3.7	4.3	6.8	Franklin CA High Yld. Muni I
LONG (GEN.)	3.3	6.2	8.0	Loomis Sayles Bond
INTERM. GOVT.	3.0	4.8	5.8	Lexington GNMA Income
LONG GOVERNMENT	−1.9	5.4	8.3	Hancock Sovereign U.S. Gov. A
ALL BOND FUNDS	5.4	5.2	7.2	
TAXABLE FUNDS	6.5	5.9	7.6	
TAX-FREE FUNDS	3.7	4.3	6.7	

*Pretax returns, includes reinvestment of dividends and capital gains   DATA: MORNINGSTAR INC.

well-heeled investors who suffer with high tax rates to buy their tax-exempt bonds. Lowering tax rates would make it more difficult to issue new bonds and would likely shrink the value of existing ones. In fact, the fading of the flat tax threat actually boosted municipal bonds somewhat, helping to offset some of the damage of higher interest rates.

Most of the municipal bond funds that earned three up-arrows for overall performance were either short-term funds with very low price volatility or long-term funds with yields so high they overcame the greater volatility. Among the shorter-term funds winning top honors are several repeats from years past—Calvert Tax-Free Reserves Limited Term A, Dreyfus Short-Intermediate Municipal Bond, and Fidelity Spartan Short-Intermediate Municipal Fund. The Dreyfus fund also earned a category rating of three up-arrows, which makes it the best of the short-term funds.

The long-term muni winners include familiar names like T. Rowe Price Tax-Free High-Yield and Van Kampen American Capital High-Yield Municipal Fund A. Both of those funds also earned three up-arrows in the category. That makes them extra special winners.

In the muni market, a bond can be creditworthy without being rated. That's because many smaller bond issuers find it cheaper to pay a higher interest rate on a bond than pay for the ratings agencies like Moody's Investor Service and Standard & Poor's to rate them. So portfolio managers and analysts who do their own credit analysis can often find unrated bonds at yields much higher than they would be if they were rated.

Sit Tax-Free Income Fund, a fund taking top honors both in the overall ratings and the category ratings, has an unusual approach. The fund earns high returns without buying junk or unrated bonds. Instead, the funds loads up on tax-exempt housing bonds. "The stated maturity on these bonds may be 17 years, but because they're backed by mortgages, they typically pay back much sooner," says Debra A. Sit, one of the fund's two portfolio managers. "As a result, you get a long-term yield with a shorter maturity bond."

Investing in these sorts of bonds helps keep the fund's NAV volatility down at very low levels. During 1996, a volatile year for the bond market, the fund's net asset value never lost more than 3 percent and it finished the year only one cent lower than it started.

Closed-End Funds

After the spectacular gains made in the stock market over the past year, a real bargain is hard to find—unless you shop among the closed-end funds. Many of these quirky funds, which invest like mutual funds but are bought and sold like stocks, have racked up stellar investment results in the last couple of years yet still trade at prices that are discounts to their net asset values. (Remember what we said in Chapter 2: The price at which a closed-end fund trades is what the market will bear, not the value of its portfolio.) The closed-end fund market is the last place on Wall Street where you can buy $1 in assets for 90 cents.

Many closed-end bond funds trade at discounts to their net asset value as well. That's akin to buying a bond at a discount. A fund that pays a dividend equal to 6 percent of its NAV is actually paying 6.7 percent to the investor who buys the fund at a 10 percent discount to its NAV. To the yield-conscious investor, every tenth of a percentage point counts. The biggest discounts in the closed-end universe belong to the categories that are most out of favor—government bond funds and investment-grade municipal funds. Many of the high-yield bond funds trade at significant premiums.

The closed-end fund Scoreboard helps to identify the best investment opportunities. The Scoreboard reports on how each fund's portfolio performed—the net asset value return—and how the fund shares fared. The three-year NAV return is the basis for BW's risk-adjusted ratings. In the latest Scoreboard, 7 equity and 10 bond funds earned three-up-arrow ratings for overall performance (Table 8-7).

There's no better case for shopping among the closed-end funds than the top-rated Europe Fund. During 1996, the fund's portfolio earned a 35.3 percent total return, its shares 34.8 percent. Either way, the Europe Fund trounced the 30.9 percent return earned by Scudder Greater Europe Growth Fund, the best-performing European equity fund in the Mutual Fund Scoreboard.

The fund's secret? "Simply stock selection," says portfolio manager Consuelo Brooke of Mercury Asset Management International in London. Perhaps more remarkable is that the fund earned its high returns without hedging against the strengthening dollar. Says Brooke, "We deal with the stronger dollar by investing in exporters which benefit from it." Despite the excellent results, the Europe Fund still traded on the Big Board at an 11.7 percent discount in March 1997. Or consider Pilgrim America Bank & Thrift, a specialized fund investing in the banking and savings and loan industries. Even with robust performance that beats many of its mutual fund peers, the fund traded at a 14 percent discount, also in March 1997.

Another gem among the closed-end funds is Central Securities. The mid-cap value fund earned a 23.3 percent average annual NAV return for the 1994–1996 period. That's 50 percent better than the 15.4 percent average annual return for the mid-cap value mutual funds. It's also 2 percentage points better than Goldman Sachs Growth & Income Fund A, the best mid-cap value mutual fund over the three-year period. The word is getting out: The fund, which sold at a discount during 1996, went to a 1.5 percent premium in early February of 1997. At that price, a good closed-end can still be a good deal—it's somewhat like buying a mutual fund with a low load. But a month later, the fund traded up to a 7.8 percent premium—which now makes it a fund to watch rather than to buy. If the premium slips, you may want to swoop in and buy some shares.

Wilmot H. Kidd, portfolio manager of Central Securities, attributes the fund's success to patience. "We don't buy stocks because we think they're going to do well in the next three-to-six months," says Kidd. "We're willing to hold three-to-five years." Such a strategy results in a fairly concentrated portfolio—the top 10 holdings make up 59 percent of the assets. But Kidd says he's not uncomfortable with that because the top holdings themselves are diverse, including stocks in the insurance, energy, and semiconductor industries. At year-end 1996, Intel Corp. was the largest single investment, but another major holding was Plymouth Rock Insurance, which is not even a public company. The fund was one of the original backers of the specialty insurers when it was launched a decade ago. That's not the kind of investment you usually find in a conventional mutual fund.

If you study the closed-end fund universe, you will also find many funds managed by the same people who run mutual funds. The top-performing Salomon Brothers Fund shares a portfolio manager with the open-end Salomon Brothers Investors Fund. Both are large-cap blend funds and had nearly identical returns over the last one- and three-year periods. The main

difference: The closed-end trades at a 7.8 percent discount (in March 1997). The mutual fund charges loads, which can add as much as 5 percent to the cost.

Michael Kagan, one of the portfolio managers on both funds, does not make bets on the economy or the market, but only on companies selling at below-average valuations. The biggest holding in early 1997 was the Canadian National Railroad. Why? "The company is starting to go through the same sort of restructuring that the U.S. railroads did several years ago," says Kagan. "They're cutting back unprofitable lines, trimming headcounts, and raising rates. That worked for the U.S. railroads, and it's going to work for them."

Another investing theme for Kagan is pricing power—investing in companies which can raise prices and make them stick. One example of that now is the upscale hotel—like Marriott and Hilton. Because of a shortage of first-class hotel rooms, they're able to raise rates.

Some of the highest premiums among the closed-ends belong to the bond funds. Consider Cigna High-Income Shares, a top-rated fund, sold at 12.1 percent above its NAV in early 1997. The income generated by its portfolio was so great that the yield still came to 9.5 percent. Morgan Stanley High-Yield Fund, another top fund,

TABLE 8-7

TOP-PERFORMING CLOSED-END FUNDS

These funds have earned three upward-pointing arrows, the highest rating for risk-adjusted total return for the 1994–96 period.

	Average annual total return*	Risk	Investment category
EQUITY FUNDS			
CENTRAL SECURITIES	23.3%	Low	Mid-cap Value
EUROPE FUND	21.0	Low	Europe
FIRST FINANCIAL	35.7	Low	Financial
PILGRIM AMERICA BANK & THRIFT	25.6	Low	Financial
QUEST FOR VALUE INCOME	12.0	Very low	Large-cap Blend
SALOMON BROTHERS FUND	20.9	Very low	Large-cap Blend
SOUTHEASTERN THRIFT & BANK	26.7	Very low	Financial
BOND FUNDS			
APEX MUNICIPAL	6.6%	Very low	Muni. Ntl. Long
CIGNA HIGH-INCOME SHARES	11.8	Very low	High Yield
COLONIAL MUNICIPAL INCOME	5.9	Very low	Muni. Ntl. Long
DREYFUS STRATEGIC MUNICIPALS	5.9	Very low	Muni. Ntl. Long
KEMPER STRATEGIC MUNI. INC.	6.2	Very low	Muni. Ntl. Interm.
MFS MUNICIPAL INCOME	6.2	Very low	Muni. Ntl. Long
MORGAN STANLEY HIGH-YIELD	11.8	Low	High Yield
MUNICIPAL HIGH-INCOME	7.1	Very low	Muni. Ntl. Long
NUVEEN CALIF. MUNI. VALUE	4.8	Very low	Muni. S.S. Interm.
PUTNAM HIGH-YIELD MUNI.	5.9	Low	Muni. Ntl. Long

*1994–96, pretax return based on appreciation of net asset value plus reinvestment of dividends and capital gains
DATA: MORNINGSTAR INC.

may look like a better buy, with a 1.7 percent premium. But the income thrown off by that fund was less, and so the current yield was 8.9 percent. The moral: Don't look at the premium alone.

Still, before paying a 10 percent premium for a high-yield closed-end fund, take another look at the high-yield bond mutual funds, especially the top-performing funds such as Northeast Investors. If you still want to consider closed-ends, consider the multisector bond funds. Most of these funds have a good portion of their assets in high-yield bonds, yet they trade at double digit discounts to NAV. That translates into current yields that are nearly as high as those on the high-yield funds that sell at big premiums. If the market gets slammed, the funds selling at premium could be the ones most at risk for a price decline.

New for 1997: Up-and-Coming Funds

It wasn't that long ago that $100 million was considered a pretty good-sized mutual fund. But as hundreds of billions of dollars poured into funds during this decade, the definitions of large and small have changed. A $100 million fund today is barely on the mutual fund radar screen.

Of course, the world doesn't need more funds—only better ones. And surprisingly, many of these smaller funds have excellent returns. The reason many are so small is that they have no marketing or advertising budgets, and so they carry on in relative obscurity. Some others belong to well-known fund families, but have been overshadowed by their larger brethren. And some are small only because they're still new and their track records are still short.

To find these up-and-coming funds, we used Principia for Mutual Funds, a software package developed and sold by Morningstar Inc., which has voluminous data on mutual funds. We screened the database for the top equity funds with at least one year's track record, as well as small funds with good risk-adjusted returns over the last three-year and five-year periods. Defining a small fund as anything under $130 million—the cut-off for funds in the Mutual Fund Scoreboard—we came up with these 50 contenders (Table 8-8). In most cases, the results are no fluke. Many are run by veteran institutional investors with proven track records who manage

money for pension funds and foundations. To obtain further information on these funds, call the telephone numbers in the table.

Smaller funds, especially if they're run by experienced money managers, can be shrewd investments. They're far more nimble than the megafunds, and can buy stocks without necessarily bumping up the price and sell quickly if necessary. Smaller funds do have one drawback: They sometimes have higher expense ratios because they have fewer assets over which to spread the costs.

Among the standouts is the White Oak Growth Stock Fund, with $54 million in assets. The fund has returned an average 29 percent total return per year over the last three years using a high-octane strategy that nonetheless has been only slightly more volatile that the overall stock market. Because of its size, the fund doesn't have to spread its money over hundreds of stocks. Instead, portfolio manager James D. Oelschlager is able to concentrate on his best stock picks. The fund's nearly fully invested, and he holds just 22 stocks. Some 65 percent of the fund's total assets are in high-tech winners such as Intel, Cisco Systems, and 3Com.

The fund may be small, but Oak Associates Ltd., the fund's management company, is no piker. The Akron (Ohio) investment firm also manages $5 billion in assets for large institutional investors such as the California and Oregon state pension systems and for numerous corporations. As for the mutual fund, says Oelschlager, it's relatively unknown because it has not been marketed to anyone other than his acquaintances who asked him to invest their money. "It was much easier to set up a fund for family and friends than manage a bunch of individual accounts," Oelschlager says.

White Oak is not the only "friends and family" fund on the up-and-comers' list. There's the $126 million Torray Fund, which buys what many others shun—companies that are in Wall Street's doghouse. Portfolio manager Robert E. Torray is a patient investor, who finds quality companies and sticks with them until they come into favor—and he'll wait four or five years. He bought Citicorp at 8 (in March 1997, it was 125) and IBM Corp. at less than 50 (in March 1997, it was 145). The fund has a 20.7 percent average annual return over the last five years, about 5 percentage points better than the S&P 500. In total, Torray manages $2.3 billion in pension assets.

Some institutional money managers, such as Susan M. Byrne of Westwood Equity Fund

Funds with $100 million are barely on the radar screen.

TABLE 8-8

UP-AND-COMING FUNDS TO WATCH

Fund	Investment category	Assets ($Million)	Sales charge	Expense ratio	Avg. annual total return(*) 1996	1994–96	1992–96	Phone number
RETIREMENT SYS. EMERGING GRTH.	Small-cap Growth	$7.1	No load	1.85	27.7%	25.3%	23.6%	800-772-3615
PAINEWEBBER FINL. SVCS. GRTH. A	Financial	78.2	4.50%	1.37	28.6	23.5	23.6	800-647-1568
DAVIS FINANCIAL A	Financial	106.9	4.75	1.18	31.5	23.5	23.5	800-279-0279
STATE ST. RESEARCH GLOB. RES. A	Natural Resources	53.8	4.50	1.75	70.3	25.9	23.0	800-882-0052
TORRAY	Mid-cap Value	126.0	No load	1.25	29.1	25.8	20.7	800-443-3036
SPECTRA	Mid-cap Growth	17.1	No load	NA	19.5	22.3	20.4	800-711-6141
IDS PRECIOUS METALS A	Precious Metals	98.5	5.00	1.61	34.3	15.0	20.2	800-328-8300
FIRST AMERICAN SPECL. EQTY. A	Mid-cap Blend	21.3	4.50	1.09	31.9	19.1	19.1	800-637-2548
SHELBY	Small-cap Growth	110.4	No load	1.33	14.0	16.5	19.0	800-752-1823
OMNI INVESTMENT	Small-cap Value	36.3	No load	1.64	25.6	19.1	18.6	800-223-9790
EV TRADITIONAL WORLD HEALTH	Health	54.8	4.75	2.21	18.3	21.3	18.4	800-225-6265
TOCQUEVILLE A	Mid-cap Blend	44.5	4.00	1.57	23.6	16.3	17.6	800-697-3863
WESTWOOD EQUITY RETAIL	Large-cap Blend	38.1	No load	1.50	26.8	21.1	17.1	800-937-8966
FIRST AMERICAN STOCK A	Large-cap Value	27.7	4.50	1.00	29.1	21.0	17.1	800-637-2548
MUHLENKAMP	Mid-cap Value	39.9	No load	1.35	30.1	17.1	17.0	800-860-3863
RETIREMENT SYS. CORE EQUITY	Large-cap Growth	10.3	No load	0.90	24.4	21.5	16.9	800-772-3615
TEMPLETON CAPITAL ACCUMULAT.	World	116.7	9.00	1.00	23.0	13.2	16.6	800-292-9293
STAGECOACH EQUITY VALUE A	Mid-cap Value	19.5	4.50	1.18	26.3	15.5	16.5	800-222-8222
HARRIS INS. EQUITY A	Large-cap Value	7.8	4.50	0.96	24.9	18.3	16.2	800-982-8782
CLOVER CAPITAL EQUITY VALUE	Small-cap Blend	93.1	No load	1.10	22.9	20.1	15.9	800-932-7781
VONTOBEL U.S. VALUE	Large-cap Value	69.9	No load	1.50	21.3	19.4	15.8	800-527-9500
LOOMIS SAYLES GROWTH & INC.	Mid-cap Value	44.0	No load	1.20	21.1	17.5	15.7	800-633-3330
HANCOCK INDEP. EQUITY A	Large-cap Blend	31.0	5.00	0.94	21.2	17.6	15.7	800-225-5291
HAVEN	Mid-cap Blend	69.3	No load	1.53	27.4	17.1	15.4	800-844-4836
PIMCO ADV. EQUITY-INCOME A	Large-cap Blend	24.0	5.50	1.25	25.3	15.5	15.4	800-426-0107
WHITE OAK GROWTH STOCK	Large-cap Growth	54.0	No load	0.97	32.3	29.0		800-932-7781
COMPASS SMALL CAP GRTH. INV. A	Small-cap Growth	29.7	4.50	1.20	31.1	26.5		888-426-6727
DREYFUS LARGE COMPANY VALUE	Large-cap Value	51.6	No load	0.83	31.4	23.0		800-645-6561
DREYFUS SMALL COMPANY VALUE	Small-cap Value	23.8	No load	0.91	34.2	21.7		800-645-6561
DAVIS REAL ESTATE A	Real Estate	26.7	4.75	1.43	37.1	20.4		800-279-0279
SMITH BREEDEN EQUITY PLUS	Large-cap Blend	8.9	No load	0.90	24.4	20.1		800-221-3138
THOMPSON PLUMB GROWTH	Large-cap Blend	12.6	No load	2.00	32.2	20.1		608-831-1300
BILTMORE SPECIAL VALUES A	Small-cap Value	8.0	4.50	1.29	37.0	19.9		800-994-4414
FRANKLIN REAL ESTATE SECS. I	Real Estate	77.3	4.50	0.67	32.5	19.7		800-342-5236
PACIFIC ADVISORS SMALL CAP	Small-cap Value	8.4	5.75	2.49	43.7	17.5		800-282-6693
EXCELSIOR LT. SUPPLY OF ENERGY	Natural Resources	33.8	4.50	0.96	38.4	17.4		800-446-1012
HEARTLAND VALUE PLUS	Small-cap Value	49.2	No load	1.54	33.8	16.5		800-432-7856
INTERACTIVE INV. TECH. VALUE	Technology	35.1	No load	NA	60.6			888-883-3863
WARBURG PINCUS SMALL VAL. COM.	Small-cap Blend	97.7	No load	NA	56.2			800-927-2874
NEEDHAM GROWTH	Mid-cap Blend	14.4	No load	NA	51.6			800-331-3186
MORGAN STANLEY LATIN AMER. A	Latin America	18.4	4.75	2.11	47.4			800-282-4404
PREMIER GROWTH & INCOME B	Domestic Hybrid	45.7	4.00**	NA	47.3			800-554-4611
GT GLOBAL NATURAL RES. B	Natural Resources	69.1	5.00**	2.87	46.5			800-824-1580
VAN ECK GLOBAL HARD ASSETS A	Natural Resources	22.3	4.75	NA	45.7			800-826-1115
CGM REALTY	Real Estate	110.2	No load	1.00	44.1			800-345-4048
ROBERTSON STEPHENS PARTNERS	Small-cap Value	116.4	No load	2.41	43.2			800-766-3863
ROBERTSON STEPHENS GLOB. NAT.	Natural Resources	119.1	No load	2.60	41.2			800-766-3863
LINDNER/RYBACK SM.-CAP. INV.	Small-cap Value	13.7	No load	1.22	41.2			314-727-5305
CRM SMALL CAP VALUE	Small-cap Value	57.8	No load	1.49	39.0			800-276-2883
DREYFUS AGGRESSIVE VALUE	Mid-cap Growth	33.6	No load	NA	38.9			800-645-6561

*Pretax return, includes appreciation plus reinvestment of dividends and capital gains
**Deferred sales charge

DATA: MORNINGSTAR INC.

Retail Class, decided not to wait for the fund mavens to discover them. She started marketing the fund two years ago and managed to get its assets up from $16 million to $38 million. Of course, good returns are the best marketing plan, and that she has. This fund, a blend of large-cap stocks, competes in a pretty crowded fund category, yet it beat the S&P 500 over the last one, three, and five years.

The $9 million Smith Breeden Equity Plus Fund is another market-beating bantam-size fund. Portfolio manager John Sprow calls it an "enhanced index fund," which means he's trying to beat the S&P 500 index by about 1 percentage point a year. That doesn't sound like much, but it's a hurdle that many funds can't clear.

Sprow takes an unorthodox approach. Rather than invest in the stocks that are in the index, he buys stock-index futures with a small part of the fund and invests the rest in mortgage-backed securities, which provide a much higher yield than stocks. Over the last three years, the fund returned about 0.40 percent a year more than the index. The fund has been in business since 1992.

Two highly rated small funds that follow more conventional investment philosophies are managed by the Retirement Systems Group Inc., a pension consulting firm. Despite its relative obscurity—the fund management company specializes in running bank pension plans—two of its seven funds have excellent records. The $10 million RSI Core Equity Fund has beaten the S&P consistently over the last few years by focusing on out-of-favor large-cap stocks, says manager James P. Coughlin. Its sister fund, the $7 million RSI Emerging Growth, produced an even better record by investing in small-cap growth stocks. The fund earned a 23.6 percent average annual total return for the 1992–1996 period. That's over 8 percentage points better than the index and the average small-cap growth fund.

Not all managers of the tiny funds are obscure. The $17 million Spectra Fund is managed by David Alger, who also runs six other funds totalling $7.3 billion in assets sold mainly by stockbrokers and insurance companies. Spectra was closed to new investors until January 1996 and is the only no-load fund managed by his firm, Fred Alger Management Inc.

True to Alger's aggressive investment style, Spectra focuses on high-growth stocks—32 percent of the fund is in technology. The fund can also sell stocks short, though Alger says he has not yet done so. Although Spectra failed to beat the market in 1996, it has an excellent long-term record. "We've been reluctant to send out flares [about no-load Spectra] because it might antagonize our brokers," says Alger.

Well, Mr. Alger, the word is out—about Spectra and about other gems among the small funds. With investors' insatiable appetite for mutual funds, these funds won't be under wraps for very long.

The BUSINESS WEEK
Mutual Fund Scoreboard

Equity Funds

MUTUAL FUND SCOREBOARD

How to Use the Tables

▲ ▲ ▲	SUPERIOR
▲ ▲	VERY GOOD
▲	GOOD
AVG	AVERAGE
▼	BELOW AVERAGE
▼ ▼	POOR
▼ ▼ ▼	VERY POOR

BUSINESS WEEK RATINGS
Overall ratings are based on five-year risk-adjusted returns. They are calculated by subtracting a fund's risk-of-loss factor (see RISK) from historical pretax total return. To get a positive rating, the fund must beat the S&P 500 on a risk-adjusted basis. Category ratings are based on risk-adjusted returns of the funds in that category. The ratings are as follows:

MANAGEMENT CHANGES
⌂ indicates the fund's manager has held the job at least 10 years; ⌂ indicates a new manager since Dec. 31, 1995.

S&P 500 COMPARISON
The pretax total returns for the S&P 500 are as follows: 1996, 22.9%; three-year average (1994-1996), 19.7%; five-year average (1992-96), 15.2%; 10-year average (1987-96), 15.3%.

CATEGORY
Each U.S. diversified fund is classified by market capitalization of the stocks in the portfolio and by the nature of those stocks. If the median market cap is greater than $5 billion, the fund is large-cap; from $1 billion to $5 billion, mid-cap; and less than $1 billion, small-cap. "Value" funds are those whose stocks have price-to-earnings and price-to-book ratios lower than that of the S&P 500. "Growth" funds have higher than average p–e's and p–b's. "Blend" funds are those in which the ratios are about average. Hybrids mix stocks and bonds, and possibly other assets. World funds generally include U.S. stocks, foreign funds do not. Sector and regional foreign funds are as indicated.

FUND (COMPARES RISK-ADJUSTED PERFORMANCE OF EACH FUND AGAINST ALL FUNDS)	OVERALL RATING	CATEGORY (COMPARES RISK-ADJUSTED PERFORMANCE OF FUND WITHIN CATEGORY)	RATING	SIZE ASSETS $MIL.	% CHG. 1995-6	FEES SALES CHARGE (%)	EXPENSE RATIO (%)	1996 RETURNS (%) PRE-TAX	AFTER-TAX	YIELD
AARP BALANCED STOCK & BOND		Domestic Hybrid		445.9	61	No load	0.88	13.2	11.9	2.8
AARP CAPITAL GROWTH	▼	Large-cap Blend	▼▼▼	877.2	24	No load	0.90	20.6	17.4	0.9
AARP GROWTH & INCOME ⌂	▲▲▲	Large-cap Blend	▲▲▲	4606.5	41	No load	0.69	21.6	19.4	2.5
ACORN ⌂	▲	Small-cap Growth	▲▲▲	2853.7	19	No load	0.57	22.6	19.2	0.7
ACORN INTERNATIONAL		Foreign		1771.7	39	No load	1.20	20.7	20.0	0.6
AIM AGGRESSIVE GROWTH	▼	Small-cap Growth	▲▲	2724.0	18	5.50‡	1.08†	14.3	12.7	0.0
AIM BALANCED A	AVG	Domestic Hybrid	▼	333.7	263	4.75	1.43†	19.3	17.6	2.5
AIM BLUE CHIP A (a) ⌂	AVG	Large-cap Growth	▲▲	158.0	115	5.50	1.26†	23.8	18.6	0.4
AIM CHARTER A	AVG	Large-cap Blend	▼▼	2804.2	35	5.50	1.17†	19.6	17.3	1.4
AIM CONSTELLATION A	▼	Mid-cap Growth	AVG	11915.2	62	5.50	1.20†	16.3	15.2	0.0
AIM GLOBAL AGGRESSIVE GROWTH A		World		1032.6	335	4.75	2.11†	23.5	23.5	0.0
AIM GLOBAL GROWTH B		World		142.5	425	5.00**	2.64†	19.3	19.3	0.0
AIM GLOBAL UTILITIES A	▼	Utilities	▼	162.9	–4	5.50	1.21†	13.9	12.7	3.5
AIM GROWTH B		Mid-cap Growth		280.4	103	5.00**	2.13†	17.6	16.1	0.0
AIM INTERNATIONAL EQUITY A		Foreign		1223.5	73	5.50	1.67†	19.0	18.1	0.1
AIM SUMMIT		Mid-cap Blend	▼▼	1305.6	24	8.50	0.71	19.9	16.9	0.2
AIM VALUE A	▲	Mid-cap Blend	▲	5128.4	51	5.50	1.12†	14.5	12.9	1.4
AIM WEINGARTEN A	▼▼	Mid-cap Blend	▼▼	5109.9	12	5.50	1.20†	17.7	14.0	0.3
ALGER CAPITAL APPRECIATION		Mid-cap Growth		156.0	215	5.00**	3.43†	13.8	13.6	0.0
ALGER GROWTH ⌂	▼	Mid-cap Growth	AVG	288.8	67	5.00**	2.07†	12.3	11.3	0.0
ALGER MIDCAP GROWTH		Mid-cap Growth		138.9	130	5.00**	2.34†	12.0	11.3	0.0
ALGER SMALL CAPITALIZATION ⌂	▼▼▼	Mid-cap Growth	▼▼▼	582.6	18	5.00**	2.11†	4.2	–0.5	0.0
ALLIANCE A ⌂	▼	Large-cap Blend	▼▼	958.5	7	4.25	1.08†	17.5	12.9	0.3
ALLIANCE GROWTH & INCOME A	AVG	Large-cap Blend	AVG	588.2	23	4.25	1.05†	24.1	19.5	1.5
ALLIANCE GROWTH B	▲	Large-cap Blend	AVG	2717.2	62	4.00**	2.05†	22.3	21.2	0.0
ALLIANCE INTERNATIONAL A	▼▼	Foreign	▼	193.4	12	4.25	1.72†	7.2	5.2	0.6
ALLIANCE PREMIER GROWTH B		Large-cap Blend		406.9	70	4.00**	2.43†	23.3	21.2	0.0
ALLIANCE QUASAR A	▼	Small-cap Growth	▲	249.7	58	4.25	1.79†	32.6	27.3	0.0
ALLIANCE TECHNOLOGY B		Technology		665.7	137	4.00**	2.48†	18.5	18.3	0.0
ALLIANCE WORLDWIDE PRIVATIZATION A		Foreign		529.4	–25	4.25	1.87†	23.1	18.9	1.2
AMCAP ⌂	▼	Large-cap Growth	▲	3784.1	7	5.75	0.71†	14.2	11.1	0.8
AMCORE VINTAGE EQUITY		Large-cap Blend		252.2	29	No load	1.09†	21.4	20.2	0.4
AMERICA'S UTILITY		Utilities		143.2	–11	No load	1.21	5.5	4.2	3.8
AMERICAN BALANCED ⌂	▲▲	Domestic Hybrid	▲▲	3941.3	29	5.75	0.67†	13.2	10.2	3.6
AMERICAN CENT. BALANCED (b)	▼	Domestic Hybrid	▼▼▼	878.4	5	No load	0.98	12.6	9.4	2.6
AMERICAN CENT. EQUITY GROWTH (c) ⌂	AVG	Large-cap Value	▼▼▼	274.3	72	No load	0.71	20.1	17.9	1.6
AMERICAN CENT. EQUITY INCOME (d)		Mid-cap Value		187.2	93	No load	0.98	23.3	19.6	2.7
AMERICAN CENT. GLOBAL GOLD (e)	▼▼▼	Precious Metals	▼	433.5	–20	No load	0.61	–2.8	–4.4	0.5
AMERICAN CENT. INCOME & GROWTH (f)	▲▲	Large-cap Value	AVG	715.1	91	No load	0.67	23.9	20.9	1.9
AMERICAN CENT. UTILITIES (g)		Utilities		144.6	–33	No load	0.75	4.5	3.3	3.7
AMERICAN CENT. VALUE (h)		Mid-cap Value		1548.2	137	No load	0.97	24.3	20.8	1.5
AMERICAN CENT.-20THC. GIFTRUST (i)	▼▼▼	Small-cap Growth	▼	874.4	45	No load	0.98	5.8	4.9	0.0
AMERICAN CENT.-20THC. GROWTH (j) ⌂	▼▼▼	Large-cap Growth	▼▼▼	4667.2	–4	No load	1.00	15.0	14.4	0.8
AMERICAN CENT.-20THC. HERITAGE (k)	▼	Mid-cap Growth	AVG	1125.5	10	No load	0.99	15.3	13.3	0.7
AMERICAN CENT.-20THC. INTL. DIS. (l)		Foreign		390.0	222	2.00*	2.00	31.2	29.6	0.2

*Includes redemption fee. **Includes deferred sales charge. †12(b)-1 plan in effect. ‡Not currently accepting new accounts. §Less than 0.5% of assets. NA=Not available. NM=Not meaningful. (a) Formerly Baird Blue Chip. (b) Formerly Twentieth Century Balanced Investors. (c) Formerly Benham Equity Growth. (d) Formerly Twentieth Century Equity-Income. (e) Formerly Benham Gold

SALES CHARGE
The cost of buying a fund. Many funds take this "load" out of the initial investment, and for ratings purposes, returns are reduced by these charges. Loads may be levied on withdrawals.

EXPENSE RATIO
Expenses for 1996 as a percentage of average net assets, a measure of how much shareholders pay for management. Footnotes indicate if the ratio includes a 12(b)-1 plan, which spends shareholder money on marketing. The average is 1.29%.

PRETAX TOTAL RETURN
A fund's net gain to investors, including reinvestment of dividends and capital gains at month-end prices.

AFTERTAX TOTAL RETURN
Pretax return adjusted for federal taxes. Assumes ordinary income and capital gains taxed at highest rate applicable in each year; uses 31% tax rate on income since 1991. Capital gains are assumed to be long-term.

YIELD
Income distributions as a percent of net asset value, adjusted for capital gains distributions.

TREND
A fund's relative performance during the four 30-month periods from Jan. 1, 1987 to Dec. 31, 1996. Boxes read from left to right, and the level of blue indicates performance relative to all other funds in that period: ■ for the top quartile; ▣ for the second quartile; ▨ for the third quartile; □ for the bottom quartile. An empty box indicates no data for that period.

TURNOVER
Trading activity, the lesser of purchases or sales divided by average monthly assets.

% CASH
Portion of fund assets not invested in stocks or bonds. A negative number means the fund has borrowed to buy securities.

% FOREIGN
Portion of funds assets invested in non-U.S. securities.

PRICE-EARNINGS RATIO
The average, weighted price-earnings ratio of stocks in a fund's portfolio, based on last 12 months' earnings.

UNTAXED GAINS
Percentage of assets in portfolio that are unrealized and undistributed capital gains. A negative figure indicates losses that may offset future gains.

LARGEST HOLDING
Comes from the latest available fund reports.

RISK
Potential for losing money in a fund, or risk-of-loss factor. For each fund, the three-month Treasury bill return is subtracted from the monthly total return for each of the 60 months in the ratings period. When a fund has not performed as well as Treasury bills, the monthly result is negative. The sum of these negative numbers is divided by the number of months. The result is a negative number, and the greater its magnitude, the higher the risk of loss. This number is the basis for BW ratings, category ratings, and the RISK column.

BEST & WORST QUARTERS
The fund's highest and lowest quarterly returns of the past five years.

AVERAGE ANNUAL TOTAL RETURNS (%)						TREND	PORTFOLIO DATA						RISK	BEST		WORST		TELEPHONE
3 YEARS		5 YEARS		10 YEARS		BW 10-YEAR	TURNOVER	CASH	FOREIGN	P-E	UNTAXED	LARGEST HOLDING	LEVEL					
PRETAX	AFTERTAX	PRETAX	AFTERTAX	PRETAX	AFTERTAX	ANALYSIS		%	%	RATIO	GAINS (%)	COMPANY (% ASSETS)		QTR	%RET	QTR	%RET	
Less than three years of data available							Low	3	11	22	17	Xerox(1)						800-322-2282
12.3	10.8	11.5	9.8	13.3	11.4		Average	2	12	21	38	Hewlett-Packard(3)	High	II 95	10.8	I 94	-8.1	800-322-2282
18.2	16.2	15.9	14.2	13.9	12.0		Low	2	15	22	34	Xerox(3)	Low	II 95	8.8	I 94	-3.3	800-322-2282
11.1	8.7	17.6	15.5	16.1	13.5		Low	2	20	26	43	Newell(2)	Average	IV 92	16.0	I 94	-5.5	800-922-6769
8.1	7.9						Low	8	98	25	23	WM-Data Cl B(3)						800-922-6769
23.8	22.9	24.9	24.0	18.8	17.4		Average	6	2	38	28	Cascade Communs.(1)	High	IV 92	26.4	II 92	-12.5	800-347-4246
15.0	13.8	14.0	13.0	11.4	9.7		Average	9	13	27	10	Gucci Group(1)	Average	II 95	11.0	II 92	-4.1	800-347-4246
19.6	17.0	12.9	11.0	13.8	12.6		Average	5	7	25	18	General Electric(4)	Average	I 95	9.1	I 92	-4.1	800-347-4246
15.8	13.3	11.4	9.6	15.1	12.4		High	2	9	26	17	FNMA(2)	Average	II 95	11.1	I 92	-4.1	800-347-4246
16.9	15.8	16.6	16.0	19.2	16.5		Average	7	5	33	24	Cisco Systems(1)	High	IV 92	19.6	I 92	-9.3	800-347-4246
Less than three years of data available							Average	4	52	29	14	Bank Intl, Indonesia(1)						800-347-4246
Less than three years of data available							Average	4	62	26	8	Hang Seng Bank(1)						800-347-4246
8.9	7.5	9.4	7.5				Average	2	30	19	9	Ameritech(3)	Average	IV 96	10.0	I 94	-7.8	800-347-4246
13.8	12.2						Average	6	5	30	15	FORE Systems(1)						800-347-4246
10.2	9.3						Average	6	100	26	18	HSBC Holdings (HK)(1)						800-347-4246
16.3	14.0	12.2	9.9	14.3	11.9		High	3	5	28	27	Nike(1)	High	II 95	13.8	I 92	-6.4	800-347-4246
16.8	15.5	17.1	15.4	18.4	15.6		High	21	17	22	11	Ameritech(2)	Average	II 95	12.2	II 94	-4.2	800-347-4246
16.5	12.7	9.6	7.3	15.1	13.0		High	6	11	29	24	SLMA(2)	High	II 95	12.5	I 92	-7.6	800-347-4246
25.7	25.3						Very high	-5	8	39	9	Cisco Systems(3)						800-992-3863
15.2	14.0	15.4	14.0	15.7	14.4		High	5	6	31	13	Cisco Systems(3)	High	II 95	17.5	II 94	-6.4	800-992-3863
18.2	17.2						High	4	6	36	11	Service International(3)						800-992-3863
14.0	11.7	11.7	9.7	18.5	16.4		High	4	5	43	36	Cascade Communs.(3)	Very high	II 95	22.8	II 92	-10.9	800-992-3863
15.6	10.9	15.2	11.2	14.7	10.2		Average	3	4	24	22	Philip Morris(5)	Average	II 95	13.5	I 94	-3.8	800-227-4618
17.9	14.6	13.5	10.4	13.3	8.6		High	3	3	22	31	AT&T(4)	Average	II 95	11.5	I 94	-4.0	800-227-4618
15.6	14.8	16.9	15.2				Average	4	5	27	16	Cisco Systems(6)	Average	IV 92	14.4	I 94	-3.5	800-227-4618
7.6	5.5	8.4	6.9	7.6	4.7		Average	0	100	28	10	DDI(2)	High	I 93	8.7	III 92	-6.9	800-227-4618
19.0	16.8						High	3	3	23	13	Philip Morris(7)						800-227-4618
22.0	16.3	16.7	13.0	13.4	10.3		High	7	6	32	27	Nine West Group(3)	High	I 96	18.8	II 92	-10.5	800-227-4618
29.9	28.0						Average	13	5	39	12	Cisco Systems(5)						800-227-4618
Less than three years of data available							Low	0	96	19	17	Pharmacia & Upjohn(3)						800-227-4618
13.6	10.7	11.8	9.0	13.5	10.6		Low	11	4	28	30	Medtronic(4)	Average	II 95	9.6	I 94	-3.0	800-421-4120
18.9	18.0						Low	1	1	24	28	Hewlett-Packard(2)						800-438-6375
6.6	5.3						Low	5	1	16	6	Potomac Electric Power(4)						800-487-3863
13.0	10.7	12.0	9.6	11.9	9.1		Low	16	6	19	13	Phillips Petroleum(2)	Very low	I 95	7.5	I 94	-3.7	800-421-4120
11.0	8.5	6.6	4.9				Average	5	3	32	15	HFS(2)	Average	II 95	8.6	I 92	-6.7	800-345-2021
17.3	15.1	13.4	11.4				High	1	0	18	21	S&P 500 Index (Fut)(3)	Average	II 95	9.6	I 92	-5.3	800-331-8331
Less than three years of data available							High	3	2	20	11	Giant Food Cl A(4)						800-345-2021
-4.0	-4.6	7.9	7.5				Low	0	74	44	18	Barrick Gold(14)	Very high	II 93	34.3	IV 94	-17.6	800-331-8331
19.1	16.5	15.2	13.2				Average	1	1	18	18	S&P 500 Index (Fut)(4)	Low	II 95	9.4	I 94	-4.5	800-331-8331
8.5	7.1						Average	2	6	17	3	Bell Atlantic(5)						800-331-8331
19.7	16.6						High	3	3	20	11	Giant Food Cl A(4)						800-345-2021
18.4	16.6	20.8	18.5	21.8	19.5		High	3	9	50	21	PMT Services(5)	Very high	IV 92	28.8	II 92	-15.0	800-345-2021
10.9	7.7	6.3	3.7	13.9	11.2		High	5	7	31	12	Newbridge Networks(4)	High	II 95	12.1	IV 95	-8.4	800-345-2021
11.0	9.2	12.7	10.7				High	0	14	30	21	Conseco(3)	High	III 95	11.8	II 92	-7.9	800-345-2021
Less than three years of data available							High	0	99	26	16	Getinge Industrier Cl B(3)						800-345-2021

Equities Index. (f) Formerly Benham Income & Growth. (g) Formerly Benham Utilities Income. (h) Formerly Twentieth Century Value. (i) Formerly Twentieth Century Giftrust Investors. (j) Formerly Twentieth Century Growth Investors. (k) Formerly Twentieth Century Heritage Investors. (l) Formerly Twentieth Century Intl. Emerging Grth.   DATA: MORNINGSTAR, INC., CHICAGO, IL.

MUTUAL FUND SCOREBOARD

FUND	OVERALL RATING (COMPARES RISK-ADJUSTED PERFORMANCE OF EACH FUND AGAINST ALL FUNDS)	CATEGORY (COMPARES RISK-ADJUSTED PERFORMANCE OF FUND WITHIN CATEGORY)	RATING	ASSETS $MIL.	% CHG. 1995-6	SALES CHARGE (%)	EXPENSE RATIO (%)	PRE-TAX	AFTER-TAX	YIELD
AMERICAN CENT.-20THC. INTL. GROWTH (m) AVG		Foreign	▲▲	1364.8	8	No load	1.77	14.4	11.1	0.0
AMERICAN CENT.-20THC. SELECT (n)	▼▼	Large-cap Blend	▼▼	4060.5	2	No load	1.00	19.2	16.0	0.8
AMERICAN CENT.-20THC. ULTRA (o)	▼▼	Large-cap Growth	▼▼▼	18418.6	27	No load	1.00	13.9	12.0	0.0
AMERICAN CENT.-20THC. VISTA (p)	▼▼▼	Mid-cap Growth	▼▼▼	2236.1	26	No load	0.99	7.6	5.3	0.0
AMERICAN GAS INDEX	AVG	Natural Resources	▲	228.7	7	No load	0.85	20.8	19.7	3.0
AMERICAN MUTUAL	▲▲	Large-cap Value	AVG	7981.7	15	5.75	0.59†	16.2	13.2	3.1
AMERICAN NATIONAL GROWTH	▼	Large-cap Blend	▼▼	152.8	13	5.75	0.98	17.6	16.3	0.9
AMERICAN NATIONAL INCOME	▲	Large-cap Blend	AVG	165.8	18	5.75	1.12	16.5	14.9	2.3
AMSOUTH BALANCED	▲	Domestic Hybrid	AVG	356.7	12	4.50	0.98	9.7	7.3	3.5
AMSOUTH EQUITY	▲	Large-cap Value	▼▼	397.9	18	4.50	1.02	15.8	13.5	1.6
ARIEL APPRECIATION	AVG	Small-cap Blend	AVG	146.3	5	No load	1.36†	23.7	21.9	0.3
ARTISAN INTERNATIONAL		Foreign		191.5	NM	No load	2.50	34.4	34.1	0.0
ARTISAN SMALL CAP		Small-cap Blend		296.1	10	No load‡	2.00	11.9	9.6	0.0
BABSON ENTERPRISE	▲▲	Small-cap Value	AVG	191.6	-5	No load‡	1.09	21.3	16.5	0.0
BABSON GROWTH	▲	Large-cap Growth	▲	311.2	15	No load	0.85	21.8	17.4	0.6
BABSON VALUE	▲▲▲	Large-cap Value	▲▲▲	783.7	154	No load	0.98	22.7	21.7	1.3
BARON ASSET	▲	Small-cap Growth	▲▲▲	1326.3	276	No load	1.40†	22.0	21.9	0.0
BARON GROWTH & INCOME		Small-cap Growth		244.0	494	No load	1.50†	27.7	27.2	0.5
BERGER 100	▼▼	Mid-cap Growth	▼	2003.8	-7	No load	1.42†	13.7	9.4	0.0
BERGER GROWTH & INCOME (q)	AVG	Large-cap Blend	▼▼	320.9	-8	No load	1.56†	15.6	11.6	1.3
BERGER SMALL COMPANY GROWTH		Small-cap Growth		782.0	37	No load	1.68†	16.8	15.3	0.0
BERNSTEIN EMERGING MKTS. VALUE		Diversified Emerging Mkts.		297.2	206	2.00*	1.92	7.1	6.9	0.4
BERNSTEIN INTERNATIONAL VALUE		Foreign		3370.7	55	No load	1.31	17.5	15.2	5.5
BERWYN INCOME	▲▲▲	Domestic Hybrid	▲▲▲	137.2	15	No load‡	0.73	14.0	10.7	6.3
WILLIAM BLAIR GROWTH	AVG	Mid-cap Growth	▲▲	501.6	38	No load	0.65	18.0	16.7	0.1
BNY HAMILTON EQUITY-INCOME		Large-cap Blend		203.4	20	No load	1.00†	19.6	16.5	1.9
BRANDYWINE 25,000	▼	Mid-cap Growth	▲	6546.9	55	No load	1.06	24.9	23.6	0.0
BT INVESTMENT EQUITY 500 INDEX		Large-cap Blend		447.5	62	No load	0.25	22.8	21.9	1.8
BT INVESTMENT EQUITY APPREC.		Mid-cap Growth		154.7	41	No load	1.00	9.6	7.6	0.7
BT INVESTMENT INTL. EQUITY		Foreign		197.8	131	No load	1.50	21.3	20.5	0.9
BT INVESTMENT SMALL CAP		Small-cap Growth		192.0	18	No load	1.25	6.9	4.7	0.0
CALVERT SOCIAL INV. MANAGED A	AVG	Domestic Hybrid	▼▼	602.9	5	4.75	1.26†	9.0	6.3	2.4
CALVERT STRATEGIC GROWTH A		Domestic Hybrid		137.4	1	4.75	2.29†	14.3	12.6	0.0
CALVERT WORLD VALUE INTL. EQ. A (r)		World		200.3	5	4.75	1.79†	12.0	11.3	0.3
CAPITAL INCOME BUILDER	▲▲	Domestic Hybrid	▲	5809.2	21	5.75	0.72†	17.6	15.5	4.4
CAPITAL WORLD GROWTH & INCOME		World		5213.0	40	5.75	0.88†	21.6	19.3	2.9
CARDINAL	AVG	Large-cap Value	▼▼▼	238.3	3	4.50	0.70†	19.4	14.3	1.0
CENTURY SHARES	AVG	Financial	▼▼	270.8	1	No load	0.94	17.2	15.5	1.4
CGM CAPITAL DEVELOPMENT	▼▼	Mid-cap Blend	▼▼▼	615.8	18	No load‡	0.85	28.1	22.0	0.2
CGM MUTUAL	AVG	Large-cap Value	▼▼▼	1182.8	2	No load	0.91	23.7	18.9	2.1
CHESAPEAKE GROWTH		Small-cap Blend		501.4	18	3.00‡	1.42	10.8	9.1	0.0
CHICAGO TRUST ASSET ALLOCATION		Domestic Hybrid		162.5	3	No load	NA†	16.6	15.1	2.8
CHICAGO TRUST GROWTH & INCOME		Large-cap Blend		215.2	17	No load	1.09†	25.4	24.5	0.7
CITIZENS INDEX		Large-cap Growth		161.9	31	No load	1.82†	23.1	22.7	0.4
CLIPPER	▲	Large-cap Value	▼	542.8	35	No load	1.11	19.4	17.0	1.2
COHEN & STEERS REALTY SHARES	▲▲	Real Estate		2036.4	157	No load	1.12	38.5	36.3	4.1
COLONIAL A	▲*	Mid-cap Value	▼	799.7	17	5.75	1.16†	16.7	14.2	1.6
COLONIAL GLOBAL UTILITIES A	AVG	Utilities	▲	174.9	-18	5.75	1.29†	12.7	11.5	3.4
COLONIAL GROWTH SHARES A	AVG	Mid-cap Blend	AVG	270.6	37	5.75	1.12†	20.5	16.5	0.0
COLONIAL NEWPORT TIGER A		Pacific ex-Japan		575.3	194	5.75	NA†	10.9	10.8	0.5
COLONIAL U.S. FUND FOR GROWTH B		Large-cap Blend		341.3	31	5.00**	2.20†	18.8	16.1	0.0
COLONIAL UTILITIES B		Utilities		729.2	-15	5.00**	1.96†	5.2	4.2	3.2
COLUMBIA BALANCED	▲▲	Domestic Hybrid	▲▲	672.6	38	No load	0.69	11.8	8.7	3.5
COLUMBIA COMMON STOCK	▲▲	Large-cap Blend	▲▲	536.8	50	No load	0.80	20.9	16.0	1.0
COLUMBIA GROWTH	AVG	Large-cap Blend	▲▲	1064.1	25	No load	0.75	20.9	15.9	0.5
COLUMBIA SPECIAL	▼	Mid-cap Growth		1585.3	15	No load	0.98	13.0	7.3	0.0
COMMERCE GROWTH		Mid-cap Growth		225.3	51	3.50	1.11	22.5	20.1	0.6
COMMON SENSE GROWTH & INCOME I	AVG	Large-cap Blend	▼	1004.6	26	8.50	0.96	17.9	13.6	1.6
COMMON SENSE GROWTH I	AVG	Large-cap Growth	▲	3189.0	37	8.50	1.00	18.9	16.1	1.0
COMPOSITE BOND & STOCK A	▲▲	Large-cap Value	AVG	266.0	20	4.50	1.02†	13.6	10.5	3.3
COMPOSITE GROWTH & INCOME A	▲	Large-cap Value	▼	194.2	37	4.50	1.07†	22.3	19.7	0.9
COMPOSITE NORTHWEST A	▼▼	Mid-cap Blend	▼▼	191.3	19	4.50	1.10†	22.6	19.6	0.0
COMSTOCK PARTNERS CAP VAL. A (s)	▼▼▼	International Hybrid	▼▼	179.0	-29	4.50	1.69†	-5.7	-7.4	6.4
COMSTOCK PARTNERS STRATEGY O	▼	International Hybrid	▼	157.7	-37	4.50‡	1.23†	-0.9	-3.1	7.3
CRABBE HUSON EQUITY PRIM.	▲▲	Mid-cap Value	AVG	405.5	-6	No load	1.40†	11.7	9.3	0.3
CRABBE HUSON SPECIAL PRIM.	AVG	Small-cap Blend		435.6	-53	No load	1.40†	5.9	5.0	1.0
DAVIS N.Y. VENTURE A	AVG	Large-cap Value	▼▼	2658.8	48	4.75	0.87†	26.5	24.8	1.0
DEAN WITTER AMERICAN VALUE	▼	Large-cap Growth	▼	3099.5	30	5.00**	1.61†	10.5	7.4	0.0
DEAN WITTER CAPITAL APPRECIATION		Small-cap Growth		325.2	180	5.00**	NA†	23.1	23.1	0.0
DEAN WITTER CAPITAL GROWTH	▼▼	Mid-cap Blend	▼▼▼	499.4	-3	5.00**	1.89†	10.7	5.7	0.0

*Includes redemption fee. **Includes deferred sales charge. †12(b)-1 plan in effect. ‡Not currently accepting new accounts. §Less than 0.5% of assets. NA=Not available. NM=Not meaningful.
(m) Formerly Twentieth Century Intl. Equity. (n) Formerly Twentieth Century Select Investors. (o) Formerly Twentieth Century Ultra Investors. (p) Formerly Twentieth Century Vista Investors.
(q) Formerly Berger 101. (r) Formerly Calvert World Values Global Equity A. (s) Formerly Dreyfus Capital Value A (Premier).

3 Yr Pretax	3 Yr Aftertax	5 Yr Pretax	5 Yr Aftertax	10 Yr Pretax	10 Yr Aftertax	Turnover	Cash %	Foreign %	P-E Ratio	Untaxed Gains %	Largest Holding Company (% Assets)	Risk Level	Best QTR	Best %RET	Worst QTR	Worst %RET	Telephone
6.8	5.3	12.8	11.2			High	0	98	28	15	Sandoz (Reg)(5)	Average	IV 93	18.3	IV 94	−5.9	800-345-2021
10.4	7.2	8.1	5.3	11.7	8.9	High	2	6	29	21	Tyco International(3)	High	II 95	8.8	I 92	−7.3	800-345-2021
14.7	13.3	13.3	12.4	20.2	18.1	Average	1	5	35	30	Cisco Systems(6)	Very high	IV 92	19.1	II 92	−11	800-345-2021
18.1	16.5	11.2	9.1	15.2	13.6	High	4	4	52	30	PairGain Technologies(7)	Very high	III 94	18.4	II 92	−10.2	800-345-2021
12.5	11.3	13.1	11.7			Very low	2	NA	18	24	PanEnergy(5)	Average	I 93	15.1	IV 93	−7.0	800-343-3355
15.3	12.5	13.6	10.8	12.8	10.0	Low	19	1	19	30	DuPont(2)	Low	I 95	7.5	I 94	−3.2	800-421-4120
15.6	12.9	10.1	7.1	12.3	8.9	Low	4	4	23	22	PepsiCo(2)	Average	I 95	8.4	I 92	−7.5	800-231-4639
14.1	11.5	11.2	8.5	12.4	9.4	Average	6	1	21	21	PepsiCo(3)	Low	I 95	8.1	I 94	−4.1	800-231-4639
10.5	8.4	10.9	9.0			Low	2	3	22	15	AmSouth Prime Obligations(3)	Very low	I 95	7.4	I 94	−2.5	800-451-8379
14.0	12.1	14.1	12.3			Low	0	3	22	23	Gannett(2)	Low	I 95	9.3	I 94	−2.8	800-451-8379
12.1	9.9	11.5	10.0			Low	1	NA	22	40	Rouse(5)	Average	IV 92	11.7	I 94	−4.8	800-292-7435
Less than three years of data available							2	100	18	9	Astra Cl B(3)						800-344-1770
Less than three years of data available							1	3	22	13	Zale(3)						800-344-1770
13.1	9.4	15.9	12.3	14.0	10.9	Very low	5	3	19	25	Helen of Troy(2)	Low	I 92	13.8	II 92	−4.3	800-422-2766
16.8	13.8	13.9	11.5	12.3	9.1	Low	2	1	26	42	American Home Products(3)	Low	I 95	8.7	I 94	−3.1	800-422-2766
18.3	17.2	18.6	17.3	14.6	13.1	Very low	8	8	17	16	Apple Computer(3)	Low	I 95	9.7	IV 94	−1.7	800-422-2766
21.0	20.7	20.0	19.5			Low	0	2	31	13	Manor Care(11)	Average	I 96	14.8	II 92	−8.6	800-992-2766
Less than three years of data available						Average	1	4	30	11	Manor Care(7)						800-992-2766
8.8	6.9	11.1	10.0	18.1	16.0	High	6	5	34	40	Conseco(3)	High	IV 92	18.2	II 94	−10.8	800-333-1001
9.2	7.7	11.0	10.0	11.9	10.1	High	9	6	29	30	Boeing(3)	Average	II 95	9.0	IV 94	−6.2	800-333-1001
21.1	20.6					Average	10	5	43	32	ACC(2)						800-333-1001
Less than three years of data available							3	NA	20	−7	So. Africa Iron & Steel Indl.(3)						212-756-4097
9.6	8.2					Low	2	100	23	12	Hitachi(3)						212-756-4097
10.9	8.2	14.2	11.1			Low	6	14	21	7	Callon Petroleum(2)	Very low	I 92	10.6	IV 94	−2.5	800-992-6757
17.5	15.8	15.1	12.9	15.7	12.3	Low	2	7	32	30	First Data(3)	Average	III 93	9.5	I 92	−5.0	800-742-7272
13.6	11.9					Average	4	8	23	20	Boeing(2)						800-426-9363
19.3	16.8	19.2	16.9	19.2	17.0	Very high	1	3	31	23	Intel(4)	High	IV 92	20.5	II 92	−8.6	800-656-3017
19.4	18.5					Very low	2	2	24	22	General Electric(3)						800-730-1313
16.0	15.0					High	10	8	37	15	Green Tree Financial(2)						800-730-1313
13.6	12.6					Average	8	100	24	18	ING(2)						800-730-1313
26.5	24.8					High	4	3	45	19	Transaction Sys. Architects A(2)						800-730-1313
9.3	6.6	8.3	6.1	9.4	7.3	High	2	5	26	11	Albertson's(2)	Low	II 95	7.2	I 94	−3.4	800-368-2748
Less than three years of data available						Very high	36	5	55	16	Vantive(4)						800-368-2748
6.8	5.7					Average	11	99	26	6	Sun Hung Kai Properties(3)						800-368-2748
12.9	10.9	12.8	10.9			Low	24	26	17	16	American Home Products(4)	Very low	IV 96	9.8	I 94	−5.8	800-421-4120
14.3	12.6					Low	9	66	20	18	ING(2)						800-421-4120
13.8	10.0	11.4	8.4	11.8	9.1	Low	3	6	23	29	Cincinnati Financial(4)	Low	IV 96	7.9	IV 94	−4.3	800-848-7734
15.0	13.4	14.0	12.4	13.4	11.0	Very low	1	NA	15	67	American Intl. Group(9)	Average	IV 96	12.4	IV 93	−8.6	800-321-1928
11.7	8.9	16.1	12.3	19.2	14.6	Very high	3	6	24	28	Jones Apparel Group(6)	High	II 92	21.7	IV 94	−14.8	800-345-4048
11.5	9.0	12.4	9.7	13.8	10.6	Very high	22	NA	24	16	Citicorp(7)	Average	IV 96	12.8	I 92	−5.3	800-345-4048
15.6	14.2					High	1	6	24	19	System Software Assoc.(3)						800-525-3863
Less than three years of data available							7	NA	28	7	Gillette(2)						800-992-8151
19.5	19.0					Very low	7	NA	26	17	Royal Dutch Petroleum (NY)(4)						800-992-8151
Less than three years of data available						Very low	0	0	25	24	Coca-Cola(7)						800-223-7010
19.1	16.7	16.9	14.1	15.0	12.0	Low	25	2	24	29	FHLMC(12)	Average	II 95	12.7	I 94	−4.8	800-776-5033
18.6	16.8	18.9	16.7			Low	8	NA	29	11	Public Storage(5)	Average	I 93	20.5	IV 93	−6.9	800-437-9912
13.7	11.0	13.7	11.4	12.3	9.9	Average	5	13	18	22	Oracle(3)	Low	II 95	9.0	I 94	−2.4	800-248-2828
7.4	5.9	9.5	7.8			Average	0	45	16	5	Korea Electric Power (ADR)(3)	Low	I 93	8.7	I 94	−4.3	800-248-2828
17.4	14.1	14.6	11.4	14.7	10.9	High	6	NA	27	27	Safeway(3)	Average	II 95	11.4	II 92	−4.8	800-248-2828
Less than three years of data available							5	100	19	11	HSBC Holdings (HK)(5)						800-248-2828
14.8	12.3					Average	2	0	21	24	Merck(3)						800-248-2828
7.8	6.5					Very low	0	NA	15	−4	Nynex(4)						800-248-2828
11.9	9.7	11.6	9.6			High	3	2	22	11	American Home Products(2)	Very low	I 93	6.3	I 94	−2.5	800-547-1707
17.3	14.7	15.6	13.5			Average	1	2	22	19	Service International(3)	Low	III 95	8.4	I 94	−2.6	800-547-1707
16.9	13.6	15.1	11.8	15.8	12.0	High	1	5	27	23	Warnaco Group Cl A(4)	Average	IV 92	12.5	II 92	−5.4	800-547-1707
14.3	10.5	15.6	12.0	18.1	15.3	Very high	7	6	32	20	ADC Telecomm.(1)	High	IV 92	19.7	II 92	−8.6	800-547-1707
Less than three years of data available							3	NA	23	31	Mobil(4)						800-305-2140
16.0	11.9	12.8	9.7			High	6	9	24	24	Texaco(2)	Average	I 95	9.7	I 94	−3.9	800-544-5445
15.6	12.2	12.6	9.4			Very high	4	6	25	16	Van Kampen Am. Sm. Cap(4)	Average	II 95	10.5	I 92	−2.8	800-544-5445
13.4	11.2	11.9	9.9	10.6	8.4	Low	11	3	21	20	FNMA(1)	Very low	II 95	8.2	I 94	−3.5	800-543-8072
18.6	16.7	14.6	12.6	12.1	9.8	Low	1	5	24	30	Lockheed Martin(2)	Low	I 95	8.1	IV 94	−1.5	800-543-8072
15.2	14.0	10.2	9.2	15.0	14.3	Very low	3	NA	26	40	Microsoft(2)	High	I 96	9.3	IV 92	−9.0	800-543-8072
−4.2	−5.5	−2.4	−3.6	5.5	3.7	Average	58	67	30	−46	Ashanti Goldfld (144A)(2)	High	IV 93	5.7	IV 92	−8.7	800-554-4611
−0.1	−2.0	3.6	1.4			High	1	63	17	−13	Vaal Reefs Expl. & Mng.(1)	Average	IV 93	7.7	IV 94	−3.6	800-645-6561
12.0	10.3	15.6	13.9			High	2	7	28	12	USG(3)	Low	IV 93	8.9	IV 94	−1.9	800-541-9732
9.5	8.2	18.7	17.7			High	32	5	30	−2	Integrated Health Services(5)	High	I 92	19.3	II 92	−7.3	800-541-9732
20.4	18.4	17.8	15.8	17.4	14.1	High	8	1	20	29	American Express(3)	Average	II 95	12.3	I 92	−5.8	800-279-0279
13.6	11.3	12.6	10.6	14.9	12.9	Very high	0	5	32	9	Intel(3)	High	III 95	13.4	II 94	−7.2	800-869-3863
Less than three years of data available							0	5	37	NA	Technology Solutions(2)						800-869-3326
12.1	10.4	5.0	3.4			Low	0	NA	30	28	Computer Associates Intl.(3)	High	IV 92	10.2	I 92	−7.3	800-869-3863

DATA: MORNINGSTAR, INC., CHICAGO, IL.

MUTUAL FUND SCOREBOARD

FUND (COMPARES RISK-ADJUSTED PERFORMANCE OF EACH FUND AGAINST ALL FUNDS)	OVERALL RATING	CATEGORY (COMPARES RISK-ADJUSTED PERFORMANCE OF FUND WITHIN CATEGORY)	RATING	SIZE ASSETS $MIL.	% CHG. 1995-6	FEES SALES CHARGE (%)	EXPENSE RATIO (%)	1996 RETURNS (%) PRE-TAX	AFTER-TAX	YIELD
DEAN WITTER DEVELOPING GROWTH	▼▼▼	Mid-cap Growth	▼▼	775.2	36	5.00**	1.77†	12.3	7.7	0.0
DEAN WITTER DIVIDEND GROWTH ◆	▲	Large-cap Blend	▲▲	12151.2	30	5.00**	1.31†	19.3	18.2	2.0
DEAN WITTER EUROPEAN GROWTH	▲	Europe	▲▲▲	1371.0	54	5.00**	2.23†	28.9	26.1	0.6
DEAN WITTER GLOBAL DIV. GROWTH		World		2913.9	30	5.00**	1.97†	16.9	14.2	0.9
DEAN WITTER GLOBAL UTILITIES		Utilities		354.2	0	5.00**	1.87†	13.2	12.9	1.0
DEAN WITTER HEALTH SCIENCES		Health		471.0	31	5.00**	2.30†	1.2	-0.5	0.0
DEAN WITTER INFORMATION		Communications		277.8	99	5.00**	NA†	-0.2	-0.2	0.0
DEAN WITTER MID-CAP GROWTH		Mid-cap Growth		364.8	80	5.00**	2.05†	14.5	12.0	0.0
DEAN WITTER NATURAL RES. DEV.	AVG	Natural Resources	▲	236.1	57	5.00**	1.90†	27.0	22.3	0.2
DEAN WITTER PACIFIC GROWTH	▼▼	Diversified Pacific		1640.4	12	5.00**	2.45†	4.8	4.3	1.6
DEAN WITTER STRATEGIST	AVG	Domestic Hybrid	▼	1370.5	9	5.00**	1.63†	15.3	12.0	2.0
DEAN WITTER UTILITIES	AVG	Utilities	▼	2682.9	-19	5.00**	1.65†	5.0	3.7	3.8
DEAN WITTER VALUE-ADDED MKT. EQ.	▲	Mid-cap Blend	AVG	1110.9	38	5.00**	1.51†	17.1	16.3	0.6
DEAN WITTER WORLDWIDE INVMT.	▼▼	World	▼▼	473.0	-5	5.00**	2.41†	6.3	4.3	0.0
DELAWARE A	▲	Domestic Hybrid	▲	506.5	-1	4.75	0.97†	13.9	10.1	3.1
DELAWARE DECATUR INCOME A	▲▲	Large-cap Blend	▲▲	1580.7	13	4.75	0.87†	20.3	14.9	3.2
DELAWARE DECATUR TOTAL RET. A	▲▲	Large-cap Blend	▲▲	660.5	20	4.75	1.19†	20.0	15.6	2.1
DELAWARE DELCAP A ◆	▼▼	Mid-cap Growth	▼	860.4	0	4.75	1.35†	13.8	9.9	0.0
DELAWARE TREND A ◆	▼	Small-cap Growth	AVG	481.3	21	4.75	1.31†	10.7	8.0	0.0
DELAWARE VALUE A	▲	Small-cap Value	AVG	202.2	12	4.75	1.48†	22.1	17.0	0.5
DG EQUITY		Large-cap Blend		457.8	27	3.50	0.94	17.6	16.6	0.9
DODGE & COX BALANCED	▲▲▲	Domestic Hybrid	▲▲	3349.7	86	No load	0.57	14.8	13.3	3.3
DODGE & COX STOCK	▲▲	Large-cap Value	▲	2227.6	81	No load	0.60	22.3	21.0	1.6
DREYFUS	▼	Large-cap Blend	▼▼	2711.7	2	No load	0.74	15.9	12.4	0.7
DREYFUS APPRECIATION	AVG	Large-cap Growth	▲▲▲	876.7	90	No load	0.92	25.7	25.3	1.0
DREYFUS BALANCED ◆		Domestic Hybrid		292.2	49	No load	1.00	11.6	9.5	2.6
DREYFUS CORE VALUE INV.	▲	Large-cap Value	▼▼	488.9	22	No load	1.13†	21.4	15.6	0.8
DREYFUS GROWTH & INCOME	▲▲	Mid-cap Blend	▲▲	2008.7	8	No load	1.06	14.4	9.8	1.7
DREYFUS GROWTH OPPORTUNITY	▼▼	Large-cap Blend	▼▼	464.4	14	No load	1.04	22.3	18.0	0.8
DREYFUS MIDCAP INDEX	AVG	Mid-cap Blend	AVG	184.1	43	1.00*	0.50	18.5	16.6	1.2
DREYFUS NEW LEADERS ◆	AVG	Small-cap Blend	▲	795.6	31	1.00*	1.19	17.3	15.0	0.0
DREYFUS S&P 500 INDEX	▲	Large-cap Blend	▲	653.3	60	1.00*	0.55	22.3	20.7	1.6
DREYFUS THIRD CENTURY	▼	Large-cap Growth	▼	562.4	34	No load	1.11	24.3	19.5	0.2
ECLIPSE FINANCIAL EQUITY	AVG	Small-cap Value	▼	170.7	-2	No load	1.14	29.9	21.3	0.8
ENTERPRISE GROWTH A ◆	AVG	Large-cap Growth	▲	196.1	60	4.75	1.60†	32.6	30.6	0.3
EUROPACIFIC GROWTH ◆	AVG	Foreign	▲▲▲	15726.6	44	5.75	0.95†	18.6	17.0	1.6
EV MARATHON GREATER CHINA GROWTH		Pacific ex-Japan		288.9	-5	5.00**	2.47†	15.1	15.0	0.4
EV TRADITIONAL GROWTH	▼▼	Large-cap Blend	▼▼▼	136.3	1	4.75	0.98†	18.2	15.5	0.5
EV TRADITIONAL INVESTORS	▲	Domestic Hybrid	AVG	223.5	-6	4.75	0.95†	13.8	9.7	2.8
EV TRADITIONAL TOTAL RETURN	▼	Utilities	▼▼	398.5	-13	4.75	1.19	7.0	3.8	5.7
EVERGREEN Y ◆	AVG	Mid-cap Blend	AVG	877.3	36	No load	1.15	17.6	16.6	0.7
EVERGREEN BALANCED Y	▲	Domestic Hybrid	AVG	748.7	-8	No load	0.62	11.7	7.9	4.1
EVERGREEN FOUNDATION Y	▲▲	Domestic Hybrid	▲▲	807.8	30	No load‡	1.07	11.5	10.1	3.3
EVERGREEN GROWTH & INCOME Y ◆	▲▲	Mid-cap Blend	▲▲	441.9	215	No load	1.27	23.8	23.0	0.8
EVERGREEN TOTAL RETURN Y ◆	AVG	Mid-cap Value	▼	856.6	-7	No load	1.19	12.9	11.2	5.1
EVERGREEN VALUE A ◆	▲	Large-cap Value	▼	328.1	12	4.75	0.90†	13.9	13.6	1.7
EXCELSIOR EQUITY A (t)	AVG	Mid-cap Blend	AVG	307.9	79	4.50	1.05	19.9	18.3	0.5
EXCELSIOR INCOME & GROWTH (u)	▲▲▲	Mid-cap Blend	▲▲▲	134.9	13	4.50	1.05	18.9	16.7	2.2
FAM VALUE	AVG	Small-cap Value	▼	253.6	-5	No load	1.25	11.2	10.3	0.7
FEDERATED AMERICAN LEADERS A (v)	▲	Large-cap Blend	AVG	604.9	46	5.50	1.16	19.4	16.8	0.9
FEDERATED EQUITY-INCOME A (w)	▲▲	Large-cap Value	▲▲	376.3	106	5.50	1.03	22.2	19.4	2.6
FEDERATED GROWTH STRAT. A	▼	Mid-cap Blend	▼▼	393.6	60	5.50	1.10	23.3	19.8	0.1
FEDERATED MAX-CAP INSTL. ◆	▲	Large-cap Blend	▲	953.1	30	No load	0.31	22.8	21.5	1.9
FEDERATED MINI-CAP ◆		Small-cap Blend		157.9	18	No load	0.73	15.3	12.4	1.0
FEDERATED INTL. EQUITY A	▼▼	Foreign		156.5	-14	5.50	1.57	5.8	5.1	0.0
FEDERATED MGD. GROWTH INSTL.		Domestic Hybrid		136.2	94	No load	1.00	10.5	8.6	3.3
FEDERATED STOCK & BOND A (x)	▲▲	Domestic Hybrid	▲	138.8	1	No load	1.07	13.7	9.5	3.1
FEDERATED STOCK ◆	▲	Large-cap Value	▼	839.8	26	No load	1.01	21.2	16.9	1.4
FEDERATED UTILITY A (y)	AVG	Utilities	AVG	761.5	-7	5.50	1.15	11.9	9.1	3.3
FIDELITY ADVISOR BALANCED T (z) ◆	AVG	Domestic Hybrid		2877.6	-18	3.50	1.46†	8.4	7.2	3.1
FIDELITY ADVISOR EQUITY GROWTH T (aa) ◆		Large-cap Growth		3439.5	64	3.50	1.54†	16.2	15.1	0.4
FIDELITY ADVISOR EQUITY INCOME T (bb) ◆		Large-cap Growth		1652.9	73	3.50	1.47†	14.6	13.2	1.3
FIDELITY ADVISOR FOCUS NAT. RES. T (cc) ◆	▲	Natural Resources	▲▲▲	648.6	105	3.50	1.84†	30.5	28.3	0.1
FIDELITY ADVISOR GROWTH OPPORT. T (dd)	▲▲▲	Large-cap Blend	▲▲▲	15527.9	42	3.50	1.58†	17.7	15.9	1.5
FIDELITY ADVISOR OVERSEAS T (ee) ◆		Foreign	AVG	1038.6	29	3.50	1.90†	12.4	10.8	1.0
FIDELITY ADVISOR STRAT. OPPORT. T (ff) ◆	AVG	Large-cap Blend	▼	563.2	-8	3.50	1.61†	1.5	-1.4	0.8
FIDELITY ASSET MANAGER ◆	▲▲	Domestic Hybrid	▲	10971.9	-2	No load	0.93	12.7	10.1	3.6
FIDELITY ASSET MANAGER: GROWTH ◆	▲	International Hybrid	▲	3377.8	17	No load	1.01	17.6	14.7	2.5
FIDELITY ASSET MANAGER: INCOME ◆		Domestic Hybrid		588.4	-2	No load	0.80	7.8	5.5	5.1
FIDELITY BALANCED	▼	Domestic Hybrid		3919.2	-20	No load	0.79	9.3	7.8	4.6

*Includes redemption fee. **Includes deferred sales charge. †12(b)-1 plan in effect. ‡Not currently accepting new accounts. §Less than 0.5% of assets. NA=Not available. NM=Not meaningful. (t) Formerly UST Master Equity. (u) Formerly UST Master Income & Growth. (v) Formerly American Leaders A. (w) Formerly Liberty Equity-Income A. (x) Formerly Stock & Bond. (y) Formerly Liberty Utility A. (z) Formerly Fidelity Advisor Income & Growth A. (aa) Formerly Fidelity Advisor Equity Growth A. (bb) Formerly Fidelity Advisor Equity Income A. (cc) Formerly Fidelity Advisor Global Resources A. (dd) Formerly Fidelity Advisor Growth Opport. A. (ee) Formerly Fidelity Advisor Overseas A. (ff) Formerly Fidelity Advisor Strategic Opport. A.

Equity Funds

DATA: MORNINGSTAR, INC., CHICAGO, IL.

3 YEARS PRETAX	3 YEARS AFTERTAX	5 YEARS PRETAX	5 YEARS AFTERTAX	10 YEARS PRETAX	10 YEARS AFTERTAX	TREND BW 10-YEAR ANALYSIS	TURNOVER	CASH %	FOREIGN %	P-E RATIO	UNTAXED GAINS (%)	LARGEST HOLDING COMPANY (% ASSETS)	RISK LEVEL	BEST QTR	BEST %RET	WORST QTR	WORST %RET	TELEPHONE
16.5	14.0	15.1	13.2	13.4	12.4		High	0	4	39	28	HFS(2)	Very high	IV 92	22.9	II 92	−15.0	800-869-3863
15.9	15.1	13.5	12.7	13.5	12.1		Very low	2	2	21	38	Gillette(2)	Low	I 95	9.3	I 94	−4.8	800-869-3863
19.7	17.4	18.7	17.2				Average	5	99	23	27	Hennes & Mauritz Cl B(2)	Average	III 93	11.9	III 92	−6.5	800-869-3863
14.5	12.7						Low	1	68	22	13	Northrop Grumman(2)						800-869-3863
Less than three years of data available							Low	4	69	19	12	Australian Gas Light(3)						800-869-3863
15.4	14.0						High	3	6	41	29	Dura Pharmaceuticals(2)						800-869-3863
Less than three years of data available								5	12	38	NA	MFS Communications(1)						800-869-3863
Less than three years of data available							Very high	−2	3	36	13	Nike(2)						800-869-3863
15.8	13.0	14.2	12.0	12.3	10.3		Average	5	10	28	23	Exxon(3)	Average	I 93	10.8	IV 94	−5.7	800-869-3863
−3.5	−4.3	12.8	12.2				Average	1	99	23	3	Cheung Kong Holdings(3)	Very high	IV 93	35.6	I 94	−18.4	800-869-3863
12.0	9.4	10.3	8.1				Very high	10	1	24	13	Pier 1 Imports(1)	Low	I 95	6.9	I 94	−2.5	800-869-3863
7.0	5.5	8.3	6.8				Very low	1	10	18	19	Williams(2)	Average	I 93	7.8	I 94	−6.4	800-869-3863
14.8	14.2	13.9	13.4				Very low	3	2	22	29	NorAm Energy($)	Average	I 95	8.8	I 94	−2.7	800-869-3863
1.1	0.1	6.1	5.1	7.3	5.5		Average	2	73	28	11	Hutchison Whampoa(1)	High	IV 93	11.5	IV 94	−7.8	800-869-3863
12.3	9.6	11.8	9.1	11.6	8.4		High	2	10	23	17	Philip Morris(4)	Very low	IV 96	6.4	I 94	−2.1	800-523-4640
16.6	12.9	14.8	11.1	12.3	8.8		Average	1	9	20	18	McGraw-Hill(2)	Low	I 95	9.8	I 94	−3.8	800-523-4640
17.7	14.3	15.2	11.6	13.1	10.4		Average	1	10	20	19	McGraw-Hill(3)	Low	I 95	10.7	I 94	−3.8	800-523-4640
11.8	8.5	9.8	7.6	15.0	13.3		Average	9	5	30	32	Healthsouth(3)	High	IV 92	15.2	II 92	−11.6	800-523-4640
12.4	10.3	16.3	13.6	17.2	14.6		Average	13	5	34	19	CUC International(4)	High	IV 92	19.7	II 92	−9.3	800-523-4640
12.0	9.6	13.9	12.1				Average	7	1	20	24	AmeriCredit(1)	Low	IV 92	11.9	IV 94	−4.9	800-523-4640
17.4	16.1						Very low	6	NA	25	25	McDonald's(4)						800-748-8500
14.5	12.8	14.0	12.3	13.2	11.0		Low	4	8	19	11	Dayton Hudson(2)	Very low	II 95	8.0	I 94	−1.2	800-621-3979
19.7	18.2	17.6	16.1	15.4	13.7		Very low	7	7	19	22	Dayton Hudson(3)	Low	I 95	9.7	I 94	−0.7	800-621-3979
11.1	6.4	9.0	5.5	10.8	7.2		Very high	1	7	27	14	Amerada Hess(3)	Average	I 95	8.8	I 92	−2.9	800-645-6561
21.6	21.0	13.5	13.0	14.8	13.4		Very low	4	6	23	27	Coca-Cola(5)	Average	II 95	9.7	I 94	−5.2	800-645-6561
13.2	11.1						Very high	0	6	27	8	Corning(2)						800-645-6561
18.2	13.9	14.9	11.3	12.2	8.3		Average	2	15	23	24	Philip Morris(2)	Average	II 95	9.5	I 92	−2.6	800-645-6561
10.7	8.3	14.1	12.3				High	13	5	26	20	Time Warner(2)	Low	IV 92	8.8	IV 94	−3.7	800-645-6561
13.7	8.9	7.5	3.5	11.4	7.8		Very high	4	4	25	14	NorAm Energy(3)	High	I 95	10.1	I 92	−9	800-645-6561
14.0	12.1	13.5	11.9				Low	0	0	25	18	U.S. Robotics(1)	Average	IV 92	11.7	I 94	−3.8	800-645-6561
15.0	12.5	14.3	11.7	14.4	12.3		High	6	3	30	22	Mentor(2)	Average	III 93	11.6	II 92	−7.1	800-645-6561
19.0	16.9	14.7	12.9				Very low	0	3	23	24	S&P 500 (Fut)(7)	Low	I 95	9.6	I 94	−3.9	800-645-6561
16.0	12.3	10.9	8.2	13.5	10.4		High	11	2	27	28	BankAmerica(3)	High	I 95	11.0	I 92	−5.6	800-645-6561
14.0	10.3	15.7	12.1				Average	2	4	17	34	Ingles Markets Cl A(1)	Average	IV 92	15.3	II 94	−6.2	800-872-2710
22.5	20.8	16.7	14.8	16.5	13.6		Average	4	2	32	39	Intel(4)	High	II 95	14.8	II 92	−7	800-432-4320
10.6	9.2	13.4	12.4	13.7	11.9		Low	12	100	23	19	Mannesmann(2)	Average	III 93	10.9	III 92	−3.8	800-421-4120
−2.0	−2.1						Low	0	99	18	8	Hutchison Whampoa(5)						800-225-6265
13.5	11.1	8.4	6.3	12.0	9.3		High	3	14	25	33	Astra Cl A Free(4)	High	IV 92	9.0	II 93	−5.5	800-225-6265
13.2	10.4	11.4	8.4	11.5	8.2		Average	4	16	23	28	Astra Cl A Free(3)	Very low	II 95	8.1	I 92	−3.1	800-225-6265
6.2	3.9	6.9	4.2	8.1	4.9		High	7	9	18	21	Frontier(4)	Average	I 93	10.5	I 94	−7.6	800-225-6265
17.6	15.1	13.4	11.4	12.3	9.8		Low	19	1	24	37	Clear Channel Communs.(3)	Average	IV 92	12.4	II 92	−5.1	800-807-2940
11.5	8.8	10.7	8.5				Low	6	1	20	18	General Electric(1)	Very low	II 95	7.1	I 94	−2.9	800-807-2940
12.7	11.1	14.7	12.9				Low	13	0	22	7	Intel(2)	Low	II 95	9.5	I 94	−3.7	800-807-2940
18.7	17.3	16.9	15.4	14.6	12.7		Low	19	2	25	14	FNMA(3)	Low	I 95	10.5	I 94	−4.2	800-807-2940
9.4	7.4	10.2	7.8	8.8	6.3		High	3	20	18	−1	Hanson (ADR)(3)	Low	I 93	7.6	I 94	−6.8	800-807-2940
16.9	13.4	13.5	10.7	13.4	10.9		Average	2	NA	19	20	General Mills(3)	Low	I 95	10.4	I 94	−2.8	800-807-2940
15.7	13.9	16.0	14.4	13.6	12.1		Low	6	5	26	22	Mellon Bank(3)	Average	IV 92	10.6	I 94	−5.6	800-446-1012
13.9	12.2	16.3	14.8				Low	4	18	23	24	United Meridian(3)	Very low	II 95	10.5	IV 94	−3.4	800-446-1012
12.5	11.5	12.3	11.5	12.9	12.1		Very low	4	NA	18	23	Conmed(7)	Average	IV 92	18.0	II 92	−4.9	800-932-3271
17.9	16.1	15.4	13.4	13.2	10.7		Average	5	4	22	21	Mobil(3)	Average	I 95	9.2	IV 94	−2.8	800-341-7400
16.3	14.4	15.7	13.9	13.2	10.3		High	4	8	21	10	H.J. Heinz(3)	Low	I 95	9.5	I 94	−4.1	800-341-7400
15.0	11.2	12.0	9.5	13.8	11.2		High	7	10	29	22	SunAmerica(2)	Average	III 95	12.0	I 94	−5.8	800-341-7400
19.3	16.8	14.8	12.5				Average	3	3	24	16	General Electric(3)	Low	I 95	9.6	I 94	−3.9	800-341-7400
12.3	10.5						Low	10	0	25	17	Iomega($)						800-341-7400
4.2	2.5	6.9	5.7	6.4	3.9		High	0	100	31	7	Nippon Comsys(1)	High	III 93	9.4	III 92	−7.9	800-341-7400
Less than three years of data available							High	4	31	24	5	AT&T(1)						800-341-7400
11.7	8.8	9.6	7.0				Average	2	5	22	16	Philip Morris(1)	Very low	II 95	6.8	I 94	−2.8	800-341-7400
17.8	15.0	15.6	12.9	12.6	10.0		Average	3	6	22	37	Philip Morris(3)	Average	II 95	9.2	IV 94	−3.4	800-341-7400
8.9	6.5	10.2	8.0				Average	1	6	16	12	FPL Group(4)	Low	IV 96	10.0	I 94	−7.2	800-341-7400
5.5	4.4	8.9	7.4				Very high	3	8	20	1	Philip Morris(3)	Low	I 93	8.0	I 94	−3.1	800-522-7297
17.0	15.9						High	10	3	28	16	General Electric(2)						800-522-7297
17.4	16.1						Average	11	3	21	16	Philip Morris(3)						800-522-7297
18.0	16.8	20.7	19.1				High	5	20	29	20	Bre-X Minerals(3)	Average	I 93	13.1	IV 94	−7.2	800-522-7297
17.2	15.7	17.8	16.2				Average	9	11	20	17	Philip Morris(6)	Low	II 95	11.4	IV 94	−1	800-522-7297
7.6	6.9	11.0	10.5				Average	13	97	25	11	Veba(3)	High	I 93	13.9	III 92	−7.9	800-522-7297
9.2	7.4	12.1	9.9	11.9	9.5		High	3	11	19	14	Whole Foods Market(5)	Average	II 95	10.3	I 94	−6.5	800-522-7297
7.6	6.0	11.6	9.9				High	17	16	21	21	FNMA(4)	Very low	IV 93	7.2	I 94	−4.8	800-544-8888
9.3	8.0	14.7	13.4				High	12	38	22	23	Philip Morris(4)	Low	IV 93	8.0	IV 94	−5.1	800-544-8888
7.5	5.7						High	41	13	20	10	FNMA(2)						800-544-8888
6.0	4.7	8.9	7.0	10.6	8.3		Very high	1	13	19	1	Philip Morris(2)	Very low	I 93	8.3	I 94	−3.2	800-544-8888

MUTUAL FUND SCOREBOARD

FUND	OVERALL RATING (COMPARES RISK-ADJUSTED PERFORMANCE OF EACH FUND AGAINST ALL FUNDS)	CATEGORY (COMPARES RISK-ADJUSTED PERFORMANCE OF FUND WITHIN CATEGORY)	RATING	SIZE ASSETS $MIL.	% CHG. 1995-6	SALES CHARGE (%)	EXPENSE RATIO (%)	PRE-TAX	AFTER-TAX	YIELD
FIDELITY BLUE CHIP GROWTH	▲	Mid-cap Growth	▲▲▲	9569.7	23	3.00	0.95	15.4	13.0	0.8
FIDELITY CANADA	▼▼	Foreign	▼	143.6	−18	4.00*	1.08	16.0	9.4	0.6
FIDELITY CAPITAL APPRECIATION	▲▲	Mid-cap Blend	▲▲	1653.7	−1	3.00	1.06	15.1	12.3	0.6
FIDELITY CONTRAFUND	▲▲	Mid-cap Blend	▲▲	23797.9	60	3.00	0.96	21.9	19.0	0.8
FIDELITY DESTINY I	▲▲▲	Large-cap Value	▲▲▲	4903.2	15	8.67	0.65	18.6	15.2	2.1
FIDELITY DESTINY II	▲▲▲	Large-cap Value	▲▲	2797.2	27	8.67	0.78	17.9	15.2	2.0
FIDELITY DISCIPLINED EQUITY	AVG	Large-cap Blend	AVG	2099.0	−2	No load	0.75	15.1	12.8	1.0
FIDELITY DIVERSIFIED INTL.	▼	Foreign	AVG	737.6	116	No load	1.12	20.0	18.9	1.0
FIDELITY DIVIDEND GROWTH		Mid-cap Blend		2345.2	343	No load	0.99	30.1	29.3	0.4
FIDELITY EMERGING GROWTH	▼▼	Mid-cap Growth	▼	1854.1	48	3.75*	1.09	15.8	15.0	0.0
FIDELITY EMERGING MARKETS	▼▼▼	Diversified Emerging Mkts.		1282.7	18	4.50*	1.28	10.0	9.5	1.5
FIDELITY EQUITY-INCOME	▲▲▲	Large-cap Value	▲▲▲	14258.9	36	No load	0.67	21.0	18.8	2.3
FIDELITY EQUITY-INCOME II	▲▲▲	Large-cap Value	▲▲▲	15238.4	27	No load	0.75	18.7	16.4	2.1
FIDELITY EUROPE CAPITAL APPREC.		Europe		185.3	3	4.00*	1.36	25.9	22.3	1.6
FIDELITY EUROPE	AVG	Europe	▲	749.8	50	4.00*	1.18	25.6	23.2	0.9
FIDELITY EXPORT		Small-cap Blend		397.5	4	3.75*	1.00	38.6	36.7	0.0
FIDELITY FIFTY		Mid-cap Growth		147.4	−6	3.00	0.99	15.8	13.8	0.6
FIDELITY	▲▲	Large-cap Blend	▲▲	4450.8	38	No load	0.60	19.8	17.0	1.4
FIDELITY GROWTH & INCOME	▲▲▲	Large-cap Blend	▲▲▲	23896.5	61	No load	0.74	20.0	18.3	1.4
FIDELITY GROWTH COMPANY	▼	Large-cap Growth		9272.6	48	No load	0.95	16.8	15.3	0.7
FIDELITY HONG KONG & CHINA		Pacific ex-Japan		167.1	NM	4.50*	NA	41.0	40.4	1.0
FIDELITY INTL. GROWTH & INCOME	▼	International Hybrid	▼	1063.4	13	No load	1.18	12.7	11.6	1.5
FIDELITY INTL. VALUE		Foreign		275.5	278	No load	1.72	9.6	8.7	0.9
FIDELITY JAPAN		Japan		286.9	−24	4.00*	1.15	−11.2	−11.2	0.1
FIDELITY LATIN AMERICA		Latin America		530.5	12	4.50*	1.41	30.7	30.0	1.8
FIDELITY LOW-PRICED STOCK	▲▲▲	Small-cap Value	▲▲▲	5664.3	69	4.50*	1.04	26.9	23.9	1.0
FIDELITY MAGELLAN	AVG	Mid-cap Blend	AVG	53988.7	1	3.00	0.92	11.7	7.1	1.2
FIDELITY MARKET INDEX	▲	Large-cap Blend	▲	1597.5	132	0.50*	0.45	22.6	21.3	1.7
FIDELITY MID-CAP STOCK		Mid-cap Blend		1695.1	46	No load	1.00	18.1	15.4	0.2
FIDELITY NEW MILLENNIUM		Mid-cap Growth		1252.9	111	3.00‡	1.18	23.2	22.2	0.0
FIDELITY OTC	AVG	Mid-cap Growth	▲▲	3387.2	44	3.00	0.82	23.7	19.5	0.2
FIDELITY OVERSEAS	▼▼	Foreign	▼	3252.8	35	No load	1.05	13.1	11.1	1.1
FIDELITY PACIFIC BASIN	▼▼▼	Diversified Pacific		500.2	7	4.00*	1.32	−2.8	−2.9	0.5
FIDELITY PURITAN	▲▲▲	Domestic Hybrid	▲▲▲	18501.7	18	No load	0.72	15.2	11.4	3.3
FIDELITY REAL ESTATE INVMT.	AVG	Real Estate		1721.6	143	0.75*	0.95	36.2	34.6	4.0
FIDELITY RETIREMENT GROWTH	AVG	Mid-cap Blend	AVG	4045.9	−1	No load	0.99	8.3	4.6	1.3
FIDELITY SEL. AIR TRANSPORT	▼▼▼	Specialty-Misc.		131.5	40	3.75*	1.41	1.2	0.9	0.0
FIDELITY SEL. AMERICAN GOLD	▼▼▼	Precious Metals	▲▲	354.8	13	3.75*	1.39	19.9	19.3	0.0
FIDELITY SEL. BIOTECHNOLOGY	▼▼▼	Health	▼▼	635.0	−25	3.75*	1.43	5.6	2.2	0.1
FIDELITY SEL. COMPUTERS	AVG	Technology	▲▲	664.0	33	3.75*	1.38	31.5	29.7	0.0
FIDELITY SEL. DEVELOP. COMMUN.	▼▼	Communications		275.3	−7	3.75*	1.51	14.6	14.6	0.0
FIDELITY SEL. ELECTRONICS	▲▲▲	Technology	▲▲▲	1565.2	75	3.75*	1.22	41.7	41.7	0.0
FIDELITY SEL. ENERGY	▼▼	Natural Resources		239.7	82	3.75*	1.63	32.4	30.2	0.5
FIDELITY SEL. ENERGY SERVICE		Natural Resources	AVG	562.8	121	3.75*	1.58	49.0	47.6	0.0
FIDELITY SEL. FINANCIAL SVCS.	▲▲	Financial	AVG	337.5	34	3.75*	1.41	32.1	29.7	0.8
FIDELITY SEL. FOOD & AGRICULTURE	▲	Specialty-Misc.		252.8	5	3.75*	1.42	13.3	11.1	0.5
FIDELITY SEL. HEALTH CARE	▼▼	Health	▲▲	1242.3	−14	3.75*	1.30	15.4	10.5	0.6
FIDELITY SEL. HOME FINANCE	▲▲▲	Financial	▲▲▲	794.3	35	3.75*	1.32	36.8	34.5	0.8
FIDELITY SEL. MEDICAL DELIVERY	▼▼▼	Health	AVG	182.9	−10	3.75*	1.62	11.0	7.3	0.0
FIDELITY SEL. NATURAL GAS		Natural Resources		153.1	77	3.75*	1.67	34.3	33.6	0.1
FIDELITY SEL. PREC. METALS & MIN.	▼▼▼	Precious Metals	▲	258.8	−16	3.75*	1.52	5.4	5.3	0.3
FIDELITY SEL. REGIONAL BANKS	▲▲▲	Financial	▲	510.6	58	3.75*	1.40	35.7	33.6	0.9
FIDELITY SEL. RETAILING	▼▼	Specialty-Misc.		222.9	464	3.75*	1.92	20.9	20.8	0.0
FIDELITY SEL. SOFTWARE & COMP.	▼	Technology	▲	401.5	14	3.75*	1.47	21.6	18.9	0.0
FIDELITY SEL. TECHNOLOGY		Technology	AVG	491.3	23	3.75*	1.39	15.6	13.6	0.0
FIDELITY SEL. TELECOMMUNICATIONS	AVG	Communications		437.0	−3	3.75*	1.52	5.2	1.3	0.6
FIDELITY SEL. UTILITIES GROWTH	AVG	Utilities	AVG	255.7	−18	3.75*	1.38	11.4	8.6	1.5
FIDELITY SMALL CAP STOCK		Small-cap Blend		538.0	10	3.00	0.99	13.6	12.5	0.1
FIDELITY SOUTHEAST ASIA		Pacific ex-Japan		795.6	20	4.50*	1.10	10.2	9.0	1.1
FIDELITY STOCK SELECTOR	AVG	Large-cap Blend	▼	1601.9	27	No load	1.00	17.1	14.4	0.9
FIDELITY TREND	▼	Mid-cap Blend		1333.9	5	No load	0.82	16.9	14.5	0.7
FIDELITY UTILITIES	AVG	Utilities	▲▲▲	1267.9	−16	No load	0.77	11.4	9.5	2.8
FIDELITY VALUE	▲▲▲	Mid-cap Value	▲	7080.1	23	No load	0.96	16.9	13.2	0.9
FIDELITY WORLDWIDE	AVG	World	▲	932.6	43	No load	1.16	18.7	17.5	1.1
59 WALL ST. EUROPEAN EQUITY	AVG	Europe	AVG	146.3	22	No load	1.24	19.3	16.8	1.1
59 WALL ST. PAC. BASIN EQUITY	▼▼▼	Diversified Pacific		153.8	29	No load	1.24	−0.7	−1.6	0.8
FIRST EAGLE FUND OF AMERICA	▲▲▲	Mid-cap Value	▲	171.4	26	No load	1.90	29.3	23.9	0.0
FIRST INVESTORS BLUE CHIP A	AVG	Large-cap Blend	▼	223.2	31	6.25	1.49†	20.6	18.4	0.8
FIRST INVESTORS GLOBAL A	▼	World	▼	250.3	10	6.25	1.83†	14.4	10.5	0.6
FIRST INVESTORS SPECIAL SIT. A	▼	Small-cap Growth	AVG	149.8	19	6.25	1.60†	11.6	9.9	0.0

*Includes redemption fee. **Includes deferred sales charge. †12(b)-1 plan in effect. ‡Not currently accepting new accounts. §Less than 0.5% of assets. NA=Not available. NM=Not meaningful.

3 YEARS PRETAX	3 YEARS AFTERTAX	5 YEARS PRETAX	5 YEARS AFTERTAX	10 YEARS PRETAX	10 YEARS AFTERTAX	TREND BW 10-YEAR ANALYSIS	TURNOVER	CASH %	FOREIGN %	P-E RATIO	UNTAXED GAINS (%)	LARGEST HOLDING COMPANY (% ASSETS)	RISK LEVEL	BEST QTR	BEST %RET	WORST QTR	WORST %RET	TELEPHONE
17.6	15.7	16.6	14.2				Very high	6	3	26	10	Philip Morris(3)	Average	II 95	11.9	I 92	−5.3	800-544-8888
6.8	4.7	8.2	6.9				Average	5	85	26	38	BCE(5)	High	I 93	11.4	IV 94	−8.7	800-544-8888
11.9	8.9	16.8	14.2	15.4	12.9		Average	6	7	25	11	General Electric(3)	Low	I 93	10.9	III 92	−3.4	800-544-8888
18.0	16.1	18.3	16.1	20.3	18.5		Very high	6	17	27	15	Schlumberger(2)	Low	II 95	13.8	IV 94	−3.2	800-544-8888
19.2	15.6	19.8	15.7	18.1	14.1		Average	4	10	21	41	FNMA(7)	Low	II 95	12.3	IV 94	−0.8	800-752-2347
18.7	15.9	19.6	16.5	18.9	15.7		Low	8	11	21	35	FNMA(6)	Low	II 95	12.0	IV 94	−0.7	800-752-2347
15.2	12.8	14.6	12.3				Very high	9	0	21	15	Travelers Group(4)	Average	III 95	10.8	I 94	−1.5	800-544-8888
12.7	11.4	11.0	10.1				High	9	97	23	14	Veba(1)	High	I 93	14.4	I 92	−9.1	800-544-8888
23.1	21.8						High	5	3	27	15	Philip Morris(3)						800-544-8888
16.3	15.4	15.3	13.7				High	4	1	39	18	Cisco Systems(3)	High	IV 92	19.9	II 94	−10.2	800-544-8888
−4.4	−4.7	11.0	10.6				Average	2	100	21	7	Telebras (ADR)(5)	Very high	IV 93	39.7	IV 94	−18.1	800-544-8888
16.9	14.5	17.3	15.3	13.5	10.7		Low	6	14	20	24	Philip Morris(3)	Low	I 93	8.9	I 94	−3.2	800-544-8888
15.7	13.7	17.0	15.1				Average	8	10	23	18	British Petroleum (ADR)(3)	Low	I 93	8.5	IV 94	−2.2	800-544-8888
15.6	14.2						Very high	7	100	23	18	Sandoz (Reg)(3)						800-544-8888
16.6	15.3	14.5	13.5	12.1	11.3		Low	7	100	21	31	Canal Plus(2)	Average	II 92	10.8	IV 92	−5.8	800-544-8888
Less than three years of data available							Very high	2	9	33	18	Anchor Gaming(6)						800-544-8888
16.8	14.9						High	4	3	27	11	Midcap 400 Index (Fut)(6)						800-544-8888
17.8	15.2	16.0	13.2	14.5	11.5		High	7	6	24	22	General Electric(3)	Low	III 95	9.4	I 94	−2.5	800-544-8888
18.5	16.5	17.2	14.8	17.3	14.7		Average	9	6	24	21	Philip Morris(4)	Very low	III 95	8.8	I 94	−2.7	800-544-8888
16.8	15.4	14.9	13.1	17.4	15.6		High	10	3	28	19	General Electric(2)	Average	II 95	16.0	II 92	−5.5	800-544-8888
Less than three years of data available								3	100	18	7	HSBC Holdings (HK)(12)						800-544-8888
7.1	6.1	9.9	9.1	9.2	8.5		High	7	99	24	7	Veba(1)	Average	I 93	11.4	IV 92	−4.5	800-544-8888
Less than three years of data available							High	2	97	26	6	Volvo Cl B(3)						800-544-8888
0.4	0.2						Average	2	100	36	−11	Fuji Photo Film(3)						800-544-8888
−5.7	−6.0						Average	6	100	19	−13	Grupo Carso Cl A1(4)						800-544-8888
18.4	15.3	20.8	18.0				Average	17	24	17	15	Bank of Montreal(1)	Low	IV 92	12.0	IV 94	−1.3	800-544-8888
14.5	11.8	14.9	11.8	16.2	13.0		High	2	12	24	7	Caterpillar(2)	Average	II 95	15.8	II 94	−4.5	800-544-8888
19.3	18.2	14.8	13.9				Very low	0	3	23	18	General Electric(3)	Low	I 95	9.6	I 94	−3.9	800-544-8888
Less than three years of data available							Very high	4	4	28	12	Cytec Industries(2)						800-544-8888
23.6	22.1						High	7	4	33	18	U.S. Robotics(3)						800-544-8888
18.5	16.4	15.7	13.0	17.0	14.2		High	4	3	33	21	Intel(4)	Average	II 95	15.5	II 94	−6.8	800-544-8888
7.7	6.7	9.2	7.7	8.9	6.7		Average	13	97	25	15	Veba(3)	High	I 93	12.2	III 92	−11.0	800-544-8888
−3.9	−5.0	6.1	5.2	5.4	4.7		Average	2	100	32	−3	Fuji Photo Film(3)	Very high	II 93	18.7	I 92	−9.6	800-544-8888
12.5	9.8	14.8	11.7	12.5	9.4		High	9	7	21	7	Philip Morris(4)	Very low	I 93	9.1	IV 94	−1.8	800-544-8888
15.5	13.9	15.7	14.2	11.8	10.0		Average	7	NA	26	11	Duke Realty Investments(6)	Average	IV 96	19.0	IV 93	−5.6	800-544-8888
10.4	7.1	12.7	8.0	14.6	10.6		High	6	14	26	12	ITT(3)	Average	IV 92	11.1	I 94	−2.9	800-544-8888
8.1	6.9	12.0	11.0	9.9	8.8		Very high	11	1	20	2	Continental Airlines(8)	Very high	II 95	23.7	III 96	−18.9	800-544-8888
4.1	3.9	14.3	14.2	8.6	8.5		Average	3	67	51	28	Newmont Mining(9)	Very high	II 93	32.5	IV 94	−15.8	800-544-8888
8.8	7.6	3.1	1.7	17.1	15.8		Average	9	15	38	16	Amgen(10)	Very high	IV 92	14.3	I 93	−19.3	800-544-8888
33.9	31.7	30.4	28.6	18.7	17.6		High	3	0	35	16	Intel(9)	Very high	II 95	25.7	IV 95	−11.9	800-544-8888
15.7	12.4	19.0	16.5				Very high	4	11	40	10	Newbridge Networks(4)	Very high	III 94	21.4	IV 95	−14.0	800-544-8888
41.2	38.9	36.5	34.0	20.0	19.0		Very high	4	1	36	16	Intel(9)	High	II 95	36.3	IV 95	−11.2	800-544-8888
17.3	15.9	13.4	12.3	11.3	10.1		High	16	32	31	20	Royal Dutch Petroleum (ADR)(6)	High	I 93	16.3	IV 93	−9.5	800-544-8888
28.3	26.9	21.4	20.6	11.2	10.8		Very high	9	10	34	23	Schlumberger(8)	High	I 93	23.2	IV 93	−12.1	800-544-8888
23.3	21.2	25.8	23.0	15.7	13.9		High	5	NA	17	22	Allstate(6)	Average	IV 92	17.2	IV 94	−6.3	800-544-8888
18.0	15.9	13.6	11.6	19.2	17.0		High	10	1	27	13	General Mills(9)	Average	III 94	10.1	I 92	−4.2	800-544-8888
26.9	23.5	11.6	9.0	19.8	17.4		Average	11	20	30	30	Bristol-Myers Squibb(6)	High	III 94	16.2	I 92	−13.1	800-544-8888
29.2	26.3	34.1	31.7	21.9	19.4		Average	14	NA	19	21	Chase Manhattan(3)	Average	IV 92	21.1	IV 94	−10.6	800-544-8888
20.7	18.1	10.0	8.1	18.3	16.7		High	3	NA	26	25	Healthsouth(8)	Very high	III 94	19.1	I 93	−18.3	800-544-8888
17.7	17.4						Average	5	10	37	15	Enron(5)						800-544-8888
0.3	0.1	10.8	10.4	6.3	5.9		Average	2	78	40	14	Newmont Mining(9)	Very high	II 93	33.7	IV 94	−10.9	800-544-8888
25.9	23.9	27.0	24.0	20.9	18.7		High	6	6	16	20	BankAmerica(5)	Average	IV 92	18.7	IV 94	−7.2	800-544-8888
8.7	8.7	12.1	11.2	16.8	15.1		Very high	3	2	26	9	Melville(10)	High	IV 92	14.7	II 92	−6.7	800-544-8888
21.3	18.9	26.3	23.4	20.2	18.1		Very high	14	3	40	16	Microsoft(8)	Very high	III 94	21.6	II 94	−17.5	800-544-8888
22.7	20.0	20.9	18.2	16.4	14.9		High	7	2	41	12	Ascend Commun.(10)	Very high	II 95	22.1			800-544-8888
12.5	9.9	16.3	13.9	17.9	16.3		Average	7	8	31	9	MFS Commun.(10)	Average	III 95	13.1	I 94	−4.3	800-544-8888
11.5	9.8	11.5	9.1	11.9	9.9		Average	1	7	23	15	Pacific Telesis Group(6)	Average	IV 96	10.5	IV 93	−6.2	800-544-8888
11.6	10.6						Very high	5	0	22	14	Ross Stores(3)						800-544-8888
−1.1	−1.6						High	6	100	21	8	Sun Hung Kai Properties(8)						800-544-8888
17.2	14.7	16.2	14.1				Very high	9	12	23	13	Travelers Group(4)	Average	III 95	13.6	II 92	−2.0	800-544-8888
10.1	6.9	13.2	10.3	13.2	10.5		Very high	3	2	26	18	Philip Morris(3)	Average	IV 92	11.6	I 94	−6.2	800-544-8888
11.3	9.1	12.1	10.0				High	2	3	22	18	GTE(5)	Average	III 95	10.0	I 92	−4.8	800-544-8888
16.9	14.6	19.0	17.0	14.3	12.5		High	4	10	25	20	Wal-Mart Stores(2)	Low	III 95	8.6	IV 94	−1.5	800-544-8888
9.4	8.4	13.7	12.7				Average	7	75	22	11	Huhtamaki (144A)(2)	Average	I 93	11.8	IV 94	−2.5	800-544-8888
10.2	8.2	12.9	10.7				Average	6	100	22	14	Vodafone Group(3)	Average	IV 93	13.0	I 94	−6.0	800-625-5759
−6.9	−9.0	8.4	6.6				Average	5	100	28	−4	Seoul Trust(3)	Very high	IV 93	36.7	I 94	−16.4	800-625-5759
19.8	16.3	21.5	18.2				Average	0	NA	20	26	Tejas Gas(4)	Average	IV 92	14.5	IV 94	−5.6	800-451-3623
16.1	13.8	12.4	10.6				Low	9	4	24	25	General Electric(3)	Average	I 95	8.6	I 92	−3.6	800-423-4026
9.1	7.0	8.7	7.4	12.4	10.9		Average	6	73	25	21	Canadian Pacific(2)	Average	III 93	8.2	I 94	−5.6	800-423-4026
10.0	8.6	13.5	12.0				Average	13	11	31	16	Systemsoft(3)	High	IV 92	18.6	II 94	−7.5	800-423-4026

MUTUAL FUND SCOREBOARD

FUND	OVERALL RATING (COMPARES RISK-ADJUSTED PERFORMANCE OF EACH FUND AGAINST ALL FUNDS)	CATEGORY (COMPARES RISK-ADJUSTED PERFORMANCE OF FUND WITHIN CATEGORY)	RATING	SIZE ASSETS $MIL.	% CHG. 1995-6	FEES SALES CHARGE (%)	EXPENSE RATIO (%)	1996 RETURNS (%) PRE-TAX	AFTER-TAX	YIELD
FIRST OMAHA EQUITY		Large-cap Blend		256.3	24	No load	0.99	15.8	12.9	2.1
FIRST PRIORITY GROWTH INVMT. (gg) ♌		Large-cap Blend		169.8	13	4.75	1.03†	22.2	20.1	0.8
FLAG INV. TELEPHONE INCOME A ♁	AVG	Communications		506.0	3	4.50	0.93†	13.4	11.0	2.3
FLAG INV. VALUE BUILDER A		Domestic Hybrid		250.6	36	4.50	1.31†	24.6	23.7	2.1
FORTIS ADVANT. ASSET ALLOC. A	AVG	Domestic Hybrid	▼▼	145.6	8	4.75	1.50†	12.0	9.5	2.6
FORTIS CAPITAL A ♁	▼	Large-cap Growth	▼	299.8	8	4.75	1.21†	18.6	14.8	0.1
FORTIS GROWTH A ♁	▼▼▼	Mid-cap Growth	▼▼▼	693.4	8	4.75	1.09†	17.2	14.3	0.0
FOUNDERS BALANCED ♌	▲▲▲	Domestic Hybrid	▲▲▲	394.0	202	No load	1.23†	18.8	16.5	2.4
FOUNDERS BLUE CHIP ♌	AVG	Large-cap Blend	AVG	535.9	44	No load	1.17†	24.4	19.8	1.1
FOUNDERS DISCOVERY	▼▼	Small-cap Growth	▼	250.7	15	No load	1.58†	21.2	18.6	0.0
FOUNDERS FRONTIER	▼	Mid-cap Growth	AVG	350.9	6	No load	1.53†	14.3	11.6	0.0
FOUNDERS GROWTH	▼	Mid-cap Growth	▲	1032.1	58	No load	1.24†	16.6	14.1	0.1
FOUNDERS PASSPORT		Foreign		179.0	260	No load	1.76†	20.1	19.8	0.2
FOUNDERS SPECIAL ♌	▼▼	Mid-cap Growth	▼	364.6	−6	No load	1.29†	15.3	13.5	0.0
FOUNDERS WORLDWIDE GROWTH	▼	World	AVG	342.1	50	No load	1.56†	14.0	12.8	0.3
FOUNTAIN SQ. MID CAP A		Mid-cap Blend		142.4	126	4.50	1.00†	17.7	15.1	0.3
FOUNTAIN SQ. QUALITY GROWTH A		Large-cap Blend		275.7	155	4.50	1.00†	23.8	22.0	0.7
FPA CAPITAL ♁	▲	Small-cap Value	AVG	492.9	40	6.50‡	0.87	37.8	34.7	0.9
FPA PARAMOUNT ♁	▲	Domestic Hybrid	AVG	683.1	19	6.50‡	0.87	29.4	27.1	1.5
FRANKLIN BALANCE SHEET INVESTMENT	▲▲▲	Small-cap Value	▲▲▲	693.4	54	1.50‡	1.17†	17.5	14.5	1.4
FRANKLIN CA GROWTH I	▲▲	Mid-cap Blend	▲	168.2	262	4.50	0.71†	30.4	29.5	0.6
FRANKLIN EQUITY I	AVG	Mid-cap Blend	▼	419.9	22	4.50	0.95†	23.0	21.6	0.6
FRANKLIN EQUITY INCOME I	▲▲	Large-cap Value	▲	266.5	40	4.50	1.00†	12.7	10.9	3.8
FRANKLIN GLOBAL HEALTH I		Health		147.1	356	4.50	0.73†	16.5	15.7	0.2
FRANKLIN GLOBAL UTILITIES I		Utilities		175.6	37	4.50	1.04†	15.0	11.7	2.5
FRANKLIN GOLD I ♁	▼▼▼	Precious Metals	AVG	349.3	−2	4.50	0.95†	1.0	−0.8	0.7
FRANKLIN GROWTH I ♁	AVG	Large-cap Growth	▼	1118.6	39	4.50	0.87†	16.7	16.1	1.0
FRANKLIN INCOME I ♁	▲▲	Domestic Hybrid	▲▲	7061.7	14	4.25	0.70†	10.5	7.8	7.6
FRANKLIN MUTUAL BEACON Z (hh) ♁	▲▲▲	Mid-cap Value	▲▲▲	4935.7	38	No load‡	0.72	21.2	17.5	2.5
FRANKLIN MUTUAL DISCOVERY Z (ii)		Small-cap Value		2965.2	117	No load‡	0.99	24.9	21.6	2.4
FRANKLIN MUTUAL QUALIFIED Z (jj) ♁	▲▲▲	Mid-cap Value	▲▲	4306.6	44	No load‡	0.72	21.2	17.8	2.5
FRANKLIN MUTUAL SHARES Z (kk) ♁	▲▲▲	Mid-cap Value	▲▲	6552.3	25	No load‡	0.69	20.8	17.0	2.4
FRANKLIN RISING DIVIDENDS I	AVG	Mid-cap Value	▼▼	303.7	11	4.50	1.40†	23.4	21.0	1.1
FRANKLIN SMALL CAP GROWTH I		Small-cap Growth		739.2	201	4.50	0.97†	27.1	25.6	0.3
FRANKLIN UTILITIES I	▼	Utilities	▼▼▼	2401.5	−17	4.25	0.73†	2.0	−0.8	5.2
FREMONT GLOBAL	▲	International Hybrid	▲	597.0	19	No load	0.88	14.0	9.2	3.2
FREMONT U.S. MICRO-CAP		Small-cap Growth		142.9	NM	No load	2.04	48.7	47.0	0.0
FUNDAMENTAL INVESTORS ♁	▲▲	Large-cap Blend	▲	7165.4	51	5.75	0.70†	20.0	17.2	1.5
GABELLI ASSET ♁	▲▲	Mid-cap Blend	▲	1081.6	−1	No load	0.95†	13.4	10.3	0.5
GABELLI GROWTH	AVG	Large-cap Growth	▲▲	623.4	18	No load	1.44†	19.4	16.5	0.1
GABELLI SMALL CAP GROWTH	▲	Small-cap Blend	▲▲▲	216.7	−5	No load	1.58†	11.9	8.6	0.0
GABELLI VALUE	AVG	Mid-cap Blend	▼	461.2	−5	5.50	1.50†	8.7	6.0	0.0
GALAXY EQUITY GROWTH RETURN A	AVG	Large-cap Blend	AVG	170.9	46	3.75	1.45	20.5	18.3	0.4
GALAXY EQUITY INCOME RETURN A	▲	Large-cap Blend	▲	134.7	48	3.75	1.49	16.5	13.3	1.7
GALAXY EQUITY VALUE RETURN A	▲	Large-cap Value	▼	137.8	32	3.75	1.49	21.1	16.9	0.8
GALAXY II LARGE CO. INDEX RETURN	▲	Large-cap Blend	▲	352.5	64	No load	0.40	22.6	21.3	1.7
GALAXY II SMALL CO. INDEX RETURN	AVG	Mid-cap Blend	AVG	326.3	18	No load	0.40	19.7	17.2	1.4
GAM INTERNATIONAL A	AVG	International Hybrid	AVG	1010.1	81	5.00	1.57	9.0	8.8	0.4
GATEWAY INDEX PLUS ♁	▲▲	Large-cap Blend	▲▲	194.4	10	No load	1.19	10.5	10.2	1.1
GINTEL ♁	▼	Mid-cap Blend	▼	157.9	63	No load	2.30	31.0	27.3	1.8
GLOBAL UTILITY B	AVG	Utilities	▲	190.8	−14	5.00**	2.06†	13.3	10.8	2.7
GOLDMAN SACHS ASIA GROWTH A		Pacific ex-Japan		269.6	60	5.50	1.77†	8.0	8.0	0.1
GOLDMAN SACHS CAPITAL GROWTH A	▲	Mid-cap Value	▼	878.6	−1	5.50	1.36†	21.4	17.7	0.7
GOLDMAN SACHS GROWTH & INC. A		Mid-cap Value		573.6	39	5.50	1.20†	26.1	22.6	1.5
GOLDMAN SACHS INTL. EQ. A		Foreign		521.7	72	5.50	1.52†	18.8	18.4	0.0
GOLDMAN SACHS SEL. EQ. A	AVG	Large-cap Blend	▼▼	209.5	81	5.50	1.25†	21.4	19.9	0.7
GOLDMAN SACHS SMALL CAP EQ. A		Small-cap Blend		205.2	−13	5.50	1.41†	21.8	20.1	0.0
GOVETT SMALLER COMPANIES A ♌		Small-cap Growth		293.2	−43	4.95	1.95†	−10.6	−15.3	0.0
GRADISON-McDONALD ESTAB. VALUE ♁	▲▲	Mid-cap Value	AVG	422.2	25	No load	1.15†	19.3	16.2	1.4
GROWTH FUND OF AMERICA	▼	Large-cap Growth	AVG	9675.3	23	5.75	0.75†	14.8	13.0	0.6
GT GLOBAL AMER. GROWTH A ♌	AVG	Small-cap Blend	AVG	344.2	−12	4.75	1.46†	15.7	13.8	0.0
GT GLOBAL EMERGING MKTS. A		Diversified Emerging Mkts.		209.7	−16	4.75	2.12†	5.3	5.3	0.1
GT GLOBAL EUROPE GROWTH A	▼▼	Europe	▼▼	469.5	0	4.75	1.83†	19.6	19.3	0.0
GT GLOBAL GROWTH & INCOME B		International Hybrid		398.9	8	5.00**	2.35†	16.1	15.2	2.5
GT GLOBAL HEALTH CARE A ♌	▼▼▼	Health	AVG	520.3	0	4.75	1.85†	23.8	21.4	0.0
GT GLOBAL INTL. GROWTH A	▼▼	Foreign	▼▼▼	198.9	−32	4.75	1.70†	9.3	6.2	0.0
GT GLOBAL NEW PACIFIC A	▼▼▼	Pacific ex-Japan		384.6	4	4.75	1.89†	20.0	16.0	0.0
GT GLOBAL TELECOMMUN. A		Communications		1095.5	−19	4.75	1.77†	5.2	2.8	0.0
GT LATIN AMERICA GROWTH A	▼▼▼	Latin America		192.8	−1	4.75	2.11†	17.0	17.0	0.0
GUARDIAN PARK AVENUE A ♁	▲▲	Large-cap Blend	▲▲▲	1396.9	44	4.50	0.81	26.5	22.3	1.0

*Includes redemption fee. **Includes deferred sales charge. †12(b)-1 plan in effect. ‡Not currently accepting new accounts. §Less than 0.5% of assets. NA=Not available. NM=Not meaningful.
(gg) Formerly First Priority Equity Invmt. (hh) Formerly Mutual Beacon. (ii) Formerly Mutual Discovery. (jj) Formerly Mutual Qualified. (kk) Formerly Mutual Shares.

184

3 YEARS PRETAX	3 YEARS AFTERTAX	5 YEARS PRETAX	5 YEARS AFTERTAX	10 YEARS PRETAX	10 YEARS AFTERTAX	TREND BW 10-YEAR ANALYSIS	TURNOVER	CASH %	FOREIGN %	P-E RATIO	UNTAXED GAINS (%)	LARGEST HOLDING COMPANY (% ASSETS)	RISK LEVEL	BEST QTR	BEST %RET	WORST QTR	WORST %RET	TELEPHONE
16.4	14.1						Low	19	NA	18	8	Ingersoll-Rand(4)						800-662-4203
15.2	13.3						High	1	1	27	21	General Electric(5)						800-433-2829
12.3	10.1	13.5	11.6	14.6	12.3		Low	1	9	26	37	SBC Communications(8)	Average	III 95	13.8	I 94	-5.7	800-767-3524
18.1	16.9						Low	3	6	20	23	Conseco(5)						800-767-3524
10.7	8.9	9.9	8.2				Average	2	3	31	29	Green Tree Financial(2)	Low	II 95	8.0	I 94	-3.5	800-800-2638
13.9	12.2	10.1	8.2	12.7	10.3		Low	11	4	33	54	Mattel(5)	High	II 95	10.7	IV 95	-3.2	800-800-2638
10.5	8.9	8.5	7.0	13.7	11.8		Low	8	2	39	54	Cisco Systems(4)	Very high	II 95	13.9	II 94	-12.3	800-800-2638
14.7	12.2	14.3	11.7	12.4	9.7		Very high	8	11	22	10	Ingles Markets Cl A(2)	Very low	III 95	8.0	I 92	-2.5	800-525-2440
17.3	13.5	13.0	9.0	13.7	9.4		Very high	9	16	22	21	Bally Entertainment(3)	Average	I 96	9.4	I 92	-6.6	800-525-2440
13.7	11.1	13.4	11.6				High	14	4	40	25	Geoworks(3)	Very high	IV 92	19.8	II 94	-10.9	800-525-2440
15.1	12.3	14.1	11.9				High	7	14	36	29	Watson Pharmaceuticals(3)	High	IV 92	16.3	I 94	-7.1	800-525-2440
17.9	15.4	16.5	13.9	16.6	13.8		High	16	8	34	23	Intel(4)	High	IV 92	14.9	II 94	-10.3	800-525-2440
10.2	10.1						Low	19	96	27	9	Noritsu Koki(2)						800-525-2440
11.3	8.2	11.6	8.5	15.5	11.9		Very high	18	24	35	14	Parametric Technology(3)	High	IV 92	13.8	I 94	-8.6	800-525-2440
10.4	9.4	12.1	11.4				Average	16	85	30	15	Ladbroke Group(2)	Average	IV 93	15.3	I 94	-5.1	800-525-2440
14.6	13.6						Low	5	NA	25	16	Adaptec(5)						800-334-0483
17.7	16.8						Low	5	NA	26	19	Intel(4)						800-334-0483
28.2	26.1	24.5	22.2	21.4	18.8		Low	22	NA	18	38	Green Tree Financial(8)	High	IV 92	22.5	II 92	-11.7	800-982-4372
16.8	14.0	16.1	13.2	16.9	13.3		High	31	3	22	28	IBM(5)	Low	I 96	11.0	IV 94	-2.2	800-982-4372
15.8	13.9	18.9	17.1				Low	20	11	15	14	Christiania Bank & Kredit(5)	Very low	IV 92	12.3	IV 94	-4.3	800-342-5236
30.9	28.1	22.6	20.5				Average	14	4	30	10	Intel(2)	Average	IV 92	16.5	II 92	-10.6	800-342-5236
17.3	14.8	12.7	10.0	11.7	9.2		Average	7	9	26	26	Intel(3)	Average	II 95	12.0	II 92	-2.9	800-342-5236
12.2	10.2	13.5	11.4				Low	6	16	17	9	Christiania Bank & Kredit(3)	Very low	I 93	8.1	I 94	-4.7	800-342-5236
27.2	25.4						Average	8	11	36	5	Astra Cl B(3)						800-342-5236
10.1	7.8						Average	6	42	19	15	Hellenic Telecomm.(4)						800-342-5236
-1.7	-2.9	5.6	4.6	8.0	6.7		Low	7	82	41	18	Barrick Gold(9)	Very high	II 93	27.3	IV 92	-11.0	800-342-5236
18.5	17.9	12.9	12.3	14.4	13.5		Very low	19	1	25	39	Computer Sciences(3)	Average	I 95	9.4	I 94	-6.5	800-342-5236
7.9	5.0	11.9	9.0	11.3	7.8		Low	8	7	14	6	Central & Southwest(1)	Very low	I 93	8.0	I 94	-5.2	800-342-5236
17.2	14.6	19.5	17.0	16.2	13.6		Average	23	31	24	17	Chase Manhattan(5)	Very low	I 93	9.2	IV 94	-2.4	800-342-5236
18.5	16.0						Average	20	60	21	16	Getinge Industrier Cl B(2)						800-342-5236
17.5	14.3	19.6	16.5	15.6	12.3		Average	23	32	24	18	Chase Manhattan(6)	Very low	III 95	9.7	I 94	-1.6	800-342-5236
17.7	14.0	19.1	15.8	15.4	12.0		Average	21	23	24	22	Chase Manhattan(8)	Very low	III 95	11.1	I 94	-2.8	800-553-3014
15.1	13.9	10.2	9.3				Low	3	2	18	37	TrustCo Bank New York(3)	Low	IV 96	11.2	I 94	-7.1	800-342-5236
25.4	23.1						Average	10	6	29	11	Barrett Resources(2)						800-342-5236
5.6	3.4	7.5	5.4	9.0	6.7		Very low	4	0	14	9	Florida Progress(4)	Average	IV 95	8.7	I 94	-9.9	800-342-5236
9.2	6.7	10.4	8.4				Average	28	42	27	14	European Investment Bank(1)	Very low	II 95	7.0	I 94	-5.6	800-548-4539
Less than three years of data available							High	26	3	28	17	Micrel(5)						800-548-1639
17.7	15.0	16.3	13.9	14.9	12.1		Low	6	11	23	22	Texas Instruments(2)	Low	II 95	9.5	I 94	-2.6	800-421-4120
12.3	10.0	14.6	12.8	15.6	13.6		Low	4	10	24	36	Time Warner(2)	Low	IV 92	8.5	I 94	-2.9	800-422-3554
15.3	11.3	12.2	9.5				High	3	1	26	28	Home Depot(3)	Average	II 95	10.2	I 94	-5.8	800-422-3554
10.8	8.4	15.0	13.2				Very low	0	3	22	39	Neiman-Marcus Group(4)	Average	IV 92	12.1	I 94	-3.6	800-422-3554
10.0	6.8	15.9	12.6				Average	0	7	25	26	Media General Cl A(14)	Average	III 93	16.7	I 94	-6.0	800-422-3554
18.2	16.7	13.0	12.0				Very low	10	NA	25	28	Thermo Electron(3)	Average	II 95	10.3	I 94	-3.6	800-628-0414
16.2	14.0	12.7	11.0				Low	13	NA	20	21	Ford Motor(4)	Low	I 95	8.8	I 94	-3.4	800-628-0414
17.0	13.5	14.7	12.1				Average	7	3	20	19	S&P Depository Receipts(4)	Low	II 95	8.5	I 94	-1.8	800-628-0414
19.3	17.9	14.8	13.6				Very low	9	3	23	28	S&P 500 (Fut)(4)	Low	I 95	9.5	I 94	-3.9	800-628-0414
15.3	13.5	13.9	12.5				Very low	6	1	25	34	Midcap (Fut)(6)	Average	IV 92	11.2	I 94	-3.7	800-628-0414
8.4	5.5	18.8	16.2	15.5	11.2		Low	-1	100	18	2	Henderson Land Devel.(4)	Average	IV 93	28.2	I 94	-10.6	800-426-4685
9.0	7.9	7.9	6.8	9.9	7.6		Very low	5	1	24	18	General Electric(7)	Very low	III 94	4.6	I 94	-2.6	800-354-6339
12.8	10.9	12.8	10.9	10.5	8.4		Average	18	2	20	35	Capstead Mortgage(19)	High	III 96	10.4	I 94	-9.5	800-243-5808
8.3	6.4	10.9	8.9				Low	2	46	21	18	AT&T(3)	Average	II 92	9.7	I 92	-6.1	800-225-1852
Less than three years of data available							Average	4	99	23	3	Swire Pacific Cl A(4)						800-526-7384
14.7	10.6	16.3	12.8				Average	6	4	20	23	Philip Morris(4)	Average	IV 92	15.7	IV 94	-5.0	800-526-7384
21.2	19.2						Average	6	3	17	17	Philip Morris(4)						800-526-7384
9.6	8.2						Average	5	98	27	17	Fresenius Medical Care(3)						800-526-7384
18.5	16.8	13.4	11.6				Low	0	4	21	20	Exxon(3)	Average	II 95	11.4	I 92	-4.7	800-526-7384
4.1	3.1						Average	1	NA	19	14	Movado Group(6)						800-526-7384
24.8	21.2						Very high	6	7	45	22	Adtran(2)						800-225-2222
14.8	12.7	15.0	13.2	13.1	11.1		Low	29	2	19	31	Sun Microsystems(4)	Low	I 93	9.2	II 94	-3.5	800-869-5999
14.2	12.3	12.9	11.4	14.7	12.6		Low	16	8	27	37	FNMA(3)	Average	II 95	12.6	II 92	-2.8	800-421-4120
18.1	14.9	18.7	15.7				Average	2	5	26	9	Philip Morris(5)	High	IV 92	25.6	II 92	-7.9	800-824-1580
-4.4	-4.8						High	3	98	15	-4	Panamerican Beverages(2)						800-824-1580
7.4	7.0	7.1	6.8	7.7	6.4		High	5	100	27	-9	Gucci Group (NY) (Reg)(6)	High	IV 93	8.7	III 92	-12.0	800-824-1580
8.4	7.3						Average	4	77	20	15	Sun Alliance Group(2)						800-824-1580
19.4	16.5	8.6	7.0				High	12	20	38	37	Amgen(6)	Very high	III 94	14.9	I 93	-14.9	800-824-1580
1.5	-0.8	5.8	4.3	8.5	7.2		Average	-1	99	27	20	Amway Japan(6)	High	IV 93	10.6	I 95	-9.9	800-824-1580
1.2	-0.8	8.9	7.3	11.5	8.1		Average	4	100	24	19	New World Development(8)	Very high	IV 93	23.9	I 94	-18.0	800-824-1580
3.0	1.2						Average	6	68	28	13	DDI(5)						800-824-1580
-4.9	-5.7	5.1	4.1				High	3	100	22	-22	Vale do Rio Doce(3)	Very high	III 94	31.0	I 95	-31.0	800-824-1580
18.7	16.2	19.4	17.1	16.0	13.1		Average	6	2	26	26	General Electric(3)	Low	IV 92	13.7	I 94	-2.9	800-221-3253

DATA: MORNINGSTAR, INC., CHICAGO, IL.

MUTUAL FUND SCOREBOARD

FUND	OVERALL RATING (COMPARES RISK-ADJUSTED PERFORMANCE OF EACH FUND AGAINST ALL FUNDS)	CATEGORY (COMPARES RISK-ADJUSTED PERFORMANCE OF FUND WITHIN CATEGORY)	RATING	SIZE ASSETS $MIL.	SIZE % CHG. 1995-6	FEES SALES CHARGE (%)	FEES EXPENSE RATIO (%)	1996 RETURNS (%) PRE-TAX	1996 RETURNS (%) AFTER-TAX	1996 RETURNS (%) YIELD
GUINNESS FLIGHT CHINA		Pacific ex-Japan		308.2	459	1.00*	1.98	34.4	33.2	1.1
HANCOCK EMERGING GROWTH B ♙	▼▼	Small-cap Growth	▼	454.5	10	5.00**	2.11†	13.0	12.3	0.0
HANCOCK GLOBAL TECHNOLOGY A ♟	▼▼	Technology	AVG	173.1	12	5.00	1.67†	12.5	11.1	0.0
HANCOCK GROWTH & INCOME A ♙	AVG	Large-cap Blend	▼	163.2	26	5.00	1.17†	22.2	18.7	0.9
HANCOCK GROWTH A	▼▼	Large-cap Growth	▼	275.4	14	5.00	1.48†	20.4	17.1	0.0
HANCOCK REGIONAL BANK B ♟	▲▲▲	Financial	▲▲	2845.6	96	5.00**	2.09†	28.4	27.7	1.1
HANCOCK SOVEREIGN INVESTOR A ♟	▲	Large-cap Blend	AVG	1429.5	12	5.00	1.14†	17.6	15.1	1.7
HANCOCK SPECIAL EQUITIES B		Small-cap Growth		996.0	81	5.00**	2.20†	3.0	3.0	0.0
HANCOCK SPECIAL OPPORT. B ♙		Mid-cap Growth		252.9	69	5.00**	2.30†	28.0	22.1	0.0
HARBOR CAPITAL APPRECIATION	▼	Large-cap Growth	AVG	1681.7	70	No load	0.75	19.9	18.8	0.1
HARBOR INTERNATIONAL	AVG	Foreign	▲▲▲	4318.6	25	No load‡	1.04	20.1	18.9	1.3
HARBOR INTERNATIONAL GROWTH		Foreign		645.6	339	No load	1.21	32.0	31.1	0.5
HEARTLAND SMALL CAP CONTRAR.		Small-cap Value		263.0	207	No load	1.44†	18.9	17.4	0.1
HEARTLAND VALUE ♟	▲▲▲	Small-cap Value	▲▲	1627.1	37	No load‡	1.29†	21.0	18.8	0.2
HOMESTEAD VALUE	▲▲	Mid-cap Value	AVG	237.3	61	No load	0.84	17.9	16.7	1.8
HOTCHKIS & WILEY EQUITY-INC.	▲	Large-cap Value	▼	203.8	25	No load	0.98	17.4	13.5	2.8
HOTCHKIS & WILEY INTL.	AVG	Foreign	▲▲	521.8	433	No load	1.00	18.3	17.4	1.7
HSBC GROWTH & INCOME (ll)	AVG	Large-cap Blend	▼	140.7	113	5.00	0.94†	17.9	15.7	1.0
IAI EMERGING GROWTH	▼▼	Mid-cap Growth	▼▼	617.6	1	No load‡	1.24	7.0	2.3	0.0
IAI MIDCAP GROWTH		Mid-cap Growth		140.3	23	No load	1.25	16.6	13.8	0.0
IAI REGIONAL	AVG	Mid-cap Blend	▼	565.2	-2	No load	1.25	15.7	10.7	0.4
IDEX GLOBAL A (mm)		World		144.0	59	5.50	1.97†	26.8	23.5	0.0
IDEX GROWTH A (nn)	▼▼	Large-cap Growth	▼▼	593.9	19	5.50	1.84†	17.1	13.6	0.0
IDS BLUE CHIP ADVANTAGE A	▲	Large-cap Growth	AVG	619.0	174	5.00	0.96	21.6	19.9	1.1
IDS DISCOVERY A	▼▼▼	Mid-cap Growth	▼▼	804.5	20	5.00	1.00	25.1	20.7	0.2
IDS DIVERSIFIED EQUITY-INC. A	▲▲▲	Large-cap Value	▲▲	1389.8	19	5.00	0.94	18.7	15.6	2.7
IDS EQUITY SELECT A ♟	AVG	Mid-cap Blend	▼	804.5	18	5.00	0.84	24.5	19.8	0.4
IDS EQUITY VALUE B	▲▲	Large-cap Value	AVG	1467.7	-3	5.00**	1.69†	20.9	17.2	1.7
IDS GLOBAL GROWTH A	▼▼	Foreign	▼▼	940.4	40	5.00	1.39	14.9	12.0	3.1
IDS GROWTH A	AVG	Large-cap Growth	AVG	2356.6	49	5.00	0.93	24.5	23.6	0.0
IDS INTERNATIONAL A	▼▼	Foreign	▼▼	937.3	16	5.00	1.39	9.4	7.4	1.5
IDS MANAGED ALLOCATION A (oo)	▼	Large-cap Blend	▼▼	2496.0	-4	5.00	0.83	12.2	7.8	2.4
IDS MUTUAL A ♟	▲	Domestic Hybrid	AVG	2886.6	7	5.00	0.83	13.6	10.5	3.6
IDS NEW DIMENSIONS A	AVG	Large-cap Growth	▲▲	6784.8	39	5.00	0.94	24.4	23.1	0.6
IDS PROGRESSIVE A	▲▲	Small-cap Value	▲	389.2	12	5.00	1.04	17.8	15.6	0.9
IDS STOCK A	AVG	Large-cap Blend	AVG	2410.3	16	5.00	0.79	19.4	17.2	1.8
IDS STRATEGY AGGRESSIVE B	▼▼	Mid-cap Growth	▼	828.4	-13	5.00**	1.85†	18.2	16.4	0.0
IDS UTILITIES INCOME A	AVG	Utilities	▲▲	694.3	3	5.00	0.89	14.4	12.5	3.0
INCOME FUND OF AMERICA ♟	▲▲▲	Domestic Hybrid	▲▲▲	16192.2	18	5.75	0.62†	15.2	12.0	5.2
INDEPENDENCE ONE EQUITY PLUS		Large-cap Blend		161.4	75	No load	NA	24.5	23.7	1.6
INVESCO ADV. EQUITY C (pp)	▲	Large-cap Blend	AVG	137.4	21	1.00**	2.28†	17.2	17.1	0.2
INVESCO ADV. FLEX C (qq)	▲▲	Domestic Hybrid	▲	489.8	23	1.00**	2.28†	13.6	11.5	1.7
INVESCO ADV. MULTIFLEX C (rr)		Small-cap Value		266.8	52	1.00**	2.50†	17.0	15.8	1.0
INVESCO BALANCED		Domestic Hybrid		134.2	53	No load	1.29†	14.7	11.8	2.7
INVESCO DYNAMICS	▼	Mid-cap Growth	▲▲	856.2	37	No load	1.14†	15.7	12.5	0.1
INVESCO EMERGING GROWTH	▼▼	Small-cap Growth	AVG	268.0	26	No load	1.48†	11.6	10.4	0.0
INVESCO EUROPEAN	▼	Europe	▼	326.0	48	No load	1.40	29.7	27.1	0.3
INVESCO GROWTH ♙	▼	Large-cap Blend	▼▼	651.3	22	No load	1.06†	21.0	16.4	0.5
INVESCO INDUSTRIAL INCOME	AVG	Domestic Hybrid	▼	4290.8	1	No load	0.93†	16.7	13.6	2.7
INVESCO PACIFIC BASIN	▼▼▼	Diversified Pacific		153.8	-20	No load	1.52	-1.2	-1.5	0.0
INVESCO STRAT. ENERGY	▼▼▼	Natural Resources	▼▼	233.1	137	No load	1.53	38.8	35.7	0.2
INVESCO STRAT. FINANCIAL SVCS ♙	▲▲	Financial	▼	622.2	44	No load	1.26	30.3	26.5	2.2
INVESCO STRAT. GOLD	▼▼▼	Precious Metals	▼	229.6	41	No load	1.32	40.6	29.7	0.0
INVESCO STRAT. HEALTH SCIENCE ♙	▼▼▼	Health	▼	936.2	-10	No load	1.15	11.4	6.8	0.1
INVESCO STRAT. LEISURE ♙	AVG	Specialty-Misc.		237.5	-9	No load	1.29	9.1	8.2	0.2
INVESCO STRAT. TECHNOLOGY ♟	▼	Technology	AVG	838.5	46	No load	1.12	21.8	17.4	0.2
INVESCO STRAT. UTILITIES ♙	AVG	Utilities	▲▲▲	157.4	5	No load	1.18	12.8	9.5	2.8
INVESCO TOTAL RETURN	▲▲	Domestic Hybrid	▲▲	1227.4	60	No load	0.95	13.1	11.8	3.4
INVESCO VALUE EQUITY	▲	Large-cap Value	▼▼	251.8	44	No load	0.97	18.5	17.1	1.8
INVESTMENT CO. OF AMERICA ♟	▲	Large-cap Blend	AVG	30875.5	20	5.75	0.60†	19.4	17.3	2.0
IVY GROWTH A	▼	Large-cap Blend	▼▼▼	288.6	5	5.75	1.59†	17.2	14.1	0.7
IVY INTERNATIONAL A ♟	▼	Foreign	▲	952.3	102	5.75	1.52†	19.7	19.0	0.5
JANUS BALANCED ♙		Domestic Hybrid		219.7	58	No load	1.32	15.3	11.8	NA
JANUS ENTERPRISE		Small-cap Growth		721.8	45	No load	1.23	11.7	10.3	NA
JANUS ♟	▲	Large-cap Blend	AVG	15890.3	27	No load	0.86	19.6	15.8	NA
JANUS GROWTH & INCOME	▼	Large-cap Growth	AVG	1100.5	74	No load	1.17	26.0	22.7	NA
JANUS MERCURY		Mid-cap Growth		2061.3	29	No load	1.12	17.7	13.5	NA
JANUS OLYMPUS		Mid-cap Growth		412.9	406	No load	NA	21.7	21.4	NA
JANUS OVERSEAS		Foreign		955.4	638	No load	1.73	28.8	28.1	NA
JANUS TWENTY	▼▼	Large-cap Growth	▼	4070.7	33	No load	0.99	27.9	21.8	NA

*Includes redemption fee. **Includes deferred sales charge. †12(b)-1 plan in effect. ‡Not currently accepting new accounts. §Less than 0.5% of assets. NA=Not available. NM=Not meaningful. (ll) Formerly Mariner Total Return Equity. (mm) Formerly Idex ll Global A. (nn) Formerly Idex ll Growth A. (oo) Formerly IDS Managed Retirement A. (pp) Formerly EBI Equity. (qq) Formerly EBI Flex. (rr) Formerly EBI MultiFlex.

3 YEARS PRETAX	3 YEARS AFTERTAX	5 YEARS PRETAX	5 YEARS AFTERTAX	10 YEARS PRETAX	10 YEARS AFTERTAX	BW 10-YEAR ANALYSIS	TURNOVER	CASH %	FOREIGN %	P-E RATIO	UNTAXED GAINS (%)	LARGEST HOLDING COMPANY (% ASSETS)	RISK LEVEL	BEST QTR	BEST %RET	WORST QTR	WORST %RET	TELEPHONE
Less than three years of data available							Very low	3	100	17	7	Sun Hung Kai Properties(10)						800-915-6565
16.5	16.3	14.7	14.5				Low	5	4	32	45	Ascend Communs.(3)	High	IV 92	19.6	II 92	–13.7	800-225-5291
21.8	19.8	20.3	17.8	13.8	11.7		Average	12	4	36	32	Computer Associates Intl.(5)	Very high	II 95	24.7	II 92	–9.3	800-225-5291
15.2	13.5	12.2	10.1	12.9	10.4		Average	0	NA	23	35	McDonnell Douglas(5)	Average	II 95	10.0	I 94	–6.4	800-225-5291
12.3	10.7	11.2	9.2	13.0	10.4		Average	7	NA	39	42	Adaptec(2)	High	IV 92	13.3	I 94	–7.8	800-225-5291
23.7	22.8	27.4	25.8	20.9	18.4		Very low	16	NA	18	22	Wells Fargo(3)	Low	IV 92	15.5	IV 94	–9.3	800-225-5291
14.2	12.7	11.1	9.7	12.2	9.9		Average	5	NA	22	26	General Electric(5)	Low	I 95	8.1	I 94	–4.1	800-225-5291
16.0	15.8						Average	4	9	50	22	Cascade Communs.(4)						800-225-5291
15.7	13.8						High	10	10	37	29	Benton Oil & Gas(3)						800-225-5291
19.5	18.9	16.1	14.5				Average	2	12	32	17	Intel(4)	High	II 95	15.9	II 92	–5.1	800-422-1050
13.7	12.6	16.4	15.5				Very low	5	99	22	32	Lukoil (144A)(4)	Average	IV 93	13.9	II 92	–4.1	800-422-1050
14.8	14.4						Average	4	100	20	15	Granada Group(5)						800-422-1050
Less than three years of data available								0	11	22	11	Interdigital Communs.(4)						800-432-7856
16.9	15.2	22.0	19.9	16.1	13.8		Low	11	4	19	19	ICN Pharmaceuticals(4)	Average	IV 92	21.4	II 92	–8.1	800-432-7856
17.4	16.1	16.5	15.4				Very low	10	4	19	22	Chase Manhattan(2)	Low	I 95	9.1	IV 94	–2.1	800-258-3030
15.0	12.3	15.0	12.6				Low	0	2	18	20	Allegheny Teledyne(5)	Average	I 95	10.2	I 94	–4.7	800-346-7301
11.2	10.1	14.3	13.3				Very low	4	100	19	4	ANZ Banking Group(2)	Average	IV 93	15.3	III 92	–6.9	800-346-7301
15.1	13.1	12.8	10.4	12.8	10.3		Average	3	1	21	14	General Electric(3)	Average	I 95	9.1	I 94	–4.3	800-634-2536
17.0	14.6	17.6	15.7				Average	8	4	50	34	Corporate Express(3)	Very high	IV 92	25.5	II 92	–13.7	800-945-3863
15.8	13.7						Low	6	8	27	21	Danka Business Sys. (ADR)(4)						800-945-3863
15.6	12.0	11.8	8.9	14.5	10.9		Average	13	NA	22	18	Baxter International(3)	Average	II 95	7.8	I 94	–2.7	800-945-3863
15.4	13.6						High	3	83	28	27	IBM(4)						800-851-9777
16.5	13.8	10.6	8.8	17.2	14.5		High	15	9	38	32	Ascend Communs.(4)	High	II 95	16.7	I 92	–7.1	800-851-9777
18.9	16.4	15.0	12.7				High	5	1	24	16	NationsBank(4)	Average	IV 95	8.3	I 94	–3.1	800-328-8300
10.9	7.3	10.2	7.6	12.6	10.1		Very high	3	4	31	25	OfficeMax(3)	High	IV 92	17.5	II 92	–11.5	800-328-8300
12.7	10.5	15.4	13.3				High	5	5	19	16	Philip Morris(2)	Very low	I 93	9.2	IV 94	–4.0	800-328-8300
13.6	10.7	13.2	10.5	13.8	10.7		Average	4	4	25	35	Tyco International(2)	Average	IV 92	10.6	I 94	–5.8	800-328-8300
14.0	11.7	14.2	11.7	13.9	11.0		Average	6	10	17	25	General Electric(2)	Low	IV 96	8.5	I 94	–3.8	800-328-8300
4.2	2.9	9.0	8.0				Average	14	92	24	11	Generale des Eaux(1)	High	IV 93	12.8	IV 94	–9.6	800-328-8300
21.9	20.0	16.3	13.7	16.7	12.4		Low	6	3	32	37	Tellabs(4)	High	IV 92	13.8	II 92	–5.7	800-328-8300
5.7	4.2	8.1	6.8	7.5	5.7		Average	7	100	27	11	Sandoz (Reg)(2)	High	IV 93	11.0	I 92	–5.8	800-328-8300
8.5	5.6	9.9	7.1	13.8	11.3		Average	5	32	26	16	NationsBank(2)	Average	III 94	8.8	I 94	–6.0	800-328-8300
11.3	8.7	11.7	8.8	11.6	8.2		Low	8	12	18	14	General Electric(1)	Very low	I 95	7.2	I 94	–3.8	800-328-8300
17.8	16.5	14.5	13.0	17.8	15.1		Average	9	2	30	35	Cisco Systems(4)	Average	IV 92	11.2	II 92	–4.2	800-328-8300
13.4	11.4	14.5	12.5	10.7	7.9		Average	7	10	20	19	Allied Group(2)	Low	IV 92	9.4	I 94	–2.6	800-328-8300
13.4	10.9	12.7	9.7	13.9	10.2		Average	5	13	25	21	General Electric(2)	Low	I 95	7.1	IV 94	–3.5	800-328-8300
14.1	12.8	9.7	8.1	12.5	11.0		High	14	3	42	44	Cisco Systems(4)	High	III 95	12.9	II 94	–7.7	800-328-8300
9.5	7.6	11.5	9.2				Average	3	20	20	12	BCE(2)	Low	IV 96	9.5	I 94	–6.4	800-328-8300
13.2	10.7	13.1	10.6	12.2	9.3		Low	8	6	19	16	Atlantic Richfield(2)	Very low	I 95	7.2	I 94	–4.5	800-421-4120
Less than three years of data available								3	1	23	NA	General Electric(6)						800-334-2292
16.2	14.8	12.6	10.6	13.0	10.2		Low	4	7	21	28	Computer Associates Intl.(3)	Low	I 95	8.6	I 94	–3.0	800-554-1156
13.3	11.5	11.6	10.0				Very low	2	10	19	21	Unilever (NY)(2)	Very low	I 95	7.8	I 94	–3.9	800-554-1156
12.1	11.3						Average	5	23	22	14	Public Storage(1)						800-554-1156
19.6	17.2						Very high	11	28	24	11	Forcenergy Cl B(4)						800-525-8085
16.0	11.6	16.0	12.8	15.8	13.1		Very high	3	12	36	19	Cisco Systems(4)	High	IV 92	19.3	II 92	–8.1	800-525-8085
11.8	8.9	16.7	14.9				Very high	9	11	46	18	Saville Systems (ADR)(3)	High	IV 92	22.8	II 92	–10.9	800-525-8085
14.4	12.4	11.5	10.2	9.4	8.5		High	5	99	29	24	Tomra Systems(2)	High	IV 96	10.1	III 92	–6.8	800-525-8085
12.6	8.5	11.7	8.0	13.0	10.0		High	1	8	30	19	Intel(5)	Average	IV 92	8.9	II 92	–6.2	800-525-8085
12.6	10.1	11.0	8.6	14.8	11.9		Average	3	6	23	21	Bank of New York(2)	Low	I 93	9.0	I 92	–4.0	800-525-8085
2.5	1.1	5.8	4.8	6.6	5.1		Average	2	100	29	9	HSBC Holdings (HK)(3)	Very high	I 93	10.8	I 92	–11.2	800-525-8085
15.6	14.5	9.3	8.7	8.1	7.3		Very high	14	22	31	15	Flores & Rucks(5)	High	I 93	18.6	IV 93	–12.4	800-525-8085
19.7	17.4	20.8	17.5	19.5	17.3		High	4	2	16	20	Conseco(6)	Average	IV 92	18.6	I 94	–5.7	800-525-8085
4.6	1.8	12.6	10.8	3.8	2.9		Average	–4	81	44	25	Bre-X Minerals(9)	Very high	I 96	46.2	IV 94	–21.3	800-525-8085
21.4	18.8	7.1	5.7	21.3	19.5		High	5	9	40	33	Oxford Health Plans(5)	Very high	III 95	19.5	I 93	–22.0	800-525-8085
6.3	4.3	15.0	12.9	17.2	14.6		Average	5	21	28	10	Time Warner(2)	Average	III 93	19.8	I 94	–5.6	800-525-8085
23.2	19.4	20.6	17.6	20.5	18.3		Very high	19	9	36	23	American General Finance(5)	High	IV 92	23.6	II 92	–9.8	800-525-8085
8.4	6.5	11.3	8.5	10.9	8.4		Very high	13	6	18	10	Public Service Colorado(4)	Low	II 93	8.8	I 94	–6.3	800-525-8085
14.2	13.0	13.0	11.5				Low	4	11	19	13	Compaq Computer(2)	Very low	II 95	7.9	I 94	–2.9	800-525-8085
17.2	15.4	13.3	11.6	13.6	11.4		Low	7	4	20	25	Boatmen's Bancshares(2)	Average	I 95	8.4	I 94	–2.8	800-525-8085
16.0	14.0	13.3	11.4	13.9	11.6		Low	8	10	23	32	Philip Morris(3)	Low	II 95	8.7	I 94	–3.7	800-421-4120
13.1	11.0	11.3	8.4	11.7	9.0		Average	4	24	25	24	Cabletron Systems(1)	Average	III 95	9.0	IV 94	–3.5	800-456-5111
11.9	11.1	15.8	15.0	15.5	14.2		Very low	7	100	22	19	Lukoil (144A)(4)	High	IV 93	12.9	III 92	–5.7	800-456-5111
13.7	11.1						Very high	9	14	24	15	Wells Fargo(4)						800-525-8983
15.7	14.1						Very high	7	16	46	27	Fastenal(8)						800-525-8983
15.3	13.2	12.7	10.7	16.4	13.5		High	22	18	29	27	Electronic Data Systems(5)	Low	II 95	9.0	I 92	–2.7	800-525-8983
17.8	15.3	12.9	11.2				Very high	5	10	28	21	Wells Fargo(4)	Average	III 95	11.8	I 92	–6.6	800-525-8983
21.9	18.9						Very high	13	19	37	18	Wells Fargo(5)						800-525-8983
Less than three years of data available								7	3	41	NA	Nike(8)						800-525-8983
Less than three years of data available							Very high	27	99	27	15	Rentokil Group(4)						800-525-8983
17.6	13.7	11.4	8.9	16.6	14.2		High	2	6	28	23	Wells Fargo(11)	High	II 95	14.3	I 92	–8.1	800-525-8983

DATA: MORNINGSTAR, INC., CHICAGO, IL.

MUTUAL FUND SCOREBOARD

FUND	OVERALL RATING	CATEGORY	RATING	ASSETS $MIL.	% CHG. 1995-6	SALES CHARGE (%)	EXPENSE RATIO (%)	PRE-TAX	AFTER-TAX	YIELD
	(COMPARES RISK-ADJUSTED PERFORMANCE OF EACH FUND AGAINST ALL FUNDS)		(COMPARES RISK-ADJUSTED PERFORMANCE OF FUND WITHIN CATEGORY)						1996 RETURNS (%)	
JANUS VENTURE	▼	Small-cap Growth	▲	1705.5	−5	No load‡	0.91	8.0	5.3	NA
JANUS WORLDWIDE	▲	World	▲▲▲	5046.3	155	No load	1.23	26.4	24.2	NA
JAPAN	▼▼▼	Japan		383.7	−30	No load	1.21	−10.9	−11.2	1.0
KAUFMANN 🧍	▼	Small-cap Growth	▲▲	5274.0	67	0.20*	2.17†	20.9	19.5	0.0
KEMPER BLUE CHIP A	▼	Large-cap Growth	AVG	215.9	36	5.75	1.30†	27.7	21.1	1.1
KEMPER GROWTH A 🧍	▼▼	Large-cap Growth	▼▼	1797.1	5	5.75	1.07†	16.3	8.2	0.0
KEMPER INTERNATIONAL A	▼	Foreign	AVG	373.8	23	5.75	1.57†	17.1	14.9	1.0
KEMPER RETIREMENT II	AVG	Domestic Hybrid	▼▼▼	168.5	−3	5.00‡	0.94	10.7	5.9	4.4
KEMPER RETIREMENT IV		Domestic Hybrid		136.5	−9	5.00‡	0.95	9.5	5.2	3.4
KEMPER SMALL CAP EQUITY A 🧍	▼▼	Small-cap Growth	▼	632.4	12	5.75	1.08†	14.1	11.4	0.0
KEMPER TECHNOLOGY A	▼▼	Technology	▼	1007.1	14	5.75	0.88†	20.6	15.5	0.0
KEMPER TOTAL RETURN A		Domestic Hybrid	▼▼▼	1900.7	6	5.75	1.12†	16.3	11.2	2.6
KEMPER-DREMAN HIGH RETURN A	▲▲	Large-cap Value	▲	382.7	397	5.75	1.25†	28.8	27.3	1.4
KEMPER-DREMAN SMALL CAP A 🧍		Small-cap Value		143.3	587	5.75	1.25†	29.6	28.6	0.4
KEYSTONE BALANCED (K-1) 🧍	▲	Domestic Hybrid	▼	1570.8	7	4.00**	1.71†	15.8	13.8	2.4
KEYSTONE GLOBAL OPPORT. B 🧍		World		351.7	28	5.00**	2.38†	2.8	1.2	0.0
KEYSTONE GROWTH & INC. (S-1)	AVG	Large-cap Blend	▼▼	265.8	19	4.00**	1.84†	21.1	17.0	0.7
KEYSTONE INTERNATIONAL	▼	Foreign	▲	161.3	20	4.00**	2.42†	13.7	13.7	0.0
KEYSTONE MID-CAP GROWTH (S-3)	▼	Mid-cap Growth	AVG	305.5	2	4.00**	1.73†	8.2	5.1	0.0
KEYSTONE OMEGA A	▼	Mid-cap Growth	AVG	154.8	15	5.75	1.37†	11.3	8.2	0.0
KEYSTONE PRECIOUS METALS HLDG. 🧍	▼▼▼	Precious Metals		169.9	−10	4.00**	2.26†	2.5	1.3	0.0
KEYSTONE SMALL CO. GROWTH (S-4) 🧍	▼▼	Mid-cap Growth	▼▼	1784.1	−10	4.00**	1.72†	0.8	−2.2	0.0
KEYSTONE STRAT. GROWTH (K-2)	▼	Mid-cap Growth	▲	516.9	−1	4.00**	2.00†	12.0	8.4	0.0
LANDMARK BALANCED A	AVG	Domestic Hybrid	▼▼	230.5	−6	4.75	1.02†	7.6	5.2	3.0
LANDMARK EQUITY A	AVG	Large-cap Blend	▼▼	229.1	7	4.75	1.05†	13.8	11.7	0.6
LEGG MASON INTL. EQUITY PRIM. (ss)		Foreign		167.5	156	No load	2.25†	16.6	15.6	0.4
LEGG MASON SPEC. INVMT. PRIM. 🧍	▼	Small-cap Blend		964.4	35	No load	1.96†	28.7	26.9	0.0
LEGG MASON TOTAL RETURN PRIM.	▲	Large-cap Value	▼	344.7	42	No load	1.95†	31.1	29.2	2.2
LEGG MASON VALUE PRIM. 🧍	▲▲	Large-cap Value	AVG	1976.1	47	No load	1.82†	38.3	36.4	0.5
LEXINGTON CORPORATE LEADERS	▲▲	Large-cap Value	AVG	391.7	53	No load	0.58	22.4	20.8	4.5
LEXINGTON GROWTH & INCOME	▲	Large-cap Blend	▲	200.2	44	No load	1.09†	26.5	24.1	0.7
LEXINGTON WORLDWIDE EMG. MKTS.	▼▼	Diversified Emerging Mkts.		256.5	−1	No load	1.88	7.4	7.4	0.0
LINDNER DIVIDEND INV. 🧍	▲▲▲	Domestic Hybrid	▲▲▲	2281.5	9	No load	0.60	11.5	8.7	6.1
LINDNER GROWTH INV. 🧍	▲	Small-cap Value	AVG	1495.1	6	No load	0.63	21.0	16.8	1.4
LKCM SMALL CAP EQUITY		Small-cap Blend		187.6	53	No load	1.00	27.0	24.7	0.4
LONGLEAF PARTNERS	▲▲▲	Mid-cap Blend	▲▲▲	2300.1	23	No load‡	1.01	21.0	17.3	1.5
LONGLEAF PARTNERS REALTY 🧍		Real Estate		156.0	NM	No load	NA	40.7	40.4	0.4
LONGLEAF PARTNERS SMALL-CAP	▲▲	Small-cap Value	▲	252.2	85	No load	1.30	30.6	28.7	0.1
LOOMIS SAYLES SMALL CAP VALUE (tt)	AVG	Small-cap Blend	▼	142.4	57	No load	1.25	30.4	25.6	0.6
LORD ABBETT AFFILIATED A (uu) 🧍	▲▲	Large-cap Value	AVG	6409.5	21	5.75	0.63†	20.1	16.8	2.2
LORD ABBETT DEVELOPING GR. A	▼▼	Small-cap Growth	AVG	292.3	50	5.75	1.03†	22.3	17.9	0.0
LORD ABBETT MID-CAP VALUE (vv)	AVG	Mid-cap Value	▼▼	257.8	13	5.75	1.27†	21.2	18.4	1.1
MAINSTAY CAPITAL APPREC. B	▼	Mid-cap Growth	AVG	1341.1	57	5.00**	1.70†	18.6	18.2	0.0
MAINSTAY EQUITY INDEX A	▲	Large-cap Blend	AVG	225.6	106	3.00	1.10†	21.9	19.9	2.3
MAINSTAY TOTAL RETURN B	AVG	Domestic Hybrid	▼▼▼	1029.6	20	5.00**	1.70†	12.7	11.5	1.3
MAINSTAY VALUE B	▲▲	Mid-cap Value	AVG	1018.8	44	5.00**	1.80†	21.1	18.3	0.9
MAIRS & POWER GROWTH 🧍	▲▲▲	Mid-cap Blend	▲▲▲	150.2	113	No load	0.99	27.8	26.7	1.1
MANAGERS INTL. EQUITY	▲	Foreign	▲▲▲	259.2	85	No load	1.58	12.7	11.8	0.7
MANAGERS SPECIAL EQUITY 🧍	AVG	Small-cap Growth	▲▲▲	250.0	111	No load	1.44	24.8	22.8	0.0
MARKETWATCH EQUITY		Large-cap Blend		231.9	89	4.50	1.35†	23.7	22.8	0.9
MARSHALL EQUITY-INCOME		Large-cap Value		231.4	74	No load	1.01	21.2	18.3	2.4
MARSHALL INTERNATIONAL STOCK 🧍		Foreign		170.0	63	No load	1.54†	19.7	18.6	2.2
MARSHALL MID-CAP STOCK		Mid-cap Growth		161.0	49	No load	1.01	20.6	17.7	0.0
MARSHALL STOCK 🧍		Large-cap Blend		236.1	−14	No load	0.98	14.7	9.7	1.2
MARSHALL VALUE EQUITY		Mid-cap Value		175.1	−14	No load	0.96	13.9	8.8	1.4
MASSACHUSETTS INV. GROWTH STOCK A	▼▼	Large-cap Growth	▼▼	1341.6	19	5.75	0.73†	22.8	14.7	0.0
MASSACHUSETTS INV. A	▲	Large-cap Blend	▲	2752.4	33	5.75	0.70†	25.9	22.5	1.3
MATHERS 🧍	▼	Domestic Hybrid	▼▼▼	171.6	−26	No load	0.98	−0.1	−1.1	3.5
MENTOR GROWTH B 🧍	AVG	Small-cap Growth	▲▲	390.5	46	4.00**	2.08†	21.0	16.2	0.0
MENTOR STRATEGY B		Mid-cap Growth		302.8	28	4.00**	2.08†	17.7	14.9	0.0
MERGER	▲▲▲	Mid-cap Blend	▲▲▲	473.8	93	No load‡	1.41†	10.0	7.1	1.2
MERIDIAN 🧍	▼	Small-cap Growth	▲	377.9	1	No load	0.96	11.2	8.2	1.1
MERRILL LYNCH BASIC VALUE B	▲▲	Large-cap Value	▲	3720.2	29	4.00**	1.61†	16.6	14.6	1.6
MERRILL LYNCH CAPITAL B	▲	Domestic Hybrid	AVG	5249.5	10	4.00**	1.58†	11.5	8.7	2.9
MERRILL LYNCH DEV. CAP. MKTS. B		Diversified Emerging Mkts.		308.9	57	4.00**	2.56†	12.2	11.6	1.5
MERRILL LYNCH DRAGON B		Pacific ex-Japan		1175.5	19	4.00**	2.41†	12.4	12.3	0.0
MERRILL LYNCH EUROFUND B	▼	Europe	▼	776.4	2	4.00**	2.15†	24.0	18.4	2.7
MERRILL LYNCH FUND FOR TOMORROW D		Large-cap Blend		237.1	6	5.25	1.33†	13.7	9.8	0.9
MERRILL LYNCH FUNDAMENTAL GROWTH B		Large-cap Growth		149.5	83	4.00**	2.16†	17.7	15.1	0.0
MERRILL LYNCH GLOBAL ALLOC. B	▲▲▲	International Hybrid	▲▲	8984.6	27	4.00**	1.93†	15.0	11.9	4.9

*Includes redemption fee. **Includes deferred sales charge. †12(b)-1 plan in effect. ‡Not currently accepting new accounts. §Less than 0.5% of assets. NA=Not available. NM=Not meaningful. (ss) Formerly Legg Mason Global Equity Prim. (tt) Formerly Loomis Sayles Small Cap. (uu) Formerly Affiliated. (vv) Formerly Lord Abbett Value Appreciation.

3 YEARS PRETAX	AFTERTAX	5 YEARS PRETAX	AFTERTAX	10 YEARS PRETAX	AFTERTAX	TREND BW 10-YEAR ANALYSIS	TURNOVER	CASH %	FOREIGN %	P-E RATIO	UNTAXED GAINS (%)	LARGEST HOLDING COMPANY (% ASSETS)	RISK LEVEL	BEST QTR %RET	WORST QTR %RET	TELEPHONE
12.9	10.1	11.0	8.5	15.8	13.2		High	6	8	38	27	Wisc. Central Transport(6)	High	III 95 14.7	II 92 −3.6	800-525-8983
16.9	15.0	17.5	16.1				High	11	87	28	22	Rentokil Group(5)	Average	IV 93 12.7	III 92 −4.1	800-525-8983
−3.8	−4.6	−1.7	−2.6	3.5	0.0		Average	4	100	38	−7	Nichiei(6)	Very high	I 94 16.8	I 92 −15.2	800-535-2726
21.7	21.0	18.9	18.4	19.3	18.9		Average	9	8	37	34	HFS(4)	High	IV 92 22.4	II 92 −12.3	800-237-0132
16.9	13.6	10.3	7.9				High	3	4	25	25	Ryder System(2)	Average	II 95 8.2	I 92 −5.1	800-621-1048
13.0	9.1	7.6	5.0	14.4	11.3		High	16	5	27	33	Ceridian(2)	High	IV 92 10.9	II 92 −7.6	800-621-1048
8.3	6.8	10.4	9.2	9.4	7.3		High	5	100	30	20	Ciba-Geigy(3)	High	III 93 12.0	III 92 −8.7	800-621-1048
8.4	4.9	8.1	5.2				Average	4	3	27	19	Monsanto(1)	Low	II 95 7.7	I 92 −5.6	800-621-1048
8.6	6.3						Average	3	3	27	13	Monsanto(1)				800-621-1048
13.1	10.0	11.1	8.4	14.0	10.8		Average	15	6	35	34	LCI International(2)	High	III 93 14.4	II 92 −11.1	800-621-1048
24.2	19.2	16.2	12.2	15.5	11.5		High	2	4	39	28	Cisco Systems(4)	High	II 95 18.7	II 92 −4.5	800-621-1048
9.9	7.2	8.7	6.0	10.9	8.5		High	5	4	25	18	Philip Morris(2)	Average	II 95 7.9	II 94 −5.4	800-621-1048
23.2	22.2	19.6	18.7				Low	24	0	20	14	FNMA(6)	Average	IV 92 12.2	IV 94 −5.3	800-621-1048
23.6	22.0						Average	15	3	15	12	Bally Entertainment(5)				800-621-1048
12.0	10.3	9.9	8.0	10.5	8.2		High	1	2	22	26	General Electric(4)	Low	I 95 6.9	I 94 −4.4	800-343-2898
8.7	8.2						Average	5	54	31	9	Shohkoh Fund(2)				800-343-2898
14.5	11.1	10.6	7.8	11.4	8.7		High	1	7	26	27	General Electric(3)	Average	II 95 9.4	I 94 −4.7	800-343-2898
5.9	4.6	9.7	8.8	6.2	4.8		Average	4	98	27	24	Canon(4)	Average	IV 93 10.9	IV 94 −4.3	800-343-2898
11.9	7.9	9.9	6.7	11.5	8.3		High	4	4	34	18	HFS(3)	High	III 95 11.4	II 92 −4.3	800-343-2898
12.9	10.6	12.3	9.6	16.0	12.5		High	4	5	33	10	General Electric(4)	High	III 93 12.4	II 92 −5.6	800-343-2898
−4.3	−4.8	8.9	8.5	6.2	5.6		Average	2	78	40	23	Euro-Nevada Mining(5)	Very high	II 93 35.3	IV 94 −14.2	800-343-2898
11.2	8.3	13.6	10.3	14.9	11.9		High	13	NA	37	18	Ensco International(2)	Very high	IV 92 21.3	II 92 −11.3	800-343-2898
11.8	8.2	11.4	8.4	11.8	8.7		High	3	15	29	22	General Electric(4)	High	IV 92 13.9	IV 94 −4.2	800-343-2898
8.9	7.2	8.4	7.1				Very high	8	NA	28	13	Electronic Data Systems(1)	Low	I 95 6.4	I 94 −3.7	800-721-1899
13.1	11.4	11.8	10.7				Average	5	NA	26	25	Pfizer(3)	Average	IV 92 9.2	I 94 −4.1	800-721-1899
Less than three years of data available								3	99	23	7	Lloyds TSB Group(1)				800-577-8589
11.1	10.2	14.4	13.4	14.6	13.2		Low	3	12	22	27	America Online(5)	High	IV 92 17.7	IV 94 −8.2	800-577-8589
16.7	14.9	15.7	14.1	12.2	10.4		Low	3	10	16	24	IBM(5)	Average	IV 96 12.5	IV 94 −8.6	800-577-8589
25.5	24.2	19.6	18.7	14.4	13.0		Low	5	9	19	49	FNMA(7)	Average	II 95 14.5	I 94 −2.0	800-577-8589
19.1	16.0	16.9	14.1	14.9	10.7			1	NA	20	28	Mobil(9)	Average	I 95 11.0	I 94 −5.1	800-526-0056
14.5	11.7	13.8	10.6	11.0	7.5		High	8	2	25	18	Diamond Offshore Drilling(4)	Average	IV 92 9.0	IV 94 −3.7	800-526-0056
−4.5	−5.0	8.1	7.2	8.4	5.8		High	5	100	21	−3	Lukoil(3)	High	IV 93 31.8	IV 94 −12.7	800-526-0056
9.4	6.6	12.8	10.0	11.2	8.1		Low	3	8	19	7	NorAm Energy(2)	Very low	I 93 6.9	IV 94 −2.7	314-727-5305
13.0	9.8	14.3	11.8	13.0	10.2		Average	4	18	27	34	Alliant Techsystems(3)	Average	I 93 8.8	IV 94 −2.4	314-727-5305
Less than three years of data available								11	NA	27	18	Kirby(2)				817-332-3235
18.9	16.5	19.9	17.5				Very low	16	6	24	21	Knight-Ridder(11)	Very low	I 95 11.4	IV 94 −4.9	800-445-9469
Less than three years of data available								15	14	26	NA	Trizeo(10)				800-445-9469
17.1	15.1	15.4	14.2				Low	3	6	26	23	White River(11)	Low	IV 92 13.9	II 92 −7.0	800-445-9469
16.5	13.9	17.4	14.5				High	13	1	22	24	Patriot Amer. Hospitality(2)	High	IV 92 17.8	II 92 −13.2	800-633-3330
18.0	14.5	15.9	12.7	13.3	9.8		Average	3	3	22	24	MCI Communications(3)	Low	IV 96 8.7	I 94 −3.5	800-874-3733
23.7	19.0	15.6	12.1	13.7	11.2		Average	4	2	25	42	JLG Industries(5)	High	II 95 19.0	II 92 −13.3	800-874-3733
13.9	10.9	13.8	11.0	11.9	8.6		Average	4	6	21	20	Snap-On(4)	Average	IV 92 9.3	IV 94 −4.5	800-874-3733
16.4	16.2	14.8	14.5	16.0	15.0		Low	5	5	29	28	HFS(3)	High	IV 92 23.3	II 92 −11.4	800-522-4202
18.4	17.1	14.0	13.0				Very low	5	4	24	21	General Electric(3)	Low	I 95 9.2	I 94 −4.2	800-522-4202
12.1	11.2	10.0	9.1				Very high	4	3	29	24	3Com(2)	Average	IV 92 9.3	II 92 −4.9	800-522-4202
15.7	14.0	16.0	14.1	14.4	12.7		Average	13	3	18	20	IBM(3)	Low	IV 92 11.4	IV 94 −4.3	800-522-4202
25.9	24.6	19.4	18.1	17.2	15.3		Very low	6	NA	22	50	Medtronic(6)	Average	III 95 16.7	I 94 −3.8	800-304-7404
10.2	9.2	14.0	13.2	10.9	8.9		Average	10	98	23	12	Sony(2)	Average	IV 93 10.5	IV 94 −3.4	800-835-3879
17.9	15.6	17.4	14.9	17.8	14.9		Average	9	1	33	26	National Education(3)	Average	IV 92 14.8	II 92 −4.4	800-835-3879
18.1	17.3						Low	1	NA	20	27	State Street Boston(3)				800-232-9091
17.0	15.1						Average	19	1	21	18	General Electric(4)				800-236-8560
Less than three years of data available								16	NA	20	9	Telefonica de Espana(2)				800-236-8560
15.0	13.3						High	3	8	34	24	Kohl's(3)				800-236-8560
12.9	10.5						Average	1	4	23	21	General Electric(3)				800-236-8560
13.4	10.5						Average	15	12	24	14	Horsham(3)				800-236-8560
13.7	8.7	12.4	8.1	14.2	10.2		Average	8	3	21	34	Microsoft(5)	High	IV 92 15.3	I 94 −8.3	800-637-2929
20.2	16.7	15.5	11.3	15.5	11.4		Average	3	7	22	33	Philip Morris(3)	Low	I 95 9.2	I 92 −4.0	800-637-2929
0.2	−1.2	1.2	0.0	7.4	4.5		Average	9	NA	23	−11	Conseco(7)	Average	II 95 4.0	IV 94 −3.0	800-962-3863
17.2	13.7	16.6	13.4	13.5	11.5		Average	13	1	34	33	Career Horizons(2)	High	III 95 13.9	II 92 −7.8	800-382-0016
12.8	11.9						High	21	3	27	26	JLG Industries(2)				800-382-0016
10.4	8.3	10.8	8.7				Very high	15	8	37	7	Bally Entertainment(4)	Very low	II 93 5.5	II 92 −1.2	800-343-8959
11.0	9.4	12.3	11.0	14.3	12.4		Low	26	3	31	26	Vivra(3)	High	IV 92 18.3	II 92 −8.1	800-446-6662
15.7	14.0	15.4	13.8				Very low	17	9	18	24	Citicorp(3)	Low	I 93 10.0	I 94 −2.1	800-637-3863
13.6	10.6	11.4	8.9				Average	4	27	16	9	YPF (ADR)(2)	Low	II 95 8.2	I 94 −2.1	800-637-3863
Less than three years of data available								2	98	17	4	Korea Mobile Telecom(5)				800-637-3863
−0.2	−0.5						Low	3	100	19	22	Cheung Kong Holdings(4)				800-637-3863
12.8	9.1	11.9	9.7				Average	2	100	17	22	STET(2)	High	IV 93 10.6	III 92 −9.0	800-637-3863
Less than three years of data available								10	22	27	24	Schering-Plough(4)				800-637-3863
Less than three years of data available								15	8	27	27	Johnson & Johnson(4)				800-637-3863
11.0	8.6	12.7	10.5				Low	22	45	21	9	Stora Kopparberg Cl A(1)	Very low	II 95 9.1	IV 94 −3.0	800-637-3863

DATA: MORNINGSTAR, INC., CHICAGO, IL.

MUTUAL FUND SCOREBOARD

FUND	OVERALL RATING (COMPARES RISK-ADJUSTED PERFORMANCE OF EACH FUND AGAINST ALL FUNDS)	CATEGORY (COMPARES RISK-ADJUSTED PERFORMANCE OF FUND WITHIN CATEGORY)	RATING	SIZE ASSETS $MIL.	% CHG. 1995-6	FEES SALES CHARGE (%)	EXPENSE RATIO (%)	1996 RETURNS (%) PRE-TAX	AFTER-TAX	YIELD
MERRILL LYNCH GLOBAL UTIL. B	AVG	Utilities	AVG	335.5	−15	4.00**	1.68†	13.3	11.5	2.6
MERRILL LYNCH GROWTH B (ww)	AVG	Mid-cap Growth	▲▲▲	3087.2	52	4.00**	1.84†	28.4	25.7	1.9
MERRILL LYNCH HEALTHCARE B	▼▼▼	Health	▲	210.7	46	4.00**	2.55†	10.7	7.0	6.3
MERRILL LYNCH INTL. EQUITY B		Foreign		803.1	−13	4.00**	2.09†	6.0	4.8	1.0
MERRILL LYNCH LATIN AMER. B	▼▼▼	Latin America		518.9	9	4.00**	2.71†	24.3	23.6	2.4
MERRILL LYNCH PACIFIC B	▼▼	Diversified Pacific		1299.3	25	4.00**	1.96†	5.0	2.9	5.5
MERRILL LYNCH PHOENIX B	AVG	Small-cap Blend	▲	397.9	−1	4.00**	2.26†	20.5	11.2	5.3
MERRILL LYNCH SPEC. VALUE B	AVG	Small-cap Value	▼▼	374.3	16	4.00**	2.15†	22.6	17.0	4.5
MERRILL LYNCH TECHNOLOGY B		Technology		466.9	−27	4.00**	2.34†	3.2	1.1	3.6
MFS CAPITAL GROWTH B	AVG	Large-cap Blend	▼	431.0	−2	4.00**	2.14†	16.2	9.1	0.0
MFS EMERGING GROWTH B	▼▼	Mid-cap Growth	▼	3655.3	78	4.00**	2.08†	13.9	13.7	0.0
MFS GROWTH OPPORTUNITIES A	▼	Mid-cap Growth	▲	835.5	16	5.75	0.87†	21.9	18.2	0.0
MFS MANAGED SECTORS A		Mid-cap Blend		232.8	18	5.75	1.43†	17.2	13.5	0.0
MFS RESEARCH A	▲	Mid-cap Growth	▲▲▲	1138.2	102	5.75	0.91†	24.3	22.7	0.0
MFS TOTAL RETURN A	▲▲	Domestic Hybrid	▲▲	2739.5	16	4.75	0.91†	14.6	11.1	3.9
MFS VALUE A	▲	Mid-cap Blend	▲	427.5	84	5.75	1.35†	16.7	13.9	0.2
MFS WORLD ASSET ALLOCATION B		International Hybrid		143.4	51	4.00**	2.10†	14.5	11.9	1.8
MFS WORLD EQUITY B	AVG	World	▲	201.6	27	4.00**	2.55†	19.5	16.5	0.0
MFS WORLD GROWTH B		World		290.4	15	4.00**	2.45†	12.5	11.0	0.0
MFS WORLD TOTAL RETURN A	▲	International Hybrid	AVG	136.2	18	4.75	1.77†	15.4	13.3	1.9
MIDAS	▼▼▼	Precious Metals	▲▲▲	200.7	NM	1.00*	2.25†	21.2	21.2	0.0
MONETTA	▼▼▼	Small-cap Growth	▼▼	211.5	−42	No load	1.36	1.6	1.6	0.0
MONTAG & CALDWELL GROWTH N		Large-cap Growth		196.2	301	No load	NA†	32.7	32.4	0.0
MONTGOMERY ASSET ALLOC. R		Domestic Hybrid		141.8	17	No load	1.42	12.9	9.5	2.0
MONTGOMERY EMERGING MKTS. R		Diversified Emerging Mkts.		912.5	7	No load	1.72	12.3	12.2	0.5
MONTGOMERY GLOBAL COMM. R		Communications		165.4	−25	No load	2.01	8.0	6.5	0.0
MONTGOMERY GROWTH R		Mid-cap Growth		994.9	16	No load	1.35	20.2	15.8	0.7
MONTGOMERY MICRO CAP R		Small-cap Blend		298.7	10	No load‡	1.75	19.1	16.9	0.0
MONTGOMERY SMALL CAP R	▼▼	Small-cap Growth	AVG	220.9	−7	No load‡	1.24	18.7	13.5	0.0
MONTGOMERY SMALL CAP OPPORT. R (xx)		Small-cap Blend		200.2	NM	No load	1.50	37.3	37.3	0.0
MORGAN STANLEY ASIAN GROWTH A		Pacific ex-Japan		208.7	14	4.75	1.88†	3.0	2.4	0.0
NATIONWIDE	AVG	Large-cap Blend	▼	995.8	18	4.50	0.63	23.9	21.3	1.6
NATIONWIDE GROWTH	AVG	Large-cap Blend	▼	687.2	14	4.50	0.66	16.7	14.2	1.0
NAVELLIER AGGRES. SMALL CAP EQ.		Small-cap Growth		190.5	77	3.00‡	1.75	15.4	15.4	0.0
NEUBERGER & BERMAN FOCUS	▲	Large-cap Value	▼▼	1179.0	15	No load	0.89	16.2	14.5	0.7
NEUBERGER & BERMAN GENESIS	▲	Small-cap Value	AVG	298.7	152	No load	1.28	29.9	29.4	0.0
NEUBERGER & BERMAN GUARD	▲	Large-cap Value	▼	5473.1	25	No load	0.82	17.9	16.0	1.0
NEUBERGER & BERMAN MANHATTAN	▼	Mid-cap Blend	▼▼	531.7	−11	No load	0.98	9.9	6.0	0.0
NEUBERGER & BERMAN PARTNERS	▲▲	Mid-cap Blend	▲	2218.3	34	No load	0.84	26.5	22.9	0.8
NEW ECONOMY	AVG	Mid-cap Growth	▲▲	4132.5	17	5.75	0.88†	12.9	10.7	0.8
NEW ENGLAND BALANCED A	▲▲	Domestic Hybrid	▲	219.5	12	5.75	1.36†	17.1	14.1	2.6
NEW ENGLAND CAPITAL GROWTH A		Large-cap Growth		141.3	14	5.75	1.61†	17.1	13.7	0.0
NEW ENGLAND GROWTH A	▼▼	Large-cap Growth	▼▼▼	1299.4	8	6.50‡	1.20†	20.9	18.1	0.3
NEW ENGLAND GROWTH OPPORT. A	AVG	Large-cap Blend	AVG	167.0	11	5.75	1.38†	17.2	11.7	0.8
NEW ENGLAND STAR ADVISERS B		Mid-cap Growth		366.1	67	4.00**	2.57†	18.1	15.2	0.0
NEW ENGLAND VALUE A	▲	Large-cap Value	AVG	299.3	24	5.75	1.37†	26.3	21.8	0.6
NEW PERSPECTIVE	AVG	World	▲	12895.0	39	5.75	0.82†	17.3	15.5	1.7
NEW USA GROWTH (yy)		Mid-cap Growth		211.4	8	5.00	2.69†	20.9	12.1	0.0
NICHOLAS	▲	Mid-cap Blend		4063.7	16	No load	0.74	19.8	17.0	0.6
NICHOLAS II	AVG	Small-cap Blend	AVG	792.4	14	No load	0.62	19.4	16.2	0.7
NICHOLAS LIMITED EDITION	AVG	Small-cap Blend	▲▲	231.9	37	No load	0.90	21.8	18.0	0.1
NICHOLAS-APPLEGATE CORE C		Mid-cap Growth		180.1	6	1.00**	2.14†	15.2	12.1	0.0
NICHOLAS-APPLEGATE EMG. GROWTH C		Small-cap Growth		224.4	17	1.00**	2.35†	17.6	14.2	0.0
NICHOLAS-APPLEGATE GROWTH EQ. B	▼▼	Mid-cap Growth	▼	193.9	−33	5.00**	2.27†	15.5	11.0	0.0
NORTHERN GROWTH EQUITY		Large-cap Growth		289.1	50	No load	1.00	17.8	16.1	0.4
NORTHERN INTL. GROWTH EQUITY		Foreign		179.4	11	No load	1.25	5.0	3.7	0.7
NORTHERN SMALL CAP GROWTH		Small-cap Value		193.4	36	No load	1.00	18.9	17.1	0.5
OAKMARK	▲▲▲	Mid-cap Value	▲▲▲	4195.0	27	No load	1.18	16.2	14.1	1.0
OAKMARK INTERNATIONAL		Foreign		1232.8	57	No load	1.32	28.0	27.6	1.0
OAKMARK SMALL CAP		Small-cap Value		316.5	NM	2.00*	1.61	39.8	39.8	0.0
OBERWEIS EMERGING GROWTH	▼▼▼	Small-cap Growth	▼▼	190.6	41	No load	1.73†	23.2	20.7	0.0
OLD WESTBURY INTERNATIONAL		Foreign		135.8	33	4.50	1.50†	21.3	20.8	1.3
111 CORCORAN EQUITY		Large-cap Blend		147.7	449	4.50	1.25†	21.4	20.7	0.9
OPPENHEIMER A	AVG	Large-cap Blend	AVG	289.0	12	5.75	1.26†	20.1	16.6	2.4
OPPENHEIMER ASSET ALLOC. A	▲	Domestic Hybrid	AVG	274.4	9	5.75	1.15†	17.2	14.2	3.6
OPPENHEIMER CAPITAL APPREC. A (zz)	AVG	Mid-cap Growth	▲▲	929.3	23	5.75	1.03†	28.0	24.2	0.5
OPPENHEIMER DISCIP. ALLOC. A (aaa)	▲	Domestic Hybrid	AVG	236.1	8	5.75	1.17†	9.6	5.8	3.3
OPPENHEIMER DISCIP. VALUE A (bbb)	▲	Large-cap Value	AVG	190.2	60	5.75	1.22†	18.4	15.7	0.8
OPPENHEIMER DISCOVERY A	▼▼	Small-cap Growth	▼	1110.8	32	5.75	1.33†	14.8	12.5	0.0
OPPENHEIMER EQUITY-INCOME A		Domestic Hybrid	AVG	2353.0	13	5.75	0.89†	20.1	17.6	3.8

*Includes redemption fee. **Includes deferred sales charge. †12(b)-1 plan in effect. ‡Not currently accepting new accounts. §Less than 0.5% of assets. NA=Not available. NM=Not meaningful. (ww) Formerly Merrill Lynch Growth for Investment B. (xx) Formerly Montgomery Small Cap II. (yy) Formerly New USA Mutual. (zz) Formerly Oppenheimer Target A. (aaa) Formerly Connecticut Mutual Total Return A. (bbb) Formerly Connecticut Mutual Growth A.

3 YRS PRETAX	3 YRS AFTERTAX	5 YRS PRETAX	5 YRS AFTERTAX	10 YRS PRETAX	10 YRS AFTERTAX	TURNOVER	CASH %	FOREIGN %	P-E RATIO	UNTAXED GAINS (%)	LARGEST HOLDING COMPANY (% ASSETS)	RISK LEVEL	BEST QTR	BEST %RET	WORST QTR	WORST %RET	TELEPHONE
7.5	6.1	10.7	9.4			Very low	2	53	17	16	Telecom Italia Mobile(3)	Average	IV 96	9.6	I 94	−7.5	800-637-3863
20.5	18.6	20.1	18.0			Low	24	9	31	24	Apache(5)	High	III 92	12.9	II 92	−7.9	800-637-3863
15.9	13.3	8.8	6.5			High	9	36	30	17	Ciba-Geigy (Reg)(6)	High	III 95	13.6	I 93	−12.1	800-637-3863
3.3	2.4					Average	9	100	25	4	Murata Manufacturing(3)						800-637-3863
−7.6	−8.1	5.4	4.9			Low	1	98	20	15	Telebras (ADR)(5)	Very high	IV 93	32.6	I 95	−29.9	800-637-3863
4.7	3.5	6.7	5.6			Low	9	100	28	14	Murata Manufacturing(6)	High	I 93	10.7	I 92	−11.4	800-637-3863
10.4	5.9	16.7	12.7			Average	9	11	26	2	Amdahl(4)	Average	I 92	19.2	IV 94	−7.0	800-637-3863
15.1	12.0	14.9	12.5			Average	7	4	24	16	PXRE(3)	Average	IV 92	14.8	II 92	−5.6	800-637-3863
10.7	8.6					High	1	14	40	−10	Informix(8)						800-637-3863
17.1	12.6	12.6	9.3	14.5	12.3	Average	15	13	24	27	Tyco International(6)	Average	I 95	9.5	II 93	−3.5	800-637-2929
18.4	18.2	18.1	17.7	19.7	19.4	Low	2	5	38	29	HFS(7)	Very high	IV 92	20.8	II 92	−11.2	800-637-2929
16.3	12.8	14.5	11.5	12.8	9.4	High	1	7	31	27	Intel(5)	High	II 95	10.5	I 94	−5.6	800-637-2929
14.9	10.8					High	1	1	28	22	Telephone & Data Sys.(10)						800-637-2929
19.9	17.6	18.4	15.8	15.6	12.4	Average	5	13	29	24	Philip Morris(2)	Average	III 95	10.6	IV 94	−4.1	800-637-2929
12.3	9.7	12.4	10.0	12.0	9.4	High	6	12	19	25	United Technologies(1)	Very low	II 95	7.3	I 94	−2.8	800-637-2929
18.0	15.2					High	16	14	24	18	Harrah's Entertainment(4)	Average	III 95	13.7	IV 94	−6.2	800-637-2929
Less than three years of data available						Very high	22	72	24	11	Powergen(7)						800-637-2929
10.5	8.2	12.1	10.3	11.9	10.7	Average	6	66	24	23	Powergen (Reg)(3)	Average	IV 93	10.6	IV 94	−3.4	800-637-2929
9.8	8.4					High	4	56	34	12	HFS(4)						800-637-2929
10.4	8.6	11.4	9.4			High	9	65	23	13	Philip Morris(1)	Very low	IV 93	7.3	I 94	−3.6	800-637-2929
11.2	10.2	20.5	19.0	10.8	9.7	Average	−3	72	42	15	Greenstone Resources(6)	Very high	II 93	36.6	IV 94	−16.9	800-400-6432
6.9	5.2	5.3	3.9	12.5	10.2	Very high	8	2	34	1	Transocean Offshore(2)	High	III 95	12.5	I 93	−6.6	800-666-3882
Less than three years of data available							4	NA	32	14	Procter & Gamble(4)						800-992-8151
Less than three years of data available						Very high	4	3	28	15	HFS(5)						800-572-3863
−2.0	−2.5					High	5	98	20	6	Bangkok Bank Ser 2(2)						800-572-3863
3.0	2.5					High	1	75	30	20	Global Tele-Systems(4)						800-572-3863
21.6	19.1					High	17	7	30	25	HFS(8)						800-572-3863
Less than three years of data available						Average	12	3	25	21	AMRE(4)						800-572-3863
13.1	9.8	14.6	12.0			Average	3	7	31	38	WorldCom(5)	High	IV 92	18.4	II 94	−10.2	800-572-3863
Less than three years of data available							3	NA	34	−4	Sanmina(4)						800-572-3863
−2.1	−2.5					Low	4	100	20	4	Cheung Kong Holdings(4)						800-282-4404
17.5	14.8	12.2	9.9	14.0	11.0	Low	1	NA	21	41	Warner-Lambert(6)	Low	III 95	8.9	I 92	−5.3	800-848-0920
15.1	12.7	12.5	10.6	12.6	10.2	Low	11	6	23	28	Intel(4)	Average	II 95	9.2	I 94	−2.7	800-848-0920
Less than three years of data available						High	4	2	36	18	PairGain Technologies(4)						800-887-8671
16.9	15.0	17.6	15.3	14.9	11.9	Low	0	7	20	37	Neiman-Marcus Group(5)	Average	II 95	12.5	I 94	−3.2	800-877-9700
17.5	16.4	16.4	15.2			Low	5	1	21	27	BMC Industries(3)	Average	IV 92	12.7	II 92	−7.0	800-877-9700
16.1	14.8	16.4	14.9	15.5	12.9	Low	4	5	20	28	Chrysler(3)	Average	II 95	11.4	I 94	−2.7	800-877-9700
11.5	8.8	12.4	9.0	12.7	9.8	Average	−3	10	26	28	First USA(3)	High	IV 92	14.6	IV 94	−5.8	800-877-9700
18.8	15.5	18.1	14.8	14.7	11.4	High	5	10	19	27	Price/Costco(3)	Average	IV 96	11.5	I 94	−4.4	800-877-9700
8.9	7.0	14.6	12.6	15.1	12.3	Low	13	27	26	25	Tele-Comm. TCI Grp. Cl A(3)	Average	IV 92	14.6	I 94	−8.0	800-421-4120
12.9	10.6	13.4	11.4	10.2	8.0	Average	3	5	19	16	EMC(2)	Very low	II 95	8.7	I 94	−3.1	800-225-7670
14.6	12.8					Average	3	1	36	26	Microsoft(2)						800-225-7670
15.8	12.4	10.0	7.5	14.6	11.3	Very high	0	5	23	18	Citicorp(8)	High	II 95	20.8	I 92	−8.5	800-225-7670
16.9	13.2	13.5	10.8	12.7	9.3	Average	0	2	18	25	Exxon(4)	Average	IV 96	10.3	I 94	−3.6	800-225-7670
Less than three years of data available						High	10	10	31	18	Cisco Systems(2)						800-225-7670
18.1	15.1	17.2	14.5	12.5	9.2	Average	4	9	20	30	Carnival Cl A(2)	Low	IV 96	10.9	I 94	−3.8	800-225-7670
13.3	11.4	13.9	12.4	13.8	11.5	Low	14	64	24	30	Philip Morris(2)	Average	IV 93	9.2	I 94	−1.7	800-421-4120
18.6	14.1					Very high	17	2	38	32	Intel(4)						800-222-2872
16.4	13.8	13.5	11.4	14.0	11.8	Low	6	2	22	40	FNMA(4)	Low	IV 92	10.2	I 94	−4.7	800-227-5987
15.7	12.9	12.5	10.3	13.4	11.5	Low	4	7	28	54	Keane(6)	Average	I 96	12.0	II 92	−4.2	800-227-5987
15.4	12.1	14.4	11.6			Low	3	4	28	41	Keane(6)	Average	I 96	15.0	II 92	−6.7	800-227-5987
11.7	10.7					High	3	5	38	31	Gucci Group (NY) (Reg)(2)						800-551-8043
14.6	13.4					High	6	4	36	33	Aspect Telecomm.(1)						800-551-8043
10.5	8.5	11.7	9.6			High	6	8	36	30	WorldCom(2)	High	IV 92	16.2	II 92	−8.2	800-225-1852
Less than three years of data available						Average	6	3	31	17	Johnson & Johnson(4)						800-595-9111
Less than three years of data available						Very high	8	99	28	2	Nikkei 300 Stock Index Fund(4)						800-595-9111
Less than three years of data available						Average	4	3	21	12	Thiokol(1)						800-595-9111
17.3	15.4	25.7	24.1			Low	9	6	22	31	Philip Morris(6)	Very low	IV 92	15.4	I 94	−4.2	800-625-6275
8.0	6.3					Average	5	100	19	7	National Australia Bank(5)						800-625-6275
Less than three years of data available						Low	6	3	15	14	U.S. Industries(6)						800-625-6275
19.2	17.9	16.2	15.2			Average	1	4	35	37	JLG Industries(4)	Very high	IV 92	22.4	II 92	−20.4	800-323-6166
3.3	3.0					Average	3	99	20	11	Swire Pacific Cl A(3)						800-545-1074
Less than three years of data available							2	4	21	14	Columbia/HCA Healthcare(3)						800-422-2080
14.4	11.2	13.3	10.8	11.6	8.6	Low	10	23	22	34	Intel(4)	Low	I 95	8.4	IV 94	−2.3	800-525-7048
12.3	9.4	12.1	9.9			Low	8	25	22	21	Chase Manhattan(2)	Very low	I 95	6.7	I 94	−3.2	800-525-7048
20.1	16.4	14.7	12.2	13.4	10.9	Average	17	5	27	34	Microsoft(3)	Average	IV 92	12.7	II 92	−3.6	800-525-7048
10.0	7.3	11.1	8.2	11.8	8.9	Average	22	1	18	12	Xerox(1)	Very low	II 95	6.5	I 94	−2.5	800-525-7048
17.1	14.7	16.8	13.8	15.5	12.3	Average	11	1	18	24	Xerox(3)	Low	IV 92	10.5	I 94	−2.3	800-525-7048
11.7	9.7	13.9	12.5	17.7	16.0	High	21	4	38	32	LCI International(1)	Very high	IV 92	24.4	II 92	−11.4	800-525-7048
14.3	12.1	12.8	10.6	12.1	9.4	Average	7	4	19	22	Chase Manhattan(4)	Low	IV 96	9.4	I 94	−3.7	800-525-7048

MUTUAL FUND SCOREBOARD

FUND	OVERALL RATING (COMPARES RISK-ADJUSTED PERFORMANCE OF EACH FUND AGAINST ALL FUNDS)	CATEGORY	RATING (COMPARES RISK-ADJUSTED PERFORMANCE OF FUND WITHIN CATEGORY)	SIZE ASSETS $MIL.	% CHG. 1995-6	FEES SALES CHARGE (%)	EXPENSE RATIO (%)	1996 RETURNS (%) PRE-TAX	AFTER-TAX	YIELD
OPPENHEIMER GLOBAL EMG. A	▼▼▼	World	▼▼▼	153.4	19	5.75	1.76†	19.4	19.4	0.0
OPPENHEIMER GLOBAL A	▼▼	World	▼▼	2610.2	20	5.75	1.17†	17.5	15.9	1.3
OPPENHEIMER GOLD & SPEC. MIN. A	▼▼▼	Precious Metals	▲	151.0	−4	5.75	1.38†	6.1	6.0	0.2
OPPENHEIMER GROWTH A	AVG	Large-cap Growth	▼	1312.8	29	5.75	1.06†	23.5	19.5	1.3
OPPENHEIMER MAIN ST. INC. & GR. A	▲▲	Mid-cap Blend	▲▲	3590.1	46	5.75	0.99†	15.7	13.2	1.3
OPPENHEIMER QUEST GLOB. VAL. A	▲	World	▲▲	194.5	21	5.75	1.88†	16.3	15.2	0.0
OPPENHEIMER QUEST OPPORT. A	▲▲▲	Large-cap Value	▲▲▲	1021.6	137	5.75	1.69†	22.8	21.8	0.4
OPPENHEIMER QUEST VALUE A	▲	Large-cap Value	AVG	450.8	53	5.75	1.68†	25.6	23.6	0.4
OPPENHEIMER TOTAL RETURN A	AVG	Large-cap Value	▼	1825.2	18	5.75	0.92†	19.7	15.4	1.8
OPPENHEIMER VALUE STOCK A ⚖	▲	Large-cap Value	AVG	147.8	8	5.75	1.28†	19.4	17.8	1.6
PACIFIC EUROPEAN GROWTH	▼▼	Foreign	▼	146.0	−9	4.00	1.55†	−1	−3.4	3.4
PACIFIC HORIZON AGGRES. GROWTH A	▼▼▼	Small-cap Growth	▼▼▼	210.9	21	4.50	1.51	14.1	6.5	0.0
PAINEWEBBER BALANCED A	AVG	Domestic Hybrid	▼▼	162.9	−4	4.50	1.26†	14.8	11.1	3.1
PAINEWEBBER GLOBAL EQUITY A	▼	World	▼	318.3	−4	4.50	1.71†	14.8	13.8	0.0
PAINEWEBBER GROWTH & INCOME A	▼	Large-cap Blend	▼▼	310.2	21	4.50	1.20†	23.8	19.5	3.5
PAINEWEBBER GROWTH A ⚖		Mid-cap Growth	AVG	213.5	8	4.50	1.28†	14.2	11.7	0.7
PARKSTONE SMALL CAP INV. A		Small-cap Growth		164.0	61	4.50	1.54†	27.6	22.1	0.0
PARNASSUS ⚖	▼	Small-cap Value	▼▼▼	268.2	4	3.50	1.02	11.7	10.7	0.0
PASADENA GROWTH A ⚖	▼▼	Large-cap Growth	▼▼	426.9	3	5.50	1.60	22.5	20.1	0.0
PASADENA NIFTY FIFTY A	▼	Large-cap Growth	AVG	145.5	19	5.50	1.90	26.5	24.6	0.0
PAX WORLD ⚖	AVG	Domestic Hybrid	▼▼	518.5	9	No load	0.97†	10.4	7.8	3.2
PBHG CORE GROWTH		Mid-cap Growth		455.7	NM	No load	1.50	32.8	32.8	0.0
PBHG EMERGING GROWTH		Small-cap Growth		1518.2	139	No load	1.47	17.1	16.0	0.0
PBHG GROWTH ⚖	▼	Mid-cap Growth	▲	5931.2	192	No load	1.48	9.8	9.8	0.0
PBHG LARGE CAP GROWTH		Mid-cap Growth		154.6	585	No load	1.50	23.4	23.4	0.0
PBHG SELECT EQUITY		Mid-cap Growth		580.1	363	No load‡	1.50	28.0	27.6	0.0
PBHG TECHNOLOGY & COMMUN.		Technology		562.6	NM	No load	1.50	54.4	53.6	0.0
PELICAN	▲▲	Mid-cap Value	▲	186.1	10	No load	1.10	20.7	19.0	1.7
PENN SQUARE MUTUAL A ⚖	▲	Large-cap Blend	▲	328.0	10	4.75	0.96†	18.7	14.0	1.4
PENNSYLVANIA MUTUAL ⚖	▲	Small-cap Value	AVG	456.1	−28	1.00*	0.98	12.8	7.2	1.3
PHOENIX AGGRESSIVE GROWTH A (ccc)	AVG	Mid-cap Growth	▲▲	233.8	15	4.75	1.29†	11.1	6.6	0.0
PHOENIX BALANCED A	AVG	Domestic Hybrid	▼▼	1830.6	−23	4.75	1.02†	8.6	4.5	2.7
PHOENIX EQUITY OPPORT. A	▼	Mid-cap Growth		201.4	−2	4.75	1.25†	11.7	8.3	0.0
PHOENIX GROWTH A ⚖	AVG	Large-cap Growth	▲▲▲	2373.1	0	4.75	1.20†	14.7	9.1	0.7
PHOENIX INCOME & GROWTH A	▲	Domestic Hybrid	AVG	467.0	−7	4.75	1.18†	12.7	8.8	3.8
PHOENIX MID CAP A (ddd) ⚖	▼	Mid-cap Growth	AVG	429.3	−12	4.75	1.42†	8.6	4.9	0.0
PHOENIX SMALL CAP A		Small-cap Growth		179.0	517	4.75	1.50†	30.0	29.9	0.0
PHOENIX STRAT. ALLOCATION A (eee) ⚖	AVG	Domestic Hybrid	▼	309.7	−14	4.75	1.21†	8.8	5.4	1.7
PHOENIX WORLDWIDE OPPORT. A	▼	World	AVG	143.2	11	4.75	1.60†	15.0	12.5	0.4
PILGRIM AMERICA MAGNACAP A	▲	Large-cap Blend	AVG	257.3	11	5.75	1.68†	18.5	17.9	0.5
PIMCO ADV. EQUITY-INCOME C	▲▲	Large-cap Blend	▲▲	257.3	40	1.00**	2.00†	24.4	19.6	0.7
PIMCO ADV. GROWTH C	▼	Large-cap Growth	AVG	1530.7	17	1.00**	1.86†	17.5	13.2	0.0
PIMCO ADV. INNOVATION C		Technology		149.8	114	1.00**	2.06†	22.7	22.2	0.0
PIMCO ADV. INTERNATIONAL C	▼▼	Foreign	▼▼▼	198.4	−3	1.00**	2.16†	5.8	4.8	0.0
PIMCO ADV. OPPORTUNITY C	▼▼	Small-cap Growth	AVG	749.0	3	1.00**‡	1.88†	11.4	7.0	0.0
PIMCO ADV. TARGET C		Mid-cap Growth		1012.6	24	1.00**	1.93†	15.7	11.8	0.0
PIONEER A	▲▲	Large-cap Blend	▲▲	2896.0	18	5.75	0.94†	19.7	17.1	1.3
PIONEER CAPITAL GROWTH A	▲▲	Small-cap Value	▲	1396.3	46	5.75	1.14†	11.7	10.2	0.3
PIONEER EQUITY-INCOME A	▲▲	Large-cap Value	▲▲	352.7	26	5.75	1.27†	12.8	10.6	2.4
PIONEER GROWTH A ⚖	▼▼	Mid-cap Growth	▼	277.5	28	5.75	1.21†	27.0	23.9	0.0
PIONEER II A	▲	Mid-cap Value	AVG	6003.8	15	5.75	0.90†	22.0	18.8	1.0
PIONEER INCOME A	▲	Domestic Hybrid	AVG	276.3	−2	4.50	1.11†	9.9	8.0	5.8
PIONEER INTERNATIONAL GROWTH A		Foreign		378.7	21	5.75	1.98†	11.3	8.8	0.7
PIONEER MID-CAP A (fff) ⚖	▼	Mid-cap Value	▼▼▼	1018.0	−3	5.75	0.88†	13.5	10.5	0.8
PIONEER SMALL COMPANY A		Small-cap Blend		239.3	347	5.75	NA†	24.2	21.8	0.0
PIPER EMERGING GROWTH	▼▼	Mid-cap Growth	AVG	298.4	19	4.00	1.18†	11.8	8.9	0.0
PIPER GROWTH	▼	Large-cap Blend	▼▼▼	184.0	5	4.00	1.24†	18.7	15.5	0.4
PREFERRED GROWTH		Large-cap Growth		381.9	−2	No load	0.86	18.7	14.0	0.0
PREFERRED INTERNATIONAL		Foreign		209.5	54	No load	1.31	17.2	15.8	2.4
PREFERRED VALUE		Large-cap Blend		307.2	34	No load	0.85	25.3	23.7	1.1
PREMIER AGGRESSIVE GROWTH A (ggg)	▼▼	Mid-cap Growth		471.2	−13	4.50	1.50	−2.4	−2.4	0.0
PREMIER VALUE A (hhh)	▼▼	Mid-cap Blend	▼▼▼	222.0	1	5.75	1.27	18.1	13.1	0.8
T. ROWE PRICE BALANCED	▲▲	Domestic Hybrid	▲	876.0	44	No load	0.95	14.6	13.1	3.4
T. ROWE PRICE BLUE CHIP GROWTH		Large-cap Blend		539.7	268	No load	1.25	27.8	27.3	0.7
T. ROWE PRICE CAPITAL APPRECIATION	▲▲▲	Mid-cap Value	▲▲	959.9	11	No load	0.97	16.8	13.6	3.9
T. ROWE PRICE DIVIDEND GROWTH		Large-cap Blend		209.5	148	No load	1.10	25.4	23.5	2.1
T. ROWE PRICE EQUITY INDEX	▲	Large-cap Blend	▲	807.7	77	1.00*	0.45	22.7	21.4	1.8
T. ROWE PRICE EQUITY-INCOME ⚖	▲▲▲	Large-cap Blend	▲▲▲	7818.1	50	No load	0.85	20.4	18.2	2.8
T. ROWE PRICE EUROPEAN STOCK	AVG	Europe	▲	765.1	44	No load	1.12	25.9	24.9	1.5
T. ROWE PRICE GROWTH & INCOME	▲▲▲	Large-cap Blend	▲▲▲	2488.8	42	No load	0.84	25.6	23.5	2.2

*Includes redemption fee. **Includes deferred sales charge. †12(b)-1 plan in effect. ‡Not currently accepting new accounts. §Less than 0.5% of assets. NA=Not available. NM=Not meaningful. (ccc) Formerly Phoenix U.S. Stock A. (ddd) Formerly Phoenix Capital Appreciation A. (eee) Formerly Phoenix Total Return A. (fff) Formerly Pioneer Three. (ggg) Formerly Premier Capital Growth A. (hhh) Formerly Premier Strategic Investing A.

3 YEARS PRETAX	3 YEARS AFTERTAX	5 YEARS PRETAX	5 YEARS AFTERTAX	10 YEARS PRETAX	10 YEARS AFTERTAX	TREND BW 10-YEAR ANALYSIS	TURNOVER	CASH %	FOREIGN %	P-E RATIO	UNTAXED GAINS (%)	LARGEST HOLDING COMPANY (% ASSETS)	RISK LEVEL	BEST QTR	BEST %RET	WORST QTR	WORST %RET	TELEPHONE
-2.9	-2.9	-6.8	-6.9				High	3	67	28	14	Reinsurance Australia(2)	Very high	IV 92	18.0	I 93	-19.2	800-525-7048
9.9	7.7	10.2	8.3	12.7	10.0		High	1	71	28	26	Nintendo(3)	High	IV 93	16.5	I 92	-6.2	800-525-7048
-0.6	-0.7	7.4	7.2	10.2	8.6		Low	6	70	38	17	Newmont Mining(5)	Very high	IV 93	28.2	IV 94	-11.4	800-525-7048
19.5	15.8	14.7	12.0	13.8	11.4		Low	33	4	22	34	Green Tree Financial(2)	Average	IV 92	12.0	II 92	-3.3	800-525-7048
14.2	12.9	21.5	19.2				High	17	3	27	15	S&P 500 (Fut)(4)	Average	IV 92	27.1	I 92	-6.4	800-525-7048
13.2	11.0	13.1	11.1				Average	7	65	22	22	Citicorp(3)	Low	II 95	9.2	IV 94	-1.5	800-525-7048
22.3	21.3	18.5	17.6				Low	16	2	17	17	Wells Fargo(7)	Low	II 95	14.5	I 94	-0.7	800-525-7048
20.2	17.9	16.9	15.0	14.1	12.0		Low	17	15	18	31	ACE(6)	Low	I 95	11.1	I 94	-2.5	800-525-7048
12.8	10.3	14.5	11.9	14.6	11.4		Average	16	4	27	23	Healthsouth(2)	Average	IV 92	12.9	II 92	-5.7	800-525-7048
17.1	15.6	13.9	12.3	12.9	11.2		Very low	10	NA	21	31	Bristol-Myers Squibb(3)	Low	I 95	7.6	I 94	-2.9	800-525-7048
0.4	-1.7	8.7	7.4				Average	1	100	30	3	Toshiba(2)	High	IV 93	20.0	III 92	-15.0	800-866-7778
13.1	6.7	8.8	4.5	15.5	12.4		High	6	8	32	25	ENVOY(2)	Very high	III 95	19.4	I 92	-14.7	800-332-3863
8.4	4.9	9.2	6.3				High	10	5	23	7	Ceridian(2)	Low	II 95	7.4	II 94	-5.8	800-647-1568
8.4	6.9	11.5	10.4				Average	1	70	24	5	Total CI B(3)	Average	IV 93	11.1	IV 94	-5.6	800-647-1568
15.8	12.8	9.5	7.6	11.6	9.5		High	14	4	22	33	Loral(2)	Average	III 95	9.4	I 92	-5.7	800-647-1568
10.8	9.1	11.0	9.5	14.5	12.7		Average	4	11	33	46	Republic Industries(4)	High	IV 92	15.0	I 94	-7.0	800-647-1568
22.0	17.9						Average	5	1	46	55	McAfee Associates(3)						800-451-8377
8.0	6.5	15.1	13.1	12.6	10.8		Low	5	NA	26	-4	Liz Claiborne(7)	High	IV 92	24.1	IV 95	-10.9	800-999-3505
14.5	13.5	7.6	7.0	13.9	13.3		Average	1	7	30	41	Gillette(4)	High	II 95	8.7	II 92	-6.5	800-648-8050
17.9	17.3	11.1	10.7				Low	2	6	28	37	Gillette(4)	Average	I 95	8.9	I 94	-4.9	800-648-8050
13.5	11.6	7.8	6.1	10.8	8.1		Low	11	NA	23	15	Merck(5)	Low	IV 95	9.1	I 94	-3.7	800-767-1729
Less than three years of data available								13	NA	46	5	U.S. Filter(2)						800-433-0051
29.1	28.1						High	21	NA	49	24	Legato Systems(2)						800-433-0051
20.0	20.0	26.6	25.2	21.3	17.7		Average	11	NA	46	19	Ascend Communs.(2)	Very high	IV 92	42.3	II 94	-12.6	800-433-0051
Less than three years of data available							High	13	NA	41	6	Cisco Systems(2)						800-433-0051
Less than three years of data available							Very high	16	NA	52	11	FORE Systems(4)						800-433-0051
Less than three years of data available								15	5	47	13	Parametric Technology(4)						800-433-0051
17.3	15.3	16.7	14.6				Average	7	9	22	21	Eastman Kodak(3)	Low	IV 96	9.5	I 94	-2.5	617-330-7500
15.4	12.2	13.5	10.6	13.1	10.0		Low	7	5	25	28	General Electric(3)	Low	I 95	9.0	I 94	-2.4	800-523-8440
10.0	5.8	11.5	8.1	11.4	8.1		Very low	5	3	16	47	Standard Register(1)	Low	IV 92	8.3	II 92	-2.6	800-221-4268
17.4	13.5	14.2	11.0	12.9	9.7		Very high	3	6	44	21	Evergreen Media Cl A(3)	Average	II 96	14.3	I 94	-2.7	800-243 4361
8.5	6.0	7.8	5.6	10.7	8.1		Very high	2	4	26	9	Monsanto(1)	Low	III 95	5.8	I 94	-3.7	800-243-4361
12.4	9.4	13.4	9.6	12.3	8.2		Very high	0	10	36	19	TCF Financial(3)	Average	II 96	10.8	I 94	-5.2	800-243-4361
14.8	11.5	10.5	8.2	13.0	10.2		High	14	13	28	25	WMX Technologies(2)	Low	III 95	10.3	I 94	-3.1	800-243-4361
9.2	6.4	10.8	8.1	11.5	8.6		High	12	7	30	11	Perkin-Elmer(4)	Very low	II 95	6.9	I 94	-4.0	800-243-4361
11.0	7.7	10.2	7.8				Very high	8	12	39	12	Newbridge Networks(3)	Average	III 95	10.9	I 94	-4.7	800-243-4361
Less than three years of data available								8	5	44	5	Coherent(3)						800-243-4301
7.9	5.7	8.9	6.5	10.8	8.3		Very high	16	9	27	9	Cisco Systems(3)	Very low	II 95	5.4	I 94	-2.5	800-243-4361
9.8	6.7	13.5	11.5	7.8	5.9		Very high	11	74	29	21	Ensco International(2)	Average	IV 93	14.4	IV 94	-4.8	800-243-4361
18.6	17.6	14.5	13.1	13.0	11.1		Low	5	NA	24	53	AFLAC(4)	Low	I 95	11.6	II 93	-1.4	800-334-3444
14.7	12.2	14.5	12.6				Very high	4	6	22	21	Sonat(3)	Low	III 93	10.5	IV 94	-4.1	800-426-0107
14.1	10.9	10.9	8.2	14.5	11.9		High	9	NA	29	32	Intel(3)	Average	II 95	10.6	I 92	-4.0	800-426-0107
Less than three years of data available							High	10	7	45	24	Cisco Systems(5)						800-426-0107
0.9	0.4	5.2	4.4	7.0	5.6		High	7	100	32	9	Daiwa Securities(2)	High	I 93	9.4	IV 94	-8.8	800-426-0107
14.5	10.6	21.3	18.2	20.6	17.5		High	11	5	37	37	DSP Communications(4)	Very high	IV 92	22.2	II 94	-13.6	800-426-0107
15.8	13.2						High	6	6	39	29	Gucci Group(4)						800-426-0107
14.7	11.9	14.4	12.0	12.7	9.8		Low	0	3	21	37	Schering-Plough(3)	Low	IV 96	7.8	I 94	-2.8	800-225-6292
18.8	16.6	20.3	18.0				Average	21	5	20	12	20th Century Industries(2)	Average	IV 92	21.4	II 92	-8.0	800-225-6292
13.7	11.9	15.0	13.3				Very low	1	NA	17	15	Schering-Plough(4)	Very low	III 95	9.2	I 94	-3.3	800-225-6292
17.1	11.9	12.0	8.6	15.3	12.5		High	5	4	28	11	Intel(5)	High	III 94	18.0	II 92	-14.9	800-225-6292
15.1	11.9	14.7	11.4	12.5	9.3		Average	1	11	16	34	Arrow Electronics(4)	Low	IV 96	12.4	I 94	-5.9	800-225-6292
8.7	6.5	8.8	6.4	10.0	7.4		Low	1	NA	20	6	Pacific Telesis Group(2)	Very low	IV 96	6.6	I 94	-3.0	800-225-6292
4.2	2.9						Very high	7	99	20	9	Korea Mobile Telecom.(3)						800-225-6292
8.5	5.9	12.3	9.9	11.8	9.1		Average	0	NA	29	39	Ascend Communs.(4)	Average	IV 92	11.5	II 94	-5.1	800-225-6292
Less than three years of data available								22	NA	NA	NA	NA						800-225-6292
14.0	12.0	13.5	12.3				Average	3	2	34	35	Tommy Hilfiger(3)	High	IV 92	17.2	II 94	-8.2	800-866-7778
13.7	10.4	9.7	7.6				Low	0	3	27	35	AlliedSignal(6)	High	I 96	8.3	I 94	-4.2	800-866-7778
14.7	12.7						Average	1	10	33	33	Intel(4)						800-662-4769
10.0	8.9						Low	4	100	18	12	Bank of Nova Scotia(3)						800-662-4769
20.1	18.9						Low	9	4	18	34	Monsanto(4)						800-662-4769
0.3	-1.0	4.2	2.0	8.2	5.5		High	-9	14	36	4	Teva Pharmaceutical (ADR)(6)	High	I 95	6.7	I 94	-4.6	800-554-4611
9.0	6.1	7.5	5.1	13.2	10.8		Very high	0	5	25	14	Jones Apparel Group(3)	High	III 93	10.4	II 92	-7.2	800-554-4611
11.9	10.3	11.3	9.4	11.0	8.0		Very low	6	22	24	14	General Electric(1)	Very low	I 95	7.1	I 94	-3.9	800-638-5660
21.1	20.6						Low	13	4	26	17	General Electric(2)						800-638-5660
14.1	11.3	13.5	11.2	13.4	10.2		Average	13	7	26	20	Centerior Energy(3)	Very low	I 95	6.4	IV 94	-1.2	800-638-5660
19.1	17.2						Average	12	13	23	17	FNMA(2)						800-638-5660
19.3	18.0	14.8	13.7				Very low	6	4	24	19	General Electric(3)	Low	I 95	9.7	I 94	-3.9	800-638-5660
18.8	16.5	17.1	14.8	14.5	11.7		Low	10	8	22	21	General Electric(2)	Very low	I 95	8.1	I 94	-2.8	800-638-5660
16.9	16.1	13.9	13.3				Very low	6	100	21	30	Wolters Kluwer(4)	Average	IV 93	9.4	IV 92	-6.8	800-638-5660
18.0	16.0	16.4	14.5	13.6	11.1		Low	7	4	25	27	Corning(3)	Low	IV 96	9.0	I 94	-4.0	800-638-5660

MUTUAL FUND SCOREBOARD

FUND (COMPARES RISK-ADJUSTED PERFORMANCE OF EACH FUND AGAINST ALL FUNDS)	OVERALL RATING	CATEGORY (COMPARES RISK-ADJUSTED PERFORMANCE OF FUND WITHIN CATEGORY)	RATING	SIZE ASSETS $MIL.	% CHG. 1995-6	FEES SALES CHARGE (%)	EXPENSE RATIO (%)	1996 RETURNS (%) PRE-TAX	AFTER-TAX	YIELD
T. ROWE PRICE GROWTH STOCK	▲	Large-cap Blend	▲	3430.8	24	No load	0.80	21.7	19.0	0.7
T. ROWE PRICE HEALTH SCIENCE		Health		194.0	162	No load	NA	26.8	25.6	0.0
T. ROWE PRICE INTL. DISCOVERY	▼▼	Foreign	▼▼	322.4	6	2.00*	1.50	13.9	13.6	0.4
T. ROWE PRICE INTL. STOCK	▼	Foreign	AVG	9340.9	39	No load	0.88	16.0	15.1	1.3
T. ROWE PRICE JAPAN	▼▼▼	Japan		147.0	−29	No load	1.32	−11	−11	0.0
T. ROWE PRICE LATIN AMERICA		Latin America		211.0	41	2.00*	1.82	23.4	22.7	1.3
T. ROWE PRICE MID-CAP GROWTH		Mid-cap Growth		1021.0	287	No load	1.25	24.8	23.9	0.0
T. ROWE PRICE NEW AMERICA GROWTH	▼	Mid-cap Growth	▲	1440.2	40	No load	1.07	20.0	17.2	0.0
T. ROWE PRICE NEW ASIA	▼▼	Pacific ex-Japan		2181.7	16	No load	1.11	13.5	13.3	0.7
T. ROWE PRICE NEW ERA	▲	Natural Resources	▲▲	1467.7	35	No load	0.79	24.3	21.6	1.4
T. ROWE PRICE NEW HORIZONS	AVG	Mid-cap Growth	▲▲	4363.4	53	No load‡	0.90	17.0	14.0	0.0
T. ROWE PRICE OTC SECURITIES	▲	Small-cap Blend	▲▲▲	415.6	49	No load	1.11	21.1	18.2	0.5
T. ROWE PRICE PERS. STRAT. BAL.		Domestic Hybrid		179.7	859	No load	1.05	14.2	12.5	2.9
T. ROWE PRICE SCIENCE & TECH.	AVG	Technology	▲▲	3291.8	44	No load	1.01	14.2	10.8	0.0
T. ROWE PRICE SMALL-CAP VAL.	▲▲▲	Small-cap Value	▲▲	1409.8	51	1.00*‡	0.98	24.6	22.8	1.1
T. ROWE PRICE SPECTRUM GROWTH	▲▲	Large-cap Blend	▲▲	2104.1	55	No load	0.00	20.5	18.1	1.3
T. ROWE PRICE VALUE		Mid-cap Value		197.9	325	No load	1.10	28.5	25.9	1.6
PRINCOR CAPITAL ACCUMULATION A	▲	Large-cap Blend	AVG	467.0	28	4.75	0.69†	23.4	18.3	1.5
PRINCOR EMERGING GROWTH A	AVG	Small-cap Blend	▲▲	245.6	51	4.75	1.32†	19.1	18.0	0.3
PRINCOR GROWTH A	AVG	Mid-cap Blend	▼	247.5	31	4.75	1.08†	12.2	11.7	0.8
PRINCOR WORLD A	▼	Foreign	▲	186.3	41	4.75	1.45†	23.8	22.0	1.2
PRUDENTIAL ALLOC. BALANCED B	AVG	Domestic Hybrid	▼	429.5	−3	5.00**	1.95†	15.7	13.2	1.7
PRUDENTIAL ALLOC. STRATEGY B	AVG	Domestic Hybrid	▼▼	220.7	−18	5.00**	2.08†	11.0	7.9	1.1
PRUDENTIAL EQUITY B	▲▲	Large-cap Value	▲	2629.7	22	5.00**	1.66†	17.1	13.6	1.8
PRUDENTIAL EQUITY-INCOME B	▲	Mid-cap Value	AVG	979.0	5	5.00**	1.78†	21.0	18.8	2.2
PRUDENTIAL EUROPE GROWTH B		Europe		137.8	12	5.00**	2.28†	23.2	22.0	0.0
PRUDENTIAL GLOBAL GENESIS B	▼	World	▼▼	131.3	−12	5.00**	2.17†	9.2	6.6	0.0
PRUDENTIAL JENN GROWTH B (iii)		Large-cap Growth		260.5	128	5.00**	NA†	13.6	13.6	0.1
PRUDENTIAL MULTI-SECTOR A	AVG	Mid-cap Blend	AVG	221.8	−1	5.00	1.23†	19.5	15.9	0.2
PRUDENTIAL PACIFIC GROWTH B		Diversified Pacific		303.7	−13	5.00**	2.21†	1.8	1.1	0.0
PRUDENTIAL SMALL COMPANIES B (jjj)	AVG	Small-cap Value	▼▼	390.8	13	5.00**	1.99†	23.0	17.6	0.0
PRUDENTIAL UTILITY B	AVG	Utilities	▲	2139.1	−9	5.00**	1.63†	21.2	18.1	2.1
PRUDENTIAL WORLD GLOBAL B (kkk)	▼	World	▼	336.6	28	5.00**	2.19†	18.2	15.7	0.2
PUTNAM ASIA PACIFIC GROWTH A	▼	Diversified Pacific		244.6	50	5.75	1.54†	5.8	4.7	3.5
PUTNAM ASSET ALLOC.: BAL. A		Domestic Hybrid		372.5	94	5.75	1.32†	17.6	15.1	2.6
PUTNAM ASSET ALLOC.: CONS. A		Domestic Hybrid		228.0	199	5.75	1.22†	11.2	9.1	3.3
PUTNAM ASSET ALLOC.: GROWTH A		Mid-cap Blend		245.4	73	5.75	1.49†	18.6	16.8	1.4
PUTNAM BALANCED RETIREMENT A	▲▲	Domestic Hybrid	▲▲	502.7	4	5.75	1.15†	16.3	10.4	4.0
PUTNAM CAPITAL APPREC. A		Mid-cap Blend		283.7	126	5.75	1.29†	30.1	27.7	0.6
PUTNAM DIVERSIFIED EQUITY B		Mid-cap Growth		218.1	61	5.00**	2.09†	15.9	13.4	1.0
PUTNAM EQUITY INCOME A	▲▲	Large-cap Value	▲	577.8	43	5.75	1.13†	21.3	20.4	2.4
PUTNAM EUROPE GROWTH A	AVG	Europe	▲▲	188.3	89	5.75	1.47†	22.7	20.3	1.2
PUTNAM FUND FOR GROWTH & INCOME A	▲▲	Large-cap Blend	▲▲▲	12305.5	43	5.75	0.89†	21.8	18.8	2.2
GEORGE PUTNAM OF BOSTON A	▲▲	Domestic Hybrid	▲	1830.9	55	5.75	0.95†	16.3	13.2	3.8
PUTNAM GLOBAL GROWTH A	▼	World	AVG	2318.4	30	5.75	1.28†	16.6	14.2	2.4
PUTNAM GLOBAL NATURAL RES. A (lll)	▼	Natural Resources	▼	197.0	29	5.75	1.13†	19.2	16.9	0.8
PUTNAM GROWTH & INCOME II B		Large-cap Value		777.1	163	5.00**	NA†	20.2	17.9	1.3
PUTNAM HEALTH SCIENCES A	▼▼	Health	▲	1289.3	13	5.75	1.10†	12.4	11.3	0.2
PUTNAM INTL. GROWTH A (mmm)	▼	Foreign	▲	302.4	422	5.75	1.74†	16.2	15.7	1.0
PUTNAM INTL. NEW OPPORT. B		Foreign		703.1	752	5.00**	2.72†	15.9	15.9	0.0
PUTNAM INVESTORS A	AVG	Large-cap Blend	AVG	1323.8	29	5.75	1.03†	21.4	17.4	0.5
PUTNAM NEW OPPORTUNITIES A	▼	Mid-cap Growth		5962.6	152	5.75	1.11†	10.8	10.6	0.0
PUTNAM NEW VALUE A		Mid-cap Value		196.7	NM	5.75	NA†	24.5	23.9	0.7
PUTNAM OTC EMERGING GROWTH A	▼▼	Small-cap Growth	AVG	1838.4	84	5.75	1.11†	4.6	2.6	0.0
PUTNAM UTILITY GROWTH & INCOME B		Utilities		637.2	4	5.00**	1.87†	14.7	11.6	3.1
PUTNAM VISTA A	AVG	Mid-cap Growth	▲▲▲	1677.6	68	5.75	1.07†	22.4	20.3	0.0
PUTNAM VOYAGER A	▼	Mid-cap Growth	▲▲	8633.1	44	5.75	1.03†	12.8	10.8	0.0
PUTNAM VOYAGER II A		Mid-cap Growth		350.3	326	5.75	1.10†	7.7	7.7	0.0
RAINIER CORE EQUITY		Mid-cap Value		220.1	212	No load	1.29†	23.3	20.6	0.7
RIGHTIME BLUE CHIP	▲▲	Domestic Hybrid	▲	289.3	14	4.75	2.17†	10.9	7.3	1.1
RIGHTIME	▲	Domestic Hybrid	▼	162.2	4	No load	2.47†	8.6	2.0	1.1
ROBERTSON STEPHENS CONTRAR.		World		1070.0	110	No load	2.54†	21.7	21.3	0.0
ROBERTSON STEPHENS EMG. GROWTH	▼▼▼	Small-cap Growth	▼▼▼	197.8	25	No load	1.64†	21.6	16.9	0.0
ROBERTSON STEPHENS GR. & INC.		Mid-cap Growth		320.0	134	No load	1.94†	24.2	23.2	2.5
ROBERTSON STEPHENS VAL. + GR.		Mid-cap Growth		660.8	−42	No load	1.45†	14.1	11.9	0.0
ROYCE MICRO-CAP	▲▲▲	Small-cap Value	▲	141.4	45	1.00*	1.94	15.5	13.5	0.1
ROYCE PREMIER	▲▲▲	Small-cap Value	▲▲	316.8	5	1.00*	1.25	18.1	15.8	1.2
ROYCE VALUE	▲	Small-cap Value	▼	145.6	−13	1.00*	1.76†	14.0	9.0	0.2
RYDEX NOVA		Large-cap Blend		360.5	62	No load	1.31	25.5	25.5	0.0
RYDEX OTC		Large-cap Growth		174.5	475	No load	1.33	43.1	43.1	0.0

*Includes redemption fee. **Includes deferred sales charge. †12(b)-1 plan in effect. ‡Not currently accepting new accounts. §Less than 0.5% of assets. NA=Not available. NM=Not meaningful. (iii) Formerly Prudential Jennison B. (jjj) Formerly Prudential Growth Opportunity B. (kkk) Formerly Prudential Global B. (lll) Formerly Putnam Natural Resources A. (mmm) Formerly Putnam Overseas Growth A.

3 YEARS PRETAX	3 YEARS AFTERTAX	5 YEARS PRETAX	5 YEARS AFTERTAX	10 YEARS PRETAX	10 YEARS AFTERTAX	TREND BW 10-YEAR ANALYSIS	TURNOVER	CASH %	FOREIGN %	P-E RATIO	UNTAXED GAINS (%)	LARGEST HOLDING COMPANY (% ASSETS)	RISK LEVEL	BEST QTR	BEST %RET	WORST QTR	WORST %RET	TELEPHONE
17.2	14.8	14.5	12.4	13.3	10.7		Average	4	26	26	40	FHLMC(4)	Low	II 95	8.2	I 94	-4.1	800-638-5660
Less than three years of data available								8	12	30	NA	United HealthCare(4)						800-638-5660
0.2	-0.5	6.5	6.0				Average	5	99	24	4	China Trust Commerc. Bank(1)	High	IV 93	15.1	III 92	-9.3	800-638-5660
8.6	7.4	11.6	10.5	11.2	8.2		Very low	4	99	25	21	Wolters Kluwer(2)	High	IV 93	12.1	IV 94	-4.2	800-638-5660
-0.3	-0.9	0.7	-0.2				Low	2	98	37	-16	Mitsubishi Heavy Industries(4)	Very high	I 94	17.0	IV 93	-13.5	800-638-5660
-5.5	-5.8						Low	5	97	16	-17	Telefonos de Mexico L (ADR)(5)						800-638-5660
20.8	19.8						Average	8	4	33	15	ADT(2)						800-638-5660
17.0	15.4	15.7	14.4	15.9	14.6		Average	3	2	32	37	HFS(4)	High	IV 92	16.2	II 92	-9.7	800-638-5660
-1.6	-2.8	13.6	12.4				Average	5	99	20	10	Hutchison Whampoa(4)	Very high	IV 93	33.9	I 94	-20.2	800-638-5660
16.4	14.2	13.2	11.0	12.1	9.7		Low	8	21	30	35	Mobil(4)	Average	I 96	9.7	I 92	-5.6	800-638-5660
22.2	19.0	19.7	16.2	16.3	13.3		Average	6	2	38	36	Paychex(2)	High	IV 92	19.2	II 92	-10.1	800-638-5660
17.5	14.2	16.9	12.7	12.3	8.9		Average	11	2	25	33	Richfood Holdings(3)	Average	IV 92	15.1	II 92	-7.2	800-638-5660
Less than three years of data available							Average	2	22	25	1	General Electric(2)						800-638-5660
27.2	24.1	24.9	21.8				High	21	9	36	24	Intel(4)	High	IV 92	22.0	I 94	-7.8	800-638-5660
16.7	14.8	18.8	17.3				Low	13	2	20	24	Electro Rent(2)	Low	I 92	11.1	II 92	-4.7	800-638-5660
16.7	14.3	15.6	13.3				Very low	0	31	19		T. Rowe Price Gr. Stk.(23)	Low	III 95	8.3	I 94	-3.2	800-638-5660
Less than three years of data available							Average	7	8	22	11	FMC(2)						800-638-5660
17.7	14.8	13.9	11.0	12.5	9.9		Average	2	1	25	18	WMX Technologies(3)	Low	IV 96	8.1	I 94	-3.9	800-451-5447
18.1	17.3	16.3	15.7				Very low	12	2	27	29	Intel(2)	Average	IV 92	12.6	II 92	-4.9	800-451-5447
15.6	14.7	12.9	11.6	14.4	12.6		Very low	6	5	26	32	Boston Scientific(3)	Average	I 95	9.4	II 92	-3.2	800-451-5447
9.4	8.0	14.1	12.9	9.7	7.2		Low	4	99	16	21	Roussel Uclaf(2)	High	IV 93	15.3	II 92	-8.7	800-451-5447
9.2	7.4	9.6	7.6				High	8	5	27	22	Cisco Systems(3)	Low	II 95	6.8	I 94	-3.9	800-225-1852
8.4	6.1	8.2	5.9				Very high	16	2	23	15	Cisco Systems(2)	Low	II 95	7.7	I 94	-4.3	800-225-1852
15.8	13.5	16.2	14.1	14.4	12.1		Low	11	5	17	24	Chrysler(3)	Low	I 93	9.3	I 94	-3.0	800-225-1852
13.2	11.0	13.6	11.5				Average	1	7	21	12	IBM(5)	Low	I 93	11.1	IV 94	-3.6	800-225-1852
Less than three years of data available							Average	11	100	25	27	Rexel (France)(4)						800-225-1852
3.0	2.1	11.7	11.0				Average	2	69	19	27	Baan(3)	High	III 93	17.1	IV 94	-6.5	800-225-1852
Less than three years of data available								1	8	33	NA	Boeing(3)						800-225-1852
14.3	10.9	13.4	10.0				High	4	6	25	12	Cisco Systems(5)	Average	III 94	10.8	IV 94	-4.9	800-225-1852
-1.2	-1.6						Average	0	100	27	7	Guoco Group(5)						800-225-1852
13.4	10.5	15.8	12.9	13.1	11.1		Average	0	1	17	17	Methode Electronics Cl A(2)	Average	IV 92	11.2	II 92	-5.4	800-225-1852
11.4	9.3	11.7	9.6	11.5	9.2		Very low	2	21	19	28	Sonat(4)	Average	IV 96	12.2	I 94	-5.0	800-225-1852
8.5	7.0	12.3	11.4	8.3	7.3		Average	0	79	25	50	Nokia(2)	High	IV 93	14.7	IV 94	-5.7	800-225-1852
2.7	1.5	12.8	12.0				Average	3	98	27	5	HSBC Holdings (UK)(3)	High	IV 93	21.8	I 92	-5.4	800-225-1581
Less than three years of data available							High	1	24	26	14	NationsBank(1)						800-225-1581
Less than three years of data available							High	1	30	26	9	NationsBank($)						800-225-1581
Less than three years of data available							Average	1	20	27	18	NationsBank(1)						800-225-1581
12.5	10.1	12.3	9.8	11.1	7.5		High	2	6	21	10	Weyerhaeuser(1)	Very low	II 95	7.1	I 94	-3.1	800-225-1581
22.9	21.6						Average	5	12	19	22	General Electric(3)						800-225-1581
Less than three years of data available							Average	0	33	27	17	Thermo Electron(1)						800-225-1581
18.3	17.2	15.1	13.9	11.8	8.6		Average	5	6	20	1	Weyerhaeuser(2)	Low	I 95	8.9	I 94	-3.5	800-225-1581
16.6	15.4	15.4	14.4				Average	4	97	19	19	Pharmacia & Upjohn(3)	Average	IV 93	11.6	III 92	-5.1	800-225-1581
18.4	15.9	16.2	13.8	14.5	10.9		Average	2	4	21	21	Warner-Lambert(2)	Low	I 95	9.6	I 94	-4.0	800-225-1581
14.7	12.1	12.5	9.9	12.2	8.7		High	4	3	19	13	Weyerhaeuser(1)	Very low	I 95	7.8	I 94	-3.7	800-225-1581
9.9	8.2	11.9	10.7	10.6	8.6		Average	5	67	27	17	Getronics(1)	Average	IV 93	9.2	III 92	-3.8	800-225-1581
13.0	11.9	11.9	9.5	12.1	10.1		Average	2	16	25	16	Exxon(4)	High	I 93	11.9	IV 93	-9.9	800-225-1581
Less than three years of data available								3	4	21	NA	Bankers Trust New York(3)						800-225-1581
23.9	22.9	11.2	10.0	17.0	15.0		Very low	6	11	30	47	Johnson & Johnson(7)	High	III 94	18.3	I 92	-12.1	800-225-1581
9.9	9.4	13.0	12.5				Average	3	99	24	3	Ito-Yokado(1)	Average	IV 93	16.3	III 92	-6.7	800-225-1581
Less than three years of data available							Low	6	98	24	7	Telecom Italia(3)						800-225-1581
17.4	13.7	15.5	11.5	14.4	9.5		High	4	2	29	31	Citicorp(3)	Average	II 95	11.1	I 94	-3.8	800-225-1581
18.8	18.6	22.8	22.4				Low	7	6	40	16	HFS(2)	High	IV 92	26.1	II 92	-8.5	800-225-1581
Less than three years of data available								5	7	23	NA	Dayton Hudson(3)						800-225-1581
18.6	15.9	19.9	17.0	17.3	15.1		Very high	3	6	47	27	Cascade Communs.(2)	High	III 95	20.9	II 92	-9.4	800-225-1581
11.3	9.3						Average	2	7	19	15	Sprint(5)						800-225-1581
18.0	16.3	17.8	15.1	16.0	13.0		High	1	3	37	27	HFS(2)	Average	III 95	13.8	I 94	-6.0	800-225-1581
16.7	14.9	15.6	14.0	17.6	15.1		Average	3	7	35	31	HFS(2)	High	IV 92	13.8	I 94	-6.3	800-225-1581
17.5	16.7						Average	4	7	39	6	HFS(2)						800-225-1581
Less than three years of data available							High	3	2	23	4	General Electric(3)						800-248-6314
13.5	9.9	10.3	8.1				Low	100	4	23	15	S&P 500 Option (Put)(47)	Very low	II 95	8.8	II 92	-2.0	800-242-1421
11.6	7.3	9.4	6.2	10.6	7.7		Very low	100	7	26	3	Fidelity Magellan(7)	Low	III 95	10.0	II 92	-4.1	800-242-1421
14.6	14.2							6	60	24	22	Inco(6)						800-766-3863
16.4	12.9	10.5	8.4				Very high	7	1	50	24	Affiliated Comp. Svcs. A(3)	Very high	IV 92	21.6	II 92	-17.2	800-766-3863
Less than three years of data available								0	5	28	13	Compuware(1)						800-766-3863
26.1	25.1						Very high	1	1	31	21	Compaq Computer(5)						800-766-3863
12.5	11.3	17.9	15.8				Low	2	4	18	11	Sevenson Environ. Svcs.(2)	Low	IV 92	13.3	II 92	-3.6	800-221-4268
12.9	11.2	14.7	13.2				Average	12	3	17	15	Standard Register(3)	Very low	IV 92	10.9	I 94	-1.1	800-221-4268
10.0	7.1	11.3	8.7	10.8	8.1		Very low	6	3	17	39	Standard Register(1)	Low	IV 92	8.7	I 94	-3.4	800-221-4268
21.6	20.7						Very low	0	NA	NA	7	S&P 500 Futures Mar. '97 (50)						800-820-0888
Less than three years of data available							Very high	0	NA	34	-6	Microsoft(13)						800-820-0888

DATA: MORNINGSTAR, INC., CHICAGO, IL.

MUTUAL FUND SCOREBOARD

FUND	OVERALL RATING (COMPARES RISK-ADJUSTED PERFORMANCE OF EACH FUND AGAINST ALL FUNDS)	CATEGORY	RATING (COMPARES RISK-ADJUSTED PERFORMANCE OF FUND WITHIN CATEGORY)	SIZE ASSETS $MIL.	% CHG. 1995-6	FEES SALES CHARGE (%)	EXPENSE RATIO (%)	1996 RETURNS (%) PRE-TAX	AFTER-TAX	YIELD
RYDEX URSA		Large-cap Blend		298.7	153	No load	1.39	–12.4	–12.4	0.0
SAFECO EQUITY NO LOAD	▲▲	Large-cap Blend	▲▲	853.1	38	No load	0.79	25.0	20.4	1.4
SAFECO GROWTH NO LOAD	▼▼	Small-cap Blend	▼▼▼	196.1	7	No load	1.02	22.9	18.2	0.0
SAFECO INCOME NO LOAD 🧍	▲▲▲	Large-cap Value	▲▲	290.3	26	No load	0.86	24.0	19.4	2.9
SALOMON BROS. CAPITAL	▼	Mid-cap Blend	▼▼	136.6	31	No load	1.36	33.3	26.1	0.7
SALOMON BROS. INVESTORS O	▲▲	Large-cap Blend	▲▲	518.4	21	No load‡	0.69	30.4	25.9	1.2
SALOMON BROS. OPPORTUNITY 🧍	▲▲	Large-cap Value	AVG	158.8	13	No load	1.18	19.6	17.9	1.4
SCHRODER INTERNATIONAL INV. (nnn)	▼	Foreign	▲	188.2	–9	No load	0.91	12.8	5.3	4.6
SCHWAB INTERNATIONAL INDEX		Foreign		259.9	33	0.75*	0.85	9.1	8.7	1.4
SCHWAB 1000	▲	Large-cap Blend		1908.8	79	0.50*	0.49	21.6	21.1	1.3
SCHWAB SMALL CAP INDEX		Small-cap Blend		220.9	60	0.50*	0.68	15.5	15.3	0.4
SCOUT STOCK 🧍	AVG	Mid-cap Value	▼	178.9	22	No load	0.85	10.7	8.7	2.5
SCUDDER CAPITAL GROWTH	▼	Large-cap Blend	▼▼	1810.5	16	No load	0.98	19.6	16.0	0.7
SCUDDER DEVELOPMENT	▼▼▼	Small-cap Growth	▼▼	971.5	11	No load	1.24	10.0	6.9	0.0
SCUDDER GLOBAL DISCOVERY (ooo)	AVG	World	AVG	362.5	43	No load	1.69	21.5	19.8	0.6
SCUDDER GLOBAL 🧍		World		1409.3	11	No load	1.34	13.7	11.7	0.9
SCUDDER GOLD	▼▼▼	Precious Metals	▲▲▲	184.3	57	No load	1.50	32.1	25.5	0.0
SCUDDER GREATER EUROPE GROWTH		Europe		150.7	243	No load	1.50	30.9	30.5	0.3
SCUDDER GROWTH & INCOME 🧍	▲▲▲	Large-cap Blend	▲▲▲	4218.2	37	No load	0.80	22.2	20.1	2.4
SCUDDER INTERNATIONAL 🧍	▼	Foreign	AVG	2644.9	12	No load	1.14	14.6	12.9	2.6
SCUDDER LATIN AMERICA		Latin America		636.9	24	No load	2.08	28.3	27.9	1.2
SCUDDER PACIFIC OPPORT.		Pacific ex-Japan		344.3	–9	No load	1.74	6.5	6.4	0.1
SCUDDER QUALITY GROWTH	▼	Large-cap Growth	▼	217.9	17	No load	1.17	18.2	15.5	0.0
SECURITY EQUITY A 🧍	▲	Large-cap Blend	▲	623.1	30	5.75	1.04	22.7	19.6	0.5
SELECTED AMERICAN	AVG	Large-cap Value	▼▼▼	1378.1	49	No load	1.09†	30.7	28.3	0.8
SELIGMAN CAPITAL A	▼▼	Mid-cap Growth	▼	259.5	20	4.75	1.09†	16.7	13.4	0.0
SELIGMAN COMMON STOCK A	AVG	Large-cap Blend	▼	656.3	7	4.75	0.93†	15.4	12.4	2.1
SELIGMAN COMMUNICATIONS & INFO. A	▼▼	Technology	▼	2414.7	24	4.75	1.61†	11.9	10.6	0.0
SELIGMAN FRONTIER A	▼	Small-cap Growth	▲	497.2	48	4.75	1.56†	11.3	9.5	0.0
SELIGMAN GROWTH A	▼	Large-cap Growth	AVG	675.1	13	4.75	0.94†	21.1	18.6	0.0
SELIGMAN HENDERSON GLOB. SM. A		World		376.1	217	4.75	1.83†	16.8	15.3	0.0
SELIGMAN HENDERSON GLOB. TECH. A		Technology		551.3	17	4.75	1.91†	14.3	14.3	0.0
SELIGMAN INCOME A	▲▲	Domestic Hybrid	▲	296.3	–7	4.75	1.00†	8.2	6.5	4.9
SENTINEL BALANCED A 🧍	▲	Domestic Hybrid	▼	287.6	6	5.00	1.27†	12.1	10.4	3.0
SENTINEL COMMON STOCK A	AVG	Large-cap Blend	AVG	1256.4	17	5.00	1.09†	20.8	17.3	1.4
SEQUOIA 🧍	▲▲	Large-cap Value	AVG	2581.5	18	No load‡	1.00	21.7	19.4	0.4
1784 GROWTH & INCOME		Large-cap Growth		375.2	38	No load	0.94†	23.6	22.7	0.6
1784 INTERNATIONAL EQUITY		Foreign		433.5	77	No load	1.13†	13.7	13.3	0.8
SIERRA EMERGING GROWTH A	▼	Small-cap Growth	▲	206.2	–12	5.75	1.68†	8.5	6.1	0.0
SIERRA GROWTH & INCOME A	AVG	Large-cap Blend	▼▼	156.2	–11	5.75	1.56†	21.6	17.0	0.4
SIERRA GROWTH A		Mid-cap Growth		142.2	–12	5.75	1.76†	17.2	12.5	0.1
SIFE TRUST I	▲▲	Financial	AVG	769.1	25	5.00	1.03	27.4	20.9	5.6
SIT MID CAP GROWTH (ppp) 🧍	▼▼	Mid-cap Growth	▼	375.3	0	No load	0.77	21.9	16.6	0.0
SKYLINE SPECIAL EQUITIES	▲▲▲	Small-cap Value		218.7	25	No load	1.51	30.4	24.4	0.0
SMALLCAP WORLD	AVG	Small-cap Growth	▲▲	7073.4	48	5.75	1.09†	19.8	16.8	0.4
SMITH BARNEY AGGRES. GROWTH A 🧍	▼▼	Mid-cap Growth	▼▼	281.9	–4	5.00	1.30†	2.7	2.0	0.0
SMITH BARNEY APPRECIATION A 🧍	AVG	Large-cap Blend	AVG	2152.4	13	5.00	1.02†	19.3	16.0	1.4
SMITH BARNEY EQUITY INCOME A 🧍	▲	Large-cap Blend	AVG	669.7	9	5.00	1.02†	16.1	11.8	2.2
SMITH BARNEY FUNDAMENTAL VAL. B		Large-cap Value		772.5	36	5.00**	2.09†	18.7	17.0	0.6
SMITH BARNEY GROWTH & INCOME B		Large-cap Blend		133.7	21	5.00**	1.65†	18.2	17.4	1.1
SMITH BARNEY MANAGED GROWTH B		Small-cap Value		466.4	57	5.00**	1.94†	15.5	14.0	0.0
SMITH BARNEY PREM. TOT. RET. B	▲▲▲	Large-cap Value	▲▲	2320.1	25	5.00**	1.62†	20.1	17.7	6.2
SMITH BARNEY SECURITY & GROWTH		Domestic Hybrid		235.9	–21	4.00‡	1.02	8.8	5.2	3.2
SMITH BARNEY SPEC. EQUITIES B	▼▼▼	Mid-cap Growth	▼▼▼	384.5	125	5.00**	2.04†	–6.4	–7	0.0
SMITH BARNEY STRAT. INVESTOR B	▲	Domestic Hybrid	AVG	211.9	–5	5.00**	1.94†	11.4	8.6	2.2
SMITH BARNEY UTILITIES B	▼	Utilities		1244.5	–26	5.00**	1.55†	1.9	–0.2	4.9
SMITH BARNEY INTL. EQUITY A 🧍	▼▼	Foreign	▼	514.8	5	5.00	1.29†	13.6	13.6	0.1
SOGEN INTERNATIONAL 🧍	▲▲▲	International Hybrid	▲▲▲	3776.7	45	3.75	1.25†	13.6	11.4	4.1
SOGEN OVERSEAS		Foreign		850.3	57	3.75	1.37†	14.5	12.2	4.4
SOUND SHORE 🧍	▲▲▲	Mid-cap Value	▲▲	131.5	94	No load	1.15	33.7	29.4	0.8
SOUTHTRUST VULCAN STOCK		Large-cap Blend		241.3	40	4.50	0.87	23.2	20.1	1.4
SSGA EMERGING MARKETS (qqq)		Diversified Emerging Mkts.		148.1	83	No load	1.28†	14.9	14.4	1.0
SSGA MATRIX EQUITY (rrr)		Large-cap Value		314.9	49	No load	0.66†	23.7	20.6	1.6
SSGA S&P 500 INDEX (sss)		Large-cap Blend		860.7	62	No load	0.18†	22.7	20.5	2.0
STAGECOACH ASSET ALLOC. A 🧍	▲	Domestic Hybrid		1143.4	6	4.50	0.90†	11.7	8.3	3.5
STAGECOACH CORPORATE STOCK A 🧍	▲	Large-cap Blend	▲	407.2	24	No load	1.01†	21.7	20.4	1.1
STAGECOACH DIVERSIFIED INC. A		Large-cap Blend		153.5	92	4.50	1.10†	22.1	19.5	2.1
STAGECOACH GROWTH & INC. A	AVG	Large-cap Blend	▼	286.1	62	4.50	1.18†	21.7	19.2	0.6
STAGECOACH LIFEPATH 2020 RET. (ttt)		Domestic Hybrid		139.7	24	No load	1.20†	13.1	11.3	2.1
STAGECOACH LIFEPATH 2040 RET. (uuu)		Large-cap Blend		179.0	42	No load	1.20†	18.3	16.4	1.1

*Includes redemption fee. **Includes deferred sales charge. †12(b)-1 plan in effect. ‡Not currently accepting new accounts. §Less than 0.5% of assets. NA=Not available. NM=Not meaningful. (nnn) Formerly International Equity. (ooo) Formerly Scudder Global Small Company. (ppp) Formerly SIT Growth. (qqq) Formerly Seven Seas Emerging Markets. (rrr) Formerly Seven Seas Matrix Equity. (sss) Formerly Seven Seas S&P 500 Index. (ttt) Formerly Stagecoach LifePath 2020. (uuu) Formerly Stagecoach LifePath 2040.

3 YR PRETAX	3 YR AFTERTAX	5 YR PRETAX	5 YR AFTERTAX	10 YR PRETAX	10 YR AFTERTAX	TURNOVER	CASH %	FOREIGN %	P-E RATIO	UNTAXED GAINS (%)	LARGEST HOLDING COMPANY (% ASSETS)	RISK LEVEL	BEST QTR	BEST %RET	WORST QTR	WORST %RET	TELEPHONE
Less than three years of data available						Very low	0	NA	NA	−11	S&P 500 Puts Mar. '97 (82)						800-820-0888
19.9	16.5	19.8	16.9	16.7	13.5	Average	6	5	24	19	Chase Manhattan(5)	Average	IV 92	14.4	II 92	−7.3	800-426-6730
15.1	9.6	12.6	8.9	14.6	11.0	High	1	1	32	21	Seagate Technology(7)	Very high	IV 92	21.6	II 92	−15.6	800-426-6730
16.9	13.8	14.9	12.4	11.4	8.9	Average	0	4	25	23	Philip Morris(3)	Very low	IV 96	8.9	IV 94	−3.0	800-426-6730
15.6	10.8	13.6	10.1	12.0	8.8	Very high	4	11	22	23	Sears Roebuck(3)	High	I 96	11.1	II 94	−9.3	800-725-6666
20.4	16.6	16.7	12.6	14.1	10.2	Average	6	17	23	33	SmithKline Beecham (ADR)(3)	Low	IV 96	9.4	I 92	−2.8	800-725-6666
17.7	15.9	15.9	14.1	13.6	11.4	Very low	15	12	17	57	Chubb(11)	Low	IV 96	11.3	I 94	−1.7	800-725-6666
7.9	2.9	12.1	9.0	9.4	7.1	Average	1	99	25	24	Ito-Yokado(3)	Average	IV 93	13.2	IV 94	−3.9	800-344-8332
9.0	8.6					Very low	3	100	30	11	NT&T(2)						800-526-8600
18.4	17.8	14.6	14.0			Very low	0	1	24	33	General Electric(3)	Low	I 95	9.4	I 94	−4.0	800-526-8600
12.6	12.5					Low	1	0	27	17	USA Waste Services(1)						800-526-8600
10.8	8.1	10.0	7.7	10.9	8.4	Low	22	NA	24	12	IBM(1)	Low	I 95	7.1	I 94	−1.7	800-422-2766
12.4	9.3	12.8	9.8	14.1	11.0	High	2	7	19	16	FNMA(2)	Average	II 95	11.3	I 94	−8.7	800-225-2470
16.2	13.3	10.9	8.4	14.7	12.4	Average	2	3	38	42	Cintas(3)	Very high	II 95	17.7	II 94	−13.1	800-225-2470
9.7	8.8	12.8	12.0			Average	8	59	29	24	IHC Caland(3)	Average	I 93	11.3	IV 94	−4.9	800-225-2470
9.5	8.3	12.5	11.4	12.8	11.6	Low	2	77	23	28	Hoechst(2)	Low	III 93	8.6	IV 94	−4.4	800-225-2470
11.5	7.5	15.0	12.4			Low	2	80	44	5	Precious Metals(19)	Very high	I 96	36.5	IV 94	−11.5	800-225-2470
Less than three years of data available						Low	6	97	23	17	Telecom Italia Mobile(2)						800-225-2470
18.0	15.9	15.8	13.6	14.3	11.3	Low	4	16	21	26	Xerox(3)	Low	II 95	8.5	I 94	−3.3	800-225-2470
7.6	6.2	10.6	9.3	9.9	7.4	Average	4	98	25	22	AEGON(2)	Average	III 93	10.5	IV 94	−4.6	800-225-2470
1.6	1.0					Average	5	94	16	2	Perez Companc Cl B(5)						800-225-2470
−3.7	−3.8					Average	4	98	21	3	First Pacific(4)						800-225-2470
15.6	13.5	10.5	9.1			High	4	5	29	23	General Electric(3)	High	II 95	9.4	I 92	−7.8	800-225-2470
18.3	15.6	16.0	12.7	15.9	12.2	Average	5	6	24	28	Bristol-Myers Squibb(2)	Average	IV 92	10.1	I 94	−3.6	800-888-2461
20.4	18.6	14.3	11.1	14.9	12.1	Low	0	1	21	29	American Express(3)	Average	IV 96	13.0	I 92	−4.3	800-243-1575
14.2	10.6	11.7	8.4	13.7	10.6	High	9	3	30	39	Travelers Group(3)	High	IV 92	11.5	II 94	−11.6	800-221-2783
13.2	10.4	12.0	9.6	11.9	8.7	Average	9	11	22	30	General Electric(2)	Average	I 95	8.5	I 94	−4.7	800-221-2783
29.5	27.0	28.1	24.6	22.5	18.3	Average	8	3	30	0	Cisco Systems(5)	Very high	II 95	29.8	IV 95	−14.4	800-221-2783
17.6	15.3	18.9	15.4	16.2	13.7	Average	3	2	30	7	CalEnergy(2)	High	IV 92	23.4	II 92	−9.8	800-221-2783
14.4	11.4	12.1	8.6	13.2	9.7	High	2	10	29	33	First Data(3)	Average	IV 92	12.6	II 94	−5.3	800-221-2783
17.4	15.9					Average	6	63	29	13	CalEnergy(2)						000-221-2450
Less than three years of data available						Average	10	42	28	−5	Cisco Systems(3)						800-221-2783
7.3	5.3	11.0	8.8	9.4	6.7	High	1	53	16	6	Carlton Communications(2)	Very low	II 95	7.3	I 94	−4.0	800-221-2783
10.6	9.0	9.5	7.8	10.1	8.0	High	10	2	21	18	General Electric(2)	Very low	I 95	6.6	I 94	−3.7	800-282-3863
17.1	14.1	13.2	10.7	13.1	10.4	Low	3	2	22	50	General Electric(3)	Average	I 95	8.2	I 94	−4.7	800-282-3863
21.2	20.1	16.6	14.9	16.0	13.8	Low	9	NA	19	55	Berkshire Hathaway(28)	Average	III 95	11.6	II 96	−2.1	800-686-6884
17.2	16.6					Average	4	18	32	29	J.D. Wetherspoon(4)						800-252-1784
Less than three years of data available						Low	5	100	28	10	Nutricia Verenigde Bedrijven(2)						800-252-1784
12.7	11.2	15.1	13.5			Very high	0	13	41	29	Paging Network(6)	High	III 95	15.6	I 94	−5.9	800-222-5852
16.9	13.6	12.8	10.0			Average	1	4	23	19	Union Pacific(2)	Average	I 95	9.6	I 94	−2.5	800-222-5852
17.1	14.2					Very high	15	10	31	24	Amgen(4)						800-222-5852
23.4	18.9	22.4	19.0	15.4	12.5	High	14	NA	17	40	J.P. Morgan(4)	Average	IV 92	14.0	IV 94	−8.5	800-524-7433
17.5	13.8	11.5	9.2	15.9	13.7	Average	4	8	36	45	Parametric Technology(4)	High	III 95	18.8	II 92	−8.6	800-332-5580
13.6	10.1	20.7	17.2			Average	7	1	18	29	Furon(3)	Average	IV 92	22.2	IV 94	−3.3	800-458-5222
12.6	9.9	14.6	12.4			Average	14	38	27	23	Wisc. Central Transport(1)	Average	III 93	11.2	IV 94	−3.9	800-421-4120
11.1	9.6	11.1	10.2	14.2	12.4	Very low	4	0	31	35	Intel(8)	Very high	IV 92	16.4	II 92	−9.0	800-451-2010
15.2	12.4	11.9	9.8	13.3	11.4	Average	13	2	22	34	Eastman Kodak(4)	Low	I 95	8.8	I 92	−3.0	800-451-2010
14.0	11.0	13.1	10.2	11.6	8.7	Average	14	3	22	28	Monsanto(3)	Low	I 95	8.6	I 94	−4.5	800-451-2010
15.1	12.3					Average	22	9	26	17	BankAmerica(3)						800-451-2010
13.6	12.7					Low	6	4	23	27	Hewlett-Packard(4)						800-451-2010
Less than three years of data available							14	5	25	4	Forest Laboratories Cl A(2)						800-451-2010
14.6	12.2	13.5	11.0	12.6	9.6	Average	15	20	19	20	Philip Morris(5)	Very low	IV 96	9.3	I 94	−0.8	800-451-2010
Less than three years of data available						Low	0	12	30	10	Cray Research(2)						800-451-2010
12.5	12.0	15.4	15.0	10.3	9.5	High	6	3	43	24	Starbucks(4)	Very high	IV 92	23.8	II 92	−13.8	800-451-2010
10.6	8.5	10.6	8.6			Average	15	8	22	18	Lockheed Martin(2)	Very low	II 95	7.5	I 94	−2.2	800-451-2010
6.2	4.3	7.5	5.4			Average	3	NA	16	6	Texas Utilities(4)	Average	II 95	8.6	I 94	−7.4	800-451-2010
2.0	1.8	10.3.	10.1	10.9	9.7	Average	0	100	26	17	L.M. Ericsson (ADR)(2)	High	IV 93	19.2	IV 94	−8.1	800-451-2010
10.3	8.6	12.9	11.4	12.5	9.9	Very low	22	61	23	15	Buderus(1)	Very low	I 93	7.9	IV 94	−3.4	800-334-2143
11.3	10.0					Very low	14	100	23	10	Randstad Holding(2)						800-334-2143
20.3	17.2	18.8	15.5	14.8	11.8	Average	6	11	19	29	Compuware(4)						800-551-1980
18.2	16.5					Average	14	2	20	24	Sun Microsystems(4)						800-239-7470
Less than three years of data available						Very low	2	99	19	4	Telebras(5)						800-647-7327
16.4	13.8					High	1	0	22	14	Intel(3)						800-647-7327
19.4	17.8					Low	0	4	24	20	S&P 500 Index (Fut)(6)						800-647-7327
11.9	9.4	11.5	9.1	11.7	10.5	Low	0	3	24	24	General Electric(1)	Low	II 95	9.1	I 94	−4.2	800-222-8222
18.4	17.1	13.9	12.8	13.9	13.3	Very low	0	2	24	53	General Electric(3)	Low	I 95	9.4	I 94	−4.0	800-222-8222
16.7	15.0					Average	12	6	22	20	Household International(4)						800-222-8222
16.1	14.3	14.0	12.5			Average	15	11	27	22	L.M. Ericsson (ADR)(4)	Average	II 95	8.7	I 94	−3.6	800-222-8222
Less than three years of data available						Average	0	24	24	12	Daimler-Benz (ADR)(2)						800-222-8222
Less than three years of data available						Low	1	20	24	15	Daimler-Benz (ADR)(2)						800-222-8222

DATA: MORNINGSTAR, INC., CHICAGO, IL.

MUTUAL FUND SCOREBOARD

FUND	OVERALL RATING (COMPARES RISK-ADJUSTED PERFORMANCE OF EACH FUND AGAINST ALL FUNDS)	CATEGORY (COMPARES RISK-ADJUSTED PERFORMANCE OF FUND WITHIN CATEGORY)	RATING	SIZE ASSETS $MIL.	SIZE % CHG. 1995-6	FEES SALES CHARGE (%)	FEES EXPENSE RATIO (%)	1996 RETURNS (%) PRE-TAX	1996 RETURNS (%) AFTER-TAX	1996 RETURNS (%) YIELD
STAR RELATIVE VALUE	▲▲	Large-cap Value	▲	248.7	82	4.50	1.06†	26.5	25.2	1.5
STATE ST. RESEARCH CAPITAL B		Mid-cap Growth		378.5	64	5.00**	2.01†	6.8	6.8	0.0
STATE ST. RESEARCH CAP. APPREC. A ⚏	▼▼	Mid-cap Growth	▼▼	374.2	12	4.50	1.40†	5.8	4.4	0.0
STATE ST. RESEARCH INVMT. B ⚏		Large-cap Blend		261.6	58	5.00**	1.53†	20.2	14.2	0.5
STATE ST. RESEARCH MGD. ASSETS B		Domestic Hybrid		244.1	36	5.00**	2.00†	19.2	16.0	1.8
STEIN ROE BALANCED (vvv) ⚏	▲	Domestic Hybrid	AVG	257.4	13	No load	1.05	17.1	13.6	3.2
STEIN ROE CAPITAL OPPORT. (www)	▼	Mid-cap Growth	▲	1423.9	328	No load‡	1.22	20.4	20.4	0.0
STEIN ROE GROWTH & INCOME (xxx)	▲▲	Large-cap Blend	▲▲	241.2	59	No load	1.18	21.8	20.1	1.4
STEIN ROE GROWTH STOCK (yyy)	▼	Large-cap Growth	▲	443.4	18	No load	1.08	20.9	18.4	0.3
STEIN ROE INTERNATIONAL (zzz)		Foreign		140.5	54	No load	1.51	8.4	7.7	0.7
STEIN ROE SPECIAL (aaaa)	AVG	Mid-cap Blend	AVG	1149.6	1	No load	1.18	18.8	16.3	0.0
STEIN ROE SPECIAL VENTURE (bbbb)		Small-cap Blend		158.0	123	No load	1.25	28.6	25.3	0.0
STEIN ROE YOUNG INVESTOR (cccc)		Large-cap Growth		271.3	547	No load	1.21	35.1	33.8	0.1
STI CLASSIC CAPTL GROWTH INV.		Large-cap Blend		197.2	12	3.75	1.80†	19.5	13.3	0.2
STI CLASSIC VAL. INC. STOCK INV.		Large-cap Blend		144.1	28	3.75	1.30†	19.1	14.2	1.9
STRONG AMERICAN UTILITIES		Utilities		134.8	14	No load	1.20	8.4	5.8	3.1
STRONG ASSET ALLOCATION	▲	Domestic Hybrid	AVG	271.4	1	No load	1.20	10.5	6.8	4.1
STRONG COMMON STOCK	▲▲	Mid-cap Blend	▲▲	1243.7	17	No load‡	1.20	20.5	15.4	0.5
STRONG DISCOVERY	▼▼	Mid-cap Growth	▼	513.8	–14	No load	1.40	1.5	–1.3	6.2
STRONG GROWTH		Mid-cap Growth		1308.2	104	No load	1.40	19.5	18.7	0.1
STRONG INTERNATIONAL STOCK		Foreign		296.3	38	No load	1.70	8.2	5.7	2.4
STRONG OPPORTUNITY	▲▲	Mid-cap Blend	▲	1769.6	33	No load	1.30	18.1	14.6	0.7
STRONG SCHAFER VALUE (dddd) ⚏	▲▲▲	Mid-cap Value	▲	514.2	176	No load	1.27	23.2	21.9	0.8
STRONG SMALL CAP ⚏		Small-cap Growth		157.1	NM	No load	NA	22.7	22.1	1.6
STRONG TOTAL RETURN		Large-cap Growth		759.1	7	No load	1.10	14.1	8.9	1.4
SUNAMERICA BALANCED ASSETS B	AVG	Domestic Hybrid	▼▼	169.5	0	4.00**	2.12†	8.3	4.9	1.1
SUNAMERICA SMALL CO. GROWTH A	▼	Small-cap Growth	AVG	163.2	66	5.75	1.53†	14.9	13.8	0.0
TCW/DW CORE EQUITY		Large-cap Blend		773.2	2	5.00**	1.82†	19.0	16.5	0.0
TCW/DW LATIN AMERICAN GROWTH		Latin America		248.8	6	5.00**	2.98†	22.0	22.0	0.0
TCW/DW SMALL CAP GROWTH		Small-cap Growth		303.7	129	5.00**	2.57†	13.7	13.7	0.0
TEMPLETON DEVELOPING MKTS. I	▼	Diversified Emerging Mkts.		3206.0	49	5.75	2.10†	22.5	21.4	1.1
TEMPLETON FOREIGN I	AVG	Foreign	▲▲	10678.2	46	5.75	1.12†	18.0	16.5	2.6
TEMPLETON GLOBAL OPPORT. I ⚏	AVG	World	AVG	590.0	16	5.75	1.52†	24.2	22.0	2.3
TEMPLETON GLOBAL REAL ESTATE I (eeee)	AVG	Real Estate		135.1	8	5.75	1.51†	20.5	19.4	2.8
TEMPLETON GLOBAL SMALL CO. I (ffff)	AVG	World	AVG	1635.1	16	5.75	1.27†	22.1	18.6	1.4
TEMPLETON GROWTH I	▲	World	▲▲▲	9394.6	29	5.75	1.09†	20.6	18.4	2.4
TEMPLETON WORLD I ⚏	AVG	World	▲▲	6685.3	12	5.75	1.03†	21.5	18.6	2.4
THIRD AVENUE VALUE	▲▲▲	Domestic Hybrid	▲▲▲	644.7	96	No load	1.21	21.9	20.9	2.2
TOWER CAPITAL APPRECIATION A	AVG	Large-cap Blend	AVG	191.4	24	4.50	1.25†	23.2	19.5	0.9
TWEEDY, BROWNE AMERICAN VAL.		Mid-cap Value		277.6	65	No load	1.39	22.5	21.2	1.1
TWEEDY, BROWNE GLOBAL VALUE		World		1211.3	51	No load	1.60	20.2	17.7	3.7
UNITED ACCUMULATIVE A ⚏	AVG	Large-cap Blend	▼	1285.2	6	5.75	0.80†	12.3	8.8	1.3
UNITED CONTINENTAL INCOME A	▲	Domestic Hybrid		511.7	4	5.75	0.89†	9.7	6.3	3.0
UNITED INCOME A ⚏	AVG	Large-cap Blend	AVG	4850.4	22	5.75	0.83†	20.5	18.6	0.9
UNITED INTERNATIONAL GROWTH A ⚏	▼▼	Foreign	▼	847.8	21	5.75	1.25†	18.2	17.1	0.8
UNITED NEW CONCEPTS A	▼▼	Mid-cap Growth	AVG	547.8	21	5.75	1.19†	4.7	3.4	0.4
UNITED RETIREMENT SHARES A	▲	Domestic Hybrid	AVG	641.6	11	5.75	0.89†	9.8	6.6	3.0
UNITED SCIENCE & TECHNOLOGY A ⚏	▼▼	Technology	▼▼	980.6	18	5.75	0.93†	8.5	6.7	0.0
UNITED SVCS. GOLD SHARES	▼▼▼	Precious Metals	▼▼▼	153.3	–13	0.10*	1.54	–25.5	–26.3	3.6
UNITED SVCS. WORLD GOLD	▼▼▼	Precious Metals	▲	225.5	22	0.10*	1.51	19.5	17.5	5.8
UNITED VANGUARD A	▼	Large-cap Growth		1288.6	2	5.75	1.09†	7.7	3.0	0.6
USAA AGGRESSIVE GROWTH	▼▼▼	Small-cap Growth	▼▼	712.7	61	No load	0.74	16.5	15.9	0.0
USAA CORNERSTONE STRATEGY ⚏	▲▲	Mid-cap Blend	▲	1151.2	21	No load	1.15	17.9	15.9	2.8
USAA GROWTH & INCOME		Large-cap Blend		499.6	87	No load	0.95	23.0	21.5	1.4
USAA GROWTH & TAX STRATEGY	▲	Domestic Hybrid	AVG	173.7	16	No load	0.82	11.1	9.2	3.5
USAA GROWTH	AVG	Large-cap Growth	AVG	1335.2	25	No load	1.01	17.8	12.5	1.6
USAA GROWTH STRATEGY		Mid-cap Growth		133.7	344	No load	1.66	22.1	20.6	1.0
USAA INCOME STOCK	▲	Large-cap Value	▼	1915.2	21	No load	0.72	18.7	15.7	4.4
USAA INTERNATIONAL	AVG	Foreign	▲▲	504.2	43	No load	1.19	19.2	17.9	1.0
USAA WORLD GROWTH		World		265.5	19	No load	1.27	19.1	16.9	0.9
VALUE LINE	AVG	Mid-cap Growth	AVG	348.9	10	No load	0.83	22.5	18.8	0.5
VALUE LINE INCOME	AVG	Domestic Hybrid	▼	147.2	2	No load	0.93	17.4	12.4	2.9
VALUE LINE LEVERAGED GR. INV.	▼▼	Mid-cap Growth	AVG	371.1	10	No load	0.88	22.3	19.0	0.0
VAN ECK GOLD/RESOURCES A	▼▼▼	Precious Metals	AVG	138.0	–12	5.75	1.81†	2.5	2.5	0.0
VAN ECK INTL. INVEST GOLD A ⚏	▼▼▼	Precious Metals	▼▼	450.9	–11	5.75	1.42	–9.4	–9.8	0.6
VAN KAMPEN AMER. CAP. COMSTOCK A	AVG	Large-cap Blend	AVG	1250.4	16	5.75	0.96†	22.3	16.6	1.5
VAN KAMPEN AMER. CAP. EMG. GR. A	▼▼	Mid-cap Growth	AVG	1652.3	43	5.75	1.10†	17.9	16.5	0.0
VAN KAMPEN AMER. CAP. ENTERPR. A	AVG	Mid-cap Growth	▲▲	1319.9	29	5.75	0.98†	23.5	21.4	0.5
VAN KAMPEN AMER. CAP. EQ.-INC. B		Large-cap Blend		632.2	54	5.00**	1.75†	14.6	12.3	1.6
VAN KAMPEN AMER. CAP. GR. & INC. A	▲	Large-cap Blend		584.9	47	5.75	1.15†	18.1	15.3	1.5

*Includes redemption fee. **Includes deferred sales charge. †12(b)-1 plan in effect. ‡Not currently accepting new accounts. §Less than 0.5% of assets. NA=Not available. NM=Not meaningful. (vvv) Formerly SteinRoe Total Return. (www) Formerly SteinRoe Capital Opportunities. (xxx) Formerly SteinRoe Prime Equities. (yyy) Formerly SteinRoe Growth Stock. (zzz) Formerly SteinRoe International. (aaaa) Formerly SteinRoe Special. (bbbb) Formerly SteinRoe Special Venture. (cccc) Formerly SteinRoe Young Investor. (dddd) Formerly Schafer Value. (eeee) Formerly Templeton Real Estate Securities I. (ffff) Formerly Templeton Smaller Companies Growth I.

3 YEARS PRETAX	3 YEARS AFTERTAX	5 YEARS PRETAX	5 YEARS AFTERTAX	10 YEARS PRETAX	10 YEARS AFTERTAX	TREND BW 10-YEAR ANALYSIS	TURNOVER	CASH %	FOREIGN %	P-E RATIO	UNTAXED GAINS (%)	LARGEST HOLDING COMPANY (% ASSETS)	RISK LEVEL	BEST QTR	BEST %RET	WORST QTR	WORST %RET	TELEPHONE
18.7	17.8	16.1	15.3				Low	1	4	21	25	Bristol-Myers Squibb(5)	Low	IV 96	11.0	I 94	−3.3	800-677-3863
11.6	10.7						Very high	2	6	39	15	HFS(5)						800-882-0052
10.6	8.6	12.6	10.2	16.4	14.5		Very high	−1	7	39	16	HFS(5)	Very high	IV 92	19.9	II 92	−8.7	800-882-0052
14.8	11.1						Low	2	11	27	34	Shell Trans/Trading (ADR)(3)						800-882-0052
10.7	9.0						High	9	25	28	13	Ford Motor(1)						800-882-0052
11.2	8.8	10.8	8.2	10.8	7.9		Average	7	14	18	27	Citicorp(3)	Low	I 96	6.2	IV 94	−3.2	800-338-2550
22.0	21.5	18.8	18.5	14.7	12.9		Low	13	4	51	15	HFS(4)	High	I 96	13.8	IV 96	−9.4	800-338-2550
16.6	14.4	14.5	12.4				Very low	18	4	23	29	Monsanto(3)	Low	IV 92	8.4	I 94	−3.2	800-338-2550
16.4	13.2	11.9	9.3	14.1	11.6		Average	5	7	33	47	Home Depot(4)	Average	III 95	10.1	I 94	−5.8	800-338-2550
Less than three years of data available							Average	2	NA	23	4	Bladex (ADR)(2)						800-338-2550
10.9	8.6	13.4	11.1	15.1	12.0		Low	10	9	26	39	Borders Group(4)	Average	IV 92	10.0	I 94	−6.7	800-338-2550
Less than three years of data available							Average	5	13	30	23	AmeriSource Health Cl A(5)						800-338-2550
Less than three years of data available							High	11	5	34	16	Outdoor Systems(3)						800-338-2550
12.7	9.9						High	7	3	25	NA	Chase Manhattan(2)						800-428-6970
18.4	14.7						High	7	11	23	−2	ITT Industries(2)						800-428-6970
13.1	11.3						High	5	7	17	11	Ameritech(10)						800-368-1030
9.9	7.2	9.4	6.6	8.9	5.7		Very high	4	28	32	7	Intergroup(2)	Very low	II 95	6.6	I 94	−2.1	800-368-1030
16.7	13.2	19.1	16.5				High	12	9	26	20	Nokia Cl A (ADR)(1)	Average	IV 92	13.5	II 92	−7.5	800-368-1030
8.9	6.0	10.0	7.1				Very high	6	5	37	−7	Flores & Rucks(5)	High	IV 92	17.8	II 92	−6.8	800-368-1030
25.5	24.7						Very high	3	5	42	17	Danka Business Sys. (ADR)(2)						800-368-1030
4.7	3.1						High	4	99	26	−4	Gemina-Gen Mobil Inter Azion(1)						800-368-1030
15.8	13.5	17.1	15.4	14.8	12.8		High	14	14	26	19	AVX(1)	Average	IV 92	10.8	IV 94	−2.8	800-368-1030
16.5	15.1	18.4	16.6	16.3	14.0		Low	2	19	15	21	Owens-Illinois(3)	Low	IV 96	11.8	IV 94	−3.6	800-368-1030
Less than three years of data available								11	3	43	NA	Harman Intl. Industries(2)						800-368-1030
12.6	10.2	12.0	10.3	10.6	8.0		Very high	3	2	35	17	Monsanto(3)	Average	III 93	9.1	II 92	−5.9	800-368-1030
10.2	7.7	10.0	6.8	10.0	7.5		Very high	5	6	24	19	Mobil(2)	Average	III 95	7.1	I 92	−4.9	800-858-8850
21.8	19.2	19.9	17.5				Very high	6	5	40	23	Flanders (144A)(2)	High	IV 92	20.2	II 92	−8.0	800-858-8850
11.0	10.2						Average	0	3	31	33	Intel(5)						800-526-3143
−9.5	−9.7						Average	2	99	17	−27	Telebras(10)						800-526-3143
20.2	20.2						High	5	4	45	33	Cascade Communs.(2)						800-526-3143
4.0	2.9	12.1	11.2				Very low	12	100	16	10	Cheung Kong Holdings(3)	High	IV 93	21.2	IV 94	−8.5	800-292-9293
9.6	7.7	12.5	10.7	15.2	12.8		Low	16	99	17	8	Sony(1)	Average	IV 93	12.0	III 92	−6.5	800-292-9293
10.4	7.5	14.7	12.2				Low	10	67	18	18	Bimantara Citra (For)(2)	Average	III 93	10.8	IV 94	−6.1	800-292-9293
5.6	4.8	10.3	9.5				Low	3	32	21	5	Weeks(5)	Average	I 93	13.5	IV 94	−5.8	800-292-9293
11.1	8.4	13.4	10.3	11.4	8.1		Low	15	72	17	23	News International(3)	Average	I 93	10.9	IV 94	−6.6	800-292-9293
13.4	10.5	15.0	12.2	14.2	11.2		Low	8	66	18	15	Ford Motor(1)	Average	IV 93	9.7	IV 94	−4.1	800-292-9293
14.2	10.7	15.5	12.0	13.0	9.5		Low	5	62	18	19	Merrill Lynch(2)	Average	IV 93	10.0	IV 94	−4.8	800-292-9293
16.5	15.7	18.9	17.9				Very low	30	1	15	23	First American Financial(4)	Very low	I 93	14.4	IV 94	−3.2	800-443-1021
18.2	15.9	13.6	10.9				Average	3	3	22	30	General Electric(2)	Average	II 95	9.9	I 92	−5.3	800-999-0124
18.4	17.8						Very low	7	14	19	19	FHLMC(4)						800-432-4789
11.6	10.5						Low	10	82	23	17	Unilever (Netherlands)(3)						800-432-4789
14.8	11.4	13.5	10.2	12.6	8.8		Very high	5	8	23	12	SmithKline Beecham (ADR)(4)	Average	IV 92	10.6	I 94	−2.1	800-366-5465
10.9	8.5	11.3	9.2	9.9	7.3		Average	6	5	24	18	Electronic Data Systems(2)	Low	II 95	7.1	IV 94	−1.8	800-366-5465
15.3	13.8	14.5	13.3	14.8	12.3		Low	2	6	22	42	Intel(3)	Average	II 95	12.3	IV 94	−2.5	800-366-5465
9.2	7.0	13.5	11.7	10.9	8.6		Average	8	100	20	17	Skandinaviska Enskild Bk. A(3)	High	IV 93	17.4	III 92	−7.7	800-366-5465
16.0	14.5	12.6	11.6	14.2	12.7		Low	29	NA	43	33	Cisco Systems(5)	High	III 95	14.6	II 92	−7.0	800-366-5465
10.8	8.2	11.6	9.3	11.7	9.1		Average	8	6	24	20	Gillette(2)	Very low	II 95	7.4	I 94	−2.0	800-366-5465
22.8	21.1	14.1	12.6	16.6	14.3		Low	10	2	47	50	Ascend Communs.(8)	Very high	II 95	19.1	I 92	−10.4	800-366-5465
−19.0	−19.8	−10.2	−11	−7.6	−8.9		Low	−33	81	33	−126	Southvaal Hldgs. (ADR)(16)	Very high	II 93	41.0	IV 95	−22.1	800-873-8637
4.8	4.2	15.8	15.4	6.1	5.4		Low	1	75	38	20	Barrick Gold(10)	Very high	II 93	36.5	IV 94	−15.5	800-873-8637
12.6	9.5	11.0	9.0	11.8	8.8		Average	20	21	29	38	FNMA(3)	High	II 95	13.2	II 92	−4.4	800-366-5465
20.2	18.5	11.5	9.5	13.1	11.0		Average	2	4	42	35	HBO(2)	Very high	IV 92	18.5	II 92	−13.9	800-382-8722
11.4	9.3	12.7	11.0	10.7	9.3		Low	7	32	24	16	B.F. Goodrich(1)	Low	I 93	10.1	I 94	−2.4	800-382-8722
17.9	16.7						Low	4	6	22	18	B.F. Goodrich(3)						800-382-8722
9.9	8.2	9.6	7.9				Very high	13	NA	20	13	J.C. Penney(2)	Very low	I 95	7.0	I 94	−3.5	800-382-8722
17.2	13.0	13.7	10.3	13.2	10.2		Average	3	10	22	3	RJR Nabisco Holdings(5)	Average	III 94	12.1	I 94	−4.9	800-382-8722
Less than three years of data available								2	20	29	7	Philip Morris(2)						800-382-8722
14.9	12.4	12.8	10.5				Low	4	NA	17	13	J.C. Penney(4)	Low	IV 96	9.7	I 94	−4.0	800-382-8722
9.8	8.8	13.1	12.2				Average	5	99	24	14	Elf Aquitaine (ADR)(2)	Average	IV 93	13.8	I 95	−5.2	800-382-8722
10.6	9.4						Average	4	71	25	17	Canon(1)						800-382-8722
15.6	12.0	11.6	8.1	14.8	11.4		Average	17	4	29	34	Newbridge Networks(2)	High	IV 92	10.4	II 92	−6.3	800-223-0818
12.3	9.6	9.3	6.3	10.6	7.6		Average	4	3	29	17	HBO(2)	Low	II 95	6.7	II 92	−5.5	800-223-0818
17.3	14.9	12.8	10.4	14.3	11.2		Average	14	3	31	43	SunAmerica(3)	High	II 95	12.6	II 92	−9.4	800-223-0818
−3.4	−3.4	8.9	8.9	4.1	4.0		Very low	2	66	43	−17	Plutonic Resources(9)	Very high	II 93	35.9	IV 94	−14.5	800-826-1115
−6.5	−7.4	4.3	3.4	3.9	2.7		Very low	2	75	41	40	Middle Witwatersrand(6)	Very high	II 93	39.1	IV 92	−13.5	800-826-1115
17.1	11.3	13.3	8.3	13.5	9.6		High	2	10	22	19	Bristol-Myers Squibb(3)	Low	I 95	10.6	I 94	−3.1	800-421-5666
16.6	14.8	16.6	14.8	17.2	15.0		Average	5	3	40	35	HBO(2)	High	IV 92	18.5	II 92	−10.2	800-421-5666
18.2	15.2	14.7	11.2	14.8	11.0		High	3	3	26	21	Philip Morris(4)	Average	II 95	11.6	I 94	−3.2	800-421-5666
13.6	11.6						High	3	9	24	12	Texaco(2)						800-421-5666
16.4	13.3	14.9	11.8	13.8	10.9		High	9	11	24	15	Texaco(2)	Low	I 95	9.5	I 94	−3.1	800-421-5666

DATA: MORNINGSTAR, INC., CHICAGO, IL.

MUTUAL FUND SCOREBOARD

FUND	OVERALL RATING (COMPARES RISK-ADJUSTED PERFORMANCE OF EACH FUND AGAINST ALL FUNDS)	CATEGORY (COMPARES RISK-ADJUSTED PERFORMANCE OF FUND WITHIN CATEGORY)	RATING	SIZE ASSETS $MIL.	% CHG. 1995-6	FEES SALES CHARGE (%)	EXPENSE RATIO (%)	1996 RETURNS (%) PRE-TAX	AFTER-TAX	YIELD
VAN KAMPEN AMER. CAP. PACE A 🧍	AVG	Large-cap Growth	▲▲	2774.7	14	5.75	0.94†	20.6	17.1	0.9
VAN WAGONER EMERGING GROWTH		Small-cap Growth		638.2	282	No load	NA†	26.9	26.9	0.0
VAN WAGONER MICRO-CAP		Small-cap Growth		140.7	658	No load	NA†	24.5	24.5	0.0
VAN WAGONER MID-CAP		Mid-cap Growth		137.7	NM	No load	NA†	23.9	23.9	0.0
VANGUARD ASSET ALLOCATION	▲▲	Domestic Hybrid	▲	2596.9	45	No load	0.47	15.7	12.7	3.8
VANGUARD BALANCED INDEX		Domestic Hybrid		826.2	40	No load	0.20	14.0	12.5	3.5
VANGUARD EQUITY-INCOME	▲▲	Large-cap Value	▲	1425.0	29	No load	0.42	17.4	15.2	3.4
VANGUARD EXPLORER	▼	Small-cap Blend	▼▼	2263.7	37	No load	0.63	14.0	12.3	0.5
VANGUARD HORIZON AGGRES. GROWTH		Mid-cap Value		153.2	105	1.00*	0.38	25.1	22.8	1.4
VANGUARD INDEX EXTENDED MKT.	AVG	Small-cap Blend	▲	2098.8	38	No load	0.25	17.6	15.1	1.2
VANGUARD INDEX 500	▲	Large-cap Blend	▲	30331.9	75	No load	0.20	22.9	22.0	1.8
VANGUARD INDEX GROWTH		Large-cap Growth		786.9	190	No load	0.20	23.8	23.0	1.3
VANGUARD INDEX SMALL CAP STOCK	AVG	Small-cap Blend	AVG	1713.4	76	No load	0.25	18.1	15.5	1.3
VANGUARD INDEX TOTAL STOCK MKT.		Large-cap Blend		3530.9	125	No load	0.25	21.0	20.2	1.6
VANGUARD INDEX VALUE		Large-cap Value		1015.7	105	No load	0.20	21.8	19.9	2.2
VANGUARD INTL. EQ. EMG. MKT.		Diversified Emerging Mkts.		637.1	172	No load	0.60	15.8	15.3	1.4
VANGUARD INTL. EQ. EUROPEAN	AVG	Europe	AVG	1594.7	57	No load	0.35	21.3	20.3	2.2
VANGUARD INTL. EQ. PACIFIC	▼▼▼	Japan		977.5	18	No load	0.35	−7.8	−8.1	0.9
VANGUARD INTL. GROWTH 🧍	▼	Foreign	▲	5568.7	51	No load	0.56	14.7	13.2	1.1
VANGUARD LIFESTRAT. CONSERV. GROWTH		Domestic Hybrid		462.5	111	No load	0.00	10.4	8.4	4.3
VANGUARD LIFESTRAT. GROWTH		Large-cap Blend		628.7	189	No load	0.00	15.4	14.0	2.5
VANGUARD LIFESTRAT. INCOME		Domestic Hybrid		151.5	25	No load	0.00	7.7	5.4	5.4
VANGUARD LIFESTRAT. MOD. GROWTH		Large-cap Blend		825.7	252	No load	0.00	12.7	11.0	3.3
VANGUARD QUANTITATIVE 🧍	▲	Large-cap Value	▼	1285.4	41	No load	0.47	23.1	19.8	1.7
VANGUARD SPEC. ENERGY 🧍	▼	Natural Resources	AVG	847.9	67	1.00*	0.48	34.0	32.9	1.1
VANGUARD SPEC. GOLD & PREC. MET.	▼▼▼	Precious Metals	AVG	496.5	−10	1.00*	0.60	−0.8	−1.5	1.8
VANGUARD SPEC. HEALTH CARE 🧍	AVG	Health	▲▲▲	2661.7	81	1.00*	0.45	21.4	20.2	1.2
VANGUARD SPEC. UTILITIES INCOME		Utilities		658.6	−13	No load	0.41	5.3	3.8	4.4
VANGUARD STAR	▲▲	Domestic Hybrid	▲▲	5863.4	21	No load	0.00	16.2	13.1	3.5
VANGUARD TAX-MGD. CAPITAL APPREC.		Large-cap Growth		517.4	104	2.00*	0.20	20.9	20.7	0.7
VANGUARD TAX-MGD. GROWTH & INC.		Large-cap Blend		234.5	138	2.00*	0.20	23.0	22.4	1.8
VANGUARD U.S. GROWTH	AVG	Large-cap Growth	▲▲▲	5532.0	53	No load	0.43	26.1	23.4	1.0
VANGUARD/MORGAN GROWTH	AVG	Large-cap Blend	▼	2053.8	40	No load	0.48	23.3	19.9	0.8
VANGUARD/PRIMECAP 🧍	AVG	Mid-cap Blend	AVG	4204.0	30	No load	0.58	18.3	17.3	0.7
VANGUARD/TRUSTEES' EQ. INTL. 🧍	▼	Foreign	AVG	916.6	−7	No load	0.47	10.2	4.1	2.5
VANGUARD/TRUSTEES' EQ. U.S.	AVG	Large-cap Blend	▼	157.7	15	No load	0.56	21.3	15.4	1.5
VANGUARD/WELLESLEY INCOME 🧍	▲	Domestic Hybrid	AVG	7012.7	−2	No load	0.34	9.4	6.8	5.5
VANGUARD/WELLINGTON	▲▲	Domestic Hybrid	▲	16189.7	28	No load	0.33	16.2	13.5	3.9
VANGUARD/WINDSOR	▲▲	Large-cap Value	▲	16738.1	23	No load‡	0.29	26.4	22.9	2.3
VANGUARD/WINDSOR II 🧍	▲▲	Large-cap Value	▲▲	15700.0	43	No load	0.39	24.2	21.7	2.5
VICTORY BALANCED A		Domestic Hybrid		281.6	30	4.75	0.98	14.5	12.6	2.8
VICTORY DIVERSIFIED STOCK A	▲	Large-cap Blend	▲	594.9	34	4.75	0.92	24.7	20.4	1.1
VICTORY GROWTH		Large-cap Growth		154.4	38	4.75	1.07	24.9	23.4	0.4
VICTORY SPECIAL VALUE A		Mid-cap Value		298.8	44	4.75	1.04	18.9	16.6	0.5
VICTORY STOCK INDEX 🧍		Large-cap Blend		305.8	72	4.75	0.55	22.1	20.7	1.8
VICTORY VALUE		Large-cap Blend		394.8	24	4.75	0.99	22.4	20.4	1.2
VISTA CAPITAL GROWTH A	AVG	Small-cap Value	▼▼	784.9	8	4.75	1.37†	24.2	20.4	0.2
VISTA GROWTH & INCOME A	▲	Large-cap Value	▼▼	1628.4	8	4.75	1.32†	19.7	16.6	1.3
VISTA SMALL CAP EQUITY A		Small-cap Blend		151.8	185	4.75	1.50†	28.8	28.3	0.0
VONTOBEL EUROPACIFIC	▼	Foreign	AVG	149.9	16	No load	1.53	17.0	13.9	3.1
WADDELL & REED GROWTH B		Domestic Hybrid		243.4	40	3.00**	2.14†	2.4	1.5	0.0
WADDELL & REED TOTAL RETURN B		Large-cap Blend		291.7	75	3.00**	1.99†	18.1	17.9	0.0
WARBURG PINCUS CAP. APPREC. COMM.	▲	Mid-cap Blend	AVG	464.9	82	No load	1.12	23.3	19.8	0.5
WARBURG PINCUS EMG. GR. COMM	▼	Small-cap Growth	▲	1151.8	107	No load	1.26	9.9	9.8	0.0
WARBURG PINCUS EMG. MKT. COMM.		Diversified Emerging Mkts.		212.4	852	No load	1.00†	9.9	9.8	0.2
WARBURG PINCUS GR. & INC. COMM. 🧍	AVG	Mid-cap Blend	▼	460.9	-53	No load	1.21	-1.2	-1.3	0.4
WARBURG PINCUS INTL. EQ. COMM.	▼	Foreign	AVG	2953.0	33	No load	1.39	10.6	9.3	2.2
WARBURG PINCUS POST-VENTURE		Small-cap Growth		165.2	476	No load	1.65†	17.3	17.3	0.0
WASATCH AGGRESSIVE EQUITY 🧍	▼▼	Small-cap Growth	AVG	219.2	−25	No load‡	1.50	5.2	3.8	0.0
WASHINGTON MUTUAL INVESTORS 🧍	▲▲	Large-cap Value	AVG	25374.5	35	5.75	0.66†	20.2	17.7	2.4
WEITZ VALUE		Mid-cap Blend		260.7	75	No load	1.35	18.7	16.8	0.6
WESTCORE MIDCO GROWTH 🧍	▼▼	Mid-cap Growth	AVG	628.8	15	No load	1.08	17.0	12.7	0.0
WINTHROP AGGRESSIVE GROWTH A (gggg)	▲	Small-cap Value	▼	237.3	11	4.75	1.64†	14.6	13.3	0.4
WPG TUDOR 🧍	▼▼	Small-cap Growth	▼	182.3	10	No load	1.30	18.8	10.5	0.5
WRIGHT INTL. BLUE CHIP EQUITY	▼	Foreign	AVG	268.9	13	No load	1.29†	20.7	18.6	0.6
WRIGHT SELECTED BLUE CHIP EQUITY 🧍	AVG	Mid-cap Value	▼▼	205.8	−5	No load	1.04†	18.6	14.9	1.0
YACKTMAN		Mid-cap Blend		755.6	33	No load	0.91†	26.0	21.5	1.6
ZWEIG APPRECIATION A	▲	Mid-cap Value	▼	275.9	1	5.50	1.63†	15.4	11.0	0.9
ZWEIG MANAGED ASSETS C		Domestic Hybrid		426.2	−19	1.25**	2.29†	9.0	7.0	2.7
ZWEIG STRATEGY C		Domestic Hybrid		621.3	17	1.25**	1.97†	12.1	9.6	0.7

*Includes redemption fee. **Includes deferred sales charge. †12(b)-1 plan in effect. ‡Not currently accepting new accounts. §Less than 0.5% of assets. NA=Not available. NM=Not meaningful. (gggg) Formerly Winthrop Focus Aggressive Growth.

3 YEARS PRETAX	3 YEARS AFTERTAX	5 YEARS PRETAX	5 YEARS AFTERTAX	10 YEARS PRETAX	10 YEARS AFTERTAX	TREND BW 10-YEAR ANALYSIS	TURNOVER	CASH %	FOREIGN %	P-E RATIO	UNTAXED GAINS (%)	LARGEST HOLDING COMPANY (% ASSETS)	RISK LEVEL	BEST QTR	BEST %RET	WORST QTR	WORST %RET	TELEPHONE
15.5	11.4	12.3	8.1	12.5	8.9		Very high	2	9	25	25	American Cap Small Cap(4)	Average	II 95	10.5	I 94	-3.6	800-421-5666
Less than three years of data available								1	2	45	NA	U.S. Robotics(4)						800-228-2121
Less than three years of data available								5	2	42	NA	NuCo2(2)						800-228-2121
Less than three years of data available								6	2	48	NA	Xylan(4)						800-228-2121
15.3	13.0	13.3	11.2				Average	25	4	24	25	General Electric(1)	Low	II 95	10.5	I 94	-4.6	800-662-7447
13.0	11.6						Low	1	0	25	16	General Electric(1)						800-662-7447
16.6	14.8	14.7	12.8				Low	7	1	21	30	Bristol-Myers Squibb(3)	Low	I 95	9.6	I 94	-6.6	800-662-7447
13.2	11.2	13.6	11.6	12.9	11.2		Average	14	1	29	23	Air Express International(1)	High	IV 92	15.5	II 92	-7.6	800-662-7447
Less than three years of data available								High	1	NA	21	18	Atmel(2)						800-662-7447
15.6	14.2	14.8	13.6				Low	2	1	27	29	Berkshire Hathaway(2)	Average	IV 92	11.6	II 92	-3.5	800-662-7447
19.6	18.6	15.1	14.1	15.0	13.8		Very low	0	3	24	24	General Electric(3)	Low	I 95	9.7	I 94	-3.8	800-662-7447
20.7	20.0						Low	1	2	29	13	General Electric(6)						800-662-7447
14.8	13.1	16.3	14.7	12.5	10.4		Low	3	0	25	19	Battle Mountain Gold($)	High	IV 92	14.1	II 92	-6.6	800-662-7447
17.9	17.1						Very low	2	0	25	16	General Electric(2)						800-662-7447
18.4	16.9						Low	0	1	18	15	Exxon(4)						800-662-7447
Less than three years of data available								Very low	5	100	21	5	Telekom Malaysia(2)						800-662-7447
14.7	13.8	13.5	12.7				Very low	3	100	21	23	Royal Dutch Petrol. (Neth)(3)	Average	II 92	10.8	III 92	-5.2	800-662-7447
2.3	2.0	3.5	3.1				Very low	2	100	38	7	Toyota Motor(3)	Very high	II 93	17.3	I 92	-18.8	800-662-7447
9.9	9.0	12.6	11.8	10.1	8.1		Low	1	98	25	21	Ciba-Geigy (Reg)(3)	Average	IV 93	12.5	I 92	-5.1	800-662-7447
Less than three years of data available								Very low	5	NA	25	5	Vanguard F/I S-T Corp.(26)						800-662-7447
Less than three years of data available								Very low	0	18	25	7	Vanguard Index Tot. Stk. Mkt.(50)						800-662-7447
Less than three years of data available								Very low	0	NA	24	1	Vanguard F/I S-T Corp.(32)						800-662-7447
Less than three years of data available								Very low	0	NA	25	5	Vanguard Index Tot. Stk. Mkt.(35)						800-662-7447
18.5	16.2	15.2	12.7	15.2	13.3		Average	5	2	20	23	General Electric(3)	Average	II 95	9.4	I 94	-4.1	800-662-7447
18.2	17.1	17.3	15.7	15.0	12.7		Low	8	27	32	22	Unocal(3)	High	I 93	21.3	IV 93	-0.9	800-662-7447
-3.6	-4.2	6.9	6.3	6.1	5.0		Very low	8	81	34	15	Euro-Nevada Mining(5)	Very high	II 93	31.3	IV 94	-12.6	800-662-7447
24.5	22.8	16.3	14.5	20.0	17.8		Very low	11	23	30	28	Bristol-Myers Squibb(5)	Average	III 94	14.7	I 93	-7.9	800-662-7447
8.9	7.1						Low	2	8	17	7	Pinnacle West Capital(4)						800-662-7447
14.2	11.7	12.8	10.6	12.1	9.4		Very low	18	NA	23	18	Vanguard/Windsor II(27)	Very low	II 95	7.6	I 94	-3.1	800-662-7447
Less than three years of data available								Very low	0	0	28	15	Coca-Cola(2)						800-662-7447
Less than three years of data available								Very low	0	3	24	14	General Electric(3)						800-662-7447
21.9	20.5	12.9	11.9	14.8	12.8		Average	6	8	28	35	Coca-Cola(4)	Average	II 95	10.5	I 92	-4.9	800-662-7447
18.1	15.7	14.2	11.6	14.6	11.2		Average	9	8	28	26	Cisco Systems(2)	Average	II 95	11.8	I 94	-4.0	800-662-7447
21.3	20.3	18.1	17.1	15.0	13.8		Very low	7	9	29	30	Intel(5)	Average	II 95	13.9	II 92	-2.9	800-662-7447
8.4	4.9	8.7	6.2	10.5	6.6		Average	1	100	24	19	Total Petroleum Cl B(3)	High	I 93	10.0	I 92	-5.5	800-662-7447
15.8	13.2	14.1	11.8	12.8	9.8		Average	1	0	23	26	Philip Morris(3)	Average	III 95	9.9	II 94	-5.2	800-662-7447
10.5	8.0	10.9	8.4	11.1	8.3		Low	3	3	20	9	Bristol-Myers Squibb(2)	Very low	II 95	8.6	I 94	4.6	800-662-7447
15.4	13.4	13.5	11.5	12.6	10.2		Low	2	6	19	24	General Electric(2)	Low	II 95	8.6	I 94	-3.9	800-662-7447
18.0	14.5	18.0	14.9	14.0	10.3		Low	10	7	23	30	Chrysler(6)	Average	II 95	11.3	IV 94	-3.1	800-662-7447
19.4	17.2	16.7	14.7	14.6	12.2		Low	7	3	18	36	Chase Manhattan(5)	Low	III 95	10.2	I 94	-4.5	800-662-7447
12.4	10.8						Average	2	7	21	12	BankAmerica(2)						800-539-3863
20.6	16.7	16.2	12.9				Average	1	2	23	20	General Electric(2)	Low	I 95	9.9	I 94	-3.4	800-539-3863
17.8	16.6						High	3	NA	24	26	General Electric(4)						800-539-3863
15.2	13.8						Average	4	2	22	19	Ucar International(2)						800-539-3863
18.9	17.7						Very low	14	4	23	18	S&P 500 (Fut)(12)						800-539-3863
17.9	16.3						Low	3	1	20	23	Texaco(3)						800-539-3863
14.4	12.5	15.3	13.9				Average	10	2	22	21	Eckerd(2)	Average	IV 92	12.6	II 92	-6.3	800-648-4782
13.8	11.9	13.9	12.4				Average	8	7	21	21	American Home Products(1)	Low	IV 92	9.6	II 92	-3.1	800-648-4782
Less than three years of data available								Average	7	4	28	19	Russell 2000 (Fut)(4)						800-648-4782
7.1	5.6	11.0	10.1	7.9	7.4		Average	7	99	27	27	Roche Holding (Div Cert)(3)	High	IV 93	14.6	III 92	-7.5	800-527-9500
15.1	14.4						Low	37	NA	42	19	Cascade Communs.(3)						913-236-2000
14.5	14.4						Low	9	1	22	17	Intel(3)						913-236-2000
18.3	15.0	15.6	12.8				High	9	3	23	23	General Motors(4)	Average	I 95	9.5	I 94	-5.6	800-927-2874
16.6	15.9	16.0	15.1				Average	7	7	35	18	Synopsys(3)	High	III 95	17.1	II 92	-8.9	800-927-2874
Less than three years of data available									3	100	17	5	Novus Petroleum(4)						800-927-2874
8.6	7.7	13.5	11.3				High	3	19	32	14	Newmont Mining(7)	Average	II 93	17.9	III 96	-5.2	800-927-2874
6.9	5.8	12.1	11.3				Low	2	100	25	8	Banco Santander (Reg)(2)	High	IV 93	17.3	IV 94	-7.1	800-927-2874
Less than three years of data available								Low	8	1	46	16	McAfee Associates(3)						800-927-2874
12.5	10.9	12.9	11.4	14.0	12.6		Average	4	1	29	21	National Health Investors(6)	High	IV 92	15.7	II 92	-12.0	800-551-1700
19.5	17.1	16.0	14.0	14.4	12.2		Low	4	NA	20	31	DuPont(4)	Low	II 95	10.4	I 94	-5.0	800-421-4120
14.0	12.0	15.1	13.3	13.2	11.4		Average	5	NA	24	19	Wells Fargo(7)	Low	II 95	11.3	I 94	-6.7	800-232-4161
13.9	11.7	13.0	11.0	16.5	13.6		Average	1	5	39	35	Oxford Health Plans(5)	High	IV 92	15.2	IV 92	-9.1	800-392-2673
11.0	9.8	14.5	12.2	13.3	10.4		Low	2	NA	19	12	First American (TN)(2)	Average	III 93	8.9	IV 94	-3.6	800-225-8011
14.8	10.7	12.5	8.6	13.8	10.1		High	0	11	41	22	Starbucks(3)	Very high	IV 92	17.4	II 94	-10.2	800-223-3332
10.5	9.7	10.7	10.1				Very low	0	100	21	27	Gas Natural SDG(1)	Average	IV 93	10.1	III 92	-5.2	800-888-9471
14.2	11.4	9.8	7.3	12.1	9.2		Average	3	NA	17	25	Sun Microsystems(1)	Average	III 95	8.0	I 92	-4.6	800-888-9471
21.4	18.6						Average	14	NA	21	21	Philip Morris(11)						800-525-8258
12.0	9.6	12.0	10.3				Average	15	10	15	27	AMR(1)	Low	III 95	9.5	II 92	-4.4	800-444-2706
6.6	5.0						Very high	32	54	25	4	PepsiCo(2)						800-444-2706
11.7	10.2						High	15	9	16	13	BankAmerica(2)						800-444-2706

DATA: MORNINGSTAR, INC., CHICAGO, IL.

Bond Funds

MUTUAL FUND SCOREBOARD

How to Use the Tables

BUSINESS WEEK RATINGS
Overall ratings show how well a fund performed compared with other rated funds and relative to the level of risk it took. Risk-adjusted performance is determined by subtracting a fund's risk-of-loss factor (see below) from its historic total return. Performance calculations are based on the five-year time period between Jan. 1, 1992, and Dec. 31, 1996. For overall ratings, funds are divided into taxable and tax-exempt funds. Funds are also rated against others in their categories (see below). Ratings are based on a normal statistical distribution within each group and awarded as follows:

♠ ♠ ♠	SUPERIOR
♠ ♠	VERY GOOD
♠	GOOD
AVG	AVERAGE
♦	BELOW AVERAGE
♦ ♦	POOR
♦ ♦ ♦	VERY POOR

RISK
The risk-of-loss factor is the potential for losing money in a fund, calculated as follows: The monthly Treasury bill return is subtracted from the fund's total return for each of the 60 months in the rating period. When a fund has not performed as well as Treasury bills, the result is negative. The sum of these negative numbers is then divided by the number of months in the period. The result is a negative number, and the greater its magnitude, the higher a shareholder's risk of loss.

PERFORMANCE COMPARISON
The tables provide performance data over three time periods. Here are equivalent total returns for the Lehman Brothers bond indexes during those periods:

	GOVT./CORP.	MUNI.
1996	2.9%	4.4%
3-year average (1994-96)	5.8%	5.2%
5-year average (1992-96)	7.2%	7.3%

FUND CATEGORIES
General bond funds are classified long-term (CL), intermediate-term (CI), short-term (CS), and ultra-short (UB); government funds, long (GL), intermediate (GI) and short (GS); municipal funds, national long (ML), national intermediate (MI), single-state long (SL), single-state intermediate (SI), and short (MS); specialized funds, convertible (CV), high yield (HY), international (IB), and multisector (MU).

SALES CHARGE
The cost of buying a fund, commonly called the "load." Many funds take loads out of initial investments, and for ratings purposes, performance is reduced by these charges. Loads on withdrawals can take two forms. Deferred charges decrease over time. Redemption fees are imposed whenever investors sell shares. Funds with none of these charges are called "no-load."

EXPENSE RATIO
Fund expenses for 1996 as a percentage of average net assets. The measures show how much shareholders pay for fund management. Footnotes indicate 12(b)-1 plans, which allocate shareholder money for marketing costs. The average expense ratio is 1.03% for taxable funds, 0.80% for tax-free funds.

TOTAL RETURN
A fund's net gain to investors, including reinvestment of dividends and capital gains at month-end prices.

YIELD
Income distributions during 1996 expressed as a percent of net asset value, adjusted for capital gains.

MATURITY
The average maturity of the securities in a fund's portfolio, weighted by market value.

TREND
A fund's relative performance during the five 12-month periods from Jan. 1, 1992, to Dec. 31, 1996. The boxes read from left to right, and the level of blue in each box tells how the fund performed relative to other funds during the period: ■ for the top quartile; ■ for the second quartile; ▣ for the third quartile; and ☐ for the bottom quartile. An empty box indicates that a fund is not rated for that time period.

TELEPHONE NUMBERS
See index on page 212.

FUND (COMPARES RISK-ADJUSTED PERFORMANCE OF EACH FUND AGAINST ALL FUNDS)	OVERALL RATING	CATEGORY (COMPARES FUND WITHIN CATEGORY)	RATING	SIZE ASSETS $MIL.	% CHG. 1995-96	FEES SALES CHARGE (%)	EXPENSE RATIO (%)	TOTAL RETURN (%) 1 YR.	3 YR.	5 YR.	PORTFOLIO YIELD (%)	MATURITY (YEARS)	TREND 5-YEAR ANALYSIS
TAXABLE													
AARP GNMA & U.S. TREASURY	AVG	GS	AVG	4826.1	–8	No load	0.6	4.5	5.0	5.5	6.5	6.1	
AARP HIGH-QUALITY BOND	♦	CI	♦	502.0	–8	No load	0.9	2.8	4.8	6.3	5.7	10.1	
ADVANCE CAPITAL I RETIREMENT INCOME		CL		170.8	23	No load	0.8†	4.5	6.8		7.4	17.1	
AIM HIGH-YIELD A	♠♠♠	HY	♠	1264.1	44	4.75	1.0†	15.4	9.9	13.3	9.4	8.0	
AIM INCOME A	AVG	MU		284.8	14	4.75	1.0†	8.6	7.2	8.8	7.1	11.6	
AIM INTERMEDIATE GOVERNMENT A	♦	GI	AVG	173.7	–1	4.75	1.1†	2.4	4.7	5.5	6.8	6.8	
AIM LTD. MATURITY TREAS. RET.	♠	GS	♠♠♠	377.0	21	1.00	0.5†	4.7	4.9	5.0	5.2	1.5	
ALLIANCE BOND CORPORATE BOND B		CL		419.2	40	3.00**	1.9†	9.3	6.4		7.9	18.8	
ALLIANCE BOND U.S. GOVERNMENT B	♦♦♦	GI	♦♦	558.5	–26	3.00**	1.7†	–0.4	3.0	4.7	7.0	7.0	
ALLIANCE GLOBAL DOLLAR GOVT. B		IB		83.0	14	3.00**	2.4†	38.3			7.8	18.5	
ALLIANCE MORTGAGE SECURITIES INCOME		GI		478.8	–35	3.00**	2.4†	3.5	3.4		6.3	NA	
ALLIANCE MULTI-MARKET STRATEGY B	♦♦♦	IB	♦♦♦	85.7	–22	3.00**	2.3†	15.2	1.5	2.2	8.3	2.1	
ALLIANCE NORTH AMER. GOVT. INC. B		IB		1309.3	9	3.00**	3.3†	23.1	3.3		11.4	12.1	
ALLIANCE SHORT-TERM MULTI-MARKET A	♦♦♦	CS	♦♦♦	388.7	28	4.25	1.3†	13.4	2.9	3.3	8.7	1.3	
AMCORE VINTAGE FIXED-INCOME		CI		90.3	10	No load	1.0†	2.8	4.5		5.6	4.4	
AMERICAN CENT.-BENHAM ADJ. RATE GOVT. (a)	♠	GS	♠	247.8	–21	No load	0.6	5.8	4.4	4.4	5.6	4.8	
AMERICAN CENT.-BENHAM EURO. GOVT. (b)		IB		252.6	0	No load	0.8	6.4	10.3		6.1	6.2	
AMERICAN CENT.-BENHAM GNMA (c)	♠	GI	♠♠♠	1130.8	2	No load	0.6	5.2	6.2	6.6	6.9	7.8	
AMERICAN CENT.-BENHAM INT. TREAS. (d)	AVG	GS	AVG	337.0	10	No load	0.5	4.1	4.9	5.9	5.6	1.9	
AMERICAN CENT.-BENHAM LONG BOND (e)	♦	CI	♦	136.6	–10	No load	0.8	2.5	5.6	6.5	6.2	10.2	
AMERICAN CENT.-BENHAM LONG TREAS. (f)		GL		127.5	22	No load	0.7	–1.4	5.0		6.2	26.0	
AMERICAN CENT.-BENHAM SHORT GOVT. (g)	AVG	GS	AVG	344.9	–12	No load	0.7	4.6	4.8	4.6	5.9	3.0	
AMER. CENT.-BENHAM TARGET 2000 (h)	♦♦	GI		272.8	–9	No load	0.5	1.6	4.4	7.0	6.3	4.3	
AMER. CENT.-BENHAM TARGET 2005 (i)	♦♦♦	GL	AVG	252.2	10	No load	0.6	–2.4	5.5	8.3	6.0	10.3	
AMER. CENT.-BENHAM TARGET 2010 (j)	♦♦♦	GL	♦	117.7	–2	No load	0.7	–4.3	6.2	10.0	6.1	19.8	

* Includes redemption fee. ** Includes deferred sales charge. † 12(b)-1 plan in effect. ‡ Not currently accepting new accounts. NA = Not available. NM = Not meaningful.
(a) Formerly Benham Adjustable Rate Govt. Secs. (b) Formerly Benham European Government Bond. (c) Formerly Benham GNMA Income. (d) Formerly Benham Treasury Note. (e) Formerly Twentieth Century Long-Term Bond. (f) Formerly Benham Long-Term Treasury & Agency. (g) Formerly Twentieth Century U.S. Govts. Short-Term. (h) Formerly Benham Target Maturities 2000. (i) Formerly Benham Target Maturities 2005. (j) Formerly Benham Target Maturities 2010.
DATA: MORNINGSTAR, INC., CHICAGO, IL.

MUTUAL FUND SCOREBOARD — Bond Funds

FUND (COMPARES RISK-ADJUSTED PERFORMANCE OF EACH FUND AGAINST ALL FUNDS)	OVERALL RATING	CATEGORY (COMPARES FUND WITHIN CATEGORY)	RATING	SIZE ASSETS $MIL.	% CHG. 1995-96	FEES SALES CHARGE (%)	EXPENSE RATIO (%)	TOTAL RETURN (%) 1 YR.	3 YR.	5 YR.	PORTFOLIO YIELD (%)	MATURITY (YEARS)	TREND 5-YEAR ANALYSIS
AMER. CENT.-BENHAM TARGET 2015 (k)	▼▼▼	GL	▼	125.8	–11	No load	0.7	–6.5	7.0	9.5	5.9	20.2	
AMER. CENT.-BENHAM TARGET 2020 (l)	▼▼▼	GL	▼▼	889.7	23	No load	0.6	–8.8	6.6	10.6	6.0	29.0	
AMERICAN HIGH-INCOME	▲▲	HY	▼	1671.2	38	4.75	0.9†	13.8	9.2	11.8	8.5	5.8	
AMERISTAR LTD. DURATION INCOME INV. (m)		CS		98.2	–6	3.00	0.9†	4.2			5.8	NA	
AMSOUTH BOND	▼	CI	▼▼	136.3	33	3.00	0.8	2.6	5.5	6.7	6.0	9.3	
ARMADA INTERMEDIATE GOVT. INSTL. (n)		GI		90.8	3	4.00	0.9†	3.5			5.9	5.5	
ASSET MANAGEMENT ADJUSTABLE RATE	▲	GS	▲▲▲	749.9	–17	No load	0.5†	6.0	5.6	5.2	6.0	3.4	
ASSET MGMT. INTERM. MORTGAGE SEC.	AVG	GS	▲	87.5	–51	No load	0.4†	2.9	4.8	5.9	6.5	4.6	
ASSET MGMT. SHORT U.S. GOVT. SEC.	▲	GS	▲▲	175.6	4	No load	0.5†	3.6	5.0	5.5	6.1	2.2	
ATLAS U.S. GOVT. & MORTGAGE SEC. A	AVG	GI	▲	223.7	–12	3.00	1.0†	4.5	5.3	6.2	6.7	NA	
BABSON BOND L	AVG	CI	AVG	137.1	–15		1.0	3.2	5.0	6.8	7.0	13.0	
BERNSTEIN GOVT. SHORT DURATION	▲	GS	▲	134.0	–9	No load	0.7	3.9	4.8	4.9	5.1	1.8	
BERNSTEIN INTERMEDIATE DURATION	AVG	CI	AVG	1594.1	26	No load	0.6	3.4	5.7	6.9	5.7	7.7	
BERNSTEIN SHORT DURATION PLUS	▲	CS	▲▲	550.4	3	No load	0.7	4.6	5.1	5.4	5.2	2.7	
WILLIAM BLAIR INCOME	AVG	CS	AVG	149.9	2	No load	0.7	3.1	5.4	6.2	5.9	4.0	
BLANCHARD FLEXIBLE INCOME		MU		176.8	–23	No load	1.6†	5.8	4.9		6.2	6.7	
BLANCHARD S-T FLEXIBLE INCOME		CS		151.4	669	No load	1.4†	6.7	5.5		5.4	NA	
BOND FUND OF AMERICA	▲	CI	▲▲	7002.4	11	4.75	0.7†	6.7	6.2	8.8	7.4	6.9	
CAPITAL WORLD BOND	AVG	IB	▲▲	815.3	17	4.75	1.1†	6.3	8.4	8.4	5.5	6.1	
CARDINAL GOVERNMENT OBLIGATIONS	▲	GI	▲▲▲	132.9	–11	4.50	0.8	5.7	6.1	5.8	7.3	NA	
CHICAGO TRUST BOND		CI		84.3	15	No load	0.8†	3.8	5.8		5.9	12.5	
COLONIAL FEDERAL SECURITIES A	▼▼	GL	▲	999.7	–19	4.75	1.2†	1.0	4.6	6.4	6.6	9.7	
COLONIAL HIGH-YIELD SECURITIES A	▲▲▲	HY	▲▲	523.3	12	4.75	1.2†	12.2	9.6	13.8	8.7	8.0	
COLONIAL INCOME A	AVG	CL	▲▲	129.7	–10	4.75	1.1†	3.6	6.1	7.8	7.0	10.6	
COLONIAL STRATEGIC INCOME B		MU		706.7	10	5.00**	2.0†	9.4	7.7		7.1	9.9	
COLONIAL U.S. GOVERNMENT A	▼	GI	AVG	874.6	–23	4.75	1.1†	2.8	5.1	5.2	6.3	6.9	
COLUMBIA FIXED-INCOME SECURITIES	AVG	CI	AVG	356.4	13	No load	0.7	3.4	5.9	7.2	6.5	5.9	
COMMERCE BOND		CI		153.6	51	3.50	0.9	2.2			6.1	NA	
COMMON SENSE GOVERNMENT I	▼▼	GI	▼▼	278.3	–16	6.75	0.8	1.8	4.1	5.5	6.6	6.7	
COMPOSITE INCOME A	▼	CL	AVG	86.7	–11	4.00	1.1†	3.5	6.2	7.4	6.6	13.1	
COMPOSITE U.S. GOVERNMENT SEC. A	▼▼	GI	▼	138.2	–22	4.00	1.0†	2.5	5.2	6.0	6.0	11.2	
DEAN WITTER CONVERTIBLE	▲	CV	▼	245.8	22	5.00**	2.0†	17.0	11.1	11.4	4.2	NA	
DEAN WITTER DIVERSIFIED INCOME		MU		778.7	36	5.00**	1.4†	8.4	6.4		9.5	5.0	
DEAN WITTER FEDERAL SECURITIES	▼▼	GI		699.6	–17	5.00**	1.5†	0.9	4.4	5.8	6.3	8.1	
DEAN WITTER HIGH-INCOME SECURITIES		HY		936.3	136	4.00**	1.6†	13.5			10.3	7.5	
DEAN WITTER HIGH-YIELD SECURITIES	▲▲▲	HY	▲	468.8	5	5.50	0.8	13.3	7.2	15.0	12.5	6.1	
DEAN WITTER INTERMEDIATE INCOME	▼	CI	▼	192.8	17	5.00**	1.6†	3.1	4.3	5.8	5.5	NA	
DEAN WITTER SHORT-TERM U.S. TREAS.	AVG	GS	AVG	299.4	3	No load	0.8†	3.9	4.1	4.5	5.4	2.8	
DEAN WITTER U.S. GOVT. SECURITIES	▼	GI	▲	6422.4	–19	5.00**	1.2†	3.2	5.1	5.7	6.3	9.0	
DEAN WITTER WORLD WIDE INCOME	AVG	IB	▲	111.6	–17	5.00**	1.9†	12.3	8.3	7.5	10.0	NA	
DELAWARE DELCHESTER A	▲▲	HY	▼▼	999.1	–2	4.75	1.1†	12.4	6.9	10.8	9.8	6.0	
DELAWARE LIMITED-TERM GOVT. A	▼	GS	▼▼	463.6	–29	3.00	1.0†	3.7	3.4	4.2	6.8	3.3	
DELAWARE U.S. GOVERNMENT A	▼▼	GI	▼▼	154.7	–21	4.75	1.2†	2.8	3.3	4.8	7.3	7.5	
DG GOVERNMENT INCOME		CI		240.2	30	2.00	0.7	2.5	4.9		5.8	8.0	
DG LIMITED-TERM GOVERNMENT INCOME		CS		82.4	–11	2.00	0.7	4.4	4.7		5.5	1.7	
DODGE & COX INCOME	AVG	CI	▲	532.8	76	No load	0.5	3.6	6.6	7.7	6.3	11.1	
DREYFUS 100% U.S. TREAS. INTERM.-TERM	AVG	GI	▲▲	191.6	–2	No load	0.8	3.1	4.7	6.4	6.0	4.4	
DREYFUS 100% U.S. TREAS. L-T	▼▼	GL	▲▲▲	136.0	–7	No load	0.3	0.9	4.6	7.5	6.8	16.4	
DREYFUS 100% U.S. TREAS. S-T	▲	GS	▲▲	187.6	0	No load	0.7	4.1	4.9	5.8	6.1	2.4	
DREYFUS A BONDS PLUS	AVG	CL	▲	605.4	–1	No load	0.9	2.6	5.0	7.6	6.1	7.8	
DREYFUS GNMA	AVG	GI	▲▲	1310.2	–9	No load	1.0†	4.4	5.3	5.9	6.4	22.5	
DREYFUS SHORT-INTERMEDIATE GOVT.	▲	GS	▲▲	561.2	–2	No load	0.7	4.0	5.1	5.9	6.0	2.3	
DREYFUS SHORT-TERM INCOME		CS		214.4	8	No load	0.8	6.2	5.7		6.9	3.1	
DREYFUS STRATEGIC INCOME	▲	MU	AVG	293.5	–9	No load	1.0	6.6	6.5	8.6	7.0	8.4	
EATON VANCE INCOME OF BOSTON	▲▲▲	HY		154.0	36	3.75	1.1†	13.7	9.0	12.6	9.8	7.1	
EV MARATHON HIGH-INCOME	▲▲	HY	AVG	590.3	21	5.00**	1.8†	13.8	8.4	11.9	9.0	7.1	
EV MARATHON STRATEGIC INCOME	▼	MU	▼▼	131.0	–9	3.00**	2.2†	18.2	8.6	7.1	7.6	NA	
EV TRADITIONAL GOVT. OBLIGATIONS	AVG	GS	▼	303.3	–16	3.75	1.9†	4.5	5.3	6.1	7.6	4.3	
EVERGREEN U.S. GOVERNMENT B		GI		155.6	–17	5.00**	1.8†	2.3	4.5		5.8	8.7	
EXCELSIOR MANAGED INCOME (o)	▼▼	CL		187.4	113	4.50	1.0	0.6	5.2	6.7	5.9	13.0	
FEDERATED ADJ. RATE U.S. GOVT. F (p)	▲	GS		224.2	–30	1.00**	1.0†	5.9	4.6	4.4	5.5	1.2	
FEDERATED ARMS INSTITUTIONAL	▲	GS	▲▲▲	597.8	–22	No load	0.6	6.5	5.1	4.7	5.9	1.2	
FEDERATED BOND FORTRESS	▲▲	CI	▲▲▲	279.7	29	2.00**	1.0	5.4	7.0	10.5	7.2	11.3	
FEDERATED FUND FOR U.S. GOVT. A (q)	▼	GI	AVG	1226.3	–11	4.50	1.0	4.2	5.3	5.3	6.4	6.5	
FEDERATED GOVT. INCOME SEC. F (r)	AVG	GI	▲▲	1840.7	–22	2.00**	1.0	4.0	5.4	5.4	6.6	NA	
FEDERATED HIGH-INCOME BOND A (s)	▲▲▲	HY	AVG	600.9	16	4.50	1.2	13.5	10.0	12.9	8.9	6.2	
FEDERATED HIGH-YIELD	▲▲▲	HY	AVG	887.4	43	No load	0.9	13.5	9.5	12.1	9.3	6.3	
FEDERATED INCOME INSTITUTIONAL	AVG	GI	▲▲	841.1	–16	No load	0.6	4.7	5.9	5.9	6.7	6.0	
FEDERATED INTERM. INCOME INST. (t)		CI		123.7	88	No load	0.6	3.3	6.7		6.3	8.9	
FEDERATED INTERNATIONAL INCOME A	▼	IB	AVG	195.1	15	4.50	1.3†	10.8	7.5	9.2	7.7	8.3	

*Includes redemption fee. **Includes deferred sales charge. †12(b)-1 plan in effect. ‡Not currently accepting new accounts or deposits. NA=Not available. NM=Not meaningful.
(k) Formerly Benham Target Maturities 2015. (l) Formerly Benham Target Maturities 2020. (m) Formerly ValueStar Sh.-Int. Duration Bond Inv. (n) Formerly Inventor Intermediate Govt. Sec. A.
(o) Formerly UST Master Managed Income. (p) Formerly Fortress Adjustable Rate U.S. Govt. (q) Formerly Fund for U.S. Government Sec. A. (r) Formerly Government Income Securities.
(s) Formerly Liberty High-Income Bond A. (t) Formerly Intermediate Income Inst.   DATA: MORNINGSTAR, INC., CHICAGO, IL.

MUTUAL FUND SCOREBOARD — Bond Funds

FUND (COMPARES RISK-ADJUSTED PERFORMANCE OF EACH FUND AGAINST ALL FUNDS)	OVERALL RATING	CATEGORY (COMPARES FUND WITHIN CATEGORY)	RATING	SIZE ASSETS $MIL.	SIZE % CHG. 1995-96	FEES SALES CHARGE (%)	FEES EXPENSE RATIO (%)	TOTAL RETURN (%) 1 YR.	TOTAL RETURN (%) 3 YR.	TOTAL RETURN (%) 5 YR.	PORTFOLIO YIELD (%)	PORTFOLIO MATURITY (YEARS)	TREND 5-YEAR ANALYSIS
FEDERATED LTD. TERM A (u)	▲	CS	▲	111.1	−18	1.00	1.1†	5.0	5.0	5.7	6.0	2.5	
FEDERATED S-T INCOME INST.	▲	CS	▲	228.7	18	No load	0.6	5.4	5.2	5.4	6.4	1.9	
FEDERATED STRATEGIC INCOME B (v)		MU		131.9	NM	5.50**	1.0†	11.6			8.0	8.1	
FIDELITY ADVISOR EMRG. MKT. T (w)		IB		78.3	118	3.50	1.5†	40.3			6.2	14.9	
FIDELITY ADVISOR GOVT. INVMT. T (x)	▼	GI	AVG	214.7	−3	3.50	0.9†	2.1	4.9	6.1	6.1	8.4	
FIDELITY ADVISOR HIGH-YIELD T (y)	▲▲▲	HY	▲▲	1775.8	40	3.50	1.1†	13.3	10.0	14.6	9.2	6.5	
FIDELITY ADVISOR INTERMEDIATE BOND T (z)		CI		262.3	12	2.75	0.9†	3.4	4.2		6.4	6.1	
FIDELITY ADVISOR SHORT FIXED-INC. (aa)	▲	CS	AVG	403.2	−25	1.50	0.9†	4.6	3.5	5.5	6.3	2.1	
FIDELITY ADVISOR STRAT. INCOME T (bb)		MU		98.7	91	3.50	1.4†	12.9			7.0	7.2	
FIDELITY CAPITAL & INCOME	▲▲▲	HY	▲▲	2162.8	−7	1.50*	1.0	11.4	7.5	14.7	8.5	6.6	
FIDELITY CONVERTIBLE SECURITIES	▲▲	CV	AVG	1119.6	7	No load	0.7	15.1	10.5	14.2	4.2	NA	
FIDELITY GINNIE MAE	▲	GI	▲▲	793.1	−2	No load	0.8	4.9	6.2	6.3	6.5	NA	
FIDELITY GLOBAL BOND	▼▼▼	IB	▼▼	121.7	−38	No load	1.2	3.5	−2.6	3.3	5.6	NA	
FIDELITY GOVERNMENT SECURITIES	▼	GI	▲	972.5	−2	No load	0.7	2.1	4.5	6.7	6.9	8.2	
FIDELITY INTERMEDIATE BOND	AVG	CS	▼	3079.7	9	No load	0.7	3.7	4.6	6.4	6.5	4.7	
FIDELITY INVMT. GRADE BOND	AVG	CI	AVG	1455.4	17	No load	0.8	3.0	4.1	7.2	6.6	8.1	
FIDELITY MORTGAGE SECURITIES		GI	▲▲▲	521.3	7	No load	0.7	5.4	7.9	7.2	6.4	6.7	
FIDELITY NEW MARKETS INCOME		IB		305.8	76	1.00*	1.2	41.4	8.4		7.2	NA	
FIDELITY SHORT-INTERM. GOVERNMENT	AVG	GS	AVG	121.5	−9	No load	0.8	4.1	4.7	4.8	6.2	3.3	
FIDELITY SHORT-TERM BOND	▲	CS	AVG	995.6	−17	No load	0.7	4.8	3.3	5.3	6.5	2.1	
FIDELITY SPARTAN GINNIE MAE	▲	GI	▲▲▲	442.6	−1	No load	0.6	5.0	6.5	6.4	6.5	7.2	
FIDELITY SPARTAN GOVT. INCOME	AVG	GI		276.9	11	No load	0.6	2.6	5.3	6.1	6.6	8.6	
FIDELITY SPARTAN HIGH-INCOME	▲▲▲	HY	▲▲▲	1717.3	59	1.00*	0.8	14.2	11.8	15.6	8.4	6.4	
FIDELITY SPARTAN INVMT. GRADE BOND		CI		359.9	123	No load	0.7	3.1	5.1		6.3	7.9	
FIDELITY SPARTAN LTD. MAT. GOVT.		GS		712.9	−14	No load	0.6	4.1	5.5	5.8	6.7	5.0	
FIDELITY SPARTAN SHORT-TERM BOND (cc)		CS		319.8	−33	No load	0.7	5.0	3.3		6.6	2.2	
FIRST INVESTORS FUND FOR INCOME A	▲▲▲	HY	▲	431.5	1	6.25	1.2†	13.4	10.3	13.1	8.6	NA	
FIRST INVESTORS GOVERNMENT A	▼▼▼	GI	▼▼▼	186.8	−14	6.25	1.4†	3.6	4.7	4.8	5.8	NA	
FIRST INVESTORS HIGH-YIELD A	▲▲▲	HY	▲	201.7	8	6.25	1.5†	13.4	10.2	13.2	9.0	NA	
FIRST OMAHA FIXED-INCOME		CI		80.9	7	No load	0.8	0.9	5.0		4.5	8.5	
FIRST PRIORITY FIXED-INCOME INVMT.		CI		148.0	−5	4.75	1.0†	3.6	4.4		5.4	7.5	
FORTIS ADVANTAGE HIGH-YIELD A	▲▲	HY	▼▼▼	118.2	5	4.50	1.2†	11.3	6.5	11.2	10.1	7.4	
FORTIS U.S. GOVERNMENT SEC. E	▼▼	GI	▼▼	355.7	−22	4.50‡	0.8†	3.4	4.0	5.2	6.6	7.5	
FOUNTAIN SQ. QUALITY BOND A		CI		89.0	22	4.50	0.8†	1.9	4.5		5.6	11.8	
FPA NEW INCOME	▲▲	CI	▲▲▲	375.5	61	4.50	0.6	7.1	7.5	8.8	6.0	4.9	
FRANKLIN ADJ. U.S. GOVT. SEC.	▼	GS	▼▼	382.8	−22	2.25	0.6†	6.2	4.4	3.7	5.9	1.0	
FRANKLIN AGE HIGH INCOME I	▲▲▲	HY	▲	2487.4	20	4.25	0.7†	14.2	10.1	12.9	9.1	8.3	
FRANKLIN CONVERTIBLE SEC. I	▲▲	CV	AVG	139.0	53	4.50	1.0†	16.3	12.4	14.7	4.3	6.5	
FRANKLIN GLOBAL GOVT. INCOME I	▼▼	IB	▼	136.8	−13	4.25	0.9†	10.8	6.5	7.4	7.1	5.9	
FRANKLIN SHORT-INTERM. GOVT. I	AVG	GS	▼	197.9	−6	2.25	0.7†	4.0	4.2	5.4	5.6	2.2	
FRANKLIN TAX-ADV. U.S. GOVT.	▼	GI	AVG	336.1	−17	4.25	0.6†	4.1	5.7	6.5	6.7	NA	
FRANKLIN TEMPLETON HARD CURRENCY	▼▼▼	IB	▼▼▼	117.1	−8	3.00	1.1†	−7	4.3	3.9	4.8	0.3	
FRANKLIN U.S. GOVT. SEC. I	AVG	GI	▲▲	10001.8	−10	4.25	0.6†	4.6	5.9	6.4	7.3	24.3	
GALAXY II U.S. TREAS. INDEX RET.	AVG	GI	▲	114.3	−11	No load	0.4	2.2	5.1	6.5	6.3	8.3	
GLOBAL GOVERNMENT PLUS A	▲	IB	▲▲▲	125.9	−45	4.00	1.1†	14.0	10.4	9.8	6.9	6.4	
GLOBAL TOTAL RETURN A	AVG	IB	▲▲	229.9	−39	4.00	1.0†	13.0	9.8	9.1	7.0	5.9	
GOLDMAN SACHS GLOBAL A	▲	IB	▲▲▲	200.6	−15	4.50	1.2†	9.4	6.9	8.1	5.5	NA	
GRADISON-MCDONALD GOVT. INCOME	▼	GI	▲	162.8	−12	2.00	0.9†	3.5	5.3	6.0	6.0	6.0	
GT GLOBAL GOVT. INCOME A	▼▼▼	IB	▼▼	231.9	−35	4.75	1.1†	6.1	1.8	6.2	6.3	6.6	
GT GLOBAL HIGH-INCOME B		IB		268.5	20	5.00**	2.4†	35.9	9.2		7.1	11.8	
GT GLOBAL STRATEGIC INCOME B		IB		336.8	−7	5.00**	2.1†	20.3	3.3		6.3	12.8	
HANCOCK GOVERNMENT INCOME A		GI		386.1	−18	4.50	1.2†	2.2			7.1	9.4	
HANCOCK HIGH-YIELD BOND B	▲▲	HY	▼	280.2	49	5.00**	1.9†	15.2	7.4	11.2	9.4	6.4	
HANCOCK LIMITED-TERM GOVT. A	AVG	GS	▼	176.0	−11	3.00	1.4†	3.4	4.3	4.9	5.8	3.8	
HANCOCK SOVEREIGN BOND A	AVG	CI	AVG	1416.1	−8	4.50	1.1†	4.1	6.5	7.8	7.3	13.8	
HANCOCK SOVEREIGN U.S. GOVT. A		GL		324.4	−14	4.50	1.2†	1.4	4.8		6.7	9.1	
HANCOCK STRATEGIC INCOME A	▲▲	MU	▲▲	407.3	15	4.50	1.0†	11.7	8.7	9.5	8.6	8.3	
HARBOR BOND	▲	CI	▲▲	288.3	24	No load	0.7	4.9	6.4	8.1	6.2	10.3	
HARBOR SHORT DURATION	▲	CS	▲▲▲	177.3	46	No load	1.8	6.3	5.5	5.1	8.1	1.3	
HOMESTEAD SHORT-TERM BOND	▲	CS	▲	79.7	28	No load	0.8	5.2	5.3	5.8	5.7	2.9	
HOTCHKIS & WILEY LOW DURATION		CS		170.3	8	No load	0.6	5.8	7.9		6.2	2.9	
HSBC FIXED-INCOME (dd)		CL		104.9	20	4.75	0.9†	2.1	5.3		5.9	14.0	
IAI BOND	▼	CI	▼▼	82.5	5	No load	1.1	4.1	4.8	6.7	5.5	14.9	
IDS BOND A	▲	CI	▲▲	2637.8	3	5.00	0.8	5.0	7.0	9.4	6.9	7.7	
IDS EXTRA INCOME A	▲▲	HY	▼	2413.3	25	5.00	0.9	14.4	8.8	13.0	9.1	7.6	
IDS FEDERAL INCOME A	AVG	GS	AVG	1168.2	8	5.00	0.9	4.2	5.8	6.0	6.3	8.5	
IDS GLOBAL BOND A	AVG	IB	▲	714.3	22	5.00	1.3	7.7	6.9	9.3	5.2	10.3	
IDS SELECTIVE A	AVG	CI	▼	1372.7	−9	5.00	0.9	2.6	5.9	7.9	6.5	7.3	
INTERMEDIATE BOND FUND OF AMERICA	▼	CI	▼▼	1416.0	−8	4.75	0.8†	4.2	4.8	6.0	6.5	4.4	
INVESCO HIGH-YIELD	▲▲	HY		437.9	27	No load	0.9	14.1	8.5	11.1	8.6	7.8	

*Includes redemption fee. **Includes deferred sales charge. †12(b)-1 plan in effect. ‡Not currently accepting new accounts or deposits. NA=Not available. NM=Not meaningful.
(u) Formerly Limited Term A. (v) Formerly Strategic Income B. (w) Formerly Fidelity Advisor Emerging Mkts. Inc. A. (x) Formerly Fidelity Advisor Govt. Investment A. (y) Formerly Fidelity Advisor High-Yield A. (z) Formerly Fidelity Advisor Limited-Term Bond A. (aa) Formerly Fidelity Advisor Short Fixed-Income A. (bb) Formerly Fidelity Advisor Strategic Income A. (cc) Formerly Fidelity Spartan Short-Term Income. (dd) Formerly Mariner Fixed-Income.

DATA: MORNINGSTAR, INC., CHICAGO, IL.

FUND	OVERALL RATING	CATEGORY	RATING	ASSETS $MIL.	% CHG. 1995-96	SALES CHARGE (%)	EXPENSE RATIO (%)	1 YR.	3 YR.	5 YR.	YIELD (%)	MATURITY (YEARS)
INVESCO SELECT INCOME	▲▲	CL	▲▲▲	269.7	3	No load	1.0†	4.9	7.7	9.0	7.1	9.8
INVESTORS TRUST GOVERNMENT B	▼▼▼	GI	▼▼▼	702.0	-35	5.00**	1.8†	2.1	1.7	3.7	6.4	8.2
ISI TOTAL RETURN U.S. TREAS.	▼▼	GL	▲	188.1	-10	4.45	0.8†	0.2	5.4	6.8	6.5	13.9
IVY BOND A	AVG	CI	▲	97.2	-8	4.75	1.5†	8.1	6.6	8.5	7.5	13.0
JANUS FLEXIBLE INCOME	▲▲	MU	▲▲	625.0	1	No load	0.9	6.4	7.8	10.1	NA	7.5
JANUS HIGH-YIELD		HY		238.2	NM	No load	1.0	24.1			8.7	6.9
KEMPER ADJ. RATE U.S. GOVT. A	AVG	GS	AVG	84.8	-32	3.50	1.2†	4.7	4.2	4.7	5.3	3.8
KEMPER DIVERSIFIED INCOME A	▲▲	MU	▲▲▲	520.7	3	4.50	1.1†	8.6	7.8	12.2	8.3	9.2
KEMPER GLOBAL INCOME A	▼	IB	AVG	86.3	-16	4.50	1.3†	5.9	7.7	6.2	6.5	6.8
KEMPER HIGH-YIELD A	▲▲▲	HY	AVG	3032.2	18	4.50	0.9†	13.5	9.4	13.0	9.5	7.7
KEMPER INC. & CAPITAL PRESERV. A	AVG	CI	AVG	494.0	-11	4.50	0.9†	2.0	6.2	7.6	6.9	13.6
KEMPER SHORT-INTERM GOVT. B	▼	GS	▼▼▼	156.5	-22	4.00**	2.0†	2.2	3.4	4.1	5.9	2.3
KEMPER U.S. GOVT. SEC. A	▼	GI	AVG	3966.2	-15	4.50	0.7†	2.8	5.7	5.6	7.4	8.9
KEMPER U.S. MORTGAGE A		GI		1868.8	-10	4.50	1.0†	2.7	5.4		7.4	8.9
KEYSTONE DIVERSIFIED BOND (B-2)	▲	CI	▲	547.7	-25	4.00**	1.8†	6.2	4.3	7.2	6.7	13.3
KEYSTONE HIGH-INCOME (B-4)	▲	HY	▼▼▼	590.5	-13	4.00**	1.9†	10.6	2.2	9.7	8.3	8.4
KEYSTONE QUALITY BOND (B-1)	▼▼	CL	▼▼	215.2	-30	4.00**	1.9†	1.7	4.0	4.9	5.2	10.9
KEYSTONE STRATEGIC INCOME B		MU		121.5	-16	5.00**	2.1†	10.1	2.8		7.1	10.0
KIEWIT INTERMEDIATE-TERM BOND		CI		117.4	-8	No load	0.5	3.4			6.2	6.4
KIEWIT SHORT-TERM GOVERNMENT		GS		140.7	-10	No load	0.3	4.5			5.9	NA
LEGG MASON GLOBAL GOVT. PRIM.		IB		161.2	5	No load	1.8†	8.2	8.8		5.9	7.7
LEGG MASON HIGH-YIELD PRIM.		HY		232.9	116	No load	1.5†	14.9			8.7	7.6
LEGG MASON INVESTMENT GRADE PRIM.	AVG	CI	AVG	91.7	8	No load	0.9†	4.3	6.1	7.2	6.3	9.0
LEGG MASON U.S. GOVT. I/T PRIM.	AVG	GS	▲	294.6	27	No load	0.9†	4.5	5.4	5.8	5.9	5.8
LEXINGTON GNMA INCOME	▲	GI	▲▲▲	133.7	2	No load	1.0	5.7	6.3	6.4	7.4	13.0
LOOMIS SAYLES BOND	▲▲▲	CL	▲▲▲	538.2	113	No load	0.8	10.3	11.8	14.3	6.8	19.1
LORD ABBETT BOND-DEBENTURE A	▲▲	HY	▼▼	1744.4	30	4.75	0.8†	11.2	7.9	11.1	9.2	9.1
LORD ABBETT GLOBAL INCOME A	▼	IB	AVG	194.7	-18	4.75	1.0†	6.2	6.6	7.2	7.3	NA
LORD ABBETT U.S. GOVT. SEC. A	▼▼▼	GI	▼▼	2528.4	-24	4.75	0.9†	1.7	4.0	5.6	8.1	9.4
MAINSTAY CONVERTIBLE B	▲▲	CV	▲	796.9	87	5.00**	2.1†	11.4	10.6	13.7	3.7	6.1
MAINSTAY GOVERNMENT B	▼▼	GI		783.5	-21	5.00**	1.7†	1.3	4.4	4.6	5.8	9.0
MAINSTAY HI-YIELD CORP. BOND B	▲▲▲	HY	▲▲▲	2439.4	52	5.00**	1.6†	15.6	12.0	15.8	7.9	5.6
MARKETWATCH INTERM. FIXED-INCOME		CI		99.2	173	4.50	1.1†	2.0	4.3		5.6	7.6
MARQUIS GOVT SECURITIES A		GI		160.3	12	3.50	0.7	3.7	5.1		5.6	7.7
MARSHALL GOVERNMENT INCOME		GI		157.2	37	No load	0.9	3.0	5.4		6.5	4.1
MARSHALL INTERMEDIATE BOND		CI		431.6	21	No load	0.7	2.4	4.7		6.0	4.1
MARSHALL SHORT-TERM INCOME		CS		104.0	19	No load	0.5	5.0	5.2		6.4	2.0
MERRILL LYNCH ADJ. RATE SEC. B	AVG	GS	▲	118.8	15	4.00**	1.6†	6.2	4.7	3.9	5.3	3.9
MERRILL LYNCH AMERICAS INCOME B		IB		163.4	58	4.00**	2.1†	33.8	12.7		8.2	NA
MERRILL LYNCH CORP. HIGH-INCOME B	▲▲▲	HY	▲	4528.6	30	4.00**	1.3†	11.6	8.1	12.0	8.6	6.3
MERRILL LYNCH CORP. INTERM.-TERM B		CI		213.1	-7	1.00**	1.1†	2.4	4.9		5.9	5.2
MERRILL LYNCH CORP. INVMT. GRADE B	▼	CI	▼▼▼	713.3	4	4.00**	1.3†	1.4	4.4	6.2	5.9	9.9
MERRILL LYNCH FEDERAL SEC. D		GI	AVG	951.3	-1	4.00	0.9†	4.6	5.2	5.7	6.4	7.0
MERRILL LYNCH GLOBAL BOND B	▼	IB	AVG	347.5	-36	4.00**	1.6†	5.6	3.7	5.8	5.1	NA
MERRILL LYNCH S/T GLOBAL INCOME B	▼▼▼	CS	▼▼	239.4	-36	4.00**	1.7†	4.5	2.4	2.0	5.6	NA
MERRILL LYNCH WORLD INCOME B	▲	MU	▼	988.2	-20	4.00**	1.6†	10.2	6.3	7.3	6.8	NA
MFS BOND A	AVG	CI	AVG	560.2	5	4.75	1.0†	3.9	6.5	7.9	7.1	10.0
MFS GOVERNMENT LTD. MATURITY A	AVG	GS	▼	225.8	-9	2.50	0.9†	2.9	4.1	5.1	6.2	1.9
MFS GOVERNMENT MORTGAGE A	▼	GI	AVG	523.5	-10	4.75	1.2†	3.2	5.5	5.8	6.5	7.8
MFS GOVERNMENT SECURITIES A	▼	GI	AVG	300.2	-11	4.75	0.8†	0.8	5.2	6.5	6.5	8.0
MFS HIGH-INCOME A	▲▲	HY	AVG	643.3	8	4.75	1.0†	12.6	8.7	12.4	8.7	7.8
MFS INTERMEDIATE INCOME B	▼▼	MU	▼▼	166.3	-28	4.00**	2.2†	3.8	3.8	4.6	5.4	5.8
MFS LIMITED MATURITY A		CS		98.9	2	2.50	1.0†	4.9	5.5		7.1	3.0
MFS WORLD GOVERNMENTS A	▼▼	IB		271.3	-20	4.75	1.5†	5.4	4.4	6.4	2.2	5.3
NATIONWIDE BOND	▼▼▼	CL	▼▼▼	130.5	-6	4.50	0.7	1.5	5.1	6.8	6.6	10.9
NEUBERGER & BERMAN LTD. MAT.	AVG	CS	AVG	239.6	-21	No load	0.7	4.5	4.8	5.3	6.1	3.3
NEUBERGER & BERMAN ULTRA SHORT	▲	UB		82.4	-15	No load	0.7	4.8	4.6	4.1	5.6	1.7
NEW ENGLAND ADJ. RATE U.S. GOVT. A	▲	GS	▲▲▲	223.1	-32	1.00	0.7†	5.8	5.0	4.8	5.7	2.5
NEW ENGLAND BOND INCOME A	AVG	CI	▼	190.0	-5	4.50	1.1†	4.6	6.6	7.8	7.0	11.0
NEW ENGLAND GOVT. SEC. A	▼▼	GI	▼▼	121.5	-18	4.50	1.4†	0.8	4.6	5.9	6.5	10.3
NEW ENGLAND LTD.-TERM U.S. GOVT. A	▼	GS	▼▼▼	275.8	-24	3.00	1.2†	4.4	4.2	4.9	7.1	5.1
NEW ENGLAND STRATEGIC INCOME B		MU		92.8	139	4.00**	1.7†	13.7			7.0	19.2
NICHOLAS INCOME	▲▲	HY	AVG	185.7	15	No load	0.6	12.4	9.2	10.2	8.4	6.5
NORTHEAST INVESTORS	▲▲▲	HY	▲▲▲	1354.8	68	No load	1.0	20.2	12.9	15.9	9.0	7.3
NORTHERN FIXED-INCOME		CI		114.5	20	No load	0.9	2.6			5.5	12.0
NORTHERN U.S. GOVERNMENT		GS		171.7	20	No load	0.9	3.1			5.0	NA
NORTHSTAR GOVT. SECURITIES T (ee)	▼▼	GL	AVG	112.2	-26	4.00**‡	1.3†	0.3	3.6	7.7	6.3	25.9
NORTHSTAR HIGH TOTAL RETURN B (ff)		HY		401.8	228	5.00**	2.3†	15.1			9.3	NA
NORTHSTAR HIGH-YIELD T (gg)	▲▲▲	HY	▲▲	124.7	-11	4.00**‡	1.3†	14.5	8.4	14.1	9.0	7.1
111 CORCORAN BOND		GI		89.2	-1	4.50	0.9	3.9	5.9		6.6	5.8

*Includes redemption fee. **Includes deferred sales charge. †12(b)-1 plan in effect. ‡Not currently accepting new accounts or deposits. NA=Not available. NM=Not meaningful.
(ee) Formerly Northstar Advantage Government Sec. T. (ff) Formerly Northstar Advantage High Total Ret. B. (gg) Formerly Northstar Advantage High-Yield T.

DATA: MORNINGSTAR, INC., CHICAGO, IL.

MUTUAL FUND SCOREBOARD — Bond Funds

FUND	OVERALL RATING	CATEGORY	RATING	ASSETS $MIL.	% CHG. 1995-96	SALES CHARGE (%)	EXPENSE RATIO (%)	1 YR.	3 YR.	5 YR.	YIELD (%)	MATURITY (YEARS)
OPPENHEIMER BOND A	▼	CI	▼	192.2	14	4.75	1.3†	4.9	5.6	6.8	7.3	NA
OPPENHEIMER BOND FOR GROWTH M (hh)	▲▲▲	CV	▲▲▲	266.1	12	3.25	1.6†	9.6	10.9	16.8	4.5	6.5
OPPENHEIMER CHAMPION INCOME A	▲▲▲	HY		389.6	39	4.75	1.2†	13.4	9.1	12.9	8.7	NA
OPPENHEIMER HIGH-YIELD A	▲▲	HY	AVG	1142.1	3	4.75	1.0†	14.3	8.7	12.0	9.0	9.4
OPPENHEIMER LTD.-TERM GOVT. A	AVG	GS	AVG	433.2	16	3.50	0.9†	4.9	5.2	5.6	6.9	2.8
OPPENHEIMER STRATEGIC INCOME A	▲	MU	▲	3667.1	12	4.75	1.0†	12.6	7.5	9.8	8.6	4.5
OPPENHEIMER U.S. GOVT. A	AVG	GI	▲	481.2	–8	4.75	1.1†	4.3	5.8	6.1	7.1	5.0
OVERLAND EXPRESS U.S. GOVT. INC. A	▼▼	GI	▼▼	77.2	153	4.50	0.9†	–0.1	4.3	5.8	6.2	11.1
OVERLAND EXPRESS VAR. RATE GOVT. A		GS	▼▼	394.0	–40	3.00	0.8†	4.4	2.7	3.4	5.4	1.4
PACIFIC HORIZON CAPITAL INCOME A	▲▲	CV	▲▲	290.8	24	4.50	1.2	19.5	11.8	15.8	3.2	9.1
PACIFIC HORIZON U.S. GOVT. A	▼	GI	AVG	77.3	–16	4.50	1.2	4.2	4.2	5.4	6.4	NA
PAINEWEBBER GLOBAL INCOME A	▼	IB	▲	540.1	–14	4.00	1.3†	7.1	5.3	6.2	6.8	5.0
PAINEWEBBER HIGH-INCOME A	▲▲	HY	▼▼▼	243.4	4	4.00	0.9†	17.3	4.7	11.8	9.1	7.3
PAINEWEBBER INVMT. GRADE INC. A	AVG	CL	▲	223.4	–14	4.00	1.0†	3.7	5.4	7.6	6.7	15.2
PAINEWEBBER LOW DUR. U.S. GOVT. C		GS		117.6	–32	0.75**	1.8†	4.7	3.1		5.0	23.0
PAINEWEBBER U.S. GOVT. INC. A	▼▼▼	GI	▼▼▼	330.7	–23	4.00	1.0†	0.7	1.8	3.6	6.0	14.2
PAYDEN & RYGEL GLOBAL F/I A		IB		658.6	13	No load	0.5	5.8	6.6		7.5	5.8
PAYDEN & RYGEL SHORT BOND A		CS		107.1	446	No load	0.4	3.7	5.1		5.4	1.8
PERMANENT PORTFOLIO TREASURY BILL	▲	UB		106.3	–8	No load	0.8	4.3	4.2	3.5	4.7	0.2
PHOENIX CONVERTIBLE A	▼	CV	AVG	207.8	–8	4.75	1.2†	11.2	9.2	10.1	3.6	NA
PHOENIX HIGH-YIELD A	▲▲	HY	▼▼	525.4	4	4.75	1.2†	17.2	8.3	12.5	8.8	8.1
PHOENIX MULTI-SECTOR FIXED-INC. A	▲	MU		175.7	4	4.75	1.1†	13.6	8.3	10.5	7.0	10.3
PHOENIX U.S. GOVT. SEC. A	▼	GI	AVG	203.0	–15	4.75	1.0†	1.9	4.9	6.1	5.3	8.5
PIONEER AMERICA INCOME A	▼	GI	AVG	144.7	–11	4.50	1.0†	2.3	4.5	5.8	6.6	7.7
PIONEER BOND A	▼	CI		99.8	–9	4.50	1.2†	1.9	4.9	6.8	7.0	13.4
PIPER ADJ. RATE MORTGAGE SEC.		UB		234.4	–46	1.50	0.6†	6.8	0.4		5.8	NA
PIPER GOVERNMENT INCOME	▼▼▼	GI	▼▼▼	80.0	–22	4.00	1.1†	4.2	4.3	5.5	6.6	NA
PIPER INTERMEDIATE BOND (ii)	▼▼▼	GI	▼▼▼	117.5	–59	2.00‡	1.0†	4.3	–2.7	3.7	8.7	25.6
PREFERRED FIXED-INCOME		CI		131.1	101	No load	0.9	3.0	5.8		5.8	12.7
PREMIER GNMA A	AVG	GI	▲	111.6	–17	4.50	1.0	4.3	5.3	6.1	6.2	NA
T. ROWE PRICE GNMA	AVG	GI	▲▲	927.6	3	No load	0.8	3.1	6.1	6.2	7.0	8.7
T. ROWE PRICE HIGH-YIELD	▲▲	HY	▼▼	1325.2	8	1.00*	0.9	11.6	5.9	10.7	9.0	7.7
T. ROWE PRICE INTL. BOND	AVG	IB	AVG	969.5	–5	No load	0.9	7.1	8.2	9.2	5.7	7.5
T. ROWE PRICE NEW INCOME	AVG	CI	AVG	1688.3	1	No load	0.8	2.4	5.8	6.3	6.7	9.3
T. ROWE PRICE SHORT-TERM BOND	AVG	CS	▼▼	446.9	–4	No load	0.7	3.9	3.4	4.4	6.0	2.3
T. ROWE PRICE SHORT-TERM U.S.	AVG	GS	AVG	95.8	–9	No load	0.7	4.3	4.8	4.2	5.9	2.8
T. ROWE PRICE SPECTRUM INCOME	▲▲	CI	▲▲▲	1356.0	37	No load	0.0	7.7	8.0	8.9	6.3	8.2
T. ROWE PRICE U.S. TREAS. INTERM.	AVG	GI	AVG	193.6	6	No load	0.7	2.4	5.1	5.9	6.2	4.7
PRINCOR BOND A	▼	CL	AVG	113.1	3	4.75	1.0†	2.3	6.2	7.9	6.8	10.6
PRINCOR GOVT. SEC. INCOME A	▼▼	GI	▼	256.4	–4	4.75	0.8†	3.9	5.6	6.4	6.3	9.6
PRUDENTIAL DIVERSIFIED BOND B		CI		136.0	60	5.00**	1.5†	5.2			6.3	11.6
PRUDENTIAL GLOBAL LTD. MAT. A	▼▼	IB	▼	81.5	125	3.00	1.2†	12.5	5.3	4.8	6.2	3.4
PRUDENTIAL GOVT. INCOME A	▼	GI		890.6	–5	4.00	1.0†	1.4	5.2	6.1	6.7	8.7
PRUDENTIAL GOVT. SHORT-INTERM. TERM	AVG	GS	▼	180.9	–14	No load	1.0†	3.9	4.6	5.4	5.5	4.6
PRUDENTIAL HIGH-YIELD B	▲▲	HY	▼	2597.8	–4	5.00**	1.4†	12.0	8.4	11.5	8.7	8.1
PRUDENTIAL INTERM. GLOBAL INCOME A	▲	IB	▲▲▲	166.0	–9	3.00	1.4†	11.0	8.4	8.9	5.9	6.6
PRUDENTIAL MORTGAGE INCOME B	▼	GI	AVG	96.0	–24	5.00**	1.9†	3.4	4.9	5.0	5.7	7.7
PRUDENTIAL STRUCT. MATURITY B		CS		94.5	–21	3.00**	1.5†	3.7	4.5		6.0	3.2
PUTNAM AMERICAN GOVT. INC. A	▼	GI		1742.3	–20	4.75	0.9†	2.3	5.5	5.7	6.3	9.0
PUTNAM CONVERT. INCOME-GROWTH A	▲▲▲	CV	▲▲	940.1	19	5.75	1.2†	17.8	12.7	15.2	4.4	7.8
PUTNAM DIVERSIFIED INCOME B		MU		2230.6	16	5.00**	1.8†	8.1	6.1		6.4	7.9
PUTNAM FEDERAL INCOME A	▼▼	GI	▼▼	370.4	–14	4.75	1.1†	2.0	5.5	5.5	6.0	9.7
PUTNAM GLOBAL GOVERNMENTAL INC. A	▼▼▼	IB	▼	340.3	–8	4.75	1.3†	9.5	4.6	6.3	7.1	11.0
PUTNAM HIGH YIELD ADVANTAGE A	▲▲	HY	▼	1094.4	23	4.75	1.1†	10.6	7.6	12.3	9.2	7.0
PUTNAM HIGH YIELD A		HY	AVG	3263.2	7	4.75‡	1.0†	12.7	8.2	12.4	9.1	7.2
PUTNAM INCOME A	▲	CI	▲	1049.9	9	4.75	1.1†	4.0	6.4	8.2	6.5	9.7
PUTNAM INTERM. U.S. GOVT. INC. A		GI		141.8	144	3.25	1.2†	3.7	5.6		5.9	6.1
PUTNAM U.S. GOVT. INCOME A	▼	GI	▲	2395.1	–18	4.75	0.9†	3.9	5.6	5.8	6.5	7.0
SALOMON BROS. HIGH-YIELD BOND B		HY		105.8	946	5.00**	2.0†	21.2			9.0	11.3
SCHWAB SHORT/INTERM. GOVT. BOND	AVG	GS	▼	131.5	–16	No load	0.5	4.0	3.9	5.1	6.1	2.6
SCOUT BOND	AVG	CI	AVG	79.8	1	No load	0.9	3.5	4.6	5.7	5.6	4.1
SCUDDER EMERGING MKTS. INCOME		IB		323.5	71	No load	1.4	34.6	13.9		8.9	NA
SCUDDER GLOBAL BOND	▼	IB	AVG	201.6	–40	No load	1.0	3.1	3.2	4.3	6.2	9.0
SCUDDER GNMA	AVG	GI	▲▲	402.9	–8	No load	0.9	4.2	5.6	5.9	6.4	8.2
SCUDDER INCOME	AVG	CI	AVG	580.4	0	No load	1.0	3.4	5.4	7.1	6.1	10.0
SCUDDER INTERNATIONAL BOND	▼▼▼	IB		359.6	–51	No load	1.3	3.5	0.9	5.1	5.8	9.0
SCUDDER SHORT-TERM BOND	AVG	CS	▼	1466.1	–19	No load	0.8	3.9	3.8	4.9	6.5	2.5
SELIGMAN HIGH-YIELD BOND A	▲▲▲	HY	▲▲▲	408.3	124	4.75	1.1†	15.0	11.8	14.9	9.6	8.5
SENTINEL BOND A	▼	CI	▼▼	97.0	–12	4.00	1.0†	1.9	5.1	7.1	6.6	6.9
SENTINEL GOVERNMENT SEC.	▼	GI		89.8	–18	4.00	1.0†	0.8	4.7	6.1	6.1	6.3

*Includes redemption fee. **Includes deferred sales charge. †12(b)-1 plan in effect. ‡Not currently accepting new accounts or deposits. NA=Not available. NM=Not meaningful. (hh) Formerly Bond Fund for Growth A. (ii) Formerly Piper Inst. Government Income.

DATA: MORNINGSTAR, INC., CHICAGO, IL.

MUTUAL FUND SCOREBOARD — Bond Funds

FUND	OVERALL RATING	CATEGORY	RATING	ASSETS $MIL.	% CHG. 1995-96	SALES CHARGE (%)	EXPENSE RATIO (%)	1 YR.	3 YR.	5 YR.	YIELD (%)	MATURITY (YEARS)	TREND 5-YEAR ANALYSIS
1784 INCOME		CI		321.6	52	No load	0.8†	2.7			6.2	11.4	
1784 SHORT-TERM INCOME		CS		145.2	93	No load	0.6†	4.3			5.8	4.0	
1784 U.S. GOVT. MED.-TERM INC.		GI		196.8	25	No load	0.8†	2.1	4.4		6.3	8.3	
SIERRA CORPORATE INCOME A	▼▼	CL	▼	248.2	−31	4.50	0.9†	0.7	4.7	7.9	7.3	19.6	
SIERRA U.S. GOVERNMENT A	▼	GI	▼	321.5	−27	4.50	1.0†	3.7	4.4	5.2	6.9	8.7	
SMITH BARNEY ADJ. RATE GOVT. A		GS		143.9	−16	4.50	1.6†	5.2	5.1		5.4	NA	
SMITH BARNEY DIVERS. STRAT. INC. B	▲	MU	AVG	2461.6	2	4.50**	1.5†	9.9	6.9	7.9	7.7	NA	
SMITH BARNEY GOVT. SEC. A		GI		388.7	−13	4.50	0.9†	1.8	3.8		6.4	7.5	
SMITH BARNEY HIGH-INCOME B	▲▲	HY	AVG	622.4	19	4.50**	1.6†	12.4	7.8	12.3	8.9	7.1	
SMITH BARNEY INVMT. GR. BOND B	▼▼	CL	▼▼	258.4	−11	4.50**	1.6†	−1	6.5	9.1	6.1	NA	
SMITH BARNEY MANAGED GOVT.	▼	GI	AVG	437.0	−15	4.50	1.0†	3.6	4.9	6.0	6.9	NA	
SMITH BARNEY SHORT-TERM U.S. A		GS	▼▼	83.2	−22	No load	1.0†	2.0	4.3	5.0	5.4	NA	
SMITH BARNEY U.S. GOVT. SEC. A	▼	GI	▲	312.5	−19	4.50	0.8†	4.0	6.1	6.3	6.5	NA	
SMITH BARNEY GLOBAL GOVT. A	▼	IB	AVG	103.2	−14	4.50	1.3†	7.5	6.0	7.4	10.1	NA	
SMITH BREEDEN SHORT DUR. GOVT. SER.		UB		188.7	−20	No load	0.8	6.3	5.5		5.6	0.5	
SOUTHTRUST VULCAN BOND		CI		89.8	7	3.50	0.9	2.4	4.2		5.8	8.6	
SSGA YIELD PLUS (jj)		UB		1001.9	−27	No load	0.4†	5.5	5.4		5.5	0.2	
STAGECOACH GINNIE MAE A	▼	GI	AVG	142.3	−14	4.50	0.8†	3.0	5.4	6.1	6.9	NA	
STAGECOACH U.S. GOVT. ALLOC. A	▼▼	GI	▼	95.7	−29	4.50	1.1†	3.5	3.4	6.7	5.4	6.0	
STAR STRATEGIC INCOME		MU		112.8	118	5.00**	NA†	5.3			7.0	NA	
STAR U.S. GOVERNMENT INCOME		GI		138.7	26	3.50	0.9†	1.7	4.4		5.9	NA	
STATE ST. RESEARCH GOVT. A	AVG	GI	▲	568.6	−13	4.50	1.1†	3.2	5.6	6.7	6.4	7.5	
STATE ST. RESEARCH HIGH-INC. A	▲▲▲	HY	▲▲	672.4	8	4.50	1.2†	16.9	8.8	13.7	8.7	8.6	
STEIN ROE INCOME	▲	CI	▲▲	337.7	63	No load	0.8	4.9	6.5	8.4	7.2	7.0	
STEIN ROE INTERMEDIATE BOND	AVG	CI	▲	312.5	0	No load	0.7	4.6	6.0	7.0	6.9	5.8	
STRONG ADVANTAGE	▲▲	UB		1417.1	43	No load	0.8	6.7	5.9	6.8	6.2	1.0	
STRONG CORPORATE BOND	▲▲	CI	▲▲▲	305.3	18	No load	1.0	5.5	9.3	10.8	6.7	11.8	
STRONG GOVERNMENT SECURITIES	▲	CI	▲	659.9	31	No load	0.9	2.8	6.0	8.0	6.0	8.2	
STRONG HIGH-YIELD BOND		HY		282.5	NM	No load	NA	26.9			8.8	6.5	
STRONG SHORT-TERM BOND	▲	CS	▲▲▲	1181.0	7	No load	0.9	6.8	5.5	6.5	7.0	2.0	
STRONG SHORT-TERM GLOBAL BOND		MU		77.6	210	No load	0.0	10.0			6.8	2.1	
SUNAMERICA DIVERSIFIED INCOME B	▼▼	CI	▼▼▼	91.5	−22	4.00**	2.1†	12.4	4.7	5.3	7.7	6.1	
SUNAMERICA HIGH-INCOME B		HY		109.6	−9	4.00**	2.1†	14.8	5.4		8.5	7.2	
SUNAMERICA U.S. GOVT. SEC. B	AVG	GI	▲▲	345.9	−31	4.00**	2.1†	2.3	5.1	4.9	5.1	NA	
TCW/DW NORTH AMERICA GOVT. INC.		IB		314.3	−49	No load	1.6†	4.0	0.6		5.3	NA	
TEMPLETON GLOBAL BOND I (kk)	AVG	IB	▲	195.2	0	4.25	1.1†	11.2	8.2	7.6	5.9	4.9	
THORNBURG LTD.-TERM U.S. A	AVG	GS	AVG	139.5	−2	2.50	1.0†	4.3	4.9	5.6	6.2	3.7	
U.S. GOVERNMENT SECURITIES	▼	GI	AVG	1192.0	−12	4.75	0.8†	2.8	4.2	6.1	7.0	7.7	
UNITED BOND A	▼	CI	▼▼▼	518.9	−8	5.75	0.7†	3.2	5.4	7.4	6.3	9.7	
UNITED GOVERNMENT SEC. A	▼▼	GI		135.3	−13	4.25	0.8†	1.8	5.3	6.6	6.2	10.1	
UNITED HIGH-INCOME A	▲▲	HY	▼	996.8	2	5.75	0.9†	11.9	8.3	11.8	8.4	6.6	
UNITED HIGH-INCOME II A	▲▲	HY	▼▼	373.8	1	5.75	1.0†	12.0	7.9	11.3	8.5	6.7	
USAA GNMA	AVG	GI	▲▲	307.0	3	No load	0.3	2.9	6.3	6.4	6.9	NA	
USAA INCOME	▼	CL	AVG	1785.0	−6	No load	0.4	1.3	6.1	7.3	6.3	13.6	
USAA SHORT-TERM BOND		CS		111.6	22	No load	0.5	5.6	5.7		6.1	2.8	
VALUE LINE U.S. GOVERNMENT	▼▼▼	GI	▼▼	203.7	−18	No load	0.7	3.9	2.0	4.4	7.0	6.9	
VAN KAMPEN AMER. CAP. CORP. BD. A	AVG	CI	▼	167.3	−4	4.75	1.1†	2.7	6.0	7.6	7.0	14.2	
VAN KAMPEN AMER. CAP. GL. GOVT. B	▼▼▼	IB	▼▼	86.5	−21	4.00**	2.3†	2.2	2.5	4.3	5.9	6.6	
VAN KAMPEN AMER. CAP. GOVT. SEC. A	▼▼	GI	▼	2175.4	−15	4.75	1.0†	1.9	4.4	5.6	6.9	7.7	
VAN KAMPEN AMER. CAP. HARBOR A	AVG	CV	▼▼	373.1	−5	5.75	1.0†	12.1	8.7	9.9	3.4	NA	
VAN KAMPEN AMER. CAP. HI-INC. A	▲▲	HY	AVG	437.4	5	4.75	1.1†	13.7	8.8	12.5	9.6	6.8	
VAN KAMPEN AMER. CAP. HI-YIELD A	▲▲	HY	▼	280.8	5	4.75	1.3†	12.5	8.5	12.0	9.1	19.2	
VAN KAMPEN AMER. CAP. U.S. GOVT. A	▼▼	GI	AVG	2553.0	−14	4.75	1.2†	4.1	5.1	5.9	7.4	7.0	
VAN KAMPEN AMER. CAP. U.S. GOVT. INC.		GI		143.8	−25	4.00**	1.9†	1.5	3.5		6.1	NA	
VANGUARD BOND INDEX INTERM.-TERM		CI		457.2	32	No load	0.2	2.6			6.5	10.5	
VANGUARD BOND INDEX SHORT-TERM		CS		326.8	57	No load	0.2	4.6			5.9	4.4	
VANGUARD BOND INDEX TOTAL	AVG	CI	▲	2952.8	23	No load	0.2	3.6	6.0	7.0	6.3	6.8	
VANGUARD CONVERTIBLE SEC.	AVG	CV	▼	166.1	−1	No load	0.8	15.4	8.3	11.4	3.6	NA	
VANGUARD FIXED-INCOME GNMA	▲	GI	▲▲▲	7398.8	7	No load	0.3	5.2	6.9	6.7	7.1	7.9	
VANGUARD F/I HIGH-YIELD CORP.	▲▲	HY	AVG	3563.5	23	1.00*	0.3	9.6	8.7	11.6	8.7	8.0	
VANGUARD F/I INTERM.-TERM CORP.		CI		616.8	71	No load	0.3	2.8	6.1		6.5	7.2	
VANGUARD F/I INTERM.-TERM U.S.	▼	GI		1270.4	6	No load	0.3	1.9	5.5	7.1	6.2	7.5	
VANGUARD F/I L/T CORP. BOND	AVG	CL	▲	3412.0	2	No load	0.3	1.2	6.6	8.8	6.9	20.0	
VANGUARD F/I L/T U.S. TREAS.	▼▼	GL	▲▲	918.0	0	No load	0.3	−1.3	6.1	8.4	6.6	21.0	
VANGUARD F/I SHORT-TERM CORP.	▲	CS	▲▲	4587.5	23	No load	0.3	4.8	5.7	6.3	6.2	2.4	
VANGUARD F/I SHORT-TERM FED.	▲	GS	▲▲	1339.2	−5	No load	0.3	4.8	5.2	5.8	6.0	2.3	
VANGUARD F/I SHORT-TERM U.S TREAS.	▲	GS	▲▲	965.8	11	No load	0.3	4.4	5.2	5.7	5.8	2.4	
VANGUARD PREFERRED STOCK	▲	CL	▲▲	297.5	−4	No load	0.4	8.5	7.9	9.0	6.8	NA	
VICTORY GOVERNMENT MORTGAGE	▼	GI	AVG	122.5	−9	4.75	0.8	4.2	5.5	6.2	6.2	16.4	
VICTORY INTERMEDIATE INCOME		CS		269.2	57	4.75	0.8	3.1	4.7		5.7	5.9	

*Includes redemption fee. **Includes deferred sales charge. †12(b)-1 plan in effect. ‡Not currently accepting new accounts or deposits. NA=Not available. NM=Not meaningful.
(jj) Formerly Seven Seas Yield Plus. (kk) Formerly Templeton Income I.

DATA: MORNINGSTAR, INC., CHICAGO, IL.

MUTUAL FUND SCOREBOARD — Bond Funds

FUND	OVERALL RATING	CATEGORY	RATING	ASSETS $MIL.	% CHG. 1995-96	SALES CHARGE (%)	EXPENSE RATIO (%)	1 YR.	3 YR.	5 YR.	YIELD (%)	MATURITY (YEARS)
VICTORY INVESTMENT QUALITY BOND		CI		153.9	21	4.75	0.9	2.5	5.2		5.9	7.3
VICTORY LIMITED-TERM INCOME	AVG	CS	▼	89.4	−48	2.00	0.8	4.0	4.5	5.0	6.2	2.0
VIRTUS U.S. GOVT. SEC. INVMT.	▼	GS	▼▼	116.2	−4	2.00**	1.0†	2.6	4.2	5.2	6.1	4.7
VISTA U.S. TREASURY INCOME A (ll)	▼▼	GI		103.4	0	4.50	0.9†	1.3	4.4	5.8	5.9	8.7
WARBURG PINCUS FIXED-INCOME	▲	CI	▲▲	158.1	31	No load	0.8	6.2	6.7	7.6	6.3	5.9
WARBURG PINCUS GLOBAL FIXED INC.	▲	IB	▲▲	142.5	78	No load	1.0	10.0	6.4	8.1	8.5	5.9
WESTERN ASSET INTL. SEC.		IB		263.4	21	No load	0.3	11.2	4.8		7.2	NA
WPG GOVERNMENT SECURITIES	▼▼	GI	▼	127.5	−26	No load	0.8	3.8	2.4	4.8	5.8	4.9
WRIGHT TOTAL RETURN BOND	▼▼	CL	AVG	91.1	−26	No load	0.8†	0.8	4.8	6.5	5.6	9.7
WRIGHT U.S. TREASURY NEAR TERM	AVG	GS	▼	132.2	−8	No load	0.8†	3.9	4.1	5.3	5.9	2.0

TAX-EXEMPT

FUND	OVERALL RATING	CATEGORY	RATING	ASSETS $MIL.	% CHG. 1995-96	SALES CHARGE (%)	EXPENSE RATIO (%)	1 YR.	3 YR.	5 YR.	YIELD (%)	MATURITY (YEARS)
AARP INSURED T/F GENERAL BOND	▼	ML	▼	1742.3	−5	No load	0.7	3.7	4.1	6.7	4.8	14.1
AIM MUNICIPAL BOND A	▲	ML		278.8	−2	4.75	0.9†	3.9	4.2	6.6	5.3	16.8
ALLIANCE MUNI. INCOME CA A	AVG	SL	AVG	460.4	−6	4.25	0.8†	4.4	5.2	7.5	5.5	25.8
ALLIANCE MUNI. INSURED NATIONAL A	▼▼	ML	▼▼▼	165.1	−1	4.25	1.0†	4.6	5.2	7.5	5.0	22.6
ALLIANCE MUNI. INCOME NATIONAL A	▼	ML		323.9	−7	4.25	0.7†	4.3	4.9	7.6	5.5	26.8
ALLIANCE MUNI. INCOME NY A	▼	SL	▼	178.7	−4	4.25	0.6†	4.3	4.3	7.2	5.6	26.7
AMER. CENT.-BENHAM CA MUNI. H-Y (mm)	▲▲	SL	▲▲▲	158.3	21	No load	0.5	5.9	5.8	7.9	5.9	21.0
AMER. CENT.-BENHAM CA T/F INS. (nn)	AVG	SL	AVG	195.3	2	No load	0.5	3.7	4.9	7.4	5.2	22.1
AMER. CENT.-BENHAM CA T/F INTERM. (oo)	▲	SI		443.4	4	No load	0.5	4.2	4.4	6.2	4.8	10.6
AMER. CENT.-BENHAM CA T/F L-T (pp)	AVG	SL	AVG	302.1	2	No load	0.5	3.6	5.1	7.4	5.4	22.6
AMERICAN HIGH-INCOME MUNI. BOND		ML		249.0	27	4.75	0.9†	6.5			5.7	10.1
ATLAS CA MUNICIPAL BOND A	▼▼	SL	▼▼	177.1	−4	3.00	0.9†	3.9	3.9	6.6	4.8	19.1
BERNSTEIN CA MUNICIPAL	▲▲	SI	AVG	310.7	39	No load	0.7	3.6	4.5	5.7	4.8	7.3
BERNSTEIN DIVERSIFIED MUNICIPAL	▲▲	MI	AVG	890.2	25	No load	0.7	3.5	4.5	5.7	4.4	7.0
BERNSTEIN NY MUNICIPAL	▲▲	SI	▲	570.1	17	No load	0.7	3.3	4.4	5.7	4.5	6.8
CALIFORNIA INVMT. TAX-FREE INCOME	▼▼	SL	▼▼	209.3	1	No load	0.6	3.1	4.3	7.2	4.9	15.2
CALVERT TAX-FREE RES. LTD.-TERM A	▲▲▲	MS	▲	512.1	12	2.00	0.7	3.9	4.0	4.2	4.2	5.8
CHURCHILL TAX-FREE OF KY A	▲	SI	AVG	223.0	−3	4.00	0.8†	4.2	4.6	6.6	5.6	15.3
COLONIAL CA TAX-EXEMPT A	▼▼	SL	▼▼	268.8	−12	4.75	0.9†	3.7	4.7	6.5	5.1	20.1
COLONIAL MA TAX-EXEMPT A	▼	SL	AVG	190.9	−9	4.75	0.9†	2.9	4.7	7.1	5.2	18.4
COLONIAL TAX-EXEMPT A	▼▼	ML	▼	2752.8	−12	4.75	1.0†	2.7	4.2	6.3	5.6	20.2
COLONIAL TAX-EXEMPT INSURED A	▼▼	ML	▼▼▼	202.7	−16	4.75	1.1†	2.3	4.1	6.1	4.9	18.6
COLUMBIA MUNICIPAL BOND	▲	SL	▲	375.7	−2	No load	0.6	3.8	4.1	5.9	5.0	13.4
COMPOSITE TAX-EXEMPT BOND A	▼	ML	▼	203.6	−11	4.00	0.8†	2.5	4.3	6.8	4.9	18.0
DEAN WITTER CA TAX-FREE INCOME	▼	SL	▼	971.3	−7	5.00**	1.3†	3.1	3.7	5.9	4.6	19.0
DEAN WITTER NY TAX-FREE INCOME	▼▼	SL	▼	191.6	−11	5.00**	1.4†	2.8	3.4	6.1	4.5	18.5
DEAN WITTER TAX-EXEMPT SECURITIES	AVG	ML	AVG	1185.3	−10	4.00	0.5	3.6	4.7	6.9	5.5	19.2
DELAWARE TAX-FREE PA A	▲▲	SL	▲▲	948.8	−6	4.75	0.9†	3.4	4.5	6.7	5.5	21.7
DELAWARE TAX-FREE USA A	▲	ML	▲▲	680.4	−12	4.75	0.9†	0.8	3.6	6.4	5.9	22.5
DREYFUS CA INTERMEDIATE MUNI.		SL		219.8	−7	No load	0.7	3.7	3.6		4.5	8.5
DREYFUS CA TAX-EXEMPT BOND	▼▼	SL	▼▼	1400.7	−8	No load	0.7	3.4	3.1	5.5	5.1	19.5
DREYFUS FL INTERMEDIATE MUNI.		SL		385.9	−9	No load	0.7	3.4	3.9		4.5	8.1
DREYFUS INSURED MUNI. BOND	▼▼▼	ML	▼▼▼	204.4	−15	No load	0.9†	2.3	2.6	5.6	5.0	23.3
DREYFUS INTERMEDIATE MUNI.	▲▲	ML	▲▲	1430.3	−8	No load	0.7	3.8	4.2	6.5	5.1	9.6
DREYFUS MA TAX-EXEMPT BOND	AVG	SL	AVG	156.6	−1	No load	0.8	4.0	4.1	6.4	5.3	23.8
DREYFUS MUNI. BOND	AVG	ML	AVG	3603.7	−8	No load	0.7	3.8	3.8	6.4	5.5	20.7
DREYFUS NJ INTERM. MUNI. BOND		SL		224.4	−3	No load	0.7	3.3	3.8		4.4	7.7
DREYFUS NJ MUNI. BOND	AVG	SL	▲	595.8	−9	No load	0.8†	3.4	3.9	6.6	5.4	19.1
DREYFUS NY TAX-EXEMPT BOND	▼	SL		1761.3	−6	No load	0.7	2.5	3.5	6.3	5.1	18.0
DREYFUS NY TAX-EXEMPT INTERM. BD	▲	SL	▲▲	364.7	−2	No load	0.8†	4.2	4.1	6.6	4.7	9.0
DREYFUS SHORT-INTERM. MUNI. BOND	▲▲▲	MS	▲▲▲	314.4	−7	No load	0.7†	4.2	3.6	4.8	4.4	2.2
DUPREE KY TAX-FREE INCOME	▲▲	SI	▲▲	312.3	6	No load	0.6	3.7	4.8	7.1	5.3	17.1
EV MARATHON CA MUNICIPALS	▼▼▼	SL	▼▼▼	349.8	−14	5.00**	1.7†	2.7	3.4	5.5	4.9	22.1
EV MARATHON CT MUNICIPALS		SL		180.9	−7	5.00**	1.6†	2.8	2.8		4.5	20.7
EV MARATHON FL MUNICIPALS	▼▼▼	SL	▼▼▼	594.5	−17	5.00**	1.5†	1.6	3.1	5.9	4.7	24.3
EV MARATHON MA MUNICIPALS	▼▼▼	SL	▼▼	260.2	−12	5.00**	1.6†	2.1	2.9	5.7	4.8	22.8
EV MARATHON MI MUNICIPALS	▼▼▼	SL	▼▼▼	163.8	−13	5.00**	1.6†	2.3	3.4	5.9	4.5	21.3
EV MARATHON NATL. MUNICIPALS	AVG	ML	AVG	2086.6	−8	5.00**	1.5†	3.6	4.5	7.6	5.5	24.0
EV MARATHON NJ MUNICIPALS		SL		369.0	−9	5.00**	1.6†	2.8	3.0	5.8	4.8	24.9
EV MARATHON NY MUNICIPALS	▼▼▼	SL	▼▼▼	576.3	−12	5.00**	1.6†	2.6	3.1	6.3	4.7	20.0
EV MARATHON NC MUNICIPALS (qq)	▼▼▼	SL	▼▼▼	166.8	−13	5.00**	1.5†	2.0	2.6	5.4	4.6	21.3
EV MARATHON OH MUNICIPALS	▼▼▼	SL	▼▼	285.8	−10	5.00**	1.6†	2.9	3.4	6.2	4.6	19.7
EV MARATHON PA MUNICIPALS	▼▼▼	SL	▼▼	422.5	−14	5.00**	1.5†	3.3	3.1	5.8	4.8	21.3
EV MARATHON VA MUNICIPALS (rr)	▼▼▼	SL	▼▼▼	174.2	−10	5.00**	1.5†	2.2	3.2	5.6	4.5	21.9
EXCELSIOR INTERM.-TERM TAX-EXEMPT (ss)	▲	ML	▲	348.9	39	4.50	0.6	4.2	4.7	6.7	4.4	8.4
FEDERATED INTERMEDIATE MUNI.	▲	MI	▼	221.6	0	No load	0.6	4.0	3.7	5.6	5.0	6.3
FEDERATED MUNICIPAL OPPORT. F (tt)	AVG	ML	AVG	370.7	−14	2.00**	1.1†	1.9	3.6	5.9	6.0	12.3
FEDERATED MUNICIPAL SEC. A (uu)		ML		616.0	−14	4.50	1.0	0.9	3.1	5.6	5.9	13.7

*Includes redemption fee. **Includes deferred sales charge. †12(b)-1 plan in effect. ‡Not currently accepting new accounts or deposits. NA=Not available. NM=Not meaningful. (ll) Formerly Vista U.S. Government Income A. (mm) Formerly Benham CA Municipal High-Yield. (nn) Formerly Benham CA Tax-Free Insured. (oo) Formerly Benham CA Tax-Free Intermediate-Term. (pp) Formerly Benham CA Tax-Free Long-Term. (qq) Formerly EV Marathon NC Tax-Free. (rr) Formerly EV Marathon VA Tax-Free. (ss) Formerly UST Master Interm.-Term Tax-Exempt. (tt) Formerly Fortress Municipal Income. (uu) Formerly Liberty Municipal Securities A.

DATA: MORNINGSTAR, INC., CHICAGO, IL.

FUND	OVERALL RATING	CATEGORY	RATING	ASSETS $MIL.	% CHG. 1995-96	SALES CHARGE (%)	EXPENSE RATIO (%)	1 YR.	3 YR.	5 YR.	YIELD (%)	MATURITY (YEARS)
FEDERATED S-T MUNI. INST.	▲▲▲	MS	▼▼	206.8	3	No load	0.5	4.0	4.0	4.3	4.2	2.4
FIDELITY ADVISOR HIGH-INCOME T (vv)	AVG	ML	AVG	456.5	−20	3.50	0.9†	3.0	3.4	6.9	5.8	17.2
FIDELITY ADVISOR MUNI. BOND INITIAL (ww)	▼	ML	AVG	944.3	−12	No load‡	0.6	4.1	4.0	6.8	5.0	12.3
FIDELITY AGGRESSIVE MUNI. (xx)	▲▲	ML	▲▲	848.9	−6	1.00*	0.6	3.6	3.9	6.8	6.2	17.3
FIDELITY CA INSURED MUNI. INCOME (yy)	▼▼	SL	▼▼	207.4	−8	No load	0.6	3.8	3.7	6.7	5.1	15.7
FIDELITY CA MUNICIPAL INCOME (zz)	AVG	SL	AVG	481.9	−5	No load	0.6	4.8	4.4	7.0	5.1	15.0
FIDELITY INSURED MUNI. INCOME (aaa)	▼	ML	▼	330.4	−7	No load	0.6	3.7	4.3	6.9	4.8	13.6
FIDELITY LIMITED-TERM MUNI. INC. (bbb)	▲▲	ML	▲▲	901.0	−4	No load	0.6	4.3	4.5	6.7	5.0	9.8
FIDELITY MA MUNICIPAL INCOME (ccc)	▲	SL		1138.1	−3	No load	0.5	3.6	4.7	7.2	5.3	15.3
FIDELITY MI MUNICIPAL INCOME (ddd)	AVG	SL	AVG	452.7	−8	No load	0.6	3.4	3.3	6.6	5.6	14.3
FIDELITY MN MUNICIPAL INCOME (eee)	▲	SL	▲	293.7	−7	No load	0.6	3.8	4.2	6.5	5.1	14.4
FIDELITY MUNICIPAL INCOME (fff)	AVG	ML	▲	1796.2	0	No load	0.6	5.0	4.1	6.7	5.3	14.4
FIDELITY NY INSURED MUNI. INCOME (ggg)	▼	SL	▼	318.1	−5	No load	0.6	3.8	4.2	6.7	4.7	12.8
FIDELITY NY MUNICIPAL INCOME (hhh)	▲	SL	▲	411.4	−5	No load	0.6	3.8	4.5	7.0	5.1	14.3
FIDELITY OH MUNICIPAL INCOME (iii)	▲	SL	▲▲	381.1	−5	No load	0.6	4.2	4.6	7.0	4.9	13.6
FIDELITY SPARTAN CA MUNI. INCOME (jjj)	AVG	SL	AVG	402.0	−1	0.50*	0.5	4.8	4.3	7.1	5.2	16.1
FIDELITY SPARTAN CT MUNI. INCOME	AVG	SL	AVG	330.1	−8	0.50*	0.6	4.2	4.3	6.8	5.1	13.2
FIDELITY SPARTAN FL MUNI. INCOME		SL		392.7	−3	0.50*	0.6	4.0	4.8		4.9	14.0
FIDELITY SPARTAN INTERM. MUNI. (kkk)		ML		211.3	−5	No load	0.5	4.6	4.4		4.7	8.0
FIDELITY SPARTAN MUNI. INCOME	▲	ML	▲	565.6	−2	0.50*	0.6	4.5	4.4	7.1	5.1	13.7
FIDELITY SPARTAN NJ MUNI. INCOME	▲	SL	▲	350.9	−4	0.50*	0.6	4.1	4.2	6.8	5.2	14.1
FIDELITY SPARTAN NY MUNI. INCOME (lll)	AVG	SL	AVG	313.7	−4	0.50*	0.5	4.3	4.4	7.2	5.1	14.3
FIDELITY SPARTAN PA MUNI. INC. (mmm)	▲▲	SL	▲▲▲	270.5	−6	0.50*	0.6	4.0	5.1	7.5	4.9	12.6
FIDELITY SPARTAN SHORT-INT. MUNI. (nnn)	▲▲▲	MS	AVG	737.2	−19	No load	0.5	3.9	4.0	5.1	4.2	3.4
FIRST INVESTORS INSURED T/E A	▼▼	ML	▼▼	1257.8	−8	6.25	1.1†	2.8	3.9	5.9	5.4	18.0
FIRST INVESTORS NY INSURED T/F A	▼	SL	▼	203.2	−5	6.25	1.2†	2.9	4.0	6.1	4.9	19.0
FLAGSHIP ALL-AMERICAN T/E A		ML		214.2	−4	4.20	0.8†	4.3	4.8	7.8	5.5	22.7
FLAGSHIP CT DOUBLE TAX-EXEMPT A	AVG	SL	AVG	210.8	1	4.20	0.7†	4.2	4.4	6.9	5.4	19.5
FLAGSHIP FL DOUBLE TAX-EXEMPT A	▼▼	SL	▼	308.6	−10	4.20	0.8†	2.6	4.1	6.8	5.3	21.5
FLAGSHIP KY TRIPLE TAX-EXEMPT A	AVG	SL	AVG	428.7	3	4.20	0.7†	3.7	4.8	7.2	5.3	20.5
FLAGSHIP LTD.-TERM TAX-EXEMPT A	▲▲▲	MI	▲▲▲	458.0	−10	2.50	0.8†	4.2	4.1	6.0	4.7	5.4
FLAGSHIP MI TRIPLE TAX-EXEMPT A	AVG	SL	AVG	254.5	−1	4.20	0.8†	3.7	4.6	7.1	5.2	18.3
FLAGSHIP MO DOUBLE TAX-EXEMPT A	AVG	SL	AVG	223.5	1	4.20	0.8†	3.8	4.3	7.0	5.2	21.3
FLAGSHIP NC DOUBLE TAX-EXEMPT A	▼	SL	▼	184.9	−5	4.20	0.9†	3.0	3.9	6.3	5.3	17.6
FLAGSHIP OH DOUBLE TAX-EXEMPT A	AVG	SL	AVG	447.8	−3	4.20	0.9†	3.3	4.4	6.6	5.3	18.1
FLAGSHIP TN DOUBLE TAX-EXEMPT A	AVG	SL	AVG	258.8	3	4.20	0.9†	3.5	4.2	6.7	5.3	19.2
FOUNTAIN SQ. OH TAX-FREE BOND A		SL		174.3	425	4.50	0.4†	3.5	4.2		4.1	8.2
FRANKLIN AL TAX-FREE INCOME I	▲▲	SL	▲▲▲	189.9	3	4.25	0.7†	4.9	5.0	7.1	5.6	20.3
FRANKLIN AZ TAX-FREE INCOME I	▲▲	SL	▲▲▲	753.9	0	4.25	0.6†	4.2	4.6	7.0	5.7	18.4
FRANKLIN CA HIGH YIELD MUNI. I		SL		174.0	119	4.25	0.4†	6.2	5.9		6.4	24.6
FRANKLIN CA INS. TAX-FREE INCOME I	▲	SL		1635.6	4	4.25	0.6†	4.1	4.7	7.1	5.4	19.5
FRANKLIN CA TAX-FREE INCOME I	▲▲	SL	▲▲	13685.9	1	4.25	0.6†	4.7	5.4	7.0	6.0	20.4
FRANKLIN CO TAX-FREE INCOME I	▲	SL	▲▲	235.1	10	4.25	0.7†	4.7	4.8	7.3	5.6	20.0
FRANKLIN CT TAX-FREE INCOME I	▲	SL	▲	180.0	8	4.25	0.7†	4.5	4.2	6.6	5.7	17.9
FRANKLIN FEDERAL TAX-FREE INCOME I	▲▲	ML	▲▲	7032.0	−2	4.25	0.6†	4.7	5.1	7.2	6.1	20.5
FRANKLIN FL TAX-FREE INCOME I	▲▲	SL	▲▲▲	1447.2	6	4.25	0.6†	4.4	5.0	7.1	5.9	18.0
FRANKLIN HIGH YIELD TAX-FREE INC. I	▲▲▲	ML	▲▲▲	4309.6	17	4.25	0.6†	6.2	6.4	8.2	6.5	19.5
FRANKLIN INSURED TAX-FREE INCOME I	▲	ML	▲▲	1666.5	−3	4.25	0.6†	4.1	4.5	6.9	5.7	18.2
FRANKLIN MD TAX-FREE INCOME I	▲	SL	▲▲	181.9	5	4.25	0.7†	3.9	5.0	7.1	5.5	18.0
FRANKLIN MA INSURED T/F INC. I	▲▲	SL	▲▲▲	310.4	4	4.25	0.7†	3.9	4.5	6.8	5.6	16.2
FRANKLIN MI INSURED T/F INC. I	▲▲	SL	▲▲	1114.2	0	4.25	0.6†	4.2	4.5	6.9	5.5	17.0
FRANKLIN MN INSAURED T/F INC. I	▲	SL	▲▲	483.7	−1	4.25	0.7†	3.5	4.2	6.4	5.5	16.8
FRANKLIN MO TAX-FREE INCOME I	▲	SL	▲▲	264.3	8	4.25	0.7†	4.7	4.8	7.2	5.5	18.3
FRANKLIN NJ TAX-FREE INCOME I	▲	SL	▲	571.3	0	4.25	0.7†	4.0	4.5	6.6	5.9	20.0
FRANKLIN NY INSURED T/F INC. I	▲	SL	▼	261.0	2	4.25	0.7†	4.3	4.3	7.2	5.6	22.4
FRANKLIN NY TAX-FREE INCOME I	▲	SL	▲▲▲	4770.7	−2	4.25	0.6†	4.1	4.5	7.3	5.9	21.5
FRANKLIN NC TAX-FREE INCOME I	▲	SL	▲	255.6	5	4.25	0.7†	4.1	4.5	6.8	5.4	19.8
FRANKLIN OH INSURED T/F INCOME I	▲	SL	▲▲	697.8	2	4.25	0.6†	4.4	4.5	6.9	5.4	18.8
FRANKLIN OR TAX-FREE INCOME I	▲	SL	▲	381.2	2	4.25	0.7†	4.3	4.5	6.6	5.4	17.8
FRANKLIN PA TAX-FREE INCOME I	▲▲	SL	▲▲▲	653.1	2	4.25	0.7†	4.5	4.9	7.2	5.7	17.5
FRANKLIN PR TAX-FREE INCOME I	▲	SL	▲	191.3	0	4.25	0.7†	5.0	4.8	6.8	5.6	20.5
FRANKLIN VA TAX-FREE INCOME I	▲▲	SL	▲▲	283.9	5	4.25	0.7†	4.2	4.7	7.0	5.6	20.0
GENERAL CA MUNICIPAL BOND	AVG	SL	AVG	302.2	−9	No load	0.8†	4.3	4.6	7.2	5.1	20.5
GENERAL MUNICIPAL BOND	AVG	ML	AVG	811.2	−16	No load	0.9†	3.1	3.9	6.9	5.4	21.4
GENERAL NY MUNICIPAL BOND		SL		312.7	−7	No load	0.9	3.1	3.7	7.0	5.1	20.1
HANCOCK CA TAX-FREE INCOME A	▼	SL	▼	294.7	−5	4.50	0.8†	4.5	4.9	7.5	5.5	22.4
HANCOCK TAX-FREE BOND A	▼	ML	▼	607.4	411	4.50	0.9†	4.2	4.3	7.7	5.7	21.5
HAWAIIAN TAX-FREE A	▲	SL	▲	659.6	−2	4.00	0.7†	3.9	4.5	6.3	5.2	15.5
IDS CA TAX-EXEMPT A	▲	SL	▼	234.9	−5	5.00	0.7	3.4	4.1	6.5	5.4	6.2
IDS HIGH-YIELD TAX-EXEMPT A	AVG	ML	AVG	5927.8	−7	5.00	0.7	2.9	4.7	6.5	6.1	21.0

*Includes redemption fee. **Includes deferred sales charge. †12(b)-1 plan in effect. ‡Not currently accepting new accounts or deposits. NA=Not available. NM=Not meaningful.
(vv) Formerly Fidelity Adv. Hi-Inc. Muni. A. (ww) Formerly Fidelity Muni. Bond. (xx) Formerly Fidelity Aggres. T/F. (yy) Formerly Fidelity CA T/F Ins. (zz) Formerly Fidelity CA T/F Hi-Y.
(aaa) Formerly Fidelity Ins. T/F. (bbb) Formerly Fidelity Ltd.-Term Muni. (ccc) Formerly Fidelity MA T/F Hi-Y. (ddd) Formerly Fidelity MI T/F Hi-Y. (eee) Formerly Fidelity MN T/F. (fff)
Formerly Fidelity Hi-Y T/F. (ggg) Formerly Fidelity NY T/F Ins. (hhh) Formerly Fidelity NY T/F Hi-Y. (iii) Formerly Fidelity OH T/F Hi-Y.   DATA: MORNINGSTAR, INC., CHICAGO, IL.

FUND (COMPARES RISK-ADJUSTED PERFORMANCE OF EACH FUND AGAINST ALL FUNDS)	OVERALL RATING	CATEGORY	RATING (COMPARES FUND WITHIN CATEGORY)	ASSETS $MIL.	% CHG. 1995-96	SALES CHARGE (%)	EXPENSE RATIO (%)	1 YR.	3 YR.	5 YR.	YIELD (%)	MATURITY (YEARS)	TREND 5-YEAR ANALYSIS
IDS INSURED TAX-EXEMPT A	▼▼	ML	▼▼	481.3	−9	5.00	0.8	2.2	3.9	6.8	5.2	5.9	[bar chart]
IDS MN TAX-EXEMPT A	AVG	SL	AVG	385.7	−7	5.00	0.7	3.6	4.4	6.6	5.8	6.6	[bar chart]
IDS TAX-EXEMPT BOND A	▼▼▼	ML	▼▼▼	1049.4	−11	5.00	0.7	2.0	3.9	6.3	5.2	6.1	[bar chart]
INVESCO TAX-FREE LONG-TERM BOND	▼	ML	AVG	238.2	−9	No load	0.9†	2.4	3.8	6.4	4.5	15.4	[bar chart]
KEMPER MUNICIPAL BOND A	▼	ML	▼	3254.9	−8	4.50	0.7†	3.3	4.9	7.3	5.3	17.6	[bar chart]
KEMPER STATE TAX-FREE INC. CA A	▼	SL	▼	1026.8	−7	4.50	0.8†	3.0	5.2	7.3	5.1	18.3	[bar chart]
KEMPER STATE TAX-FREE INC. NY A	AVG	SL	AVG	290.4	−10	4.50	0.8†	3.0	5.0	7.4	5.6	17.5	[bar chart]
KEYSTONE TAX-FREE	▼	ML	AVG	1557.9	29	4.00**	0.9†	3.1	3.7	5.9	5.0	19.7	[bar chart]
LIMITED TERM NY MUNICIPAL A	▲▲▲	SI	▲▲▲	635.6	12	2.00	0.9†	4.8	4.7	6.9	5.3	11.5	[bar chart]
LIMITED TERM TAX-EXEMPT BD. AMER.		MI		210.7	1	4.75	0.7†	4.5	4.5		4.8	5.2	[bar chart]
LORD ABBETT CA TAX-FREE INC. A	▼▼▼	SL	▼▼▼	272.3	−10	4.75	0.8†	3.4	2.8	6.2	5.4	24.9	[bar chart]
LORD ABBETT T/F INC. NATIONAL A	▼▼	ML	▼▼	627.4	−6	4.75	0.8†	4.0	3.9	6.6	5.4	23.5	[bar chart]
LORD ABBETT TAX-FREE INCOME NJ	▼	SL	AVG	185.4	−5	4.75	0.7†	4.1	4.4	7.3	5.3	22.4	[bar chart]
LORD ABBETT TAX-FREE INCOME NY A	▼▼▼	SL	▼▼▼	308.8	−8	4.75	0.8†	3.7	2.9	6.0	5.4	22.7	[bar chart]
MAINSTAY TAX-FREE BOND B	AVG	ML	AVG	496.6	−9	5.00**	1.2†	3.3	3.7	6.0	5.2	22.0	[bar chart]
MERRILL LYNCH CA MUNI. BOND B	▼▼	SL	▼	446.5	−22	4.00**	1.2†	3.9	4.0	6.4	5.0	18.7	[bar chart]
MERRILL LYNCH FL MUNI. BOND B	▼▼▼	SL	▼	185.5	−15	4.00**	1.2†	3.2	3.1	5.8	4.7	20.6	[bar chart]
MERRILL LYNCH MUNI. INSURED B	▼▼	ML	▼▼	701.0	−11	4.00**	1.2†	2.8	3.5	6.1	4.8	20.3	[bar chart]
MERRILL LYNCH MUNI. NATIONAL B	▼	ML	AVG	397.6	−5	4.00**	1.3†	4.1	4.2	6.5	5.1	22.2	[bar chart]
MERRILL LYNCH MUNI. INTERM.-TERM B	AVG	MI		169.8	−8	1.00**	1.1†	3.1	3.4	5.7	4.4	11.5	[bar chart]
MERRILL LYNCH NY MUNI. BOND B	▼▼▼	SL	▼▼	371.4	−31	4.00**	1.2†	2.9	2.6	5.7	4.8	21.2	[bar chart]
MFS CA MUNICIPAL BOND A	▼▼	SL	▼	248.2	−9	4.75	0.7†	2.9	3.8	6.6	5.3	16.8	[bar chart]
MFS MA MUNICIPAL BOND A	▼	SL	▼	244.2	−7	4.75	1.2†	2.8	4.0	6.3	5.3	18.5	[bar chart]
MFS MUNICIPAL BOND A	▼▼	ML	▼▼	1854.7	−7	4.75	0.6	1.6	3.7	6.8	5.2	19.2	[bar chart]
MFS MUNICIPAL HIGH-INCOME A	▲▲	ML	▲▲	990.7	−1	4.75	0.9	3.1	5.2	6.6	6.1	20.3	[bar chart]
MFS MUNICIPAL INCOME B	AVG	ML	AVG	257.5	−23	4.00**	2.1†	2.9	3.5	5.8	4.8	17.9	[bar chart]
MFS NC MUNICIPAL BOND A	▼▼	SL	▼▼	394.0	−7	4.75	1.2†	3.5	4.1	6.0	4.9	19.3	[bar chart]
MFS SC MUNICIPAL BOND A	▼▼	SL	▼▼	155.6	−11	4.75	1.2†	2.8	4.0	6.2	5.0	18.0	[bar chart]
MFS VA MUNICIPAL BOND A	▼▼	SL	▼▼	395.5	−10	4.75	1.2†	1.7	3.5	5.7	5.1	18.4	[bar chart]
NATIONWIDE TAX-FREE INCOME	▼	ML	▼	265.3	−1	5.00**	1.0†	3.7	3.5	6.4	4.9	19.6	[bar chart]
NEW ENGLAND MUNICIPAL INCOME A (ooo)	▼	ML	▼	181.0	−7	4.50	0.9†	4.6	4.1	6.7	5.4	21.0	[bar chart]
NEW YORK MUNI.	▼▼▼	SL	▼▼▼	197.1	−13	No load	3.6†	−7.7	−5.3	1.3	4.0	17.4	[bar chart]
NORTHERN INTERMEDIATE TAX-EXEMPT		MI		254.3	7	No load	0.9	3.4			4.0	5.3	[bar chart]
NUVEEN MUNICIPAL BOND R	▲▲▲	ML	▲▲▲	2836.3	−3	No load‡	0.6	4.3	5.7	6.8	5.3	21.4	[bar chart]
OPPENHEIMER CA MUNICIPAL A (ppp)	AVG	SL	AVG	293.0	3	4.75	1.0†	4.8	4.7	7.2	5.4	23.1	[bar chart]
OPPENHEIMER MUNICIPAL BOND A (qqq)	▼▼	ML	▼▼	589.5	−7	4.75	0.9†	5.2	4.2	7.0	5.4	21.0	[bar chart]
OPPENHEIMER NY MUNICIPAL A (rrr)	▼▼	SL	▼▼	665.8	−7	4.75	0.9†	4.2	3.8	6.7	5.5	20.4	[bar chart]
OVERLAND EXPRESS CA T-F BOND A	▲	SL	▲	239.7	−11	4.50	0.6†	4.1	5.1	7.4	5.1	16.7	[bar chart]
PACIFIC HORIZON CA T/E BD. A	▼	SL	▼	220.1	0	4.50	0.9	3.8	4.4	6.8	4.8	19.7	[bar chart]
PAINEWEBBER NATL. T-F INCOME A	▼▼▼	ML	▼▼▼	278.9	−16	4.00	0.9†	2.1	3.2	5.9	4.6	18.2	[bar chart]
PIONEER TAX-FREE INCOME A	▼	ML	▼	440.1	−7	4.50	0.9†	3.6	4.3	6.8	5.1	21.7	[bar chart]
PREMIER CA MUNICIPAL BOND A	▼	SL	▼	166.9	−10	4.50	0.9	4.0	4.7	7.1	5.0	19.8	[bar chart]
PREMIER MUNICIPAL BOND A	AVG	ML	AVG	475.1	−5	4.50	0.9	4.0	4.5	7.5	5.8	23.1	[bar chart]
PREMIER STATE MUNI. BOND CT A	AVG	SL	AVG	315.1	−6	4.50	0.9	4.5	4.4	6.9	5.3	19.7	[bar chart]
PREMIER STATE MUNI. BOND FL A	AVG	SL	AVG	207.7	−16	4.50	0.9	3.1	4.8	7.0	5.2	24.2	[bar chart]
PREMIER STATE MUNI. BOND MD A	AVG	SL	▲	273.8	−9	4.50	0.9	4.5	4.9	6.9	5.2	21.7	[bar chart]
PREMIER STATE MUNI. BOND MI A	AVG	SL	▲	162.8	−9	4.50	0.9	3.3	5.0	7.5	5.3	19.2	[bar chart]
PREMIER STATE MUNI. BOND OH A	▲	SL	▲▲	250.7	−8	4.50	0.9	4.1	4.8	7.2	5.4	18.5	[bar chart]
PREMIER STATE MUNI. BOND PA A	AVG	SL	▲	209.4	−4	4.50	0.9	3.9	5.0	7.5	5.1	20.4	[bar chart]
T. ROWE PRICE CA TAX-FREE BOND	▲	SL	▲	156.3	6	No load	0.6	4.5	5.0	7.2	5.2	17.2	[bar chart]
T. ROWE PRICE MD TAX-FREE	▲	SL	▲▲	807.8	5	No load	0.5	3.8	4.7	7.0	5.4	16.7	[bar chart]
T. ROWE PRICE TAX-FREE HIGH-YIELD	▲▲▲	ML	▲▲▲	1033.2	5	No load	0.8	5.0	5.4	7.7	5.8	19.0	[bar chart]
T. ROWE PRICE TAX-FREE INCOME	▲	ML	▲	1344.8	−4	No load	0.6	3.3	4.7	7.2	5.3	16.9	[bar chart]
T. ROWE PRICE TAX-FREE SHORT-INT.	▲▲▲	MS	▲	439.3	−3	No load	0.6	4.0	4.1	4.9	4.3	3.1	[bar chart]
T. ROWE PRICE VA TAX-FREE	▲	SL	▲	189.9	7	No load	0.7	4.1	4.9	7.3	5.2	17.4	[bar chart]
PRINCOR TAX-EXEMPT BOND A	▲	ML	▲	189.4	3	4.75	0.8†	4.6	4.6	7.1	5.4	18.9	[bar chart]
PRUDENTIAL CA MUNI. CA INCOME A	▲▲	SL	▲▲▲	154.0	−2	3.00	0.4†	4.4	6.0	8.4	5.8	18.7	[bar chart]
PRUDENTIAL MUNI. HIGH-YIELD B	▲▲	ML	▲▲	695.8	−23	5.00**	1.0†	3.2	5.1	6.9	6.1	20.0	[bar chart]
PRUDENTIAL MUNI. INSURED B	▼▼	ML	▼▼	334.7	−35	5.00**	1.1†	2.4	4.0	6.2	4.7	16.6	[bar chart]
PRUDENTIAL MUNICIPAL NJ B	▼	SL	▼	167.2	−29	5.00**	1.0†	2.3	3.6	6.2	4.7	17.3	[bar chart]
PRUDENTIAL MUNICIPAL NY A		SL	AVG	175.7	−1	3.00	0.7†	2.4	4.1	7.0	5.1	16.3	[bar chart]
PRUDENTIAL MUNICIPAL PA B	AVG	SL	AVG	152.1	−24	5.00**	1.2†	2.8	3.9	6.6	5.2	17.6	[bar chart]
PRUDENTIAL NATL. MUNICIPALS A	▼	ML	▼	502.9	−7	3.00	0.8†	2.7	4.1	6.7	5.3	18.1	[bar chart]
PUTNAM CA TAX EXEMPT INCOME A	▼	SL	▼	3174.4	−3	4.75	0.7†	3.6	4.8	7.1	5.2	22.0	[bar chart]
PUTNAM FL TAX EXEMPT INCOME A	▼▼	SL	▼▼	252.8	−7	4.75	1.0†	2.9	4.3	6.7	5.2	20.4	[bar chart]
PUTNAM MA TAX EXEMPT INC. A	AVG	SL	▲	274.4	3	4.75	1.0†	3.9	4.9	7.5	5.7	20.9	[bar chart]
PUTNAM MUNICIPAL INCOME A	AVG	ML	▲	814.2	−4	4.75	1.0†	3.2	4.7	7.4	5.8	19.3	[bar chart]
PUTNAM NJ TAX EXEMPT INCOME A	▼	SL	▼	231.5	−5	4.75	1.0†	3.6	4.1	6.7	5.3	20.7	[bar chart]
PUTNAM NY TAX EXEMPT INCOME A	▼▼▼	SL	▼▼	1844.4	−9	4.75	0.8†	3.4	3.4	6.7	5.4	20.4	[bar chart]
PUTNAM NY TAX EXEMPT OPPORT. A	▼	SL	▼	165.5	−8	4.75	1.1†	3.8	5.5	6.7	5.5	22.6	[bar chart]

*Includes redemption fee. **Includes deferred sales charge. †12(b)-1 plan in effect. ‡Not currently accepting new accounts or deposits. NA=Not available. NM=Not meaningful.
(jjj) Formerly Fidelity Spartan CA Muni Hi-Y. (kkk) Formerly Fidelity Spartan Interm. Muni. (lll) Formerly Fidelity Spartan NY Muni Hi-Yield. (mmm) Formerly Fidelity Spartan PA Muni High-Yield. (nnn) Formerly Fidelity Spartan Short-Interm. Muni. (ooo) Formerly New England Tax-Exempt Income A. (ppp) Formerly Oppenheimer CA Tax-Exempt A. (qqq) Formerly Oppenheimer Tax-Free Bond A. (rrr) Formerly Oppenheimer NY Tax-Exempt A.

DATA: MORNINGSTAR, INC., CHICAGO, IL.

MUTUAL FUND SCOREBOARD — Bond Funds

FUND	OVERALL RATING	CATEGORY	RATING	ASSETS $MIL.	% CHG. 1995-96	SALES CHARGE (%)	EXPENSE RATIO (%)	1 YR.	3 YR.	5 YR.	YIELD (%)	MATURITY (YEARS)
PUTNAM OH TAX EXEMPT INC. A	AVG	SL	▲	188.5	-4	4.75	1.0†	3.6	4.5	6.8	5.2	18.6
PUTNAM PA TAX EXEMPT INC. A	AVG	SL	▲	188.6	1	4.75	1.0†	3.7	4.9	7.3	5.3	18.8
PUTNAM TAX EXEMPT INCOME A	▼▼	ML	▼▼▼	2125.8	-9	4.75	0.8†	3.1	3.7	6.9	5.5	20.7
PUTNAM TAX-FREE HIGH YIELD B	▲▲	ML	▲▲	1441.0	-3	5.00**	1.5†	2.5	3.8		5.6	20.6
PUTNAM TAX-FREE INSURED B	▼▼	ML	▼▼	349.3	-10	5.00**	1.6†	2.7	4.0	6.0	4.8	21.0
ROCHESTER FUND MUNICIPALS	▲	SL	▲▲	2308.1	8	4.00	0.8†	5.3	4.6	7.9	6.1	21.9
SAFECO MUNICIPAL BOND NO LOAD	▼▼	ML	▼▼	481.4	-7	No load	0.5	3.2	4.8	7.1	5.4	26.5
SCUDDER CA TAX-FREE	AVG	SL	AVG	296.6	-3	No load	0.8	3.6	4.5	7.3	4.9	13.2
SCUDDER HIGH-YIELD TAX-FREE	▲	ML	▲	292.9	-3	No load	0.8	4.4	4.4	7.5	5.5	11.0
SCUDDER MANAGED MUNI. BONDS	AVG	ML	AVG	736.1	-5	No load	0.6	4.1	4.6	7.1	5.1	10.4
SCUDDER MA TAX-FREE		SL	▲▲	330.8	2	No load	0.8	4.1	4.8	7.8	5.1	9.9
SCUDDER MEDIUM-TERM TAX-FREE	▲▲	MI	AVG	649.8	-8	No load	0.7	4.0	4.7	6.8	4.7	9.3
SCUDDER NY TAX-FREE	▼▼	SL	▼	188.1	-5	No load	0.8	3.3	4.2	7.1	4.9	11.8
SELIGMAN MUNICIPAL OH A (sss)	AVG	SI	▼▼	158.6	-9	4.75	0.8†	3.8	4.4	6.6	5.3	19.0
1784 TAX-EXEMPT MED.-TERM INC.		ML		231.6	20	No load	0.8†	4.3	5.0		4.9	10.2
SIERRA CA MUNICIPAL A	▼	ML		358.1	-11	4.50	0.9†	4.4	4.1	6.9	5.5	19.4
SIERRA NATIONAL MUNICIPAL A	▼	ML	AVG	210.6	-18	4.50	0.8†	4.3	3.9	7.3	5.3	18.8
SIT TAX-FREE INCOME	▲▲▲	ML	▲▲▲	305.5	8	No load	0.8	5.7	5.8	7.1	5.6	16.6
SMITH BARNEY CA MUNICIPALS A	AVG	SL	AVG	575.0	-3	4.00	0.8†	5.7	6.4	7.9	5.2	22.2
SMITH BARNEY MANAGED MUNI. A	▲▲	ML	▲▲	1974.4	5	4.00	0.7†	5.6	6.6	9.0	5.6	22.4
SMITH BARNEY MUNI. LTD. TERM A	▲▲▲	MI	▲▲	370.9	61	2.00	0.8†	3.7	4.4	6.1	5.3	6.2
SMITH BARNEY MUNI. NATIONAL A	▲	ML	▲	366.9	-8	4.00	0.7†	3.7	5.1	7.6	5.7	19.1
SMITH BARNEY MUNI. NY A	AVG	SL	AVG	545.7	513	4.00	0.7†	4.2	5.0	7.5	5.3	21.6
SMITH BARNEY TAX-EXEMPT INC. B	▲	ML	▲	625.3	-14	4.50**	1.3†	3.9	4.0	6.4	5.1	22.3
STAGECOACH CA T/F BOND A	▼▼	SL	▼▼	293.6	-1	4.50	0.7†	3.8	4.4	7.4	5.0	13.4
STATE ST. RESEARCH TAX-EXEMPT A	▼▼	ML	▼▼	222.8	-12	4.50	1.1†	2.9	3.8	6.5	4.8	19.3
STEIN ROE HIGH-YIELD MUNICIPALS	▲	ML	▲	295.0	4	No load	0.9	4.5	5.7	6.6	6.1	17.9
STEIN ROE INTERMEDIATE MUNICIPALS	▲	ML	▲	200.5	-8	No load	0.7	4.2	4.4	6.3	4.8	8.8
STEIN ROE MANAGED MUNICIPALS	AVG	ML	AVG	612.9	-4	No load	0.7	3.8	4.6	6.6	5.3	16.8
STRONG HIGH-YIELD MUNI. BOND		ML		244.8	-8	No load	0.4	5.1	6.1		6.6	21.4
STRONG MUNICIPAL ADVANTAGE		MS		501.4	NM	No load	0.0	4.9			5.0	0.9
STRONG MUNICIPAL BOND	AVG	ML		233.8	-5	No load	0.8	2.4	2.9	6.4	5.4	20.0
TAX-EXEMPT BOND OF AMERICA	▲	ML	▲	1513.1	1	4.75	0.7†	4.6	5.3	7.3	5.3	17.9
TAX-EXEMPT FUND OF CA	▲	SL	▲	262.6	5	4.75	0.7†	4.3	5.2	7.3	5.2	11.2
TAX-FREE FUND OF CO A	▲	SL	▲▲	214.4	-2	4.00	0.6†	3.8	4.2	6.5	5.1	9.2
TAX-FREE TRUST OF AZ A	AVG	SL	AVG	394.4	0	4.00	0.7†	3.6	4.2	6.6	5.2	15.1
TAX-FREE TRUST OF OR A	AVG	SL	▲	304.8	-3	4.00	0.7†	3.7	4.4	6.2	5.1	15.1
THORNBURG INTERM. MUNI. A	▲▲▲	ML	▲▲▲	246.1	11	3.50	1.0†	4.5	4.9	7.3	5.1	7.6
THORNBURG LTD.-TERM NATL. A	▲▲▲	MS	▼	915.3	0	2.50	1.0†	4.0	4.0	5.7	4.6	3.6
UNITED MUNICIPAL BOND A	▼	ML	▼	973.0	-5	4.25	0.7†	4.1	5.1	7.8	5.2	12.0
UNITED MUNICIPAL HIGH-INC. A	▲▲▲	ML	▲▲▲	409.6	4	4.25	0.8†	6.9	6.5	8.6	6.3	10.3
USAA CA BOND	AVG	SL	AVG	439.0	6	No load	0.4	5.4	5.2	7.3	5.7	21.2
USAA TAX-EXEMPT INTERM-TERM	▲▲	ML	▲▲	1711.2	2	No load	0.4	4.5	4.9	6.9	5.6	9.3
USAA TAX-EXEMPT LONG-TERM	AVG	ML	AVG	1872.7	-2	No load	0.4	4.5	4.5	6.9	5.9	25.8
USAA TAX-EXEMPT SHORT-TERM	▲▲▲	MS	▲▲	785.9	1	No load	0.4	4.4	4.4	4.9	4.6	5.5
USAA VA BOND	▲	SL	▲▲	284.9	8	No load	0.5	5.1	4.8	7.1	5.7	19.8
VALUE LINE TAX-EXEMPT HIGH-YIELD	▼	ML	▼	201.9	-13	No load	0.6	3.5	4.0	6.2	5.1	18.1
VAN KAMPEN AMER. CAP. H/Y MUNI. A	▲▲▲	ML	▲▲▲	611.3	18	4.75‡	1.0†	5.8	6.5	7.7	6.6	19.7
VAN KAMPEN AMER. CAP. INS. T/F A	▼▼	ML	▼▼	1294.2	-5	4.75	0.9†	3.7	4.5	7.0	5.2	18.3
VAN KAMPEN AMER. CAP. MUNI INC A	▼	ML	▼	802.4	-3	4.75	1.0†	4.1	4.1	6.8	5.8	18.8
VAN KAMPEN AMER. CAP. PA T/F A	▲	SL	▲	226.9	0	4.75	1.0†	3.9	4.5	7.3	5.2	19.2
VAN KAMPEN AMER. CAP. T/F HIGH A	AVG	ML	AVG	669.9	1	4.75	1.0†	3.1	4.3	5.6	6.6	20.1
VANGUARD CA TAX-FREE INS. INTERM.		SI		350.7	64	No load	0.2	5.4			4.8	7.1
VANGUARD CA TAX-FREE INS. L/T	AVG	SL	AVG	1050.1	7	No load	0.2	5.0	5.5	7.7	5.3	12.9
VANGUARD FL INSURED TAX-FREE		SL		544.6	13	No load	0.2	4.2	5.3		5.0	12.9
VANGUARD MUNI. HIGH-YIELD	▲	ML	▲	2038.9	3	No load	0.2	4.5	5.4	7.7	5.5	13.1
VANGUARD MUNI. INSURED L/T	AVG	ML	AVG	1949.1	-3	No load	0.2	4.0	5.2	7.5	5.4	13.4
VANGUARD MUNI. INTERM.-TERM	▲▲	MI	▲	6122.9	6	No load	0.2	4.2	5.0	7.1	5.1	7.2
VANGUARD MUNI. LIMITED-TERM	▲▲▲	MS	▲	1789.3	6	No load	0.2	4.1	4.2	5.0	4.5	3.3
VANGUARD MUNI. LONG-TERM	AVG	ML	AVG	1141.8	2	No load	0.2	4.4	5.3	7.7	5.3	14.2
VANGUARD MUNI. SHORT-TERM	▲▲▲	MS	AVG	1451.8	3	No load	0.2	3.7	3.8	4.0	3.9	1.2
VANGUARD NJ TAX-FREE INS. L/T	AVG	SL	AVG	839.9	5	No load	0.2	3.2	4.7	7.3	5.3	11.4
VANGUARD NY INSURED TAX-FREE	AVG	SL	▲	944.5	9	No load	0.2	4.1	5.0	7.5	5.1	11.7
VANGUARD OH TAX-FREE INS. L/T	▲	SL	▲	214.6	8	No load	0.2	4.2	5.0	7.6	5.2	9.8
VANGUARD PA TAX-FREE INS. L/T	▲▲	SL	▲▲	1627.6	3	No load	0.2	4.3	5.1	7.6	5.4	10.4
VOYAGEUR AZ INSURED T/F A	AVG	SL	AVG	209.3	-12	3.75	0.7†	4.1	4.7	7.3	4.8	16.1
VOYAGEUR CO TAX-FREE A	AVG	SL	AVG	358.3	-9	3.75	0.8†	4.1	4.5	7.4	5.1	22.6
VOYAGEUR FL INSURED T/F A	▼	SL	▼	192.2	-21	3.75	0.5†	2.9	4.5	7.4	4.9	22.5
VOYAGEUR MN INSURED A	AVG	SL	AVG	304.9	-1	3.75	0.9†	3.8	4.0	6.8	4.9	18.6
VOYAGEUR MN TAX-FREE A	AVG	SL	▲	428.4	-6	3.75	0.9†	3.3	4.2	6.6	5.1	20.2

*Includes redemption fee. **Includes deferred sales charge. †12(b)-1 plan in effect. ‡Not currently accepting new accounts or deposits. NA=Not available. NM=Not meaningful.
(sss) Formerly Seligman Tax-Exempt OH A.

AARP INVESTMENT PROGRAM
800-322-2282

ADVANCE CAPITAL I GROUP
800-345-4783

AIM FAMILY OF FUNDS
800-347-4246

ALLIANCE CAPITAL GROUP
800-227-4618

AMCORE VINTAGE MUTUAL FUNDS
800-438-6375

AMERICAN CENTURY INVESTMENTS
800-345-2021

AMERICAN FUNDS GROUP
800-421-4120

AMERISTAR FUNDS
800-824-3741

AMSOUTH FUNDS
800-451-8379

AQUILA GROUP
800-872-5859

ARMADA FUNDS
800-622-3863

ASSET MANAGEMENT FUND (AMF)
800-527-3713

ATLAS FUNDS
800-933-2852

BABSON FUND GROUP
800-422-2766

BERNSTEIN (SANFORD C.) FUND
212-756-4097

WILLIAM BLAIR MUTUAL FUNDS
800-742-7272

BLANCHARD GROUP OF FUNDS
800-829-3863

BOND FUND OF AMERICA
See American Funds Group

CALIFORNIA INVESTMENT TRUST GRP.
800-225-8778

CALVERT GROUP
800-368-2748

CAPITAL WORLD BOND
See American Funds Group

CARDINAL GROUP
800-848-7734

CHICAGO TRUST BOND FUNDS
800-992-8151

COLONIAL GROUP
800-248-2828

COLUMBIA FUNDS
800-547-1707

COMMERCE FUNDS
800-305-2140

COMMON SENSE TRUST
800-544-5445

COMPOSITE GROUP OF FUNDS
800-543-8072

DEAN WITTER FUNDS
800-869-3863

DELAWARE GROUP
800-523-4640

DG INVESTOR SERIES
800-748-8500

DODGE & COX GROUP
800-621-3979

DREYFUS GROUP
800-645-6561

DUPREE MUTUAL FUNDS
800-866-0614

EATON VANCE GROUP
800-225-6265

EVERGREEN KEYSTONE FUNDS
800-807-2940

EXCELSIOR FUNDS
800-446-1012

FEDERATED FUNDS
800-341-7400

FIDELITY ADVISOR FUNDS
800-522-7297

FIDELITY GROUP
800-544-8888

FIRST INVESTORS GROUP
800-423-4026

FIRST OMAHA FUNDS
800-662-4203

FIRST PRIORITY FUNDS
800-433-2829

FLAGSHIP FUNDS
800-227-4648

FORTIS FUNDS
800-800-2638

FOUNTAIN SQUARE FUNDS
800-334-0483

FPA FUNDS
800-982-4372

FRANKLIN GROUP OF FUNDS
800-342-5236

FUNDAMENTAL FAMILY OF FUNDS
800-322-6864

GALAXY FUNDS
800-628-0414

GENERAL CA MUNICIPAL BOND
See Dreyfus Group

GENERAL MUNICIPAL BOND
See Dreyfus Group

GENERAL NY MUNICIPAL BOND
See Dreyfus Group

GLOBAL TOTAL RETURN A
See Prudential Mutual Funds

GLOBAL GOVERNMENT PLUS
See Prudential Mutual Funds

GOLDMAN SACHS ASSET MGMT. GRP.
800-526-7384

GRADISON-MCDONALD MUTUAL FUNDS
800-869-5999

GT GLOBAL GROUP OF FUNDS
800-824-1580

HANCOCK JOHN FUNDS
800-225-5291

HARBOR FUNDS
800-422-1050

HAWAIIAN TAX-FREE A
See Aquila Group

HOMESTEAD FUNDS
800-258-3030

HOTCHKIS & WILEY FUNDS
800-346-7301

HSBC FUND GROUP
800-634-2536

IAI FUNDS
800-945-3863

IDS GROUP
800-328-8300

INTERMEDIATE BOND FD AMERICA
See American Funds Group

INVESCO FAMILY OF FUNDS
800-525-8085

INVESTORS TRUST
800-656-6626

ISI FUNDS
800-955-7175

IVY/MACKENZIE GROUP OF FUNDS
800-456-5111

JANUS GROUP
800-525-8983

KEMPER FUNDS
800-621-1048

KEYSTONE DIVR BOND (B-2)
See Evergreen Keystone Funds

KEYSTONE HIGH-INCOME (B-4)
See Evergreen Keystone Funds

KEYSTONE QUALITY BOND (B-1)
See Evergreen Keystone Funds

KEYSTONE STRATEGIC INCOME B
See Evergreen Keystone Funds

KEYSTONE TAX-FREE
See Evergreen Keystone Funds

KIEWIT MUTUAL FUND
800-254-3948

LEGG MASON FAMILY OF FUNDS
800-577-8589

LEXINGTON GROUP
800-526-0056

LIMITED TERM TAX-EX. BD. AMER.
See American Funds Group

LOOMIS SAYLES FUNDS
800-633-3330

LORD ABBETT FAMILY OF FUNDS
800-874-3733

MAINSTAY FUNDS
800-522-4202

MARKETWATCH FUNDS
800-232-9091

MARQUIS FUNDS
800-462-9511

MARSHALL FUNDS
800-236-8560

MERRILL LYNCH GROUP
800-637-3863

MFS FAMILY OF FUNDS
800-637-2929

NATIONWIDE FUNDS
800-848-0920

NEUBERGER & BERMAN GROUP
800-877-9700

NEW ENGLAND FUND GROUP
800-225-7670

NICHOLAS GROUP
800-227-5987

NORTHEAST INVESTORS GROUP
800-225-6704

NORTHERN FUNDS
800-595-9111

NORTHSTAR FUNDS
800-595-7827

NUVEEN MUTUAL FUNDS
800-351-4100

111 CORCORAN FUNDS
800-422-2080

OPPENHEIMER FUNDS
800-525-7048

OVERLAND EXPRESS FUNDS
800-552-9612

PACIFIC HORIZON FUNDS
800-332-3863

PAINEWEBBER MUTUAL FUNDS
800-647-1568

PAYDEN & RYGEL INVESTMENT GRP.
800-572-9336

PERMANENT PORT. FAMILY OF FDS.
800-531-5142

PHOENIX FUNDS
800-243-4361

PIONEER GROUP
800-225-6292

PIPER FUNDS
800-866-7778

PREFERRED GROUP
800-662-4769

PREMIER FUNDS
800-554-4611

PRICE T. ROWE FUNDS
800-638-5660

PRINCOR FAMILY OF MUTUAL FDS.
800-451-5447

PRUDENTIAL MUTUAL FUNDS
800-225-1852

PUTNAM FUNDS
800-225-1581

ROCHESTER FUNDS
716-383-1300

SAFECO MUTUAL FUNDS
800-426-6730

SALOMON BROTHERS GROUP
800-725-6666

SCHWAB FUNDS
800-526-8600

SCOUT GROUP
800-422-2766

SCUDDER FUNDS
800-225-2470

SELIGMAN GROUP
800-221-2783

SENTINEL GROUP
800-282-3863

1784 FUNDS
800-252-1784

SIERRA TRUST FUNDS
800-222-5852

SIT GROUP
800-332-5580

SMITH BARNEY GROUP
800-451-2010

SMITH BREEDEN FAMILY OF FDS.
800-221-3138

SOUTHTRUST VULCAN FUNDS
800-239-7470

SSGA FUNDS
800-647-7327

STAGECOACH FUNDS
800-222-8222

STAR FUNDS
800-677-3863

STATE STREET RESEARCH GROUP
800-882-0052

STEIN ROE MUTUAL FUNDS
800-338-2550

STRONG FUNDS
800-368-1030

SUNAMERICA FUNDS
800-858-8850

TAX-EXEMPT BOND OF AMERICA
See American Funds Group

TAX-FREE FUND OF CO A
See Aquila Group

TAX-FREE TRUST OF AZ A
See Aquila Group

TAX-FREE TRUST OF OR A
See Aquila Group

TCW/DW FUNDS
800-526-3143

TEMPLETON GROUP
800-292-9293

THORNBURG FUNDS
800-847-0200

U.S. GOVERNMENT SECURITIES
See American Funds Group

UNITED GROUP
800-366-5465

USAA GROUP
800-382-8722

VALUE LINE MUTUAL FUNDS
800-223-0818

VAN KAMPEN AMER. CAPITAL FDS.
800-421-5666

VANGUARD GROUP
800-662-7447

VICTORY GROUP
800-539-3863

VIRTUS FUNDS
800-723-9512

VISTA MUTUAL FUNDS
800-648-4782

VOYAGEUR GROUP
800-553-2143

WARBURG PINCUS FUNDS
800-927-2874

WESTERN ASSET TRUST
818-584-4300

WPG MUTUAL FUNDS
800-223-3332

WRIGHT MANAGED INVMT. COS.
800-888-9471

FUND	RATING	CATEGORY	RISK	SIZE ASSETS $MIL.	FEES EXPENSE RATIO (%)	NAV. RET. (%) 1 YR.	NAV. RET. (%) 3 YRS.	SHARES RET. (%) 1 YR.	SHARES RET. (%) 3 YRS.	YIELD (%)	TREND 3-YEAR ANALYSIS	PREMIUM/DISCOUNT 1996 HIGH	LOW	1/31/97
ADAMS EXPRESS	▲▲	Large-cap Blend	Low	1138.8	0.5	20.8	16.2	16.2	13.1	2.6		-10.8	-17.7	-16.8
ALLIANCE GLOBAL ENVIRONMENT	▲	Specialty–Misc.	Low	96.3	1.6	32.7	15.7	35.0	12.5	0.0		-16.9	-23.1	-23.2
ARGENTINA FUND	▼▼	Latin America	High	122.9	2.0	15.7	0.4	6.1	-8.1	2.8		12.3	-10.9	-8.1
ASA LIMITED	▼▼	Precious Metals	High	323.7	0.5	-7.0	-11.2	-3.2	-7.2	4.0		11.2	-5.2	5.2
ASIA PACIFIC	▼	Pacific ex-Japan	High	279.2	1.6	8.3	-3.6	-7.2	-14.4	0.0		9.4	-17.5	-14.3
ASIA TIGERS	▼	Pacific ex-Japan	Average	256.2	1.7	8.5	-2.5	-2.0	-11.8	0.3		4.9	-18.5	-17.2
AUSTRIA FUND	AVG	Europe	Average	136.3	1.8	14.6	7.1	9.0	-1.1	1.4		-13.7	-24.6	-21.5
BAKER FENTRESS	▲	Mid-cap Growth	Low	760.7	0.7	14.7	14.6	15.5	12.5	4.2		-15.1	-22.8	-19.3
BERGSTROM CAPITAL	▲▲	Large-cap Growth	Low	151.4	0.8	8.8	18.0	11.5	13.0	2.5		-7.9	-16.9	-13.5
BLUE CHIP VALUE	▲▲	Large-cap Value	Low	107.8	1.2	21.4	19.1	39.5	19.7	1.2		3.5	-12.9	-6.4
BRAZIL FUND	▼	Latin America	High	418.0	1.6	29.5	16.7	9.6	10.9	2.4		9.4	-20.4	-16.0
BRAZILIAN EQUITY	▼	Latin America	High	100.2	1.9	27.7	12.1	4.3	4.8	0.1		32.3	-28.4	-16.1
CENTRAL EUROPEAN EQUITY	▲	Europe	Average	289.1	1.2	32.8	17.7	32.6	11.7	0.5		-17.7	-24.1	-20.0
CENTRAL FUND OF CANADA	AVG	Precious Metals	Average	81.3	NA	-6.5	-3.0	-1.2	-4.5	0.2		6.8	-3.9	-5.6
CENTRAL SECURITIES	▲▲▲	Mid-cap Value	Low	347.6	0.6	28.0	23.3	25.8	27.2	3.5		7.7	-2.5	1.5
CHILE FUND	AVG	Latin America	Average	317.0	1.5	-11.0	7.3	-16.3	1.1	3.0		-2.2	-15.4	-10.4
CHINA FUND	▼	Pacific ex-Japan	Average	177.1	2.6	34.6	-3.2	12.6	-18.5	0.8		16.6	-19.6	-17.7
CLEMENTE GLOBAL GROWTH	AVG	World	Average	61.4	1.6	6.5	2.7	0.6	-4.1	0.0		-15.8	-26.4	-25.1
COHEN & STEERS REALTY INCOME	▲▲	Real Estate	Low	30.8	1.7	33.2	15.3	40.7	16.3	4.2		13.4	0.0	20.3
CZECH REPUBLIC		Europe		91.1	2.4	29.8	NA	7.4	NA	4.2		7.6	-17.2	-12.4
DELAWARE GRP. DVD. & INC.	▲▲	Dom. Hybrid	Very Low	205.7	0.8	22.0	12.4	27.3	14.8	9.9		12.0	0.2	3.7
DELAWARE GRP. GLOBAL DVD. & INC.		Dom. Hybrid		97.0	1.1	23.3	NA	26.9	NA	10.1		8.5	-2.7	3.6
DUFF & PHELPS UTILITIES INC.	AVG	Dom. Hybrid	Average	1678.5	1.2	4.0	5.4	4.6	3.7	8.6		12.6	1.4	6.8
EMERGING GERMANY	AVG	Europe	Average	147.7	1.5	16.1	2.9	12.1	-4.7	0.0		-18.2	-27.5	-24.1
EMERGING MKTS. INFRASTRUCTURE	AVG	Div. Emg. Mkts.	Average	216.6	1.8	14.9	-0.4	4.4	-11.5	0.8		-4.5	-21.8	-17.7
EMERGING MKTS. TELECOMMUNS.	▼	Div. Emg. Mkts.	Average	151.3	1.8	13.0	2.2	10.9	-10.4	0.0		-3.5	-20.8	-16.5
EMERGING MEXICO	▼▼▼	Latin America	Very High	114.5	1.8	29.3	-16.0	22.0	-24.9	1.3		-6.4	-21.6	-17.0
ENGEX	▼	Small-cap Growth	High	15.4	3.3	-3.1	3.8	-3.1	3.4	0.0		-16.1	-31.0	-29.4
EQUUS II	AVG	Dom. Hybrid	Average	98.1	5.1	30.1	15.0	36.1	13.4	0.2		-26.3	-42.6	-30.8
EUROPE FUND	▲▲▲	Europe	Low	183.0	1.4	35.3	21.0	34.8	15.5	0.9		-5.9	-19.3	-10.1
EUROPEAN WARRANT	▼	Europe	High	122.8	2.0	55.6	8.9	45.6	1.3	0.0		-6.9	-26.5	-22.1
FIDELITY ADV. EMERGING ASIA		Pacific ex-Japan		143.5	1.8	19.3	NA	10.9	NA	3.0		-0.7	-16.1	-13.3
FIDELITY ADV. KOREA		Pacific ex-Japan		41.9	1.8	-29.2	NA	-10.6	NA	0.0		13.5	-13.3	7.3
FIRST AUSTRALIA	AVG	Pacific ex-Japan	Average	183.6	1.5	14.0	4.4	10.4	2.1	2.2		-10.5	-19.9	-16.1
FIRST FINANCIAL	▲▲▲	Financial	Low	224.8	1.2	43.0	35.7	57.2	42.4	1.1		5.9	-13.6	9.6
FIRST IBERIAN	▲	Europe	Average	89.6	1.9	37.9	17.5	45.5	10.2	0.8		-18.3	-25.4	-23.4
FIRST ISRAEL	▼▼	Foreign	High	70.4	2.2	7.0	4.1	3.9	-8.2	0.0		-4.3	-18.6	-16.4
FIRST PHILIPPINE	▼	Pacific ex-Japan	High	224.7	1.8	20.6	-2.1	20.2	-5.9	0.0		-12.1	-23.4	-19.0
FOREIGN & COLONIAL EMG. MID. EAST		Foreign		43.7	3.0	25.3	NA	27.9	NA	0.0		-9.6	-22.3	-18.7
FRANCE GROWTH	AVG	Europe	Average	205.1	1.6	25.0	10.3	13.9	-0.4	0.7		-11.6	-23.7	22.3
GABELLI EQUITY	▲	Mid-cap Blend	Low	1015.4	1.2	9.0	9.4	11.0	5.2	8.1		-3.5	-9.2	-7.4
GABELLI GLOBAL MULTIMEDIA		Communication		81.4	2.0	9.3	NA	7.5	NA	5.5		-13.4	-20.7	-19.9
GENERAL AMERICAN INVESTORS	▲	Large-cap Growth	Low	597.8	1.3	19.4	12.8	18.9	9.9	0.9		-13.5	-18.5	-13.9
GERMANY FUND	▲	Europe	Average	220.9	1.2	27.8	16.3	21.6	8.9	2.5		-12.8	-22.9	-18.7
GLOBAL HEALTH SCIENCES	▲	Health	Average	417.6	1.2	15.1	25.3	13.9	20.3	0.0		-15.4	-25.7	-20.0
GREATER CHINA FUND	▼▼	Pacific ex-Japan	High	228.2	2.4	37.7	-3.7	13.6	-13.9	0.8		7.9	-20.4	-20.9
GROWTH FUND OF SPAIN	▲	Europe	Low	270.9	1.2	32.4	18.9	27.9	14.4	1.3		-14.2	-22.2	-19.3
G.T. GLOBAL DEVELOPING MKTS.		Int. Hybrid		504.0	1.8	24.5	NA	24.7	NA	4.2		-4.2	-23.2	-19.7
G.T. GLOBAL EASTERN EUROPE (a)	AVG	Europe	Average	113.8	1.8	21.5	9.0	18.2	1.9	0.5		-5.2	-20.1	-13.0
H&Q HEALTHCARE INVESTORS	AVG	Health	Average	127.7	1.6	7.0	14.3	7.6	11.6	0.0		-5.8	-19.9	-15.1

NA = Not available.
(a) Formerly G.T. Greater Europe.

DATA: MORNINGSTAR, INC., CHICAGO, IL.

How to Use the Tables

Closed-end funds are publicly traded investment companies. Their results are measured two ways: one, by the change in net asset value (NAV), which is generated by the fund's manager; the other, by the change in the shares' market price. Total returns, which include dividends and capital gains, are shown for one- and three-year periods. The three-year figure is an average an-nual return. All returns are pretax.

BUSINESS WEEK RATING
Ratings are based on three-year risk-adjusted performance of the fund's portfolio. A rating is calcu-lated by subtracting a fund's risk-of-loss factor from total return. Equity funds are rated against each other, and to earn an above-average rating, must beat the S&P 500 on a risk-adjusted basis. For ratings, municipal bond funds are separated from other bond funds.

▲ ▲ ▲	SUPERIOR
▲ ▲	VERY GOOD
▲	GOOD
AVG	AVERAGE
▼	BELOW AVERAGE
▼ ▼	POOR
▼ ▼ ▼	VERY POOR

RISK
For each fund, the monthly Trea-sury bill return is subtracted from the monthly NAV return in each month of the rating period. When a fund has underperformed Trea-sury bills, this monthly result is negative. The sum of these nega-tive numbers is then divided by the number of months. The result is a negative number, and the greater its magnitude, the higher the risk of loss.

EXPENSE RATIO
Fund expenses for 1996 as a per-cent of average net assets. Ratio may include interest expense.

YIELD
Income earned during 1996, as a percentage of yearend NAV per share, adjusted for capital gains.

MATURITY
The average maturity of the secu-rities in a bond fund, weighted according to their market value.

TREND
A fund's relative performance during 1994, 1995, and 1996. From left to right, the level of blue in each shows how the portfolio of each fund performed relative to other funds: ■ for the top quartile; ▇ for the second quartile; ▄ for the third quartile; and ☐ for the bottom quartile. An empty box indicates no returns for that time period.

PREMIUM/DISCOUNT
The market price of closed-end funds is either less than the value of their securities, a discount, or more, a premium, to their NAVs.

FUND	RATING	CATEGORY	RISK	SIZE ASSETS $MIL.	FEES EXPENSE RATIO (%)	NAV. RET. (%) 1 YR.	NAV. RET. (%) 3 YRS.	SHARES RET. (%) 1 YR.	SHARES RET. (%) 3 YRS.	YIELD (%)	TREND 3-YEAR ANALYSIS	1996 HIGH	LOW	1/31/97
H&Q LIFE SCIENCES INVESTORS	AVG	Health	Average	111.0	1.6	3.9	9.6	2.6	7.9	0.0		-7.7	-20.4	-18.4
HERZFELD CARIBBEAN BASIN		Latin America		8.8	3.3	14.3	NA	-7.2	NA	1.6		33.1	-12.7	-13.1
INDIA FUND		Foreign		257.8	2.0	-15.3	NA	-14.0	NA	0.1		16.2	-10.2	-2.7
INDIA GROWTH	▼▼▼	Foreign	Very High	97.5	2.2	-13.2	-12.3	-12.0	-19.9	0.7		28.7	-1.0	5.0
INDONESIA FUND	▼▼	Pacific ex-Japan	Very High	49.2	2.0	14.3	-8.7	-3.7	-22.3	0.0		27.0	-11.7	12.1
IRISH INVESTMENT	▲▲	Europe	Low	82.6	1.6	28.3	22.8	25.1	18.0	1.5		0.0	-19.5	-9.5
ITALY FUND	▼	Europe	Average	102.6	1.4	21.4	5.4	16.8	-3.8	1.8		-11.0	-19.8	-15.0
JAKARTA GROWTH	▼	Pacific ex-Japan	High	47.9	1.9	10.8	-1.7	-5.6	-14.8	0.0		11.7	-14.4	-16.2
JAPAN EQUITY	▼	Japan	Average	97.1	1.0	-15.7	1.6	-24.1	-4.7	0.4		26.4	-3.8	-15.0
JAPAN OVER-THE-COUNTER EQ.	▼▼	Japan	High	80.0	1.5	-11.1	-7.6	-23.8	-12.3	0.6		21.2	-9.8	14.3
JARDINE FLEMING CHINA REGION	▼▼	Japan	High	130.2	2.2	28.3	-11.7	12.7	-21.5	0.2		5.7	-22.5	9.1
JARDINE FLEMING INDIA		Pacific ex-Japan		77.4	2.9	-14.7	NA	-21.9	NA	0.0		25.3	-8.7	-19.6
JOHN HANCOCK BANK & THRIFT OPPORT.		Financial		744.5	1.5	31.4	NA	33.2	NA	1.7		-8.7	-21.3	0.6
KOREA FUND	▼▼	Pacific ex-Japan	High	509.3	1.3	-30.2	-3.1	-30.0	-10.9	0.0		14.3	2.1	16.2
KOREA EQUITY	▼▼▼	Pacific ex-Japan	High	51.1	1.9	-33.1	-17.5	-25.8	-24.0	0.0		4.0	-9.4	7.3
KOREAN INVESTMENT	▼▼	Pacific ex-Japan	High	62.8	2.0	-31.5	-14.3	-25.9	-24.0	0.0		1.5	-10.6	5.8
LATIN AMERICA EQUITY	▼	Latin America	High	145.2	1.8	13.6	-0.2	9.2	-10.3	0.4		0.1	-19.3	-13.4
LATIN AMERICA INVESTMENT	▼	Latin America	High	150.0	1.8	13.2	0.2	8.3	-12.2	1.5		-0.6	-19.8	-14.0
LATIN AMERICAN DISCOVERY	▼▼	Latin America	High	193.3	2.2	48.3	1.2	39.6	-9.0	1.2		-1.5	-18.6	-14.7
LIBERTY ALL-STAR EQUITY	▲	Large-cap Blend	Low	973.9	1.1	21.6	16.5	16.2	11.6	0.0		0.4	-9.2	-8.1
LIBERTY ALL-STAR GROWTH	▲▲	Large-cap Blend	Very Low	46.8	1.4	18.3	10.9	9.3	4.8	0.0		-8.9	-19.9	-16.7
MALAYSIA FUND	▼▼	Pacific ex-Japan	High	241.6	1.4	21.1	-1.5	20.0	-5.4	0.0		3.8	-14.0	-8.3
MEXICO FUND	▼▼▼	Latin America	Very High	861.6	1.1	26.4	-17.0	21.2	-24.3	2.9		-7.4	-20.3	-17.2
MEXICO EQUITY & INCOME	▼▼	Latin America	Very High	137.9	1.7	27.3	-6.7	22.5	-16.8	4.3		-7.0	-22.3	-15.4
MFS SPECIAL VALUE		Small-cap Blend	Low	93.2	1.3	18.0	13.9	26.4	17.8	5.9		24.6	6.4	27.5
MORGAN FUNSHARES		Large-cap Growth		6.3	2.0	14.9	NA	5.9	NA	0.0		-7.6	-22.5	-18.7
MORGAN GRENFELL SMALLCAP	AVG	Small-cap Growth	Average	111.5	1.5	17.3	17.1	14.8	14.4	8.7		-5.0	-21.0	-12.0
MORGAN STANLEY AFRICA INVMT.		Foreign		292.8	1.8	9.3	NA	16.9	NA	0.9		-17.2	-24.5	-23.1
MORGAN STANLEY ASIA-PACIFIC		Div. Pacific		910.8	1.4	-2.8	NA	-18.6	NA	6.2		-3.2	-23.6	-18.2
MORGAN STANLEY EMG. MKTS.	▼	Div. Emg. Mkts.	Average	392.6	1.9	14.9	-3.5	-4.0	-10.9	0.7		19.1	-14.4	-6.9
MORGAN STANLEY INDIA INVMT.		Foreign		318.6	3.2	-0.9	NA	4.1	NA	0.0		24.1	-6.4	10.8
MORGAN STANLEY RUSSIA & NEW EURO.		Europe		132.9	NA	NA	NA	NA	NA	NA		-1.1	-13.3	-12.7
NATIONS BALANCED TARGET MAT.		Dom. Hybrid		57.4	1.2	10.1	NA	10.9	NA	3.9		-5.7	-18.7	-13.5
NEW AGE MEDIA	AVG	Communication	Average	222.7	1.3	1.5	13.3	1.8	7.0	0.0		-13.3	-22.9	-18.1
NEW GERMANY	AVG	Europe	Average	575.0	1.0	24.5	11.9	27.2	5.1	2.6		-18.0	-28.3	-22.5
NEW SOUTH AFRICA		Foreign		74.2	2.0	-19.8	NA	-14.5	NA	0.6		-15.4	-24.0	-18.4
PAKISTAN INVESTMENT	▼▼▼	Foreign	Very High	56.5	2.2	-27.2	-30.1	-2.4	-30.8	0.0		7.5	-16.1	1.4
PETROLEUM AND RESOURCES		Nat. Resources	Low	484.6	0.6	25.4	15.9	30.9	16.3	2.3		-5.6	-12.6	-5.5
PILGRIM AMERICA BANK & THRIFT (b)	▲▲▲	Financial	Low	252.3	1.1	34.8	25.6	37.1	24.0	1.0		-10.9	-22.9	-8.0
PORTUGAL FUND	AVG	Europe	Average	92.5	1.6	32.0	11.4	24.3	-0.1	0.6		-5.9	-23.2	-18.9
QUEST FOR VALUE CAPITAL *	▲	Large-cap Blend	Low	890.9	0.0	10.7	14.6	13.3	18.1	0.0		-3.0	-11.0	-2.3
QUEST FOR VALUE INCOME **	▲▲▲	Large-cap Blend	Very Low	890.9	0.7	12.6	12.0	7.8	6.8	12.0		4.7	-1.3	-0.5
ROC TAIWAN	▼	Pacific ex-Japan	High	394.7	2.0	25.9	3.2	-2.4	-9.3	0.0		18.6	-14.5	-14.2
ROYCE MICRO-CAP	▲▲	Small-cap Value	Very Low	113.9	1.4	15.9	14.4	13.3	8.5	1.1		-9.7	-20.2	-17.6
ROYCE VALUE	▲	Small-cap Value	Very Low	321.8	2.0	15.2	11.4	16.0	8.4	1.1		-6.8	-17.8	-14.8
SALOMON BROTHERS	▲▲▲	Large-cap Blend	Very Low	1588.4	0.4	30.2	20.9	39.2	24.1	1.9		-7.3	-17.6	-5.9
SCHRODER ASIAN GROWTH	AVG	Div. Pacific	Average	269.5	1.7	6.8	-0.4	-0.3	-8.7	0.8		0.3	-13.9	-10.2
SCUDDER NEW ASIA	AVG	Div. Pacific	Average	133.4	1.7	2.5	-4.0	-11.5	-12.8	0.2		12.7	-18.1	-13.7
SCUDDER NEW EUROPE	▲	Europe	Low	281.1	1.6	34.4	16.8	23.9	9.2	0.4		-12.7	-22.5	-20.3
SINGAPORE FUND	AVG	Pacific ex-Japan	Average	120.6	2.0	3.1	1.2	-9.3	-11.9	1.1		11.1	-10.4	-9.8
SOURCE CAPITAL	▲▲	Mid-cap Value	Very Low	328.5	0.9	22.4	14.1	24.9	13.1	7.7		2.1	-9.5	-0.6
SOUTHEASTERN THRIFT & BANK	▲▲▲	Financial	Very Low	60.5	1.3	25.0	26.7	21.9	26.4	1.7		-0.1	-19.5	-10.6
SOUTHERN AFRICA		Foreign		104.0	2.1	-3.5	NA	5.8	NA	2.7		-14.5	-24.0	-18.7
SPAIN FUND	AVG	Europe	Average	146.4	2.1	37.2	15.5	33.7	1.7	1.4		-12.9	-23.1	-22.3
SWISS HELVETIA	AVG	Europe	Average	307.2	1.4	2.0	11.0	-3.0	1.2	0.5		-8.7	-18.8	-18.6
TAIWAN FUND	▼	Pacific ex-Japan	High	385.4	2.4	36.9	9.2	8.6	-9.6	0.0		24.5	-14.1	-14.8
TCW/DW EMG. MKTS. OPPORT.		Div. Emg. Mkts.		274.4	1.7	15.1	NA	10.3	NA	0.4		4.0	-21.6	-9.8
TEMPLETON CHINA WORLD	AVG	Pacific ex-Japan	Average	327.8	1.7	40.5	3.6	30.8	-5.3	2.0		4.2	-21.6	-18.2
TEMPLETON DRAGON		Pacific ex-Japan		1044.7	1.5	38.3	NA	25.4	NA	2.1		-6.2	-21.2	-18.1
TEMPLETON EMERGING MKTS.	AVG	Div. Emg. Mkts.	Average	288.7	1.7	21.3	1.8	2.7	-2.5	0.0		37.8	-0.4	3.7
TEMPLETON RUSSIA		Europe		113.2	2.0	83.9	NA	65.8	NA	0.4		28.0	0.3	6.4
TEMPLETON VIETNAM OPPORT.		Pacific ex-Japan		116.6	1.5	12.0	NA	7.5	NA	2.6		3.0	-22.9	-17.4
THAI FUND	▼▼▼	Pacific ex-Japan	Very High	214.7	1.3	-36.0	-16.6	-25.3	-13.4	2.0		6.1	-14.1	11.9
THAI CAPITAL	▼▼▼	Pacific ex-Japan	Very High	60.1	2.3	-31.6	-16.3	-20.9	-13.9	1.1		11.0	-10.0	7.6
TRI-CONTINENTAL	▲▲	Large-cap Blend	Low	2835.0	0.6	22.6	16.2	21.6	14.1	2.5		-15.5	-19.3	-16.8
TURKISH INVESTMENT	▼▼▼	Foreign	Very High	40.8	1.9	17.4	-21.6	5.0	-25.6	2.5		27.9	-10.1	-8.8
UNITED KINGDOM	▲	Europe	Low	63.8	1.6	25.4	15.4	23.7	6.4	2.5		-14.1	-20.7	-16.2
WORLDWIDE VALUE	▲	Europe	Low	71.2	2.1	33.4	15.3	50.4	15.3	0.0		-7.6	-21.8	-11.3
ZWEIG FUND	▲▲	Dom. Hybrid	Very Low	589.1	1.2	17.3	10.6	9.6	3.2	11.2		3.8	-5.2	-3.9
ZWEIG TOTAL RETURN	▲▲	Dom. Hybrid	Very Low	638.8	1.1	6.3	6.9	4.1	-0.1	10.4		6.4	-3.5	-0.7

NA=Not available.
(b) Formerly Pilgrim Regional Bankshares. *Converts to Oppenheimer Quest Capital Value Fund, an open-end mutual fund, on Feb. 28. **Liquidated on Jan. 31.

DATA: MORNINGSTAR, INC., CHICAGO, IL.

FUND	RATING	CATEGORY	RISK	SIZE ASSETS $MIL.	FEES EXPENSE RATIO (%)	NAV. RET. (%) 1 YR.	NAV. RET. (%) 3 YRS.	SHARES RET. (%) 1 YR.	SHARES RET. (%) 3 YRS.	YIELD (%)	MAT. (YRS.)	TREND 3-YEAR ANALYSIS	1996 HIGH	LOW	1/31/97
ACM GOVERNMENT INCOME	▼▼	Multisector	High	590.1	1.3	16.9	8.2	24.7	4.4	9.9	16.2		9.0	−5.5	−0.6
ACM GOVERNMENT SECURITIES	▼▼	Multisector	High	771.0	2.0	17.6	8.1	19.8	1.3	10.8	14.4		0.5	−11.0	−6.8
ACM GOVERNMENT SPECTRUM	▼▼▼	Multisector	Very High	265.2	1.3	6.1	1.6	6.5	−4.0	10.8	15.8		1.2	−11.2	−4.5
ACM MANAGED DOLLAR INCOME	▼▼▼	International	Very High	390.1	1.1	40.5	11.7	41.2	7.2	11.0	14.9		0.5	−13.1	−8.9
ACM MANAGED INCOME	▼	Multisector	High	192.4	1.1	10.6	9.9	17.3	6.0	9.9	10.2		15.2	0.8	5.3
ACM MUNICIPAL SECURITIES INC.	▼▼	Muni. Ntl. Long	High	136.1	0.8	6.8	3.1	6.4	5.3	7.1	26.0		6.5	−2.9	2.0
ALL AMERICAN TERM	AVG	Interm. (Gen.)	Low	198.4	1.1	10.4	7.8	7.7	5.0	8.4	8.3		−7.1	−13.6	−12.3
ALLIANCE WORLD DOLLAR GOVT. II	▼▼▼	International	Very High	1055.8	1.3	34.9	8.4	30.2	5.7	10.7	19.3		5.0	−10.7	−4.9
AMERICAN GOVT. INCOME PTFL.	▼▼▼	Interm. Govt.	Very High	180.8	1.4	7.2	−0.2	1.0	−7.3	9.1	9.7		−2.0	−16.7	−11.1
AMERICAN MUNICIPAL TERM	▲	Muni. Ntl. Long	Average	96.4	0.6	3.9	5.4	9.1	7.7	5.8	16.8		−2.4	−9.3	−4.3
AMERICAN STRAT. INCOME PTFL. II	▼▼	Interm. (Gen.)	Average	254.3	1.3	6.9	5.6	10.1	0.1	9.7	15.4		−13.6	−18.9	−13.0
APEX MUNICIPAL	▲▲▲	Muni. Ntl. Long	Very Low	196.0	0.9	7.6	6.6	13.5	4.4	7.2	21.0		−3.8	−13.6	−6.4
BANCROFT CONVERTIBLE	▲	Convertibles	Average	83.3	1.2	19.3	14.1	17.4	10.6	4.0	6.7		−8.8	−16.3	−13.1
BEA INCOME	AVG	Interm. (Gen.)	Low	280.6	0.9	7.9	7.7	11.0	7.5	11.8	8.4		1.0	−12.3	−6.0
BLACKROCK 1998 TERM	▼	Short Govt.	Very Low	575.6	0.7	6.8	6.2	11.4	3.6	5.3	7.1		−4.8	−10.5	−5.2
BLACKROCK INCOME	▼	Long Govt.	Average	469.7	1.1	6.5	6.5	9.0	2.5	8.8	13.9		−12.7	−20.0	−15.8
BLACKROCK INS. MUNI. 2008	▼	Muni. Ntl. Long	High	418.9	1.0	4.6	5.6	13.7	4.9	5.5	13.4		−6.2	−13.3	−9.6
BLACKROCK INS. MUNI. TERM	AVG	Muni. Ntl. Long	Average	284.3	1.0	4.7	5.6	7.5	5.3	6.2	13.3		−3.2	−8.1	−5.7
BLACKROCK INVMT. QLTY. TERM	▼	Long Govt.	Average	328.4	0.9	3.5	7.2	4.3	2.3	7.7	13.4		−12.9	−18.7	−14.7
BLACKROCK MUNI. TARGET TERM	AVG	Muni. Ntl. Long	Average	448.8	0.9	4.3	5.3	7.4	6.0	6.0	10.4		−4.1	−8.2	−5.3
BLACKROCK N.Y. INS. MUNI. 2008	AVG	Muni. S.S. Long	High	173.6	1.1	3.7	5.2	9.6	6.5	5.7	13.1		−3.4	−8.7	−4.9
BLACKROCK N. AMER. GOVT. INC. TRUST	▼▼	International	High	422.4	1.0	14.1	9.2	14.6	5.1	7.0	12.4		−8.2	−19.0	−17.6
BLACKROCK STRATEGIC TERM		Interm. Govt.	Average	516.3	0.8	5.4	6.9	12.1	0.8	6.6	9.3		−13.5	−18.5	−12.8
BLACKROCK TARGET TERM	▼▼	Interm. Govt.	Average	929.1	0.8	5.2	5.8	8.1	3.5	6.5	7.4		−8.1	−13.5	−9.5
CIGNA HIGH-INCOME SHARES	▲▲▲	High Yield	Very Low	273.5	1.1	15.7	11.8	19.1	12.4	10.8	8.3		16.1	7.3	12.1
COLONIAL INTERMARKET INCOME I	AVG	Multisector	Low	129.9	1.0	10.3	8.3	9.6	4.4	9.5	9.7		2.0	−8.8	−7.5
COLONIAL MUNICIPAL INCOME	▲▲▲	Muni. Ntl. Long	Very Low	201.1	1.0	4.8	5.9	11.4	3.2	7.3	23.0		−0.5	−10.4	−1.0
CORPORATE HIGH-YIELD	▲	High Yield	Average	300.4	0.7	12.1	9.5	16.2	9.3	10.4	7.0		6.5	−2.2	7.9
DEAN WITTER GOVT. INCOME	AVG	Interm. Govt.	Low	439.9	0.7	5.9	7.1	7.3	4.9	7.3	9.4		−3.6	−12.1	−8.9
DREYFUS MUNICIPAL INCOME	▲	Muni. Ntl. Long	Low	195.3	0.8	4.4	4.9	14.6	4.7	6.3	23.8		2.7	−6.2	0.4
DREYFUS STRATEGIC MUNI. BOND	▲▲	Muni. Ntl. Long	Low	439.8	0.8	5.3	5.7	11.2	3.7	6.6	22.5		31.4	−4.3	4.1
DREYFUS STRATEGIC MUNICIPALS	▲▲▲	Muni. Ntl. Long	Very Low	566.8	0.9	5.1	5.9	11.2	4.0	6.8	22.7		4.3	−4.4	0.7
DUFF & PHELPS UTILITIES TAX-FREE	AVG	Muni. Ntl. Long	Average	129.7	1.4	2.1	5.6	6.8	5.9	5.6	21.6		1.1	−6.0	−0.1
DUFF & PHELPS UTILITY & CORP.	▼▼▼	Long (Gen.)	High	502.5	0.8	1.0	6.7	0.6	5.6	8.4	20.3		1.7	−9.8	−2.9
EMERGING MKTS. FLOATING RATE		International		67.5	1.7	35.2	NA	47.3	NA	9.5	13.9		5.1	−5.2	0.8
FIRST AUSTRALIA PRIME INCOME	AVG	International	High	1291.4	1.3	18.6	11.6	5.8	5.2	9.6	7.3		3.7	−15.2	−6.0
FRANKLIN PRINCIPAL MATURITY	▼▼▼	Multisector	High	194.6	3.3	16.5	5.7	15.2	6.0	6.5	5.7		0.5	−17.0	−5.2
GLOBAL HIGH INCOME DOLLAR	AVG	International	High	351.1	1.5	23.9	10.8	22.6	6.7	9.9	15.5		−8.6	−16.9	−16.3
GLOBAL PARTNERS INCOME	▲▲	International	Very High	219.5	1.3	41.7	15.3	40.9	11.0	12.1	13.0		0.6	−9.8	−9.6
GREENWICH STREET MUNICIPAL		Muni. Ntl. Long		237.1	1.1	1.1	NA	2.8	NA	5.6	22.6		−1.9	−9.0	−2.0
HIGH INCOME ADVANTAGE	▼▼	Interm. (Gen.)	Average	156.7	0.9	9.5	4.7	19.3	10.4	11.1	7.4		17.9	4.8	−7.0
HIGH INCOME OPPORTUNITY	▲	Long (Gen.)	Low	788.1	1.2	13.3	8.8	20.9	8.0	9.7	8.0		−0.5	−8.2	−12.6
INCOME OPPORTUNITIES 1999	AVG	Long (Gen.)	Average	432.6	0.7	8.1	8.2	15.6	7.8	5.6	13.4		−7.1	−13.9	−1.3
INSURED MUNICIPAL INCOME	▼▼	Long (Gen.)	Very High	301.0	1.3	3.7	4.3	3.0	0.0	6.5	27.1		−14.0	−18.7	2.4
INTERCAPITAL CALIF. INS. MUNI. INC.	▼▼	High Yield	Very High	177.5	NA	4.3	4.0	9.7	−0.8	6.1	24.7		−8.4	−15.2	18.1
INTERCAPITAL CALIF. QLTY. MUNI.	▼▼	High Yield	Very High	148.2	NA	4.1	4.8	8.9	−1.0	6.2	25.5		−10.1	−17.2	0.4
INTERCAPITAL INCOME SECURITIES	▼	Interm. Govt.	Average	210.7	0.7	5.9	7.2	3.0	1.4	8.7	24.2		−1.3	−13.4	−8.9
INTERCAPITAL INS. MUNI. INC.	▼▼	Muni. Ntl. Long	High	434.1	NA	4.8	5.1	6.7	−0.2	6.5	24.8		−12.5	−18.8	−14.9
INTERCAPITAL INS. MUNICIPAL	AVG	Muni. S.S. Long	Average	352.7	NA	4.8	5.4	5.5	3.3	6.9	25.6		−2.4	−7.4	−9.3
INTERCAPITAL QLTY. MUNI. INC.	AVG	Muni. S.S. Long	High	524.5	0.7	5.5	5.9	11.0	4.9	6.9	22.3		−3.7	−9.9	−13.2
INTERCAPITAL QLTY. MUNI. INVMT.	▲	Long (Gen.)	Average	273.4	0.7	4.7	5.2	4.3	2.2	7.2	22.3		0.4	−7.7	−12.3
INVESTMENT GRADE MUNICIPAL	AVG	Muni. Ntl. Long	High	169.6	1.7	6.4	5.6	5.8	2.0	6.6	25.6		−13.3	−18.0	−13.2
JOHN HANCOCK INCOME SEC.	▼	Muni. Ntl. Long	Average	169.0	0.8	5.0	7.1	2.5	5.0	8.2	13.2		−2.6	−9.2	−6.8
JOHN HANCOCK PATRIOT GLB. DVD.	▼	Muni. Ntl. Long	High	116.8	1.3	9.3	8.4	2.4	3.1	8.4	NA		1.3	−12.9	−5.1
JOHN HANCOCK PATRIOT PREF. DVD.	AVG	Muni. Ntl. Long	Average	98.1	1.3	10.2	9.4	13.4	9.3	8.6	NA		3.9	−3.8	−5.7
JOHN HANCOCK PATRIOT PREM. DVD. I	▼▼▼	Muni. Ntl. Long	High	140.1	1.3	6.2	6.9	13.5	10.0	8.2	NA		5.6	−3.7	−15.4
KEMPER HIGH-INCOME	▲	High Yield	Low	215.1	1.2	15.9	9.4	20.0	12.9	9.8	8.0		11.2	5.2	3.9
KEMPER INTERMEDIATE GOVT.	▼	Short Govt.	Low	268.5	1.0	2.9	5.5	9.0	3.4	8.5	9.7		−6.5	−14.7	−7.2
KEMPER MULTI-MARKET INCOME	AVG	Multisector	Low	217.1	1.0	8.9	8.5	9.6	9.2	9.1	8.3		3.4	−5.3	1.4
KEMPER STRATEGIC MUNI. INC.	▲▲▲	Muni. Ntl. Interm.	Very Low	128.0	0.8	6.3	6.2	8.0	6.7	6.5	18.3		7.7	−0.9	3.5
LATIN AMERICA DOLLAR INC.	▼	International	Very High	93.7	1.8	49.4	13.7	43.7	9.1	9.9	16.1		7.2	−11.8	−10.3
LINCOLN NATL. CONV. SEC.	AVG	Convertibles	High	120.4	1.1	22.1	13.1	24.7	9.0	4.9	8.0		−5.7	−17.8	−8.9
MANAGED HIGH-INCOME PTFL.	▲	High Yield	Low	394.2	1.2	14.9	9.6	20.3	9.0	11.4	8.2		2.5	−5.9	1.1
MANAGED MUNICIPALS PTFL.	AVG	Muni. Ntl. Long	Average	417.6	1.0	3.8	5.2	4.0	5.5	5.6	20.9		−0.7	−8.1	−1.8
MFS CHARTER INCOME	AVG	Multisector	Low	728.5	0.9	8.6	7.8	16.7	8.2	8.7	8.6		−4.9	−15.4	−8.2
MFS GOVT. MARKETS INCOME	▼	Multisector	Average	552.8	1.0	4.8	6.1	15.7	6.4	7.8	11.4		−7.3	−17.0	−10.8
MFS INTERMEDIATE INCOME	▼	Multisector	Low	1161.8	1.0	6.5	6.8	16.6	7.0	8.0	7.8		−7.6	−16.9	−12.0
MFS MULTIMARKET INCOME	AVG	Multisector	Low	740.9	1.2	9.7	8.3	19.2	9.9	8.4	10.3		−6.7	−17.3	−11.4
MFS MUNICIPAL INCOME	▲▲▲	Muni. Ntl. Long	Very Low	328.7	1.3	4.1	6.2	3.5	7.0	7.1	19.4		12.5	2.7	10.9
MONTGOMERY STREET INC. SEC.	▼	Long (Gen.)	Average	198.2	0.7	6.1	7.3	4.6	3.8	8.1	11.8		−4.2	−12.3	−9.0

NA=Not available.

DATA: MORNINGSTAR, INC., CHICAGO, IL.

FUND	RATING	CATEGORY	RISK	SIZE ASSETS $MIL.	FEES EXPENSE RATIO (%)	NAV. RET. (%) 1 YR.	NAV. RET. (%) 3 YRS.	SHARES RET. (%) 1 YR.	SHARES RET. (%) 3 YRS.	YIELD (%)	MAT. (YRS.)	TREND 3-YEAR ANALYSIS	1996 HIGH	LOW	1/31/97
MORGAN STANLEY EMG. MKTS. DEBT	▼▼▼	International	Very High	500.7	1.9	51.3	12.1	31.2	8.8	7.1	11.6		4.3	−14.5	−6.6
MORGAN STANLEY HIGH-YIELD	▲▲▲	High Yield	Low	152.7	1.1	17.5	11.8	25.9	10.6	9.7	10.5		4.2	−7.3	1.7
MUNICIPAL HIGH-INCOME	▲▲▲	Muni. Ntl. Long	Very Low	185.0	0.8	6.6	7.1	14.9	6.4	6.7	22.0		−3.4	−11.5	−0.6
MUNICIPAL PREMIUM INCOME	▲	Muni. Ntl. Long	Average	257.7	1.2	5.2	5.6	9.0	1.9	6.4	20.4		−6.3	−11.9	−8.3
MUNIENHANCED FUND	AVG	Muni. Ntl. Long	High	337.8	0.7	3.4	5.3	6.7	2.0	6.7	21.8		−6.3	−10.8	−6.4
MUNIVEST FUND	▲	Muni. Ntl. Long	Average	577.5	0.6	5.2	5.7	10.2	2.8	7.1	19.1		−2.5	−10.1	−5.2
MUNIYIELD FUND	▲▲	Muni. Ntl. Long	Average	564.3	0.6	6.4	6.6	12.5	6.7	6.8	22.1		0.3	−8.5	−2.2
MUNIYIELD CALIFORNIA	▲	Muni. S.S. Long	Average	253.0	0.7	6.3	5.8	19.8	5.8	6.3	18.4		−1.7	−14.7	−3.6
MUNIYIELD INSURED	AVG	Muni. Ntl. Long	High	695.5	0.7	4.5	5.6	7.9	2.8	6.6	23.4		−6.3	−12.1	−7.8
MUNIYIELD NEW JERSEY	AVG	Muni. S.S. Long	Average	131.7	0.7	3.3	4.8	13.3	4.3	6.2	20.6		−2.3	−10.7	−2.1
MUNIYIELD N.Y. INSURED	▼	Muni. S.S. Long	High	182.1	0.7	2.2	4.4	8.2	4.4	6.1	23.0		−1.9	−9.5	−3.2
MUNIYIELD QUALITY	AVG	Muni. Ntl. Long	High	433.7	0.7	3.8	5.0	8.1	2.6	7.1	22.1		−6.1	−13.8	−6.2
NEW AMERICA HIGH-INCOME	▲▲	High Yield	Average	76.4	1.4	16.4	11.8	16.9	12.9	10.3	8.7		7.7	−1.2	0.0
NUVEEN CALIF. INVMT. QLTY.	▲▲	Muni. S.S. Long	Low	206.0	0.8	4.9	5.3	8.2	6.4	6.2	21.2		5.2	−0.9	3.0
NUVEEN CALIF. MUNI. VALUE	▲▲▲	Muni. S.S. Interm.	Very Low	253.5	0.8	4.9	4.8	3.3	1.8	6.0	20.5		4.2	−3.8	2.4
NUVEEN INS. CALIF. PREM. INC. MUNI. 2	▼▼	Muni. S.S. Long	Very High	173.7	0.8	4.3	4.3	8.2	4.2	5.9	21.7		−4.1	−11.2	−9.2
NUVEEN INS. PREM. INC. MUNI. 2	▼▼	Muni. Ntl. Long	Very High	490.8	0.8	3.1	4.0	5.1	2.4	6.0	19.5		−9.3	−14.7	−10.8
NUVEEN INS. QLTY. MUNI.	AVG	Muni. Ntl. Long	Average	580.6	0.8	4.2	5.3	8.0	5.2	6.5	23.4		1.0	−5.8	−2.3
NUVEEN INVMT. QLTY. MUNI.	▲	Muni. Ntl. Long	Average	550.1	0.8	4.1	5.4	3.5	2.9	7.0	21.3		−0.3	−6.3	−5.0
NUVEEN MUNICIPAL ADVANT.	▲	Muni. Ntl. Long	Low	653.6	0.8	4.8	5.6	1.1	4.3	6.9	22.3		1.8	−4.7	−2.5
NUVEEN MUNI. MKT. OPPORT.	▲	Muni. Ntl. Long	Low	702.5	0.8	4.8	5.6	0.3	4.3	7.0	21.6		−0.1	−5.8	−4.6
NUVEEN MUNI. VALUE	▲▲	Muni. Ntl. Long	Very Low	1968.9	0.7	4.9	5.5	−1.9	3.0	6.6	21.8		−0.6	−11.0	−7.9
NUVEEN N.J. PREM. INC. MUNI.	AVG	Muni. S.S. Long	High	173.3	0.9	3.8	5.5	8.2	5.8	6.1	18.3		−1.7	−9.2	−0.1
NUVEEN N.Y. INVMT. QLTY. MUNI.	▲	Muni. S.S. Interm.	Average	275.4	0.8	3.1	4.2	9.0	6.1	6.2	23.4		9.6	1.7	9.0
NUVEEN N.Y. SEL. QLTY. MUNI.	▲	Muni. S.S. Long	Average	359.4	0.8	3.6	4.9	2.4	6.6	6.4	22.5		5.5	−1.2	1.5
NUVEEN PENN. PREM. INC. MUNI. 2	▼	Muni. S.S. Long	High	221.8	0.8	5.3	5.2	7.3	3.2	6.2	21.3		−3.1	−12.6	−7.8
NUVEEN PERFORM. PLUS MUNI.	▲▲	Muni. Ntl. Long	Low	892.7	0.8	5.0	5.5	−0.7	3.3	7.1	22.6		3.0	−4.5	−1.6
NUVEEN PREM. INS. MUNI. INC.	AVG	Muni. Ntl. Long	Average	297.4	0.8	3.7	5.2	6.5	4.7	6.4	21.2		−0.5	−7.1	−2.9
NUVEEN PREM. MUNI. INC.	▲▲	Muni. Ntl. Long	Average	302.2	0.8	5.8	6.3	6.3	7.6	6.8	19.9		0.7	−5.7	−0.3
NUVEEN PREM. INC. MUNI.	▲▲	Muni. Ntl. Long	Low	957.8	0.8	4.8	5.6	1.6	1.8	7.0	22.6		−2.4	−9.3	−5.1
NUVEEN QLTY. INC. MUNI.	▲	Muni. Ntl. Long	Average	821.8	0.8	5.2	5.5	7.0	5.3	6.8	22.5		0.6	−4.6	−1.0
NUVEEN SELECT QLTY. MUNI.	▲	Muni. Ntl. Long	Average	507.1	0.8	4.3	5.4	7.4	4.2	6.9	22.5		1.7	−3.9	−0.5
OPPENHEIMER MULTI-SECTOR INC.	▲	Multisector	Low	309.8	1.1	13.2	8.2	10.5	4.7	9.3	8.7		−1.3	−9.5	−7.1
PACIFIC AMER. INCOME SHARES	AVG	Interm. (Gen.)	Average	149.4	0.8	7.1	8.2	4.2	4.6	8.0	14.7		−3.5	−10.3	−6.8
PILGRIM AMER. PRIME RATE (a)	▲▲	Ultrashort	Very Low	1021.6	1.2	6.9	7.8	15.1	12.4	8.4	6.0		4.6	−4.0	3.1
PIMCO COML. MRTG. SEC.	▲	Interm. (Gen.)	Low	150.9	1	9.7	9.8	12.9	7.5	9.1	20.1		−3.4	−9.1	−3.4
PREFERRED INCOME	▲▲	Long (Gen.)	Low	153.2	1.6	13.5	10.0	23.8	9.1	7.7	NA		−5.3	−15.6	−4.6
PREFERRED INCOME OPPORT.	▲▲	Long (Gen.)	Low	140.1	1.3	13.8	10.6	23.3	6.9	7.8	NA		−5.9	−15.1	−6.8
PUTNAM HIGH INCOME CONV. & BOND	▲	Convertibles	Low	127.8	1.0	13.0	12.1	13.8	14.1	8.3	8.2		9.9	−1.0	4.1
PUTNAM HIGH YIELD MUNI.	▲▲▲	Muni. Ntl. Long	Low	196.6	1.2	5.9	5.9	8.9	6.3	6.9	23.1		11.8	4.2	11.3
PUTNAM INTERMEDIATE GOVT. INC.	▼	Multisector	Average	546.0	1.0	5.0	6.2	6.4	4.8	8.0	8.3		−8.1	−14.6	−11.1
PUTNAM INVMT. GRADE MUNI.	▼	Muni. Ntl. Long	Average	237.8	1.5	2.0	3.3	5.6	6.3	7.2	21.5		19.0	9.2	15.6
PUTNAM MANAGED MUNI. INC.	AVG	Muni. Ntl. Long	Average	444.7	1.2	3.4	4.9	11.3	8.3	6.8	20.3		13.8	5.8	11.8
PUTNAM MASTER INC.	▲	Multisector	Low	491.6	1.0	10.6	8.3	10.7	6.4	8.5	9.0		−8.6	−13.4	−10.4
PUTNAM MASTER INTERM. INC.	AVG	Multisector	Low	332.5	1.0	9.5	7.7	8.5	6.0	8.3	8.4		−8.7	−14.2	−15.4
PUTNAM MUNICIPAL OPPORT.	▲▲	Muni. Ntl. Long	Average	220.6	1.1	5.3	5.9	11.4	8.3	7.1	24.3		4.2	−3.0	3.4
PUTNAM PREMIER INCOME	AVG	Multisector	Low	1225.0	0.9	10.3	8.3	8.8	6.4	8.7	8.6		−8.8	−17.7	−9.2
PUTNAM T-F HEALTH CARE	▲▲	Muni. Ntl. Long	Very Low	198.5	0.9	7.6	6.2	14.3	4.8	6.7	21.3		−4.3	−10.5	−4.4
RCM STRAT. GBL. GOVT. INC.		International	Average	355.2	1.2	9.0	NA	13.4	NA	8.6	11.8		−10.2	−16.3	−10.6
SALOMON BROS. 2008 WORLDWIDE	▼▼	International	Very High	343.3	1.0	29.8	11.2	25.0	9.4	10.3	18.4		4.2	−10.8	−10.1
SELIGMAN SELECT MUNI.	▲	Muni. Ntl. Long	Average	159.4	0.9	4.5	5.0	7.5	6.3	6.7	23.1		7.7	−0.2	4.7
SENIOR HIGH-INCOME PTFL.	▲	High Yield	Very Low	461.7	0.9	11.0	8.0	12.1	9.9	10.0	6.8		3.8	−4.3	3.7
STRATEGIC GLOBAL INCOME	▼	International	Average	307.5	1.2	15.7	8.0	16.9	4.5	9.3	15.3		−10.5	−17.9	−14.7
TCW CONVERTIBLE SECURITIES	▼▼	Convertibles	High	271.3	0.8	12.0	9.1	10.0	10.8	9.0	9.1		13.6	−5.3	8.9
TCW/DW TERM 2000	▼▼▼	Interm. Govt.	High	459.2	0.8	6.1	5.3	11.9	−0.7	5.9	16.5		−8.7	−17.3	−9.4
TCW/DW TERM 2002	▼▼▼	Long Govt.	High	423.1	3.1	7.0	6.9	13.4	1.7	7.1	16.4		−8.2	−17.6	−11.1
TEMPLETON EMG. MKTS. INC.	▼▼▼	International	High	642.9	1.1	26.0	8.0	20.3	4.0	10.2	14.2		3.1	−11.5	−9.2
TEMPLETON GLOBAL INCOME	AVG	International	Low	1048.6	0.7	12.4	8.5	11.7	5.6	8.3	5.3		−10.5	−17.5	−15.2
TRANSAMERICA INCOME SHARES	▼	Long (Gen.)	Average	158.7	0.6	3.5	7.1	4.4	5.8	8.1	18.8		4.6	−4.0	−5.1
USF&G PACHOLDER	▲▲	High Yield	Low	86.9	0.9	20.4	10.4	13.8	7.4	9.5	8.0		7.3	−4.4	−4.8
VAN KAMPEN AMER. CAP. BOND (b)	▼▼	Long (Gen.)	Average	231.1	0.7	3.7	6.8	3.6	5.7	8.2	20.1		−4.2	−10.7	−8.0
VAN KAMPEN AMER. CAP. CA. QLTY. (c)	▲	Muni. S.S. Long	Average	160.5	1.7	5.5	5.5	15.5	6.8	6.3	21.0		−0.3	−10.0	−1.6
VAN KAMPEN AMER. CAP. INC. (d)	▲	Long (Gen.)	Very Low	122.2	0.9	8.9	8.2	12.8	8.1	8.8	10.3		−3.0	−9.8	−3.7
VAN KAMPEN AMER. CAP. MUNI. (e)	AVG	Muni. Ntl. Long	Average	590.0	1.6	5.1	5.3	5.0	1.3	7.0	20.0		−8.5	−14.7	−9.7
VAN KAMPEN AM. CAP. MUNI. OPPORT. (f)	▼	Muni. Ntl. Long	High	249.3	1.8	4.3	4.6	6.7	1.2	6.7	19.6		−9.2	−17.0	−13.4
VAN KAMPEN AMER. CAP. STRAT. SECT. (g)	▼	Muni. Ntl. Long	High	148.9	1.8	3.8	4.0	3.5	0.2	6.8	20.9		−10.2	−17.0	−14.2
VAN KAMPEN AM. CAP. TR. INS. MUNI. (h)	▼	Muni. Ntl. Long	High	157.7	NA	3.0	4.0	8.3	6.4	6.5	21.2		2.0	−5.3	−1.1
VAN KAMPEN AM. CAP. TR. INV. GR. MUNI. (i)	AVG	Muni. Ntl. Long	Average	450.8	NA	4.6	5.1	4.8	4.3	7.4	22.2		−1.1	−8.9	−6.6
VAN KAMPEN AM. CAP. VALUE MUNI. INC. (j)	▼▼	Muni. Ntl. Long	High	344.6	1.8	4.4	3.6	3.6	1.0	6.7	21.4		−11.3	−17.2	−13.0
WORLDWIDE DOLLARVEST		International		100.2	1.8	58.4	NA	45.1	NA	9.1	17.3		0.3	−18.7	−6.7

NA=Not available.
(a) Formerly Pilgrim Prime Rate. (b) Formerly American Capital Bond. (c) Formerly Van Kampen CA Quality Muni. (d) Formerly American Capital Income. (e) Formerly Van Kampen Municipal Trust. (f) Formerly Van Kampen Municipal Opp. (g) Formerly Van Kampen Strategic Sector. (h) Formerly Van Kampen Tr. Insured Muni. (i) Formerly Van Kampen Tr. Invmt. Gr. Muni. (j) Formerly Van Kampen Value Muni. Income.

DATA: MORNINGSTAR, INC., CHICAGO, IL.

INDEX

Note: Page numbers followed by *t.* refer to tables.

About the Author

Jeffrey M. Laderman is a senior writer at BUSINESS WEEK specializing in finance. He helped launch the annual BUSINESS WEEK Mutual Fund Scoreboard, writes the accompanying cover stories, and reports on the stock market and mutual funds. Mr. Laderman is a graduate of Rutgers University and has a master's degree in journalism from Columbia University. He is a Chartered Financial Analyst and a member of the New York Society of Security Analysts and the Association for Investment Management and Research.